The Cambridge Companion to
Matthew Paris

Matthew Paris is one of the most remarkable and renowned figures in the cultural history of medieval England. A career monk at the influential Benedictine abbey of St Albans, Paris, through the texts he wrote and books he made, bears witness to the rich intellectual, artistic, social and political environment of the monasteries and their lasting impact on the wider world. His compelling accounts of recent history and the lives of legendary saints and churchmen are a distinctive and valuable guide to the emergence of the English kingdom and its place in European Christendom. His accomplished and vivid artwork brings into focus both the craft skill and visual sensibility stimulated by the medieval church. This systematic survey, the first published for almost seventy years, brings together expert scholarship and offers fresh, interdisciplinary perspectives on Paris, his life's work as writer, artist, cartographer and maker of manuscript books, and its enduring legacy.

JAMES G. CLARK is Professor of History at the University of Exeter. He has written widely on the cultural, intellectual and religious life of monasteries in medieval England and their legacies after the Reformation. His books include *A Monastic Renaissance* (2004), *The Benedictines in the Middle Ages* (2011) and *The Dissolution of the Monasteries* (2021).

Cambridge Companions to History

Cambridge Companions to History provide accessible and thought-provoking introductions to key topics, eras, places and figures, invaluable to both the student and scholar. Edited by leading academics, each volume contains specially commissioned essays by a team of expert contributors from around the world, presenting cutting-edge research and suggesting new paths of inquiry for the reader. Companions are designed not only to offer a comprehensive overview of their chosen topic, but also to provoke debate and discussion. Like the highly successful Cambridge Companions to Literature and Cambridge Companions to Philosophy series, these volumes are ideal for use by students, and will be of interest also to the curious general reader.

A full list of recent titles in the series can be found at the following address: www.cambridge.org/history-companions

The Cambridge Companion to
Matthew Paris

Edited by
JAMES G. CLARK
University of Exeter

CAMBRIDGE
UNIVERSITY PRESS

Shaftesbury Road, Cambridge CB2 8EA, United Kingdom

One Liberty Plaza, 20th Floor, New York, NY 10006, USA

477 Williamstown Road, Port Melbourne, VIC 3207, Australia

314–321, 3rd Floor, Plot 3, Splendor Forum, Jasola District Centre, New Delhi – 110025, India

103 Penang Road, #05–06/07, Visioncrest Commercial, Singapore 238467

Cambridge University Press is part of Cambridge University Press & Assessment, a department of the University of Cambridge.

We share the University's mission to contribute to society through the pursuit of education, learning and research at the highest international levels of excellence.

www.cambridge.org
Information on this title: www.cambridge.org/9781108473491
DOI: 10.1017/9781108562355

© James G. Clark 2026

This publication is in copyright. Subject to statutory exception and to the provisions of relevant collective licensing agreements, no reproduction of any part may take place without the written permission of Cambridge University Press & Assessment.

When citing this work, please include a reference to the DOI 10.1017/9781108562355

First published 2026

Cover image: The death of Matthew Paris depicted in the margin of his own manuscript copy of his *Historia Anglorum*. London, British Library, Royal MS 14 C VII, fol. 218v.

A catalogue record for this publication is available from the British Library

A Cataloging-in-Publication data record for this book is available from the Library of Congress

ISBN 978-1-108-47349-1 Hardback
ISBN 978-1-108-46176-4 Paperback

Cambridge University Press & Assessment has no responsibility for the persistence or accuracy of URLs for external or third-party internet websites referred to in this publication and does not guarantee that any content on such websites is, or will remain, accurate or appropriate.

For EU product safety concerns, contact us at Calle de José Abascal, 56, 1°, 28003 Madrid, Spain, or email eugpsr@cambridge.org

Contents

		page	
	List of Figures		viii
	List of Contributors		x
	Preface		xiii
1	The Making of Matthew Paris JAMES G. CLARK		1
2	Matthew Paris and the *Chronica maiora*: Chronology, Truth and the Crisis of 1258 DAVID CARPENTER		32
3	Matthew Paris and the Plantagenet Regime JAMES G. CLARK		68
4	Matthew Paris, Europe and Christendom BJÖRN WEILER		90
5	Matthew Paris and the Secular Church PHILIPPA HOSKIN		118
6	Matthew Paris and Britain ANDY KING		144

7   Matthew Paris' Pictorial *Life of Alban*   167
    KATHRYN GERRY

8   Matthew Paris' Enthroned Virgin and Child   196
    BETH WILLIAMSON

9   The 'Becket Leaves'   201
    CECILY HENNESSY

10 Manuscript Design in Production and Transmission   208
    JESSICA COATESWORTH

11 Matthew Paris and Heraldry   240
    ADRIAN AILES

12 Matthew Paris and His Maps   244
    PAUL HARVEY

13 Matthew Paris as Scribe: Idiosyncrasy
    and Collaboration   256
    MANUEL MUÑOZ GARCÍA

14 The Vernacular Culture of Matthew Paris   272
    MARIANNE AILES

15 Afterlife   301
    JAMES G. CLARK

16 Matthew Paris' Manuscripts: Working Books
    and Artefacts in Medieval and Early Modern
    Collections   335
    ANDREW DUNNING

17 Digitising Matthew Paris: The 'Book of St Albans'
    (Dublin, Trinity College, MS 177)   368
    ESTELLE GITTINS, ALISON RAY, CAROLINE HARDING
    AND CLAIRE MCNULTY

   References   375
   Index   418

Figures

1.1 Portrait of Matthew Paris, engraving by Thomas Cecil, 1640. *page* 2
1.2 Title page of Matthew Parker's first printing of Matthew Paris' *Chronica maiora* under the title *Historia maior*, London, 1571. 3
1.3 Portrait of Matthew Paris, engraving by Hinchcliffe, 1852. 4
7.1 King Offa of Mercia setting out on expedition, dressed in crown and armour with sword and decorated shield, Dublin, Trinity College, MS 177, fol. 55^v. 172
7.2 St Germanus and St Genevieve, Dublin, Trinity College, MS 177 fol. 52^{r-v}. 173
7.3 Alban is led to the scene of his martyrdom, Dublin, Trinity College, MS 177 fol. 36^r. 177
7.4 St Alban, St Amphibalus and the informant, Dublin, Trinity College, MS 177 fols. 31^v–32^r. 178
7.5 Alban sleeps; Alban spies Amphibalus, Dublin, Trinity College, MS 177 fols. 30^v–31^r. 180
7.6 Aracle depicted as a chivalric knight, beardless, beautiful and young, Dublin, Trinity College, MS 177 fol. 37^r. 185
7.7 Alban's relics revealed to King Offa, Dublin, Trinity College, MS 177 fols. 56^v–57^r. 187
8.1 Matthew Paris' image of the Virgin Mary enthroned with the infant Christ, BL, Royal MS 14 C VII, fol. 6^r. 196
9.1 (a) The coronation of the Young Henry in Westminster Abbey. (b) The Coronation Banquet in Westminster

		Palace. The Life of St Thomas Becket, 'Tthe Becket Leaves', Wormsley Library, MS BM3750, fol. 3ʳ.	202

10.1 Heptarchy layout. (a) Manchester, Chetham's Library MS 6712, fol. 98ʳ. (b) (i) Eton College MS 123, fols. 120ᵛ–121ʳ; (ii) BL Cotton MS Nero D II, fol. 80ʳ. — 213

10.2 Titular incipits. (a) Manchester, Chetham's Library MS 6712, fol. 7ʳ. (b) Cambridge, Corpus Christi College, Cambridge, MS 26, fol. 1ʳ. — 220

10.3 Diagrammatic forms. (a) Bodleian Lat. th. b. 1, membrane 3. (b) BL Cotton MS Claudius D VI, fol. 10ᵛ. — 225

10.4 Glossed layout. (a) Henry of Huntingdon's *Historia Anglorum* BL Cotton MS Julius D VII, fols. 32ᵛ–33ʳ. (b) Glossed gospel book from St Albans, Cambridge, Trinity College, MS B.5.3, fol. 23ᵛ. — 227

10.5 (a) The 1571 printed edition used as an exemplar for one of the additions in an autograph manuscript, Cambridge, Corpus Christi College, MS 16 (II), fol. 10ᵛ. (b) *Matthæi Paris, monachi Albanensis, Angli, Historia maior à Guilielmo Conquaestore, ad vltimum annum Henrici tertij: Cum indice locupletissimo* (London: Reginald Wolf, 1571), 224. — 231

11.1 Heraldry in Matthew Paris' *Liber additamentorum*, British Library, Cotton MS Nero D I, fol. 171ᵛ. — 241

17.1 Modelling of the surface of the parchment creates a three dimensional effect for the brickwork of the abbey church, Dublin, Trinity College, MS 177 fol. 60ʳ. — 373

Contributors

ADRIAN AILES is Research Associate in the Centre for Medieval Studies at the University of Bristol.

MARIANNE AILES is Professor of Medieval French at the University of Bristol.

DAVID CARPENTER is Professor of Medieval History at King's College, London.

JAMES G. CLARK is Professor of History at the University of Exeter.

JESSICA COATESWORTH is an independent researcher.

ANDREW DUNNING is R. W. Hunt Curator of Medieval Manuscripts at the Bodleian Library, Oxford.

KATHRYN GERRY is Visiting Assistant Professor of Art History at Bowdoin College.

ESTELLE GITTINS is Archivist and Librarian at Trinity College, Dublin.

CAROLINE HARDING is photographer for the Library of Trinity College, Dublin.

PAUL HARVEY was Emeritus Professor of Medieval History at the University of Durham.†

CECILY HENNESSY is former Academic Director of Christie's Education, London.

PHILIPPA HOSKIN is Director of the Parker Library, Corpus Christi College, Cambridge, and Professor affiliated to the Faculty of Divinity, University of Cambridge.

ANDY KING is Lecturer in History at Southampton University.

CLAIRE MCNULTY is Carnegie Postdoctoral Research Fellow at the Library of Trinity College, Dublin.

MANUEL MUÑOZ GARCÍA is Lecturer in Latin Palaeography at the University of Durham.

ALISON RAY is an archivist at Lincoln College, Oxford.

BJÖRN WEILER was Professor of Medieval History at Aberystwyth University.†

BETH WILLIAMSON is Professor of Medieval Culture and Chair in the History of Art at the University of Bristol.

Preface

Matthew Paris (d. *c.* 1259) is one of only a handful of authors from medieval England whose writings have had a readership ever since their own lifetime and whose name by and large has always been known. He stands with Bede, William of Malmesbury, Geoffrey Chaucer and Thomas Malory as a primary example of the kingdom's early cultural creativity and its enduring legacy.

By his own account he was recognised as an authority on the affairs of church and crown even as he lived out his days as a Benedictine monk of St Albans Abbey. Without doubt, soon after his death in or around 1259, his chronicle of contemporary history was consulted by annalists active elsewhere in England; within a quarter of a century it was one of a number of documents kept at his monastery which were in demand as a source of reference for royal regimes.

Later, his manuscripts retained a renown at least among students of English history and the monks would show them to visitors (and allow them to copy them) on request. They prized his books for their public relations so much that from the middle years of the fifteenth century they began to give some of them away. Now Matthew's profile became fixed on the horizons of prelates and princes, enough to ensure that at the Reformation several of his books still at St Albans were preserved as a matter of priority.

The scale and scope of his coverage soon made Matthew's surviving chronicle manuscripts sought-after sources for the age of monks and popes now passed away, as likely to be quoted on the Norman Conquest as on the events of his own day. Although his writing on other subjects – saints, their miracles and the early history of his monastery – were not widely read or reproduced before the nineteenth century and his art and cartography were largely overlooked, his chronicles were set in place as the cornerstone of a national history.

Translation into French in 1840–41 by Jean-Louis Huillard Bréholles, a scholar of Europe's *grandes histoires*, confirmed his status. In the series of chronicles, memorials and public records published by the British government between 1858 and 1911 Matthew's writing featured in no fewer than fourteen of the ninety-nine volumes. In the century that followed, readers of all kinds have met Angevin England and European Christendom through him.

Now the manuscripts he made and illustrated are among the most widely reproduced and recognised and to date the only complete works of any English medieval author to be freely available digitally.

Matthew Paris' testimony on his own time and his recent past may now be more familiar to many than his whole body of work – history and hagiography, Latin and vernacular – and the scenes – a monastery and its cultural and social milieu – in which it took shape. This Companion aims to offer an introduction and guide to these connecting contexts. In spite of the onward, upward trajectory of Matthew's profile as a contemporary historian, for years the landscape around him was neglected, and when it was first explored, preconceptions about a public historian clouded the view.

Only recently, in the light of growing knowledge and understanding of monastic culture, vernacular literature, book craft and the affairs of the English and European ruling elites, has it become possible to place Matthew in circumstances which he himself might have readily recognised. Researchers whose investigations have enabled this fresh perspective have shaped this Companion. It is a sombre privilege that among the contributions is one of the final essays by Björn Weiler, whose scholarship has done so much to renew research on Matthew and high medieval historical writing and whose legacy is invaluable guidance on these narratives and their sources. Here too is Paul Harvey's last word on Matthew's maps. Originating at a symposium sponsored by St Albans Cathedral Dean & Chapter, this survey has evolved and expanded to provide a route map through Matthew Paris' world.

JAMES G. CLARK

1

The Making of Matthew Paris

Since the manuscripts of his writings first passed out of his monastery of St Albans, Matthew Paris has been regarded as a man apart. When a portion of his chronicle fell into the hands of John Russell, Bishop of Lincoln (1480–94), the prelate recognised its historical value at once and covered it with copious notes, but perhaps for that very reason, he was not readily persuaded that it came from the ancient abbey in his own diocese.[1]

Fifty years on, and after the St Albans book collection had been broken up, John Leland (1502–52), an antiquarian who had searched many of these ancient libraries, judged Matthew to be among the highest authorities for the annals of England. 'I very much favour Matthew' (*ut merito auctoritati Matthaei plurimum faveo*), he declared, distinguishing him by name instead of institutional affiliation.[2] Leland was the first reader beyond St Albans to discover the full scope of Matthew's historical endeavours, reaching from the reign of Henry III (1216–72) into the remote Saxon past and further still to the legendary landscape of King Arthur. Noting a tendency to embroider details he nonetheless recognised him as an authority (*autoritati Matthaei plurimum faveo*).[3]

John Bale (1495–1563), the first to trace church history after Henry VIII's Reformation, responded, upholding Matthew as among those 'noble' authors whose legacy was no less than the 'conservacion of Englandes antiquitees, the bewtie of our nacyon'.[4] Bale drew readers' attention not only to the breadth and depth of Matthew's testimony but also to what he regarded as its unvarnished truth. '[For] how to become a full antichrist ... in all ... ungodlynesse', he advised, 'loke [to]

Matthew Paris'.[5] Suspicious of the stories of some of the most commonplace chronicles, such as the printed *Chronicles of England* and *Polychronicon*, he asserted, 'I have Matthew Paris ... to confound them.'[6] Bale was a lifelong rebel and in Matthew he saw a like-minded critic who 'confutyth this devlyshe dreame'.[7] When twenty years later Archbishop Matthew Parker (1504–75) published a full text of his chronicle for the first time, he fixed Matthew's profile in a classical frame: fulfilling Cicero's dictum that true history is 'the light of truth', 'whatever he heard, he reported' as an independent witness never weighed down by the wickedness of the age (see Figure 1.1).[8]

The second printing of Matthew's works (1639–40) presented a portrait of him in gathered habit, hinting at a robed, classical sage about to declaim before an audience (see Figure 1.2).[9] When the

Figure 1.1 Portrait of Matthew Paris, engraving by Thomas Cecil, 1640.

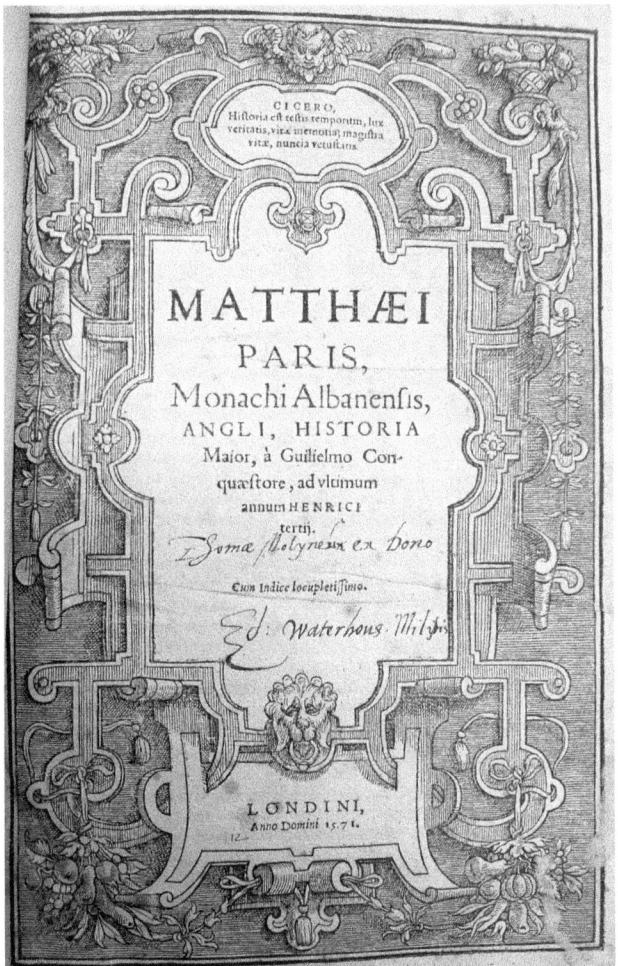

Figure 1.2 Title page of Matthew Parker's first printing of Matthew Paris' *Chronica maiora* under the title *Historia maior*, London, 1571.

engraving was redone to accompany the first English translation of his history in 1852–54, his figure was placed in a scene of an encampment of knights in coats of chain mail clutching lance, shield and sword in preparation for battle (see Figure 1.3). Now he was more than a wise commentator on current affairs. He was a reporter on the front line.[10]

The frequent reproduction of Matthew's chronicle accounts from the mid nineteenth century, far more than any monastic historian other

Figure 1.3 Portrait of Matthew Paris, engraving by Hinchcliffe, 1852.

than Bede, in full or in part, in a modernised Latin, in English and French translations has etched this profile in sharp relief. As the force of the confessional conflict of the Reformation has faded, his critical honesty has been celebrated. '[He] had the nerve to let himself go', like 'a distinguished predecessor of the Fleet Street gossip'.[11] Unstintingly opinionated and subjective, his monastic profession has been eclipsed by a populist status, representing 'healthy English prejudices' and the 'foibles of the ordinary man in the street' – in short, an everyman.[12]

The separation and transformation of Matthew Paris traces the arc of responses to the remains of England's medieval literature since the turn of the sixteenth century, passing from a prosecution witness in the Reformation trial to the preferred narrator of the nation's story. The cost of the personal reputation and public stage given to him over time, however, has been the distortion of his body of creative work and its significance in his own day and after. His annals of his kingdom and of Christendom have been allowed to eclipse his record-keeping on other subjects. His investment in narrative history has been emphasised at the expense of his equal interest in the exemplary life histories of established or emerging saints. For three centuries there was almost no acknowledgement of his writing in Norman French. The character of his outlook and commentary on his world has drawn attention without due recognition of his affiliation to his profession as monk. Likewise, the material evidence of his creativity – the number of surviving manuscripts, maps and paintings which certainly passed through his hands – too often has been described in isolation as the traces of a singular genius, not, as it surely was, one instance of the art, craft, archival and literary activity of a substantial, diverse and dynamic institutional community.

In fact, it might be suggested that the foundation for an appreciation of Matthew and the value of his work for an understanding of the political, religious and social life, art and culture of the high Middle Ages is an awareness of his monastic world. Like a growing number of those who lived under vows in his time, Matthew Paris was a career monk. So far as we know he was not entered into this life from infancy. Few were in England by the beginning of the thirteenth century. Rather, he chose his course in adolescence or early adulthood and committed himself to membership of a particular corporate body and to the national and international networks with which it identified. He may have been occupied with the routine demands of his monastic rule for as much as two decades before he devoted very much time to the making of books.

Every generation after his own has assumed that the small group of mid thirteenth-century manuscripts that name him and display his distinctive script and a rich array of illustrations, miniatures, portraits and narratives schemes amount to a more or less coherent body of work as conceived by Matthew himself. The transcriptions from some (but not all) of these books published in thirteen volumes of the Rolls Series from 1866 and 1883 framed this view with formidable scholarly authority and in the following century and further it remained the point of departure for understanding his achievement.[13] Different interpretations of evidence so familiar and seemingly resolved and entirely new discoveries have arisen only as access to manuscript collections has widened and, most recently, as digitisation has advanced comparative analysis.[14]

The claim that Matthew's writings 'have come down to us almost intact'[15] may no longer be wholly secure but there can be no doubt that above all else Matthew was the writer of which his own monastic and secular contemporaries were aware, who made histories, archival collections and lives of celebrated saints.

He compiled a chronicle of the recent past in the kingdom of England, narrating the affairs of monarchy, church and to a degree wider society, and their encounters with peoples across the sea. The surviving manuscripts show this history being edited and revised over a number of years to fulfil different purposes. Matthew aimed to maintain his narrative in a long form that recounted affairs in England and the islands of Britain alongside the wider fortunes of European Christendom. Cross-references in his edited, shorter version indicate that he identified this comprehensive account as a 'greater chronicle' (*cronica maiora* or *historia magna*). His shorter narrative was intended to spotlight England's experience, an 'History of the English' (*Historia Anglorum*). He also compiled – and partly copied in his own hand – an 'abbreviation' or precis of his chronicle (*Abbreviatio chronicorum*) presented in manuscript in the form of an annal. Matthew drew on his core narrative also to create a continuation of another history of the recent past, the 'Flowers of History' (*Flores historiarum*) begun at St Albans by his older contemporary Roger of Wendover. The nineteenth-century editors devoted their volumes to teasing apart the web of manuscripts and texts and to deducing Matthew's own rationale. Prevailing views about the keeping of records in a medieval monastery, the corporate – and public – role of chronicles about the process of compiling and copying manuscript books weighed heavily on their reading of the evidence and sometimes misled them entirely.[16]

Matthew's own commentary on his historical enterprise is very slight. What can be certain is that he wrote on the record of the recent past throughout his career in compiling texts, designing and illustrating books and he did so to see his work read and referenced in a variety of contexts in his own monastery and, surely, elsewhere.[17]

Matthew was also the compiler of an epic, five-century account of the abbots of his monastery, referred to in the earlier of the two copies made in his lifetime, the 'Deeds of the Abbots' (*Gesta abbatum*). A sequence of biographies of the twenty-three abbots down to

Matthew's own day, the largely consistent structure of the text would suggest the whole was compiled by Matthew, although it seems likely that he drew on records of earlier times, which may have included some or other form of annal or chronicle. Matthew made histories with vivid narrative, animated with dramatic scenes and exchanges of dialogue. Yet he underscored his own prose with transcripts of documents; as a companion to his 'Greater Chronicle' he compiled a register of documents which he called his 'Book of Additions' (Liber additamentorum).[18]

Another St Albans history remains at the margins of Matthew's record. A dual biography of the legendary Mercian monarchs, *The Lives of the Two Offas* (*Vitae duorum offarum*), which was entered into the manuscript, now BL, MS Nero D I, also containing the *Gesta abbatum*, is by its very subject a companion piece to Matthew's annal of abbots. The account it contains of the life of Offa II king of Mercia (757–96 CE), St Albans Abbey's legendary founder, is closely aligned to the opening passages of Matthew's *Gesta*. The text also repeats a proverbial phrase found repeatedly in Matthew's 'Greater Chronicle'.[19] It has been accepted by some modern scholars as Matthew's work[20] but its modern editor and translator concludes that he may have recovered and revised what was an older, anonymous work, acting as an 'enhancing editor'.[21]

Now, Matthew's contribution to hagiography can be more clearly focused. He wrote Latin lives of contemporary churchmen, both archbishops of Canterbury, Stephen Langton and Edmund of Abingdon, who was proclaimed a saint in 1246. His nineteenth-century editors had kept the evidence of his parallel writings in French at arm's length but there is now general agreement that he was the author of vernacular versions of the lives of St Alban, Archbishop Edmund, the penultimate Saxon king of England Edward the Confessor and the martyred Thomas Becket, Archbishop of Canterbury.[22] Perhaps surprisingly, there is no trace of a Latin life of Alban or his co-martyr Amphibalus that might be attributed to Matthew, but he is the probable compiler of the account of the translation of the relics of Amphibalus and the miracles attributed to his new shrine that is found in the Trinity College Dublin manuscript, known as the 'Book of St Albans'. The same manuscript also retains part of an account of Amphibalus and his martyrdom which may have been from Matthew's own hand.[23]

The illustrations – narrative panels, portraits, sketches and armorial blazons – that frame these manuscripts and are threaded through the margins of their text blocks have appeared to some almost too accomplished and prolific to be the possible output of a single hand. At first modern scholars inclined towards the same idea of a school, which seemed a tempting explanation overall for the form and content of these books all associated with a single monastery.[24] The communal memory of his own monastery was that Brother Matthew was indeed, in the words of the fourteenth-century chronicler Thomas Walsingham, writing in the abbey's Book of Benefactors, a 'brilliant artist' (*pictor peroptimus*).[25] Deeper study of the underlying drawing, the attitude of figures, style of clothing and scenery and the deployment of colour has strengthened the case for a single vision in design and execution.[26] Recent studies of the remarkable sequence of painted panels accompanying the *Life of St Alban* in the manuscript Trinity College, Dublin 177 – known as the 'Book of St Albans' – have tended to accept them as Matthew's.[27]

It is the illustrations to the French lives of Thomas Becket and Edward the Confessor each witnessed in a single manuscript that may rather reflect a 'school' of Matthew Paris. Perhaps these paintings were his own commission to professional artists, or they were made by such copied from or inspired by (now lost) originals of his own.[28]

Suzanne Lewis argued that the wide range of connections between pictorial illustration and narrative should give grounds for a 'new confidence' that the author of the chronicle was also a gifted illustrator.[29] She identified additional hands only contributing details to a handful of illustrations already substantially drawn in BL, MS Nero D I, Claudius D VI and Cambridge Corpus Christi College MS 26.[30] Lewis also tempered the admiration of his art, judging him 'archaic', 'awkward', 'hesitant' and deserving the favourite faint praise for an artist, 'largely self-taught'.[31]

Nonetheless, Matthew Paris can be confirmed as a creative of rare scale and scope, a writer of history and hagiography in Latin and Norman French, an archivist, artist, cartographer and a pioneering student of heraldry.[32]

The timeline for this prolific creativity remains open to debate. There is no evidence to support the traditional idea of a more or less formal succession from one generation of chronicler to another – that is, from the earlier St Albans chronicler Roger of Wendover, who died in 1235, to Matthew and then to unnamed others. Richard Vaughan regarded the last decade of Matthew's life, when he came closest to crown and courtiers, as the most productive;[33] recently it has been argued that the 'Greater Chronicle' was always a work in progress, capturing current affairs in close to real time.[34] Suzanne Lewis suggested that he took up painting 'fairly late in life' but the obvious symbiosis of text and image in his body of work would surely make this doubtful as does his use of drawing assistants for his final additions to his manuscripts.[35] Matthew's 'career', if it can be called that, was of a monk professed for life to the conventual routine and it may be more meaningful to see his creative life as an expression of that journey.

By his own testimony he entered the monastery in 1217 – a moment when it was reeling from the internal tensions brought by a new abbot and the external threats of the Barons' War – and took up his books and pens around 1235.[36] His role as a monk alongside as many as one hundred colleagues at St Albans and a similar number spread across the abbey's empire of dependent priories remained the first and foremost influence on what he created in word and image, and how.[37]

Matthew matters precisely because he was not an onlooker, still less an outsider. He was experienced in and engaged with the framework of lordship, religious and cultural authority which had been formed between church, crown and political nation; one in which monasteries, and in particular those of great age and wealth, held a privileged position. His manuscripts are our passport inside.

It was the status of St Albans Abbey in this hierarchy which above all shaped Matthew's creative work. St Albans was one of some twenty-odd monasteries tracing their origins in the remote Saxon past which had been renewed in the wake of the Conquest. The church was rebuilt – it was just a century old when Matthew made his profession there – old holdings were returned and then extended with new patronage.[38] But St Albans had not shared in further investments which the incoming Normans had offered its peers. Conspicuously, it had been overlooked by the new royalty. Acts of crown patronage and protection were rare in the century after the dedication of the new church; visits were unknown. When after his marriage (1236) Henry III and his family showed more than a passing interest in the abbey and chose to mark feasts and festivals in the church, it was a new experience for the community.[39] It was with good reason that Matthew researched the ties of their Saxon forebears to legendary monarchs such as Offa and Æthelred;[40] it was past compensation for the monastery's present neglect.

The crown's aloofness arose in large part from the troubled history of the abbey's patron saint. Alban was an ancient saint and his cult was known at the time of the Conquest to reach back to the beginnings of British Christianity.[41] But they were too remote and too thinly documented to form a strong impression on Norman patrons. Perhaps they were also too 'British'. The saints of other monasteries they restored such as Edmund (at Bury) and Edward (at Westminster), were Saxon monarchs and prelates whose histories held a natural appeal and were well recorded. Also, there was no question as to the site of their saints' relics whereas Alban's remains were claimed by churches at home (e.g. Ely) and abroad (e.g. Odense).[42]

The problems of Alban's profile were compounded by the incoming Norman abbots. Their inclination was to sidestep an inherited devotional tradition so short on substance. They spared every expense on the shrine and instead invested in pre-Conquest cults of proven popularity, such as those of Cuthbert and Wulfstan, and in those, such as Alexis of Rome, carried across from Norman calendars.[43] It was almost 100 years after the Norman takeover that a shrine for St Albans was finally completed and a hagiography was compiled.[44] The new written accounts of the saint – and a co-martyr 'discovered' after the restoration of the shrine – reached an audience outside the abbey only at the turn of the thirteenth century. The earliest surviving manuscript of a sequence of seventy-three miracle stories reported at the shrine was made circa 1200.[45] Another short sequence was collected in the manuscript containing the illustrated passion of Alban and Amphibalus made by Matthew Paris himself. This opened with the translation of Amphibalus' relics undertaken by Abbot William in 1220, a ceremony which Matthew must have witnessed just a year or so after making his own solemn profession.[46] He surely wrote aware that the cult, that is to say, a following for the saint(s) outside of the abbey's immediate circle, was still not widespread.

There is nothing to suggest the compulsion to claim association with other cults, apparent among the first Norman abbots, had receded at the beginning of the thirteenth century. It seems more than coincidence that the last story in the first sequence of miracles of St Alban should tell of the saint acting in tandem with the martyred archbishop. When Matthew wrote in his *Gesta abbatum* of the friendship of Abbot Simon with Thomas Becket, it may be he was reporting a memory which the community was keen to make known to prospective patrons.[47] He also recalled his colleague Master Walter's witness to the ceremony of the translation of the shrine at Canterbury in 1220, a sight first spoken of in his first year at the abbey.[48] Matthew's first abbot, William of Trumpington (1214–35), presented the church with a gold and silver reliquary containing the rib of Wulfstan of Worcester a century, almost to the year, after the second Norman abbot, Abbot Richard d'Aubigny, had secured a relic of the same saint.[49] Abbot William also restored the chapel of St Cuthbert and secured indulgences to mark its rededication.[50] From Laurence, erstwhile monk of Jerusalem, he procured relics of the Holy Innocents, Jerome and of the cross itself, inserted into a crucifix.[51] Matthew noted how the abbot was at pains to see the whole cycle of saints' feasts duly observed, as well as persuading his community to adopt a daily act of devotion for the Virgin Mary. Clearly struck by the cult, he painted her image showing himself in prayer.[52] Matthew's formation as a monk at this time may have impressed on him the importance of number and variety in the devotions of a great church and perhaps also of novelty. His interest in the lives of saints old and new whose relics were not yet known at St Albans – Edward the Confessor, Thomas Becket, Edmund of Canterbury, Richard of Chichester – arose not only from his associations in the outside world; it was the vocation to which he was called.

In the absence of significant or sustained interest from the crown, the establishment of the post-Conquest abbey at St Albans had rested on the tactical acts of settler lords seeking to secure a territorial profile for themselves.[53] Only one of these patrons was found among the high nobility, Robert de Mowbray, earl of Northumbria, and his domain was declared forfeit following his rebellion.[54] For the most part they represented the second rank of lordship, those rising through royal service whose estates and influence were concentrated regionally.[55]

The lasting consequences for the community of monks were the comparative isolation of the abbey of St Albans from any proprietorial interest and a commitment to a chain of dependent churches planted in their patrons' principal domains in East Anglia, the Midlands and the northern border.[56] These, which were made monastic 'cells' of the mother house, were built and endowed with notable ambition by their founding families, bequeathing to the abbot and monastic community the practical and political challenges of governing a distant empire. In his *Gesta abbatum* Matthew showed how these demands consumed the time and energy of his abbots, William and John. He also documented a developing identity, a house (*domus*) at St Albans with a growing number of satellite domains, priories and residences at London and Yarmouth (Norfolk), the source of the monastery's fish.[57] The mapper of routes across Britain and through the European mainland belonged to a monastery unusually burdened with essential journeys cross-country.[58]

At the turn of the thirteenth century, the St Albans leadership were still feeling their way towards a way of living within their network. A preference for abbots associated with families influential in these regions offered stability, although perhaps at the expense of St Albans itself. Increasingly, they wielded the weapons of visitation, legislation and personal and corporate sanctions. Matthew Paris was always aware of these tensions. He became acutely sensitive to the social status and regional origins of those in his line of sight, from fellow monks to officers of the monastery, from churchmen to courtiers. He also showed a special interest in statutory instruments of governance.[59] The unique constitution of St Albans Abbey and its cells was an uncommonly useful perspective from which to view the first English parliaments. Perhaps it provided the experience and insight which guided him through the reform in 1248 of the undisciplined Benedictine community at Nidarholm.[60]

In spite of a less exalted place on the horizons of Norman lordship, the abbey accrued a substantial endowment of estates and churches reaching across most of the eastern side of England from the Thames to the Tyne. These sources of income supported the steady growth of the St Albans community. Perhaps the peak was reached around the year 1200. Matthew reported that Abbot John of the Cell set a limit on the number of monks at 100 and for the conduct of an abbatial election the same, minimum number of monks should be present.[61] Several monasteries in the abbey's peer group of pre-Conquest foundations saw such numbers at this time – Bury, Glastonbury, Westminster – but probably none exceeded them.[62]

Generally, such large communities became increasingly stratified. Since the population in provincial settlements was small, it was inevitable that rising numbers arrived from diverse origins. At Bury St Edmund's, the abbot's chaplain, Jocelin of Brakelond, famously observed the division between the educated elite and the 'illiterate', meaning those who had made their profession without first passing through emerging universities, or even any school.[63]

The St Albans *Gesta abbatum*, which for these years records what Matthew Paris himself had heard recalled, gives the impression of differences not only of education but also regional background and social status. At the turn of the thirteenth century there was a hierarchy of monks distinguished for their advanced studies: Walter of Rheims carried the title 'Master', connecting him to a career at Paris or another nascent university. Roger of Poitiers was said to be distinguished for his command of many disciplines, grammar, logic, natural philosophy, civil and canon law; in short, the syllabus of the secular schools. Reymund, prior under Abbot John of the Cell, was known for his collection of books, among them a copy of Peter Comestor's *Scholastic History*, a guide to the study of the Bible then fast becoming a staple textbook for students of theology. His successor as prior, Alexander of Langley, Matthew remembered as an expert rhetorician, a characterisation which surely also signalled the study of the liberal arts.[64]

The toponyms of the monks of this generation – that is to say, the place names that follow their first names – do suggest a wide geographical catchment. Some surely came to St Albans after earlier careers in France whether or not it was their place of birth. Internal migration between monasteries was more common than in the later Middle Ages, and Matthew's *Gesta* records the arrival of Ralph of Stanham, erstwhile prior of Whitby Abbey.[65] Men of 'northern parts' were familiar at St Albans. Matthew knew this was the origin of Germanus, whom Abbot William sent to take up the priorate of Tynemouth.[66] When he described Abbot William's visit to Tynemouth, although not a first-hand witness, he could well imagine the antipathy between northerners and southerners (*licet generaliter sese non diligant ad invicem boreales et australes corde sincero*).[67]

His awareness of their different point of view was heightened by his passing contact with secular churchmen and royal clerks from the western side of the kingdom – far outside the abbey's territorial domain – and those whose duties carried them across the borders into Scotland and Wales. In the last years of his life, Matthew may have learned news of Wales from the long stay at St Albans of Bishop Richard of Bangor.[68]

Clerks retained in the household of the abbot extended this cosmopolitan society. Matthew recalled Nicholas, known as the Greek, whom he claimed to have assisted Bishop Grosseteste in his Latin translation of the *Testaments of the Twelve Patriarchs*.[69]

Yet the tension which above all Matthew met on entry into the community was a matter of social class. In his first years the community was still disturbed by the election of Abbot William. It was said that from the outset he, from a knightly family, showed a preference for the company of the social elite and for their lifestyle.[70] Matthew learned that senior monks had soon lamented their choice, recalling ruefully King John's response when the new abbot was named: 'Ha! He's the one that I want.'[71] Matthew's *Gesta* discovered a history of division between high-born abbots and their communities. Abbot Warin (1183–95) had been condemned by the sacrist William Martel for his self-regard and the favour he shamelessly showed to his kinfolk, however distant the connection.[72] Both Richard d'Aubigny (1100–19) and Geoffrey de Gorron (1119–46) were said to have enriched their own Norman families at the expense of the abbey.[73] Matthew took up these suspicions. He saw Abbot William embark on his visitation with a whole caravan of worldly family and friends; he counted the 100 horses lost in a year, resources of the prodigal nobility.[74] He was more of a monarch in his realm than a monk professed to the same vows as his brethren.

Matthew's portrait of William's successor, John de Hertford (1235–63), perhaps implied a shift in the superior's social status. John was of local birth; Hertford was little more than a dozen miles from St Albans. No precise measure of his family's standing was given in the *Gesta abbatum*, perhaps because there was nothing of distinction to say. It may be there was an oblique indication of it when the narrative observed how often Abbot John was bested in his battles with the local lay elite.[75]

Matthew's judgement of secular society drew on a discourse of social criticism long established inside the monastery. Perhaps it was also sharpened by personal experience. It may be more than coincidental that Matthew came to be recognised in and outside St Albans only after Abbot William's death.

The visible difference, if not also the clash between the vowed religious and the secular way of life was heightened for the St Albans monks of Matthew's generation because of cohorts of lay brothers (*monachi conversi*, as Matthew describes them) and the retained clerks who lived and worked alongside.[76] Matthew himself accepted and often admired them for their contribution to the church and the monastic community but their presence appears also to have prompted him to record and reflect on the distinctive discipline of his own kind – that is, of observant monks – in diet, dress and daily devotions.

He himself is not easily placed in this large, diverse community. The only biographical information now surviving notes his activity as a writer and artist of the books he wrote and recalls his journey to Norway, but it reveals nothing of his geographical and social origin. His family name offers no further clue. Paris can be found in the twelfth and thirteenth centuries across southern England from east to the far south-west among those who were tenants, merchants and landlords on some scale. Another St Albans monk of the same century shared the name. William Parys is named as the donor of a manuscript of the *Sentences* of Peter Lombard.[77] Thomas Fuller 'presumed [Matthew] born in [Cambridgeshire] as bred in the next county [Cheshire, in Fuller's running-order] where the name and family of Paris is right ancient'.[78] Matthew's awareness of an English proverb, 'Men seth gamen goth on wombe. Ac ich segge, gamen goth on herte [Play enters the belly but now I say play enters the heart],' which he repeats in his account of Edmund of Abingdon, might be the hint of an origin below the tier of landowners at which the Anglo–Norman vernacular was the lingua franca.[79] A passing reference to an obscure holy well of 'St Cradon' – perhaps meant to be St Cadoc – in Cornwall in one of the miracle stories he copied into the Dublin manuscript could be a hint of a West Country homeland.[80] Of course, it cannot be proved.

If he made his profession as a young adult, almost certainly he would have been among a growing number of monks at St Albans who did so. With them he would have stood apart from the leadership of the community, which by his own account was dominated by those whose scholastic titles and skills spoke of careers before they came to the monastery. Their ascendency may explain why for more than forty years Matthew himself never held any office. It is doubtful that he had studied at the same level.

He admired the learning of these masters and listened for details of the academic world out of which they came. He remembered the names of the famous clerks who fled Paris in 1229.[81] Troubled Richard of Croxley, Abbot of Westminster (1246–58), he praised for his school learning in both laws.[82] The Bishop of Lincoln's bullying of Oxford, a focus for academic learning, filled him with foreboding.[83] He even overcame his distaste for novelty to praise the mendicant friars for their learned preaching.[84]

These observations are made in the detached tone of an outsider. Yet Matthew knew current interests of his own generation of schoolmen well enough to give close attention to the testimony of John Basing, the archdeacon of Leicester under Bishop Robert Grosseteste, a pioneering scholar of the Greek language, who compiled a guide capturing the whole essence (*vis*) of Greek such that it was called the 'Greek Donatus'.[85] On one occasion he reached for one of their favourite authorities, Bernardus Silvestris' *Cosmographia*, copying his couplet on the nature of the buffalo when in 1252 Richard, earl of Cornwall (1209–72) was sent some from abroad.[86]

Nonetheless, the few glimpses given of his own sources of reference suggest reading largely outside the syllabus of these advanced schools: court poetry (Henry of Avranches), a copy of which he wrote out;[87] a handful of favourite classical tags repeated so often in different contexts as to suggest his overall stock was low;[88] and the scriptural stories and images which were the daily diet of any observant monk.

He showed the fruits of further reading so sparingly in his own writing that it does suggest he was not so much a scholar as a thoughtful browser. Describing the siege of Bedford Castle, he reached for 'architectoria', a medieval recasting of the classical 'architectura', which he would have met in an encyclopaedia of terms but not in the original manual on the subject by the classical authority, Vitruvius.[89]

Matthew may not have known the same schools from where the masters and many of the books now seen at the abbey had come, but somehow he had become well versed in the vernacular French culture of the social elite.[90] It also thrived in the reading and original writing of regular women, not least among the Benedictines at nearby Barking Abbey.[91] But other than through the work of Matthew himself there is scarcely any sign of interest in or use of vernacular languages at St Albans. In fact, there are faint traces among Benedictine men of this time elsewhere: at the end of the century, at Reading Abbey, a church and community whose exchanges with crown and court life were as close as St Albans.[92]

The meeting point between monastics and francophone secular society was the worship of their altars and shrines. Here was Matthew's own centre of gravity. The ceremonies of the church were always the frame through which he watched the comings and goings at St Albans. What he remembered of King Henry's visit to the shrine in March 1255 was his performance of devotions day and night and that his gifts of vestments were entered in the book kept for the purpose in the abbey church.[93] His point of view was sometimes sharply focused in his *Historia Anglorum*: when Richard, earl of Cornwall, embarked on Crusade, he came to the abbey and in the chapter house the community bade him farewell with their 'devout prayers' (*orationibus eorum devotus commendebat*). In the longer form of the entry in *Chronica maiora* the action of the brethren is not described.[94] The description in the St Albans *Flores* of relics taken out (or off) from the shrine for the king and the singing of a special chant carry an echo of Matthew as the committed choir monk.[95]

What he observed best of the abbots he knew first-hand was their attitude to these fundamental duties. His obituary for William of Trumpington dwells on his renewal of the fabric of the abbey church and his determination to revitalise devotions.[96] Matthew pictures him vividly, participating in the 'work of God' (*Opus Dei*), the pattern of worship required under the monastery's rule.[97] He led the chant from his stall in the choir, was to be seen there at both the break and the end of the day (Matins to Compline) and presided as celebrant at festal masses.[98] Matthew documented William's development of the liturgical calendar and customs, the introduction of a daily mass for the Virgin Mary, and associated lighting of candles and sounding of bells; and his scheme – the first in the monastery's post-Conquest history – for his own commemoration using the chant sequence for the patronal saint.[99] His written observations of William's successor, John de Hertford, were briefer but again he noted his choir acts: the provision of a precious vestment, the assign of income to the office of the sacrist and his plan for his own posthumous commemoration.[100]

Matthew's constant attention to the detail of church ceremony, timing, location, text and dynamics (procession and otherwise) leaves the impression that here was his viewpoint on the life of the abbey. It may be telling that he only remembered the speech of Abbot William when he witnessed him at the head of the community in choir, as at the reception of a cohort of novices.[101] Even happenings beyond the abbey he recalled according to the calendar of his church. Parliament was summoned, he wrote in 1246, 'on the day [the fourth Sunday in Lent] that we sing "Rejoice O Jerusalem! (Laetere Jerusalem Isaiah 66:10)"'.[102] Near the end of his life, his report of a sentence of interdict at St Albans still gave the cloister monks' view of the strange suspension of the daily offices and the compulsion to conduct the chapter meeting in whispers.[103]

His long experience of the observant routine made him a champion of custom and a defender of discipline. He was proud of his part, as he put it, in Norway reforming 'the Benedictine order in the houses of Black Monks'.[104] Although he commended the academic masters who were now monks with him, he criticised the Cistercians' creation of a college at the University of Paris. In the schools, he lamented, the rigour of the monastic order was dissipated by the wickedness of the world.[105] He welcomed Abbot William's change to the community's footwear from soft sheepskin to tooled leather as 'more honest' (*honestius*) for a monk.[106]

A lament for the laxity of monastic discipline in that day – an offence to the legacy of Benedict and Bernard (of Clairvaux, the Cistercian champion) – made near the end of the narration of John de Hertford's abbacy may be the heartfelt regret of the aged Matthew.[107] At this time of life, the hope for a return to the simple purity of ancient monastic observance seemed to be rising in Matthew. He condemned the multiplicity of orders now present in England (*ordines in Anglia ... videretur inordinata*)[108] and considered that the shame of modern monastics (*moderni*) would anger both Benedict and Bernard.[109]

Here it is worth noting in this context how he claimed Edmund of Abingdon for an observant monk. 'He maintained his abstemiousness in ... all worldly things ... assiduous in prayer ... took only the briefest sleep.'[110] He was drawn to stories which demonstrated a monastic devotion: how when a Master of Arts, Edmund built his own oratory in the parish where he was living; how he was suspicious of his scholastic syllabus, 'sinfully entrapped by his type of learning ... while moving among scholars he seemed to be not merely religious but the perfect model of the religious life'; he was 'assiduous in reading and meditation ... fervent in prayer, even constant in keeping fasts and vigils', never missed matins and came to all the offices (at Merton) 'as if he had been under an obligation to do so'. It was said he turned laymen and schoolmen to the cloister.[111] Such were the secular churchmen Matthew admired – not only Edmund but also Bishops Richard Wyche and Robert Grosseteste – who placed personal religion at the centre of their prelacy.[112]

It was a monastic outlook touched by misogyny. In spite of his interest in tracing the early history of St Albans, Matthew ignored entirely the figure of Christina of Markyate (d. c. 1155), recluse and later abbess, although her anniversary was recorded at the abbey and her hagiography was preserved, if not originated there. He scarcely noticed the communities of monastic women set under the jurisdiction of the abbot except to condemn them for their support of the incoming Dominicans.[113] Perhaps his prejudice was as much status as sex. Like many monks it seems he was sceptical of the place of professed women in the territory of the male clergy. Yet when he saw and even spoke to secular women, especially those of noble rank, he put aside monastic sensibility to praise their personal qualities, even their beauty.[114] Worthy of his attention was the Christian witness of well-born women Margaret Bisset, 'of distinguished birth and a life yet more so' (*genere praeclara, moribus clarior*) and Cecilia de Sanford, a widowed gentlewoman living under vows, 'noble in blood, nobler still in morals' (*sanguine nobilis, sed moribus nobilior*).[115]

This outlook of the observant monk was surely reinforced in Matthew – and others of his generation at St Albans – by William of Trumpington's programme of reconstruction and renewal, a transformation of the church and its cult life second only to the Norman restoration. The space for worship and the way in which it was animated through liturgical words, processions and props (i.e. relics, images) was changed by Abbot William in the opening years of Matthew's cloister career, when he himself would have been most tightly bound to the daily observant routine.[116]

It does seem likely it was sharpened also by the same abbot's commitment to the programme of reform promulgated at the fourth Lateran Council convened in 1215, at which he was present with two of the monastery's masters of the schools.[117] The canons issued at the council called for a general recovery of discipline among the clergy, regular as much as secular, to raise the quality of pastoral care of the laity and to strengthen the church's defence against heresy and the non-Christian religions of Judaism and Islam.[118] Monks were required to adopt the same arrangements for teaching as were already established in the cathedral schools, and the diverse and widespread networks of Benedictines were urged to accept a new system of centralised governance under the authority of the General Chapter.[119] What Matthew remembered of Abbot William represents him as a champion of the council's cause: his regal and rigid rule of his monks, his exemplary conduct in choir routine and his investment in the textbooks of a mainstream clerical curriculum. Perhaps it is telling that the one book for reading which the abbot commissioned for the monks was a copy of Peter Comestor's *Scholastic History*, the foundation of the emerging academic syllabus in theology.[120] He was a likely source of the works of the Paris master Robert de Courçon (d. 1219) and Jacques de Vitry (d. 1240), Bishop of Acre, chronicler of the Fifth Crusade and popular preacher of reform, which Matthew boasted proudly were to be found in the abbey book collection.[121] Abbot William instilled an understanding of the canons of 1215 sufficiently for the monks to invoke them when they elected his successor twenty years on.

Perhaps William also led the abbey into a closer association with England's Benedictine congregation. Matthew learned of the collegial friendship he had found at the council in his counterparts from Bury St Edmunds and Durham.[122] Abbot William took a leading role in the inaugural gatherings of the new General and Provincial Chapters of Benedictines which were convened in England from 1218. The second meeting of the General Chapter, summoned in September 1219, was hosted at St Albans.[123] Matthew's own identification with the network of Black Monks increased over time. When the Cistercians came to Hailes (Gloucestershire) he situated it for himself and his brethren as 'not far from Winchcombe', the ancient Benedictine abbey that stood on its border.[124] Matthew's witness to these steps in his first years at St Albans may explain the attention he gave in his later narratives not only to papal initiatives for reform, such as the injunctions of Gregory IX and Innocent IV and English missions of their legates, but also to the arrival, rule and preaching campaigns of the friars.[125] Into his last decade he continued to follow closely the rolling programme which was transforming the 'Black Order' (*de reformatione ordinis inter nigri ordinis*), complementing his chronicle entries with copies of canons collected in his 'Book of Additions'.[126]

Increasingly Matthew identified with his order as a corporate cause. He kept a watch on oppressions of the monastic, of all customary traditions, but increasingly the focus of his interest was the fortunes of the Benedictines.[127] The struggles of the monks of the Canterbury and Winchester cathedrals left him lamenting the 'disgrace and ignominy' (*dedecus et ignominiam*) of his kind.[128] When the abbot of Walden quit his office to become a friar, for Matthew it was a betrayal of the older monastic order.[129] He responded to the mendicants' reported mockery of the Benedictines as 'greedy and proud' both with criticism of their ambitious building plans and the allegation that they duped the dying out of their money, and he asserted that his own form of regular religious life was 'authentic and codified by the Church fathers' (*autenticos et a sanctis patribus constitutos*).[130] Although he disliked the friars' dismissal of Cistercian monks as '*rusticos*', he also challenged that order for its claim to precedence in the church.[131] The sacred relics of Edmund of Abingdon, he suggested, should not remain at Pontigny since 'almost all the glorious saints lie in houses of the order of Black Monks, few or none in the houses of Cistercians'.[132]

It was certainly under the influence of William of Trumpington that the monastery was made a focus for art and craftwork. His changes to the church building and its interior decoration were carried out by members of the monastic community skilled in masonry, timber work, sculpture and painting. Matthew identifies them in his *Gesta abbatum* as Matthew of Cambridge, who acted as Master of Works,[133] Walter of Colchester 'incomparable painter and sculptor', who held the office of sacrist, and Richard, identified only as 'our monk' who decorated the new guests' hall built by Abbot John de Hertford.[134] The *cartulary* of the sacrist's office made in the same period records painters (called *pictores*) present in the town of St Albans.[135] There can be little doubt that a man such as Walter who took up the monastic life was a member of a wider craft constituency well established in the vicinity of the abbey. Matthew's own practice as a painter, and perhaps his own skill, was developed in an environment in which professional craft was flourishing for as much as twenty years.

The abbot's procurement of new books for the monastery may have brought the creative and craft skills of script, rubrication, illustration and binding inside the monastery. There had been phases (if not, perhaps sustained periods) of book production at the abbey for much of the past century. Among Abbot William's predecessors, Geoffrey de Gorron and Simon (1166–83) were remembered for their personal direction of particular book projects.[136] The twelfth-century books now surviving give evidence of successive groups of copyists at work in these seventy-five years, among them some showing the skill and style associated with the best of the cross-Channel scribes and book artists active at this time.[137] The high craft of these books speaks of a professional workshop in which the monks were not, or not principally, participants, but patrons.

On the face of it, the circumstances in which new books were made seem to have been little changed when Matthew began his monastic life at St Albans. In his *Gesta abbatum*, he reported that Abbot William had presented to the convent a copy of Peter Comestor's *Scholastic History*, the writing of which had been organised by the prior, Reymund, who had ensured it was finished to perfection. He also provided a fine psalter fit for a king and an ordinal to the dependent priories at Redbourn and another of no lesser quality to Wymondham. The impression here is of particular manuscripts produced ad hoc and the implication is that professional artisans wrote them and the role of the monks themselves was to supervise their work.[138]

There are few traces of these costly commissions among the surviving dozen or so books of St Albans' provenance – certain or assumed – which date from the six decades of Matthew's lifespan. The greater number of these are shown to have been gifts made to the monastery by individual monks or their patrons. Abbot William donated a turn-of-the-century anthology of the theological writings of Hugh of St Victor. What may have been the personal, working copy of the Lombard's *Sentences* belonging to Matthew's namesake, William Parys, passed into the conventual collection. The suffragan bishop, John of Ardfert, whose presence among the monks Matthew recorded in his chronicle and in the *Gesta abbatum*, donated a manuscript of William de Montibus.[139] Perhaps these hint at a shift of emphasis in the book culture of the community, from the primary influence of the abbots' own enterprise to the independent initiative of their community, both its professed members and, as in the case of Bishop John, the network of churchmen and clerks connected with them.

There is some corroboration for this in the condition of this same sample of books which carry the annotations of readers in scripts characteristic of the first half of the thirteenth century: monks who picked them up in the book collection for studies of their own. Among them was Matthew himself.[140]

It is also suggested by the few fragments of manuscript compilations other than those with which he was involved. The largest of these has been represented as miscellany compiled and part copied by an individual monk, identified as John of Wallingford, infirmarer at St Albans during the abbacy of John de Hertford, whose portrait was painted by Matthew himself on the last leaf of a quire containing a liturgical calendar.[141] In fact it is a gathering together of texts written by several hands over a run of years; among them is the work of Matthew Paris himself. It is likely that each of them came to be made in a particular context for a particular purpose. Another is a sequence of letters from the abbacy of John de Hertford copied in a contemporary hand.[142] Now they appear among unrelated texts, but since their interest is narrowly institutional it seems almost certain that they were first intended for another location.

What may be concluded with some certainty is that William of Trumpington's abbacy saw further traffic in books generated both by acts of patronage and by personal, creative initiative. Matthew's capacity to copy a book, to devise and execute a particular design, even to illustrate it, and his impulse to practise these skills for himself was not unusual in the monastery in the first quarter of the thirteenth century.[143] Indeed, from the abbot who received his profession right across the community of monks, it may have been represented to him as the model of a monastic life.

Matthew also inherited from his seniors an interest in documenting the history of their house. He himself acknowledged that the beginning of his *Gesta abbatum* was an annal of the names and acts of the early abbots of St Albans which came to him from one Bartholomew and had belonged to Adam, cellarer during the abbacy of Robert de Gorham (1151–66).[144] This annal may itself have been a compilation of records of the reigns of particular abbots. It incorporates what appears to be a self-contained account of the constitution of the office of the abbey kitchener in the time of Abbot Geoffrey de Gorron.[145] In the half century before Matthew made his profession, an unnamed monk of St Albans had recorded another aspect of Geoffrey's abbacy, the career of the recluse Christina, whom he appointed as superior of a community of professed women at Hertford.[146] From the turn of the thirteenth century, Roger of Wendover, who held the priorate of the dependent community at Belvoir, compiled an annal aimed at developing and extending the contemporary history of the London canon, Ralph de Diceto, to recount current affairs from the perspective of St Albans.[147] Around this time it may have been John of Wallingford who began a brief annal of early British and English history to the reign of Cnut (1016–35), which is now found near the front of his miscellany.[148]

Although no abbey cartulary survives from this same period, there is evidence of active archival compilation. Matthew himself recalled how Abbot William had compiled a record of the losses the abbey suffered during the First Barons' War, writing it in his own hand (*in manu propria*).[149] A sequence of charters concerning the office of the sacrist and the altar of the co-patron saint, Amphibalus, is conserved in a composite manuscript made a century later.[150] It may be another indication of the independent copying of texts and keeping of books. Matthew may have entered a monastery with a collective awareness of history but a tradition of individual expression.[151] His colleague John of Wallingford shadowed Matthew in his watch on current affairs but he made an annal of his own.[152] Perhaps what set Matthew apart was his capacity to mobilise peers with common interests – among them John of Wallingford – to assist him in his own enterprise.[153]

The dynamics of monastic life that Matthew Paris met at St Albans in the wake of the Barons' War were matched among many of the abbey's peers. The renewal of the monastic church and its principal cults was a common enterprise. The ambition and energy of the sacrists at Bury St Edmunds, who maintained a record book for their office, a *Gesta sacristarum* from circa 1200 to 1263, echoes that of Matthew's celebrated Walter of Colchester.¹⁵⁴ At Westminster, daily Marian devotions were now introduced alongside elaborate posthumous commemorations for past abbots, possibly the very model for Trumpington and Hertford's propositions at St Albans.¹⁵⁵ The abbots of Bury and Westminster stood beside William of Trumpington at the Lateran council of 1215; in its aftermath Bury confronted the challenges its canons raised as they struggled to settle the matter of their abbot's election. Bury and other independent abbeys of Benedictines such as Evesham and Tewkesbury made the same investment in keeping of annals and related record collections.¹⁵⁶ The striking similarity in the material surviving from Bury is the independence of the compilers, who narrated accounts of their own times and collected and transcribed charters from their different positions within the community, the abbot's household, the office of the kitchener or the sacristy. Like Roger of Wendover, the Tewkesbury annalist recorded current affairs from the perspective of his own precinct.

Matthew himself appeared not only aware of this shared experience but also eager to articulate it as an identity. He reported on the causes, the gains and losses of his colleagues' communities. He commended his colleagues when he perceived the rights and privileges of monastic status to have been upheld, but he was certain to condemn them if he thought they had failed those rights and privileges. It may be that he gave voice to a corporate point of view that was more developed at St Albans than elsewhere. As Matthew recalled in the *Gesta abbatum*, Abbot John de Hertford had proposed (1253) the formation of an affinity with the Benedictines of Bury St Edmunds, Canterbury, St Augustine's, Evesham and Westminster which is not documented elsewhere and which appears to have come to nothing.¹⁵⁷

In fact, it may be that in some ideas and outlooks St Albans in the first half of the thirteenth century did still stand apart. The dominance of masters of the schools does not appear to have been typical of the hierarchy of Benedictines in the years after 1215. The traces of learning of this kind at its nearest neighbours, Bury and Westminster, are very slight; from elsewhere, there is nothing at all.¹⁵⁸ This influence, and the customary discipline Abbot William apparently advanced in the wake of the Lateran Council, which still resonated with Matthew twenty years on as he copied and recopied the canons of successive papal legates, may also help to explain the absence of any more diverse culture at the abbey. Less than twenty miles from St Albans, on the same route north, the Augustinians at Dunstable appear to have absorbed news of people and things of all kinds by word of mouth.[159] By contrast, the prompt and purpose of Matthew Paris' creativity was almost always his own monastic profession.

The lived experience of England's largest, wealthiest and most influential monasteries in the thirteenth centuries is not at all well documented. It was a period as pivotal in their development and in their imprint on religious culture and economic, social and political life as the coming of the Normans. Relations with royal, seigniorial and papal authority were perhaps more volatile and impactful than at any time until the reformation of Henry VIII. The renewal of their churches and cult practice resulted in patterns of worship which remained in place, scarcely altered, for another two centuries. The programme of papal reform began to draw them towards the learning, teaching, pastoral care and governance of the secular clergy. The majority of monastic annals and chronicles which have been preserved scarcely notice these transformations; many are little more than customised versions of more homogenous narratives. The body of records, cartularies, registers, and *Gesta abbatum* – which do remain in larger numbers – display the limitations of their genre: they describe the business of an institution but not its prevailing attitudes or outlook. Hardly any other original writing from monasteries of this period survives. Matthew Paris' manuscripts present a uniquely valuable point of entry into an otherwise very shadowy world. Of course, the scale and scope of this body of work opens a wide perspective on the years. His lack of an office gives a view from ground level. Above all, his voice, voluble and idiosyncratic, gives expression to the experience of a monastery both a part and a parcel of momentous times. As an unnamed colleague recalled in an obituary neatly inscribed in the margin of the last of his texts, Matthew Paris was an eloquent man (*vir quidam eloquens*) who wrote down a great deal (*in scriptis plenarie redegit*) in an age of great events (*gesta magnatam, tam saecularium quam ecclesiasticorum, necnon casus et eventus, varios et mirabiles*).[160] The rare monk's-eye view is what compels him still to be studied.

Notes

1. BL, Royal MS 14 C VII, fol. 1^r.
2. Hearne 1715, v. 54. For Leland's library searches, see Carley 2000, xliv.
3. Leland 1544, fol. 30^r; Hearne 1715, ii. 335, iii. 163–67. See also Chapter 16 339–40.
4. Bale 1549, fol. ff vii^v–viii^r.
5. Bale 1551, fol. li^v.
6. Bale 1551, fol. lvi^r.
7. Bale 1551, fol. xxii^r.
8. [Matthew Paris] 1571, title-page. For the antiquarian interest in Matthew's manuscripts, see Chapter 16, 339–47.
9. [Matthew Paris] 1640, frontispiece.
10. [Matthew Paris] 1639; [Matthew Paris] 1640. See Chapter 3, 68–89.
11. Smalley 1974, 161–62.
12. Smith 1913, 167; Vaughan 1958c, 264–65.
13. The Rolls Series editions are Madden 1866–69; Riley 1867–69; Luard 1872–83. For studies that followed in their wake, see Jenkins 1922, 61–67; Galbraith 1944, 23–26; Vaughan 1958c, 157; Gransden 1974b, 356–57.
14. On digitisation of Matthew Paris' manuscripts, see Chapter 17, 368–74.
15. Vaughan 1958c, 1.
16. For the differing views of their achievement, see Jenkins 1922; Galbraith 1944; Vaughan 1958c; Gransden 1974b.
17. For Matthew's contribution to and influence on the making of books, see Chapter 10, 208–39 and Chapter 13, 256–71.
18. For Matthew's *Gesta abbatum* see Riley 1867–69, i. 3–324. For his 'Additions' see Luard 1872–83, vi. 1–465; Vaughan 1958c, 81–84.
19. Swanton 2010, 23–24n185.
20. Vaughan 1958c, 47–48.
21. Swanton 2010, xxix–xxxi at xxxi. See also Gransden 1974b, 358.
22. See Chapter 14, 272–300.
23. Dublin, Trinity College, MS 177, fols. 70r–v, 73r–77r. For this manuscript see also Chapter 16, 354–55.
24. Page 1902, 275–92; Lethaby 1916, 189–96; Lethaby 1917a; Lethaby 1917b; James et al. 1924; James 1925–26, 1–26; Vaughan 1958c, 226–27.
25. BL, Cotton MS Nero D VII, fols. 50^v–51^r.
26. Vaughan 1958c, 227–34.
27. See Chapter 7, 167–95. See also Baswell 2010, 169, 176–77; Slater 2018, 203; Kauffmann 2020.
28. See Chapter 9, 201–7. See also Morgan 1988; Kauffmann 2020, 186.
29. Lewis 1987, 19.
30. Lewis 1987, 24–26.
31. Lewis 1987, 433.

32. For Matthew's map-making, see Chapter 12, 244–55. For his record of blazons of arms, see Chapter 11, 240–43.
33. Vaughan 1958c, 9, 91.
34. Greasley 2021.
35. Lewis 1987, 433.
36. Madden 1866, iii. ix n.3; BL, Cotton MS Nero D I, fol. 165^v. See also Vaughan 1958c, 1–2.
37. For the monastic population at St Albans, see Knowles and Hadcock 1971, 74–75 at 75.
38. Riley 1867–69, i. 52, 70–71.
39. Madden 1866–69, ii. 488; Luard 1872–83, iv. 358, 402, 639.
40. See, for example, the copies of these monarchs' charters Matthew entered into his 'Book of Additions' (*Liber additamentorum*) (BL Cotton MS Nero D I, fols. 74r–201v), printed in Luard 1872–83, vi. 1–8, 15–27. See also Riley 1867–69, i. 84 and Chapter 16, 357.
41. For the origins of the cult, see Laynesmith 2018.
42. Riley 1867–69, i. 12–18, 34–38.
43. Riley 1867–69, i. 70, 190, 283. The cult interest in St Alexis is indicated by the making of the illustrated, bi-lingual texts of the saint's life surviving as a quire in the St Albans Psalter, Hildesheim, Dombibliothek MS St Godehard 1, pp. 57–68. See also Chapter 7, 179–180.
44. Riley 1867–69, i. 189; McLeod 1980.
45. Now, BL, Cotton MS Faustina B IV, fols. 19vb–40va.
46. Dublin, Trinity College MS 177, fols. 73ra–77rb at 73ra.
47. Riley 1867–69, i. 184–88.
48. Luard 1872–83, iii. 59.
49. Riley 1867–69, i. 283.
50. Riley 1867–69, i. 288.
51. Riley 1867–69, i. 291.
52. Riley 1867–69, i. 284, 293. For Matthew's representation of the Virgin Mary see Chapter 8, 196–200.
53. Riley 1867–69, i. 55–58.
54. Riley 1867–69, i. 56–57.
55. Riley 1867–69, i. 6–58, 62, 67, 77–78, 95. See also the local men of property Matthew's Abbot William was obliged to appease with gifts, Riley 1867–69, i. 296–97.
56. Riley 1867–69, i. 56–57. See also Knowles and Hadcock 1971, 59, 67, 78–79, 81.
57. Riley 1867–69, i. 290.
58. For Matthew's mapping of roads and routes and his possible influence on map-making at nearby monasteries, see Chapter 12, 253–54.
59. Riley 1867–69, i. 292–95; Luard 1872–83, vi. 175–85.
60. Luard 1872–83, v. 42–45 at 45.

61. Riley 1867–69, i. 234. See also Vaughan 1953a, 4.
62. Knowles and Hadcock 1971, 61, 66, 80.
63. Butler 1949, 130.
64. For these masters turned monks, see Madden 1866–69, ii. 90; Riley 1867–69, i. 254, 258, 261, 294. See also Thomson 1982, i. 71–75.
65. Riley 1867–69, i. 260.
66. Riley 1867–69, i. 275. For a view of the catchment see also the names of monks whose obits were recorded in John of Wallingford's miscellany, BL, Cotton MS Julius D VII, fols. 112v–13v.
67. Riley 1867–69, i. 271.
68. Luard 1872–83 v. 2, 288, 432, 602. See also Chapter 6, 151, 157, 161, 165.
69. Luard 1872–83, iv. 232–33 at 233. See also Nisse 2017.
70. Riley 1867–69, i. 250, 254.
71. Riley 1867–69, i. 254.
72. Riley 1867–69, i. 195, 199.
73. Riley 1867–69, i. 71–72, 95.
74. Riley 1867–69, i. 258–59 at 259.
75. Riley 1867–69, i. 312, 329.
76. Riley 1867–69, i. 280, 290, 293.
77. BL, Royal MS 2 F VIII.
78. Fuller 1662, 156.
79. Lawrence 1996, 153.
80. 'Etiam a Cornubia scilicet a fontibus sancti Cradonis ...': Dublin, Trinity College, MS 177, fol. 74ra. For Matthew's origin see also Chapter 14, 273.
81. Luard 1872–83, iii. 168.
82. Luard 1872–83, v. 700.
83. Luard 1872–83, v. 618.
84. Madden 1866–69, iii. 40.
85. Luard 1872–83, v. 284–87 at 286.
86. Luard 1872–93, v. 275.
87. Luard 1872–83, vi. 62. The copy is Cambridge, University Library, MS Dd 11. 78. See also Vaughan 1958c, 128, 176.
88. For example, Madden 1866–69, ii. 396, 405 (Ovid, *Remedia amoris*, I. 19); Luard 1872–83, iii. 189; v. 470 (Ovid, *Amores*, I. 10. 48); iv. 61, 122 (Ovid, *Metamorphoses*, IV. 471). The recurrence of these tags in the *Vitae duorum Offarum* further ties the text to Matthew: [Matthew Paris] 1640, 6.
89. Luard 1872–83, iii. 86.
90. See Chapter 14, 272–300.
91. Auslander 2012.
92. Coates 1999, 74.
93. Luard 1872–83, v. 489–90.
94. Madden 1866–69, ii. 437; Luard 1872–83, iv. 43–44 at 43.
95. Luard 1890, ii. 431.

96. Riley 1867–69, i. 303–4.
97. For the template of the monastic *Opus Dei*, see Fry 1980, 203–17, 249. Also see Riley 1867–69, i. 303–4.
98. Riley 1867–69, i. 303–4.
99. Riley 1867–69, i. 292.
100. Riley 1867–69, i. 313, 321–22.
101. Riley 1867–69, i. 304.
102. This was the opening phrase of the entry antiphon for the mass on the fourth Sunday in Lent: Luard 1872–83, iv. 511.
103. Luard 1872–83, v. 590.
104. Madden 1866–69, iii. 40–41 at 41.
105. Madden 1866–69, iii. 57.
106. Riley 1867–69, i. 293.
107. Riley 1867–69, i. 367–68.
108. Luard 1872–83, v. 631.
109. Madden 1866, iii. 111.
110. Lawrence 1996, 122.
111. Lawrence 1996, 123–25, 140–41.
112. For Matthew's view of the secular church, see Chapter 5, 118–43.
113. Riley 1867–69, i. 387. Yet he noted the profile of Europeans Elisabeth of Thuringia and Hildegard of Bingen: see Chapter 4, 110.
114. Luard 1872–83, iii. 624.
115. Madden 1866, ii. 413, 468; Luard 1872–83, iv. 200; v. 235–36. See also Slater 2018, 192–93.
116. Riley 1867–69, i. 281–88.
117. Riley 1867–69, i. 261–63 at 261–62. For Abbot William and the St Albans' view of the council see also Chapter 5, 120, 134.
118. For Matthew's response to the affairs of the secular church and of Christendom as a whole, see Chapter 4, 90–117, and Chapter 5, 118–43.
119. Tanner, Alberigo and Jedin 1990, i. 230–71 at 240–41. See also the survey provided in Gransden 2007, 199–203.
120. The manuscript is now BL, Royal MS 4 D VII. The *Historia scholastica* is followed by the *Liber exceptionum* of Richard of St Victor.
121. Liebermann 1879, 323–29 at 328.
122. Riley 1867–69, i. 262.
123. Pantin 1931–37, i. 15.
124. Luard 1872–83, v. 86.
125. Madden 1866–69, ii. 398, 400, 413–14; Luard 1872–83, iii. 499–517; iv. 292–94, 410–12, vi. 234–49. See also Robson 2024, 43–48.
126. Madden 1866–69, iii. 59.
127. Madden 1866–69, iii. 129.
128. Madden 1866–69, ii. 449; Luard 1872–83, iv. 108.
129. Luard 1872–83, iv. 164.

130. Luard 1872–83, iv. 279–80.
131. Luard 1872–83, iv. 279–80.
132. Lawrence 1996, 160.
133. Riley 1867–69, i. 280–81, 285.
134. Riley 1867–69, i. 314.
135. BL, Cotton MS Julius D III, fos. 46v–47r; Clark 2020, 211–12.
136. Riley 1867–69, i. 94, 192; Thomson 1982, i. 20–27, 51–62.
137. Thomson 1982, i. 32–33, 54–56, 60–62, 75–76 (illustrations).
138. Riley 1867–69, i. 294. See also Thomson 1982, i. 72. The copy of Peter Comestor may be identified as now BL, Royal MS 4 D VII.
139. Riley 1867–69, i. 282, 285, 288.
140. Vaughan 1953b, 390–92. Matthew's marginal notation is found in BL, Cotton MS Vitellius A XX (Chronicle), BL, Royal MS 13 D V (Geoffrey of Monmouth and William of Malmesbury), BL, Royal MS 13 E VI (Ralph de Diceto) and Oxford, Corpus Christi College, MS 2 (Bible).
141. BL, Cotton MS Julius D VII, fol. 42r. See also Vaughan 1958c, 229–30; Lewis 1987, 390, 419–20, 425. See also Chapter 2, 34–37 and Chapter 10, 226–27.
142. Oxford, Bodl., MS Digby 20, fols. 105^r–109^r.
143. See also Chapter 10, 208–39 and Chapter 13, 256–71.
144. Riley 1867–69, i. 4. See also Clark and Preest 2019, 8–9.
145. Riley 1867–69, i. 73–75.
146. Talbot 1987, 5–10 at 6.
147. The manuscript containing Ralph de Diceto is now BL, Royal MS 13 D VI. For outlines of the work of Roger of Wendover, see Vaughan 1958c, 21–34; Gransden 1974b, 315–19.
148. BL, Cotton MS Julius D VII, fols. 10r–33v; Vaughan 1958a ix–xv; Vaughan 1958c, 154.
149. Riley 1867–69, i. 296.
150. Now BL, Cotton MS Julius D III, fols. 46v–47r at 46v, 47v–48v at 48r. See also Clark 2020, 211–12.
151. For Matthew's approach as an annalist, see also Chapter 2, 32–67.
152. BL, Cotton MS Julius D VII, fols. 46v–110r; Vaughan 1958b. For the differences between them see Chapter 2, 34–35.
153. See Chapter 2, 34–37.
154. Gransden 2007, 218–20; Gransden 2015, 35–37, 102–15.
155. Harvey 2003, 5–8.
156. Luard 1864–69, i. 43–180 (Tewkesbury); Gransden 1974b, 111–13 (Evesham), 405n13, 407 (Tewkesbury); Sayers and Watkiss 2003 (Evesham).
157. Riley 1867–69, i. 391–94.
158. Gransden 2015, 221–28 at 221.
159. Luard 1864–69, iii. 3–408; Webster and Preest 2018; Webster 2020, 161; Gransden 1974b, 295, 297–99; Webster 2020, 161.
160. Riley 1867–69, i. 394–395.

DAVID CARPENTER

2
———

Matthew Paris and the *Chronica maiora*
Chronology, Truth and the Crisis of 1258

Matthew Paris' reputation as an historian stands or falls on his *Chronica maiora*.[1] This extraordinary work provides a highly detailed account of contemporary events from 1234–35 to Paris's death in 1259. It is centred on England but has much too about Britain and the wider world.[2] Paris owed a great debt to his predecessor at St Albans, Roger of Wendover. Indeed, the *Chronica maiora*, until 1234–35, is essentially a copy, although with many additions and alterations, of Wendover's *Flores historiarum*.[3] Yet in terms of sheer weight of material, Paris' work dwarfs Wendover's and that of all the other historians working in the period. The *Flores historiarum*, in the twenty-two years between 1212 and 1233, averages 18 pages a year in the printed Rolls Series edition. The *Chronica maiora*, in the twenty-two years between 1236 and 1258, achieves a yearly average of 77.[4] After the *Chronica maiora*, the monastic chronicle which covers this period in most detail is that of Dunstable priory. It does so in 68 printed pages, as opposed to the *Chronica maiora*'s 1,689.[5] If one adds in the accompanying documents which Paris copied into a separate volume (his *Liber additamentorum*), then the *Chronica maiora* between 1236 and 1258 is roughly the same length as all twelve of the chronicles, covering the *whole* of the thirteenth century, in the Rolls Series *Annales Monastici* edition. As V. H. Galbraith commented, 'medieval history on this scale is unique'.[6]

Galbraith pointed to the range of interests which lay behind the gigantic scale of Paris' work and paid tribute to his 'humanity', which meant he was interested in the whole of human life, not just the doings of an elite.[7] Richard Vaughan likewise wrote of Paris' 'interest in human beings and in the ordinary episodes of daily life', 'a rare and valuable quality', he thought, 'among medieval chroniclers'.[8] Neither Vaughan nor Galbraith, however, had a very positive view of Paris as an historian. Vaughan believed him 'basically unreliable as a historical source'. Galbraith thought his additions to Wendover's account of John's reign were 'not merely worthless, but very misleading'.[9] Part of the trouble lay in the way Paris' understanding and accuracy were blurred by his prejudices, notably those against foreigners and against the demands of royal and papal government.[10] Vaughan also felt that Paris was simply not very bright. He was a man of 'limited intelligence and fixed ideas'. 'Posterity, in fact, has been tricked by the scope of his writings ... into regarding him as the greatest historian of his age, instead of the quidnunc that he was.'[11]

Vaughan's monograph, *Matthew Paris*, remains a tour de force, indispensable in unravelling the chronology of Paris' various works and establishing the relationship between them.[12] Since it appeared in 1958, a great deal more of value has been published, including, in 2009, a major article by Björn Weiler on Paris' conception of the historian's task.[13] What, however, neither Vaughan nor subsequent scholars have done in any detail is to consider how Paris collected and wrote up his information and why he ordered it in such a chronological fashion.[14] It is these questions of methodology and approach, lying at the heart of the *Chronica maiora*, which I will discuss in the first part of this chapter before going on to explore, in a way complimentary to Weiler's, Paris' attitude to truth and the pressures which made him, as he would have thought, depart from it. Finally, I will look at Paris' last phase and in particular, his account of the revolution of 1258–59. It is often suggested that this reveals Paris' waning powers as he entered old age. I will argue, on the contrary, that it shows Paris' powers at their height.

Behind the great length of the *Chronica maiora* lies the whole way Paris collected and arranged his information. Although the text after 1234–35 is a fair copy written up Paris sometimes years later than the events described, he rarely arranged his material in any kind of continuous narrative.[15] Instead, the *Chronica maiora* is divided up into chapters, some only a few lines long, some a few pages, most somewhere between the two, and each usually hinging on some new piece of information. These chapters are then arranged for the most part chronologically. Many indeed start with a date, so 1257 begins with

Christmas (as do all Paris' years) and then has events dated by reference to Holy Innocents' Day (28 December), the octave of St Stephen (2 January), Christmas, epiphany (6 January), the feast of the conversion of St Paul (25 January), the approach of Lent (21 February), the fifth ides of February (9 February), the fifth nones of March (3 March), the seventh ides of March (9 March) and so on and so on.[16] Between these precisely dated chapters are others tied into the chronological framework through beginning with words such as 'during these times', 'at the same time' and 'in these days'.[17]

What makes the *Chronica maiora* so overwhelming in terms of scale is both the level of detail in the chapters and their chronological frequency, so that there can be several in a single month and more than 100 in a year. Another key feature is that Paris made no attempt to break up the chronological sequence of the chapters in the cause of arranging them thematically. Instead, a chapter on one subject may be interleaved with others about different matters altogether. Because the chapters occur so often, this means that even events which lasted for no more than a few weeks or months, like an embassy, a parliament or a military campaign, can be broken up into a series of discrete and non-consecutive chapters. It is this bulletin-like approach which makes the *Chronica maiora* sometimes appear like a cross between a daily, weekly and monthly newspaper.[18]

Given the considerable time lag that sometimes opened up between the fair copy of the *Chronica maiora* and its record of events, as Vaughan appreciated, Paris must have made notes of information almost as soon as it came in.[19] In no other way could he have maintained his level of detail. Between the notes and the fair copy, there was an intervening stage in which the notes were expanded into a draft more or less the same as the final fair copy. Something of the process is probably reflected in the cases where, by some slip, the *Chronica maiora* seems to preserve both an early draft and a later, fuller account of the same event.[20] It may be reflected too in the odd disjunctions between the *Chronica maiora* and the chronicle of Paris' friend and fellow St Albans monk, John of Wallingford, a chronicle based on the *Chronica maiora*, but with a good deal of information not found within it.[21] Both give an account, under 1256, of how workmen were overcome by foul air escaping from a drain they were digging out in London. There are a few words in common – '*quidam fossores*', '*calamos/calamum aqueductus*', '*fulgur ... de terra/de terra fulgur*' – but, apart from that, the language is different.[22] Since Wallingford's account is no shorter than Paris' and indeed adds both the date and locality of the event (it happened on the vigil of St Thomas in West Cheap), it is clear that he was not simply abbreviating the *Chronica maiora*. Rather, this may be a case where the words in common are drawn from the initial notes of the event with Paris and Wallingford then writing up their own separate versions.

The final draft behind the *Chronica maiora* was probably written on a series of separate leaves and it was from these, shuffled into chronological order, that the *Chronica maiora* itself was ultimately copied. This would explain how, through the misplacing of a leaf, a chapter sometimes appears out of sequence, and how, through the failure to discard leaves containing earlier drafts, there can sometimes be two accounts of the same event.[23] It would also explain, through the accidental dropping out of a leaf, how there is material in John of Wallingford's chronicle completely absent from Paris'. Thus, it is Wallingford who gives a detailed account in 1253 of Geoffrey de Lusignan's mistreatment of one of the king's cooks. Paris by contrast, omits the episode, although he knew about it (it features in his *Liber additamentorum*) and it was just the kind of thing which normally set him going. That he had written about it and had somehow mislaid the leaf (as opposed to this just being Wallingford's own work) is suggested by another curious fact, namely that, at this precise point, Paris also omits the start of a 'colloquium' of the bishops which met in the octave of the Epiphany at London. Instead, the bishops materialise in his narrative without any explanation of how they got there. This was surely because the leaf which had the assault on the king's cook also contained or was attached to the account of the London colloquium, and so in missing the one, Paris also missed the other.[24]

Whatever the precise process, by its end Paris had produced a text which could be copied with little alteration into the *Chronica maiora*. In other words, the final stage was one not of composition but of copying, the cursive hand of the leaves being transformed into the formal hand of the book.[25] The best proof that the draft was much the same as the book lies in the last section of the *Chronica maiora* for 1258–59, which was written out not by Paris himself but by one of his assistants.[26] This assistant made it absolutely clear in the obituary he penned of Paris that he was merely the copyist not the author, yet what he provided is a full text, absolutely characteristic of everything which had gone before.[27] That text must therefore have come from a full and finished Parisian draft. Doubtless the timescale in which Paris moved from notes to final draft varied, but it could be short. Indeed, since the text of the *Chronica maiora* seems to continue to just before Paris' death, he was writing up the draft promptly and fully right down to his end.[28] This promptitude is confirmed by a passage near the close of the *Chronica maiora* where Paris expresses uncertainty as to whether Richard of Cornwall, returning to England, had taken an oath to accept the reforming enterprise, only for the immediately succeeding chapters to give precise information about such an oath.[29] The passage expressing ignorance must have been written soon after the first news came in; otherwise it would have been overtaken by the arrival of more exact intelligence. It survives because Paris did not emend his draft (although he might have done so had he lived), and the copyist simply put down what was before him.[30] When Paris himself came back to the drafts to write up the *Chronica maiora*, he could certainly emend them in the light of subsequent events, but the work of copying could also be a fairly mindless process, hence the various mistakes and repetitions.[31] Since many of these were probably carried over from the final draft, it is clear that the latter was not checked, or not checked carefully enough.[32]

Paris did not labour alone. Vaughan identified no fewer than fifteen scribes who helped in copying out his various works.[33] His assistants also helped with the collection of information, manifestly so for the period in the second half of 1248 when Paris was absent in Norway. Despite this, the *Chronica ajora* has a verbatim (and often quoted) record of a speech the king made to Parliament. It also states that papal envoys saw the king at Windsor on the feast of the exaltation of the Holy Cross (14 September), a detail which must have been noted at the time.[34] One of Paris' assistants was John of Wallingford, whose chronicle, largely copied from the *Chronica maiora*, was written out in his own hand and ran from the earliest times down to 1258 (the year of his death). John put his name to the work but modestly said it was simply 'excerpted from the work of diverse historians'.[35] At the very least he was an able abridger for the whole of his chronicle would not run to much more than 200 printed pages. Another St Albans monk was certainly an able historian, for the continuation of the *Chronica maiora* from Paris' death down to 1261 provides an independent and highly valuable account of these years.[36]

The scriptorium at St Albans, with Paris surrounded by his assistants, may suggest parallels with Chartwell when Churchill was producing one of his historical works. Whether Paris' assistants, like Churchill's, ever supplied draft chapters for the master just to touch up, we will never know. The modesty with which Wallingford described his own work, and the self-effacing nature of the continuator – he refused to give his name and was unworthy, he said, even to unlatch the shoe of his great predecessor – hardly suggests this happened on any scale. Just how unique Paris' efforts were and how central to the *Chronica maiora* is revealed by what happened after his death. The continuator was an able and diligent man. His account of 1260, his only full year, covers 21 printed pages and has 35 chapter headings, but this pales before Paris' last full year, 1258, which takes up 67 pages and has 104 headings.[37] The continuator was neither collecting information as frequently as Paris, nor writing it up in such abundance. His account of Henry III's visit to France to ratify the 1259 treaty runs to about 3 pages. Paris' account of the visit in 1254 runs to 10.[38] Equally striking is what happened after the continuator died or retired in 1261, for there was no one at St Albans to take his place. The *Flores historiarum*, which preserves the continuator's work, was carried on between 1261 and 1265 not at St Albans but at Pershore Abbey. Historical writing at St Albans was dead for more than a generation.[39] Paris' labours were unique. When he laid down his pen at the end of 1250, as it turned out temporarily, he understandably reflected in a poem on the 'rest' he would now enjoy.[40]

Sheer volume, of course, is nothing without accuracy. How accurate is the *Chronica maiora*? It is here that a yawning gap opens up in Parisian studies. There has been no attempt to fact check the *Chronica maiora* between 1234 and 1259 against the voluminous government records and other sources of the period. Vaughan, indeed, admittedly with much else to do, cited not a single government record in his footnotes. Instead, Paris' accuracy has been tested merely as a by-product of other studies. The result has often been to confirm Vaughan's views of Paris' unreliability.[41] His mistakes range from minor slips over dates and details to complete misunderstandings of events.[42] Here the fact that Paris sometimes commented with the benefit of hindsight was not always helpful. Thus, his knowledge that the Castilian threat to Gascony in 1253–54 never materialised led him to allege, quite unfairly, that it was more or less invented by the king to extort money from his subjects.[43] Most egregious of all are examples where Paris, to suit his own agenda, seems simply to have made things up. In 1252, for example, he narrated a furious quarrel between Henry III and the master of the house of the Hospitallers in Clerkenwell. In Paris' story, Henry threatened to revoke the order's charters, using powers equivalent to those of the pope, while the master complained bitterly of the king's injustices. The only record evidence at this time, however, bears on a dispute not with the Templars of Clerkenwell but with the London house of St Thomas of Acre. This argument raised issues quite different from the challenge to rights enshrined in charters. One cannot help suspecting that Paris had heard vaguely of a quarrel involving one of the crusading orders in London, and, on that basis, had invented the confrontation with the Templars. His purpose in so doing was to illustrate his oft-repeated claim (largely unfounded) that the king was resorting to papal methods to annul the rights of his subjects' enshrined charters.[44]

How Paris might have justified such inventions, we will see later. Here I would stress that Paris' errors and embellishments were very far from the whole story. Quite often the wonder is not that he got things wrong, but that he recorded them at all. No one else did. Not all the criticism, moreover, seems fair. J. C. Holt, for example, showed how muddled he was about Magna Carta. Yet when Paris, in the 1250s, at last obtained an authentic text of the 1215 Charter, he laboured to revise the version he had inherited from Wendover in its light. One should also make a distinction between the *Chronica maiora* where Paris is merely elaborating Wendover, and the *Chronica maiora* when it is Paris' own and his methods of collection have come into play. If one works through a year of the *Chronica maiora*, correlating its information with other sources, one gains a powerful sense of how conscientiously Paris captures information as it comes in. Thus in 1257 Paris tells of how, on the feast of the conversion of St Paul (25 January), the bishop-elect of Winchester, John of Gatesden, and Peter des Rivaux were sent as envoys to France to prolong the truce. Sure enough, the patent rolls show that on 12 January the three were issued with letters of credence for their mission.[45] Two chapters later, Paris says that 'around this same time' the queen was conceded the Longespee wardship. The letters patent to that effect were dated 3 January.[46] Three chapters on Paris records 'in the same year' the election and the king's acceptance of a new bishop of Coventry. This was correctly placed for local material shows the election took place at the end of January while the letter patent restoring the temporalities was issued on 17 February.[47] Paris begins the next chapter, describing the rising of the Welsh, with an 'at the same time', which would indicate that it occurred in the early months of 1257, exactly the dating found in the *Annales Cambriae*.[48] Paris also mentions the attempted mediation of Richard of Cornwall, something confirmed by a letter patent of 10 February.[49] These facts are but the harvest of a couple of months. Paris kept up collecting them in the same painstaking, tolerably accurate fashion for a quarter of a century.[50]

Paris has not merely a record of factual accuracy. He can also show a genuine understanding both of situations and of people. He appreciated very well the ties between England and Gascony and the importance of Bordeaux.[51] According to Beverley Smith, in a recent study, he 'makes numerous informed references to the problems that confronted Henry III in Wales [and] often reveals a perceptive appreciation of the significance of the events he describes'.[52] Paris' much criticised tendency to blow both hot and cold about individuals arose not from incomprehension or hypocrisy, but from a recognition that human beings are complex individuals capable of both good and evil.[53] The whole structure of the *Chronica maiora* enabled, as we will see, each action to be judged on its merits. Nor were the merits and demerits Paris detected always bars to understanding. Insofar as they coincided with the attitudes and imperatives of the age, as they often did, they helped rather than hindered his diagnosis. One may feel Paris captures some of the essence of both Louis IX and Simon de Montfort.[54] His picture of Henry III himself is both nuanced and, in part, convincing. Paris certainly excoriates Henry's simplicity and generosity to foreigners, but these were indeed very notable characteristics of the king. Paris also admires Henry's piety and even sometimes praises the astuteness and wisdom of his secular conduct. In one passage, he has Henry wishing to end the oppressions of the sheriff's 'pia ductus intentione', which catches exactly the monarch's good, if often ineffective intentions. That this observation (in the *Historia Anglorum*) replaced one which was probably far more critical suggests a real advance in Paris' understanding of the king.[55]

Paris' incomprehension and unreliability is not the only reason he has fallen foul of later commentators. They have also disliked the way he wrote history in series of chronological bulletins. 'A man with strong views on current evils', wrote Galbraith, 'he saw a certain drift in events which he could better have expressed if it had then been possible to group his facts under subjects instead of the rigid chronological summary imposed upon him'.[56] Vaughan observed that 'Matthew made no attempt to organize his chronicle, as, for instance, did William of Malmesbury, in the form of a coherent narrative covering a period of years: instead he collected all the information he could obtain, and recorded it in rough chronological order.'[57] Paris was certainly familiar with Malmesbury's work.[58] In his own saints' lives, moreover, although they could be divided into chapters, he did not write the chronological bulletin type history found in the *Chronica maiora*; indeed he did not have the material to do so.[59] Had he adopted a more reflective, thematic approach, he could have freed himself from the awful labour of recording events almost on a daily basis. Even if addicted to that, he could at least have shuffled his leaves into themes and thus told the story of connected events in one sequence instead of breaking them up.

So why did Paris write as he did? The obvious answer is that he was simply employing the chronological, bulletin-like method he inherited from Roger of Wendover, a method shared with many other medieval chroniclers. Clearly there is truth in that for the pattern of the *Chronica maiora* is indeed that of Wendover's *Flores historiarum* writ large.[60] Yet it is quite wrong to think that Paris was just mindlessly following the path of his predecessor. On the contrary, he believed deeply in correct chronology and laboured to maintain it. Thus under 1239 he indicated the proper place for an out-of-sequence chapter with the following note: 'this election [to the bishopric of Chester] took place before the birth of Edward [the king's son]; it should be transferred therefore and inserted here', the here referring to where the chapter was to go.[61] Paris was perfectly aware that he was telling stories in stages for he frequently informed readers that there would be a further instalment in due course.[62] On one occasion, he even went on to justify his method, observing that 'those things which are connected together can by no means be narrated together'.[63] 'Why not?' one might demand, but the answer is very clear for Paris believed passionately that events in history must be put in their proper 'order' or 'time'. Thus he sometimes said not merely that a later 'sermo' would tell more about a story, but that it would do so 'in its time' or 'in its order' or in its 'place and time'.[64] When, by contrast, Paris occasionally connected events together in defiance of chronology, by, for example, joining together what happened earlier and later in a year, he felt the need to justify himself: 'these things happened when the year had proceeded a good way; the order, however, is distorted but changed out of necessity; for where there is pain, there the finger'.[65] Given the amount of 'pain' ('dolor') around, that Paris did this so rarely shows how strongly he believed in telling history in its proper chronological sequence.[66] To do that was part of what the great labour of the *Chronica maiora* was about.

It was not a labour for its own sake. Paris stood in a Christian tradition dating back to Bede which saw the historian's task as that of presenting a gallery of good and bad examples.[67] These examples were themselves situated within an historical framework created by God working his purpose out, a purpose being realised both on a great apocalyptic scale (for Paris believed the last days might be near) and in the events of daily life, where God rewarded good deeds and punished bad.[68] Paris therefore had a profound reverence for events themselves for they were God's events. From them, posterity could learn about divine judgement and the consequences of good and bad actions. Thus Paris said he had written the *Chronica maiora* 'for the utility of subsequent posterity, for the love of God and for the honour of the blessed Alban protomartyr of the English, lest age and oblivion destroys the memory of modern events'.[69] Paris wrote these lines at the end of 1250, having taken the decision, subsequently reversed, to end his great work. When some years later, he recalled that decision, he was even more explicit about why he had written:

> For it is good, to the praise of God, to preserve in writing the events of notable things, in order that those coming after by reading may be

> warned to avoid evil things which deserve punishment, and encouraged to do good things which God will fully reward.

The sentiments are, of course, conventional but they were deeply felt.[70] It was not for Paris to impose his own order on events. He did not 'presume to determine the future'.[71] It might, after all, be unclear how things fitted into God's plan, or whether someone's motives were pure or perverted. Only God, as Paris said, knew the secrets of men's hearts. Mere mortals had to await 'the judgement and proof of subsequent actions'.[72] In following those actions and allowing each to be judged on its merits, the structure of the *Chronica maiora* was perfectly adapted. That was equally true where Paris felt God's hand was clear. Thus he was able to conclude one chapter about the exactions of king and pope by observing that 'a following *sermo* will elucidate more fully in its time' how, 'by a just judgement of God', such plunder brought absolutely no advantage.[73] Likewise, his treatment of Louis IX's crusade in a series of separated chapters, many of them dealing with the extortions and pride of the French, allowed him to remind readers again how a '*sequens sermo*' would reveal God's punishment of such conduct.[74]

Paris' belief that history was God's history therefore did not mean he was excluded from commenting upon it when he felt called upon to do so, which was not infrequently. Indeed, Paris' judgements and their passionate expression are both the most arresting feature of the *Chronica maiora*, and also, for many later historians, the most unfortunate.[75] This is because, so it is said, they both blurred Paris' understanding and undermined his honesty, leading him to invent speeches and alter documents, hence in good measure Vaughan's damning comment that he was 'basically unreliable as an historical source'.[76] Paris seems also convicted of hypocrisy since he appears perfectly aware of the historian's need to be truthful. In a well-known passage he lamented that

> the condition of historians is hard since if true things are said, men are provoked; if falsities are committed to their writings, God, who separates truth tellers from flatterers, does not accept it.[77]

Yet does not this passage both help us understand Paris' alleged transgressions and provide what, in Paris' eyes, would have been their justification? For the 'truth' Paris was talking about here was not 'truth' in terms of factual accuracy (although that was certainly important), but truth in the sense of the historian's duty to avoid flattery and to distinguish between right and wrong. What was likely to annoy 'man' was not some mistake over a date but passages in which Paris cried out against the oppressions of king, pope, archbishops, friars and foreigners. If, in this cause, Paris added to a document or elaborated a speech, that was to tell the truth not to tamper with it. Thus the passage Paris inserted into a letter of the patriarch of Constantinople to the pope, the most grievous tampering with a document which Vaughan detected, precisely began by affirming the need to be truthful. The patriarch, 'so that we may arrive at the very pith of the truth', thus tells the pope that 'many powerful and noble men would obey you, if they did not fear the unjust oppressions ... which you practice'.[78]

As Björn Weiler has put it, Paris' 'desire to offer a moral interpretation ... required him to present events in a manner that made their deeper meaning, their ethical value and message, discernible to his readers ... In order to fulfill this function, it was at times required of those writing history that they press home moral lessons, that they go beyond what actually happened to elicit the deeper meaning of events'.[79]

Did Paris, in his own time, feel under pressure to tone down his opinions? It is easy to dismiss his lament about the truth being provocative as no more than one of his 'sententious platitudes'.[80] Yet it actually follows lines in which Paris confessed that he had indeed omitted material 'although true and manifest', 'lest the truth breeds enemies which often happens'.[81] It was also in similar terms that Paris explained his decision to give up writing the *Chronica maiora* at the end of 1250.

> Here brother Matthew proposed to terminate his Chronicles on account of certain imminent dangers. For if true things are said of the powerful and commended to writing, wars (*bella*) are bred for him [Matthew]; if things are passed over in silence, or good things are written for bad, the whole work will be mutilated, and vehemently condemned and discarded as flatteries, adulation and falsities.[82]

Paris then went on to reflect bitterly on how he had been labouring in a barren field amidst man's ingratitude before expressing the hope, in the passage quoted earlier, that his work would nonetheless benefit posterity by showing how God rewards good and punishes evil. All this comes in Paris' *Abbreviatio chronicorum*, which he wrote 'very likely' after 1255.[83] That he still felt moved to write so fully and emotionally about the abandonment of his work (more fully indeed than in the *Chronica maiora* and the *Historia Anglorum*) shows how deeply he felt about the issue.[84] Had his writings indeed brought down 'wars' upon his head? And did those wars force him to retreat? The answer to these questions brings us to another remarkable feature of his historical writing, namely the way in which he went back over his criticisms and, in some cases either excised them or toned them down. Historians have usually advanced two explanations for Paris' revisions. One is that he was preparing copies of his work for presentation to the king. The other is that he came to feel more sympathy for the king and some of his other targets as he got to know them better and as he approached old age.[85] These views are not mutually exclusive but they do reflect very differently on Paris as a historian. In the second case, he changes his mind but retains his integrity; in the first, he stands accused, on his own terms, of displeasing God by omitting truths and writing falsities.

There was nothing impossible about Paris changing his mind. He could acknowledge purely factual mistakes and recognise that stories he had once believed were untrue.[86] He may genuinely have come to take a more sympathetic view of Henry III, as we have seen. There is, however, nothing in the *Chronica maiora* to suggest that Paris ever changed his mind in so substantial and settled a fashion as to necessitate the scale of revisions which he actually carried out.[87] Writing in 1258, near the end of his career, he still catalogued the abuses of Henry's rule and cried out against his simplicity.[88] Even the acknowledgement that Henry was personally a 'rex Christianissimus' was put in the mouth of a hated royal official, Simon Passelewe, who was trying to exact money from St Albans.[89]

The earliest revisions Paris carried out were, in fact, quite openly prudential since their stated aim was to remove from the *Chronica maiora* passages which might give 'offence'. Thus Paris went through the text, Vaughan suggests around 1250, and wrote 'vacat' and sometimes 'vacat quia offendiculum' against a whole series of passages which were to be omitted in another copy of the *Chronica maiora* then being prepared.[90] On one occasion, the marginal annotation even acknowledged that the passage to be omitted was true: 'vacat non quia falsum sed provocans'.[91] Paris had clearly not changed his views. When the clerk had made a mess of the new copy by failing to exclude all the marked passages, thus rendering it useless for public inspection, he put many of them back in at the foot of the page, doubtless on Paris' instruction.[92] Paris, of course, when he resumed the *Chronica maiora* after the break in 1250, continued in exactly the same vein as before.[93] Paris' second attempt at revision was to his *Historia Anglorum*, the abbreviation of the *Chronica maiora* which he probably wrote between 1250 and 1255. This he bowdlerised even more thoroughly than he had the *Chronica maiora*, writing in his own hand new versions of offending passages either over erasures or on slips of vellum pasted above the original text.[94] He was even prepared to conceal how far subsequent events had revealed God's judgement. Thus he cut an observation in 1242 that 'the end of the affair, *finis negotii*' showed how much the king's attempt to get money from the church had displeased God.[95]

Most of the passages omitted in the attempted revisions of the *Chronica maiora* and the *Historia Anglorum* were attacks on the king, his relations (especially Archbishop Boniface), the friars and the pope. It may well be that Paris' aim in making the expurgations was to provide a fair copy which could be presented to the king, or safely inspected by him and his court when they came to St Albans. In 1247, Henry had asked Paris to record the great ceremony in which he had brought a phial of Holy Blood to Westminster.[96] He was thus well aware that a chronicle, which recorded his doings, existed at St Albans, where of course he and Paris often met. Many magnates and ministers were equally well informed, for they too often gave Paris information.[97] What on earth would have happened had Henry asked to inspect Paris' work? It was not even as though the opprobrious comments were buried in the text. They were up there in red in the chapter headings. Had Henry seen the annal for 1247, he would have loved the wholly positive account of the ceremony of the Holy Blood.[98] He would have loved too the heading proclaiming 'the firm faith of the king during the illness of Edward his son'. But he would have been appalled had he turned on a folio and seen 'How the lord king enriched his brothers to such an extent that he pauperized himself. Not surprisingly the word 'pauperized' was deleted in one of the revisions.[99] If Henry or his courtiers had actually read the *Chronica maiora*, the consequences would have been explosive. That Paris appreciated the danger is suggested by passages marked up for revision with the comment 'warning since offensive'. Once he refused to name the king's evil counsellors on the grounds that to do so would be 'unsafe'.[100] Another passage, related to the king's ministers, was to be deleted 'since offensive to friends'.[101] The *Chronica maiora* was surely kept locked well away during royal visits. Well might Paris refer to the '*bella*' he could suffer by telling the truth.

Were these '*bella*' raised most directly by forces within St Albans itself? Paris said that he had written the *Chronica maiora* 'for the love of God and the love of the blessed protomartyr St. Alban'.[102] The monks of St Albans were clearly the first and primary audience for the work. They had backed it with abundant resources.[103] But were they troubled by the results? There was firstly the danger, as we have said, that the king or some other victim would actually want to see what had been written. The consequences of that would have been as disastrous for St Albans as for Matthew himself. Another problem was that the *Chronica maiora* threatened to be un-exportable. There was, of course, a long tradition of chronicles passing between religious houses, with one house copying that of another. Yet the *Chronica maiora*, in Vaughan's words, never 'seems to have passed into general circulation' and was 'was virtually unknown outside St Albans'.[104] Vaughan thought this was 'extraordinary'. It was not extraordinary at all. There was no way the monks were going to export what could only get them into trouble.

The same fate, and for the same reason, nearly overtook the only one of Paris' chronicles which did have a substantial afterlife. This was his *Flores historiarum*. Paris had written the *Flores*, a highly abridged version of the *Chronica maiora*, for Westminster Abbey. The section between 1241 and 1249 is in his own hand and has a several original passages about the Abbey. Some of the chronicle would have appealed to Henry. Thus Paris told how he was building the new abbey 'in the manner of a most Christian king'.[105] Yet there were other passages in a very different vein. Paris could not restrain himself. He included venomous remarks from the *Chronica maiora* and sometimes added to them. 'These things I have been led to write about, that the inconstancy of a womanly king might be known to posterity,' he declared.[106] This was not the sort of thing which could be sent to Westminster Abbey of all places. Nor was it. Paris gave up adapting the *Flores* around 1250, a natural point for it to go to Westminster. But he never sent it, probably appreciating that it would be unacceptable. Instead, the text seems to have languished at St Albans till the early 1260s, when it was obtained by Pershore Abbey. It was only later in that decade that it finally reached Westminster by, which time Paris' offensive passages had lost topicality and were anyway buried beneath later material.[107]

Not everyone at St Albans was worried about Paris' tone. John of Wallingford in his own chronicle echoed his master's sentiments entirely. Paris' continuator was another matter. He admired Paris intensely, yet his own work between 1259 and 1261 was far less strident.[108] While enthusiastic about the reform of the realm, he set out fully and fairly the complaints the king made against his council in 1261.[109] He also, more remarkably, made no criticisms of the pope although he had ample opportunities to do so.[110] Striking too is the role he played in the second and final revision of the *Chronica maiora*, which Vaughan dates to near the end of Paris' life. This revision was more extensive than the earlier effort since it involved not the marking up of passages for deletion, but the rewriting of them altogether, much as in the *Historia Anglorum*. Vaughan believed that Paris made these changes at the end of his life because he felt his previous criticisms had been unjust, but, as we have seen, there is nothing in the *Chronica maiora* to suggest such a change of heart.[111] The great majority of the changes, moreover, were made not by Paris himself but by his continuator.[112] Since at least one of them can actually be dated to after Paris' death, that may be true of others.[113] The changes are not out of line with those Paris himself had made to the *Historia Anglorum*, but that the continuator carried on making them suggests that he was genuinely worried by the accusations in the *Chronica maiora*.

Paris, therefore, fearful of outside reaction and under pressure from within, *was* on occasion prepared to please man and tone down his writings; hence perhaps the troubled way in which he recalled his decision to abandon the *Chronica maiora* in 1250. Nonetheless, he bent to the world with the greatest reluctance. The *Chronica maiora* remained to the end a sustained critique of the age. Over twenty-five years, Paris assaulted evil, praised good and testified to the truth as he saw it, trying where possible to trace the working out of God's plan. If he had known how far his views have offended some later historians, he might well have shaken his head and reflected that in telling the truth he had indeed provoked man. The material for Paris' critique was provided by his massive record of events, arranged chapter by chapter in chronological order. Paris was certainly capable of adorning the tale in the cause, as he would have seen it, of bringing out important truths. But a comprehensive analysis and fact-check of the *Chronica maiora* would testify to his colossal labours and establish his reputation as a hugely informed and often perceptive chronicler of his times.[114] In Paris' mind the record and critique were inseparable. Both make the *Chronica maiora* a unique work of history.

In the final part of this chapter I will turn to the last phase of Paris' life and thus to his account of the revolution of 1258–59.[115] In the *Chronica maiora*, the beginning of the revolution at the Westminster Parliament of April and May 1258 is written up in Paris' own hand, as, to this point, is the whole of the *Chronica maiora's* final volume, which begins in 1254 and is now preserved in the British Library.[116] Soon after the Westminster Parliament, however, in fact from just before the start of the Oxford Parliament in June, a new hand takes over, copying out the remainder of the *Chronica maiora* from what, as we have seen, must have been very full Parisian drafts. The last chapter transcribed was that recounting the execution of Walter de Scotteny at the end of May 1259. The presumption is that Paris died soon afterwards.[117]

Vaughan himself was critical of Paris' performance in this last phase: 'it is clear that Matthew understood very little of the nature and significance of the baronial reform movement, and still less of the events of 1258'.[118] There are certainly odd gaps in Paris' account, but the explanation for these, as will be seen, is more complex than simply a lack of understanding. In fact, Paris' account of the revolution often shows remarkable knowledge and insight, as well as exemplifying some of the points of technique we have already discussed. It also brings out another facet of Paris as a historian, not so far discussed, namely the importance he attached to documents and his desire to preserve them.[119]

Paris gives a characteristic account of the Westminster Parliament in April and May 1258. Although it lasted all told for less than a month, he divides his narrative, which takes up five printed pages, into four separate chapters.[120] The first two are consecutive, but between the second and the third and the third and the fourth are chapters dealing with other events, most of them either dated by Paris to this period or datable to it from other sources.[121] Paris' account of the parliament is factually valuable for it preserves otherwise unknown but perfectly believable confrontations between William de Valence, on one side, and Simon de Montfort and Richard de Clare on the other.[122] It also gives Paris the opportunity to point to the truth as he sees it, with the result that it is difficult to distinguish his own critique of Henry's rule with that offered at the parliament. When Paris comes, however, in the final chapter, to the king's actual capitulation, he leaves the reader with a sense of anticlimax. Paris builds up with a long list of accusations hurled at Henry and then continues:

> The king however, coming to himself, although late, since he understood the truth of the accusations, humbled himself, declaring that he had too often been bewitched by evil counsel, and he promised under a great oath, on the altar and feretory of Saint Edward, that, fully and openly correcting his former errors, he would readily comply with his native-born subjects.[123]

By itself, as an explanation of the king's capitulation, this can hardly be complete. After all, Henry had faced vocal criticisms at parliament after parliament in the 1240s and 1250s and had never before acknowledged their truth and given way to reform. Why did he do so now? At the time two explanations were offered. The official one, given in letters patent issued by the king on 2 May, and later in a baronial letter to the pope, was that the king had agreed to reform of the realm quite willingly in return for the prospect of a tax to prosecute the Sicilian business.[124] The second reason, unofficial, was that the king had been coerced into submission by an armed march on his hall at Westminster, which left him for a moment fearing he was a prisoner. Since this account, in the annals of Tewkesbury Abbey, is circumstantial and probably from a newsletter, it carries conviction.[125] Yet Paris says nothing about such an episode. Why?

One reason might be the effects of age, something which nearly all commentators seem to detect in Paris. 'But it is fair to note that Matthew was at this time an old man, no doubt with failing powers,' wrote Vaughan as some excuse for the account of 1258.[126] Well, steady on! At this time Paris was around sixty, much the same age as I am now.[127] That may, of course, serve to confirm the hypothesis of decline, but many historians do excellent work in their sixties and indeed later than that. Life expectancy in the thirteenth century was much shorter than it is today, but there is no reason to think that the aging process, especially for well-fed Benedictine monks, was much different.[128] This does not rule out the possibility that Paris was increasingly impeded by ill health, but the evidence for that is hardly convincing. Madden and Vaughan drew attention to the decline in his handwriting, but while it may become looser in his later works, it remains perfectly legible, even in the last example which we have from a document copied after March 1259.[129] Sometimes the trouble seems merely to be more that Paris needed a new nib or a darker ink. There is also nothing in the fact that the last part of the *Chronica maiora* was copied out by another scribe.[130] That Paris remained perfectly able to write, we have just seen. Most probably he had simply fallen behind in making the fair copy of the *Chronica maiora*, as he had often done before, with the result that it was written up by another scribe after his death. In any case, whatever Paris' physical state, the last part of the *Chronica maiora* shows no decline in energy or quality. The sixty-seven printed pages of 1258 place it in a mid table eleventh in the twenty-two years post 1235. Post 1248, when Paris started to copy documents into his *Liber additamentorum* rather than into his main text, it comes in fourth.[131] Indeed, there is more about 1258 than there is for any year between 1253 and 1257. If the text contains mistakes and repetitions, these had been equally characteristic of his earlier work.[132] Paris, moreover, was assiduous to the end in collecting information and writing it up into draft chapters. One of the last things he wrote, the account of the quarrel in 1259 between Simon de Montfort and Richard de Clare, shows him at his most informed and his most vivid.[133]

Why then did Paris give so sketchy an account of the king's capitulation in 1258? The barons had good reason for keeping the march on the king's hall quiet since it conflicted with their claim of royal consent,

consent which meant no justification for revolution was necessary since none had taken place. But I find it unbelievable that Paris was ignorant of this dramatic event, which must have been widely known however much the barons wished to conceal it. Rather I would suggest a different explanation. Far from failing to appreciate the significance of what had happened, he appreciated it all too well. What had taken place was a unique act of violence against the king. Paris had written about rebellions against Henry III before, expanding Wendover's account of Richard Marshal's in 1233–34, but that was both a long time ago, and had not involved any direct assault on the king. Indeed, Richard Marshal had been careful to respect the king's person.[134] Where he saw it clearly, Paris believed in drawing out the truth, but here, in 1258, he was unsure where the truth lay. Had the barons, as the chronicler Thomas Wykes later put it, 'gathered together against their lord and king and anointed of the Lord'?[135] Even in 1258, Paris would have acknowledged that Henry's almsgiving, masses and general religiosity weighed heavily in the balance against his faults.[136] He did not deserve to be treated like King John. But if then Paris was troubled by the political morality of the king's coercion, why did he not say so? The answer is that this would have delegitimised the reform of the realm in which he intensely believed. Paris therefore preferred to cover up what had actually happened and go along with the official version that Henry had accepted reform perfectly freely.[137]

There is one other factor which helps explain Paris' emasculation of the Westminster Parliament. When he wrote up his account he had no idea that things were going to turn out all right. Instead, he feared the country was on the brink of a civil war. He ended the section about the parliament by telling how a group of leading magnates, 'taking precautions for themselves, confederated together; and since they vehemently feared the traps and snares of the aliens, and greatly suspected the nets of the king, they went about protected by arms and horses and a copious company'.[138] Had Paris known that the barons would soon be firmly in the saddle with Henry now going along 'willingly, *gratanter*' with their reforms, he might have been readier to acknowledge how the revolution had begun.[139] God would then have bestowed his blessing on baronial methods. But when he wrote his account of the Oxford Parliament Paris did not know.

There are several reasons for thinking that Paris wrote up his account of the Westminster Parliament very soon afterwards and certainly before the reassuring events at Oxford and Winchester in June and July. The *Chronica maiora*, in its last years, had sometimes lagged considerably behind events. The section around May 1257 was probably written as late as March 1258.[140] Yet there is no sign of any time lag in the narrative of the Westminster Parliament. Nothing in it shows any knowledge of later events. This is not because Paris, in writing up the *Chronica maiora*, had stopped looking forward. Indeed, just before the Westminster Parliament, he observed that a '*sequens sermo*' would reveal the resistance to the papal envoy, Mansuetus. This, however, merely pointed on a few chapters to the events in late April and early May.[141] There is indeed one telling sign that Paris, when writing up the *Chronica maiora* for April, did *not* know about events in the coming July. In the chapter immediately before that on Mansuetus, he told how Lord Edward, in order to raise money, had given lands to William de Valence in return for some of his superfluous treasure. He then observed that for both of them this was a bad omen, in William's case because it suggested he would be despoiled of his superfluities. Would Paris have written as tamely and vaguely as that had he known that, within three months, Valence would be expelled from the kingdom and stripped not merely of his superfluities but of everything he had?[142]

Paris therefore missed the violent denouement of the Westminster Parliament because he was troubled by its propriety and meaning.[143] Is that concern even reflected in his handwriting? It is certainly a remarkable fact that the tendentious account of the king's capitulation is one of the most illegible parts of the *Chronica maiora*, with the ink faint and the pen scratchy, as though Paris just wanted to get it down as soon as possible.[144] His fears for the future may also explain why he decided to bring the *Chronica maiora* right up to date at this point.[145] Having done so in early May, he added nothing for at least a couple of months, as though he was anxiously waiting on events. The entry after the parliament cannot have been written till early July since it tells of how the north winds blew throughout April, May and the greater part of June, destroying hope of future crops.[146] That Paris was so worried is a tribute to his perception as an historian, for it shows he understood the nature of these revolutionary events. In thinking that the kingdom was close to civil war he was almost certainly correct.[147]

Beyond the immediate crisis, there continue to be odd gaps in Paris' record of 1258–59. At the Oxford Parliament, he described the oath to support the baronial enterprise and the appointment of Hugh Bigod as justiciar by the nobles, but he has nothing about the council of fifteen and its power to select the king's ministers and control his seal, which lay at the heart of baronial control. Instead, there is just the vague statement that the king swore 'willingly' to comply with the counsels of the magnates.[148] Yet Paris cannot be blamed for these lacunae for the precise authority of the council was never publicly proclaimed, almost certainly because it was considered too revolutionary to be openly acknowledged.[149] What is striking, and testimony to Paris' belief in the importance of documents, is that he was clearly frustrated by this failure to proclaim the reforms. 'However, they [the barons] still did not plan to publish what had been decided,' he grumbled, having told how (in July 1258) the Londoners were asked if they would adhere to the '*statutis baronum*'.[150] When Paris did get documents from this period he made sure to preserve them. The writ commissioning the inquiry of the four knights was gummed into the *Liber additamentorum*, while the baronial letter of explanation to the pope was copied out in his own hand, as was also the draft legislation of March 1259 on suit of court.[151] In a heading he appended to the latter in the *Liber additamentorum*, one senses both his pleasure at having some '*statuta baronum*' to record and his relief at the consensus which produced them:

> This is the new provision of the magnates of England published at the New Temple in the month of March in the forty-third year of the reign of King Henry III for the common utility of all the kingdom and the king, by whose consent and will that provision and publication proceeded.[152]

As Vaughan noted, this provision is the last example we have of Paris' hand. To the end, he remained as assiduous in copying out documents as he did composing the drafts of the *Chronica maiora*. Indeed, the provision of March 1259 was probably the last thing Paris did write for (as Paul Brand observes) it breaks off at the bottom of a page in midsentence, with the following page left blank.[153] Fittingly, it looks as though it was in the act of writing that Paris was struck down. The provision of March 1259 is scarcely the most riveting of documents, and perhaps the initial excitement of getting the text followed by the boredom of actually copying it out hastened Paris' demise![154] But in copying it out at all, he set a standard his successor could not meet since, as the blank page shows, the latter made no attempt to finish off the document.[155]

Paris' account of 1258–59 stands up in other ways. When set against the official record, he clearly exaggerated the brutality of the attack on Shere in Surrey by the men of the bishop-elect of Winchester. But official records themselves can mislead, and Paris' account of the way Henry refused justice to the victim of the attack, John Fitzgeoffrey, may well be more accurate than that found in the plea roll of the new justiciar, with its need to justify the revolution. Paris thus has an emollient Henry begging John to withdraw his complaint and not bring scandal on the bishop. The plea roll, by contrast, alleges that he simply 'did not wish to hear him'.[156] Later, Paris' account of Richard of Cornwall's return to England early in 1259 is confirmed by record evidence.[157] He is also well informed about the fall of William de Valence's steward, William de Bussey, and Bussey's role in the killing of a boy at Trumpington in Cambridgeshire.[158] If Paris speculates wildly about the crimes of the Jew Elyas le Evesk, he at least knew about Elyas' conversion to Christianity.[159] Paris appreciated the vigour with which the realm was being reformed. 'The magnates of England', he wrote, in one of his very last chapters, 'attended in salutary fashion to the reforms ("*statutis*") which they had started, assiduous and confederated together in wholly abolishing evil customs and injuries and corrupt practices'.[160] In terms of detail, Paris knew about the consent of the Londoners to the revolution, the inquiry of the four knights, the activities of the justiciar, the restrictions on the sheriffs and the Ordinance of the Magnates.[161] Had he lived he would doubtless have put in something about the provisions of March 1259. His view that Henry appeared to accept the reforms 'willingly' is supported by a contemporary newsletter.[162]

All in all, Paris' narrative of 1258–59 is a remarkable achievement and one enhanced by a final jewel, namely the picture given of Simon de

Montfort. Vaughan's statement that 'of Simon de Montfort [Paris] has little to say' is simply wrong, both for the period of Henry's personal rule and even more for the revolution of 1258–59.[163] In Paris' first chapter about the Westminster Parliament, Montfort nearly comes to blows with William de Valence. In the last chapter he complains about Valence before the whole parliament and demands justice.[164] At the Oxford Parliament, having, so Paris affirms, voluntarily given up his royal castles of Kenilworth and Odiham despite spending much money on them, he threatens Valence with the loss of his head if he does not make equivalent resignations.[165] A little later, the king cries out that he fears Montfort more than all the thunder and lightning in the world, because (so Paris speculates) the earl 'vigorously and fervently prosecuted the provision, namely that they [the barons] should compel the king and all adversaries to stand by their counsels'. The confrontation itself has Paris at his most vivid and circumstantial for it occurs when Henry, going downriver from Westminster to dine, was forced by an approaching storm to disembark at the palace of the bishop of Durham on the Strand, where Montfort was staying.[166] Next year, it is Paris who preserves the acrimonious quarrel with Richard de Clare, with Montfort angrily declaring that he did not care to live with men who were oath breakers and refused to accept the '*statuta salubres*'.[167] For Paris, Montfort's presence is essential to the movement of reform, and it is gravely weakened by his absences in France.[168] No other baronial leader is given anywhere near the same prominence. Paris even shows insight into the moral imperatives which governed Montfort's personal and political life. Thus it was in this last period that he rewrote an old passage for 1238 to say that Montfort, on his return from Rome in that year, ordered 'in the name of justice' his debts to be paid and everything which his ministers had taken from the people to be restored.[169] In its concern with the oppression of the people, this mirrors exactly the terms of Montfort's will, drawn up in December 1258. It also, of course, coincides with one of the main themes of the baronial reforms.[170] Were it not for Paris' death, we would think these passages were written up with the benefit of hindsight. In fact, Paris, perceptive and prophetic, captures brilliantly the driving force and ideological stance which were soon to make Montfort the ruler of England. Paris, far from being in decline in 1258–59, was at the height of his powers.

Notes

1. I am grateful to Barbara Harvey, Margaret Howell, John Maddicott and Björn Weiler for commenting on a draft of this chapter.
2. For Paris' life, see Chapter 1 of Vaughan 1958c, reissued with supplementary bibliography (1979) [hereafter Vaughan] and the article in the *Oxford Dictionary of National Biography* by Simon Lloyd and Rebecca Reader: www.oxforddnb.com/view/article/21268. For Paris' wider concerns outside Britain, see Chapter 4, 90–117. See also Papp Reed 2022. Although Paris also wrote a *Historia Anglorum* and a *Flores historiarum*, these are, for the most part, abridgements of the *Chronica maiora*, as on an even shorter scale is his *Abbreviatio chronicorum*. For novel interpretations of his chronicling career and narrative process recently published see also Weiss 2018, Greasley 2021 and Papp Reed 2022.
3. The *Chronica maiora*, with the passages copied directly from Wendover in small type, is printed in Luard 1872–83. Kay 1969 argued that Paris took over from Wendover in the course of 1234, not 1235, as usually supposed. His hypothesis has some weight. In his *Matthew Paris*, Vaughan took the usual view that the changeover was in 1235 (28–30), but in Vaughan 1986, 8 he stated that Paris might have started in 1234 or 1235. He was presumably influenced here by Kay's paper, which he cited in the supplementary bibliography (276) to the reissue of *Matthew Paris* in 1979.
4. Luard 1872–83, iii. 334–640 (1236–39); iv. i–655 (1240–47); v. 1–728 (1248–58). Wendover's work is printed in Hewlett 1886–89. Wendover becomes original from about 1202 although the text was written up or at least revised in the 1220s. His longest year (fifty pages) is 1215, partly because of writing out papal and royal documents including, of course, a version of Magna Carta. After a fallow period in the Minority he began to write more, averaging between 1226 and 1233 twenty and a half pages per year. One wonders if he had Paris' assistance in this period. The classic study of the relationship between Wendover and Paris is Galbraith 1944. Much new light on Wendover's career is shed in Crook 2015.
5. Luard 1864–69, iii. 143–211.
6. Luard 1864–69; Galbraith 1944, 42, 24.
7. Galbraith 1944, 38.
8. Vaughan 1958c, 129. For Paris' range see also Gransden 1974b, chapter 16, 'Matthew Paris', at 361–63.
9. Galbraith 1944, 37; Vaughan 1958c, 134.
10. Vaughan 1958c, 143.
11. Vaughan 1958c, 126, 151–52. Gransden 1974b, chapter 16 is much more positive.
12. Vaughan in his book is freely and, to my mind, fairly critical of Powicke 1944. Powicke's review of Vaughan 1958, 482–85 is a masterpiece of

condescension in which from Olympian heights he puts a cocksure youngster in his place. Powicke, however, writes perceptively about Vaughan's attitude to Paris (482). Both Barbara Harvey and Hugh Lawrence have discussed with me Powicke's reaction to Vaughan.

13. Holt 1964; Gransden 1974b, chapter 16; Hilpert 1980; Lewis 1987; Le Goff 1996, 432–50; Reader 1996, chapter 7; Reader 1999; Weiler 2000; Weiler 2009. For the *Oxford Dictionary of National Biography*, see note 2 of this chapter. The most recent examination of Paris' narrative strategies is found in Kjaer 2013.
14. This is not really a theme of Powicke 1944, despite its title.
15. For the time lag, see Vaughan 1958c, 8–9, 59–61.
16. Luard 1872–83, v. 601–18.
17. Luard 1872–83, v. 611–13, 632, 643 etc. etc.
18. Alternative readings of Matthew's narrative strategy, a case for his conscious 'plotting' of subjects and themes and his projection of an authorial self are set out in Weiss 2018 and Papp Reed 2022, 25–53 at 31, 37–38.
19. What follows builds on the brief remarks found in Vaughan 1958c, 9, 136. Given the level of detail, Paris must have been taking such notes from the start in 1234–5, although, when he came to write up the fair copy, he often inserted new information and new ideas. I think Paris always intended a continuation of Wendover's *Flores Historiarum* but for a contrary view, see Greasley 2019.
20. Thus in 1257 Paris says envoys were sent to France to prolong the truces, but in another account, perhaps representing an earlier draft, he says they were sent for 'secret' reasons: Luard 1872–83, v. 611, 620. For other possible examples see Luard 1872–83, v. 114, 136 (on the Jews); v. 490–91, 496–97 (on Grosseteste's miracles); 504, 523 (on John de Gray); 649, 651 (on the king's return from Wales); 688, 695 (on the house of the Franciscans at Bury).
21. For John, see Vaughan 1958c, 66–77. See also Chapter 10, 226–27. There is no printed text of his chronicle which is found in BL Cotton MS Julius D VII. However, since John died at the St Albans cell of Wymondham in 1258, the chronicle became known locally and was copied quite fully at St Benet at Hulme and, with many more omissions, at Norwich. These chronicles have been printed: Ellis 1859; Luard 1859. Luard's text indicates in larger type the passages which are not found in Paris (and thus in effect what is original to John). Unfortunately Ellis' edition does not do this. Vaughan 1958c, prints (70–77) the original material between 1100 and 1258 which had not already appeared in the two Roll Series volumes.
A proper edition of John's chronicle would shed interesting light on the methods of writing history at St Albans even if it would not reveal hitherto unknown historical detail.

22. Ellis 1859, 188; Luard 1872-83, v. 600.
23. Vaughan 1958c, 9. See note 19 of this chapter and Luard 1872-83, v. 611-12, 618, 620-21 (on the return of the abbot of Westminster and the elect of Salisbury). For an example of a very misplaced chapter in 1258 see note 131 of this chapter.
24. Ellis 1859, 175; Luard 1872-83, v. 359-60; vi. 406; Vaughan 1958c, 72 and see his comment on 68. Another passage not found in Paris is where Henry III first swears to go on a pilgrimage to Pontigny and then changes his mind: Ellis 1859, 177. For record evidence on this see *CR 1251-3*, 433. Wallingford's chronicle also seems to be the only source for Richard of Cornwall destroying his fish weirs in accordance with Magna Carta: Luard 1859, 131.
25. For Paris' cursive hand, see Vaughan 1953, 376-94 at 387.
26. Luard 1872-83, v. 695n2.
27. Luard 1872-83, 748n1 and illustrated as the volume's frontispiece; Vaughan 1958c, 7-8. See note 27 of this chapter.
28. The final chapter of the *Chronica maiora* concludes with the statement, 'It is to be known that thus far wrote the venerable man, brother Matthew Paris.' The scribe then added that the subsequent text was by another brother, unworthy to unlatch Paris' shoe. The scribe followed this observation with a drawing of Paris on his death bed, under the rubric 'here died Matthew Paris'. This would seem to imply that Paris passed away soon after the last events recorded in the *Chronica maiora* is For the obituary see Luard 1872-83, v. 748n1, illustrated as the volume's frontispiece. The final volume of the *Chronica maiora* is preserved in the British Library as BL, Royal MS 14 C VII. For comment on the obituary, see Vaughan 1958c, 7-8 and Sir Frederic Madden's introduction to Madden 1866-69, i. xxiii, note 2.
29. Luard 1872-83, v. 732-34; for an earlier example see Vaughan 1958c, 9.
30. Paris, had he lived, might also have changed the passage where he says he will commit nothing to writing about the negotiations with France since nothing has been published: Luard 1872-83, v. 741 and see also the bottom of 740.
31. For mistakes and repetitions see Vaughan 1958c, 37-38.
32. Sometimes, however, repetitious passages are marked up for deletion: for example, Luard, 1872-83, v. 527, 564. Powicke 1959, 484, in his review of Vaughan, asked how Paris could have written up the *Chronica maiora* if all he had was notes to go on. He thus posited a lost original from which the present text was copied. In effect, as Vaughan himself would probably have pointed out, Paris' very full drafts, often done soon after events, were the lost original.
33. Vaughan 1953c, 384. For Matthew's assistants see Chapter 13, 267-68.
34. Luard 1872-83, v. 20-21, 23.

35. Vaughan 1958c, 67.
36. The implication of the obituary (see note 27 of this chapter) is that the continuation ran on in the *Chronica maiora* itself. It is not there now. The death of Paris comes at the end of the folio and the following folios are later material. However, the text of the continuation is preserved in the continuation of Paris' *Flores historiarum*: Luard 1890, ii. 426–70; see note 38 of this chapter.
37. Luard 1872–83, v. 661–729; Luard 1890, ii. 440–61.
38. Luard 1872–83, v. 467–68, 475–84; Luard 1890, ii. 437–38, 440–42, 446.
39. For the cessation of historical writing at St Albans and its later revival, see Galbraith 1937, xxix and Gransden 1982, 4–5. For the Pershore continuation, see Carpenter 2012b. The whole text between 1251 and 1265 was copied at Pershore, using down to 1259 mostly Paris' writings and between 1259 and 1261 the writings of his continuator. The chronicle then uses material from Pershore itself.
40. Luard 1872–83, v. 197–98.
41. For example, Holt 1964, 68–69, 78–79, 82, 84; Langmuir 1972, especially 463–69; Summerson 1992; Le Goff 1996, 432–50, especially 432, 434, 444–45, 450.
42. An odd example of a mistaken date concerns Henry III's visit to St Albans in the second half of 1251. Paris dated this visit to the octave of the nativity of the Virgin (15 September) whereas Henry's itinerary shows it took place between 28 and 30 August: Luard 1872–83, v. 257–58. Was this a case where Paris' notes failed to give a date, leaving him to rely on memory? For another example of a mistake concerning Henry's itinerary see Luard 1872–83, v. 51–52. Here Paris dated Henry's visit to Huntingdon to Hilary 1249. In fact, it took place in the following August.
43. Luard 1872–83, v. 423–25, 445, vi. 284n1, 287. That Henry's fears were real, if unfounded, is argued in Ellis 1952, 179–80. See also Maddicott 2010, 211–13.
44. Luard 1872–83 v. 339; *CR 1251-3*, 242–43; see Powicke 1947, 324n2; Clanchy 1968; Summerson 1992; Carpenter 1996, 78–79. Vaughan 1958c singles out (134) as 'Perhaps the most blatant example of his abuse of historical material' Paris' account of papal demands for taxation in 1244, which included speeches for and against. The whole was lifted from Roger of Wendover's account of a similar episode in 1226: Luard 1872–83, iii. 103; iv. 374–75. There are many other cases where one suspects speeches have been largely made up; for example, Richard of Cornwall's in 1238: Luard, 1872–83, iii. 477–78.
45. *CPR 1247-58*, 537; Luard 1872–83, v. 611.
46. *CPR 1247-58*, 536; Luard 1872–83, v. 612; Howell 1998, 274. Paris also mentions the queen receiving the Cantilupe wardship. This came from

Edward, which perhaps explains why there is no record evidence for the transfer.

47. *CPR 1247–58*, 542; Luard 1864–69, i. 376–80; Luard 1872–83, v. 613.
48. Williams ab Ithel 1860, 91–93; Luard 1872–83, v. 613–14.
49. *Foedera*, I, i, 354 (*CPR 1247–58*, 541).
50. In view of his usual reputation, it is surprising how often historians testify to Paris' understanding of events and reasonable accuracy: Madden 1866–69, iii, pp. xxix–xx; Vaughan 1958c, 136; Clanchy 1978, 25–48; Staniland 1986; Carpenter 1996, chapter 7; Jotischky 2004, especially 74–75, 82–83; Liu 2007; Smith 2010. I am grateful to Henry Summerson for letting me see a copy of his unpublished paper 'Issues of law in the chronicles of Matthew Paris'. Summerson shows how Paris' accounts of legal actions varied between the erroneous and the substantially true. His conclusion is that 'there are probably as many instances of record evidence largely or wholly corroborating the chronicle as there are of contradiction'. Taking Paris as a whole, I would put the balance decisively in his favour.
51. Luard 1872–83, iv. 594; v. 19, 277–78, 370.
52. Smith 2010, 31.
53. Contrast Le Goff 1996, 444–45.
54. I consider Simon de Montfort later. There is no space here to discuss Paris' treatment of Louis IX, but I cannot agree with Le Goff's very hostile account in his 1996, 432–50. It fails to recognise that Paris is a strictly contemporary witness, which makes what he says about Louis all the more valuable. It is also contradicted by the extensive use Le Goff makes of Paris' testimony.
55. Madden 1866–69, ii. 389. Paris' revisions are discussed more fully later in this chapter. For juxtaposition of praise and criticism, see Luard 1872–83, iv. 503–05, 586, 590, 594, 598; v. 55–60, with the praise (for his conduct in the Alton robbery case) sharpened in Madden 1866–69, iii. 47 and Luard 1872–83, v. 114, 130, 316–17, 319–20, 44–51, 482, 539, 567, 569, 573–74; Luard 1890, ii. 361; and see also what is said later in this chapter about the annal of 1247 and the ceremony of the Holy Blood. Paris gave a balanced account of the career of the king's leading minister, John Mansel: Liu 2007, 159–73. Lars Kjaer, however, argues that Henry manipulated his accounts of Henry's Christmases 'in a manner that aligned itself to his various authorial agendas', agendas usually hostile to the king: 'Matthew Paris and the royal Christmas', with the quotation at 154 and a qualification in note 9 to page 142.
56. Galbraith 1944, 39–40. Galbraith suspected that the annual summaries which Paris introduced into the *Chronica maiora* were an attempt to achieve 'some sort of synthesis of discrete events'. They are, however, too short to be very effective although the account of the year's weather with which they usually begin is useful.

57. Vaughan 1958c, 143. Weiler (2009, 268) too has reservations about this method.
58. Vaughan 1958c, 104, 129.
59. See, for example, his life of Edmund of Abingdon: Lawrence 1960, 222-89. The same is true of Paris' account of the abbots of St Albans in Riley 1867-69, with ii. 183-324 being Paris' own work. I have not studied them in any detail, but my impression is that Paris' *Historia Anglorum* and *Flores historiarum* follow, in abbreviated form, the pattern of the *Chronica maiora*. The *Historia Anglorum* has the same type of chapter headings. In the *Flores*, the headings become more frequent in the section between 1241 and 1249, which Paris wrote out himself. In both works one finds Paris' characteristic pointing on to future events as discussed later in this chapter; for example, Madden 1866-69, ii 465; Luard 1890, ii. 242, 312, 338.
60. As Galbraith (1944, 20) pointed out, Paris also inherited Wendover's 'constitutional' attitude.
61. Luard 1872-83, iii. 540n5.
62. For example, Luard 1872-83, iii. 471; iv. 83, 188-89, 198, 202, 628; v. 22, 74, 102, 117, 136, 439, 470, 513, 516, 622, 680, 737.
63. Luard 1872-83, v. 135-36: 'Sed quae simul contigerunt, simul minime poterunt enarrari.'
64. Luard 1872-83, v. 439, 470, 513, 516, 737.
65. Luard 1872-83, iv. 618. See also the marginal note in Luard 1872-83, iv. 56 and heading in Luard 1872-83, iv. 146 where Paris used the word 'anticipatio' to indicate that events which took place some time ago were inserted at these points.
66. For an instance where Paris, having referred to Gilbert Basset, was led to give an account of his death and other events later in the year, before returning to events in their previous chronological sequence, see Luard 1872-83, iv. 89. See also his addition about Sir Geoffrey Langley: Luard 1872-83, v. 340. Paris did, on occasion, tell stories in a continuous sequence – for example, that of alleged crucifixion by the Lincoln Jews of a Christian boy in 1255: Luard 1872-83, v. 516-19 – although more is added in 1256 (546, 552). For this episode, see Carpenter 2012a, 129-48.
67. For Paris' statement of his purpose, copied from Wendover, see Luard 1872-83, i, 1-2. For discussion, see Weiler 2009, 258-62, 267-68. For Bede's example see Campbell 1986, especially 10-19.
68. For signs of the last days see Luard 1872-83, iv. 603-04; v. 302, 35, 175-77, 261.
69. Luard 1872-83, v. 197.
70. 'Bonum quippe est ad Dei laudem eventus rerum notabilium scribendo perpetuare, ut subsequentes legendo castigentur, mala quae digna sunt ultione devitando, et bona quae Dominus plene remunerat operando':

Madden 1866–69, iii. 319–20. This is from Paris' *Abbreviatio chronicorum*. The passage in which they come is discussed more fully later.
71. Riley 1867–69, ii. 324.
72. Luard 1872–83, v. 102.
73. Luard 1872–83, v. 470.
74. Luard 1872–83, v. 77, 87–88, 102, 117, 170–01. See Le Goff 1996, 440. For references to God's power and will, see Luard 1872–83, iv. 91, 100, 151, 225, 238; v. 492–93, 523.
75. For Paris' subtle arrangement of evidence to make God's judgement clear, see Kjaer 2013, for example in his account of the marriage of Henry's daughter and Alexander III of Scotland (pp. 145–48).
76. Vaughan 1958c, 130–34.
77. Luard 1872–83, v. 469–70. See Madden 1866–69, iii, xxix–xxx.
78. Vaughan 1958c, 132–33. See Weiler 2009, 274–75.
79. Weiler 2009, 275–76 and 258–62 with the quotations at 275 and 276. Likewise Clanchy observes that Paris wanted 'to give facts life and significance' in line with his didactic purpose: Clanchy 1978, 47.
80. Vaughan 1958c, 151.
81. Luard 1872–83, v. 469.
82. 'Hic quoque proposuit frater Matheus Cronica sua terminare, propter imminentia quedam pericula. Si enim de potentibus vera dicantur et scripture commendentur, bella parantur ei; si taceantur, vel bona pro malis annotentur, mutilabitur, et de blandimentis, adulationibus et falsitatibus graviter opus totale condempnabitur et redarguetur': Madden 1866–69, iii. 319 (the *Abbreviatio chronicorum*) and xxix–xxx.
83. Vaughan 1958c, 113–14.
84. Contrast Luard 1872–83, v. 197–98; Madden 1866–69, iii. 96–67.
85. Madden 1866–69, iii. xxxii–iii; Luard 1872–83, iii. xiv–xv; iv. xii–xiii; Vaughan 1958c, 123–24; Gransden 1974b, 370–71.
86. For Paris' correction of a particular factual error, see Carpenter 1990, 245n11. Paris seems initially to have believed letters from the east about Louis IX's successes but subsequent events, as he lamented, showed the stories were utterly false. See Luard 1872–83, vi. 167–69. I take it the headings pointing to the falsity of the letters were written later, as did Luard 1872–83, v. 87, 118. Paris commented (118) that the episode weakened his trust in letters.
87. In Weiler's (2009, 274) view Paris became more outspoken with age, not less.
88. Luard 1872–83, v. 676, 680–81, 68–90, 741.
89. Luard 1872–83, v. 684. For Paris' technique of expressing views through third parties, see Weiler 2009, 273–74.
90. Vaughan 1958c, 117. Examples are Luard 1872–83, iii. 265, 294, 475, 487, 490, 493, 616–18; iv. 3, 63, 228, 230–31, 252, 457–58, 505, 561.

91. Luard 1872–83, iii. 381.
92. Vaughan 1958c, 117. This is my interpretation of what happened.
93. I wonder whether there was sometimes an ironic subtext to Paris' alterations. For example (Madden 1866–69, iii. 51 and 52n3; Vaughan 1958c, 122), when Paris replaced coruscating criticism of the way the friars sold indulgences for the benefit of the crusade with 'in order that Christ's faithful should not be deprived of the advantage of the indulgence . . . [the friars] courteously received a redemption according to the means of each'.
94. Madden 1866–69, iii. xxxii–iii; Vaughan 1958c, 120–23. Vaughan 1958c (123) thought the changes were probably made between 1256 and 1259. For the contrasting accounts in the *Chronica maiora* and the *Historia Anglorum* of the wedding of Henry's daughter, Margaret, to Alexander III of Scotland in 1251, see Kjaer 2013, 145–47.
95. Madden 1866–69, ii. 461n5.
96. Luard 1872–83, iv. 644–45.
97. See Vaughan 1958c, 12–18 for an impressive list of informants.
98. It is noticeable how Paris did not spoil the positive impression by criticising the way the ceremony was linked to the knighting of William de Valence.
99. Luard 1872–83, iv. 639, 650.
100. Paris was here making a change to Wendover, who had merely said it would be wrong to include them: Luard 1872–83, iii. 220. I owe all this to Gransden 1974b, 370.
101. Luard 1872–83, v. 265, 490, 252.
102. Luard 1872–83, v. 197–98.
103. For Paris' Benedictinism and loyalty to St Albans, see Gransden 1974b, 372–74.
104. Vaughan 1958c, 154–55.
105. Luard 1890, ii. 289; see also 321 on Henry and Edmund of Abingdon.
106. Luard 1890, ii. 312.
107. Carpenter 2012b, 1365–66.
108. As Gransden observes (1974b, 377–78, 417), although here she is treating the text between 1259 and 1265 as all coming from St Albans.
109. Luard 1890, ii. 463–64. This makes one think that the continuator had access to some version of 'the lord king's grievances against his council': Treharne and Sanders 1973, nos. 30, 31 and Ridgeway 1988.
110. See most notably Luard 1890, ii. 432–34, about the pope's favour (having been misled) to the elect of Winchester and about papal taxation (described without comment).
111. Vaughan 1958c, 117–19, 124.
112. Vaughan 1958c, 118–19. Vaughan says that the hand which made the changes is that which finished the *Chronica maiora*. It is thus the hand which wrote out the obituary of Paris. Assuming this is the hand of the

composer of the obituary, not just that of the copyist, and assuming also that the composer was identical with Paris' continuator (which the obituary itself implies), then it was the continuator who was responsible for putting in the last changes to the *Chronica maiora*. No original text of the continuation survives, only a copy made, as I have argued, at Pershore Abbey (see note 38 of this chapter).

113. If the very last part of the *Chronica maiora* was copied after Paris' death, then it must have been later still that a passage in 1259 offensive to the Dominicans was marked 'vacat': Luard 1872–83, v. 742. It is also the continuator who was probably responsible for the complimentary passage about Montfort in 1258 written over an erasure (703) although it doubtless reflected Paris's views.
114. See the very just appraisal in Gransden 1974b, 356.
115. For contemporary accounts of '1258' and how far the revolutionary reforms were ever publicly proclaimed, see Carpenter 2016, 30–42. In the same volume (109–24), Kjaer's 'Writing Reform and Rebellion' explores the narrative strategies of the contemporary historians.
116. BL, Royal MS 14 C VII.
117. Luard 1872–83, v. 695n2; 747–48. In the section between the Westminster and Oxford Parliaments, which is still in Paris' hand, there is a missing leaf. I do not think this affects the hypothesis advanced later in this chapter: Luard 1872–83, v. 694n1.
118. Vaughan 1958c, 140.
119. See Gransden 1974b, 361.
120. Luard 1872–83, v. 676–78, 680–81, 688–90.
121. So for the date of Simon Passelewe's mission to Waltham, St Albans and Reading (Luard 1872–83, v. 682–68), see *CPR 1247-58*, 625. For the Franciscans arriving at Bury (Luard 1872–83, v. 688), see Gransden 1964, 23.
122. Luard 1872–83, v. 676–77; Maddicott 1994, 154.
123. Luard 1872–83, v. 689.
124. Luard 1872–83, vi, 400–01; Treharne and Sanders 1973, nos. 1, 2.
125. Luard 1864–69, i, 163–65; see Carpenter 1996, chapter 9 at 187–90.
126. Vaughan 1958c, 140n1. For other references to Paris' ageing, see Madden 1866–69, iii, xxi; Luard 1872–83, v. xv.
127. Or was when a draft of this paper was first given as a talk. One wonders how Powicke, then in his seventies, reacted to Vaughan's remark!
128. For monastic diet and life expectancy, see Harvey 1993, 127–29, from which it appears that Paris lived considerably longer than the majority of fifteenth-century Westminster monks.
129. Madden 1866–69, iii. xxi; Vaughan 1953c, 388 and plate XVII (b), (c) and (d); Vaughan 1958c, 10. My first impression, looking at Paris' last known writing, was how neat it was: BL, Cotton MS Nero D I, fol. 82^r (Luard

1872–83, vi. 496), of which (d) is a small portion. The final volume of the *Chronica maiora*, mostly in Paris' hand, is BL, Royal MS 14 C VII.
130. For the view that this reflects his waning powers, see Madden 1866–69, iii. xxi; Vaughan 1958c, 10.
131. For the effect of *Liber additamentorum*, see Vaughan 1958c, 67.
132. Luard 1872–83, v. xv and note 2; Vaughan 1958c, 37. One striking error is the placing in 1258 of the chapter recording John Mansel's foundation of a religious house at Bilsington in Kent: Luard 1872–83, v. 690–91. In fact the foundation took place in 1253. That Paris was here copying from a draft from 1253 which had somehow re-emerged is suggested by the fact (as Hui Liu has pointed out) that Mansel is described as 'provost of Beverley' whereas from 1256 Paris gives him his new title of treasurer of York. See Liu 2007, 172.
133. Luard 1872–83, v. 744–45; Maddicott 1994, 180.
134. Luard 1872–83, iii. 253.
135. Luard 1864–69, iv. 118–19. Wykes was here adapting Psalms 2:2.
136. For this view (put into the mouths of Llywelyn and Louis IX) see Luard 1872–83, iii. 290; iv. 231–32; Paris was clearly impressed by Henry's behaviour when he stayed at St Albans in March 1257 and November 1258: Luard 1872–83, v. 617–18, 724.
137. Although Paris went along with the official version and revealed nothing about how the king had been coerced, he also was silent about the bargain over Sicily. He certainly knew about the offer of help as it is contained in the barons' letter of explanation to the pope which he copied out himself (Luard 1872–83, vi. 400–01). The letter, however, was written after Paris had finished his account of the Westminster Parliament, if my arguments are correct. It is possible, therefore, that Paris did not know about the supposed bargain. Alternatively, he may just have thought it unimportant.
138. Luard 1872–83, v. 689–90.
139. Luard 1872–83, v. 695–98. By an extraordinary mistake the printed text (696) reads 'graviter' rather than 'gratanter', which is quite clearly what is written in the manuscript: BL Royal MS 14 C VII, fol. 210.
140. Luard 1872–83, v. 644 seems to point on to 663, 675.
141. Luard 1872–83, v. 679–80, 686.
142. Luard 1872–83, v. 679. After the end of the account of the Westminster Parliament, there seems to be a change of pen and ink, which is consistent with a delay before the next chapter was written: BL Royal MS 14 C VII, fol. 209^r (Luard 1872–83, v. 690). However, as mentioned in what follows, Paris' pen needed changing at this point, so too much should not be made of this.
143. For examples of Paris omitting or keeping quiet about actions which he thought shameful, see Luard 1872–83, v. 676; vi, 284n1.
144. BL Royal MS 14 C VII, fol. 209^r (Luard 1872–83, v. 689–90).

The writing begins to deteriorate from around 'Et ut brevibus concludatur'. There is a slight improvement near the end of the chapter.
145. Paris had also brought the *Chronica maiora* right up to date at the end of 1250: see Vaughan 1958c, 60–61. See Powicke's criticism of Vaughan here in his review of *Matthew Paris* (Powicke 1959, 483).
146. Luard 1872–83, v. 690.
147. Carpenter 1996, 195–96.
148. Luard 1872–83, v. 695–98.
149. The nearest to any proclamation is Treharne and Sanders 1973, no. 7. For further discussion see Carpenter 2016.
150. Luard 1872–83, v. 704.
151. Luard 1872–83, vi. 396–97, 400–07, 496; Vaughan 1958c, 182–83.
152. Luard 1872–83, vi. 496. Paul Brand wonders whether Paris was here copying from a writ, but that he felt moved to do so is itself significant: Brand 2003, 32–33.
153. BL, Cotton MS Nero D I, fol. 82^r (Luard 1872–83, vi. 496); Vaughan 1958c, 10; Brand 1992, 336. The illustration in Vaughan 1953c, plate XVII (d) is of the final part.
154. For the whole of what was copied by Paris (Luard conspicuously failed to publish the whole text), see Brand 1992, 337–39.
155. The continuator did copy out the administrative and political part of what later historians call 'The Provisions of Westminster': Madden 1866–69, iii, xxiii, note 2; Luard 1872–83, vi. 512; Treharne and Sanders 1973, 148–57.
156. Luard 1872–83, v. 708–09; TNA, Just 1, 1187, m.1. For the episode, see Stewart 2000. I have argued that what even in Paris' account amounted to a denial of justice was one of the sparks which set off the revolution at the Westminster Parliament: Carpenter 1996, 192–93. I still think this is true, but it should be noted that Paris himself (Luard 1872–73, v. 708–09) only recorded the incident later in his narrative when John brought his complaint before the justiciar.
157. Paris (Luard 1872–83, v. 733) said one fear was that Richard would bring back the Lusignans to England and this is confirmed by *CPR 1258–66*, 10.
158. Luard 1872–83, v. 737–39; TNA, Just 1/82, mm.24d, 36; Just 1/83, mm.13, 22. See Carpenter 1996, 327–28 and Hershey 2000.
159. Luard 1872–83, v. 730; TNA, 1187, m.10. This episode is discussed and Paris' errors are pointed out in Summerson, 'Issues of law in the chronicles of Matthew Paris'.
160. See Luard 1872–83, v. 746; see also 704, 705. For a similar appreciation of this vigour, see the end of the newsletter in Treharne and Sanders 1973, 96–97.
161. Luard 1872–83, v. 704, 714–16, 720, 744–45.
162. Treharne and Sanders 1973, 95 (where Henry is said to beg that none but Englishmen shall stay around him).

163. Vaughan 1958c, 149. Vaughan was right, however, in seeing that Paris regarded Montfort as a 'naturalis'.
164. Luard 1872–83, v. 676–77, 689; Maddicott 1994, 154.
165. Luard 1872–83, v. 697; Maddicott 1994, 160–01. As Maddicott observes, 'In Paris's account of the Oxford parliament, written soon after the event and long before Montfort had emerged as supreme leader in 1263, he is the only one of the reforming magnates whose particular activities are mentioned.' Maddicott also points out (163) that Paris is the only source for Henry, Montfort's eldest son, pursuing the Lusignans to France: Luard 1872–83, v. 703.
166. Luard 1872–83, v. 706; Maddicott 1994, 150.
167. Luard 1872–83, v. 744–45; Maddicott 1994, 180.
168. Luard 1872–83, v. 737, 744–45; Maddicott 1994, 177, 191, 357.
169. This is written over an erasure in Madden 1866–69, ii, 409. The Latin is 'Jussitque omnibus debitoribus suis omnia, quae abstulerunt ministri eius a plebe, sub specie justiciae, restitui et de injuria satisfieri.' For the date of the changes to the *Historia Anglorum*, see Vaughan, 1958c, 123. For another passage in which Paris may reflect Montfort's ideas, see Maddicott 1994, 87.
170. Maddicott 1994, 175–76, 166–70.

3

Matthew Paris and the Plantagenet Regime

On 13 October 1247, Matthew Paris met monarchy in person for the first time in his life.[1] Probably he was already in his sixth decade.[2] He had been recording the acts and reported words of royalty for more than ten years, but what he had known at first-hand were largely the effects of royal authority, especially as it touched St Albans and the surrounding region. The drama of public affairs, and the performance of kingship itself, was brought to him by word of mouth, such as the exceptional ceremony (*solempnitate inaudita et incomparabilia*) of the royal wedding in 1236.[3] Now, in the king's presence at Westminster Abbey, he held a position on the principal public stage. The occasion was the Henry III's observance of the feast of the translation of St Edward the Confessor, whose sacred value was leavened dramatically by the presence of a vial of the blood of Christ brought from the Holy Land just days before and now offered to England's premier church of St Peter.[4]

Before this moment Matthew had seen the king only at a distance as a member of the monastic community at St Albans when Henry III marked there the feasts of St Barnabas (11 June) and St Thomas (21 December) three years before.[5] He did not explain how he came to be invited as a witness to the ceremony at Westminster; quite probably it arose from the corporate tie between the two royal abbeys rather than from the personal intervention of the king.[6] Still, the encounter began a connection between the Benedictine monk and the monarch which continued for the remainder of Matthew's active career. Nine months or so after their meeting at Westminster Matthew was sent to Norway in answer to a request from another monarch, Haakon IV, for assistance in the reform of the royal monastery at Nidarholm. Matthew's mission may have been prompted by his part in the affairs of another monastery, Holm (Norfolk), but the Norwegian's own affinity with King Henry may have further enhanced his renown.[7] Back in England Matthew may have again spoken directly with the king when he celebrated Easter at St Albans in April 1251; weeks later he was with the royal household at Winchester where he heard horrifying tales of those returning from the Holy Land.[8] Then, after a passage of six years, towards the end of Lent in 1257, the king stayed for a week at St Albans, and in the royal apartments, at table and in the private chambers, Matthew was, so he claimed, always at his side.[9] Their conversation was friendly – *amicabiliter* – and turned to subjects spiritual and eternal as King Henry reflected on monarchs made saints.[10] These may have been their final exchanges. The king returned to St Albans in November 1258 and witnessed the convent's ceremony for the feast of St Katherine's but now Matthew did not cross his path.[11] It is possible to perceive a change in his coverage of the crown thereafter. In the last columns of the chronicle certainly compiled by Matthew, the king and his acts are described with the same degree of detachment which had marked the first part of his narrative covering events three decades before.

Remarkably, Matthew took a parallel path towards a personal acquaintance with two other members of the royal family. Queen Eleanor of Provence was present with her husband at Westminster in 1247. It was surely their first meeting, and from here Matthew grew to know her personally, together with the king, separating her from his critique of her uncle, William of Savoy and Henry's half-brother, William de Valence, whose influence he decried.[12] Matthew witnessed Eleanor's lasting grief (*funus fraternum deflevit tempore diuturno*) at Savoy's loss.[13] Presenting her with his *Estoire de Seint Edouard*, he gave her more than conventional praise: she was generous and wise, naturally, but also kindly (franchise: *Estoire*, l. 56) and of a like mind (*commun voler*: *Estoire*, l. 68) with her husband, traits which would be most visible at first-hand.[14] It was a signal of a sincere attachment that the queen presented an altar hanging personally to Matthew, not, as might be for a general act of patronage, to the abbot and convent of St Albans.[15]

Matthew also came to know the king's eldest surviving brother, Richard, earl of Cornwall. He may have seen him at close quarters before he first spoke to the king and queen, when the earl entered the chapter house at St Albans in 1240 and entreated the monks for their prayers (*a conventu suffragia petiit orationum*).[16] Perhaps it was Richard himself who told him how calm Henry had seemed at his wedding (*cum summo conamine totum se exhibuit serenum et jocundum*).[17] For almost twenty years Matthew followed Richard's travels through the kingdom and beyond, gathering tales not of a prince but of a personality regal and prodigal but also conspicuously devout.[18] The show-stopping performance, staged (1241) by Emperor Frederick at Rome, of two Saracen girls dancing on rolling spheres, was surely shared with him personally by the earl.[19] No doubt Richard also told him of his present (1252) of breeding buffalo[20] and he may have confided to Matthew his conviction that his recovery from an 'obscure and serious' sickness (1247) came through the intercession of St Edmund of Abingdon.[21] Certainly, the cost to him in cash of the creation of Hailes Abbey (Gloucestershire), the staggering sum of 10,000 marks, spent 'if only (*utinam*) that it might please God', reads like a candid aside.[22] It may have been the end of their exchanges. There is no indication of a meeting between them in the later fifties. In fact, in his final years Matthew appeared more equivocal about him: bitterly, he exposed him as the agent of his brother in securing a secret (clam) bribe from the abbey's cellarer.[23] When, in 1257, Richard's sea voyage was postponed he remarked tartly that he found time to tyrannise St Albans,[24] although months later Matthew put his hope in him again as famine threatened livelihoods and life itself.[25]

In the train of the royal family, Matthew met those nobles, knights, prelates and clerical officials who brought form and function to the royal regime. These representatives of the 'political nation' were not unknown in monasteries, particularly the hierarchy of ancient, wealthy cult churches most attractive to courtly patrons. But typically only the monastic superior and perhaps some of their senior officeholders might do more than watch them from a distance as they paid their respects at the high altar or the patronal shrine. Although he held no such office himself, it does appear Matthew Paris came into direct contact with some of these figures even before he found himself in the king's presence. It may be that his melodramatic account of the rebel Falkes de Breauté's impassioned repentance before the bishop of London, Eustace of Fauconberg, was told him by the prelate himself, although there is no record of a visit to St Albans during his brief tenure of the see. Here Matthew is not his own best witness; the source he named in the *Historia Anglorum* version of the anecdote was the bishop of Coventry, Alexander de Stavenby.[26]

Matthew's early reports of the exploits of John Mansel, the king's clerk whom King Henry appointed chancellor in 1246, would suggest they had been on personal speaking terms for several years before. Matthew's breathless account of Mansel's wounding at Vérines in 1243, being brought back to life by the attentions of medics and his merits deserving to be counted among the first of England surely came from the horse's mouth.[27]

Hubert de Burgh, the earl of Kent and the king's justiciar, was certainly known to Matthew before he himself was welcomed to Westminster, Winchester or elsewhere. A committed choir monk such as Matthew may have come closer than others to the earl when his teenage daughter, Margaret, was buried at the abbey in 1236.[28] But it was Matthew's association with a local secular clerk, Laurence of St Albans, that led him into an audience with de Burgh. An explanatory note in the margin of the manuscript of his narrative known as *Historia Anglorum* recalls that Hubert told of his escape from Devizes Castle in 1233 'at London and in the presence of Laurence of St Albans'.[29]

Matthew's entry into the regime's own arenas from 1247 transformed his first-hand encounters. Now he spoke with senior prelates from across the kingdom, such as Robert Grosseteste of Lincoln and Richard Wyche of Chichester.[30] It seems it was only when he was a recognised presence on their own ground that he gained the acquaintance of crown agents, barons of the exchequer, such as Alexander Swereford, and justices of the King's Bench such as Roger Thurkleby; now too his watch over John Mansel became almost an obsession.[31]

The arc of Matthew's experience of the Angevin regime makes him a unique observer in his time. Monastic chroniclers were almost always well informed because the successful administration of their monasteries depended on the reception and transmission of information, written and oral, official and unofficial. Many of their houses were well placed in the landscape to watch the whole caravan of crown and court when it passed by. Yet none of those whose annals have survived from the first half of the thirteenth century saw the king and the political nation at such close quarters, nor did any of their annalists know them at first-hand. Matthew's immediate peer group, the compilers of contemporary chronicles at Bury St Edmund's, Coggeshall, Dunstable and Tewkesbury, wove their narratives from the uneven threads of reports that reached them.[32] Even the increasing royal favour shown to Westminster seems to have failed to inspire any monk to apply pen to parchment.[33] In fact, no account of current or recent affairs had offered such a witness on the principal subjects for almost a century. William of Malmesbury was disingenuous in describing himself as 'remote from the mysteries of the court', although even his personal experience was more with prelates than with princes.[34] In fact, the only English writer with knowledge of the cloister life to report on royalty as a present witness was the unnamed author of the life of Edward the Confessor (*Vita Ædwardi regis*) who may have been in the service of his queen.[35] Eyewitness reports, of his own or of others shared with him, were the lifeblood of Matthew's writing on worldly affairs. For the acts of the church and its clergy he collected documents in general circulation in much the same way as his peers in other monasteries, but for the Angevin regime he told his own tale.

In the face of monarchy, Matthew the monk was in awe. Watching the procession of the Holy Blood at Westminster, his eye was caught by the king's glittering throne. Golden from head to foot (*veste deaurata ... et coronula aurea*), the king was glorious (*gloriose*), glorified.[36] What then he saw for himself he had long imagined: for the train of Princess Isabel in 1235 he had pictured the very riches of the kingdom in procession. The coronation of Queen Eleanor the following year conjured an extraordinary solemnity (*solempnitate inaudita et incomparabili*); at the sight of the royal procession he thought the crowd was surely struck dumb (*stuporem ... generaret*).[37] He was alone among contemporary annalists to recall the flowers strewn at Henry's first coronation.[38] When the king came to Winchester to celebrate the feast of the Confessor (1243), Matthew marvelled at the mobilisation of a multitude from the outer reaches of the kingdom (*coacti sunt multi de ultimis finibus regni*) and the proud wonder with which they welcomed him (*fastu et superstitione est receptus*).[39]

The marvel of this and perhaps of any monarchy for Matthew was not a matter of principle or of physical might but of materiality. Royalty commanded the treasure of a kingdom. Royal riches (*regales divitias*) were the ultimate measure of quality of the finest things, such as the psalter which Abbot William presented to Redbourne Priory.[40] As might be expected of a monk who had documented the holy relics of his own church, Matthew was especially fascinated by the sacred objects of this kingship: Curtana, Edward the Confessor's sword carried in procession at Henry's second coronation;[41] and the ring from Rome so beautiful, as Matthew saw for himself, it caused the king's heart to soar.[42] He pictured the entry of the blood of Christ into London with a canopy painted in red and gold.[43]

The unmistakable mark of monarchy was the crown. He opened the new chapter of Henry's reign with crowns; in one copy two crowns, one placed on the young man's head, another, gilded, surmounting the royal coat of arms; in another he added the legend '*corona regis Henrici*'.[44] The 1243 truce between Henry III and Louis IX was pictured as a handshake between the two crowns of England and France.[45] Matthew placed Henry's crown in the parade of majesty that passed through Christendom. He sketched their crowns when they came to them;[46] Emperor Frederick he showed in majesty on his seal.[47] When he knighted his half-brother William de Valence in 1247 Matthew viewed the king in close-up, 'seated gloriously on his royal throne' and garlanded with a golden coronet.[48]

Familiar with the abundant and fine furnishings of a great institution, he was also excited by the excess of royal trappings, the countless cups of Princess Isabel's dowry dinner service, the weight of robes and the train of mounts most 'sought-after' (*desiderabilibus*) and 'speedy' (*veredariis*) which passed by, with glinting tack, in each procession.[49] When the king came with Prince Edward to the shrine of St Alban (1252) Matthew counted out their offerings: four necklaces, three cloths and two rings together with twelve gold bezants (*talenta*).[50] Here Crassus, celebrated as Rome's richest man, was reborn.[51] Their colours, quality and cost also caught his craftsman's eye. He was keen to record that the king's new reliquary for the Confessor's shrine was fashioned from the 'purest gold' by London smiths 'hand-picked' (*electis*) for the purpose. Likewise, he pictured the Conqueror first furnishing the shrine with a pall of 'fine gold and silver' (*D'or fin e de argent*).[52] The richness of royalty returned him to the dictum of Ovid: 'the skill surpassed the substance' (*materiam superabat opus*).[53]

Yet Matthew's attention was held equally by the humanity of monarchy. Henry, as he reflected in his life of Edmund of Abingdon, remained an 'earthly king'.[54] At close hand what impressed above all was the intensity of his emotions. He was a ruler ruled by his heart.[55] His anger 'blazed', building to a 'frenzy' of feeling when seized with a suspicion of 'patent plotters' (*propatulo proditorem*).[56] Bystanders could be terrified. It also propelled him to cunning plotting of his own (*rex iratus ad alia se convertit astutiae argumenta*).[57] Then, just as suddenly, he might succumb to a nervous collapse and act like a child, inconsolable, impossible to talk round (*nullis verborum ambagibus circumventus ab incepto proposito retardaretur*).[58] Sight of the son – and perhaps the recollections of the older generation – inspired an image of the father: confronted with Magna Carta, Matthew imagined King John became a madman (*more furiosi*) grinding his teeth, rolling his eyes (*frendere dentibus, oculis torvis intuitum retorquere*), his body given over to uncontrollable gestures (*inordinatorum gestuum*).[59]

Kings were people but kingship was still a sacred principle. In spite of his increasing dismay at Henry himself, it seems Matthew never wavered from his investment in his office. The cloister monk looked on the performance of monarchy as he might the liturgy. To the abbey's account of the king's first coronation he added only that it was done 'solemnly, with canticles'.[60] In his first recorded conversation with the king, Matthew was convinced that regality carried a real presence: 'Lord, the dignity of this glorious scene will hold fast in the memory' (*Etiam domine, quia dignum retineri, vere gloriosa dieta ideo hic peracta est*). Although he never named it a divine right he was in no doubt of its ultimate source. He expanded Roger of Wendover's report of Henry's first coronation to emphasise its sacramental aspect: as an act of 'solemn anointing' (*unguentes coronaverunt solempniter*).[61] Historically, he traced an apostolic succession of rulers who were holy saints, martyrs and confessors, charged like a priesthood itself to overcome 'our threefold enemies ... the flesh, the devil and the world'.⁶² His *Lives of the Two Offas* celebrated monarchs who were veritably monastic in their devotions, such as Wermund, father of the first Offa, who 'looked for leisure for prayer and contemplation', exchanging the 'material weapons' of the earthly prince to confront 'spiritual enemies'.⁶³ Matthew kept a watch on his own King Henry's votive acts, observing both a monarch's orchestration of ritual (*jussit ... exequias ... celebrari*) and the prayerful solemnity of the ordinary devotee (*cum summo honore et reverentia ac timore accipiens*).⁶⁴ His portraits painted them following the template of Christ in majesty. Only the Lord God, by His righteous judgement (*sed justo Dei judicio*) held the power to bring about any change in their fortune.⁶⁵ As David Carpenter has phrased it, Matthew was impressed by the 'golden weight' of a worshipping king.⁶⁶

Matthew's view of England's monarchy was not based on any particularly rare or privileged awareness of its written records. When he began to keep an account of current affairs, the monastery had been collecting and curating archives for more than a century. Perhaps the first systematic cartulary recording their dealings with crown and church had been compiled by the monks in the years around 1100.⁶⁷ Then, still struggling with the aftershocks of the Conquest, the monks kept a narrow focus on the immediate interests of the abbey, its properties and the rights associated with them and its position under the governance of the church. In the thirteenth century there was no significant change in this outlook. Before Matthew, Roger of Wendover had reached out for copies of episcopal and papal deeds, but for royal affairs he had relied on second-hand authorities such as Ralph de Diceto, Roger Howden and William of Newburgh. Matthew himself followed suit. Almost all of the authentic documents which he entered verbatim into his narrative originated in the institutions of the church. The royal deeds which came directly into his hands were those at any rate coming into the archive concerning challenges to or confirmations of the abbey's corporate rights. The largest sequence, which he reproduced in his 'Book of Additions' (*Liber additamentorum*), concerned the crown's interventions in a dispute with the bishop and monks of Durham over the advowson of parish churches within their jurisdiction.⁶⁸ His narration of the first meetings of King Henry's parliament incorporates details of date, location and ceremonial do draw from formal records, but these were widely known and his reports of proceedings, of the king's anger (*ira maxima*) and of his magnates' suspicions of a tightening noose suggest his best resource was the testimony of those who were there.[69] Reporting the first parliament meetings, Matthew worried that words and deeds would be lost to oblivion (*ne oblivio ... deleret*).[70] Only his notice of some exchequer records and the abbey's transcripts of the 1215 and 1225 charters indicate a good catch of current documents, and these were collated clumsily by Roger of Wendover or another of his generation and Matthew himself chose not to (or could not) untangle them.[71]

Matthew's increasing familiarity with the leading figures of the political nation did not significantly expand his sources of written evidence. He was given sight of the records of the royal exchequer perhaps by Alexander Swereford. He was aware that they held details of the coronation ceremony; a selection of the documents he transcribed was also among those for which the exchequer kept registered copies.[72] Yet what he took and made most of from these well-placed, professional contacts was knowledge at one remove from the main concerns of the regime, such as the embassy to Morocco allegedly dispatched by King John; some of it was simply arcane, such as Swereford's story of King Offa of Mercia, St Albans Abbey's legendary founder.[73] What Matthew owed above all to the regime's principal actors was an impression of the performance of monarchy, ceremonial, devotional and martial. Matthew Paris' informants did not make him a documentary historian but a vivid dramatist.

Matthew's view of kingship was not founded on current affairs at all but drawn from the history and legend of the Bible and classical antiquity. Both informed his profile of Edward the Confessor: he was Solomon yet with echoes of Caesar, Darius, Menelaus and Priam.[74] His own King Henry and his family each found their ancient avatar. Henry III was Lycurgus in the face of the Gascons;[75] his brother, Richard of Cornwall, Octavian; Countess Margaret of Flanders, Medea; Beatrice of Provence, Niobe.[76] But in picturing kingship in action, perhaps inevitably, a lifetime choir monk, biblical idioms always rose in him first. King Henry's grandfather Richard had 'fought the good fight' as had Timothy. Henry himself he said was stirred by the Holy Spirit; when William the Marshal died he lamented the death of a good man 'like David ... for the fate (*casum*) of Jonathan and Saul'.[77] When he turned against Richard of Cornwall, he was wont to see him as 'another Jacob', a 'sly usurper' (*alter Jacob et subtilis supplantator*).[78] In fact, all of the actors in the royal regime and all of their dramas he set in a biblical scene. Henry's Poitevan counsellors were the 'hawkers' (*institores*) and 'moneylenders' (*numularios*) confronting Christ in the temple.[79] Louis of France held his spear (*lanceam*) before Hubert de Burgh like another Saul (Samuel 18:10).[80] Henry's subjects suffered his taxation as the 'pillage of the people' of Zion (Isaiah 61:8).[81] Yet to pass judgement as narrator, Matthew took up what few – so it appears – wise words of the ancients he could always call to mind: repeatedly he reached for a saying he believed to be from Seneca the Elder – that a man's enemy dies doubly for the loss of his free will – to elevate Roger of Wendover's earlier report of the death of Eustace the Monk (1217) as well as his own of the imperial chancellor Pietro della Vigna (1249) and the anti-king of Germany, William II (1256).[82]

Beyond the royal family, public figures were, like the characters of scripture and the classics, scarcely more than expressions of virtue and vice. Matthew saw the psalmist's proverbial betrayer, 'as crooked as a bow' (Psalm 77: 57), repeatedly reborn: in the king's justiciar, Stephen of Segrave; in England's delegates at the Council of Lyons; in the citizens of London; and in no lesser person than the Holy Roman Emperor himself, Frederick II.[83] In Simon de Montfort he saw three classical archetypes combined: perfect manhood (Paris), warrior (Mars) and public servant (Cato).[84] When the Caursines peddled loans he saw Juvenal's men, whose condemnation was a self-inflicted wound.[85] The kingdom's prelates were latter-day prophets 'blessed', 'most reverent' (*sanctissimus*) 'men of God' (*homines Dei*) confounded only by those in thrall to he who is 'the common enemy of man'. Nobility was a worldly status, not a state of being, and it was almost inevitable that those at these heights would lay bare their true character, as they did when (1244) the king's clerk, John of Gatesden, dared to marry above himself.[86] Christendom's enemies conspired to do evil things (*facinora*), just as Jason or Nicanor (2 Maccabees 4:19, 8:34). Muslims were Ovid's villains for whom 'vice was their stock-in-trade'.[87] Their fates were likewise proverbial: narrating the public battles between the church in England and the papacy, Matthew's first point of reference was the prophecies of Isaiah in the case of

Cardinal Otto (1241), John Bretache (1246), the papal subsidy (1250) and Innocent IV's assault on episcopal sees (1253).[88] He reached for the words of the prophet – 'Destroyer, you will be destroyed' – to dispatch Falkes de Breauté to his ignominious end and again for the nameless 'wicked' (*impiis*) who knew no peace (*non est pax*: Isaiah 48:22) after the troubled times of John had passed.[89] Choosing to be reconciled to the king, Gilbert the Marshal followed Ovid's dictum that 'to give requires good sense'.[90] Henry's own commanding candour fulfilled the same poet's picture of 'order, prayers and promises combined'.[91]

Yet there were moments when Matthew held up another template to these contemporary scenes. In the performance of public life he also recognised the characters and dramas of romance. There is no copy of poetry or prose on a secular subject among the surviving St Albans books which could have been known to Matthew, although they were seen there in later generations. But they are found elsewhere in the Benedictine network in and around his lifetime: the *Lais* attributed to Marie de France were at Reading Abbey before 1300, an anthology of romances was seen at Dover in 1389 and a copy of *Guy of Warwick* was listed among donations to the library at Ramsey Abbey some time after 1350.[92]

Matthew knew the language, form and metres of texts like these well enough to use them in his lives of the saints. His characterisations of his living subjects hint at a liking as much for their tropes as for their underlying themes. Knights offered exemplars of manhood. Prince Louis was a twenty-four-hour warrior tireless in the face of the enemy (*die ac nocte infatigabiliter insultibus armatorum impetivit*).[93] Of all Hugh Neville's adventures in the Holy Land, it was his overpowering of a lion that Matthew chose as the principal scene. He emphasised not only prowess but also physique: Harold Godwinson had been 'powerful, strong and large' (*De cors fu seins, forz e pleners*),[94] William the Marshal 'invincible'.[95] He remarked on their aesthetic: Gilbert de Umfraville was an extraordinary bloom (*flos singularis*).[96] Earl Richard's retinue 'twinkled' (*micante*).[97] Saer de Quincy was the 'most beautiful' of all.[98] For good knights, Matthew also claimed cultivations. He drew attention to the 'education' of Baldwin de Vere and John of Lexington.[99] Paulin Piper was a 'clerical knight or knightly clerk' (*miles literatus sive clericus militaris*).¹⁰⁰ Richard de Clare was 'youthful and elegant' yet also 'eloquent and expert in the laws of the land'.¹⁰¹ To the marriage of Edward the Confessor and Edith came the accomplished 'knights of bravery and youth who ... shiver their lances ... sing, dance and [play the] fiddle' (*Valetz de force e juvente ... de mener ces dances/Chantent, balent e vielent*).¹⁰²

Presiding over this knighthood was their king: his own Henry he pictured as Merlin's lynx;¹⁰³ reaching far into the past he recalled Offa II of Mercia as 'a great champion' and 'a brave heart ... favoured by Mars'.¹⁰⁴ Like ladies of the *Lais* their queens were archetypes of all the virtues and devise of women: Queen Eleanor was 'flower of virtue and honour', the 'fountain of perfection' (*flurs/De dames par bens e honurs ... Ki funtaine es d'afeitement*).¹⁰⁵ Offa II's Thryth was 'beauty', 'grace' and 'eloquence' but also hidden 'secret snares'.¹⁰⁶

Women in the ambit of crown and court were also exemplary characters of a courtly drama. Beatrice of Provence was a 'rare' (*expectabilis*) and 'wondrous beauty' (*mirae pulchritudinis mulierem*) of perfect civility and prudence;¹⁰⁷ Alice de Lusignan, the countess of Surrey, was a youthful 'flower' blighted prematurely.¹⁰⁸ Even three-year-old Princess Katharine was mute but 'most beautiful'.¹⁰⁹

He pictured these real-life figures of recent and distant past in scenes reminiscent of romance. The knights of Henry III entered a hall showing the serried shields of heroes past, which set them trembling with a fearful awe.¹¹⁰ At Malden, Matthew could not fail to notice that they gathered at a round table.¹¹¹ For feats of arms he conveyed spectacle – trumpets and horns, bolting horses¹¹² – vivid violence – blood-drenched swords, a skull pierced through the marrow¹¹³ – and a trace of supernatural power – physicians conjuring breath out of a broken body, a sword 'devouring' its prey.¹¹⁴ At the last, they fell like legends, lances snapped and shields dropped, shattered and turned downward, '*clipei prostrati*'.¹¹⁵

Monastic life was anchored by the authority of texts and Matthew himself remained close bound as he watched performances on the public stage. Still, through his first-hand encounters he did come to discover and to a degree to absorb the different ideas, identities and language which increasingly defined the lived experience of public affairs. Early in his record of current affairs he turned from traditional terms for the lordship of the realm, magnates, nobles (*magnates, nobiles*) and took up 'baronage' (*barnagium*), a noun not seen in the annals kept in the rest of the monastic network.[116] On the horizon of his *Gesta abbatum* likewise there were 'barones', there described as marauders who left 'monachos' with nowhere to hide.[117] Matthew was also quick to accept 'parliament' as the name for the meeting of the king and his lords, clerical and lay. He labelled the meeting of winter 1236–37 both a 'council' and a 'great parley' but between 1242 and 1246 he settled on 'general parliament'.[118] The term does appear in the entries made in the annals of the abbeys at Burton-on-Trent and Tewkesbury, but the date of their compilation is unclear.[119] Matthew wrote as he saw and heard at the time. Now also he described the obligation of the king and his baronage as to the 'commonweal(th)' of the kingdom, for which he used the Latin 'respublica'.[120] The subsidy of 1237 was a threat to the 'well-being' (*utilitatem*) of the 'commonweal'; Stephen Segrave he condemned as no 'friend' to the 'commonweal', while London's claim on the king was 'as good for the commons of the city as for the commonweal'.[121]

His general view of the nature of good government carried with it an understanding of particular customs. The king governed in accordance with due custom and tradition (*ab antiquo*).[122] Counsel was to be taken from those born to the role, 'gentlemen of legitimate line, especially those of royal blood' (*Li gentil hume natural/Numee ment due sanc real*).[123] Their 'assent and consent' was required for any act contemplated by the crown, and it should be 'complete', 'unanimous' or 'universal' (*consensu universalis*); to have to persuade (*ad consensum flectere*) was contemptible.[124] The crown cannot act only in its own interest and at will since by tradition it bears the dual responsibility for wealth (*dapsilitate*) and the defence of the realm.[125]

Perhaps he gave an oblique glance at this present challenge in his history of the two Kings Offa when he reflected 'management of the chief men of the kingdom demanded special skill', commending Offa I for 'distributing [his] spoils ... to his chief men with royal generosity' and always 'taking good advice'.[126]

He captured the principles of this political nation – emerging and established – and also something of its personality. King Henry's excessive generosity to the Poitevans provoked onlookers to sarcastic laughter (*inde ridentibus immo derisorie cachinnnantibus*).[127] Seasoned household knight and king's justice Sir Thomas de Moulton Matthew remembered as a great man, 'a mighty warrior' in the 'flush of his youth' and later a 'learned lawyer'.[128] Geoffrey de Lizzino, a Poitevan chaplain, so beguiled Henry and his courtiers that he seemed to be more like a player than a priest.[129] Such self-interest and indulgence led this king's court to resemble the worst excesses of Rome (*et facta est curia regalis Romanse consimilis*).[130]

Yet neither his own first-hand observations nor the testimony of his informants led him towards original insights into the regime. Although he described King Henry's conduct over charters of liberty, the administration of royal justice and taxation as deceitful, unjust even tyrannical, he dwelt more on failings of character than on flaws in policy. He represented the adult Henry as irascible like his father and as prodigious in his appetite for riches as the Poitevans under whose influence he so fatally fell. In passing, he perceived an impulse in the young king to restore good order in his realm (*emendatio regni sui*), fleeting recognition of his need for good counsel and latterly of his being held captive by his own high-handedness and greed.[131] But he did not turn to a discussion of the practice of kingship as he did on the performance of prelacy in his lives of Edmund of Abingdon and Stephen Langton.

Likewise, he was less inclined to appraise the mechanics of government offices than the character of those that held them. Hugh de Pateshull he commended for his virtues – good faith and honesty – but his view of his contribution to the 'workings' (*secretum*) of the exchequer were superficial: he recalled only that Hugh kept good care of the receipts and seal (of office).[132] Both William de Haverhill and Philip Lovell were praised for their personal qualities as treasurers, 'diligence' in service, prudence and generosity, verdicts not very far removed in fact from Matthew's measures of a good abbot.[133]

Matthew's close watch on the people of the royal regime was not matched in the annals of any of his peers. He stood still further apart by recording something of the wider realm and its people as a whole. A professed monk who travelled outside his own precinct nonetheless, he shared his first-hand experience of winding roads, dales, hills and wild woods (*tot viarum diverticula, tot dumeta, tot latibula, tot silvae*).[134] He noticed the sergeants-at-arms in the train of the king and his courtiers and recalled how the restriction on market stalls at Westminster meant vendors were caught in the rain.[135] In a provincial landscape he saw commoners, husbandmen, labourers and traders in the fields and streets (*mercatores, populares agricolae*).[136] And he kept, or liked to suggest that he kept, his ear close to the ground. 'Many and various murmurs and grumbles' were heard, so he claimed, when King Henry planned a further campaign in Wales.[137] He passed on the troubles caused by the devalued currency that were the talk of provincial market places.[138] Murrain outbreaks in Norfolk and in southern counties he thought worth mentioning.[139] When friars preached for a fresh crusade, he noticed how the crowds came out for them as keenly as they did at Rogationtide.[140] Matthew even gave a voice to the blacksmith set to fetter Hubert de Burgh, giving the 'everyman' view that he was 'the greatest' [of courtiers] and the most loyal'.[141]

Here the people were not objects of the king's will or the work of his government; they were subjects who acted and spoke for themselves. Matthew was inclined also to give them a distinct, national identity. All annalists of his time recognised the different peoples of Christendom, but no other so clearly focused on the sources of that nationhood. Englishness was territorial: the speech he gave Thomas of Hortington before the Muslim emir told of an abundant land with well-tended fields, pasture and woods.[142] Foreigners were from overseas (*transmarinis*), a world apart.[143] A tournament he pictured as a contest between the English and 'foreigners'.[144] Even a common monastic status did not stop Matthew from scathing criticism of the Cluniac prior of Thetford (Norfolk), whose fondness for drink was extreme 'even by French standards'.[145] The most conspicuous sign was language, and Englishmen looked for it at home and abroad. When a demon appeared to Stephen Langton in Italy, Matthew was at pains to note that it spoke not in English but '*in lingua patria: nun pas pur toi Cristianelle*'.[146] Above all, it was a matter of natural descent – that is, ethnicity – the English were the true 'natives' (*naturales*).[147]

It was Henry III's challenge to this national community that became the crux of Matthew's criticism of the king. He called out his prodigious anger and greed in the tone of any preacher's homily; it was Henry's offences in the face of the kingdom's natural order that prompted his unprecedented expressions of outrage. Good fortune was won by 'his

English' (*cum suits Anglicis*), just as he brought on himself an ill fame (*in quo facto rex suam non mediocriter denigravit famam*).[148] The favour the king showed to the Poitevan clique in 1242 riled, Matthew wrote, 'the faithful of England' (*Anglorum fidelium*).[149] It was the native baronage (*naturales barones*) and English prelacy who were the 'natural counsellors of his court'. The foreigners given bishoprics were woefully ignorant, not least of English and its idioms.[150] At the end of his life, Matthew focused on their status more clearly still: they were the '*optimates*' of England, the born leaders of the *res publica*.[151] There was implicit criticism in his celebration of the Confessor as a king who conferred his castles on 'his own subjects, gentlemen of birth, and vassals' (*ducs, as cuntes e baruns ... ses natureus/Gentilz de nesaunce e feus*).[152] Henry's preferred favourites, territorial ambitions and papal submission robbed his subjects of the royal protection that was their birthright, and it lost him the love (*diligens*) of his native people (*hominum naturalium*).[153]

Matthew was more than a detached observer of the English cause. He represented the interest of a provincial society which in the wake of the war of 1215–17 and then in the face of King Henry's demands reached out for the rights which had been promised in so any hard-won charters. He watched closely the crown's appointment of county officials[154] and made an exemplary story of the gratuitous greed of William de Insula, the sheriff of Northampton, and his eleventh-hour escape from the capital punishment so conspicuously his due.[155] When the king dismissed sheriffs suspected of corruption, it won him rare praise from Matthew.[156] The incessant demands of justices in the eyre and sheriffs led him to the conclusion that the current oppressions of the crown were as much the result of home-grown agents as foreigners (*tam indigenarum quam exterorum*).[157] The monk shared his neighbourhood's hostility towards the *escheator* Adam Fitzwilliam, a man, he wrote, who was 'monied but wishing to be more so' (*nummosus quidem, sed nummosior esse cupiens*),[158] and he joined them in championing those, such as knights in distant Shropshire, who refused to 'carry the Lord king's yoke' (*noluerunt colla subdere novae domini regis constitutioni*).[159]

Matthew was not slavish towards knightly society. He pictured St Albans and its dependent priories as imperilled by those with territory and influence. Robert Fitzwalter, he reflected, was like an earl (*comes*) commanding a wide swathe of property and people.[160] His true affiliation was to those who acted as advocates and benefactors in the service of his own church, men such as the 'judicious and thoughtful' Laurence de Therbrugge and the 'most pious' William de Sisseverne.[161] The exceptions to his rule of thumb for royal officials were those such as the king's clerk and special councillor Robert of Sotindon, and justiciar Henry of Bath, who had proved themselves 'protectors' of St Albans.[162]

Matthew always viewed the state of the nation from St Albans. The occasion of the royal wedding was an opportunity to offer his St Albans readership the proof of the precedence of their abbot, just as Alban, the protomartyr, is first among all England's martyrs.[163] When he last spoke directly to his troubled king, he could not resist raising with him what mattered most to the monastery itself, the loss of their claim on the manor of Aldenham to their rivals at Westminster Abbey.[164]

Matthew Paris reported on the affairs of the world as might be expected of any lifetime resident of a monastery. Historians have perhaps been beguiled by the length and lively language of his chronicle and by his versatility as a writer in Latin and French in poetry and prose to be persuaded that he was a commentator ahead of or even out of the culture of his community and time. In fact, his final judgment, in his *Gesta abbatum* account of his own abbot, John de Hertford, was not that of an intimate of royalty or an erstwhile guest at court but a member of the clergy: this was a king who thirsted for the spoliation of the church (*sitienter desideravit ecclesiam irrestaurabiliter praegravare*).[165] His descriptions of secular society, as much as of his own monastic milieu, were rooted in the biblical idioms and images of the observant Benedictine. Indeed, it seems he was not strongly inclined to turn to the resources of secular learning and literature which were close at hand at St Albans. His use of the Latin classics was confined to a few favourite tags which appear almost as a mnemonic in the columns of the chronicle. He found little or no advantage in the abbey's position to make use of the formal acts of the crown and the developing institutions of government. If he turned to any other authority to animate his annal it was the French tales of romance familiar to so many of his subjects. Of course, such a blend of clerical biblicism and courtly imagery might explain the monk's personal appeal to a pious king and his family. It is his direct witness of their world, their behaviour, the words they spoke and the value that some of them may have expressed which distinguishes his annals from what survives of the writings of his peers. Matthew made sense of his world as he had been formed to do as a Benedictine monk, but he saw and heard it as any one of us would.

Notes

1. Luard 1872–83, iv. 644.
2. For Matthew's date of birth see Vaughan 1958c, 1–2.
3. Luard 1872–73, iii. 336. See also Madden 1866, ii. 386. The brief description does not bear out Richard Vaughan's suggestion that Matthew saw the wedding for himself: Vaughan 1958c, 3.
4. For this episode see Vincent 2001, 2–5; Carpenter 2021–23, 474–78.
5. Luard 1872–83, iv. 358, 402.
6. Vaughan 1958c, 3; Vincent 2001, 2.
7. Madden 1866, iii. 40–41; Luard 1872–83, v. 36. See also Weiler 2012.
8. Luard 1872–83, v. 129–30, 233–34, 253–54.
9. Luard 1872–83, v. 617.
10. Luard 1872–73, v. 617.
11. Luard 1872–73, v. 724.
12. '*Magistrum regis Angliae*': Luard 1872–73, iii. 623; v. 229.
13. Luard 1872–73, iii. 623.
14. Wallace 1983, 2–3.
15. Luard 1872–73, vi. 391.
16. Luard 1872–72, iv. 43, 146. For a discussion of their relationship see also Hilpert 1981, 90–96, 114–18.
17. Luard 1872–72, iv. 283.
18. Luard 1872–72, iv. 42–47, 138–48, 180–81, 229; v. 97–99, 109–12, 292–93, 629–30, 640, 732–35.
19. Luard 1872–72, iv. 147.
20. Luard 1872–72, v. 275.
21. Luard 1872–72, iv. 632.
22. Luard 1872–83, v. 262.
23. Riley 1867–69, i. 346.
24. Luard 1872–83, v. 627. For Matthew's view of Earl Richard see also Chapter 4, 95–96.
25. Luard 1872–83, v. 673–74.
26. Madden 1866, ii. 265–66.
27. Luard 1872–83, 236–37 at 237.
28. Luard 1872–83, vi. 389.
29. Madden 1866, ii. 359n. See also Luard 1872–83, iii. 249.

30. Madden 1866, iii. 135; Luard 1872–83, iv. 643–44; v. 369.
31. Luard 1872–83, v. 211, 317; vi. 519. See also Chapter 2, 60, nn. 50, 55, and Chapter 6, 150.
32. For these texts see Luard 1864–69, i. 43–180; iii. 3–408; Webster and Preest 2018; Stevenson 1875; Gransden 1964. For Dunstable see also Webster 2020. The Coggeshall annal may have been compiled in real time but not from a proximity to the crown: Carpenter 1998.
33. There is no indication of an impulse to compile a contemporary history at Westminster until late in the reign of Henry III: Gransden 1974b, 453.
34. William of Malmesbury, *Gesta regum*, V, prologue, 2; Mynors, Thomson and Winterbottom 1998–99, i. 708–09.
35. Barlow 1992, xliv–xlv.
36. Luard 1872–83, iv. 644.
37. Luard 1872–83, iii. 320, 337.
38. Luard 1872–83, iii. 58.
39. Luard 1872–83, iv. 255.
40. Riley 1867–69, i. 294.
41. Luard 1872–83, iii. 337–38.
42. Luard 1872–83, v. 515.
43. Cambridge, Corpus Christi College, MS 16 (II), fol. 216ra, lower margin.
44. Cambridge, Corpus Christi College, MS 16 (II), fol. 23ra, upper and lower margins; Cambridge Corpus Christi College, MS 26, fol. 106^v, lower margin.
45. Cambridge Corpus Christi College MS 16 (II), fol. 16rb, right-hand margin. See also Luard 1872–83, iv. 242.
46. For example, Cambridge Corpus Christi College MS 16 (II), fols. 22rb, right-hand margin (Coronation of Otho IV); 68va, left-hand margin (Coronation of Louis IX); 217va, left-hand margin (Haakon IV).
47. Cambridge, Corpus Christi College MS 16 (II), fol. 127^r.
48. Luard 1872–83, iv. 644.
49. Luard 1872–83, iii. 319–20, 369; iv. 255. Matthew's observation on the princess' plate were among his early additions to Wendover's narrative.
50. Luard 1872–83, v. 320.
51. Luard 1872–83, v. 274.
52. *Estoire de Seint Aedward*, ll. 4666–67; Wallace 1983, 131.
53. Luard 1872–83, iii. 320. See also his account of the enrichment of the Confessor's shrine, iv. 157. The quotation is from Ovid's *Metamorphoses*, Book 2, line 5.
54. Lawrence 1996, 133.
55. Lawrence 1996, 146.
56. Luard 1872–83, v. 530.
57. Riley 1867–69, i. 374.

58. Luard 1872–83, iv. 184. For Matthew's view of King Henry's capricious behaviour see also Chapter 4, 93–94.
59. Luard 1872–83, ii. 611.
60. Luard 1872–83, iii. 2.
61. Luard 1872–83, iii. 1.
62. *Estoire de Seint Aedward*, ll. 3, 7, 21, 23; Wallace 1983, 1.
63. Swanton 2010, 15–16.
64. Luard 1872–83, iv. 402, 641.
65. Luard 1872–83, v. 470.
66. Carpenter 2020, 715. See also 283–85.
67. See Keynes 1993.
68. Luard 1872–83, vi. 150–51, 175, 233–34, 255–57, 267–68, 286–89, 320–23, 326–32, 340–41, 343–48, 352–53, 376–82, 393–94, 396–97. See also Gransden's discussion on his difference from Wendover, Gransden 1974, 359, 363–4, 368–9.
69. Luard 1872–83, iv. 362–63, 622–23 at 622 vi. 516, 518, 520; v. 223; Madden 1866, ii. 8, 131, 135, 349, 426, 430; iii. 33.
70. Luard 1872–83, iv. 185.
71. Coxe 1841–44, iii. 302–15; iv. 103–4; Luard 1872–83, ii. 588–606 at 589–604; vi. 251–52, 518. See also Hilpert 1981, 62–89; Holt 1964, 69, 76, 82, 85–86.
72. Vaughan 1958c, 17–18.
73. Luard 1872–83, ii. 559–64; vi. 519.
74. *Estoire de Seint Aedward*, ll. 746–47; Wallace 1983, 22.
75. Luard 1872–83, v. 409.
76. Luard 1872–83, v. 439, 477, 537, 602.
77. Luard 1872–83, iii. 290.
78. Luard 1872–83, v. 18–19 at 18.
79. Luard 1872–83, iv. 191.
80. Luard 1872–83, iii. 4, 325.
81. Luard 1872–83, v. 6.
82. Luard 1872–83, iii. 27; v. 69, 551.
83. Luard 1872–83, iii. 187; iv. 69, 479; v. 128, 183.
84. Luard 1872–83, iii. 57.
85. Luard 1872–83, iii. 328–29 at 329. See also Chapter 5, 121, 123, 127.
86. Luard 1872–83, iv. 403.
87. Luard 1872–83, iii. 352; iv. 377; v. 114–15, 519.
88. Luard 1872–83, iv. 84–85 at 85, 588–89; v. 171, 206, 403.
89. Riley 1867–69, i. 269, 70.
90. Luard 1872–83, iv. 56. Matthew used the same saying in his account of Abbot Wulnoth: Riley 1867–69, i. 16.
91. Luard 1872–83, iv. 61.

92. Sharpe et al. 1996, 402 (B68. 491); Coates 1999, 74, 162; Stoneman 1999, 99–100 (BM1. 170). For the courtly literature, notably *chansons de geste*, which may have influenced Matthew's writing see Chapter 14, 283–96.
93. Luard 1872–83, iv. 202.
94. *Estoire de Seint Aedward*, ll. 4501–02. See also ll. 4307–08, 4508–09; Wallace 1983, 121, 127.
95. Luard 1872–83, iii. 43.
96. Luard 1872–83, iv. 415.
97. Luard 1872–83, v. 97.
98. Luard 1872–83, iii. 60&n. See also Madden 1866, ii. 243.
99. Luard 1872–83, iii. 378; v. 610.
100. '*Miles literatus*' he also applied to Robert de la Hoo: Luard 1872–83, v. 345.
101. Luard 1872–83, v. 362.
102. *Estoire de Seint Aedward*, ll. 1213–18; Wallace 1983, 35.
103. Luard 1872–83, iv. 511; v. 451.
104. Swanton 2010, 65–66.
105. *Estoire de Seint Aedward*, ll. 53–54, 63, 69; Wallace 1983, 2–3.
106. Swanton 2010, 47–48, 91–92.
107. Luard 1872–83, iii. 335; iv. 261.
108. Luard 1872–83, v. 551.
109. Luard 1872–83, v. 632.
110. Luard 1872–83, v. 480.
111. Luard 1872–83, v. 318.
112. Luard 1872–83, v. 145; Swanton 2010, 9–10.
113. Luard 1872–83, v. 159, 315; Madden 1866, ii. 147, 182, 391 Swanton 2010, 9–10.
114. Luard 1872–83, iv. 29, 612; v. 80, 132, 284, 660; Swanton 2010, 9–10.
115. Luard 1872–83, iv. 491; Madden 1866, ii. 510.
116. Luard 1872–83, v. 21, 540.
117. Riley 1867–69, i. 267.
118. Luard 1872–83, iii. 380; iv. 180, 185, 362, 511, 518, 557, 560; Madden 1866, ii. 393, 490–91; iii. 5. In his *Gesta abbatum* Matthew first named Parliament when noting Abbot John's summons in 1254: Riley 1867–69, i. 341.
119. Luard 1864–69, i. 116 (1240); 143 (1251), 278 (1246).
120. Luard 1872–83, iii. 410.
121. Luard 1872–83, iii. 383, 410; iv. 94, 169.
122. Luard 1872–83, iii. 610; iv. 217.
123. *Estoire de Seint Aedward*, ll. 590–91; Wallace 1983, 17.
124. Luard 1872–83, v. 50, 601.
125. Luard 1872–83, v. 50.
126. Swanton 2010, 22, 34, 111–12.
127. Luard 1872–83, iv. 254.

128. Luard 1872–83, iv. 49.
129. Luard 1872–82, v. 329.
130. Luard 1872–83, v. 199.
131. *Et bene credimus, quia hoc apparet ex regis aviditate et egestate, quod clanculo captus fuit et retentus fuit*: Luard 1872–83, v. 21.
132. Luard 1872–83, iii. 296.
133. Luard 1872–83, v. 320.
134. Luard 1872–83, v. 369.
135. Luard 1872–83, v. 29, 333.
136. Luard 1872–83, iii. 519; iv. 198, 490; v. 316.
137. Luard 1872–83, v. 677.
138. Madden 1866, iii. 35; Luard 1872–83, v. 15–16.
139. Madden 1866, iii. 124; Luard 1872–83, v. 321.
140. Luard 1872–83, v. 73.
141. Luard 1872–83, iii. 227–28. See also Madden 1866, ii. 348.
142. Riley 1867–69, i. 237.
143. Luard 1872–83, iii. 244. See also Chapter 4, 95–96.
144. Luard 1872–83, v. 265.
145. Luard 1872–83, v. 31.
146. Liebermann 1879, 323–29 at 324.
147. Luard 1872–83, iii. 241; iv. 64.
148. Riley, 1867–69, i. 374; Luard 1872–83, v. 683.
149. Luard 1872–83, iv. 191.
150. Luard 1872–83, v. 184.
151. Luard 1872–83, iii. 411; v. 689.
152. *Estoire de Seint Aedward*, ll. 2496–2501; Wallace 1983, 71.
153. Luard 1872–83, iv. 64; v. 229.
154. Luard 1872–83, iii. 363; v. 577–81. See also Maddicott 1984.
155. Luard 1872–83, v. 577–81.
156. Luard 1872–83, iii. 363.
157. Luard 1872–83, iv. 34, 186–87; v. 370–71.
158. Riley 1867–69, i. 306.
159. Luard 1872–83, v. 410–11 at 410.
160. Riley 1867–69, i. 220–21.
161. Riley 1867–69, i. 225.
162. Luard 1872–83, v. 28, 223, 394.
163. Luard 1872–83, iii. 337.
164. Luard 1872–83, v. 129–30.
165. Riley 1867–69, i. 374.

BJÖRN WEILER

4

Matthew Paris, Europe and Christendom

The title of this chapter is one that Matthew Paris would probably have found difficult to understand. It implies, for instance, a juxtaposition between England and the European mainland – or 'Continent' – that reflects a modern British way of thinking, not that of a thirteenth-century monk. Matthew Paris' manner of engaging with that mainland echoed the very different cultural parameters within which he moved. There was, for instance, not much of a language barrier: most of Matthew's correspondents, in England as elsewhere, would have communicated either in Latin or distinct yet mutually accessible versions of French.[1] Similarly, Matthew as well as his contemporaries would have formed part of pan-European networks – family connections would see to it that they did, as would membership of a religious community or trading networks.[2] They similarly shared an outlook on the world around them, a common approach to perceiving and interpreting what they observed. Of course, not all of this was unique to the thirteenth century: similar ties exist in a modern context. What was important, however, was the degree to which Matthew Paris formed part of a wider European cultural, religious, political, social and economic community, not the fact that he did.

This circumstance has implications for how we may approach Matthew's relationship with, his perception and his concept of that wider European community. Here, I would like to focus on two closely related aspects of that relationship: what did Matthew know about Europe, and how did he use this information?[3] Matthew's *Chronica Maiora* remains a key document for our understanding of Europe during his lifetime. Yet it also stands in splendid isolation amidst numerous lives of English saints and several revisions of the *Chronica* that focused more narrowly on English affairs. What does this mean for Matthew's reporting of events on the mainland? What, in his eyes, was the news that mattered, that merited recording and interpreting? Matthew also selected the information he reported for the specific purpose of instructing and enlightening his audience. What did he mean by that? Second, what can the answers to these questions tell us about Matthew's concept of Europe? This is a more complex question then it may at first appear. When referring to Europe in a modern context, we normally refer to a geographical entity as well as a set of norms and values, of institutional, political and cultural principles. 'Europe', to quote Robert Bartlett, 'is both a region and an idea'.[4] However, Matthew barely used the term 'Europa'. When he did, he often used it interchangeably with the term 'Occident', denoting a geographical more than a cultural or political unit.[5] Once Matthew sought to express cultural or religious affinities, he preferred Christendom (*Christianitas*). What, though, did this mean in practice? What was the geographical scope of Matthew's engagement with Europe, and what was its cultural framework?

It is perhaps worth reminding ourselves just how wide the range of Matthew's reporting was, and how varied the type of information he collected. Matthew recorded, for instance, the relics brought back to Aachen by Charlemagne in 800;[6] the dispute between Eric and Abel over the Danish throne in the 1240s;[7] the legend of King Abgar of Edessa;[8] an account of Armenia as conveyed by visitors from that region in 1252 (including news as to where Noah's Ark might be found, and the legend of the Wandering Jew);[9] or how the daughter of the (Greek Orthodox) archbishop of Athens, being well versed in the liberal arts, could foretell natural disasters.[10] The list could easily be extended, but it already points to the geographical scope of the chronicler's reporting (in this case, France, Germany, Greece, Asia Minor and Scandinavia). It also points to the kind of information he was interested in, to his kaleidoscopic view of the world around him (with miracles and curious tales existing alongside references to the Bible and accounts of contemporary high politics).[11] Yet it would be mistaken to assume that there was no order to the materials he collected. Matthew produced a compendium of worthwhile information, of entertaining as well as instructive anecdotes, but also of strange occurrences that defied easy interpretation, whose meaning might become apparent only at some point in the future, and which for that very reason merited recording.[12] The writing of history, as Matthew had explained at the outset of both the *Chronica* and the *Historia Anglorum*, was a serious task, one that could guide an audience to a better understanding of God's plan for humankind, that would take that audience further along the path to eternal salvation. Historical writing did so both in a traditional sense by offering models of good deeds to emulate, and of bad ones to shun, but also by providing the means through which signs and wonders could be deciphered.[13]

This also meant that events had to be interpreted, their meaning made evident to those perusing Matthew's writings. Simple recording was not enough. What does this mean for Matthew's reporting of events on the mainland? On a most elementary level, he selected information with an eye, first, on how it might illustrate moral and political truths directly related to contemporary English affairs, and, second, on how it would illuminate the place of England within the wider world of Latin Christendom. The former expressed itself chiefly in a tendency to attribute to foreign regions political mechanisms and norms that Matthew felt were missing, or were not upheld with sufficient rigour, in England. In 1253, for instance, Matthew reported how the king of Castile had greatly expanded his lands, whereas English lordship was in tatters. The Spanish king, out of pity and friendship, sent an embassy to England to remind Henry III of the secret of successful kingship: to be a lamb to one's people and a lion to one's foes – not, it is implied, the other way round.[14] More frequently, such criticism centred on the king's refusal to take the advice and counsel of his barons and his favouritism towards foreign relatives. Such criticism often worked by direct reference: when Matthew reported on the marriage between the king's sister Isabella and Emperor Frederick II in 1235, he also established a clear contrast with King Henry III's marriage to Eleanor of Provence in 1236. Matthew emphasised that the emperor had sent home Isabella's English companions, as she should be educated in the customs and laws of her new realm.[15] This set the scene for how Matthew subsequently referred to the wedding.[16] In 1238, Earl

Richard of Cornwall was said to have castigated the king for failing to follow the example of Frederick II: the emperor had sent home his wife's foreign companions instead of showering them with lands and estates; the king of France similarly did not alienate the royal domain to satisfy the greed of his foreign in-laws.[17] Matthew revisited the theme when reporting on Richard of Cornwall's career as emperor-elect: after the earl's coronation in 1257, his son and various English nobles returned because, it was believed, the Germans, unlike the English, did not want their king to bend his will in the manner of reeds to the counsel of aliens.[18] Events abroad provided an opportunity for direct comment on those at home.

Matthew sketched implicit contrasts too. It seems, for instance, that in Matthew's eyes even the Mongols derived at least some of their strength from their habit of killing any foreigner approaching their camps when they held councils or dealt with matters of importance.[19] That those in power were obliged to take the advice and counsel of their subjects was a central theme in Matthew's writing, one that permeated texts as diverse as his Life of Edward the Confessor, or his – largely fictitious – account of the Saxon king Offa.[20] It certainly mattered as a means of evaluating historical events. When, in the entry for the year 1257, Matthew listed the chief peers of France, he also commented on the Norman claim to the English throne: when Edward the Confessor appointed Duke William the Bastard of Normandy as his heir, this act lacked legitimacy, as Edward had proceeded without consulting his barons.[21] Things were different abroad, even among the infidel and the schismatic. When in 1229 the Knights Templar sent a treasonous letter to the sultan of Egypt (al-Kamil), inviting him to prepare a trap for a crusading Emperor Frederick II, al-Kamil thus deliberated at length with his advisors before formulating his response,[22] and when in 1237 the Byzantines rejected plans for a union with the Latin Church (as they abhorred the venality and corruption of the papal court), the decision was made after a Byzantine prelate had reported back to the Greek nobility on his experiences at the court of Rome.[23] These episodes – and examples from Latin Christendom could also be adduced – win much of their potency from the contrast with the English king's refusal to take proper advice. In 1238 Henry III thus oversaw the clandestine marriage between his sister and an upstart French adventurer (Simon de

Montfort), several earlier promises notwithstanding.[24] As his brother Richard pointed out, he had promised that he would not make such decisions without first consulting his barons,[25] and when in 1254 Henry was offered the kingdom of Sicily on behalf of his youngest son, Edmund, rather than taking the advice of his barons, he accepted the kingdom without hesitation, and then, so Matthew told us, rolled around on the floor in the fashion of an idiot.[26]

Of course, Matthew had been as little privy to al-Kamil's secret council as to Henry III's display of undue exultation, and we may safely assume that he had no eyewitness accounts to draw on either. What mattered was the moral and political message these episodes conveyed. The chronicler fleshed out bare news in a manner in which they could serve to highlight deeper truths. This was not always a conscientious strategy – many of the references to foreign rulers taking guidance are incidental, made in passing, and are not constructed as a central point of the narrative. Matthew fashioned events as he expected them to have unfolded. Even so, there was a clear contrast. Matthew Paris wrote the history of Europe because it merited recording in its own right, but also because it provided a means with which to comment on the deeds of his English contemporaries. In doing so, Matthew was no different from almost any other writer of history in the thirteenth century. It does mean, however, that his modern readers have to be aware of the degree to which he often filtered events so as to provide moral lessons for his audience, the extent to which he so frequently – and especially when dealing with matters outside England – described events as he thought they ought to have occurred, and not necessarily as they did occur.

It would at the same time be mistaken to assume that Matthew used the wider world exclusively as a mirror of morals. It also mattered as the stage on which Englishmen excelled, where they performed many and valiant deeds and proclaimed the greater glory of the English nation. When in 1229 Frederick II restored Jerusalem to Christian control, this was thus not the emperor's doing, but that of the bishop of Winchester who had accompanied him,[27] and when in 1247 an imperial army besieged Parma, this was, above all, divine punishment because the bishop of London had been robbed while staying in the city a few years before.[28] Similarly, the king apart, most Englishmen who ventured onto the wider European scene quickly became famous for excelling at their tasks: Matthew Paris (the Norwegians even secured a papal mandate to obtain his services),[29] Richard of Cornwall (who ransomed failed crusaders wherever he turned,[30] sought to restore peace between pope and emperor,[31] and, once elected king of the Romans, freed towns and regions from manifold exactions),[32] and William Longespée, one of the few true crusading heroes of the thirteenth century.[33] The theme surfaces elsewhere in Matthew's writing too. In the *Vitae Duorum Offarum*, Offa II successfully warded off and even won grudging respect from Charles Martel and Charlemagne.[34] In the *Estoire*, his life of Edward the Confessor, Matthew similarly included a tale about the barbarous customs of the empire and the more civilised mores of England: after an English princess (Gunnilda), married an emperor, she was accused of adultery and had to purge her name through trial by combat. Having proven her innocence with the aid of a dwarf, she repudiated her husband and returned home to a glorious welcome.[35] English virtue was triumphant once more.

Yet Matthew was also wary of that wider world. Just because rulers abroad did things better, this did not mean that, given the opportunity, they would not seek to destroy, conquer and subdue the island or its inhabitants. Much as Matthew praised Richard of Cornwall, for instance, he also felt that Richard was in danger of falling prey to greedy foreigners.[36] Equally, if not duped or tricked by deceitful aliens, Englishmen were often brought low by envious ones. This sentiment seems to have underpinned the episode about Gunnilda in the *Estoire*. It was also evident in Matthew's account of Cardinal Robert Sumercote, a gracious, amicable and wise man, Matthew claims, who, rumour had it, was poisoned because he was English, and because he would have made a capable pope.[37] Similarly, the deposition of Stephen of Lexington as abbot of Clairvaux in 1257 had been triggered by the intrigues of an envious Frenchman.[38] That the plotter was French was no coincidence: among the peoples of Europe, the French had most frequently inflicted suffering and humiliation on the English.[39] In fact, being envious of the English, combined with arrogance and a desire to dominate others, was, in Matthew's eyes, the natural state of the French.[40] It was because of that arrogance, in turn, that the king of Norway refused to join the crusade of Louis IX,[41] and, alongside the ties, both ancient and modern, that bound together Germany and England, a shared language, and Richard of Cornwall's many qualities (and great treasure), it was the fear of choosing an arrogant Frenchmen that made the Germans elect the earl to be their king.[42] However, while the French were haughtier and more supercilious than others, in Matthew's eyes pride and arrogance were traits common to all foreigners. The Germans were rash and proud (and frequently got into fights with each other),[43] and the Norwegians were an impetuous and indiscreet people who disliked injustice as much as they spurned modesty.[44]

All this certainly made Germans and Norwegians difficult company to keep, but the combination of greedy, impetuous and ambitious foreigners with a weak and ineffectual king also posed political dangers. Matthew explained as much when in 1244 he described how one of Frederick II's envoys sought to convince the English barons not to back the pope against the emperor. According to Matthew, only a narrow stretch of sea separated England from the lands of the emperor, and the imperial emissary had warned that, by granting financial aid to the *curia*, the king and barons would find themselves in wars that would 'scratch them to their bones'. More importantly, the chronicler continued, offering financial aid to the pope would mean fighting the English (as the emperor's English wife had borne him a son), and would deprive Henry of the means to avenge the humiliation and suffering the French had so frequently inflicted upon his people.[45] When, on hearing the complaints of his barons and prelates, Henry eventually did complain to Pope Innocent IV, he did so in his habitually soft and gentle fashion, with the result that the pontiff sought to wrest Wales from Henry's grasp.[46] Matthew may have exaggerated the threat posed by foreigners, but he also reflected widespread fears. In 1232, for instance, the king's former justiciar Hubert de Burgh had been accused of seeking to deliver England into the hands of Frederick II.[47] When interpreting Merlin's prophecy, Matthew identified Frederick II as the man who, jointly with the Scots, would expel the English from Britain and restore it to Welsh rule.[48] When in 1236/37 imperial envoys visited Ireland to collect the empress' dowry, this caused palpable unease at court.[49] In 1240, rumours of an imminent Danish invasion began to circulate.[50] In fact, when Matthew recorded the death in that year of both Valdemar II of Denmark and his only son, he felt that their demise meant that Edward the Confessor protected England against the threat of renewed Danish tyranny.[51] England, in short, was surrounded by those envious of the accomplishments of its people and desirous to exploit the weakness of its king.

Matthew's attitude towards the lands beyond the Channel was certainly ambivalent. It was not, however, internally inconsistent. He did not advocate that Henry III adopt the rashness, greed and ambition of his neighbours. What distinguished the English as a people from their neighbours were their humility, piety and courage.[52] These qualities expressed themselves not only in the numerous valiant deeds performed by Englishmen abroad, but also in the many saints who peopled the island (which, in the *Chronica*, far outnumber those on the mainland), and by the fact that the miracles Matthew reported occurred mostly in England. The kingdom was clearly blessed with and deserving of divine benevolence. This good will, in turn, was at least partly merited by the unwillingness or even inability of the English to be as arrogant, rash and greedy as their neighbours. What Matthew did demand, however, was that the kingdom's ruler abide by universal norms of political behaviour, that he acknowledge, encourage and protect the virtuous nature of his people, that he take the advice of his native barons, and that he shun the counsel of corrupt and greedy aliens. For if he failed to do so, he would weaken the virtues of his people and would deliver them into the eager hands of their rivals and foes.

Matthew Paris was not, however, a thirteenth-century British Europhobe, nor was he, in more academic terms, a proponent of English exceptionalism, of the belief that England was deeply and profoundly different from an elusive norm uniformly adhered to east of Dover. The English may have excelled and their king may have failed miserably at upholding virtuous principles of political and moral conduct, but these principles were shared by Englishmen, Frenchmen, Germans, Norwegians and Castilians alike. It was simply the case that the English were also better at shunning the vices common to their neighbours. Moreover, as we have seen, even Greek schismatics and Muslims upheld such common principles. The circumstance is worth keeping in mind, not the least because it points to another major preoccupation of the chronicler, one that both reflected and transcended his concern for the standing and welfare of the English.

England was, after all, part of a wider cultural and political community, its fortunes inextricably tied to that community. That community was of course Christendom, and it is to Matthew's definition of Christendom and its wider relationship with England that we should now turn.

When reporting the death of Sultan al-Kamil of Egypt in 1238, Matthew described him in terms of an ideal, quasi-Christian ruler: the sultan had freed many slaves, given lavish gifts to hospices for Christian pilgrims and performed many other deeds of charity; although a pagan he was truthful, merciful, generous and, as far as the customs of his people and the suspicions of his neighbours permitted, a Christian. In fact, Emperor Frederick II had hoped to convert him to Christianity.[53] Alongside the vigorous defence of a ruler's kingdom and the abhorrence of alien counsel, al-Kamil's were the virtues of a truly good prince.[54] We also need to keep in mind, however, Matthew's otherwise visceral hatred of Muslims, Byzantines and non-Latin Christians.[55] He thus described Mohammed as the puppet of a corrupt Nestorian monk who fed him heretical ideas out of which Mohammed spun the Koran,[56] and the first patriarch of Constantinople as the product of an unnatural union between a harlot and an antipope.[57] It is perhaps also worth setting Matthew's obituary for al-Kamil alongside those he composed for other Muslim rulers. Saladin died a miserable death, appropriately ending a life that was a scourge to others;[58] and his brother, an inveterate villain, the tyrant of Asia, died of grief over a crusading victory and went straight to hell.[59] Clearly, there were limits as to just how far Muslim rulers could serve as moral exemplars. What was different about al-Kamil?

To answer this question we need to ponder what else Matthew had to say about the ruler of Egypt. Al-Kamil first appeared on the chronicler's horizon with the Fifth Crusade and the siege of Damietta. Having been forced to retreat before the advancing crusaders, he sent an envoy to treat for peace, offering to return Jerusalem to Christian control provided the siege of Damietta was lifted. After the crusaders rejected the offer, al-Kamil defeated them in battle but still agreed to an eight-year truce, and showed great concern for the Christian wounded and captives.[60] Al-Kamil appears for a second time in the context of Emperor Frederick II's crusade of 1228/29. Frederick had been excommunicated in 1227 by Pope Gregory IX when he failed yet again to fulfil the vow, first made in 1216, to lead a campaign to the Holy Land. The emperor set sail regardless, but, on landing in Jerusalem, was met with deep hostility by the Latin patriarch and the military orders.[61] Al-Kamil, Matthew reports, on hearing of Frederick's arrival, provided him with presents and eventually ceded Jerusalem to his control.[62] Most important in the present context are the motivations and thoughts that Matthew attributed to al-Kamil and the contrast he frequently painted between the Muslim ruler and the crusading Latins. In 1219, al-Kamil had been moved to offer a truce because he felt that the God of the Christians was strong and that, to stay in power, he must return to God what by right belonged to God. Al-Kamil also trusted in the fact that the greed and ambition of the Christians would turn their God against them.[63] Events proved him right. Matthew reported al-Kamil as expressing similar sentiments in 1228 in the context of an alleged plot by the Templars. Frederick, eager to visit the place where St John had once baptised Christ, was to be accompanied by only a small force. The Templars sent a secret message to al-Kamil, inviting him to capture or even kill the emperor. The sultan in turn was horrified at the treacherous nature of the Christians, especially of those donning religious habits. Taking the advice of his councillors (who suggested that the plot could be used to sow discord among the Christians), al-Kamil passed the Templars' letter to Frederick.[64] It is important to note just how important the events of 1228 were to Matthew. When in 1246 the Templars sent envoys to the sultan of Egypt to request the return of Christian captives, the sultan refused their request: they had shown just how treacherous and untrustworthy they were when they sought to betray Frederick.[65] And when recounting in 1250 the chief events of the previous fifty years, Matthew Paris referred again to the events of 1228 as a token of the popes' hatred for Frederick.[66] Quite clearly this was not a minor incident, but one that to Matthew encapsulated fundamental truths.

How does all of this contextualise Matthew's obituary for al-Kamil? The ruler of Egypt served a function in relation to Latin Christendom as a whole, which Latin Christendom (and men like al-Kamil) served in relation to Henry III. That is, he was an ideal moral type: he was more upstanding, pious and concerned to do good than many a Christian.

Moreover, he recognised a truth that many of the Latins failed to see and that was central to Matthew's understanding of the world: the importance of Jerusalem for Christendom, the moral and political obligations its protection laid upon true Christians. This connection was not merely a matter of ensuring a Christian presence – after all, Saladin had allowed mass to be said in Jerusalem, but this did not spare him eternal damnation.[67] Al-Kamil, by contrast, did not merely tolerate Christians in Jerusalem, but ceded it to them. Only the corruption, treachery and infighting of the Christians allowed him to keep the city. The crusaders at Damietta, the Templars and papal allies during Frederick II's crusade, showed themselves guilty of the very mistakes, though on a much grander scale, for which Matthew had also maligned King Henry III, and they succumbed to the very vices against which the English king proved unable or unwilling to protect his people.

The defence of the Holy Land and the propagation of the Christian faith were central pillars of that broader community of values and norms of which Matthew Paris perceived England to be a part. This is evident even in the design of Matthew's manuscripts: the famous map of the pilgrimage route to Jerusalem, for instance, prefaces the Cambridge manuscript of the *Chronica*. It is also evident in the fact that so many of the events Matthew described were related to crusading or to the challenges facing Latin Christendom. Croatians and Bulgarians thus made an appearance because of their adherence to various heresies,[68] Bohemia, Hungary, Poland, Russia and Persia because of the Mongol invasions.[69] India in turn registered because it was from there that the legendary Prester John was to lead an army against Muslims and Mongols,[70] and Armenia because of the Armenian visitors to St Albans, their account of Noah's Ark, the legend of the Wandering Jew and the devastating impact of the Mongol invasions.[71] The Armenian case is, of course, indicative of the degree to which the information Matthew provided was dependant on lines of exchange and contact, on news actually reaching St Albans. It is also indicative, however, of the kind of information Matthew was interested in, of what he deemed worth recording. The focus on crusading and the overall affairs of Christendom are after all equally evident in his reporting on regions much closer to England. The archbishops of Cologne in Germany, for instance, chief agents in dealings between the rulers of

England and those of the Holy Roman Empire,[72] had their deeds recorded either because of their dealings with England or because of their crusading endeavours.[73] The same was true of the dukes of Bavaria and Austria – in the latter case, Matthew was, it seems, unaware of attempts in 1225 to arrange a marriage between the English king and the duke's daughter.[74] The kings of Hungary in turn appeared either as victims of the Mongols or as participants in campaigns to free Jerusalem,[75] and even major places of commerce like Marseilles were mentioned primarily in the context of crusading.[76] In short, the crusades defined the geographical horizon of much of Matthew's reporting.

That dimension also mattered as a means of evaluating political actions. It was, for instance, a means by which sins could be atoned. When in 1246 James of Aragon had the bishop of Gerona's tongue torn out (because he spoke too freely against the king), James merited forgiveness at least in part because of his successful campaigns against the Muslims of Iberia.[77] James was, however, unusual, not because of the severity of his crimes, but because the sin followed the atonement. More typical were the cases of Peter des Roches, the bishop of Winchester, and Emperor Frederick II. Peter was by no means one of Matthew's heroes. In fact, the chronicler did not hold back with invective against the bishop, who in 1232–34, as leader of the king's Poitevin favourites, had triggered what was perhaps the most serious crisis of Henry's early adult reign.[78] However, on reporting the prelate's death in 1238, Matthew wrote a glowing obituary in which he made no reference to Peter's political role in England. Instead he focused on his participation in the emperor's crusade, his successful attempts at mediating between pope and emperor and his numerous religious foundations.[79] That is, participation in the delivery of Jerusalem outweighed otherwise grave and serious failings. As far as Frederick II was concerned, Matthew's attitude was famously complex, oscillating between admiration and unease, praise and condemnation. He certainly did not refrain from criticising Frederick's cruelty and hubris.[80] Yet when reporting the emperor's death in 1250, the chronicler stressed the emperor's piety and the fears that his death caused to both crusaders and the Christians in the Latin East.[81] In fact, Matthew's sympathies swayed towards Frederick whenever the emperor offered to lead a campaign to Jerusalem, and when Matthew recounted the chief events of the half century between 1200 and 1250, the papal–imperial conflict was reported so as to stress the corruption and greed of the papal court and the damage it caused to the affairs of Christendom.[82] Matthew's obituaries were not marked by an unwillingness to speak hurtful truths, to respect the memory and forgive the flaws of those recently deceased: he did not refrain from sending men to hell or purgatory if he felt their past actions merited such suffering. There is, however, a general pattern that those who saw to the affairs of Christendom would be forgiven for their transgressions, political and otherwise.[83]

Advancing Latin Christendom was also a token of successful royal lordship. King Valdemar II of Denmark was thus singled out because he had fought pagans all his life and had established six bishoprics.[84] The rulers of Christian Iberia equally excelled at spreading the Christian faith: Matthew recounted the exploits of James of Aragon (who took Ceuta)[85] and Ferdinand of Castile – who conquered Cordoba, Valencia and Seville, Majorca and Minorca.[86] In fact, Valdemar's and Ferdinand's campaigns were so important to Matthew that in 1250 he listed them among the chief events to have taken place during the past fifty years.[87] The latter notice is worth dwelling on, as it illustrates how and why crusading was also a means with which to pass moral comment. News of the Danish and Castilian conquests thus followed reference to Henry III's inability to regain the lands lost by his father, and were in turn followed by references to the popes' hatred for Frederick II, the emperor's eagerness to fight in the Holy Land notwithstanding; the Templars' plot of 1228; and how Innocent IV had only been able to become pope because his more capable rival had been murdered.[88] The relative crusading fervour of other rulers was an embarrassment to the English king – Henry failed to match the valiant efforts of his people (and it is worth noting that many English excelling on the wider European scene did so because of their crusading efforts). English crusading excellence highlighted Henry's shortcomings in other ways too. There was a reason Alfonso X of Castile, who had already made two Muslim kings his subjects, gave Henry III advice on how to be a good king. Similar sentiments perhaps shine through in Matthew's statement that James of Aragon and Ferdinand of Castile had instilled fear in Louis IX.[89] The only time an Englishmen triggered such emotions was when Richard of Cornwall became king of the Romans.[90] Similarly,

James of Aragon, his various faults notwithstanding, was both valiant and able to see through papal machinations.[91] That is, successfully pursuing the expansion and defence of Christendom was a token of good kingship. It expressed adherence to shared norms of political behaviour, to the exercise of prudence, generosity and valour. Meek and ineffectual kings did not make good crusaders.

Showing concern for the affairs of Christendom was also part of a wider set of duties and obligations. Nowhere is this more evident than in Matthew's depiction of the papal court. In fact, he is famous for the vitriol he heaped upon those popes active during his lifetime, and it was perhaps this vitriol that made him so popular among Protestant authors of the sixteenth and seventeenth centuries. What matters here, though, are the values that Matthew claimed were violated by these pontiffs, foremost among them that individual popes, through their corruption and greed, had deterred many a Muslim or Byzantine from becoming Catholic. This was implied in the case of al-Kamil, but it was also the very reason given by the Byzantines who in 1238 rejected plans for a union of the churches because they were horrified at the curia's corruption. In fact, the only success in reconciling schismatics to the church was achieved by one of the early Dominicans, who in the 1230s convinced the Nestorian Christians of Armenia to foreswear their errors. This also occurred long before the friars became themselves papal allies and their subsequent moral decline.[92]

Such failings were closely linked to the issue of heresy, which posed an even greater challenge to Christendom than Islam or schismatic Christians in the East. Matthew's reporting on the subject was extensive. He dealt with Arianism,[93] Donatism[94] and Pelagianism,[95] the major challenges to Catholic Christianity in antiquity.[96] It was, however, in reporting the affairs of his own age that Matthew provided his most detailed coverage.[97] To Matthew, heretics were worse than Saracens,[98] and he fully supported their forceful persecution: he penned a poem in praise of Simon de Montfort the elder, leader of the Albigensian crusade,[99] believed that the annihilation of the Stedinger peasants in the 1230s was a sign of divine backing for those fighting them[100] and applauded the efforts at exterminating heretics in general (be it by burning them at the stake or by burying them alive).[101] Yet heresy was not just a matter of heterodox beliefs, but also of actions that violated basic social and moral norms. Matthew thus recounted with some glee how bankers in London were persecuted for heresy (because of their usury),[102] and notice should be taken of the various unorthodox practices that he ascribed to the citizens of Milan: the town was a hotbed of Albigensians, Patarenes, Satanists and bankers.[103]

His concept of heterodoxy thus applied by no means only to those already outside the church. When describing the death of Robert Grosseteste, Matthew included a speech allegedly given by the bishop in which he offered a very specific definition of heresy: it was chosen by human reason, contrary to scripture, taught in public and tenaciously defended. Grosseteste elaborated: as *heresy* was a Greek word while *election* (having been singled out to administer divine grace) was Latin, it was all the more scandalous that members of the Roman curia appointed to benefices and official positions those unsuitable for the care of souls. Granting, for instance, authority to someone too young for the priesthood was a decision driven by human desires of patronage based on family relationship or shared origin; it contravened scripture, as the Bible had prohibited appointing those as shepherds who were unsuitable to fight off wolves; it was public, as such appointments were made with properly sealed letters; and it was tenaciously defended, as those opposing such actions were suspended, excommunicated and attacked. Yet those who failed to oppose these sins were themselves guilty of heresy: they condoned rather than combated those undermining the faith. This was especially true of the Dominicans and Franciscans. In fact, it would be fair to say that both the pope and the friars would suffer eternal death, unless they rectified these violations of orthodox practice and belief.[104]

How far this speech was Grosseteste's rather than Matthew's is difficult to ascertain. It certainly reflected several of the chronicler's bugbears. In addition to the papal trade with benefices (the appointment of curial officials to receive the income attached to tithes and other sources of revenue, originally intended to provide sustenance for those engaged in pastoral care),[105] Grosseteste thus inveighed against the spurious reasons Innocent IV gave for revoking the privileges of his predecessors[106] and the protection he extended to usurers and bankers.[107] It comes as no surprise, therefore, that Matthew reported on three occasions that Innocent IV had been dispatched if not to hell, then at least to purgatory.[108] It needs, of course, to be taken into account that he wrote these passages at about the time when Henry III had accepted the Sicilian throne on behalf of his son Edmund, which resulted in unprecedented financial demands on the English church. Consequently, Matthew's commentary became ever more bitter. Yet this was not the first time that Matthew criticised the papal court for its heterodox practices and allies. In 1236, Matthew first reported approvingly that the emperor would not fight in the Holy Land while false Christians remained at large in his domains and then wondered why the papal curia – who ought to be a father to the faithful and a hammer to the infidel – was so eager to protect them.[109] In 1244, Master Martin, a papal envoy, was much maligned: he demanded palfreys and gifts from abbots, suspending those who refused, and viewed vacant bishoprics and benefices primarily as a means of enriching the papal court.[110] That same year, Matthew inserted a long list of papal extortions, very much foreshadowing the complaints later attributed to Robert Grosseteste, while in Syria pagans had overrun Jerusalem and killed many Christians, so Matthew, the papal court was concerned mostly with exploiting the church. Cathedrals and abbeys had been endowed to provide for the poor and the kingdom, not for the papal court; being so instrumental in defending the papal court (by using the funds of English churches), the kingdom was also exposed to foreign threats (as papal wealth had to be destroyed at its source). At the same time, the pope deprived the king of the funds he needed to recover his own inheritance and had sacrificed the rights of England to satisfy his greed and ambition.[111]

These examples contextualise Matthew's concept of heresy as any action that ran counter to basic moral and social norms embedded in scripture. Banking, for instance, fell under heresy because it violated biblical prohibitions against usury, but also – and this is worth noting – because it caused untold suffering to those already poor and powerless.[112] Heresy furthermore required condemnation because it caused physical, economic and social harm to society: in 1236 the curia's antics jeopardised the battle against heresy, in 1244 it prevented Christians from coming to the aid of the Holy Land, and in his account of the year 1250, Matthew reported heavy floods and stormy seas as a sure token of divine wrath at the greed and corruption of Innocent IV.[113] Finally, the curia was symptomatic of a wider malaise: wealth and secular might would lead those astray who were not Benedictine monks.

In 1238 Robert le Bougres, a Dominican in charge of persecuting heretics in France and Flanders, thus descended slowly into tyranny: a man of decent learning, Matthew reported, successful in the office of preaching, he put on trial numerous heretics. However, he soon abused his powers and put to death many innocents and many who were either of a simple mind or inarticulate.[114] Robert did not start out with the intention of doing evil. However, the excessive pursuit of virtue turned into a sin as great if not greater than the vices it was initially meant to combat. A like trajectory could be witnessed in the case of the Dominicans and Franciscans: both started out as movements renowned for their poverty and piety as well as their moral uprightness (in 1233 they had thus exhorted King Henry III to mend his ways and to take the counsel of his native subjects).[115] However, when they were soon after (in 1234) granted the right to preach the cross and sell crusading indulgences, they collected so many funds and signed up so many who were unsuitable for the business of fighting that they ultimately cooled enthusiasm for the Holy Land.[116] It was sad to see, Matthew remarked a few years later, how the friars had gone into steeper decline more quickly than any other new order: where similar movements had taken forty or fifty years to decline, they took barely twenty-five.[117] In short, proximity to economic and political power corrupted those not steeled and hardened by their exposure to the proper disciplines of the monastic life.

As a result, such clergy allowed heresy to spread, endangered the unity of Christendom and failed to aid the Holy Land. They also encouraged the spread of tyranny because they proved themselves unable to offer the moral leadership and admonition that, in Matthew's eyes, it was the main duty of members of the church to provide. There was a reason Matthew, on recording in the *Historia Anglorum* the death of Innocent III in 1216, remarked that Innocent suffered a judgement of divine wrath, perhaps even eternal damnation, because of the treachery he had committed against the English barons and the king of France.[118] What Matthew referred to was that in 1215 Innocent had first encouraged the barons and the French to resist King John, and then sided with the king after all (a reference to the issuing of

Magna Carta and its subsequent annulment by the pope). That is, Innocent succumbed to greed, envy and the lust for power. Wise kings like James of Aragon, Louis IX of France or Hakon of Norway quickly learned how to avoid getting ensnared in the schemes of a corrupt and venal church. Weak and foolish ones like Henry III remained not only ineffective, unable or unwilling to put an end to Roman extortions, but also lacked the moral sense to rule their kingdom effectively and wisely.

They required wise and prudent clerics to guide them, and it is worth noting that, in Matthew's eyes, those clerics were most worthy of veneration who stood up to royal power, who did not shy away from thrusting their advice on an unwilling king. St Alban, Edward the Confessor and the two Offas apart, Matthew's hagiographical oeuvre centred on archbishops – Thomas Becket, Stephen Langton and Edmund Rich – who forcefully resisted royal and papal power, who forced the monarch to abide by common rules of appropriate moral and political conduct. Yet admonishing the king was not the prerogative of saintly prelates alone. By way of example, it is worth pondering how Matthew constructed his complaints about papal extortions voiced in 1244: interspersed with grievances about grasping papal agents and a supine king were several instances of bishops who spoke out forcefully, who reminded their king of the norms and values, customs and practices that he was meant to uphold and by which he was meant to abide.[119] By exploiting the church rather than reprimanding the king, the pope failed to do his duty by the people given into his care. It was left to the English prelates to perform that function instead. Such admonition, moreover, was by no means limited to the running and organisation of the church alone. Matthew thus held former students of Edmund Rich in high esteem, not the least because they kept resisting the king's demands for taxation.[120] In 1244 bishops were among those, so Matthew reported, who demanded that a commission be appointed to ensure that the terms of Magna Carta be kept,[121] and in 1253 they took a leading role in demanding a reissue of Magna Carta.[122] Offering moral and spiritual guidance extended to the affairs of the realm as a whole. This also brings us back to Matthew's obituary for Peter des Roches. The bishop had made amends not only by having been to the Holy Land, but also by berating the king for his undue patronage of foreigners. That des Roches only fulfilled his proper episcopal function once expelled from power only confirmed Matthew's wider attitude towards the relationship between clergy and secular might. Wealth corrupted. Only exceptional individuals and institutions of sufficient age and robustness could withstand the allure of worldly riches.

The Benedictines were one such institution. They may have been wealthy, but their wealth served a purpose, and, unlike in the case of newer orders, did not lure them into corruption and moral decline. Their wealth served to finance what in a modern context would be called the social and economic fabric of the realm: bridges, granaries, hospitals and roads. They were the kingdom's keepers both spiritually and materially. There were, of course, proud, corrupt and greedy monks, but they only made shine all the more brightly the religious fervour of their brethren. Most importantly, though, Benedictines had an apostolic pedigree (they followed the rule of St Benedict).[123] Their longevity and fervour reflected those hallowed origins and thus point to another essential feature of Matthew's understanding of Christendom: it was the duty of all Christians to preserve, defend and restore a tradition of Christianity rooted in and sanctified by the history of the church. In 1244 Master Martin not only violated the curia's duty to preserve the liberty of the church, but also aimed to overturn its venerable apostolic order: when Augustine had preached in England, and when King Athelstan (as well as many of his peers and successors) had granted estates for the foundation of bishoprics, Matthew had the English prelates argue, they had established a principle of organisation that was now being threatened for no other reason than to enrich a greedy and profligate pope. Innocent IV and his agents undermined the foundations of Christendom not only by consorting with heretics and by their corruption and greed and lust for worldly power, but also by betraying the origins of their own power and that of the community entrusted to their care. It thus comes as no surprise that one of Matthew's most frequent complaints about the pope – voiced also by Grosseteste – was that Gregory IX and Innocent IV reserved the right to overturn the grants and privileges of their predecessors: they sought to break the chain of apostolic succession, claiming for themselves a degree of authority that placed them above the apostles themselves. They added arrogance and hubris to corruption, avarice and greed.

Looking back to an ideal status quo ante, to a normative status rooted in and ennobled by the patina of history, remained a central feature of Matthew's thinking. It formed, for instance, a key element in his rejection of authority. Abbots who curtailed the liberties of monks, bishops who intruded in the running of exempt abbeys and royal councillors who sought to weaken ancient liberties all threatened to undermine the basic ordering of Christian society. This does not mean that Matthew rejected innovation per se: sometimes liberties had to be enshrined anew (as in the case of Magna Carta, notwithstanding its relationship with the coronation charter of Henry I), and new means had to be found to counter new challenges or to pursue established goals (like the recovery and defence of the Holy Land). Yet they all aimed to preserve or seek to restore an ideal ordering of society rooted in the long course of Christian history.

That hallowed tradition was, however, under threat. It was besieged as much by Muslims, Mongols, Byzantines and heretics as by inept kings, rapacious pontiffs and mendacious friars. The sense of threat in turn may help to contextualise Matthew's frequent invocation that the end of the world was nigh.[124] Do those invocations make him a firm believer in an imminent apocalypse? Probably not (though more work will need to be done on the subject). On a practical level, there would have been little point to produce as monumental a work as the *Chronica*.[125] Few authors of extensive histories believed the world was to end in their own lifetime. The apocalypse need not, of course, be a bad thing (it would, after all, herald the return of Christ), but it would militate against the kind of labour Matthew undertook to trace and record the sum of human history. It is more likely that Matthew believed that the end of the world would come, but that he also sought to provide his readers with a means of preparing for that event. Matthew also knew his Bible and church fathers well enough to understand that the end of days could not be predicted. He was a monk steeped in Christian thought, not a born-again zealot. There were signs and wonders that could foretell great changes, but their meaning would all too often become apparent only to later generations.[126] It was for this reason, as he had explained in the *Chronica*, that Matthew wrote history: posterity would be able to make sense of the events he recorded.[127] Consequently, Matthew's references to the imminent end of days were perhaps expression not of certain belief, but of criticism and unease: rather than warding off or delaying the apocalypse, or preparing their flock for its coming, Innocent IV and his ilk acted so as to make it all too likely that God in his righteous wrath would destroy them and those around them. The world might end because those appointed to be its guardians had become its oppressors. In this sense, Matthew's references may also constitute a spur to action: the coming of the apocalypse was not to be awaited in passive stupor, but demanded active preparation, offered a last chance for moral and religious renewal.[128]

It was not, however, all gloom and doom. In his summary of the chief events occurring between 1200 and 1250, Matthew thus interspersed tales about internal oppression, a corrupt papal court, the rise and fall of the Dominicans or the fall of Jerusalem with signs of hope and renewal: the Beguines of Cologne; the emergence of new saints in Elisabeth of Thuringia, Robert of Knaresborough, Edmund Rich, Roger of London and Hildegard of Bingen; the rebuilding of Westminster Abbey; or the arrival in England of the relic of the Holy Blood.[129] In fact, Matthew had inserted various references to Elisabeth of Thuringia in Roger of Wendover's text[130] and later feted her alongside Hildegard of Bingen.[131] Furthermore, miracles were performed by Edmund Rich,[132] the archdeacon Thomas of Northumberland,[133] Richard of Chichester[134] and Eric of Denmark.[135] Christendom, as we have seen, was expanded by Hakon of Norway, Ferdinand of Castile, James of Aragon and Valdemar of Denmark and heresy suppressed by Simon de Montfort. Yet that list of hopeful signs also indicated wider concerns. Almost all the miracles reported thus occurred in England, mostly at Lincoln and Chichester,[136] though also at Redbourn (worked by St Amphibalus),[137] Leicester (where a female recluse spent seventy years without eating)[138] or Clare (where a woman regained the ability to walk).[139] The miracles similarly did not lack a critical edge: when the Cistercian monks of Pontigny felt burdened by the number of pilgrims to the shrine of St Edmund, they cut off one of the saint's arms. For this they incurred great shame – observers, so Matthew, compared their actions unfavourably to the Benedictines' more respectful treatment of saintly remains – and miracles ceased: the brethren had succumbed to greed and hubris.[140] Equally, Matthew included a series of pious but warning legends: a voice warned the agents of a corrupt archbishop of York that everything that belonged to the prelate did in fact belong to the devil;[141] also at York, the devil warned those visiting a priest who was mighty in preaching but secretly avaricious that all the dying man's property belonged to him.[142] Not without reason, it seems, had Matthew noted in the margins of his manuscript that these tales were '*impertinens sed utile*', impertinent but useful.

All of which brings us back to key themes in Matthew's approach towards and concept of Europe. To some extent, Henry's failures as much as the successes of his subjects formed part of a recurrent pattern by no means confined to England. They reflected both the ideals and the norms of a community of Christians – the defence of the Holy Land, piety, generosity and an abhorrence of tyranny – and the less-than-perfect reality of Matthew's experience – where envy, greed and a lust for power endangered not only the internal peace of Christendom, but its very existence. What Matthew sought to offer was an account both of these dangers and of the means by which they could be met – hence his invective against violations of basic moral, political and religious norms, but hence also his desire to record both valiant and virtuous deeds and the existence of holy men and women. What all this also means was that Matthew perceived that wider community as one of religion and morals, not just geography. The geographical limits of Christendom mattered little – except as something to be expanded and defended – and would, in any case, have included the newly Latinate Nestorians of Armenia and the subjects of Prester John in India just as they would have excluded the pagans of Frisia and Lithuania or the Muslims of Iberia and Sicily. More important was the complex relationship between that wider community, its fears and values, its challenges, defeats and successes, and England. That relationship in turn played itself out as much in concrete actions, such as valiant deeds in Outremer, as it did on a moral and religious plane, in the ability or inability, the willingness or reluctance of individual players to abide by basic principles of moral and political conduct, of adhering to the essential norms that defined Christendom. England, while at times a shining beacon of Christian virtue, was only one part of a much larger community. To sketch the history of that community and England's part within it was a central focus of Matthew's writing. It is only by keeping in mind that complex relationship that we will also understand Matthew's concept of Europe.

Notes

1. Crane 1997; Wogan-Browne et al. 2009; Trotter 2011.
2. Matthew 1997; Weiler and Rowlands 2002; Matthew 2005.
3. On this occasion, it will not be possible to set Matthew alongside other thirteenth-century writers of universal history. He was, after all, part of a broader, trans-European trend. This will have to remain the subject of a separate investigation, which would also have to explore the networks of communication on which Matthew drew.
4. Bartlett 1993, 1.
5. This section draws on the work of Klaus Oschema, who is preparing a more detailed study of the concept of 'Europe' in medieval historical writing, and who kindly provided me with his annotated list of references to *Europe* and *Occident* in the Latin chronicles of Matthew Paris. Madden 1866–69, i. 241–42 (the French, like many other people of Europe, descended from the Trojans); 262 (the bishop of Winchester's wealth was without parallel in Europe); ii. 279–80 (the Hellespont constitutes the border of Europe); Luard 1872–83, i. 5 (Sem received Asia, Cham Africa, and Japhet Europe), 13 (the early apostle divide their preaching zones in Europe and Africa), 106 (the British king Aviragus' fame spread across Europe); ii. 45–46 (Urban II's crusades preaching, distinguishing between geographical zones of Europe, Africa and Asia), 155, 180 (Trojan descent of the Franks, Hellespont); iv. 118–19 (Frederick II on the Mongols sweeping Europe after having swept Asia); 119–20 (news spread across Europe), 612 (pope sends his legates to the four quarters of Europe); v. 439 (all of Europe was thrown into turmoil because of the curia's desire for luxury).
6. Luard 1872–83, i. 82.
7. Luard 1872–83, iv. 93; v. 221–22.
8. Luard 1872–83, ii. 177.
9. Luard 1872–83, v. 341 (see also Luard 1872–83, iii. 163, 357).
10. Luard 1872–83, v. 285–86.
11. In fact, the miscellaneous nature of Matthew's reporting has frequently been commented upon: Vaughan 1958c, 143–44; Gransden 1974b, 363–64.
12. Weiler 2009, 258–62.
13. Luard 1872–83, i. 1–2.
14. Luard 1872–83, v. 399–400.
15. Luard 1872–83, iii. 325.
16. Further underlined by later, considerably more outspoken comments: Luard 1872–83, iii. 362, 387, 388, 411, 413, 471, 476.
17. Luard 1872–83, iii. 477.
18. Luard 1872–83, v. 653.

19. Luard 1872–83, iv. 388.
20. Weiler 2009, 273–74; see also Riley 1867–69, i. 254–57; and, generally, see Vaughan 1958c, 139–41.
21. Reader 1996, 118–47; Luard 1872–83, v. 606–07.
22. Luard 1872–83, iii. 178–79.
23. Luard 1872–83, iii. 470.
24. Luard 1872–83, iii. 470.
25. Luard 1872–83, iii. 473.
26. Luard 1872–83, v. 457–58.
27. Luard 1872–83, iii. 490. On the historical context see Giles 1987; Vincent 1996, 229–58.
28. Luard 1872–83, iv. 637–38.
29. Luard 1872–83, v. 44.
30. Luard 1872–83, iv. 143–44.
31. Luard 1872–83, iv. 148–49.
32. Luard 1872–83, v. 695–98.
33. Lloyd and Hunt 1991.
34. [Matthew Paris] 1640, with separate pagination, 12–16. On the text: Grüner 1907; Vaughan 1958c, 189–94.
35. Wallace 1983, ll. 506–31; an English translation is available in Fenster and Wogan-Browne 2008, 60.
36. Luard 1872–83, v. 625–26.
37. Luard 1872–83, iv. 168; v. 194.
38. Luard 1872–83, v. 651.
39. Luard 1872–83, v. 604–07.
40. See for instance Luard 1872–83, v. 23, 307. It even made them bring shame on themselves when in 1242 they started attacking English merchants: after all, as the chronicler explained, the French had initially received their name from granting refuge and protection to the poor, oppressed and huddled of Christendom. Luard 1872–83, iv. 198–99.
41. Luard 1872–83, iv. 650–52.
42. Luard 1872–83, v. 603.
43. Luard 1872–83, v. 603.
44. Luard 1872–83, iv. 651.
45. Luard 1872–83, iv. 313.
46. Luard 1872–83, iv. 315–16, 323–24, 398–400. See also for a similar use of the papal court as legitimising mechanism Pryce and Insley 2005, no. 253. For papal attempts to take advantage of Henry's weakness see also Luard 1872–83, iv. 448; v. 189.
47. Carpenter 1980.
48. Luard 1872–83, i. 208. In the Rolls Series edition, Frederick has been misidentified as Frederick Barbarossa.
49. Maxwell-Lyte 1916–64, 265; *TR*, no. 55.

50. Luard 1872–83, iv. 9.
51. Luard 1872–83, iv. 92.
52. See for instance the remarks made by Robert Sumercote: Luard 1872–83, iv. 5, 64.
53. Luard 1872–83, iii. 383–84.
54. Matthew's image of kingship will require a study of its own, but the virtues here assigned to the sultan were also those of other idealised kings. See for instance the *Vitae duorum Offarum* and the portrayal of Charlemagne (especially Luard 1872–83, v. 562) and Richard the Lionheart (Luard 1872–83, iii. 215–17), in addition to the examples of Ferdinand of Castile and – within limits – Valdemar of Denmark.
55. See for instance his lives of Mohammed: Luard 1872–83, iii. 344–52, 354–61. Powell 2001.
56. Luard 1872–83, iii. 352.
57. Luard 1872–83, iii. 470; Jotischky 2004.
58. Luard 1872–83, ii. 383.
59. Luard 1872–83, iii. 39. See also for other examples Luard 1872–83, v. 107, 203.
60. Luard 1872–83, iii. 45–46, 48–50, 52–54, 65, 68–70.
61. For the emperor's crusade see Hechelhammer 2004.
62. Luard 1872–83, iii. 160, 173–74, 176.
63. Luard 1872–83, iii. 52–53.
64. Luard 1872–83, iii. 178–79.
65. Luard 1872–83, iv. 525–26.
66. Luard 1872–83, v. 193–94.
67. Luard 1872–83, iii. 216.
68. Bulgaria: Luard 1872–83, ii. 49, 57 (dubious behaviour during the First Crusade); iii. 78, 361, 460, 520 (their heresies, though Matthew equates them with the Albigensians). Croatia: iii. 78 (election of a Cathar antipope).
69. Poland: Luard 1872–83, iv. 109, 110, 115, 387; v. 439 (the duke wrongly listed as one of the imperial electors). Russia: Luard 1872–83, iii. 460 (in a letter by the patriarch of Constantinople on lands of orthodox adherence); Mongols: iv. 113, 387, 635; v. 193 (chief events 1200–50). Hungary: Luard 1872–83, iii. 639; iv. 114, 120, 274 298, 547. Bohemia: Luard 1872–83, iv. 109, 110, 115, 455. Persia: Luard 1872–83, i. 55 (Persian kings before Alexander the Great); iv. 299 (Mongol invasion of 1244); vi. no. 48 (Mongol invasions). See also Zsuzsanna Papp Reed's view of Matthew's development of a 'subplot' concerning the Mongol threat: Papp Reed 2022, 25–53 at 31,–37–38.
70. Prester John: Luard 1872–83, ii. 316; iii. 398; vi. 115 (the Mongols killing Prester John). India: i. 415 (King Alfred sends alms to St Thomas in India); iii. 398 (Prester John rules in India); v. 217 (Emperor Frederick had allies even in India).

71. Luard 1872–83, iii. 161, 163, 164; v. 341 (Ark and Wandering Jew); iv. 390, 547; v. 340 (Mongols).
72. Stehkämper 1971.
73. Luard 1872–83, ii. 54; iii. 32. The exceptions were Heribert of Cologne (i. 484–86) and Anno II (ii. 4), both active in the eleventh century.
74. Austria: Luard 1872–83, ii. 216, 384–85, 395, 397, 408–10 (Leopold V – Richard the Lionheart's infamous foe); iii. 9, 14, 35–36, 38–39, 47 (Leopold VI during the Fifth Crusade); iv. 114, 272–74, 407 (Frederick II and the Mongols); Zöllner 1966. Bavaria: Luard 1872–83, iii. 67–69; iv. 107, 114.
75. Luard 1872–83, ii. 54 (Coloman during the First Crusade); iii. 9, 13, 14 (Andrew II during the Fifth Crusade).
76. Luard 1872–83, ii. 362–63, 366; iii. 67, 305, 366, 616; iv. 29, 44; v. 23–24, 256 (referring to the crusades of Richard the Lionheart, the Fifth Crusade, those of Richard of Cornwall and St Louis respectively). See also Bamberg (iii. 9) or Messina (ii. 366–67).
77. Luard 1872–83, iv. 578. He received forgiveness from the papal court. However, unusually, Matthew did not credit corruption, bribery or greed for the pope's forgiveness, but the king's campaigns in Iberia.
78. The most detailed modern narratives of the revolt and its background are Vincent 1996, 337–39, 375–428, 438–40; Smith 2001, 14–20; Carpenter 2003, 312–17; Clanchy 2006, 194–212.
79. Luard 1872–83, iii. 489–90.
80. Weiler 2008, 70–71.
81. Luard 1872–83, v. 190, 216–18. On Matthew's obituary and its context see Weiler 2008, 73–74, 79–83.
82. Luard 1872–83, v. 193–94.
83. Weiler 2008, 75–79.
84. Luard 1872–83, iv. 92.
85. Luard 1872–83, iii. 366–67, 385.
86. Conquests: Luard 1872–83, iii. 334, 384, 529; v. 25, 193, 232. Death notice: v. 232, 311.
87. Luard 1872–83, v. 193.
88. Luard 1872–83, v. 193–94.
89. Luard 1872–83, iv. 204 (in the context of the abortive Poitevin campaign of 1242, and as they were related to Henry III).
90. Luard 1872–83, v. 626.
91. In 1245 he had refused to let Innocent IV seek refuge in his lands due to the corruption of the papal curia: Luard 1872–83, iv. 410, 422.
92. See for instance Robert Grosseteste's definition of heresy as reported by Matthew Paris: Luard 1872–83, v. 402. See also Thomson 1977, 3–34. For the interest of Matthew Paris among Protestant authors see Chapter 15, 317.
93. Luard 1872–83, i. 159, 164.
94. Luard 1872–83, i. 159, 164.

95. Luard 1872–83, i. 175–76 (Matthew stressing that the heresy had originated among the Britones – that is, the Welsh), 178, 183–86, 189.
96. See also for other heresies Luard 1872–83, i. 164, 175, 177.
97. Especially the Albigensian Cathars: Luard 1872–83, ii. 310, 554–57, 566; iii. 57, 78, 106, 110, 267, 520; iv. 231; v. 4, 23, 195. He seems to have viewed Albigensians as peculiar to the counties of Provence and Toulouse, referring to those Cathars in Flanders and France as Patarenes: Luard 1872–83, iii. 361, 375, 520; iv. 271–72. See also v. 246–54 (the Shepherds' Crusade).
98. Luard 1872–83, iii. 375.
99. Luard 1872–83, iii. 57.
100. Luard 1872–83, iii. 267.
101. Luard 1872–83, iii. 361, 520.
102. Luard 1872–83, v. 245.
103. Luard 1872–83, iii. 375.
104. Luard 1872–83, v. 401–02.
105. For a case study see Egger 2002.
106. Luard 1872–83, v. 403–04.
107. Luard 1872–83, v. 404–07.
108. Luard 1872–83, v. 429–30, 470–72, 491–92.
109. Luard 1872–83, iii. 375. He similarly tells an intriguing story that occurred in 1244: Innocent IV was touring France to promote the emperor's excommunication. A parish priest in Paris then jokingly told his parish that there was animosity between pope and emperor. He did not know how it had started, but he would excommunicate whoever had first injured the other and absolve the injured party. The clue was in the respective responses of Innocent and Frederick: the latter laughed and gave the priest many gifts; the former punished him most severely. Luard 1872–83, iv. 406–07.
110. Luard 1872–83, iv. 284–85.
111. Luard 1872–83, iv. 311–14, 365–71, 374–76, 379. For Matthew's view of the papacy and papal court see also Chapter 5, 120–21, 129–31.
112. Luard 1872–83, iii. 331–32, 410, 422, v. 245.
113. Luard 1872–83, v. 176–77.
114. Luard 1872–83, iii. 520.
115. Luard 1872–83, iii. 251.
116. Luard 1872–83, iii. 287.
117. Luard 1872–83, iii. 332–3; iv. 279–80, 511–12. He returned to the theme in his summary of key events between 1200 and 1250: Luard 1872–83, v. 194–95.
118. Madden 1866–69, ii. 215.
119. Luard 1872–83, iv. 286, 294–98, 349–55. For Matthew's focus on the politics of prelacy see also Chapter 5, 119–20.

120. See his coverage of Sewal of York: Luard 1872–83, v. 653, 678–79, 691–92, and Richard de Wyche of Chichester, Luard 1872–83, v. 5, 369, 380, 384, 419, 496–97.
121. Luard 1872–83, v. 362–66.
122. Luard 1872–83, v. 373–75.
123. Also useful: Bocquet 1995. For Matthew's commentary on the Benedictines see also Chapter 1, 20–21, and Chapter 5, 136.
124. Luard 1872–83, iv. 603–04; v. 30–31, 46–47, 176–77.
125. For a somewhat different view see Connolly 2009.
126. This may have to be viewed alongside Matthew's wide reading in visionary literature, extending even to Hildegard of Bingen (Luard 1872–83, iv. 280). The subject requires an exploration of its own. In the meantime, though centring on Matthew's attitude towards Joachim of Fiore, see Hilpert 1985.
127. Luard 1872–83, i. 1–3. For Matthew and posterity see also Chapter 15, 301–2.
128. I owe this point to Matthew Gabriele. See also Gabriele 2003; Holdenried 2006.
129. Luard 1872–83, v. 192–97.
130. Luard 1872–83, iii. 37, 51.
131. Luard 1872–83, iv. 82.
132. Luard 1872–83, iv. 632; v. 113–14, 120.
133. Luard 1872–83, v. 383–85.
134. Luard 1872–83, v. 380, 384, 419.
135. Luard 1872–83, v. 221–22.
136. Luard 1872–83, v. 419–20, 496–97.
137. Luard 1872–83, iii. 16.
138. Luard 1872–83, iii. 101.
139. Luard 1872–83, iii. 312.
140. Luard 1872–83, v. 113–14.
141. Luard 1872–83, iii. 298–300.
142. Luard 1872–83, iii. 300–01.

5

Matthew Paris and the Secular Church

In 1244 Matthew Paris' *Chronica maiora* noted with resignation the decline of the English church. Would, Matthew said, that it could return to the days of St Augustine, when bishops were appointed with chapters, either secular or monastic, and suitable incomes for their maintenance, in order to praise God and to give alms to the poor.[1] A few years earlier, in 1237, he had also referred to the decline of the English church. Once the mirror of the Western church in its ideal form, it now found itself preyed upon by the degenerate and ignorant.[2]

In claiming that the church was in serious decline, Matthew viewed it as he did other mid thirteenth-century institutions whose failures he tracked as part of his eschatological concerns.[3] His scrutiny of religious leaders – of popes, bishops and parish clergy – had much in common with his treatment of secular authorities. Like kings and barons, religious leaders provided the examples of good and bad behaviour that Paris promised his readers in his prefaces to the *Chronica maiora* and the *Historia Anglorum*. These examples would give his readers a blueprint for working towards salvation.[4] In his saints' lives Matthew presented ideal types of clergy and it was against these ideals that he measured the action of the clergy in his chronicles. Often Matthew found the clergy wanting – a sign that the church was in need of serious reform. The sort of reform Matthew sought was not, however, entirely that which the historian of the thirteenth-century church might expect. The church reform movement as expressed in the Fourth Lateran Council (Lateran IV) of 1215 provided Matthew with a blueprint for the ideal churchman. These standards were not, however, always the measures that Matthew chose. Instead, Matthew emphasised different values. These were specific to the English context: a reflection of demands for reform made by the English episcopate. In Matthew's treatment of the church we get a glimpse of monastic uncertainty about central, papal reform and understand something of Matthew's focus on national identity.

Unsurprisingly, Matthew's model clergy are seen most clearly when in the *vita* of saints, describing the lives and conduct of bishops and parish clergy who were appropriate candidates for canonisation. Ideal bishops, in Matthew's eyes, were men who fulfilled pastoral duties in a spirit of personal penance and humility: they acknowledged their dependence upon God to perform their pastoral duties. These duties included not just preaching and teaching, but also the bishops' obligation to advise and guide kings and, in particular, to speak out on behalf of the church, upholding its law and status and protecting its liberties from secular encroachment. In Paris' *Vita Sancti Edmundi* he provides a clear pattern of a good bishop.[5] Much of the information in this *vita* was reshaped or copied from earlier lives of the archbishop, particularly that by Eustace of Faversham, and the posthumous character of Edmund was not primarily formed by Matthew.[6] However, he added his own emphasis and information. When the monks of Canterbury come to elect their new archbishop, Edmund is represented as the perfect choice: Matthew depicts the monks commenting that they were able to think of no one else who possessed all the necessary qualities.[7] Edmund is a learned man educated at Oxford and Paris and known for his effective preaching and teaching.[8] As archbishop of Canterbury he is described as travelling through his diocese, continuing to teach and preach. He is also a humble man, reluctant to accept the archbishopric until he is told that if he refuses it then another much less suitable candidate may accept to the detriment of the diocese.[9] Matthew describes Edmund as frugal in his habits, eating little and dressing simply.[10] His piety is also emphasised. He was 'always occupied, praying or meditating, correcting books, hearing confessions, resolving theological questions or giving judgment in legal disputes'.[11] He does not neglect his duty to offer guidance to the king: in 1234, during William Marshal the Younger's uprising, he admonishes Henry III and seeks a peaceful conclusion to the conflict.[12] The bishop's duty to protect and oversee the English church is also emphasised in Matthew's reshaping of the myth of Edmund's exile which Eustace introduced into his *vita*. Eustace claims that Edmund's last journey was undertaken because Edmund, limited in his exercise of his pastoral office by outside forces and unable to liberate the church, chose to copy St Thomas Becket by going into exile.[13] Matthew adds a further – though, as Lawrence points out, a largely implausible – detail into the story. His Edmund is driven abroad by the vexations of the papal legate Otto and by the harm he suffered from 'the mightier of the kingdom whom, out of respect for pope and king, I do not consider it proper or safe to accuse by name'.[14] Matthew also expands upon Eustace of Faversham's comparison between Edmund and his famous saintly predecessor, Thomas Becket, whose murder was understood to have resulted from his support for the rights of church and, by the 1230s, for the rights of the state too.[15] Becket spent his exile at the Cistercian abbey of Pontigny, where Edmund's body was later buried: Matthew reports that miracles began to be performed at his grave within less than a year.[16]

Matthew's life of St Alban deals not only with the saint himself, but also with Amphibalus, the missionary priest who converted him.[17] Amphibalus is central to St Alban's own story. He converts St Alban through his preaching and teaching, beginning by telling Alban the story of the Garden of Eden, linking it to the incarnation of Jesus Christ, and then describing the life, death and resurrection of Jesus. He is also presented as a model of a priest. When Amphibalus' teaching at first angers Alban, Amphibalus is said to have shown humility in his response, spending the night suitably in prayer.[18] Later, when Alban the convert substitutes himself so he is executed in Amphibalus' place, the respited priest perseveres in his missionary work, going to his native land of Wales, where he preaches sermons on the Trinity, hears confessions and baptises. He performs his pastoral duty diligently until he too is finally martyred.[19]

The life of St Alban concludes with a journey to the court at Rome. Rome in Matthew's *vitae* is sometimes portrayed as a place where deceit and greed are ascendant. In the *Gesta abbatum* Abbot William of Trumpington, attending Lateran IV in 1215, is forced to make a present of 100 marks to the papacy.[20] In St Edmund of Abingdon's *vita* papal overreaching is said to take the archbishop abroad in 1240.[21]

Matthew, however, also had in his imagination an ideal Rome which he described in the lives of both St Alban and King Edward the Confessor. This perfect Rome is the embodiment of holiness, the central location for dispensing Christian judgment, justice and mercy. It is where Christians can go to confess and be absolved, as Amphibalus' murderers do and as Edward the Confessor, the holy king, hoped to do too. It is also the place where sainthood can be validated – the life of St Alban ends with a description of how those who had experienced miracles through the intervention of Alban and Amphibalus took a written account of their experience to submit to the authority of Rome.[22]

In his chronicles Matthew measured the contemporary clergy of his day against these standards. This was not always to their detriment. Thirteenth-century clergy, both great and humble, could provide the good as well as the bad examples Matthew had promised his readers. Clergy are shown actively supporting the liberties of church and kingdom. In the *Chronica* Matthew records the occasions when reissues of Magna Carta were further strengthened by the bishops, using the solemn process of excommunication, as in 1253.[23] He also describes individual bishops standing up for the rights of both the English people and the English church. Matthew tells us that Roger Niger, the bishop of London, even in his old age opposed the Caursine moneylenders who had impoverished many.[24] Roger's successor as the bishop of London, Fulk Basset, also provides for much of his episcopate an example of Matthew's good bishop. At his election he is described as upstanding and educated. In 1250 Matthew shows him opposing Boniface of Savoy, the archbishop of Canterbury, who is infringing the rights of the church through his claims of visitation and the amount he demands as procuration (payments in money or kind to maintain a bishop and his household during visitation), giving the detail that Fulk continues to stand against the archbishop's oppression even when the king supports the archbishop.[25] In 1255 Matthew put Fulk at the centre of opposition to new demands being made on the church for money, coming now from Master Rustand, the papal *nuncio*, who had been sent to England to levy vast sums (135,500 marks at least) for the papal coffers. Fulk is described as leading the opposition, declaring he would rather be beheaded than give in to such demands, whilst his colleague Walter de Cantilupe, the bishop of Worcester, is recorded as saying that he would rather be hanged.[26] Fulk, says Matthew, is a shield of the church.[27] That he is not described as a potential saint is a result of his lack of enthusiasm for the baronial rebellion under Simon de Montfort and his subsequent refusal to swear the oath of loyalty to the barons in 1258.[28] Other bishops' sanctity is also emphasised in the context of their political stance. Unlike some of his contemporaries, Matthew does not focus solely on the promotion of his own house's cult. Rather, he is especially responsive to the current dynamics of other churches and their cults, even within St Albans' own chronicles. He notes the miracles performed at the deaths – and at the tombs – of both Richard Wyche, the bishop of Chichester (d. 1253) and Robert Grosseteste, the bishop of Lincoln (d. 1253).[29] Both men are known for their pastoral care, but it is their support of the rights of the church which Matthew emphasises.[30]

Equally, the parish clergy of the chronicles are sometimes described as fulfilling their duties properly and are held up as models, particularly in passages in the *Chronica* where Matthew evidences concern about the way the friars are meddling in parish business. He records in hostile terms the Franciscans' attempts to enter the territory of large established monastic houses, and particularly their unwelcome entry into Bury St Edmunds.[31] In pastoral terms too he sees their intervention as unnecessary, suggesting that standards of parochial care are already sufficient. The most disruptive aspect of the Franciscans' practice is their hearing of confessions from parishioners: Matthew sees these extra opportunities for confession as not only unnecessary but also dangerous: they disrupt a system which is working perfectly well and allow the laity to evade their duty to make confession to their parish priests. The friars, he complains, hear confessions carelessly and are relaxed about the making of expiation by the penitent; they take money from penitents rather than giving a practical penance, which would be of more use to the penitents' souls. By offering such penances they give parishioners an opportunity to avoid their duty of confessing to their parish priest, who is able to hear them.[32] In Matthew's *Chronica* local parish priests articulate their complaints to their archdeacon, saying that the friars' interference places them in personal spiritual danger. The parish priests have a solemn personal obligation to ensure their parishioners' salvation: if parishioners are allowed to confess to the friars, parish priests become unable to fulfil this duty.[33]

So Matthew could, then, find amongst the clergy, great and humble, past and present, examples of ideal conduct demonstrating the strength of the church and its clergy when working as they should. Equally often, however, Matthew saw the English church and its clergy as in an increasing decline.[34] Matthew understood the institution itself to be weakened by theft of both spiritual and temporal rights and resources by secular and ecclesiastical authorities overreaching their proper roles. The church and its clergy who failed to live up to their obligations had two key things in common. They were – or they showed sympathy for – foreigners and they made or suffered from a wrong application of resources, either temporal or spiritual. The use of resources as a measure of behaviour, in terms of money and goods, rights and law, is a central theme in Matthew's description of the church. In 1244 his depiction of a church in decline focused around this idea: the regular giving of alms and the maintenance of the necessary possessions for its sustenance in the early days of the English church is contrasted with the situation in Matthew's own day, perceived as a general impoverishment.[35]

In this context Matthew's frequent depiction of the papacy as making the wrong use of temporal resources is unsurprising. He connects the papacy to the excesses and usury of the Caursine moneylenders (so called because of their association with the French city of Cahors) and he describes papal excesses ranging from the political to the personal. At one end is Innocent IV's personal desire for golden fringe, which he had seen on the vestments of the English. Paris had heard, no doubt from messengers who accompanied the Cistercian abbots to Rome in 1246, that the pope had greedily demanded that these abbots send him such fringe as a gift for use on his own papal vestments.[36] At the other extreme is papal ambition in international politics. Towards the end of the *Chronica* Matthew traces the pope's involvement in the Sicilian business: the attempt to obtain the rule of Sicily on behalf of the papacy, to which Henry III of England had committed himself.[37] The pope's inappropriate and avaricious desire to use England's economic and political resources for his own ends are united in the exclamation Matthew put in the mouth of the pope: 'Certainly England is our garden of delights! It is an inexhaustible well of wonderful things and from this multitude much may be extorted.'[38]

The pope's legates and *nuncio*s also serve as examples of such greed, and Matthew recounts how they misappropriated – or encouraged the misappropriation of – the church's income in England. Master Martin uses his powers to exact money from the clergy in order to provide for the pope's relatives. He tries to intervene in the appointment of a bishop of Chichester in order to 'lay his crooked fingers on the revenue for the use and benefit of the pope'. Matthew describes Martin's use of vacant churches for the pope's own candidates as theft.[39] Not only does Martin steal churches for the pope, he is also accused of stealing for himself by persuading the king to give him personal land and revenues. He demands gifts from religious houses and then repeats his demands, asking for things of more value, bringing about, Matthew says, amongst the religious, 'slavery in the Egypt of Britain'.[40] Perhaps he had in mind the requirement for abbots-elect to seek confirmation at Rome, which was (as in the case of John de Hertford) to be the pretext for a number of demands for additional gifts and levies.[41]

It is not only the papacy which is criticised for the misuse of church resources. The parish clergy of the diocese of Lincoln are criticised for their misuse of their own incomes. In 1251 a group of these men were, says Matthew, very anxious to avoid the bishop of Lincoln's demands that they be ordained to priest's orders. This aversion stemmed from the practical consideration that once ordained as priests they would be tied to a parish, limiting their networking opportunities and their opportunities for future career progression. For those Lincoln clergy not yet ordained to higher orders (as a number were), it could also limit their life choices in other ways. Marriage would, for example, become an impossibility for them.[42] So, with 'fox-like cunning', Matthew says, they collected a large sum of money to send to Rome as a bribe to persuade the papacy to give them all licences to go to study at the universities, thus removing the necessity for their ordination to higher orders.[43] Such men put ambition and personal advancement above their duty to serve their parishes. Bishops are judged in a similar way. Boniface of Savoy, the archbishop of Canterbury, is said to steal from churches during visitations, demanding procuration at such a level when he proposes to visit the monastic houses of the province of Canterbury in 1250 that his fellow bishops are said to object.[44] Boniface is also recorded as having lay waste to the woodland of the archbishopric as he leaves the country in 1245, pretending he needs the money to pay his legitimate debts when in fact he requires it to support his niece's finances.[45] The long-term assets of the diocese are stolen from his successors to fund his personal expenses.

The bishops' profligacy could be about less tangible things. Poor use of the church's resources could come about through weakness or inadequacy of their personal and managerial skills. Bishops failed in their duty when, for instance, they failed to prevent intervention by the papacy, when they failed to uphold the rights of local patrons (secular or ecclesiastical) to nominate suitable clergy for a parish church in their gift, and when they failed to uphold the rights of cathedral chapters to elect their own bishops. Matthew records occasions when, he says, the episcopate intervened appropriately to prevent the election of an unsuitable clergyman as in the *Chronica* where Robert Grosseteste's examination of Robert Passelewe's learning is said to have resulted in his rejection for the see of Chichester, paving the way for the election of the highly educated future saint Richard Wyche.[46] He also, however, records situations where the clergy were powerless to stop these interventions, as in his portrayal of the election of Boniface of Savoy at Canterbury and Aylmer of Valence at Winchester.[47] In 1245, when describing the Council of Lyon, Matthew is particularly scathing of the English bishops' failure to have accepted their petition demanding the excesses of the papacy are curbed.[48] Here they lack the personal resources which would have led to respect for the church and episcopate.

The relationship between the bishops' use of canon law and their ability to have that law upheld by requesting secular intervention was another concern for Matthew. Excommunication provided a particular example. As we have seen, the bishops could add threats of excommunication to the reissues of Magna Carta, with the double aim of guiding the behaviour of the king and upholding the liberties of the church which were established (although only in general terms) at the start of the document. Excommunication was the ultimate ecclesiastical weapon which separated people not only from day-to-day interaction with their neighbours, but also, potentially, eternally from God. However seriously or otherwise the laity took the sanction of excommunication, the episcopate should have recognised its power potential.

This power is another misused resource in Matthew's chronicles. He gives the examples of the Franciscans, who absolve people from excommunication for not fulfilling their crusading vows at the same time as commuting those vows; the papal legate, who reverses all the excommunications of Archbishop Edmund of Abingdon in 1240; the advisers, 'who work for the devil', says Matthew, and who tell the king in 1253 not to worry about being excommunicated for infringing Magna Carta since the pope would always absolve him for money; and the churchmen who were said generally in 1237 to use excommunication as a threat to get what they wanted. All were seriously misusing the church's power and spiritual resources.[49] In addition, the failure to have a sentence of excommunication upheld is another weakness of the clergy. The bishop of Lincoln, dealing with a recalcitrant clergyman, has him excommunicated, but when the excommunicate refuses to correct his behaviour the bishop is unable to enforce it by royal writ as he should have been able to since the sheriff refuses to perform his duty and arrest the excommunicate.[50] In such a case a bishop is so weak that he has lost any claim to spiritual resources and power and thus has deprived the church more generally.

Matthew often links examples of ecclesiastical misuse of resources, particularly greed over temporal goods, to the role of the foreigner in English affairs. Matthew's thoughts about an ideal church served by model clergy were very English in their reach and conception. In the *Gesta abbatum* he repeatedly criticises the Norman abbots of the late eleventh and twelfth centuries for their favour to their kin.[51] In 1244, when he looked back in the *Chronica* to the church's past, he did not, like the more general, international church reform movement, look back to the earliest history of the church but to the English church as founded by Augustine, with three bishops at Rochester, Canterbury and London, each assigned suitable sustenance by the newly converted King Ethelbert, and whose primary role was to give alms, offer hospitality and praise God.[52] Now, he complains, there is a lack of almsgiving in England and church offices are bought and sold. And to a greater or lesser extent, he feels that this has come about because foreign interests have gained a foothold in the English church. The popes and their legates have moved beyond giving counsel and leadership and now demand money in the form of taxes and presents from the English clergy, in order to support papal ambitions overseas.

Unwelcome foreign interference also came in the form of money-lending: papal and royal demands had driven bishops and religious houses to borrow money. Then there was the issue of the Lusignan and Savoyard bishops. These men were the relatives of Henry III and of his wife, Eleanor, respectively, and the favour the king showed them caused resentment amongst the barons. Their appointments were seen as theft: they had stolen position, authority and actual temporal income which would otherwise have been in the custody of English-born bishops (and by implication, more likely to have kept wealth within the country).

Throughout his chronicles, Matthew associated Italians with greed, from the Caursine moneylenders through to the pope himself.[53] Matthew's hostility to the papacy expressed a view that was widespread in mid thirteenth-century England. There was general resentment at the financial burden of papal demands, which the pope could always justify as resulting from England's agreement to pay 1,000 marks of annual tribute to the pope following the 1213 surrender of the country as a papal fief, a lingering consequence of King John's weak rule. This annual demand from the pope continued to rankle and fuelled protests in the 1230s, as considered later in this chapter. In 1235, as Matthew began to write his great chronicle, the Caursines arrived in England and, to Matthew at least, the frequent appearance of papal legates – the pope's representatives – in the country provided a local focus for English discontent. The 1240s were a period of constant dispute over papal demands for taxation and other payments from the church.[54] When Matthew complained about papal provisions – that is, the granting of English parish churches to candidates nominated by the pope rather than the church's proper patron – he was, as Kim notes, complaining not about unsuitable clergy but purely about them being foreigners.[55] The *Chronica* makes Robert Grosseteste, the bishop of Lincoln, a mouthpiece for Matthew's resentment, having him declare that these foreigners are stealing 70,000 marks from the country.[56] In 1231 Matthew described with approval the uprisings against Italian clergy who held churches in the country, when Robert Thweng, under the pseudonym of William Withers, led bands of armed men to attack, pillage and burn barns holding the incomes of these overseas clergymen, and seized some Italians. The *Historia* records that amongst a group of foreign cathedral clergy travelling between St Albans and London at this time, one London canon, Cinthius the Roman, was seized and ill-treated by armed men.[57] In all of these instances Matthew's concern was that the income of the church in England was being removed from the country: the profits of benefices were being exported overseas. Although this problem of non-local clergy sweating the assets of benefices far from their homes could have been presented as a problem for the church in general, for Matthew it was the English church which mattered. It was the losses of the English church which he emphasised.

To Matthew the draining of authority and resources from the church to the state could also be a form of theft by foreigners. Matthew had thought carefully about the relationship between church and state. They were intertwined but could also be seen as two states, each with its own separate systems of law and taxation, for example.[58] The relationship between the two needed careful balance. In 1244 Matthew's description of the ideal church in England was one which was supported by the king, who kept secular and ecclesiastical power in equilibrium. Matthew recorded instances of the state encroaching on the church's rights through, for instance, interfering in episcopal elections and in the refusal of the king to support the enforcement of excommunications issued under ecclesiastical law through the secular arm, as described earlier in this chapter. Henry III's failure to uphold the balance of church and state was, Matthew claimed, one reason that that ideal bishop, Edmund of Abingdon, horrified at the state of the English church, had gone to complain to the pope. He met, though, with no success: what else could be expected from an Italian?[59] Matthew's depiction of Henry as conspiring with or in the power of the papacy was part of an implied 'foreignness' in the king himself, evidenced in his failure to defend the church's resources for the benefit of the English.

This focus on the misuse of resources and the unwelcome presence of the foreigner in the English church's affairs as explanations for the church's decline are not in many ways a surprise. These were pervasive concerns for Matthew. The use, misuse, possession and loss of resources were the way in which he judged the moral status of his secular protagonists too, principally in his chronicles but also in his saints' lives. The king's duty to rule for others not himself, and in particular to rule on behalf of his subjects, through his distribution of resources was commonly articulated in terms of abiding by natural and divine law by the 1240s.[60] In his life of Edward the Confessor, Matthew drew a picture of a king who understood the use of resources and his obligation to give to his subjects whilst maintaining the wealth of his kingdom.[61] It was Edward whom Henry had taken as his role model as king and in whose pattern he tried to place himself before his subjects.[62] The king's gifts to his foreign relatives of what should have been given to the country was part of Matthew's evidence that Henry III did not rule well. Henry III's weakness is reflected in his lack of ability to raise income legitimately and in his misguided giving of substantial gifts to his Savoyard and Lusignan relatives, which were subsequently removed from England. Archbishop Boniface of Savoy's departure from the kingdom with wealth gained from his diocese's woodland is paralleled by Peter of Savoy's attempted journey out of England loaded down with English gold and goods which he had obtained from Henry.[63] The Jews in Paris' chronicles are presented as having have a dual purpose, an analysis which further supports Matthew's attitude to resources. They are themselves resources: they belong to the king, and as such should be used for the benefit of the country. When Henry misuses them, for example, by overtaxing them, leading the Jews to try to call in their debts across the country at high rates of interest, Matthew is clear that it is in this context that their misery must be read.[64] Yet the Jews are also depicted as misusing the resources of the country themselves. The Jews were well established in the medieval mind as embodying greed and avarice: literally worshipping money. As usurers, the interest they collected on loans was seen as actual theft of money and, in theological terms, they were condemned for the theft of time, by which interest accrued.[65] To Matthew payments of interest to the Jews were another example of how English wealth was being stolen, and the Jews' threats to leave the country – or the chance of their being expelled from England – made the possibility of their taking English money and resources out of the country every bit as real as Peter of Savoy's dash to the English Channel loaded down with gold.[66]

Just as interesting, however, as tracing the route which Matthew believed the church had taken in its mid thirteenth-century decline is observing a path which Matthew did not take in his analysis. Lateran IV and the broader reform movement of the Western church theoretically provided him with another set of measures by which the clergy and the church could be found wanting. William of Trumpington, Matthew's first abbot, had been present at Lateran IV, so Matthew could have received a first-hand account of proceedings there.[67] Yet though there are overlaps between Matthew's criticisms of the church and those of Lateran IV, the two are by no means identical. The Council and its canons were the early thirteenth-century expression, refracted by Innocent III, of the aims of the reform papacy. These focused around simony (the sale of benefices for money or, in canon law, for favours in kind), the inheritance of benefices and, related to the latter, preventing the marriage (or as the church described it concubinage) of the clergy. Overall, the papal reform movement sought to remove the church from lay control and influence and, in the process, to bring the Western church as a whole further under direct papal control. It brought the appointment of clergy at all levels – from the local parish priest to cathedral canons, monks and bishops – under the authority of their direct ecclesiastical superior and sought to ensure that appointments were made on merit. Bishops were to be responsible for authorising new clergymen, checking their learning and characters, and the laity must be prevented from making their own appointments, being allowed only to present suggestions for new parish priests to their local bishop. No church was allowed to be a hereditary holding; sons must not follow their fathers into benefices. Bishops were to be elected by the chapters of their own cathedral churches, not imposed upon them by kings, and their election should be free, without lay pressure. Clergy who infringed any of these rules in order to obtain their positions would be instantly removed, as would those responsible for obtaining their posts for them.

In 1215 Pope Innocent III had sought to give a new impetus to this reform in a great council at Rome, the first for thirty-five years, summoned to 'eradicate vices and to plant virtues, to correct faults and to reform morals, to remove heresies and to strengthen faith, to settle discords and to establish peace, to end oppression and to nurture liberty and to induce princes and Christian people to come to the aid and succour of the Holy Land'.[68] Of central importance to Innocent III were the canons issued in this council. His opening sermon mentioned reform of the church as one of the three central ways in which mankind must 'pass over' from vice to virtue, and he undertook to have the canons circulated internationally after the Council, together with an introduction which would put them in context.[69] As a whole, they expressed a revitalisation of an international ecclesiastical reform movement which had begun several centuries before. They were composed in the name of a pope who, as a cardinal, had noted the need for a reformation in the papal court itself, and whose personal devotion to his distant predecessor, St Gregory the Great, seems to have influenced his concern with episcopal authority and responsibility.[70]

English bishops issued diocesan rules – statutes – which attempted to enforce these canons throughout the thirteenth century.[71] Concern about the need for resident clergy, complaints of pluralism and of the use of parish churches principally as sources of income, the desire to separate church and state, the concern that pastoral care, particularly the hearing of confession, is not being maintained in the parish churches and anxiety about the education of the clergy are all issues which the modern historian, guided by the Council's canons, expects to see in these contemporary church sources. Yet these were not Matthew's concerns. Whilst he shared some of the pope's concerns – about simony and about the interference of the state in the church – the Council's measures for the performance of pastoral care were not his.[72] The canons of Lateran IV were not central to his understanding of the church's problems.

Matthew, in his chronicles in particular, acknowledged the existence of pluralism, of non-resident clergy and of the use of parish churches for monetary gain rather than as a focus for the salvation of souls. Yet these were not things which he saw as a concern if they neither involved foreign influence nor diminished the church's resources. This is particularly clear in his descriptions of the concerns and activity of the parish clergy. These were the men whom Lateran IV expected to undertake the majority of pastoral work and who were needed to guide the laity towards salvation. They were to hear confessions and to perform mass (requiring them to be ordained priests).[73] Yet when Matthew saw clergy who are not suitably ordained and whose focus was on the income rather than the duty of their parishes – clergy whose behaviour he could in theory use to support his position that the church was in decline – he recorded, but did not criticise, their actions. In 1245, he noted that one John de Gatesdene was knighted at Christmas following his recent marriage. Now that he was a married man and a knight he resigned all his rich benefices: as Paris said, with obvious approval, he 'gave up the danger of the cure of souls and was advanced to the level of the higher nobles'.[74] There is no suggestion that a man ordained only to lower orders (he cannot have been in higher orders if he was able to marry) had done wrong in holding benefices with cure of souls at all. In 1241 Paris recorded the story of John Mansel's presentation to the church of Thame. Mansel was the king's chancellor and Thame was one of the most valuable churches in the diocese of Lincoln (it was also connected to a prebend, but like other Lincoln prebends it had cure of souls). The king had made the appointment, only to discover that the bishop of Lincoln had already admitted a different cleric. John was persuaded to give up Thame with the argument that such a well-educated and important man would easily find himself given an even more lucrative church, and the happy ending was that John did indeed receive two very wealthy churches a short time afterwards.[75] Matthew did not seem to think that using the temporal value of a benefice – where there was cure of souls – as an inducement was wrong.

He also described the clergy as defending the holding of multiple benefices. He recorded without criticism the objection Walter de Cantilupe, the bishop of Worcester, made at the 1237 Council of London to the papal legate Otto's condemnation of pluralism. Without it, said Cantilupe, no clergyman would have a large enough income to undertake his duties of almsgiving.[76] The right use of resources was being balanced against the need for resident clergy. Only when copying a passage from the earlier life by Eustace of Faversham in his own life of St Edmund of Abingdon does Matthew issue a standard condemnation of non-residency amongst the clergy. Moreover, Matthew was not consistently concerned about other issues of the reform movement. He may have approved of John de Gatesdene's decision to resign his churches once he married, but in 1252 his obituary for the archdeacon of Leicester, Master John of Basingstoke, told another story. Master John's death was recorded as one of the disasters of 1252. Matthew wrote a detailed description of his virtues. He was a learned man, 'well experienced in the threefold and fourfold course of study', he was able to write in Greek and had invented a new form of calculation. All of these virtues he had learnt from one young woman, Constantia, identified as Master John's mistress, who was 'endowed with every virtue' and equally well educated.[77] Clearly Matthew did not think that keeping a concubine was a matter that needed serious condemnation.

The non-resident clergy Matthew described should, according to canon law, have had substitutes who were ordained priests: vicars. If Matthew assumed their existence, this might explain why he was not concerned by the idea of absentee rectors. Matthew, however, showed distinct hostility towards these men. The church reform movement was itself ambivalent about them. Whilst they could ensure the maintenance of pastoral care in parishes which would otherwise be empty, there was a suspicion that these were neither the best quality nor the most committed clergy. Their poor incomes were particularly a problem in this context. In 1222 the Council of Oxford, under the archbishop of Canterbury, Stephen Langton, had declared that vicars' incomes should be valued at five marks a year, but this could not be enforced.[78] In addition, the tithes and offerings assigned from the church to the vicar, from which he was to make his five marks, were not usually the most easily collected portion, meaning that what they actually received was probably even less. Some churchmen feared that vicars, unable to survive on their incomes, would also take on other churches, leaving some benefices with absentee vicars as well as rectors.[79] Matthew's resentment, however, was based not on the fact that vicars might neglect their duties and that pastoral care might suffer, but on the attempts made to provide them with better incomes to prevent such dereliction. In 1252, in the *Chronica*, he complained that the bishop of Lincoln had obtained a papal mandate to allow him to increase the income of vicars in churches belonging to religious houses. This, he said bitterly, was intended 'to infringe the revenues of religious men and to increase the part of the vicars'.[80] The problem here, from Matthew's point of view, was that the bishop now had the power to demand that religious houses relinquish some of the profits of churches that had been appropriated to them (that is where a religious house had become the corporate rector of a church), in order to ensure the vicars of those churches had a living wage. Matthew's concern here was not for the vicars nor with Lateran

IV standards of pastoral care. Instead he is concerned about episcopal interference in the affairs of religious houses and the effect this living wage legislation might have on their income: Matthew the monk was outraged that St Albans would, in effect, have a larger wages bill.

It is not that Matthew was unaware of the details of Lateran IV. Certainly, he detailed its canons in his writing, but that was not unusual amongst thirteenth-century chroniclers. The details of the canons seem to have received surprisingly little attention amongst attendees or their contemporaries who recorded the Council's events. Few attempted to list their contents, and even those who did tended to give up before reaching their end. The Giessen report says only, 'Then the constitutions of the lord pope were read.' The chronicler of St Martin of Tours is equally brief, whilst Aubrey of Trois-Fontaines gives up providing details after the first seventeen canons, saying only, 'and many others followed up to seventy'. Matthew's predecessor as chronicler at St Albans at the time of the Council, Roger of Wendover, got the number of canons wrong, declaring there were only sixty and then only noted that some of the prelates were pleased by the legislation and others declared it to be burdensome.[81] Paris was equally unconcerned with the details of the Council's main legislation. He recorded the universal nature of the Council and only gave detail, in the *Historia*, of the papal denunciation of Abbot Joachim's heresy.[82] He did know the contents of at least some of the canons. In discussing the election of John de Hertford as abbot of St Albans he was careful to note that the correct process, laid down by the Council, was followed in sending two monks to obtain confirmation of the new abbot's election from the pope.[83] In 1244 a new order of friars, the Friars of the Cross, entered the diocese of Lincoln, taking offerings from the people, bringing what they claimed was a papal bull declaring the order's legitimacy and challenging the authority of the local church. 'Certain wise men', said Matthew (and in the *Chronica* such a vaguely attributed comment could well have been from Matthew himself), noted that Lateran IV had forbidden new orders.[84]

Possibly Matthew, and those other monastic chroniclers, ignored the canons because it was not monastic houses, but the bishops, who were expected to police this legislation, so having copies did not seem urgent. Perhaps too the chroniclers, including Matthew, were unhappy about the Council itself. Lewis has pointed out that the picture of the Council which Matthew draws in the *Chronica* suggests two groups of men arguing wildly, in a pose similar to Matthew's drawing of the bishop of Auxerre arguing with the Pelagian heretics. They are nearly enveloped in green waves which, Lewis suggests, may refer to insults often cast at the thirteenth-century papacy such as 'the quicksands of Roman subtlety'.[85] Some of the later canons of the Council, which attempt to legislate behaviour within monastic houses and the relationship between the religious and the bishops, may not have pleased the Benedictine Matthew. There were canons about the behaviour of members of the religious orders when electing heads of houses, the practice of simony in abbeys and priories and the monastic collection of tithe.[86] The religious may also have been unhappy with the incidental results of the Council. Lateran IV, by encouraging increased episcopal control within the dioceses, seems to have given bishops a greater sense of their duty to intervene within monastic houses. The episcopal duty to visit monastic houses was already established by 1215, and Lateran IV in fact reduced the amount of procuration (support in money or kind for visiting bishops and their households),[87] but it did not diminish the duty and seems to have encouraged a regular pattern of episcopal visitation, despite frequent monastic protest, which became particularly well established in England.[88]

These visitations, and bishops' claims to a right to carry them out, were regularly opposed by Matthew. His objections to Boniface of Savoy's attempts to visit religious houses go beyond his objection to the archbishop's demands for procuration.[89] He wrote critically of episcopal intervention in religious houses. In the diocese of Lincoln, where St Albans stood, he was particularly critical of Bishop Robert Grosseteste. Paris recorded his visitations as 'acts of tyranny'. Grosseteste had unfairly deposed the abbot of Bardney, thus provoking the monks of Canterbury to excommunicate him in return.[90] During his visitation of Ramsey Abbey, Grosseteste destroyed any item which was fastened down, going through the monks' dormitory, seizing personal possessions, breaking open chests and smashing the precious items stored within them.[91] His treatment of nuns during his visitations particularly shocked Matthew: the bishop had their breasts squeezed to ensure that they were not pregnant.[92]

Paris extends his sense of episcopal injustice to secular cathedral communities. Grosseteste's claim to the right to visit his cathedral chapter and the chapter's parish churches, a long-running dispute, is recorded in detail by Matthew, including in one of the vivid vignettes which he gives in his chronicles.[93] A member of a chapter preaching about the bishop's claims in the cathedral quoted scripture declaring that even the stones would cry out against such injustice, at which point a wall in the cathedral collapsed.[94] Matthew's view of Grosseteste's demands is clear, even though the bishop's right was upheld by the papacy in 1245.

Despite his resentment of episcopal intervention, it must have been a temptation to make use of the existing standards drawn up by the church reform movement to measure the church's decline. A temptation, that is, unless Matthew also resented the reform movement's claims and demands more generally. He understood the implications of papal strictures: he saw the pervasive influence of Gregory IX's 1237 statutes for the reform of the Benedictine Order, and his *Liber Additamentorum* provides a detailed account of the statutes' reception in England.[95] Although Matthew added nothing to Wendover's description of Lateran IV, he did leave a description of a council held by the papal legate, Otto, in 1237, intended to set down legislation for the church in England based on those canons of twenty years earlier and itself part of Otto's time in England enforcing Gregory's statutes. Matthew copied out the canons of this council in the *Chronica*, and he described its events there in detail.[96]

The veracity and certainty of his account has been questioned, but if it is not historically accurate, then it is all the more likely that it represents Matthew's own attitude to the council itself.[97] The picture he drew – in both words and image – was, as Lewis has noted, one permeated with distrust and resentment.[98] At the very start of the council the prelates arrive 'greatly harassed and fatigued'. They are obeying a summons which has come from a legate whose presence in England was, said Matthew, widely resented.[99] Otto's position always appears threatening and domineering. In advance of the council he has had 'an excessively dignified and grand seat raised on beams' with steps up to it at the front of St Paul's. Here he sits at the start of the council, surrounded by elaborate hangings, and here he begins to speak with a 'trumpet-like voice'.[100]

The scene is illustrated in both the *Chronica* and the *Historia*, but Lewis has noted that the picture in the earlier *Chronica* – written more or less contemporaneously with the council itself – gives an impression of distress and uncertainty, with the legate at the left, his hand raised in admonition, sitting on a throne which seems itself unstable, whilst the bishops to the left are crowded together.[101] Unlike the bishops gathered at the Lateran Palace in 1215, who began the announcement of the canons with a pronouncement of the creed and who seem to have heard the canons in orderly fashion, the bishops of England at this council were in some disarray. Illness meant that the respected elder statesman amongst them, Robert Grosseteste, who was prepared to oppose the papacy and its messengers when necessary, and who should have begun the council with a sermon, was not present and Otto had to preach instead. On the second day the king was said to have sent his own representatives, the earl of Lincoln, John Fitzgeoffrey, and William de Raleigh, to ensure that nothing was done contrary to the dignity of king and kingdom.[102] These canons were not to benefit the church if they did not also support the crown. Nor did the assembled clergy, according to Matthew, hesitate to intervene and protest as each canon was discussed: this was the occasion when Bishop Walter de Cantilupe protested the ban on holding churches in plurality (interestingly described specifically as a canon of Lateran IV) and the legate, when he went to St Pauls to declare this canon, was so afraid of the reactions of angry beneficed clergy in the crowd that he had to be accompanied by an armed guard made up of the earls of Pembroke, Lincoln and Leicester.[103]

Matthew's objections were probably in part, as Lewis suggests, related to fears that the canons of such councils would 'threaten the large properties belonging to the great houses of the old religious orders'.[104] The resentment he records in 1252 over the increased provision for vicars in monastic churches demonstrates that this was in his mind. A closer look at other episcopal requests for reform, however, also recorded by Paris, suggest that another important issue for him was again that of the foreign church and the rights of the English church in that context. Otto's canons demonstrate an understanding of English circumstances and law, but they are the canons imposed by an international church and, particularly in their presentation by Matthew, by an unwanted Italian usurper whose presence was likely only, said the English to each other, to bring 'great loss to the kingdom'.[105] By contrast, another set of complaints about the need for reform, issued by the English episcopate and known to Matthew – known as gravamina (meaning just complaints) – were concerned with purely English concerns, with the boundaries between the jurisdictions of church and state and with the state's duty to uphold the liberties of the church. In his entry in the *Chronica* for 1239, Matthew records the earliest known of these documents,[106] versions of which were to be reissued in 1253, 1257, 1267, 1280 and 1285, in the clerical petitions of 1294, in the statements in the *Articuli Cleri* of 1314 and through the clerical complaints of 1328–29 and 1341.[107] They begin with a clear statement that the king is infringing the charter of liberties which was issued with a sentence of general excommunication against those breaking it.[108] They go on to list the complaints of the clergy.[109] They talk of the impeding of canon law by forcing the clergy to answer to secular courts and through the king's claim to decide disputes outside his own jurisdiction, concerning particular instances around tithes and church patronage, for example. In particular the king is said to be refusing to hand over clerks accused of capital crimes to the church as canon law said he should. They complain that clerical income is being withheld by the king and seized by his bailiffs. They note that the king is not observing sentences of excommunication nor the right of the clergy to call on secular powers to enforce such sentences in circumstances where the excommunicate remains obdurate. The gravamina of 1253 and 1257 include, in addition to these issues, further concern about royal intervention in the appointment of parish clergy and in the election of bishops. The 1257 statutes are given in full in the *Liber Additamentorum*.[110] In other words, these are the complaints about the state of the church, given, as Matthew did, in terms of the use of resources. They are by English prelates about English concerns and relationships. The ideal relationship of king and church which they desire was not dissimilar to Matthew's presentation of the relationship between Ethelbert and his bishops. His analysis of the problems and decline of the church is focused on the English situation.

When Matthew looked at the secular English church in the mid thirteenth century he saw an institution which had moved far from what he thought were its beginnings. In its origin it was an institution for charitable giving, prayer and praise, supported by the state, free from unnecessary claims upon it. By the late 1230s, the church and its clergy were in decline, a negative view in all likelihood coloured by Matthew's eschatological concerns of a world fast approaching dissolution and judgement. The clergy whom Matthew saw and heard about in his own day were not always the pious, educated men performing pastoral duties and living a life of simple humility, giving to others, whom Matthew depicted in his saints' lives. Nor was Rome the ideal Rome, where law and justice reigned and where pilgrims could make confession and receive absolution on their way to heaven. What Matthew believed that he saw more often than not was a world of greed, where the church in England was losing its income and rights to the desires of a greedy papacy, making demands ranging from gold fabric to large-scale taxation to fund an unnecessary and unwinnable war, a world where the clergy might make use of the pope's desire for money to obtain their own desires, misusing the income of their churches to do so. It was a world where the church's liberties and law were being infringed on all sides and the church was being weakened by an English king and pope who seemed to collude to impoverish the English.

Notes

1. Luard 1872–83, iv. 312.
2. Luard 1872–83, iii. 389.
3. In his gathering of evidence from twenty-five half centuries in his entry for 1250 in the *Chronica* and the *Historia*, the decline of the Church is one piece of evidence mentioned, Luard 1872–83, v. 192–26.
4. Luard 1872–81, i. 1–2. For an increased emphasis on the moral value of history in Matthew's preface, beyond that in his exemplars, see Weiler 2009, 259.
5. See the English translation of the prose life in Lawrence 1996, and the edition of this text in Lawrence 1960, 222–89.
6. Lawrence 1960, 30–47; Lawrence 1996, 109.
7. Lawrence 1960, 237–38; Lawrence 1996, 130.
8. Lawrence 1960, 232–33; Lawrence 1996, 126.
9. Lawrence 1960, 238; Lawrence 1996, 131.
10. Lawrence 1960, 227–28; Lawrence 1996, 122.
11. Lawrence 1960, 243; Lawrence 1996, 123–24.
12. Luard 1872–83, iii. 244–45; Lawrence 1960, 240–43; Lawrence 1996, 133–34. A similar 'ideal' admonishment is offered in the life of St Edward the

Confessor to King Harold by his archbishop, Stigand, warning him to uphold the oath he is said to have sworn to allow William to succeed to the English throne after Edward (see Fenster and Wogan-Browne 2008, 104).

13. Lawrence 1960, 217.
14. Lawrence 1960, 180–82; Lawrence 1996, 149, 168–76.
15. Lawrence 1960, 260–61; Lawrence 1996, 148–49. Matthew also drew the comparison in the *Chronica*; see Luard 1872–83, iv. 74, 328. In the *Chronica* Paris pairs the two again in 1241 when he has the two former archbishops (now both saints) appear together in a clerk's dream, where they destroy the walls that Henry III has been profligately spending on building in London (Luard 1872–83, iv. 93–94).
16. Madden 1866–69, iii, 93, 301, 326; Luard 1872–83, iv. 74; Lawrence 1960: 262–64; Lawrence 1996, 150–52.
17. Fenster and Wogan Browne 2010, 8–9.
18. Fenster and Wogan Browne 2010, 2:41–50, 5–6:102–74, 7:200.
19. Fenster and Wogan Browne 2010, 32–35:1120–1269.
20. Riley 1867–69, i. 263.
21. Lawrence 1960, 255; Lawrence 1996, 144–45.
22. Fenster and Wogan Browne 2008, 72, 76, 78; Fenster and Wogan Browne 2010, 47:17810–11, 48:1812–46.
23. Madden, 1866–69, ii. 137; Luard 1872–83, v. 375. For the possibility of wide-reaching pastoral effects from excommunications around Magna Carta, including general raised awareness of the contents of the Charter, see Hill 2016, 638–42. Such awareness would have included an understanding of the importance of maintaining the rights of the church, however they were interpreted, amongst laity and clergy.
24. Luard 1872–83, iii. 331–32.
25. Luard 1872–83, v. 121–23.
26. Luard 1872–83, v. 553.
27. Luard 1872–83, v. 747.
28. Luard 1872–83, v. 705, 747.
29. Madden 1858, 139, 147–48, 318, 327, 329–31; Luard 1872–83, v. 380, 384–85, 407, 419, 490–91, 496–97. Wyche would eventually be formally canonised, although this occurred after Matthew's death. Lawrence 2004.
30. Madden 1866–69, ii. 146; Luard 1872–83, v. 326, 351, 377–78, 400.
31. Riley 1867–69, i. 385; Luard 1872–83, iii. 332; Luard 1880, v. 688, 695, 742.
32. Luard 1872–83, iii. 332.
33. Luard 1872–83, iv. 516–17; Steckel 2015, 164–65.
34. Luard 1872–83, iii. 389; Luard 1872–83, iv. 312; Luard 1872–83, v. 192–96.
35. Luard 1872–83, iv. 312.
36. Luard 1872–83, iv. 546–47.
37. Luard 1872–83, v. 458–59, 463. For the Sicilian business see Treharne 1962, 50; Clanchy 1968, 169–72; Maddicott 1994; Weiler 2001.

38. Luard 1872–83, iv. 547.
39. Luard 1872–83, iv. 368, 375, 402, 416, 418. In the *Historia Anglorum* Matthew is clear. Master Martin has come to take money for the papacy from the English church (Madden 1866–69, i. 488–89).
40. Luard 1872–83, iv. 379.
41. Riley 1867–69, i. 309.
42. From Bishop Grosseteste's rolls of institutions to benefices we can see that clergy ordained only below the level of subdeacon could be given churches where residence was actually enforced, though they could not fulfil the duties of pastoral care there. See for example Hoskin 2015, nos. 291, 1013.
43. Luard 1872–83, v. 279. For the right of clergy who went to university not to be ordained to the priesthood as early as the 1250s, see Logan 2014, 20–22.
44. Luard 1872–83, v. 121–23.
45. Luard 1872–83, iv. 405. This was also initially recorded in the *Historia* but was pasted over and replaced with Henry III's request for prayers that he should have a son (Madden 1866–69, ii. 499n).
46. Luard 1872–83, iv. 401.
47. Madden 1866–69, i. 448–49; ii. 86, 95, 315; Luard 1872–83, iv. 15, 61, 103–04; Luard 1880, 55, 179.
48. Luard 1872–83, iv. 518, 527.
49. Luard 1872–83, iii. 389; iv. 72; v. 77, 138, 360–61.
50. Luard 1872–83, v. 109.
51. See complaints of despoiling of abbey property in favour of their kin by Abbots Paul, Richard, Geoffrey, Robert and Simon (Riley 1867–69, i. 64, 71–72, 95, 181, 194).
52. Luard 1872–83, iv. 312.
53. In 1246 he connects the papacy and the moneylenders, stating that the Caursines could only act with papal approval. Madden 1866–69, ii. 316; Luard 1876, 331.
54. Luard 1872–83, iii. 328; Lunt 1939, 599–600; Lewis 1987, 246.
55. Kim 2000, 65–70.
56. Luard 1872–83, v. 355. In the *Historia* Paris says that Grosseteste had made calculations to demonstrate the increase in such benefices in his day but gives no exact amount (Madden 1866–69, ii. 128).
57. Madden 1866–69, i. 338; Luard 1872–83, iii. 240. On these events more generally see Stevenson 1899, 94–97; MacKenzie 1929, 181–23; Vincent 1996, 303–09; Brentano 1998, 6–7.
58. For tensions in these areas in the mid thirteenth century, particularly around the arrest of clerks accused of secular crimes and the use of writs of prohibition to remove cases from the ecclesiastical courts, often leading to a legal impasse, see Gabel 1929, 30–61; Poole 1933, 239–46; Cheney 1936, 224–25; Flahiff 1941, 101–14; Flahiff 1944, 262–96; Helmholz 1981, 297–314; Helmholz 2004, 511–14.

59. Madden 1866–69, i. 402, 435; ii. 275; Luard 1872–83, iv. 14.
60. Schulz 1945; Lewis 1964; Tierney 1965; Radding 1969; Blecker 1984, 109; Nederman 1984; Nederman 1988; Harding 2002, 1445–46.
61. Fenster and Wogan-Browne 2008, 16–17.
62. Binski 1990, 346–47; Carpenter 2007, 877–80.
63. Luard 1872–83, iv. 178.
64. Madden 1866–69, i. 76, 118, 292, 322–23, 343, 496; Luard 1872–83, iii. 543; v. 441, 458.
65. Wood 2002, 161; Strickland 2007, 210–11.
66. Madden 1866–69, i. 104; ii. 320, 343; Luard 1872–83, v. 487.
67. Riley 1867–69, i. 271–73.
68. Bolton 1991, 90–97; Mellone 1999; Duggan 2008, 341.
69. Moore 2003, 231–33.
70. Egger 2004, 32–38.
71. Cheney 1941, 34–51.
72. Lateran IV canons 16, 18, 26–31, 42–46, 53–54, 56, 68–70 (Tanner 1990, 243–44, 247–49, 253–55, 258–59, 261, 266–67).
73. Lateran IV canons 14, 15, 23, 32, 63 (Tanner, Alberigo and Jedin 1990: 242–43, 246, 249, 264).
74. Luard 1872–83, iv. 403. The *Historia* does not mention John's benefices but they are recorded in Matthew's abbreviation of the *Chronica* (Madden 1866–69, i. 498; ii. 293).
75. Luard 1877, 152; Mansel was to cause difficulties in the 1250s for St Albans, supporting the royal marshal Geoffrey of Childwick in his battles against the abbey. *Gesta abbatum* (Riley 1867–69, i. 314–16).
76. Luard 1872–83, iii. 418.
77. Luard 1872–83, v. 286–87. This mistress is not recorded in the *Historia* (Madden 1866–69, ii. 119).
78. Cheney and Powicke 1964, 112.
79. See for example Robert Grosseteste, bishop of Lincoln, 1235–53, speaking to the pope in 1250. Gieben 1971, 345.
80. Luard 1872–83, v. 300.
81. Hewlett 1886–89, iii. 342; Kuttner and García y García 1964, 128, 163–64.
82. Madden 1866–69, i. 416; i. 161.
83. Riley 1867–69, i. 308.
84. Luard 1872–83, v. 612.
85. Lewis 1987, 123–24.
86. Lateran IV, canon 55, 57, 59–61 (Tanner, Alberigo and Jedin 1990, 259–63).
87. Lateran IV, canons 33–34, 65–66 (Tanner, Alberigo and Jedin 1990, 250, 264–65).
88. Cheney 1983, 1–16.
89. Madden 1866–69, ii. 59, 77, 313.

90. Luard 1872–83, iv. 246–47. In the *Historia* he mentions Grosseteste's severity at visitation but gives no detail (Madden 1866–69, ii. 108).
91. Luard 1872–83, v. 226.
92. Luard 1872–83, iv. 245–48; v. 226.
93. For the most recent description of this quarrel see Bennett 2015, 18–21.
94. Luard 1872–83, iii. 528.
95. Luard 1872–83, vi. 185, 234, 258–59, 291.
96. Luard 1872–83, iii. 420–21. Cheney and Powicke 1964, 241–59. The *Historia* makes only very brief textual reference to the Council, though it was illustrated here (Madden 1866–69, i. 413; ii. 275; the image is reproduced in Lewis 1987, 250).
97. Cheney and Powicke 1964, 279.
98. Lewis 1987, 249.
99. Luard 1872–83, iii. 416.
100. Luard 1872–83, iii. 417.
101. Lewis 1987, 250.
102. Luard 1872–83, iii. 417.
103. Luard 1872–83, iii. 417.
104. Lewis 1987, 249.
105. Luard 1872–83, iii, 417.
106. Cheney and Powicke 1964, 279–84.
107. Luard 1864–69, 305, 422; Luard 1872–83, iii. 616; v. 359; Cheney and Powicke 1964, 469, 1132–33; Gray 1966; Denton 1986; Vaughan 1958c, 70–77.
108. Cheney and Powicke 1964, 280.
109. Cheney and Powicke 1964, 281–84.
110. Luard 1872–83, vi. 353–65. The most recent edition from Matthew's text is Cheney and Powicke 1964, 539–48.

6

Matthew Paris and Britain

Matthew Paris was a historian of England. His *Chronica maiora* was conceived as a history of England, and he gave the first of his revised abbreviations of it the title *Historia Anglorum* (*The History of the English*).[1] But Matthew was concerned to set the history of England within the wider context of the history of Christendom and the world, in its allotted place in God's creation.[2] Given the enormous scope of his chronicles, and in particular the *Chronica maiora*, his coverage of England's neighbours in Britain forms only a small portion of the whole. Nevertheless, he has far more to say than any other English chronicler during Henry III's reign about Wales and Scotland – although not Ireland.[3] His works are thus hugely valuable as a source for Welsh and Scottish history; but equally, his commentary on these countries is very revealing, illuminating Matthew's purposes and agendas as a chronicler.

Like most English chroniclers, Matthew's idea of Britain was derived in large part from Geoffrey of Monmouth's *Historia regum Britanniae*, which he accepted unquestioningly.[4] The *Chronica maiora* and the *Flores historiarum* share an account of the origins of Britain, with the Trojan Brutus as its first king, lifted virtually verbatim from Geoffrey, via Roger of Wendover.[5] This had real historical weight for Matthew, for he subsequently makes a point of the Trojan descent of the Welsh in his account of their resistance to Henry III's planned expedition to Wales in 1257.[6]

Visual confirmation of Matthew's concept of Britain is provided by the four maps which he drew to accompany his various historical works, all of which show Scotland and Wales, but not Ireland.[7] One of these maps, accompanying the manuscript of the *Chronica maiora*, has a label describing the Welsh as 'descended from Brutus, who was of Trojan origin'.[8] Yet, again like many other English chroniclers, Matthew sometimes conflated Britain and the British with England and the English. This is given graphic form in the map accompanying the manuscript of the *Historia Anglorum*, probably the earliest of his surviving maps of Britain. Part of a sequence which locates England in relationship to Jerusalem, it bears the legend: 'Britain now called England, which embraces Scotland, Galloway and Wales'.[9] And this underlying assumption helped to shape Matthew's view of Britain's past as England's past. At the original end point of the *Chronica maiora* at 1250, and also in a passage recording Henry III's customary offerings to the abbey in 1256, Matthew describes St Alban as 'the protomartyr of the English' (*Anglorum prothomartirem*) – despite the fact that, as Matthew himself records elsewhere, Alban was a Briton, martyred a century before the advent of the Anglo-Saxons in Britain.[10] This reflected his concern to promote Alban as pre-eminent amongst the saints of England, alongside the royal saints Edward and Edmund and the saintly bishops Thomas Becket and Edmund of Canterbury, but it also reflected the common historical portrayal of the English as the heirs to the political and cultural legacy of the Britons.[11]

Nevertheless, as his references to the Trojan descent of the Welsh suggest, Matthew had a clear sense of the separate identities of the nations of Britain. He had a great affection for his own homeland; describing the visit to England in 1256 of the Scottish king, Alexander III, and his queen (who was herself English), he commented that they were keen to gaze upon England's 'churches, cities and castles, rivers and meadows, woods and fields, which are admired as the greatest delights amongst all kingdoms'.[12] And he was equally willing to allow such sentiments to the Welsh. Recording the election of the Welshmen Thomas Wallensis, archdeacon of Lincoln, as bishop of St Davids in 1247, 'because he was born in Wales' (*eo quod in Wallia fuerat oriundus*), he comments that: 'everyone is naturally drawn to the sweetness of his birthplace' (*ad dulcedinem originis sui quilibet naturaliter attrahitur*).[13]

Matthew was well aware of the political divisions within Wales; relating how the Welsh of North and South Wales were 'united' (*confoederati sunt*) in 1257, he commented that this was unprecedented, 'because they had always been opposed to each other'.[14] However, when he referred to Wales or the Welsh, he generally meant Gwynedd, the princes of Gwynedd and their subjects; indeed, the princes of Gwynedd are almost the only Welsh leaders he mentions in his coverage of his own times.[15] He usually describes Dafydd ap Llywelyn as Prince of North Wales,[16] but twice refers to him simply as the Prince of Wales.[17] Similarly, in the *Flores historiarum*, he twice refers to Llywelyn ap Gruffudd as Prince of Wales.[18] Thus, on occasion, Matthew appears uncritically to accept Dafydd and Llyweyln's own estimation of their authority in Wales, even though the title of 'Prince of Wales' was not formally recognised by Henry III until the sealing of the treaty of Montgomery in 1267 – several years after Matthew's death.[19] Notably, he barely mentions the English lords of the Welsh Marches as a group. In his account of Anglo–Welsh conflict in 1258, he introduces them as 'the borderers, whom we call "Marchers"' (*contermini, quos Marchisios appellamus*), a phrasing which suggests that he does not expect his readership to be familiar with the term.[20]

As for Scotland, Matthew fully accepted its status as an established kingship of long standing, albeit owing homage to the kings of England. His knowledge of Scotland, however, generally seems to have extended only to the English-speaking lowlands. The earliest of his maps lists Galloway separately alongside Scotland and Wales as a constituent part of Britain, yet generally, the Gaelic-speaking areas of Galloway and the highlands seem barely to have registered.[21] Nor did the west coast and the islands, which remained in the allegiance of the king of Norway until after Matthew's death. The one exception to this is his account of a dispute over the Isle of Man in 1248/49; Matthew seems not to have known the identity of the island, which he misplaces between the Orkneys and Scotland.[22] Similarly, Matthew has markedly little to say on Ireland, and unsurprisingly, such matters as he does touch upon all relate directly to England or the church, such as the visit of an unnamed Irish 'sub-king' (*regulus*) of Connaught to London to petition King Henry in 1240,[23] or the annulment of the election of Ralph of Norwich as the archbishop of Dublin.[24] It may be that Ireland simply did not figure in Matthew's idea of Britain, for it barely features in Geoffrey of Monmouth's *Historia regum Britanniae*, and the English lordship in Ireland was becoming increasingly peripheral to English affairs.

A major feature of English commentary on their British neighbours in the twelfth and thirteenth centuries was the characterisation of the Welsh as 'barbarians' living a pastoral lifestyle that did not conform with the social, economic and moral norms of Francophile Western Christendom. The Scots tended to be regarded with more ambivalence, owing to the anglicised culture of the English-speaking lowlands and the close links between the English and Scottish royal families.[25] Matthew does, to an extent, reflect these perceptions in his maps; for example, the description of Scotland north of the Forth ('*Scotia ultramarina*') as a 'mountainous and wooded region, begetting an uncultivated and pastoral people, due to the marsh and reeds';[26] and a label for South Wales ('*Suth Wallia*'), describing it as a 'marshy, mountainous, wooded region, and impenetrable, fit for herdsmen, with agile, uncultivated and warlike inhabitants'.[27]

Such prejudices also inform the *Chronica maiora*'s account of a rebellion in Galloway in 1236 against Alexander II, with the rebel army assembled from Galloway, the Isle of Man and Ireland. The Gaelic-speaking Galwegians had invariably been depicted by twelfth-century English writers as uncivilised savages.[28] Matthew duly characterises the 'Galwegians' (*Galewenses*) as 'barbarians' (*barbiri*) who undertook 'a certain form of divination following an abominable custom of their ancient ancestors' (*quoddam genus arriolandi . . . secundum quandam . . . antiquorum atavorum suorum abominabilem consuetudinem*), in which they mixed their blood together and drank it as a show of common purpose.[29] Here, though, Matthew may simply have been reflecting the bias of his (unknown) source for this event. He does not invariably portray the Galwegians as 'barbaric'; in his account of a later rebellion in Galloway in 1247, it is not the Galwegians whose behaviour transgresses the accepted bounds, but rather the fault lies in the rapacious lordship of the Anglo-Scottish Roger de Quincy, Earl of Winchester, against whom they are rebelling.[30] It is also striking that Matthew describes Eógan (the lord of Argyll), a Gaelic Scot from the Highlands, as a 'bold and most decorous knight' (*militem strenuum et elegantissimum*) – particularly as it is possible that Matthew may have met him in person in Norway.[31] And in general, Matthew evidently regarded the Scots as part of the Francophile mainstream; the Scots attending the wedding of Alexander III at York are depicted as behaving in a courteous, courtly manner entirely appropriate to the occasion.[32]

Indeed, Matthew employed the topos of barbarianism to rather caustic effect when he depicted Alexander II playing up the image in order to deter the papal legate Otto from visiting the Scottish church, claiming of his realm that 'ungovernable, wild men dwell there, who thirst after human blood, and whom I myself cannot tame'.[33] The notion that the king of Scots should have solemnly informed a papal legate that he could not guarantee his safety from the blood-drinking wild men who roamed unchecked through his kingdom is, of course, patently absurd. Matthew may simply have invented the story himself, or possibly he was repeating scurrilous rumour (perhaps a satirical exaggeration of a genuine warning by Alexander of the volatile political state of his realm), playing on the prejudices of an Italian cardinal travelling to the northern edges of the world. But for Matthew, the story conveyed a higher moral truth about the pusillanimity of the agents of the papacy.[34]

Matthew's stated purpose in writing his histories was to provide moral instruction. He laid out this purpose explicitly in the virtually identical prologues to the *Chronica maiora* and the *Flores historiarum* (albeit that these prologues were adapted from Robert of Torigni, via Roger of Wendover).[35] And he summed it up in a comment in the *Abbreviatio Chronicorum*, where he records his original intention to finish the *Chronica maiora* at 1250:

> It is indeed an excellent thing to perpetuate notable events in writing, for the praise of God and in order that posterity should be instructed by reading, how to avoid those things which deserve punishment, and how to engage in the good things which are rewarded by God.[36]

This moral purpose gave shape to Matthew's political agenda, which was centred around the proper exercise of kingship and lordship and the authority of the papacy, within the proper bounds of custom and law. In particular, he deplored excessive interference or arbitrary impositions, whether by kings, lords, bishops or popes. At the same time, he firmly believed that it was duty of those same kings, lords, bishops and popes to defend those rights, privileges and liberties which had rightfully descended to them by divine providence. It was also imperative that they be properly counselled in the exercise of their authority. And kings in particular, as the rulers of nations, should properly be counselled by natives. The influence of undeserving aliens was to be deplored – and Matthew deplored it with considerable enthusiasm.[37]

Matthew includes some accounts of purely domestic Scottish and Welsh events; indeed one chapter of the *Chronica maiora*, concerning the murder of Patrick, son of Thomas of Galloway, is marked out with the marginal note: 'Pertains to the history of the Scots' (*Pertinet historie Scotorum*) – probably an annotation to help with the compilation of the *Historia Anglorum*.[38] However, as a historian of England, Matthew usually viewed Scotland and Wales through the prism of their relations with England (just as he did the other nations of Western Christendom).[39] Thus, in the *Chronica maiora*, he introduces his account of Dafydd ap Llywelyn's appeal to Innocent IV for papal protection in 1244, with the comment: 'I do not think it either unrelated or irrelevant to my subject matter, nor wholly beside the point for the history of England.'[40] When he does discuss events internal to Wales or Scotland, there is usually an English angle, as with his account of rebellion in Gaelic-speaking Galloway in 1236,[41] which arose from the division of the lordship between the three daughters and co-heiresses of Alan of Galloway, and their husbands, Roger de Quincy, Earl of Winchester, John Balliol and William de Forz, son of the earl of Aumale – all of whom held extensive English estates. And it is highly likely that Matthew's account depended on a source close to one of these three.[42]

Indeed, where Matthew's informants concerning events in Scotland and Wales can be identified, they were generally English, rather than Scottish or Welsh. And as a monk of one of the oldest, wealthiest and well-connected Benedictine houses in Britain, he was very well placed to obtain such information.[43] In particular, St Albans had close links with the Anglo–Scottish borders, through its dependency of Tynemouth Priory, with its liberty comprising properties scattered across the southeast of Northumberland.[44] Tynemouth was ideally located to pick up information from Scotland, for the Anglo–Scottish border marked a political boundary, and not a cultural one, and there were strong and close societal and religious links between northern England and southern Scotland.[45] These links are highlighted by various episodes recorded by Matthew relating to the priory, and for which its monks were presumably the source. Thus he includes a notice of the death of Patrick, Earl of Dunbar (who also held estates in Northumberland), in 1248, while on crusade with Louis IX. Matthew reports that he 'was believed to have taken up the cross to be reconciled to God and St Oswin' (*qui creditur crucem assumpsisse, ut Deo et beato Oswino reconciliaretur*), as he had been involved in a dispute with the convent of Tynemouth, where the Saxon saint Oswine of Deira (d. 651 CE) was buried.[46] Similarly, Matthew notes the discovery at Tynemouth in 1257 of the bones of Malcolm III ('Canmore'), King of Scots, and his son, killed while invading Northumberland in 1093, and buried in the priory at the insistence of Robert de Mowbray.[47] Indeed, the prior of Tynemouth was, on occasion, directly involved in Anglo–Scottish affairs; Matthew praises the prior's role as an intermediary between Alexander II and Henry III, helping to bring a peaceful end to the confrontation between them in 1244.[48]

Matthew was also able to obtain news from St Albans' many visitors, not the least of them Henry III himself, who came to the abbey on a number of occasions, and his entourage would have included many who would have been able to pass on detailed information on his dealings with Scotland and Wales.[49] Matthew was personally acquainted with John Mansel, one of Henry's closest advisers, and his detailed and stirring account of Mansel's role in 'rescuing' Margaret, Queen of Scots, from the custody of her guardians in 1255 suggests that Mansel himself was his source.[50] Furthermore, Henry's visits brought news of events straight to Matthew's ears; for instance, when Henry was at the abbey in November 1259, messengers arrived to inform him of the death in a riding accident of Walter Comyn, Earl of Menteith, described by Matthew as 'the most powerful earl in Scotland'.[51] This offered a perfect example of the sudden turning of Fortune's wheel to illustrate the vain, fleeting transience of worldly wealth and glory.

Other visitors could be equally informative. In 1252 Alan de la Zouche, justiciar of Chester and the Four Cantrefs of Wales, stopped at St Albans on the way to deliver royal revenues to the treasury in London; he confidently assured his listeners that 'the whole of Wales was obediently and peacefully subjected to English laws'.[52] The details of Zouche's appointment the year before are also reported by Matthew, presumably on Zouche's own information. The latter's report on the condition of Wales was confirmed by Richard, Bishop of Bangor, who was staying at St Albans, having sought shelter there in 1248 after fleeing his war-ravaged bishopric the year before.[53] Bishop Richard would maintain his connections with St Albans after he returned to Wales, visiting the abbey again for three weeks in 1258 on his way to London as an envoy from Llywelyn ap Gruffudd. Richard proved a valuable source of information for Matthew, providing a perspective from the Welsh side, particularly as he played an occasional role in Llywelyn's government – but he also serves to illustrate the limits of Matthew's knowledge.[54] He obviously did not stop at St Albans on his way back to Llywelyn in 1258, as Matthew had to confess his ignorance of the results of his negotiations: 'what response he brought back is not known'.[55]

The limitations of Matthew's information are also clear in his account of the homage performed by Alexander III to Henry III on the occasion of his marriage. This provides the only record of the homage of Alexander (then aged just ten years old) to Henry for the lands he held of the kingdom of England. Unfortunately, while surely correct in broad outline, this was erroneous in detail, for Matthew seems to have lacked a detailed knowledge of the English holdings of the kings of the Scots. He describes the territory as 'Lothian, and the remaining lands'.[56] Lothian was not part of the kingdom of England, nor did the kings of England lay claim to it.[57] Matthew's account of the 1237 Treaty of York between Henry and Alexander II is similarly inaccurate, for he reports that the king of Scots was to receive 300 librates of land in England, when in fact the treaty specified 200 librates; and he does not name the lands which were granted, notwithstanding that they included the substantial regality of Tynedale in Northumberland, not far from Tynemouth Priory.[58] In the absence of any more up-to-date information, Matthew may simply have depended on his own reworking of Roger of Wendover, in which he recorded that Lothian had been granted to Kenneth, King of Scots, by King Edgar in 975.[59]

Matthew's views of events in Scotland and Wales were also, at least in part, influenced by the biases and agendas of his informants. A case in point is his account of the dispute in 1248–49 between Alexander II and Eógan (the lord of Argyll), over Eógan's homage to Håkon IV of Norway, which was probably shaped by his visit to Norway in 1248–49. Here, he met and conversed with Håkon IV, and may even have met Eógan, so it is surely no coincidence that his account of the affair is markedly similar to Norwegian accounts.[60] Similar factors may explain the particular animus which Matthew maintained against Dafydd ap Llywelyn, Prince of Gwynedd, whom he regarded as 'a betrayer and brother-slayer'.[61] The *Chronica maiora* has two short accounts, quite widely separated, of the conflict that broke out between Dafydd and his brother Gruffydd in 1240, after the death of their father, Llywelyn ap Iorwerth. Though differing in detail, both accounts record how Dafydd 'deceitfully' (*in dolo*) imprisoned Gruffydd, in spite of the safe conduct he had from Richard, Bishop of Bangor.[62] This was an affair of internal Welsh politics, but Matthew was able to draw on the testimony of one of the participants, Bishop Richard himself, who came to St Albans in 1248.[63] And it was presumably Richard's testimony that prejudiced Matthew against Dafydd, for Richard had excommunicated Dafydd, and subsequently denounced his conduct to Henry III, convincing him (by Matthew's account) to try to procure Gruffydd's release.[64] This view of Dafydd continued to colour Matthew's depiction of his relations with Henry; relating the confrontation that led to Dafydd's submission in 1241, Matthew describes him as 'false and injurious to many' (*fallacem et multis injuriosum*), and 'a trouble-maker in all things and a rebel' (*cavillatorem in omnibus ... et rebellem*).[65]

Matthew's approach to Scotland and Wales reflects the interconnectedness of the realms and principalities of Britain in the thirteenth century. His account of Anglo-Scottish and Anglo-Welsh relations was shaped, at least in part, by the close family connections between the kings of England and the kings of the Scots and the princes of Wales, and between the nobility of all three nations.[66] This was reflected in items such as his notice of the death in London in 1244 of Margaret, sister of Alexander II and widow of Gilbert Marshal, Earl of Pembroke; and the settlement of the marital dispute between Roger Bigod and his wife, Isabella, another of Alexander's sisters (though in this latter case, Matthew's prime focus was on Roger's obedient acceptance of the church's judgement in the matter).[67] Matthew also recorded, if only incidentally, some of the personal bonds shaping such relationships, describing Queen Eleanor's great affection for her daughter and the latter's husband, the young Alexander III, who Eleanor 'loved as an adopted son'.[68] Matthew's account of Dafydd ap Llywelyn similarly emphasises his relationship to Henry III, as the son of King John's illegitimate daughter Joan, repeatedly referring to him as Henry's 'nephew' (*nepos*). In this case, though, this was undoubtedly intended to emphasise his treachery and lack of familial loyalty to his rightful lord, for each reference to his relationship to Henry is accompanied by a pejorative epithet.[69]

As a chronicler of English history, Matthew inevitably framed his approach in England's claims to the overlordship of Wales and Scotland. For Matthew, as for his contemporaries, an important part of a king's duty was the maintenance and protection of his status and the rights properly pertaining to his realm, and he took for granted that in the case of the king of England these included homage from the king of Scots for his Scottish kingdom as well as for his English lands. Matthew describes the 1244 crisis in Anglo–Scottish relations in terms of an issue of overlordship, reporting that when King Henry was staying at St Albans in June 1244, he received news (*rumores*) that

> the king of Scotland had impudently declared that he held not even a particle of the kingdom of Scotland from the king of England; and he neither wanted to nor should.[70]

Similarly, Matthew describes how, at his wedding to Henry's daughter Margaret at York in 1251, Alexander III refused to do homage to Henry for the kingdom of Scotland, 'as his predecessors had done ... as is clearly recorded in the chronicles in many places',[71] although he did do homage for 'the tenements which he holds of the lord king of the English, specifically of the kingdom of England'.[72] In this case, however, the episode may have been intended to highlight not so much the issue of overlordship, but rather the weakness of Henry III. Henry, Matthew stated, did not pursue the matter of Alexander's homage for Scotland because he did not wish to spoil the wedding feast or to trouble 'a king so young' (*tam juvenem regem*). And so he 'dissembled for the while, quietly passing over everything'.[73] Matthew then offers a pointed comparison, for the episode is immediately followed by an account of how, when the earl marshal, Roger Bigod, claimed his right to demand Alexander's palfrey by ancient custom, Alexander firmly but diplomatically refused to accede.[74] Thus, Alexander, 'a king so young' and newly crowned, is shown to be far more capable of asserting his authority than the adult, long-reigning Henry.[75]

Matthew was equally clear in upholding the basic principle of English overlordship of Wales. His most explicit statement of this overlordship comes when it was under threat from the papacy. He recounts how, in 1244

> Pope Innocent the Fourth wished to exempt Dafydd, prince of North Wales, from his fealty to the king of England, to whose lordship he was bound in many ways, and to subject him to his own lordship.[76]

Returning to the same theme shortly after, he expresses his astonishment that the pope could have favoured Dafydd's cause, adding, with a rhetorical flourish: 'Can any Christian not know that the prince of Wales is a petty vassal of the king of England?'.[77] This is as much a negative repudiation of the pope's jurisdiction over Dafydd's relations with England as it is a positive assertion of the king of England's overlordship of Wales. Nevertheless, when war broke out between Dafydd and Henry later in the same year, Matthew's account framed it as 'the rebellion of the recalcitrant Welsh against the charters they had made and against their oaths' (*De rebellione Walensium jam contra cartas confectas et juramenta sua recalcitrantium*), and he later describes Henry's campaign against Dafydd as 'deservedly provoked' (*merito commoti*).[78]

Matthew's depiction of England's relationships with Scotland and Wales is, however, also shaped by his own very decided views on the nature and proper limits of overlordship. This is illustrated by his treatment of the events leading up to the Anglo–Scottish confrontation of 1244. He records the murder of Patrick, son of Thomas of Galloway, and his companions, who died when Walter Bisset burned down their lodgings at Haddington in 1242.[79] Bisset was exiled from Scotland by Alexander and sought shelter with Henry, claiming that he had been treated unjustly on the grounds that as the 'liege man' (*homo ligius*) of the king of England, the king of Scots did not have the right to exile any of his noblemen without the king of England's consent. Bisset went on to denounce Alexander for having given shelter to Geoffrey Marsh, a fugitive from the English lordship of Ireland, claiming that this was 'in violation of the allegiance and fealty by which he was bound to the king of England' (*in laesionem ligantie et fidelitatis qua tenetur regi Anglie*).[80] Henry was intensely angered by this and, Matthew relates, waited for 'a suitable time for retribution', adding the cliffhanger, 'as will be revealed in the account coming after'.[81]

The right to overrule a liege's judicial authority by the hearing of appeals was becoming one of the defining principles of overlordship.[82] But as Matthew frames the affair, Alexander is in the right, for he is described as 'a just and merciful man' (*vir justus et misericors*). By contrast, Bisset was an oath breaker: 'he had sworn to set out for the Holy Land, and not return, for the redemption of his soul and of those aforesaid who died by fire', but went instead to Henry's court.[83] By Matthew's moral compass, then, Bisset – and thus by extension his claims – was not justified.

The point about the proper limits of overlordship is reinforced when Matthew delivers the promised sequel (considerably later in his narrative). In 1244 Henry III raised an army and marched to the border in pursuance of a slightly different set of grievances, alleging that Geoffrey Marsh and other fugitive enemies had been received by Walter Comyn, and had fortified castles in in Galloway and Lothian 'to the prejudice of the king of England, and contrary to the charters of their ancestors' (*in prejudicium regis Anglie et contra cartas predecessorum suorum*).[84] Alexander raised an army of his own and war seemed to be in the offing, though in the event, a settlement was reached. Matthew praises Alexander in the highest of terms, describing him as 'a good, just, pious and munificent man, loved by all, by the English as well as his own, and deservedly' (*vir bonus, justus, pius, et dapsilis, ab omnibus tam Anglis quam suis diligebatur, et merito*). He goes on to describe how the Scottish knights and foot soldiers (all 100,000 of them), having confessed their sins and encouraged by preachers, had no fear of death 'because they were going to fight justly for their country' (*quia pro patria sua juste dimicaturi forent*) – with the obvious corollary that, had he invaded his vassal's land, Henry would not have been waging a just war.[85] This contrasts with Henry's invasion of Wales in the same year, which Matthew described as 'deservedly provoked'.[86] Thus the narrative presented by Matthew puts Alexander unequivocally in the right. The charter sealed by Alexander to settle the dispute, of which Matthew provides the full text, addressed Henry as his 'liege lord' (*ligius dominus noster*), and conceded 'that we will for ever preserve good faith to [Henry], and also love for him' (*quod in perpetuum bonam fidem ei servabimus pariter et amorem*), but it concedes none of the prerogatives of overlordship beyond a promise not to ally with Henry's enemies.[87]

However, despite his admiration for Alexander II, 'a wise and modest man' (*vir sapiens et modestus*), Matthew was ready to criticise him when he too overstepped the proper bounds of lordship. His account of Alexander's dispute with Eógan, Lord of Argyll, over Eógan's homage to Håkon IV for the Isle of Man in 1248–49 presents Alexander in avaricious and vindictive pursuit of a magnate rightfully upholding his service to his two lords, 'so long as the lords should not be enemies' (*dummodo non essent domini sibi adversantes*). When Alexander insists on mounting an expedition against Eógan he incurs the displeasure of God and St Columba and is struck down with a sudden mortal affliction.[88] An overbearing king being brought low by God as punishment for his oppressive conduct fits perfectly with Matthew's agenda.

Matthew used his account of the Anglo–Scottish confrontation of 1244 to suggest that it was entirely morally justifiable to take up arms against a lord, a king or an overlord who was acting beyond the proper bounds of his authority. Such conduct was explicitly described as tyranny in his account of the rebellion in Galloway in 1247, provoked by the depredations of the Anglo–Scottish Roger de Quincy, who 'tyrannically despoiled the magnates of that land, more than was customary and contrary to what was proper'.[89] Similarly, in recounting Llywelyn ap Gruffudd's wars with the English in 1256, 1257 and 1258, Matthew takes a rather different line from his accounts of Dafydd ap Llywelyn's unjustified rebellions. Of the Welsh preparations against Henry's expedition of 1257, he comments, 'their cause seemed just even to their enemies'.[90] In the *Flores historiarum*, he describes how 'Llywelyn, prince of Wales ... defended his country manfully, vigorously resisting the English to uphold his ancestral liberties'.[91] And in the *Chronica maiora*, he provides a stirring speech for Llywelyn which invokes God's aid and excoriates King Henry, Prince Edward and Sir Geoffrey Langley.[92] Langley, who made a fortune out of administrative service to Henry and Edward, was a particular bête noire of

Matthew's,⁹³ and he directly blames Langley's oppressions as 'the king's collector of dues' (*regium exactorem*) for the rising of the Welsh against Edward, 'their lord (*domini sui*)', in 1256.⁹⁴ Clearly, for Matthew, the Welsh were justly resisting 'the tyranny of Edward and his household'.⁹⁵ This favourable view of the Welsh under Llywelyn ap Gruffudd may have been based partly on reports from Richard, Bishop of Bangor, whose opinions Matthew clearly respected, but it also fitted with his own agenda, providing a counterpoint to his disapproval of Henry, Edward and their agents.⁹⁶ It is surely no coincidence that Matthew becomes more sympathetic to Welsh rebellion against Henry and Edward just as opposition was mounting against them in England.

Perhaps one of the most striking instances of Matthew's treatment of the Welsh, in particular, is in his use of them as an object lesson in their resistance to the malign influence of rapacious foreigners – even though these rapacious foreigners were, in this case, the English themselves. A case in point is Matthew's description of the preparations for war in 1257, where he says of the Welsh: 'they strove steadfastly for their ancestral laws and liberties' (*pro avitis legibus suis et libertatibus constanter ... decertabant*). This is contrasted with: 'the wretched English, who, trampled underfoot by every foreigner, allowed the ancient liberties of their kingdom to be extinguished' (*miseris Anglicis, a quolibet alienigena conculcatis, qui suas antiquas libertates regni permittunt exufflari*). Matthew's didactic purpose is here made explicit by the added rider: 'nor were they shamed by the example of the Welsh' (*nec erubescunt, exemplo Walensium informati*).⁹⁷ He thus put forward as an inspiring ideal the proud and determined resistance of the Welsh to the English who threatened their liberty, to be set against the abject failure of the English to resist the foreigners who threatened theirs. The foreigners that Matthew had in mind were the Poitevin and Savoyard relatives of Henry and his queen. Denouncing the marriage, by the queen's procurement, of Baldwin de Redvers, heir to the earldom of Devon, to Margaret of Savoy, Matthew had already condemned 'the pusillanimous English ... their indolence and supine naivety rebuked by the boldness of the Welsh'.⁹⁸

Equally pointed (although lacking the explicit comparison) is Matthew's brief account of events in Scotland in 1257. According to Matthew, Alexander III

> went shamefully and excessively awry, promoting foreigners, following their advice, and exalting and setting them above his native-born men; furious, these denizens and native-born, took the king and queen back into custody, so that he should not rush into anything worse ... carefully guarding them, for long enough until, after the example of the Germans, all the foreigners had been removed.[99]

The 'example of the Germans' was a reference to Richard of Cornwall, who sent his followers home after his coronation as king of the Germans, allegedly because 'the Germans, unlike the English, would not tolerate that their king's heart should be bent like a reed by the counsels of foreigners'.[100]

In fact, the events in Scotland were part of an ongoing factional dispute over the custody of Alexander, who was still a minor (now aged sixteen), and it was Walter Comyn, Earl of Menteith, who had seized control of Alexander from the rival faction headed by Alan Durward.[101] The only contemporary Scottish account of the affair, from the chronicle of Melrose, attributes an entirely different motivation to Comyn, and makes no mention of the promotion of foreigners, nor are Comyn's party identified as 'native born'.[102]

Alexander's promotion of foreigners and the antipathy it aroused has all the hallmarks of an invention born of Matthew's own agenda, for the only foreigner known to have received conspicuous advancement in Scotland at this time was Richard de Potton, an English cleric promoted to the see of Aberdeen.[103] It is tempting to speculate that Matthew wrote up the finished version of this chapter in 1258, for it looks as though he was projecting onto Scottish politics his view of and hopes for the revolution in the politics of England of that year (a time lag of one or two years was typical in the compiling of the final draft of the *Chronica maiora*).[104] Again, the politics of Scotland (and indeed Germany) were being presented as an *exemplum* for the edification of the English.

For the historian sitting down to analyse Matthew Paris' view of Britain, he can appear confusingly inconsistent, partly because of his strictly annalistic approach, which does not lend itself to drawing out themes; and partly owing to the various influences of his informants' viewpoints. But there is, in fact, an underlying consistency to his treatment of Scotland and Wales.

Unlike some of the historians of Edward I's reign, such as Peter Langtoft and the anonymous author of the Anglo–Norman Prose *Brut*, Matthew was not interested in justifying English claims to the overlordship of Scotland and Wales. Nor was his intention to record historical precedents of the sort which Edward I would later demand from the chronicles of various abbeys, including St Albans.[105] Matthew simply accepted English overlordship as a fact. This, however, was a period during which theories of overlordship and sovereignty, and the attendant rights of a superior lord to interfere in the government of his vassals' territories, were being developed and clarified, drawing on ideas derived from Roman law (ideas ventriloquised by Matthew through Walter Bisset).[106] Matthew, however, maintained a traditional view of a less intrusive, more symbolic model of overlordship. His strictures on the proper exercise of kingship applied equally to the exercise of overlordship. For Matthew, there was no contradiction in praising the Scots or the Welsh for resisting an improper exercise of overlordship by the king of England and then rebuking that same king for failing to enforce the acknowledgement of that overlordship, within the appropriate bounds. And by the same token, the Welsh and the Scottish political communities were to be praised for upholding their liberties against the king of England or indeed against their own rulers – and blamed when they rebelled against the properly exercised overlordship of the king of England. Equally, Matthew apportioned praise or blame to the kings of Scots and the Welsh princes (in effect, the princes of Gwynedd) according to whether they exercised their office appropriately.

For the study of medieval Britain over the longue durée, Matthew Paris is invaluable in offering a perspective from the mid thirteenth century, without the benefit of hindsight of the revolutionary changes of Edward I's reign. The *Chronica maiora* is – by far – the best informed surviving source for England's relations with Wales and Scotland in the period 1236 to 1259. Yet there is absolutely nothing in it to suggest that within twenty-five years of its end point Edward I would have conquered Wales or that, in the following decade, Edward would abolish the Scottish kingship and impose direct English rule on Scotland (albeit only briefly). To the contrary, describing the war of 1257, Matthew describes Edward as at one point considering whether to abandon Wales and the Welsh as 'unconquerable' (*indomabilibus*).[107] With hindsight, it can seem obvious that Llywelyn ap

Gruffudd's success in expanding his dominion over Wales was predicated on English weakness, and Edward I's conquest of Wales, and indeed his invasion of Scotland, can appear as the inevitable culmination of two centuries of English expansionism. Matthew Paris provides a salutary reminder that none of this seemed inevitable before the event.

Notes

I would like to thank the editor for guidance on the *terra incognita* of thirteenth-century St Albans historiography, the greatly-missed Björn Weiler for advice and for copies of several of his papers which have informed this piece, and Claire Etty for helping to shape my thoughts on Matthew Paris and for detailed and constructive criticism and editing of several drafts of the piece.

1. Madden 1866-69, i. xxxviii; Vaughan 1958c, 111-12; Weiler 2009, 269. For the sake of manageability, the current discussion will be confined to the *Chronica maiora*, the *Historia Anglorum* and the *Flores historiarum*, and will concentrate on the period 1235 to 1260, when Matthew was writing about contemporary events.
2. Weiler 2009, 257-58.
3. The extent of Matthew's coverage of Scotland, compared to that of other English chroniclers, is brought out very starkly in Anderson 1908, which provides a comprehensive collection of accounts of Scottish affairs recorded in English chronicles. Matthew furnishes a large majority of the coverage for the period 1236-61, much more than all other English chroniclers combined; Anderson 1908, 341-79. Matthew's scant coverage of Ireland is discussed later in this chapter on pages 146-47.
4. There were a few English chroniclers, before and after Matthew, who expressed some degree of scepticism over some parts of the *Historia regum Britanniae*, mostly to do with Arthur – notably Alfred of Beverley and William of Newburgh, writing in the twelfth century, and Ranulph Higden, writing in the fourteenth; Gransden 1974b, 212, 264-65; Moll 2003, 65-67.
5. Luard 1872-83, i. 21-24; Hewlett 1886-89, I, 24-27 (and compare Reeve and Wright 2007, 26-31. For Matthew's use of the *Historia regum Britanniae* in his *Flores historiarum* see Ingledew 1994, 696-700.
6. Luard 1872-83, v. 639.
7. Gilson and Poole 1928; Harvey 1992.
8. '*De Bruto propagatus, qui a Troiannus duxit originem*'; Cambridge, Corpus Christi College, 16I, fol. ivv; Gilson and Poole 1928, 6, map B.
9. '*Britannia nunc dicta Anglia, qui complectitur Scociam, Galeweiam et Walliam*', BL, Royal MS 14 C VII, fol. 5^v; Gilson and Poole 1928, 5, map D;

Harvey 1992, 104; Breen 2005. It is not clear why Galloway is listed separately from Scotland.
10. Luard 1872–83, v. 197, 574. The *Chronica maiora* records Alban as a Briton in its account of his martyrdom, *sub anno* 304 (Luard 1872–83, i. 148–54, derived from William of St Albans' *Passio S. Albani*, via Roger of Wendover); this account was copied verbatim into the *Flores Historiarum*, *sub anno* 303 (Hewlett 1886–89, i. 169–74).
11. Matthew Paris is generally accepted as the author of a Latin life of Edmund of Canterbury, and Anglo-Norman verse lives of Alban, Edward, Thomas and Edmund of Canterbury; Vaughan 1958c, 161–81.
12. *Ecclesias, civitates et castra, fluvios et prata, silvas et agros, ... quae inter omnium regnorum delicias maxime comprobantur*; Luard 1872–83, v. 573. It should be noted that, his surname notwithstanding, there is nothing to suggest that Matthew was not English born; Vaughan 1958c, 1.
13. Luard 1872–83, iv. 647. For Wallensis see Bateson and Costambeys 2004. His election is briefly noted, without comment, in Madden 1866–69, iii. 30.
14. '*Quia semper sibi ad invicem adversabantur*', Luard 1872–83, v. 645. This was a somewhat roseate view of a process which included the forceful subjugation of some of the Welsh princes by Llywelyn ap Gruffudd. This positive spin can probably be attributed to Richard, Bishop of Bangor (1236–67), who was one of Matthew's main informants on Wales: Smith 2014, 57, 100, 118; and see later in this chapter page 151 and note 53.
15. One of the very few others is Gruffydd ap Madog, lord of Bromfield, of the Powys dynasty, described by Matthew as 'one of the most powerful of the Welsh' (*Quidam ... potentissimus Walensium*), who appears as an ally of Henry's against Dafydd ap Llywelyn in 1241; Luard 1872–83, iv. 148–49. He appears again in Matthew's account of Llywelyn ap Gruffudd's campaigns in 1257, but as Gruffydd de Bromfield, and it is by no means clear that Matthew realised that this was the same man; Luard 1872–83, v. 597, 613, 646. For his career see Stephenson 2005.
16. '*Princeps Norwallie*', Madden 1866–69, iii. 14; Luard 1872–83, iv. 316, 398, 517.
17. '*Princeps Wallie*', Luard 1872–83, iv. 323–24 (while emphasising his status as a 'lowly vassal' (*vassalulum*) of the king of England); Luard 1872–83, iv. 489 (when Henry is said to have complained of the hostility of 'the prince of Wales').
18. '*Princeps Wallie*', Hewlett 1886–89, ii. 416, 435.
19. Smith 2014, 285.
20. Luard 1872–83, v. 717. Although he had already made passing references to 'marchers' (*marchisii*) in annals for 1244 and 1245; Luard 1872–83, iv. 358 (repeated verbatim in Madden 1866–69, ii. 487–88); Luard 1872–83, iv. 407.
21. See page 145 of this chapter and note 9.

22. '*Insula illa inter Orkadem et Scotiam sita est*'; Luard 1872–83, v. 88–89. Man is placed correctly (more or less) on his maps.
23. Luard 1872–83, iv. 57–58. This was Feidhlim Ua Conchobair, and Matthew makes a number of errors in his account of Feidhlim's visit; Verstraten 2003, 21.
24. Matthew provides two widely different accounts of the affair; in the *Chronica maiora*, the canons of Dublin are blamed for electing 'an entirely worldly man' (*hominem . . . penitus secularem*), but in the *Flores historiarum*, he is said to have been let down by his procurators at Rome. Luard 1872–83, v. 560; Hewlett 1886–89, ii. 416.
25. Gillingham 1993; Davies 2000, 113–41.
26. '*Regio palustris montuosa nemorosa, gentem incultam generans et pastoralem, propter mariscum et harundinetum*', BL, Cotton MS Claudius D VI, fol. 12^v; Gilson and Poole 1928, 5, map A (a similar label appears on Cambridge, Corpus Christi College, 16(I), fol. iv^v; Gilson and Poole 1928, 5, map B).
27. '*Regio palustris montuosa nemorosa, et inuia pastoribus accomoda incolas habet agiles incultos & bellicos*', BL, Cotton MS Claudius D VI, fol. 12^v; Gilson and Poole 1928, 5, map A.
28. See for instance the descriptions of Galloway ('a wild country where the inhabitants are like beasts, and . . . altogether barbarous') in a late twelfth-century life of Aelred of Rievaulx; Powicke 1950, 45–46 at 45.
29. Luard 1872–83, iii. 364–66. The rebellion is discussed by Oram 2012, 156–58, 193.
30. See pages 156 of this chapter and note 89.
31. See page 152 of this chapter and note 60.
32. For the wedding and Matthew's account of it see Staniland 1986.
33. '*Indomiti . . . et silvestres homines ibi habitant, humanum sanguinem sitientes, quos nec ego ipse valeo edomare*'; Luard 1872–83, iii. 413.
34. See the comments of Weiler 2009, 274. According to Matthew, Alexander also claimed that no legate had ever visited Scotland before, which was also patently untrue; Barrell 2005, 161.
35. Weiler 2009, 258–59.
36. Madden 1866–69, iii. 319, translated by Vaughan 1958c, 151.
37. Vaughan 1958c, 141–43; Gransden 1974b, 369.
38. Vaughan 1958c, 64–65; and see page 154 of this chapter and note 79.
39. Weiler 2009, 269–71.
40. *Nec arbitror materiae mae vel alienum fore vel impertinens, vel etiam historias regni Anglie penitus inutile*: Luard 1872–83, iv. 316 (and see page 154 of this chapter and note 76).
41. See page 147 of this chapter and note 29.
42. This is possibly a source connected with Roger de Quincy, for Matthew subsequently recounts Roger's involvement in another rebellion in

Galloway in 1247 (though this informant seems not to have altogether approved of Roger, for Matthew's account blames him for the latter rebellion; see page 147 of this chapter and note 30).
43. Gransden 1974b, 360–61.
44. For Tynemouth and its holdings see Gibson 1846–47, i. i–xvi – a work of stated pious and moral intent of which Matthew Paris would undoubtedly have approved; Craster 1907, 34–153; Holford and Stringer 2010, 203–23.
45. Stringer 1994.
46. Luard 1872–83, v. 41; and see Hodgson 1904, 61–62.
47. Luard 1872–83, v. 633. Matthew describes Mowbray as 'the founder of the church of Tynemouth' (*fundator ecclesie de Thynemutha*), whereas in fact, he granted an existing (though moribund) house to St Albans: Riley 1866–69, i. 56–57. See also Aird 2004. Further details of Malcolm's death and burial are given in the *Additamenta*; Luard 1872–83, vi. 370–71.
48. Madden 1866–69, ii. 494–95; Luard 1872–83, iv. 83; Luard 1890, ii. 280–81. The prior – unnamed by Matthew – was Richard de Parco, elected in February 1244; Smith and London 2001, 132.
49. Vaughan 1958c, 12–13.
50. Luard 1872–83, v. 504–06; Liu 2007, 159–73; Carpenter 2020, 620. For Mansel see also pages 60, 65, 71, 132, 142.
51. '*Comes in Scotia potentissimus*', Luard 1872–83, v. 724.
52. '*Tota Wallia obedienter et in pace legibus subjacet Anglicanis*', Luard 1872–83, v. 227, 288.
53. Luard 1872–83, iv. 647; v. 2; Vaughan 1958c, 12, 15. Presumably, Bishop Richard remained in touch with his diocese, even from exile.
54. Smith 2014, 114–15, 126–30.
55. '*Quid responsionis reportavit, ignoratur*', Hewlett 1886–89, ii. 435. The *Chronica maiora* has a much shorter notice of the negotiations with a rather different slant, and no mention of the bishop; Luard 1872–83, v. 704.
56. '*Laudiano videlicet et terris reliquis*', Luard 1872–83, v. 268. For background see Carpenter 2020, 522.
57. Duncan 2016, 154.
58. Stones 1970, no. 7 (40–41). Tynedale is marked on three of Matthew's maps of Britain; Gilson and Poole 1928, 10.
59. Luard 1872–83, i. 467–68; and see Duncan 2016, 154.
60. Cowan 1990; Weiler 2012.
61. '*Proditor et fratricida*', Luard 1872–83, iv. 323.
62. Luard 1872–83, iv. 8, 47–48. This may represent careless double copying of an initial rough draft when the final draft of the *Chronica maiora* was compiled (see the comments of Vaughan 1958c, 9). The two accounts are consolidated in Madden 1866–69, ii. 430; and see also Luard 1872–83, iv.

148–49; Madden 1866–69, iii. 280. For the dispute and Matthew's treatment of it see Williams 1962–64, 401–08; Smith 2014, 49–53.
63. See page 151 of this chapter and note 53.
64. Luard 1872–83, iv. 148–49.
65. Luard 1872–83, iv. 149–50. For Dafydd's submission to the king see also Carpenter 2020, 238.
66. Frame 1988; Davies 1990; Davies 2000.
67. Madden 1866–69, ii. 497–48; Luard 1872–83, iv. 396; Luard 1890, II. 283, 284 (Margaret); Luard 1872–83, v. 382–83; Hewlett 1886–89, ii. 387 (Isabella). Matthew was evidently ignorant of Isabella's name, leaving a blank in the manuscript of the *Chronica maiora*. He also refers to her, somewhat misleadingly, as 'the daughter of the king of Scotland', for she was the daughter of King William, who had died in 1214. For Bigod's dispute with her see Morris 2005, 4–5, 43–44.
68. *Quasi filium dilexit adoptivum*; Luard 1872–83, v. 501.
69. Madden 1866–69, ii. 431, 453, 482–83; Luard 1872–83, iv. 47, 323, 398, 517; Luard 1890, ii. 221, 236, 239, 274, 285; and see page 152 of this chapter and note 61.
70. '*Quod rex Scotie regi significaverat procaciter, quod nullam etiam particulam regni Scotie a rege Anglie tenuit vel tenere voluit aut debuit*': Luard 1872–83, iv. 358–59; repeated almost verbatim in Madden 1866–69, ii. 489; Luard 1890, ii. 278–79.
71. '*Sicut fecerunt predecessores . . . prout evidenter in cronicis locis multis scribitur*', Luard 1872–83, v. 268. For the marriage see also Carpenter 2020, 518–25.
72. '*Fecit igitur rex Scotie regi Anglorum homagium ratione tenementi, quod tenet de domino rege Anglorum, de regno scilicet Anglie*', Luard 1872–83, v. 268. Matthew erroneously names Lothian as being held of the kingdom of England (see page 151 of this chapter and notes 56 and 57).
73. '*Ad tempus omnia sub silentio preteriens dissimulavit*', Luard 1872–83, v. 268.
74. Matthew was much given to such telling comparisons; Weiler 2009, 272–73.
75. Luard 1872–83, v. 269. The custom pertained to Bigod's office of marshal, by which he was entitled to a gift from anyone knighted by the king; Morris 2005, 30.
76. '*Papa Innocentius quartus David principem Northwallie, domino regi Anglie multiformiter obligatum, a fidelitate regis exemptum, dominio suo voluit mancipare*', Luard 1872–83, iv. 316. Matthew also gives a brief account in Madden 1866–69, ii. 482–3. Dafydd's appeal to the pope is discussed by Richter 1970–71, 208–13.
77. '*Et quis Christianorum ignorat principem Wallie regis Anglie esse vassalulum?*', Luard 1872–83, iv. 324.

78. Madden 1866–69, ii. 487–88; Luard 1872–83, iv. 358, 398. The phrase is not reproduced in the shorter narrative of the *Historia Anglorum*. See also Carpenter 2020, 425–31.
79. Luard 1872–83, iv. 200–02. And see Oram 2012, 166–70; Young 1997, 41–43.
80. This relates to the execution for treason of William Marsh, Geoffrey's son (an incident related in lurid detail in Luard 1872–83, iv. 196–97). The *Flores historiarum* notes Geoffrey's flight to Scotland and his death in exile, but without mention of Bisset's accusations; Hewlett 1886–89, ii. 253.
81. '*Usque ad idoneum tempus retributionis, sicut sequens sermo declarabit*', Luard 1872–83, iv. 202. This textual cross-reference appears to refer forward to the Anglo-Scottish confrontation of 1244, which suggests that this part of the *Chronica maiora* must have been written up no earlier than then.
82. The hearing of appeals would be a key feature of Edward I's implementation of the overlordship of Scotland and Philip IV's of Gascony in the 1280s and 1290s: Dodd 2007, 175.
83. '*Juraverat iter se arrepturum in Terram Sanctam et irrediturum, pro redemptione anime suae et predictorum ... combustione peremptorum*': Luard 1872–83, iv. 201.
84. Carpenter 2020, 421–24. This was the same Walter Comyn whose death Matthew would record in 1259; see page 150 of this chapter and note 51.
85. Luard 1872–83, iv. 380. For these events see Oram 2012, 170–74.
86. See page 154 of this chapter and note 78.
87. Luard 1872–83, iv. 381.
88. Luard 1872–83, v. 88–89; Cowan 1990; McDonald 1997, 307; Oram 2012, 193–96.
89. '*In homines illius patrie nobiliores majori solito et secus quam decet tirannide desaeviret*', Luard 1872–83, iv. 653.
90. '*Causa ... eorum etiam hostibus eorum justa videbatur*', Luard 1872–83, v. 639–40.
91. '*Lewelinus ... princeps Wallie ... viriliter patriam defendebat, et paternas libertates sustinendo, Anglis potenter resistebat*', Hewlett 1886–89, ii. 416–17.
92. Luard 1872–83, v. 646–47. Given Matthew's contacts with the bishop of Bangor, it is not beyond the bounds of possibility that the speech is based on a genuine report of sentiments expressed by Llywelyn himself, but given Matthew's propensity for speech writing (Vaughan 1958c, 134), it is rather more probable that it is entirely his invention.
93. Madden 1866–69, iii. 322; Luard 1872–83, v. 136–37, 379–80; Luard 1890, ii. 367, 379. Matthew condemns Langley's extortions in England roundly and at some length and records Langley's malefactions in Scotland and

Wales as part of the same pattern. He recounts how Langley was appointed by Henry as one of the guardians of his daughter Margaret, Queen of Scots, in 1252, but was shortly dismissed by the Scottish nobility, who could not long tolerate his 'wilfulness' (*impetus*). Luard 1872-83, v. 136-37; and see Madden 1866-69, iii. 322; Luard 1890, ii. 379; Coss 1975; Howell 1998, 115-16, 125-26, 145-46.

94. Madden 1866-69, iii. 322; Luard 1872-83, v. 592-93. Nor was Matthew the only English chronicler to take this line; both the Tewkesbury and the Dunstable annalists also blamed Langley, amongst others, for the Welsh rising; '*Annales Prioratus de Dunstaplia*', in Luard 1864-69, iii. 200-01; '*Annales de Theokesberia*', in Luard 1864-69, i. 158; and see Smith 2014, 82-84.
95. '*Edwardi vel familie ejus tirannidem*'; Luard 1872-83, v. 594.
96. Smith 2014, 57, 100, 118.
97. Luard 1872-83, v. 639-40.
98. *Anglici pusillanimes, quorum ignaviam et supinam simplicitatem Walensium strenuitas reprehendit*; Luard 1872-83, v. 616 (omitted from *Historia Anglorum* and *Flores historiarum*). For the marriage and the queen's involvement in arranging it see Howell 1998, 53-54.
99. *Indecenter nimis deliraret, alienigenas promovendo, sequendo, et supra naturales homines suos exaltando et constituendo, ipsi indigenae et naturales indignantes, ne ad deteriora prorumperet, ipsum regem et reginam sub custodia reponentes ... custodiebant prudenter, donec omnes alienigenas exemplo Alemannorum longius amovissent*: Luard 1872-83, v. 656.
100. '*Alemanni non sustinent cor regis sui, sicut Anglici, consiliis alienigenarum more arundinis inclinari*', Luard 1872-83, v. 653. I have to thank the late Björn Weiler for advice on this German connection.
101. Brown 2004, 51-53; Carpenter 2020, 519, 523-24.
102. Translated in Anderson and Anderson 1990, ii. 585-86, 588-90.
103. Duncan 1975, 574-75.
104. Vaughan 1958c, 9-10, 77.
105. Stones 1969-70; Taylor 2017. Unfortunately, the return from St Albans does not survive, though a document summarising the most useful of the evidence records that St Albans supplied evidence of Malcolm III's homage to William I; Palgrave 1837, 136-37. Henry III did personally request Matthew (by his own account) to record the ceremony in 1247 in which Henry gave a phial of Christ's blood to Westminster Abbey (Luard 1872-83, iv. 644-65), but Henry's concern was to commemorate an act of royal piety, and not the political rights of the crown.
106. See pages 155-55 of this chapter and note 80.
107. Luard 1872-83, v. 640.

KATHRYN GERRY

7
———

Matthew Paris' Pictorial *Life of Alban*

On his way to a meeting of the Great Council, King Henry VI (r. 1422–61, 1470–71) stopped at the Abbey of St Albans, where he was shown a manuscript containing several versions of the Life of St Alban along with other documents related to Alban's cult and the history of the monastery.[1] This event is well known among manuscript scholars today because the occasion was thought worthy of a note added to the flyleaf of the manuscript, the so-called Book of St Alban, now kept at Trinity College Dublin with the shelf mark 177 (and referred to in this chapter as 'Trinity 177').[2] However, this note leaves much unsaid. Did this encounter take place in the abbot's study, where the book was apparently kept? Did the abbot offer the book or did Henry ask to see it specifically? Was Henry impressed by this book? Was this the first time he had seen it? Did he take time to look at the series of pictures recounting the conversion and martyrdom of St Alban and the rise of his cult? Did Henry look at the images of the Mercian king Offa and feel persuaded to follow his early English predecessor's example by supporting the monastery? The flyleaves of the manuscript contain other notes too, including remarks widely understood to mean that this volume and other copies of saints' lives were circulated among lay noblewomen at some distance from St Albans.[3] These tantalising snippets from the book's early life offer us important insights into how the manuscript might have been used and valued by those who made it and owned it in the centuries before the Dissolution, but tantalisation is as far as they take us, and these brief textual inscriptions raise many more questions than they answer.

For many modern readers, the very concept of a book has the text at its heart. Books are vehicles for texts, reproduced in multiple editions and printings and available in a variety of formats. But the people who made and used books before the era of mass production would have understood that each book was a unique object, and in many cases the pictures, ornament, covers, the quality of the parchment and other material components of the object might have been just as crucial as the text to an appreciation of any particular book. With that in mind, if we want to understand Matthew Paris' work we must rely not only on the texts that he composed and compiled and edited, but also on the material frameworks that he created at the same time, the manuscripts that contained those texts and directed how a reader was to engage with and understand the texts. In this chapter I will outline some of the ways in which the pictorial components of Trinity 177 might help to elucidate the purpose and meaning of the book almost 800 years after it was made.

Matthew Paris has become a staple of medieval studies, recognised as an author, artist, cartographer and historian. Aside from the historical or artistic value of any of his texts or images, part of the reason we find Matthew so fascinating today is that we have so many of his autograph works, manuscripts that he, often in collaboration with other members of the monastic community, designed, inscribed and illustrated himself. Trinity 177 is one such book, a manuscript that seems to have been planned and overseen – and in large part personally written and illustrated – by Matthew.[4] Like many of his chronicles, Trinity 177 centres on the concerns of the St Albans community, but more than many of the other manuscripts associated with Matthew, one could argue that Trinity 177 reflects a highly unified vision, in terms of both scope and purpose. Matthew certainly played a strong role in the production of his chronicles and the *Liber additamentorum*, but these manuscripts were continued beyond his death, the intention carried forward by subsequent generations, while Trinity 177 seems to have started and ended with Matthew. His sustained and material involvement in the Trinity 177 project strongly indicates that the book reflects his own intentions, and although the book was continued over the course of many years and possibly through several changes in plan, the ideas it presents are specific to Matthew's own moment.[5]

The entire manuscript, taken as a whole, is an important source for research concerning Matthew as a monk and an author, the Abbey of St

Albans and the history of the cult of Alban. The version of the Life of Alban in French verse, apparently composed by Matthew and now found in Trinity 177, and the images that he incorporated into the manuscript have received the lion's share of the scholarly attention given to this book, but the manuscript contains other texts as well, including other versions of Alban's life, hagiographical material specific to Amphibalus, Alban's confessor, liturgical material and devotional texts, and copies of charters purporting to document the foundation of the abbey.[6] With versions of the narrative composed by William of St Albans (Latin prose), Ralph of Dunstable (Latin verse) and Matthew Paris (French verse and pictorial sequence), the manuscript offers a significant opportunity to see the development of a narrative over several iterations, each subsequent version produced with clear reference to the earlier accounts. This collection of texts and images, composed by various members of the St Albans community over several generations and gathered together – curated, as it were – by one of those members, presents a unique witness to the community's understanding of the saint's cult, both historically and devotionally, in the mid thirteenth century.

Matthew apparently composed several other saints' lives as well, some of them illustrated, but the Trinity manuscript is the only one to have survived in a (mostly) intact autograph copy.[7] This is an important point when we consider the relationship between Trinity 177 and two other manuscripts containing saints' lives often attributed to Matthew's authorship: the Lives of Thomas Becket and Edward the Confessor now found in Stokenchurch, Wormsley Library MS BM 3750 (a fragment of four leaves) and Cambridge, University Library MS Ee.3.59, respectively. These two manuscripts are widely believed to be directly copied from exemplars designed and produced by Matthew Paris, a conclusion reached in part because of strong similarities shared across the three books in layout, pictorial style and use of the tinted line drawing technique, but the Wormsley and Cambridge manuscripts are likely to have been made at least a decade or two later than Trinity 177, perhaps in London, and the exact relationship between the three is far from certain.[8] These questions are compounded by larger uncertainties surrounding the production of illustrated saints' lives in the thirteenth century. A sufficient (though still small) number of surviving illustrated saints' lives from the eleventh and twelfth centuries has enabled us to establish a fairly strong understanding of the patronage, production and function of hagiographic manuscripts in a period when monastic scriptoria and libraries dominated the market.[9] The thirteenth century, however, with a growing body of lay artists and courtly readers, marks a turning point. Fewer manuscripts containing extended hagiographic narratives survive from this period. This might be due to the accidents of survival, or perhaps it reflects larger shifts in subject matter and media: secular, courtly romances displaced stories of the saints among readers, while those holy narratives instead spilled across the stained glass expanses of Gothic churches.[10] Positioned as a lynchpin between these two phases of medieval book culture, Trinity 177 can offer insights not only into the textual development of the Life of Alban and that saint's cult, but also into the composition, illustration and circulation of other saints' lives in thirteenth-century England.

In order to understand what Trinity 177 can tell us about these larger questions of devotional and book culture, however, a thorough understanding of this manuscript as a unicum is necessary, taking into account the materials used, as well as the texts, pictures and ornament included in the book. The remainder of this chapter will offer an introduction to the pictorial cycle in Trinity 177 and some of the issues and questions raised by this series of images. Researchers have offered plausible answers to some of these problems, but many remain unresolved.

An important question to ask at the start of any study of images within a manuscript is whether or not we are seeing the images as they were first created. Fading colours, overdrawing, wear, dirt and other damage can all cause significant shifts in the original appearance of images and ornament in medieval manuscripts. In the case of Trinity 177, there have been notable losses to the picture cycle and a mis-ordering of the pictures when the manuscript was rebound, so that the manuscript as we have it today is not what the earliest readers would have seen. The series of pictures in Trinity 177 appears to have originally comprised sixty-three images. Today fifty-three images survive, running in sequence across the upper portions of the page from folio 29^v through folio 63^r (not every leaf has an image).[11] Several leaves from the start of the text have been lost and a sequence of notations in a post-medieval hand numbering the images begins at '3' (fol. 29ᵛ), indicating that the lost leaves contained two images. Within the extant leaves, eight images were painted on separate pieces of parchment which were then pasted to the leaves and have since been removed and lost.[12]

Even with such changes, we can still ask what role these images were meant to play in this particular book. We are accustomed to seeing pictures within books primarily as illustrations accompanying the text. These illustrations might direct or expand a reader's understanding of the text, but most of us today see the verbal text as the primary component of the book and the pictorial content as a secondary, dependent element. The embrace of the graphic novel as a worthy format for literature in the late twentieth and early twenty-first centuries asks us to question our usual understanding of the relationship between words and pictures. Can the pictures ever stand on their own, with words playing only a supporting role? The series of images in Trinity 177 do in fact form a pictorial narrative that presents a unique version of the story. These images do, on many of the folios, accompany textual material that covers the same topic, particularly in the account of Alban's conversion and martyrdom, but the pictures carry the narrative further in time than any one of the textual accounts in the book. The series of images running along the top of the folios moves from the days of Alban and Amphibalus and the immediate aftermath of their martyrdoms (fols. 29ᵛ–50ʳ) into an account of the fifth-century visit of Germanus of Auxerre to Britain and his actions at the tomb of Alban (fols. 51ʳ–55ʳ), and then carries the reader along to the later eighth century, when the Mercian king Offa supposedly rediscovered the site of Alban's tomb, built a church on the spot and founded the monastic community of St Albans (fols. 55ᵛ–63ʳ) (see Figure 7.1).[13]

Not only does this pictorial text move beyond the verbal accounts copied into this manuscript, but it presents a version of these events that offers a different spin from the extant copies found in other sources. One notable example of this is the reordering of the events recorded in accounts of Germanus' visit to England: in other accounts, Germanus visits Alban's tomb after his defeat of the Pelagian heretics, but in this pictorial version, made at St Albans, the bishop visits Alban's tomb before his debate with the Pelagians, praying to the saint and then, because of Alban's support, defeating the enemy.[14] The images of

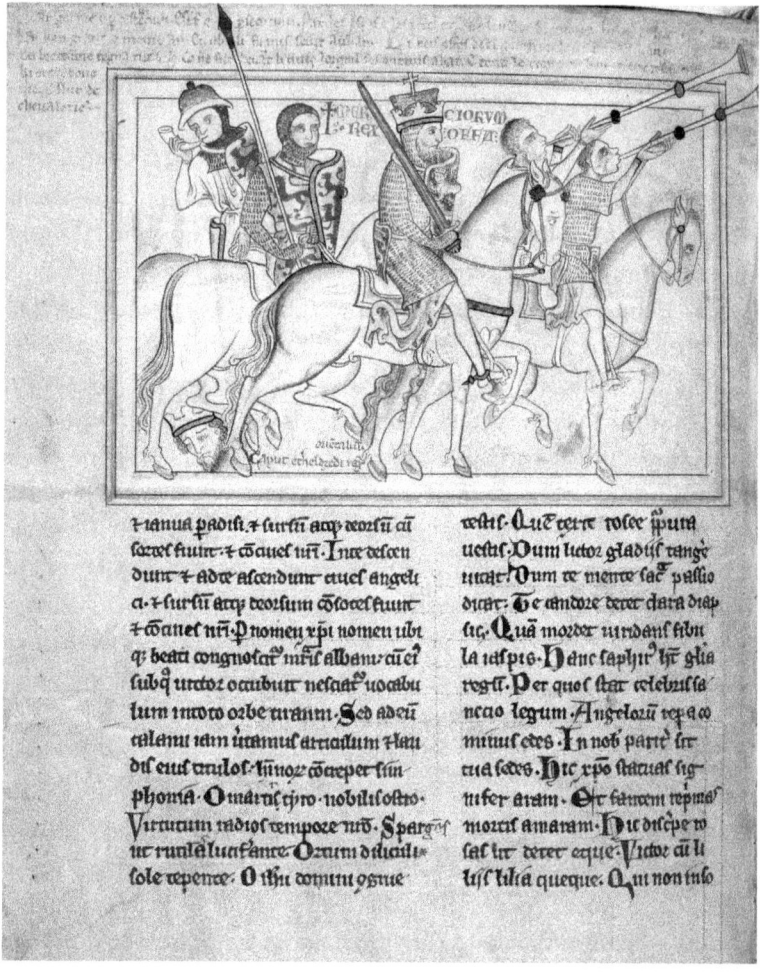

Figure 7.1 King Offa of Mercia setting out on expedition, dressed in crown and armour with sword and decorated shield, Dublin, Trinity College, MS 177, fol. 55^v. © The Library of Trinity College Dublin

Germanus also include an episode in which, prior to his departure for England, the bishop hears St Genevieve's vow of chastity and then hangs a penny around her neck (fols. 52^r, 52^v) (see Figure 7.2) with seemingly little connection to the cult of Alban. Laura Slater has proposed plausible links between Genevieve and the audience of lay noblewomen referred to in the added inscription mentioned earlier in this chapter,

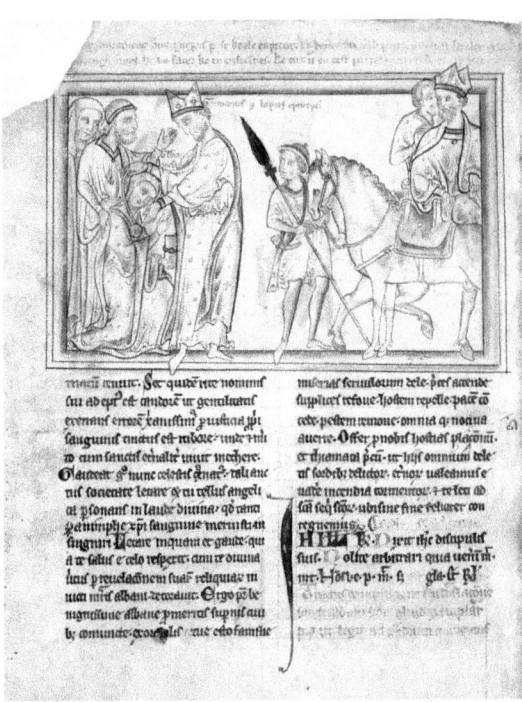

Figure 7.2 St Germanus and St Genevieve, Dublin, Trinity College, MS 177 fol. 52^{r-v}. © The Library of Trinity College Dublin

but it might be worth exploring other potential resonances between Germanus' dealings with Genevieve and his adventures in England.[15] Is the bishop's commendation of Genevieve offered as a comment on or a comparison with his subsequent recognition and promotion of Alban? Is the city of Paris being linked with St Albans? In the case of the final image of the series, in which Offa lays his foundation charter on the altar (fol. 63^r), the image appears directly above a copy of this (likely forged) charter, doing double duty as both the culmination of the narrative and a visual verification of the legal document below.[16] When we consider, then, the nature of this series of images alongside the other contents of the manuscript, the pictorial narrative emerges not as an adjunct to Matthew's text, but as a text in its own right. This Pictorial Life of Alban can thus be considered one of several versions of the story of Alban and St Albans, presented alongside narratives in Latin and vernacular French, verse and prose, legal documents and paraliturgical material, all collected in this one manuscript volume.

In this way, we can understand the pictorial narrative as a kind of translation, parallel in some ways to the versions in Latin and French, and this raises questions about the use of distinct languages and formats within this collection. Why juxtapose French and Latin, verse and prose, image and text? One answer offered for Trinity 177, and in relation to other vernacular and pictorial manuscripts of the twelfth and thirteenth centuries, is that the use of the vernacular and of images catered to a lay audience, and this argument often moves further and suggests a specifically female audience.[17] Although such an argument certainly gains a degree of support from some of the inscriptions added to the flyleaf (see earlier in this chapter), this argument does not adequately answer the question of why multiple Latin versions would be included, or why legal documents like the charter on folio 63^r would be of interest to readers who did not have a particular concern in the corporate affairs of the abbey. Furthermore, the claim that images were seen as more suitable for female readers ignores the many illustrated manuscripts copied for an almost certainly male audience, lay and otherwise.[18]

It is important to keep in mind the multilingual context of England in the centuries following the Norman Conquest. The survival rate of texts has been heavily weighted by the enduring prominence of Latin and the Norman dominance of the social, political and ecclesiastical hierarchy in the centuries following the Conquest. Nevertheless, speakers of Latin, Anglo–Norman French and English formed what Ian Short has described as a 'trilingual society' (to say nothing of the Celtic languages).[19] Martin Kauffmann has examined the Life of Alban as found in Trinity 177 alongside the illustrated Life of Edward now in Cambridge and the surviving leaves of the illustrated Life of Thomas Becket, both of which, as noted previously, are perhaps copies of exemplars drafted by Matthew Paris.[20] Kauffmann moves beyond questions of attribution to consider what we might glean from the arrangement of texts and images in these books in relation to audience and the development of reading practices in the later Middle Ages. He sees Matthew's use of captions within these manuscripts as representative of larger trends in the use of supplementary texts, and compares the use of Latin and vernacular in the three manuscripts, noting that although all three display a complex and nuanced interplay between Latin, French and pictures, there is no consistent pattern across the body of work.[21] As Kauffmann observes, the claim that a French text implies a lay audience is an oversimplification, and in fact it would be more correct to say that the choice to use French (or any vernacular in Christian Europe at this time period) expanded the potential audience of a text by removing barriers, with clerics able to read the vernacular as well as Latin. This would certainly have been the case at St Albans, where many of the monks hailed from the Anglo–Norman gentry.[22] Rather than seeing the division between vernacular and Latin as a division between audiences, Kauffmann argues that we should consider it as a marker of division between genres and levels of authority, with Latin captions reserved for the people and events of solemn sacred history.[23]

Indeed, in the Pictorial Life of Alban in Trinity 177, we can witness the potential for images and texts interacting in ways that transcend the juxtaposition of different linguistic translations within the same volume. We can certainly consider what might be gained from collecting William's twelfth-century Latin prose account in the same volume as Ralph of Dunstable's Latin verse edition and Matthew Paris' vernacular verse rendition (both largely based on William's text), with a reader being able to read the texts sequentially and cross-reference them by paging back and forth in the codex. But the interplay of pictures, Latin inscriptions, rubrics in vernacular verse and the variety of texts with which these images are paired across the sequence of thirty-three openings of the Pictorial Life offers the potential for complex multivalent readings, available in different ways to different readers and opening different paths of contemplation and ideation for those readers.

Though by no means identical, the arrangement of images and texts within the folios of the Pictorial Life of Alban is perhaps comparable in this potential to the Eadwine Psalter, a highly complex multilingual manuscript produced in the mid twelfth century at Canterbury (Cambridge, Trinity College, MS R.17.1). The Eadwine Psalter also presents a series of translations of the same text, with the literal illustrations, ultimately dependent on the Utrecht Psalter, forming a text of its own alongside the *Gallicanum*, *Romanum*, and *Hebraicum* versions of the psalms, enriched by translations from the Latin into French and English vernaculars and a Latin gloss.[24] Like Trinity 177, the Eadwine Psalter seems rooted in its local and historical setting, contextualising the text of the Psalms, crucial for any Christian audience but especially for a monastic one, by joining these multiple translations with a plan of the monastic complex at Canterbury and a portrait of a heroic monastic scribe of that house, and making a clear reference to the Utrecht Psalter, which seems to have had a great historical significance to the Canterbury community, though its exact nature is lost to us today.[25] Trinity 177 was clearly not directly based on the Eadwine Psalter, but given the close relationship, at least in the earlier Norman period, between Canterbury and St Albans, and the role that Canterbury played in the development of the St Albans library, it certainly seems possible that both institutions had access to a shared set of ideas for the potential of manuscript books to create knowledge or provoke a particular response or pattern of thought in a reader, by means of innovative arrangements of pictures, texts, translations and formats within a single volume.[26]

While we might recognise analogies between the Eadwine Psalter and Trinity 177, and we can identify more concrete links between the image cycles in Trinity 177, the 'Becket leaves', and the Cambridge Life of Edward, we must also acknowledge that, like all medieval manuscripts, Trinity 177 is a unicum, a singular combination of texts, pictures and ornament standing alone for its material qualities as much as its specific contents. Furthermore, like all manuscripts, Trinity 177 was made for a certain purpose at a particular moment in time – although its intended functions and envisioned audiences might have been multiple, the manuscript needs to be taken on its own terms. For these reasons, it is crucial that any study of this manuscript considers the precise placement and juxtaposition of images and texts, both in the larger sense of why these particular texts and images have been brought together and in the more localised cases – like that of the image of Offa presenting his charter at the altar – of the alignment of particular images with particular texts.

While the specific arrangements and pairings are unique, we can nevertheless identify characteristics in the Trinity 177 image cycle that closely align with Matthew's work more generally. One such quality is the action-driven nature of the images, with movements, gestures and compositions moving the viewer along, left to right, at a quick pace, described by Cynthia Hahn as 'almost cinematic'.[27] This can be seen, for example, in the image on folio 36^r (see Figure 7.3), where the profile

Figure 7.3 Alban is led to the scene of his martyrdom, Dublin, Trinity College, MS 177 fol. 36^r. © The Library of Trinity College Dublin

positioning of the figures shows that the group is marching in a single direction. Many of the figures gesture in this same direction with one even giving Alban a push forward, while the backward glances of Alban and the knight leading him serve to emphasise the relentless forward motion. This same sense of narrative progression is achieved with different pictorial devices in the opening across folios 31^v–32^r (see Figure 7.4): here the back-to-back pairings of the same figures in subsequent scenes, Amphibalus on folio 31^v and the informant on folio 32^r, carry the action forward and the repeated framework of the arch helps the viewer to follow the story across the full opening.

This emphasis on the chronological unfolding of the narrative in alignment with the left-to-right reading of the page and the codex can also be seen in the Lives of Becket and Edward generally believed to be

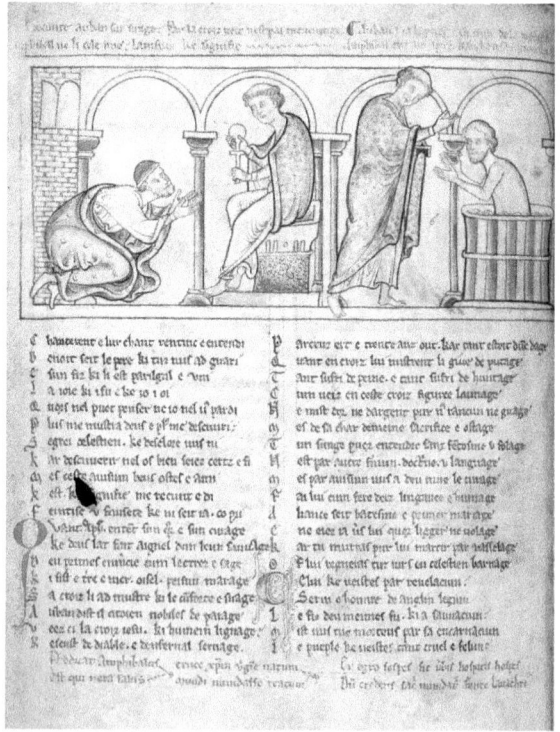

Figure 7.4 St Alban, St Amphibalus and the informant, Dublin, Trinity College, MS 177 fols. 31^v–32^r. © The Library of Trinity College Dublin

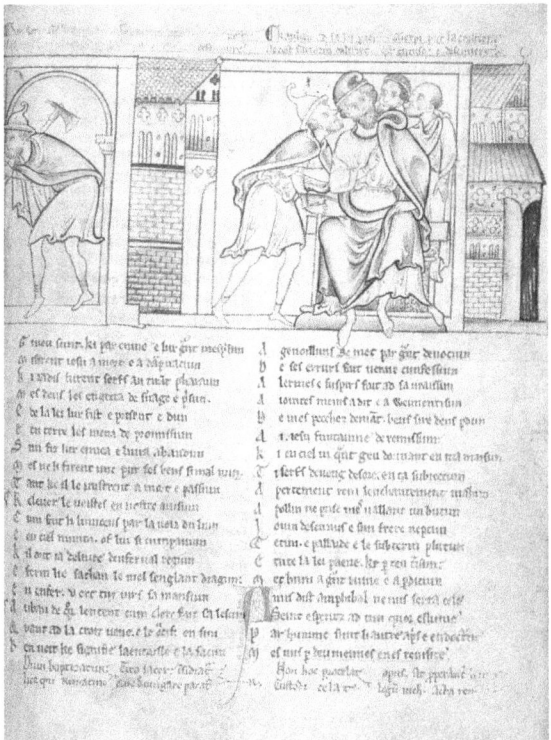

Figure 7.4 (cont.) © The Library of Trinity College Dublin

associated with Matthew Paris.[28] The *mise-en-page* employed in these image cycles is a key feature that ties Matthew's account of the Life of Alban to the Lives of Becket and Edward. In all three manuscripts, the images stretch across the top portion of the folio, often covering the full span of the leaf, but in some cases only taking up the width of a column of text, as in folio 30ᵛ in Trinity 177 (see Figure 7.5).[29] This distinctive arrangement is in contrast to some of the earlier saints' lives produced at English monasteries, such as the Life of St Edmund, circa 1130 (New York, Pierpont Morgan Library, MS M.736), which includes both full-page miniatures and historiated initials, and the Life of Cuthbert, circa 1200 (London, BL Add. MS 39943), made at Durham, which incorporates an extensive cycle of full-page miniatures.[30] On the other hand, it finds analogues with other examples, including a small booklet containing the Life of Alexis produced at St Albans in the first

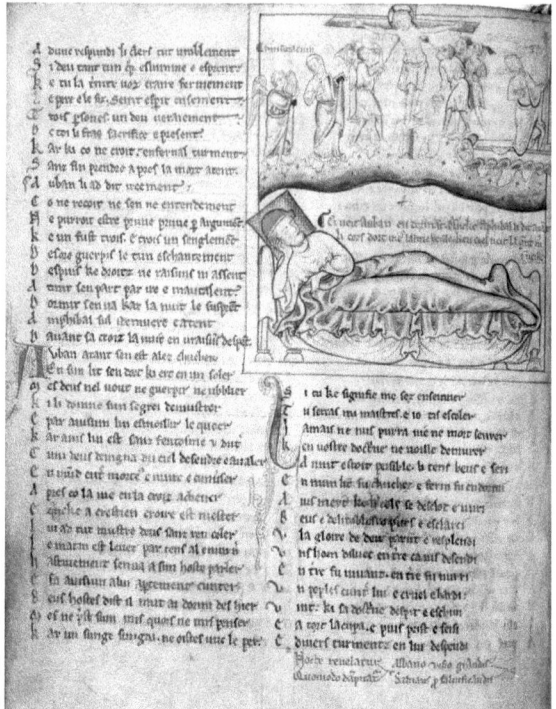

Figure 7.5 Alban sleeps; Alban spies Amphibalus, Dublin, Trinity College, MS 177 fols. 30ᵛ–31ʳ. © The Library of Trinity College Dublin

quarter of the twelfth century (now a part of the St Albans Psalter, Hildesheim, Dombibliothek, MS St Godehard 1), and, to a lesser degree, an earlier Life of Cuthbert made at Durham at the start of the twelfth century (Oxford, University College MS 165).[31]

In addition to the layout of image and text, the Alexis and the earlier Cuthbert life share with Trinity 177 the technique of tinted line drawing, a prominent feature of many of Matthew's works. By no means particular to Matthew Paris, tinted line drawing had been popular in the earlier Middle Ages, notably at St Albans in the early years of the twelfth century, but its popularity appears to have dwindled in the second half of the twelfth century. The early and mid-thirteenth century saw a resurgence of interest in this technique in a variety of genres, and Matthew, though not the originator, was at the forefront of this revival.[32] Matthew seems to have used this technique throughout his career – for example, in the

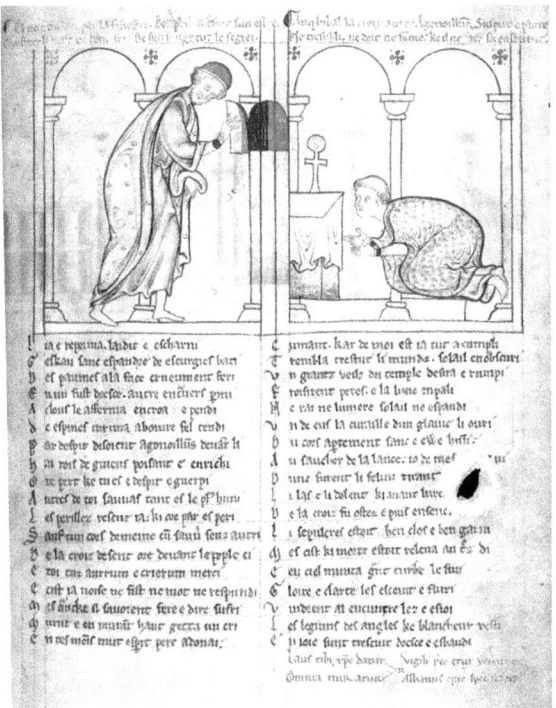

Figure 7.5 (cont.) © The Library of Trinity College Dublin

marginal illustrations found throughout the *Chronica maiora* and many of his other historiographic works – and the choice to use the same technique in the Becket and Edward lives has been one of the key points in identifying their relationship to Matthew Paris.[33] In general, the choice to use tinted line drawing has sometimes been described by researchers as a cost-cutting measure, selected when the more expensive and time-consuming technique of full painting was not affordable, or when time was short.[34] Was Matthew's decision to use this technique driven by financial concerns, saving a few pennies on pigment and producing an illustrated work in less time?[35] The use of a somewhat faster method of illustration would be in keeping with the sometimes slapdash appearance of Trinity 177, with its use of low-quality scraps of parchment in places, inconsistent formatting of the text and rubrics that sometimes look like afterthoughts, squeezed into too small of a space, as at folio 33^r, or placed within rather than above the image, as at folio 30^v.[36] This reasoning would not, however, explain why the technique was retained in the fair copies of the Becket and Edward Lives that have survived, produced apparently for patrons at the highest end of the socio-economic scale.[37] Furthermore, the use of gold in some of the images undermines the contention that the tinted line drawing technique was seen as cost-saving. Was Matthew motivated by the work of contemporaries, such as the Franciscan Brother William, whose drawing of the Apocalyptic Man was kept by Matthew and included in the so-called *Liber additamentorum*?[38] As M. A. Michael has noted, Matthew's decision to preserve this drawing and his instructions to the reader on how best to view it indicate that Matthew thought the drawing was indeed something special.[39] Did Matthew perhaps see tinted line drawing as a way to link his thirteenth-century work to the older documents held at the monastery, implying a degree of authority and authenticity by implicitly suggesting an earlier source? It is indeed the case that St Albans was one of several centres of production for tinted line drawing in the earlier twelfth century, and the technique was also associated with some of the venerated earlier books kept at Canterbury.[40] A desire to reference older monuments has also been identified as a motivation for the use of the technique in the Guthlac and Eligius Rolls, in those instances coupled with the choice to use the antiquated scroll format.[41]

The proposal that the use of the tinted line drawing technique in Trinity 177 was at least in part a conscientious attempt to link this composition with older documents and works of art is supported by a general interest on Matthew's part in the potential of material history to make the past more present. One example of this is the representation of a pagan idol in the scene on folio 34^v, in which Alban is brought before the magistrate. Did Matthew base this image on archaeological fragments of the Romano–British settlement of Verulamium? His textual account opens with a claim that the history of the saint was gleaned from images or words inscribed on the crumbling walls of the city, and the *Gesta abbatum monasterii sancti Albani*, partly authored and partly compiled by Matthew Paris, notes that Abbot Ealdred, supposedly the eighth abbot sometime in the later tenth century, was interested in the material remains of the Romano–British site of Verulamium.[42]

The abbey owned several objects dating from (or at least believed at the time to date from) this early period, as well as many treasures of more recent manufacture. Matthew seems to have put a high value on these material objects and he recognised the potential of some of these items to forge links between past and present. His emphasis in the *Gesta abbatum* on the aesthetic qualities of the architectural refurbishments and adornments carried out in his own day implies an interest in the role of materiality in the communal devotional experience, and the detail which Matthew paid to these items in his account seems to reflect the high priority placed on them by Abbot William (r. 1214–35), who carried them out.[43] Matthew's catalogue of the rings and other jewels held by the monastery further demonstrates his interest in the relational power of such precious objects. As Deirdre Carter and Judith Collard have argued, Matthew's careful and precise renderings of the abbey's collection of jewels in the *Liber additamentorum* served to reify and reinforce the relationships between the monastery and its donors that culminated in the gifts of these gemstones. Beyond a financial value, the jewels symbolised the social and political capital of the monastery, and the detailed images that Matthew created as a record of these gifts ensured that the appearance and materiality of each item would be an integral part of that record.[44]

The repeated depiction of the so-called Alban Cross in Trinity 177 accomplishes a similar goal to that of the gems in the *Liber additamentorum*, using a real object held at the monastery at the time the manuscript was made – in fact, acquired during Matthew's lifetime – to verify the events depicted and to amplify the relationship between those historical events and the thirteenth-century abbey. As discussed by Birthe Kjølbye-Biddle, the cross depicted in the Pictorial Life of Alban, with its distinctive round-headed shape, was modelled on a relic recently procured by Abbot William for the St Albans community, a cross believed to have been the very one owned by Amphibalus and given to his convert Alban.[45] Given his use of these visual references to foster a stronger connection between past and present, and to emphasise the interplay between past actions and present objects in establishing authority and re-inscribing communal memory, it is reasonable to suppose that the styles and techniques employed by Matthew in Trinity 177 were intended to do similar work.

The visual specificity that Matthew uses for these ancient items is even more striking in light of the fact that he largely follows the practice, widespread in his lifetime, of depicting historical figures in contemporary dress. In fact, as will be outlined in the remainder of this chapter, many of the images in the Pictorial Life of Alban strike a chord with significant artistic and spiritual trends of the time, reminding us that Matthew and his viewers were engaged with larger concerns of the day. This is hardly surprising in the work of a chronicler who is notable among his contemporaries for a broader scope of interest, writing about events across Europe and as far away as Asia when most of his contemporaries were content to confine their efforts to events taking place closer to home.[46] Many studies of Matthew Paris have focused on his awareness of and engagement with secular concerns of the day, and even when modern researchers do examine Matthew's interest in Church affairs, these studies tend to bring out the political, rather than the spiritual, aspects of his work.

Matthew's immersion in secular aspects of culture can also be seen in his interest in the developing genre of courtly literature, and scholars have noted a decidedly chivalric flavour in his saints' lives and some of his other writing.[47] The affinity with secular romance extends beyond the format and language of the narratives, and Hahn and Christopher Baswell have both noted the significant emphasis, visual and verbal, placed on the soldier who is converted at the scene of Alban's execution, dubbed 'Aracle' (Herakles) by Matthew in the text.[48] As Hahn has detailed, Aracle is presented in the guise of a noble knight; he is visually contrasted with the pagan aristocrats in ways that accord with the typical chivalric hero, being beautiful, beardless and young, and his conversion is depicted with a similar composition to the initiation ceremony of a knight (fols. 37^r, 38^v) (see Figure 7.6). Hahn also notes the link made in Trinity 177 between the ancient Roman period and the Christian present, again typical of romance narratives, in which the heroism of characters from ancient history and myth is often presented as a model to be emulated by medieval knights. Such cross-fertilisation between literary and visual arts can be seen in other media, too, as in the circa 1400 Nine Heroes series of tapestries now at the Metropolitan Museum of Art in New York. These pictorial hangings are based on a poetic tradition first attested in the early fourteenth century and they present Julius Caesar and Alexander the Great alongside King David

Figure 7.6 Aracle depicted as a chivalric knight, beardless, beautiful and young, Dublin, Trinity College, MS 177 fol. 37ʳ. © The Library of Trinity College Dublin

and King Arthur as courtly role models.[49] When considered in light of medieval pageantry, the use of courtly costume and gesture in the Trinity 177 pictorial narrative takes on a deeper resonance. Later medieval spectacles and celebrations often included pageants in which the distinction between the heroes of the ancient past and the chivalric knights of the present day was elided by means of costumes and heraldry, just as Matthew Paris has done in the visual account of Alban and Aracle.[50] Matthew's interest in literary romance might have been spurred on by his personal contacts within the court, as well as his immersion in the secular history of his chronicles, where similar allusions to chivalric literature can be identified.[51]

Matthew was, however, first and foremost a monk, and while it is certainly the case that some of his texts found an audience with secular elites, his work, including much of the material brought together in Trinity 177, speaks to an audience deeply concerned with the affairs of St Albans Abbey and the devotion due to their patron saint. Although more subtle than some of the textual inscriptions, a preoccupation with spiritual sight and the important role of the visual sense in understanding and communing with the divine is apparent throughout the pictorial cycle.[52] Collard has discussed the possible influence on Matthew's drawings of writers like Alexander Nequam (1157–1217), who advocated internal visualisation as a meditative process.[53] Hahn has drawn attention to the important role of sight in Matthew's Pictorial Life of Alban – for example, in the scenes of Alban witnessing Amphibalus at prayer, watching him through an arch-shaped window, just as we are watching the story through the arch-shaped frames of the images.[54] The idea that revelation can be afforded through visual experience extends to the world of dreams too. Alban is first compelled to learn from Amphibalus in a dream, and later the location of Alban's relics is revealed to Offa in a dream mediated by an angel (fols. 30^v–31^r, 56^v–57^r) (see Figures 7.5 and 7.7).[55] This account of Offa's dream in the early history of the monastery is echoed by Alban's mystical appearances in the more recent past. According to the *Gesta*, Alban appeared on several occasions in the twelfth century, verifying the sanctity of his own relics and revealing the location of Amphibalus' burial.[56]

Less palatable to modern eyes is Matthew's tendency to use visual images to confirm and reinforce prejudices against anyone outside of the world of Western European Christendom. This is not at all particular to Matthew Paris, and in fact such visual 'othering' was apparently part of the standard toolkit of thirteenth-century visual artists, as can be seen, for example, in the *mappa mundi* found in the so-called Map Psalter (BL Add. MS 28681, fol. 9^r), where the various 'races' of the world are catalogued in a series of images along the right edge of the map, showing a range of plausible and implausible physical characteristics that, in typical medieval fashion, are taken to represent interior qualities of the people thus represented.[57] In Trinity 177, this is manifest in a tendency to elide the visual characterisations of despised groups, as well as the words used to describe them. Matthew calls Alban's enemies 'Saracens', a term medieval Europeans used to describe Muslims, even though the Romano–British elite who would have been responsible for

7 Matthew Paris' Pictorial *Life of Alban*   187

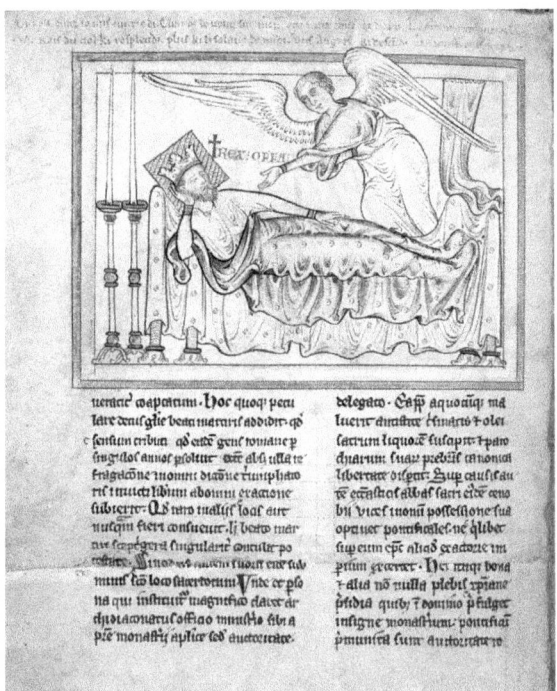

Figure 7.7 Alban's relics revealed to King Offa, Dublin, Trinity College, MS 177 fols. 56ᵛ–57ʳ. © The Library of Trinity College Dublin

arresting and executing a Christian martyr, hundreds of years before the emergence of Islam, would have been pagan in the traditional classical manner. These 'bad guys' in the manuscript are often depicted with exaggerated features and costuming, especially their headgear, similar to those often used to signify Jewish people in medieval pictorial art (fols. 32ʳ, 38ᵛ).[58] Hahn has recognised this visual conflation between different groups as another way to elide past and present, to turn the enemies of a Romano-British Alban into the enemies of thirteenth-century European crusaders.[59] We might also view this visual elision in light of Matthew's recording of the Mongol invasions of Europe. Did he perhaps have in mind statements like that of Peter des Roches (d. 1238), Bishop of Winchester, who is reported by Matthew to have advised Henry III not to side with Muslim armies in a fight against the Mongol forces invading Europe, but rather to see both Muslims and Mongols as equally contemptible, calling them both 'dogs'?[60]

Figure 7.7 (cont.) © The Library of Trinity College Dublin

Although there has been a great deal of research on Matthew Paris, and his Pictorial Life of Alban in Trinity 177, clearly many questions remain. As we continue to explore these questions and almost certainly identify others, we need to keep in mind that while historians of medieval art, text, religious practice, philosophy and science often work within the boundaries of their own disciplinary silos, Matthew Paris was not bound by those categories. He might very well not have seen his chronicles as fundamentally different from his hagiographies, or from his works on magic for that matter. Just as the boundaries he might have acknowledged between French and Latin, and perhaps even English, were more fluid than those we construct today, he might not have recognised a particularly stark divide between his use of image and text. Historians have sometimes debated the worth of Matthew's efforts by comparing his chronicles with modern notions of history writing, and art historians have sometimes been tempted to see in the immediacy of Matthew's drawings a forward-looking style, describing his work in terms that position him on the leading edge of a transition from medieval to modern.[61] We would do well to keep his identity as a monk front and centre and to remind ourselves that he was a man of his time, with a deeply held belief in the power of the divine and the efficacy of devotional practice, and without access to the knowledge and viewpoints we have at our fingertips today.

The fast pace and vivid details of Matthew's pictorial narratives make them seem exciting and action packed, and the sketch-like quality of the tinted line drawing technique lends them an immediacy that modern eyes might not often find in medieval art. But the Pictorial Life of Alban, no less than the verses it accompanies, is a carefully and thoughtfully planned statement. It may have had multiple audiences, but it presents a single viewpoint. Just as the abbot who showed it to the king a century later must have had a motive, the monk who created this pictorial narrative intended it to deliver a distinct message about the history and future of the cult of Alban. We may not be able to read much 'between the lines' of the fourteenth-century inscription on the flyleaf, but we can deduce a great deal of Matthew Paris' goals and motivations through a careful and informed analysis of his pictures.

Notes

* I am grateful to Trinity College Dublin for providing the images of MS 177 which accompany this chapter, and to the staff at that library and the British Library for making Trinity 177 and related manuscripts available to me; the research that went into this chapter was partly funded by Bowdoin College, the Institute of English Studies at the University of London, the International Center of Medieval Art and the Samuel H. Kress Foundation; the chapter is much improved by the generous comments of James Clark, Laura Cleaver and Emma Maggie Solberg, and any remaining errors in the text are entirely my own.

1. Henry VI's perusal of the manuscript is recorded on the flyleaf of folio 1ᵛ: ... *erissimus rex Henricus sextus exiens ad consilium magnum Westmonisterrii tentum hunc librum visus est et ad honorem gloriosi martiris Albani*, transcribed by Colker 1991, I, no. 177, 339–43 at 341; see also Clark 2001, 222. See also Chapters 15 and 16, 313, 337.

2. The manuscript previously had the shelf mark E. I. 40; see Colker 1991, i. 339–43 for a brief description. For a fuller account of the manuscript and some of its principal texts see Wogan-Browne and Fenster 2010, especially the contributions of C. Baswell and P. Quinn, Section 3, 169–212; the

manuscript has been fully digitised and is available at https://digitalcollections.tcd.ie/concern/works/8p58pm63q?locale=en.
3. Folio 2ʳ; there are two inscriptions in question (among several spread across the folio). M. R. James reads the first as *Usque ad pascha poteritis hunc labellum si placet retinere* and the second as *G. mittatis si placet ad dominam comitissam harundell' Isabellam vt mittat vobis librum de sancto thoma martire et sancto [ed-]wardo quem transtuli et protraxi que[mque po-]terit domina comitissa cornub[ie retinere] usque ad pentecosten* ... (James 1920, 20, 21), while Colker finds the first too faded to transcribe and gives the second of these as *Mittatis si placet ad dominam comitissam Harundell' Isabellam ut mittat uobis librum de sancto Thoma martire et s<ancto Ed>wardo quern transtuli et protra(here ?) <po>terit domina comitissa Corni<uallie ?> usque ad pentecostem*, noting that what James reads as the initial G is a paragraph sign (Colker 1991, i. 341, 342); together, these statements have sometimes been taken to indicate that this manuscript was sent to external lay readers and that some portions of the book might have been designed with this audience in mind: Slater 2018; James believed that the first of these two inscriptions indicated that this manuscript had been sent out, and that the second was a draft of a note referring to other books (James 1920, 20, 21, 24). See also Carter 2011.
4. The manuscript contains significant portions of text in a hand widely recognised as Matthew's, as well as marginal notes and corrections in his hand that indicate he was directing the other scribes at work in the book; see Baswell 2010, 191–94. Noting Matthew's tendency to contribute both scribal and artistic work to projects that he oversaw, Michelle Brown has described him as a 'desktop publisher' (Brown, forthcoming; I am indebted to Brown for sharing an advance draft).
5. The exact date of the manuscript has been the subject of much debate, with arguments made for the 1230s (or earlier) and the 1250s (though not later than Matthew's death *c.* 1259); although some questions about the manuscript might rely on a more precise date, for the purposes of this chapter, it is sufficient to note that the book was made between circa 1225 and circa 1259, and that, as Baswell and others have argued, it was likely the product of a series of revisions made over several years (see Wogan-Browne and Fenster 2010, 19, 20, and Baswell 2010, 179–81). As to Matthew's direction of the project, we might leave open the possibility of a patron or *concepteur* other than Matthew himself, but I know of no evidence to date that would support this.
6. See Colker 1991, i. 339–43 for a very brief overview, and Wogan-Browne and Fenster 2010, 1–58 for further discussion, with a concise list of contents at 16, 17.
7. Matthew is credited with composing two Latin saints' lives: Stephen Langton, Archbishop of Canterbury (fragments found in London, BL Cotton MSS Vespasian B XIII, fol. 133ᵛ, Nero D I, fol. 196ʳ and an added

leaf at fol. 19ᵛ), and Edmund Rich, Archbishop of Canterbury (London, BL Cotton MS Julius D VI, fols. 123ʳ–156ᵛ); and four vernacular saints' lives: the Alban here under discussion, a translation of his Latin Life of Edmund (known from London BL Cotton MS Vitellius D VIII, dest. 1731; a later copy is contained in a legendary held at Welbeck Abbey), Edward the Confessor (Cambridge, University Library MS Ee.3.59) and Thomas Becket (a fragment of four leaves: Stokenchurch, Wormsley Library MS BM 3750). Although not strictly hagiographical, the lives of the two Offas should be included in this list (an autograph copy survives in London, BL Cotton MS Nero D I, fols. 2ʳ–25ʳ, with some illustrations attributed to Matthew Paris and most completed by a later hand).

8. See Morgan 1988; Binski and Panayotova 2005, cat. no. 113, 248, 249; the Cambridge Life of Edward has been digitised: https://cudl.lib.cam.ac.uk/view/MS-EE-00003-00059/1; for the text see Fenster and Wogan-Browne 2008.

9. The foundational source for these manuscripts is Wormald 1952 and Cynthia Hahn's extended analysis is an essential reference: Hahn 2001.

10. Generalisations, however, run the risk of oversimplifying a complex situation: not only secular romances, but also illustrated copies of the Apocalypse were popular among lay audiences in the later Middle Ages; see Morgan and Thomson 2008, especially the essays by de Hamel (3–21) and Hunt (367–80). Another complicating factor is that many present-day authors cite the three illustrated hagiographies associated with Matthew Paris as the main (often the only) evidence for generalising statements about illustrated saints' lives in the thirteenth century. Two Lives of St Cuthbert produced circa 1200 in Durham (BL Add. MS 39943, which is rich with images, and Cambridge, Trinity College MS O.I.64, which seems to be closely based on Add. 39943 with spaces left for images that were not provided) are not often included in the discussion of thirteenth-century illustrated saints' lives, but if these two books were given as much attention as the Alban, Thomas and Edward lives, generalisations would be very different; see Morgan 1982, 58–60, and Marner 2000, especially chapter 3, 37–53.

11. An error in binding before the manuscript was foliated resulted in leaves 46 and 47 being placed out of sequence; this is corrected in most discussions of the manuscript, with the leaves referred to in the proper sequence, but with their extant foliation, so that folios 47 and 46 fall between folios 38 and 39.

12. See Quinn 2010, 195–212 for a detailed and careful description of the complex codicological state of the manuscript.

13. Note that the image was removed from folio 50ᵛ and no trace of the text remains, so it is unclear if this image was part of the Alban series or the Germanus series (see Quinn 2010, 204); for Germanus and St Albans, see Wood 2009; for Offa and St Albans, see Crick 2007, 78–84.

14. For an account of some of the discrepancies between the pictorial account and the textual version it accompanies, see McCulloch 1981; Baswell's observations also support the claim made here that the pictures could be read as a discrete version of the story (Baswell 2010, esp. 176–79); Hahn also notes that the pictures in which Matthew departs most significantly from the text 'constitute perhaps his most original contribution to the Life [of Alban]' – see Hahn 2001, 287.
15. Slater 2018.
16. For St Albans charters and their authenticity, see Crick 2007 and see also Crick's comments on Offa's role in the foundation in Crick 2001.
17. See Baswell 2010; Slater 2018.
18. Famous examples include the mid twelfth-century Winchester Psalter (BL Cotton MS Nero C IV), the early thirteenth-century Morgan Picture Bible (New York, Morgan Library, MS M. 638), the mid thirteenth-century Westminster Psalter (BL, Royal MS 2 A XXII) and the many manuscripts known to have been made for Jean, Duc de Berry in the early fifteenth century. Monks and clerics apparently also liked pictures in some of their books, as, for example, in the Eadwine Psalter, discussed later in this chapter, and it appears that most, if not all, of the earlier illuminated saints' lives were made largely for in-house use at monasteries, both male and female (see Wormald 1952; Hahn 2001).
19. Short 2003. See also Chapter 14, 272.
20. See notes 7 and 8 of this chapter.
21. Kauffmann 2020 especially 182–84, 206; he notes that this linguistic interplay was in and of itself highly appreciated within Anglo–Norman literary culture of this period.
22. According to the *Gesta abbatum monasterii sancti Albani*, within about a generation of the Conquest the older English monks had been largely replaced by Normans: Riley 1867–69, i. 66 (all subsequent references are to vol. I); an English translation is also available: Clark and Preest 2019, 146. Many of the abbots are recorded as being from noble Norman families and having close connections among the Anglo–Norman aristocracy (information about their family and connections is usually given near the start of each account).
23. Kauffmann 2020, 204–20.
24. See Gibson, Heslop and Pfaff 1992.
25. The portrait of Eadwine is on folio 283^v; the plan of the monastic compound and its waterworks is on folios 284^v–286^r; for the Utrecht Psalter (Utrecht, Bib. Rijksuniv., MS. 32) see van der Horst, Noel and Wüstefeld 1996.
26. Abbot Paul (r. 1077–93), the first abbot of St Albans installed under the Norman regime, had close ties with Archbishop Lanfranc and during his abbacy books were sent to St Albans from Canterbury and Canterbury

provided the model for liturgical and monastic customs at St Albans. See Riley 1867–69, i. 57–59, and Clark and Preest 2019, 122–24. See also Thomson 1982, i. 11–12, and Crick 2001, 82.

27. Hahn 2001, 285; Baswell 2010 uses the same term. The narrative accounts found in stained-glass windows from this period in England and France are often described in terms that emphasise their dynamic qualities, but in that case, it is the radiant colour of the illuminated glass, as well as the movement of the light itself, that occasions the comparison to modern media, and indeed while the narrative itself is a driving feature in the arrangement of image sequences within stained glass, these arrangements are usually constructed as complex geometric formulations rather than text-like, left-to-right sequences; see Caviness 1992.

28. See notes 7 and 8 of this chapter. It is worth noting that many questions remain about the precise relationships between these manuscripts and the thirteenth-century market for illustrated saints' lives more generally.

29. A similar layout was sometimes used for illustrated copies of the Apocalypse made in the mid thirteenth century and later, for example, the Dyson Perrins Apocalypse (Los Angeles, J. Paul Getty Museum, Ms. Ludwig III 1 [83. MC.72]), see Binski and Panayotova 2005, cat. no. 43, 146, 147.

30. The composite structure of M.736 makes it difficult to determine if the series of full-page miniatures was created specifically for this manuscript, and the artistic style has been linked with St Albans; see Gerry 2014. For the Cuthbert manuscript see Marner 2000.

31. For the Life of Alexis (the so-called Alexis Quire within the St Albans Psalter) see Gerry 2014; although not as close a comparison, the early twelfth-century Life of Cuthbert also incorporates a series of tinted line drawings presented in bands across the width of the page, often following a left-to-right narrative arrangement: see Baker 1978 and Gerry 2014.

32. Lacey 2018, plus figures 12.1–12.5; especially at 162. An earlier example of this renewed interest in tinted line drawing is the Guthlac Roll (BL, Harley Roll Y. 6), probably made circa 1200 at Crowland Abbey, for which see Warner 1928, Kelly 1989 and Hahn 2001, especially chapter 6, pages 172–208. The Guthlac Roll is only about half a century later than the Eadwine Psalter, and the possibility of lost intermediaries should be taken into account. For examples of the technique used in different genres both before and after circa 1200, see Holcomb 2009.

33. Many of Matthew's manuscripts were produced over the course of several years or longer, and there has been little agreement as to the date of these manuscripts, with art historians and palaeographers often disagreeing as to whether a book was made earlier or later in Matthew's career; see Baswell 2010.

34. Lacey 2018, 159, 160. Wormald (1953, 19, 20) noted that the money- and time-saving aspects of tinted line drawing would often be a motivating

factor, but he allowed that the decision in at least some cases might be ascribed to an aesthetic preference for the technique.
35. Lacey 2018, 162.
36. See Baswell 2010 and Quinn 2010.
37. See Baswell 2010, especially 181, 182. The technique was also popular in the second half of the thirteenth century in illustrated Apocalypses, again seemingly made for high-status patrons for whom cost was not likely an issue.
38. London BL Cotton MS Nero D I, fol. 156ʳ.
39. Michael 2004. Michael suggests that Matthew might have believed the image to be miraculous, an observation that is perhaps more in keeping with medieval image culture than Suzanne Lewis' proposal that this drawing, along with drawings that Lewis identifies as faithful copies of contemporary works of art, are evidence of Matthew's connoisseurial appreciation for the work of fellow artists: Lewis 1987, 418–27.
40. In addition to the Alexis Quire, this tradition is witnessed by London, BL Cotton MS Titus D XVI; see Thomson 1982 cat. no. 19, vol. 1, 91, 92, and Gerry 2020, especially 216–22. Manuscripts using the technique were produced at Canterbury Christ Church Cathedral, the tradition certainly receiving some impetus from the Utrecht Psalter (Utrecht, Bib. Rijksuniv., MS. 32); see van der Horst, Noel and Wüstefeld 1996.
41. For the Guthlac Roll, see note 32 of this chapter; the fragmentary Roll of Saint Eligius, made in northern France in the mid thirteenth century, is now housed in Paris, Musée Carnavalet, D.7075, see Holcomb 2009, cat. no. 40, 138, 139.
42. The text in Trinity 177 uses the words '*sculptum*' and '*sculpturam*' (fol. 20ʳ, col. 1, lines 23 and 24) while the AASS version, compiled from several exemplars, has '*scripturam*' – Thomas O'Donnell and Margaret Lamont give 'engravings' and 'carvings', preserving the ambiguity of the Latin: O'Donnell and Lamont 2010, 139, and see note 6, 161; McCulloch 1981, 775. The account of Ealdred is found in Riley 1867–69, i. 24 and Clark and Preest 2019, 79. This material was also discussed in Gerry 2021.
43. Gifts of the abbots, including books, reliquaries, textiles and various liturgical implements, are mentioned for each abbot, but a significant amount of text and description is given to these items in the chapter on Abbot William of Trumpington. See also Chapter 1, 17. Earlier, in the accounts of Geoffrey and Simon, the appearance, materials and construction of the shrine of the saint receive notable attention. Considering that William was abbot when Matthew first arrived at St Albans, it would not be surprising if Matthew was impressed and strongly influenced by William's priorities.
44. Carter 2022; Collard 2022b.
45. Kjølbye-Biddle, 'The Alban Cross', Henig and Lindley 2001, 85–110; see also McCulloch 1981.

46. Weiler 2009; Weiler 2019. Matthew's interest in global affairs and history is also apparent in the maps he created: Connolly 1999, 598–622; Gaudio 2000; Breen 2005; Connolly 2019 and plates I, V, VI, VIII.
47. Hahn 1990; Hahn 2004.
48. Hahn 2001, 302–06; Baswell 2010, 184–90.
49. See Cavallo 1993, 13–14, 94–124 (www.metmuseum.org/met-publications/medieval-tapestries-in-the-metropolitan-museum-of-art); Campbell 2002, 48, 49 (www.metmuseum.org/met-publications/tapestry-in-the-renaissance-art-and-magnificence).
50. Cruse 2006; the events discussed by Cruse are somewhat later than Trinity 177 – the earliest documented events that he discusses took place in the late thirteenth century.
51. See, for example, his description of Saer de Quincy in the *Chronica Maiora*: Luard 1872–83, iii. 60. I am grateful to James Clark for this observation.
52. On the role of the sense of sight in medieval theory and art, see Kessler 2019, chapter 9, especially 209–17.
53. Collard 2015, especially 176.
54. Hahn 2001, 287–302.
55. Carolyn Carty has offered significant insight into the role of dreaming in medieval conceptions of sanctity and divine revelation; see Carty 1999; Carty 2000.
56. The goldsmith monk Anketil was visited by Alban in a dream to quell any doubts about the authenticity of the relics (Riley 1867–69, i. 87; Clark and Preest 2019, 174), and Alban revealed the whereabouts of Amphibalus' relics to a local man, who then led the monks to the site (Riley 1867–69, i. 192, 193; Clark and Preest 2019, 301, 302).
57. Mittman 2015; Lindquist and Mittman 2018.
58. On the depiction of Jewish people in medieval Europe see Bale 2019, www.getty.edu/art/exhibitions/outcasts/downloads/bale_misrepresenting_jews.pdf; Strickland 2022.
59. Hahn 2001, 301.
60. Luard 1872–83, iii. 489. See also Chapter 4, 93, 97–103.
61. See, for example, Galbraith 1944; Gransden 1974b, 356–79; Lewis 1987; Michael 2004. Weiler and others have provided a useful corrective to some of the earlier viewpoints.

8

Matthew Paris' Enthroned Virgin and Child

Figure 8.1   Matthew Paris' image of the Virgin Mary enthroned with the infant Christ, BL, Royal MS 14 C VII, fol. 6ʳ. © The British Library.

The famous image of Matthew Paris kneeling in adoration, almost prostrate, before the enthroned Virgin and Child, in the opening pages of his *Historia Anglorum*, is one of the most famous images associated with the Benedictine monk-chronicler.[1] It forms a kind of 'frontispiece' to a volume that, as currently bound, contains the *Historia Anglorum* text (a shorter history of England than found in Matthew's much more extensive *Chronica maiora*), and a series of prefatory material, including itineraries, maps and drawings of the kings of England.[2] It may be that the manuscript's folios remained unbound, or at least not bound in final form, until close to his death. However, the inscription on the verso of this Virgin and Child image, offering it to the abbey of St Albans as a gift from Matthew himself, suggests that this folio was bound in to the book, or at least a part of it, before Matthew's death in 1259.[3]

The cowled figure is identified by the inscription 'Brother Matthew Paris ('Frat[er] Mathiãs Parisiensi[s]'). The image of the Virgin and Child is characterised by detailed furnishings and clothing, careful and complex drapery folds and subtle tints of colour wash – blues and reds for the Virgin's undergarment, like a 'shot' silk, yellow with red patterning for her dress and pale green with red patterning for her cloak. All of these features make this one of Matthew Paris' most accomplished works, and very probably one of his last productions. The holy figures are finely drawn with a powerful concentration on the intimate physical relationship between the mother and child. The child is cradled in the crook of the Virgin's left arm as she lifts him close to her, so that he is not sitting on her lap, but held tightly against her upper body. The intimacy is exemplified by the intense exchange of gazes between the two, the child's touching of his mother's hair with his left hand and the closeness of Christ's cheek against that of his mother. This is reminiscent of the Byzantine icon type known as the 'Eleousa' ('The Virgin of Tenderness').[4] The general comportment of the child might also be redolent of active, vibrant and childlike humanity, and perhaps somewhat suggestive of another icon type, a variant of the Eleousa, known as the Kykkotissa, in which the child's legs are particularly active. However, in trying to capture the significance of this image it is not necessarily productive to try to track precise iconographic source types. This image is perhaps not strictly an evocation of any particular icon type. It is more likely an open, suggestive, adaptable image, a tool for devotion and for flexible contemplation.

The figures' right hands touch as the Christ Child accepts the fruit offered to him by his mother. This fruit symbolises the Passion that is to come, which Christ will accept and of which the Virgin has sorrowful foreknowledge. The artist has included a further charming, but also possibly significant, detail in the shape of the Christ Child's left big toe resting on the Virgin's belt. This little detail might to some extent point the viewer of this image to think of one of the most important relics of the Virgin Mary, the Holy Girdle, which was dropped by the Virgin at the Assumption into the hand of St Thomas the Apostle. This possibility is all the more inviting given that Westminster Abbey possessed a relic of the Virgin's girdle which was one of the most revered and most highly indulgenced of the Abbey's extensive relic collection.[5] Matthew was of course very well aware of the most important of Westminster's relics, as he recorded – and illustrated – the procession led by Henry III in October 1247, when the Holy Blood was presented to the Abbey by the king.[6] Not only was Matthew present at this event, but after the ceremonies associated with the transfer of the relic, he was summoned to see the king in person (and, indeed to dine with him) and instructed to write an account of the events.

The idea of Matthew at Westminster Abbey, recording the event of the Holy Blood relic procession and embellishing that part of his *Chronica* with an image of the king holding the Blood reliquary in his hands, has sometimes encouraged commentators to consider the possibility that other images in Matthew's oeuvre might record the presence of other real artefacts or images. For instance, might this image of the Enthroned Virgin in the *Historia Anglorum* have been a rendering of a real image of the Virgin and Child?[7] It seems more likely that Matthew Paris' interests lay less in providing a record of particular revered images and more in engaging with contemporary devotional habits, including devotion to the Blessed Virgin, interest in the Body of Christ, and 'the intensity of devout gaze'.[8] To understand this Enthroned Virgin image in that way helps also better to elucidate the striking image of Matthew himself, kneeling at her feet.

This image of Matthew is often referenced as an 'author portrait', or as an 'artist portrait'.[9] In one sense it can certainly be compared with earlier images of writers, such as the famous full-page frontispiece, added apparently in the tenth century to a ninth-century manuscript now known as 'St Dunstan's Classbook', which depicts a cowled monk, Dunstan, Abbot of Glastonbury and Archbishop of Canterbury (d. 988), kneeling prostrate at the feet of Christ.[10] But neither Dunstan in the 'Classbook' frontispiece, nor Matthew in the *Historia Anglorum* image, is depicted in these images primarily as an author or artist. Matthew is not shown with any symbols of writing or image-making, as is found in other images of, for example, evangelists or in the image of Frater Rufillus, a monk of Weissenau Abbey in Ravensburg in Germany, who is depicted within an illuminated letter 'R' at the outset of the Life of St Martin of Tours on folio 244 of the Weissenau Passionary.[11] The monk-illuminator is depicted with a brush in his right hand and a container of paint on his left, together with five other pots beside and behind him, and a blade on the bench beside him. Matthew holds none of these implements of fabrication. Instead he kneels, bowing low, with his hands in front of him, gesturing towards the text that is inscribed to the left, as though he might be speaking the words: 'O happy the kisses pressed upon the lips of the nursing child when, as He often did as a crawling infant, He who is your true son of your body played with you [His mother] even as, true God begotten of God through His Father, He commanded'.[12] The origins of the text are not certain, but the imagery surrounding kissing is broadly 'sponsorial' in tone, associated with the Song of Songs, and the kisses exchanged between bride and bridegroom in that text, and associated with homilies or other texts on the Assumption of the Virgin Mary.[13] It fits, therefore, with the intimacy of the embrace between the Virgin and Child, and also suggests, in allusive tones, a devotional kiss offered by Matthew as he kneels at the Virgin's feet.[14]

Clearly this image of the author (compiler, scribe and artist) draws on the tradition of portraits of scribes humbling themselves before a holy figure. In that sense it is a representation of Matthew Paris that seeks to define his authorial presence. However, what is most important in this image is the depiction of the person who has made this image as a tool for devotion, a record of devotion and a model of devotion, engaging with it in that spirit. This is an image of Matthew Paris who, with the inscription naming him, we are encouraged to see *is* the artist of this image, but it does not principally show him *as* an artist. It shows him as a devotee. The very making of the image was almost certainly, for

Matthew, an act of devotion. This may help partly to explain the distinction between the sophistication, detail and careful handling of colour and shading in this image and the pen outline drawings that characterise the more 'documentary' illustrations to his historical chronicle writings, a distinction that has sometimes made it difficult for scholars to reach agreement about the genuine extent of Matthew's output. This image of Matthew in adoration, praying at the foot of the Virgin Mary, provides a representation that we and Matthew's contemporaries could recognise as a statement of authorial presence. But the most important essence of this image is the depiction of, indeed the very essence of, an act of humble devotion.

Notes

1. British Library, Royal MS 14 C VII, fol. 6^r.
2. Collard 2015, 154 for the contents of this manuscript.
3. 'This book was given by Brother Matthew Paris. May the souls of Matthew and all the faithful dead rest in peace. Amen.' Translation by Morgan 1982, 141.
4. From the Greek '*eleos*' (Ελεος), mercy.
5. Thompson 1902–04, 2:49; Luxford 2019, 204–30, 214–15.
6. Luard 1872–83, iv. 640–05; Vincent 2001, 1–4.
7. Lewis 1987, 424, where it is suggested that this image might be a rendering of an earlier statue at the Abbey church of St Albans.
8. Binski 1991b, 143.
9. Collard 2015, 151–82.
10. Oxford, Bodleian Library, MS Auct. F.4.32, fol. 1^r. The hand of both the drawing of Christ and of the monk, as well as the accompanying inscription have been identified with the hand of a document associated with Dunstan as Abbot of Canterbury.
11. Cologny, Fondation Martin Bodmer, MS 127. Rufillus is also depicted within an initial D on fol. 29^v of a copy of Ambrose's *Hexaemeron* now Amiens, Bibliothèque Municipale, MS Lescalopier 30, not with paints, but with a blade and a stylus or pen.
12. 'O felicia oscula lactentis labris impressa, cum inter crebra indicia reptantis infantiae, ut pote verus ex te filius tibi matri alluderet, cum verus ex Patre Deus Dei Genitus imperaret.' Translation by Collard 2015, 171, based on the edited version provided by James 1925–26, 18.
13. Binski 2006, 88–89.
14. For some of the confluences between kneeling in adoration, and kissing, see Cannon 2010.

CECILY HENNESSY

9

The 'Becket Leaves'

The coronation of the Young King Henry is one of twelve scenes on eight pages with accompanying text that have survived on four leaves, generally known as the 'Becket leaves' (see Figures 9.1a-b).[1] These may have been copied from illuminations that Matthew Paris devised. The coronation, a political and religious rite, was particularly controversial in the feud between Henry II and Thomas Becket, Archbishop of Canterbury. Contrary to English custom, Henry arranged in June 1170 for his eldest son, Henry, known from this time as the Young King, to be crowned during his father's lifetime. He called for Roger, Archbishop of York, to conduct the sacred ceremony, rather than the exiled Becket, whose right it was to do so. By the end of that year, Becket was slain at the hands of Henry II's knights, an event for which the king was eventually repentant.

The fifteen-year-old boy is shown seated on a green cushion, dressed in a blue robe, with a reddish-coloured mantle over his right shoulder and holding a rod or staff while Roger, on the right, places the crown on his head, and four other bishops stand as witnesses. This and the adjacent scene are set within a frame. The two scenes are divided by a bright red and green marble column with a painted capital and base, giving a sense of the rich colour of both cathedral and palace. In the right-hand scene, in a celebration banquet at the great hall in Westminster Palace, Henry II presents the Young King seated at the far end of a table with an elaborate covered chalice and the royal cup, and, as the verse records, tells his son that he, Young Henry, is the sole king.[2] A minstrel boy, sitting on the floor with crossed legs, adds festive

Figure 9.1a The coronation of the Young Henry in Westminster Abbey; the coronation banquet in Westminster Palace, The Life of St Thomas Becket, the 'Becket Leaves', Wormsley Library, MS BM3750, fol. 3ʳ. © The Trustees of The Wormsley Fund. Reproduced with permission from The Wormsley Estate.

harp music to the occasion, while a youth dressed in a green tunic holds a scroll with the ominous words, '*ecce maiestas nimis inclinata*', 'behold majesty too much bent low'.[3] Some early biographers of Becket omit this part of the story, perceiving Henry II's action as unfitting.[4] Its inclusion here emphasises the king's lack of judgement and the text tells how, in revenge for Henry's sin, his son will rise against him.[5] This

Figure 9.1 b, detail of Figure 9.1 a. (cont.) © The Trustees of The Wormsley Fund. Reproduced with permission from The Wormsley Estate.

took place in 1173.⁶ The poet mourns the boy's early death before he was thirty and extolls his beauty and valour.⁷

The illumination is tinted with just a few colours of wash on top of an ink drawing, defining the forms and details. This style of painting was not new, but Matthew Paris is recognised as one of its finest proponents.⁸ The artist, who it is generally agreed was not Matthew, was similarly skilled, managing to move the story on with great pace and energy, using gestures and character interactions to bring the events to life with useful annotations in red ink giving a direct and evocative narrative.

The Latin text above the miniatures gives a summary of the events depicted. The Anglo-Norman text below the miniature in rhyming couplets is in three columns and is adapted from a Latin text known as the *quadrilogus*, which was compiled at the very end of the twelfth century from four of the many current lives of Becket.⁹ Matthew's pithy verse focuses on the nub of the issues. The writing in red at the top of the centre column on folio 3 is a summary or rubric and here says, in essence, how wrong the coronation was.¹⁰

In making an illustrated edition of the life of Thomas Becket, Matthew was responding to and promoting the hugely popular cult surrounding this recent martyr. Becket's death in 1170, for which Henry II confessed some responsibility, and his stand for the church's independence against secular authority, enflamed the emotions and zeal of people from all levels of society throughout Europe and beyond, particularly after an abundance of miracles was accredited to his powers. The complete manuscript would probably have included details on the saint's early life, his rise to power, his friendship as chancellor with Henry II, his conflict over the independence of the church, the anger and poor communication which led to Becket's death and Henry's purported remorse, the extraordinary run of miracles that followed, and Thomas Becket's sanctification.

Matthew was also involved in recording the lives of four other English saints: Alban, Amphibalus, Edward and Edmund.¹¹ He probably undertook the writing of *Thomas* towards the end of the 1230s.¹² The fourteenth-century records of St Albans, Matthew's abbey, document that he 'elegantly illustrated the Lives of Saints Alban and Amphibalus, and of the archbishops of Canterbury Thomas and Edmund'.¹³ At least in some cases, he was writing these saints' lives for aristocratic women at the height of society, of whom two are mentioned in a handwritten note by him, Isabel, Countess of Arundel and Sanchia, Countess of Cornwall. A copy of *The Life of Saints Alban and Amphilabus*, written and illustrated by Matthew, survives, and, among other jottings in it is a note written in Matthew's hand asking that the Countess of Arundel send the book of St Thomas the Martyr and St Edward to the Countess of Cornwall.[14] He describes the book as '*transtuli et protraxi*' by him, possibly meaning 'translated and designed/illustrated'.[15] The book must have contained the lives of both Thomas and Edward in one volume. It may be that the book was his own personal copy, or that it was a later version loaned to the Countess of Arundel. The note does not imply that she owned it. Alternatively, someone else could have made a copy from Matthew's original. It is possible that the surviving leaves are from that book.[16] They are probably datable to circa 1240.[17]

Isabel de Warenne (1226/30–82), the Countess of Arundel, was born in 1226 or 1230 and married in 1234 at the age of eight or younger.[18] Very young marriages were not infrequent among the nobility and royalty. For instance, the Young King was aged five and his wife, Margaret of France, was aged three when they married, and his sister, Leonor, was nine at her wedding.[19] If the autograph of *Thomas* was written in the 1230s and Isabel had it or a copy of it, she could have had it from about the age of ten or twelve. *The Life of Saints Alban and Amphilabus*, in which the note about her is written, can be dated also to the first half of the 1230s, although the note is later.[20]

This perhaps throws some light on the nature of the 'Becket leaves', its images, and the book exchange between teenage girls.[21] Isabel was daughter of the Earl of Surrey and was Henry III's cousin. Sanchia, Countess of Cornwall (*c.* 1225–61), was the sister of Eleanor (1223–91), Henry III's foreign wife from Provence. Eleanor married in 1236, aged twelve or thirteen. Eleanor, at that time, may well have been the recipient of a combined book of the lives of Sts Thomas and Edward. The text and images would have introduced her to popular English hagiography.[22] Sanchia married Henry's brother, Richard, in 1243 and became Countess of Cornwall. Matthew's note asking for Isabel to give a book to Sanchia must therefore have been written in 1243 at the earliest, when Sanchia was about eighteen and may have been new to English life.[23]

Putting an emphasis on the age of these girls who were reading Matthew's books perhaps throws further light on the nature of the manuscripts. The poetry in the 'Becket leaves' has been described as doggerel, but it is evocative, the story moves quickly, the rubric gets to the point, the images are legible and entertaining and the picture titles helpful.[24] It is not surprising such a book would be popular amongst very young women, some of whom were unfamiliar with English life, encapsulating in vividly expressed verse the life of the martyr whose story had enthralled believers for the past fifty years.

Notes

1. Stokenchurch, Wormsley Library, MS BM3750, fol. 3^r. For possible original foliation see Backhouse and de Hamel 1988, 13; for description see de Hamel 1986, 33; for further discussion see Morrison and Hedeman 2010, cat. no. 49.
2. For the verse see Meyer 1885, 18.
3. Backhouse and de Hamel 1988, 31.
4. Strickland 2016, 90.
5. Meyer 1885, xviii–xix, 18–19.
6. For young Henry, Henry II and Becket see Hennessy 2023, 74–77.
7. Meyer 1885, xix.
8. Backhouse and de Hamel 1988, 15, 17.
9. By William of Canterbury, John of Salisbury, Alan of Tewkesbury and Herbert of Bosham; Backhouse and de Hamel 1988, 5; for the text see Meyer 1885. On how many leaves there were originally and their order see Backhouse and de Hamel 1988, 13.
10. Meyer 1885, 15.
11. See Binski 2024; also see Kauffmann 2020.
12. Binski 2024, 22–31. Binski dates the now-lost autograph of Thomas' life to 1236–37; see 30. For an earlier study, see Vaughan 1958c, 159–81.
13. Riley 1870–71, ii. 303; de Hamel 1986, 37; Backhouse and de Hamel 1988, 14.
14. James 1920, 20: 'Mittatis si placet ad dominam comitissam harundell Isabellam ut mittat vobis librum de sancto thoma martire et sancto edwardo quem transtuli et protraxi quemque poterit domina comitissa cornubie retinere usque ad pentecosten'; Vaughan 1958c, 170. See also Chapter 16, 337.
15. Dublin, Trinity College, MS 177, fol. 2^r.
16. Backhouse and de Hamel 1988 15, 18.

17. On date see Binski 2024, 26, 28, 30; also see Morgan 1988, 89–91, 94, who tentatively suggested the 'Becket leaves' may be earlier than Becket's now lost *Life of St. Thomas*.
18. Wogan-Browne 2001, 165.
19. On Margaret, see Hennessy 2023, 74–76 and on Leonor see Hennessy 2023, 82–84.
20. Binski 2024, 36.
21. Vaughan 1958c, 181.
22. Binski 1991, 94; Wogan-Browne 2001, 55; Binski 2024, 26. On the languages used by these women see Wogan-Browne 2001, 15–16.
23. Binski 2024, 25.
24. For doggerel see Vaughan 1958c, 181.

10

Manuscript Design in Production and Transmission

The design of medieval manuscripts has, until relatively recently, received little scholarly attention. Design is not art history, nor is it literary study, and although closely related to codicology and the archaeology of the book, its elusive qualities have deterred further research. Although manuscript design is none of these things specifically, it also relates to all of them, and this plurality calls for a different approach to their study that is from the point of view of their users and makers – as it were, a reverse engineering.

The view of 'design' as an idea and deliberate act of creation is a modern concept. A practice in which aesthetics are weighed with functionality only emerged from art and craft in the industrialisation of the eighteenth century. During this period design and production became separate entities; they were no longer tasks completed by the same hand.[1] Design history as a discipline has struggled to align itself over what is and is not 'design', as well as the periods within which we can consider deliberate design to have occurred, but increasingly emerging from this debate is a notion of design as a constant in human history.[2]

In the Middle Ages there was no separation considered when manuscripts were being produced, and those making the manuscripts, though of differing levels of skill and ability, would have frequently made design-based decisions about the books they were creating. This chapter will make the case for considering design in medieval manuscripts, to demonstrate how this methodology can be brought to bear on manuscripts from different periods and the range of conclusions that can be drawn.³ A design-based methodology can be both complementary to existing approaches and robust enough to stand alone and provide new, innovative discoveries. Moreover, design can be used to understand better the influences on manuscripts and to start to reconstruct the wider intellectual and creative communities in which manuscripts were created.

Few scholars, especially in English language studies, have taken design-based approaches to medieval manuscripts, although this area of study is gaining traction. Scholars such as Bonnie Mak and Lucie Doležalová have researched the continuity of design in specific medieval textual traditions, and others like Daniel Wakelin and Erik Kwakkel are producing innovative, design-focused research looking at usage and purpose.⁴ Design has also been utilised as a valuable tool by scholars of Anglo-Saxon England such as Janet Bately and Linda Nix, who have found this alternative approach essential for reconstructing and learning more about manuscript traditions where few of the original manuscripts survive.⁵ Design history for many, though, sits more comfortably within the era of early printing, on which the pioneering works are those of Henri-Jean Martin, Lotte Hellinga and Roger Chartier.⁶ In this regard, scholarship on fifteenth-century printing bears strong affinities to more modern, theoretical approaches to graphic design, where consideration of the printed text is key.⁷ As well as demonstrating how utilising a design-led methodology works with different types of scholarly approaches, this chapter will also study different types of book production across a broad period from 1250 to 1600. From medieval manuscript production to early printing, and back to manuscript production again in the early modern period, this chapter will also highlight the different ways in which manuscript and book design was approached from a contemporary perspective.

Examining the manuscripts and printed editions that contain Matthew Paris' works enables a better understanding of the role design decisions played in the creation of manuscripts and editions with specific functions, and of Paris' own significance for manuscript production at St Albans. In the early modern era, the printed books of Matthew Paris' work and the manuscripts copied from them demonstrate a conceptual shift in how books were considered. Paris and the works he created therefore provide a window into contemporary perspectives on history manuscripts and books, how knowledge was shared and presented, and changing attitudes towards books across the period studied.

The Manuscript Tradition of the *Flores historiarum*

The *Flores historiarum* was the first of the St Albans histories attached to the name of Matthew Paris, and it is from this base that the role of manuscript design and the transmission of design features can begin to be seen. The *Flores* was a condensed history covering the years from Creation to 1259, and it provided a useful framework from which other individuals and institutions could develop their own historiographical traditions. It is extant in twenty-nine manuscripts, in various iterations, lengths, and completeness.[8] The earliest surviving manuscript of the *Flores historiarum* is Manchester, Chetham's Library, MS 6712 [hereafter Chetham's 6712]. The manuscript consists of 297 folia of reasonable-quality parchment and measures 187 × 245 mm. This specific manuscript was made in St Albans Abbey in the first half of the thirteenth century before going to Pershore Abbey and then Westminster Abbey by the end of the century.[9] In terms of textual content, the portion written at St Albans is thought to be the work of two monks, Matthew Paris and Roger of Wendover, and five different scribes wrote the manuscript while at St Albans Abbey.[10] It is the only surviving *Flores historiarum* manuscript with a direct connection to St Albans, and is therefore one of the best-studied manuscripts in the *Flores* corpus.[11] After the manuscript left St Albans it was then continued by two scribes at Pershore Abbey and ten more at Westminster Abbey, where the manuscript became a working document that was being actively compiled.[12] Many have suggested that Chetham's 6712 was intended as a presentation copy for Westminster Abbey, and when it left St Albans Abbey this could well have been the case, but the standard of continuations added at Westminster indicate that the manuscript did not hold a similarly privileged position in that abbey's library.[13] Nevertheless, it was this movement of the first *Flores* manuscript away from St Albans Abbey that allowed for the textual and visual dissemination of this historiographical tradition.

The *Flores historiarum* manuscripts display several distinctive design features, all of which can be traced to Chetham's 6712 and subsequently replicated in a select group of other books. These include heraldry, paratextual elements, schemes of illumination and diagrammatic presentations of text. The largest and most complex feature in the *Flores* is the presentation of the Anglo-Saxon heptarchy. The Anglo-Saxon heptarchy is a list of the seven kingdoms of early medieval England – Kent, Mercia, Wessex, Northumbria, East Anglia, Essex and Sussex – and it was a common element in medieval historiography.[14] In the *Flores historiarum* it is usually included around the year 686. Most of the twenty-nine *Flores* manuscripts simply contain the heptarchy as a list written within the normal text block and give it little stress or emphasis. But in four of the manuscripts it is displayed as a distinctive eight-column grid prefaced by an introduction that spans the full width of the writing space.[15]

These design features offer a different way to group manuscripts: through the dissemination of specific features. In the case of the Anglo-Saxon heptarchy, grouping by design features draws attention to a series of manuscripts stemming from the Chetham's *Flores*, centred around Westminster Abbey and the immediate surrounding area. The eight-columned presentation of the heptarchy saw only a short-lived transmission and seems to be present in one generation of copies only, suggesting that it was not considered viable or relevant to reproduce long term. This makes the reception of this feature particularly distinctive, and the heptarchy manuscript grouping highlights connections that challenge existing patterns established on textual variation alone.

There are commonly considered to be two main textual variants of the *Flores historiarum* (defined by the later additions rather than the original text): the Merton *Flores*, originating from Windsor, Eton College library MS 123 (Eton 123), and the Westminster *Flores*, found in Chetham's 6712.[16] There is little textual variation between most of the *Flores* manuscripts – in most cases the manuscripts were copied directly from an exemplar without notable change and the key textual differences are seen in the continuations – and the core text therefore is not a reliable source of evidence to understand manuscript filiation. Studying the design of the manuscripts and the shared features seen across the corpus offers further insights into the pattern of transmission. Chetham's 6712 was the origin of all subsequent textual variants, but it was also the source of all shared visual features, and by studying these elements it is possible to understand more about where the *Flores historiarum* manuscripts were made as well as to identify particular paths of dissemination.

The first of the three further manuscripts to contain the Anglo-Saxon heptarchy is Eton 123, the second earliest *Flores* manuscript and a manuscript likely copied directly from Chetham's 6712. Both manuscripts contain the same text up to 1265, as well as very similar illumination and design, including the Anglo-Saxon heptarchy in eight columns, which suggests a very close connection.[17] Chetham's 6712 and Eton 123 are considered to form two separate textual traditions: there is a shared core text up to around 1265 but the manuscripts then contain different textual continuations, which differ increasingly as the chronology continues in each variant.[18] Although the continuations vary between these two manuscripts, we must be wary of creating theses of transmission that involve multiple 'missing' exemplars, as Vaughan suggests, when the manuscript evidence suggests otherwise.[19] Instead, as will be shown, historical texts such as the *Flores* encouraged customisation. It is far more likely that the Eton manuscript was copied from Chetham's verbatim to a certain point and that then it was customised by its future owner to match their institutional requirements.[20] Focusing on the textual difference has shaped research to such an extent that the two manuscripts are usually considered as separate entities, ignoring the close relationship in terms of design that existed between them. What the textual approach misses is the direct relationship between the Eton and Chetham's manuscripts; Chetham's 6712 must have been the exemplar for the Eton manuscript because they share specific distinctive features.

The Anglo-Saxon heptarchy in eight columns is a distinctive presentation within the *Flores* tradition that unites the manuscripts that carry it (see Figure 10.1). In its original form in Chetham's 6712 the heptarchy is introduced by a text block in a single column, with the Anglo-Saxon rulers and their chronologies presented across eight very narrow columns below. It is limited to one page in the Chetham's manuscript but varies in length in the other three manuscripts that contain it, simply due to where it begins within the text. The Eton manuscript was

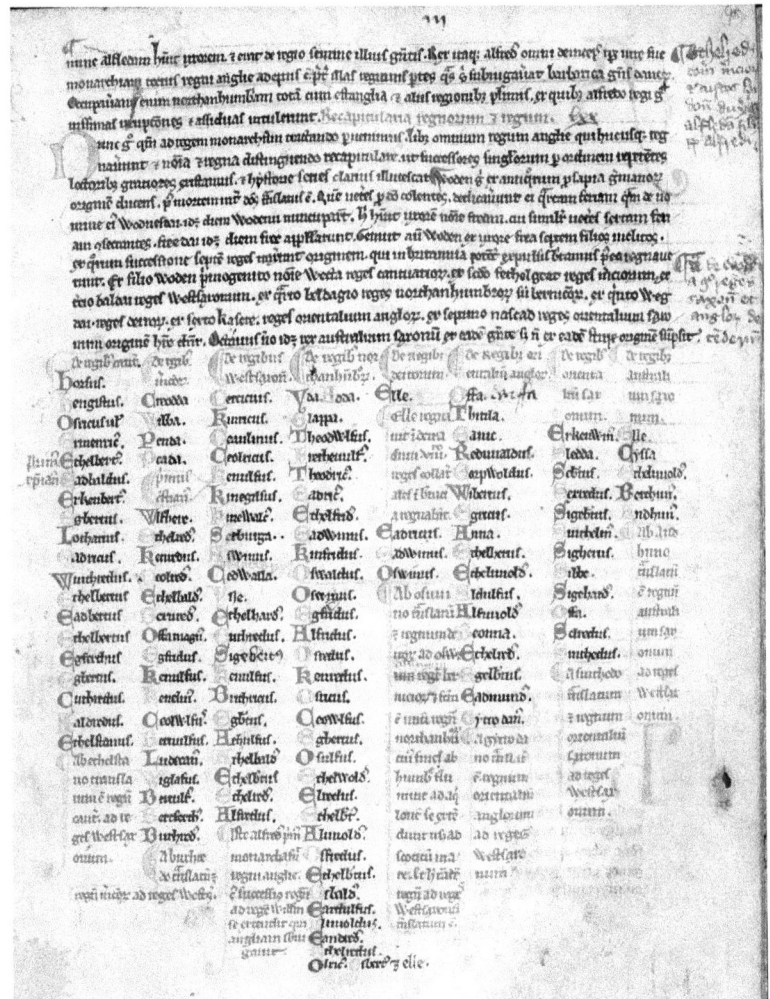

Figure 10.1 Heptarchy layout. (a) Manchester, Chetham's Library MS 6712, fol. 98ʳ. Reproduced with permission from Chetham's Library (b) (i) Eton College MS 123, fols. 120ᵛ–121ʳ; © The Provost & Fellows of Eton College; (ii) BL Cotton MS Nero D II, fol. 80ʳ. © British Library

produced in the early fourteenth century and written by one scribe up to the chronicle entry for 1290. The manuscript was then finished to a high standard by five different scribes. Like the Chetham's *Flores*, the Eton manuscript also contains illuminations for the coronations of each new king from William I onwards.[21] The heptarchy is not complete in this

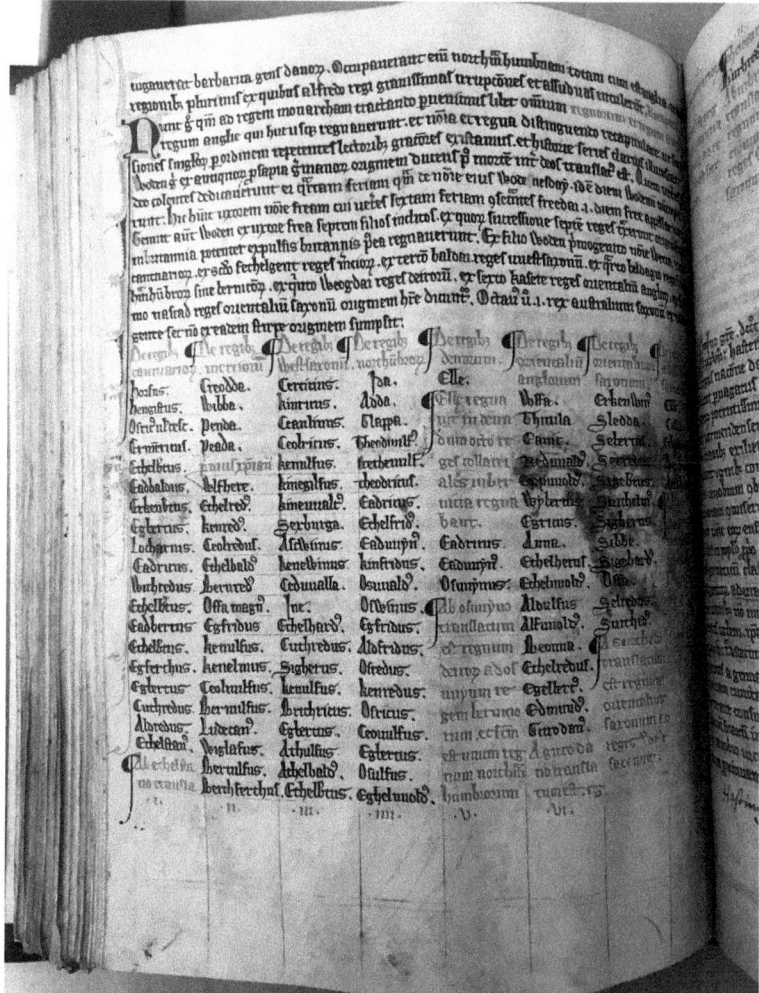

Figure 10.1 (cont.)

manuscript, missing the column for Sussex. The page size in Chetham's 6712 is actually smaller than in Eton 123, measuring 187 × 245 mm compared to Eton's 195 × 272 mm, meaning that there should have been adequate space in the manuscript for eight columns; however, in this instance the scribe has not anticipated the amount of space required and perhaps lacked the ability to adapt his script size even though he was able to split the feature across two folia. Nonetheless, in all other

Figure 10.1 (cont.)

respects the heptarchy follows the same design as the Chetham's manuscript. Combine this and other shared visual traits, such as the coronation illuminations, and a strong connection between the two manuscripts starts to emerge. Eton 123 was owned by Merton Priory, which was geographically very close to Westminster Abbey (7.5 miles as the crow flies) and it seems highly likely that Eton 123 used Chetham's

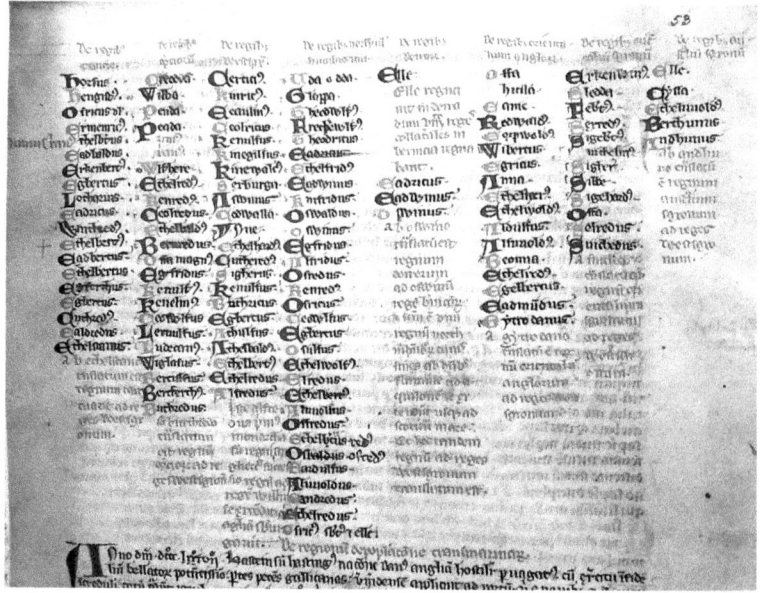

Figure 10.1 (cont.)

6712 as a direct exemplar once the manuscript was at Westminster.[22] The shared design features confirm this connection. As noted, the scribe of the Eton manuscript lacked the foresight or capacity to adapt the written space of the manuscript to contain the heptarchy on one leaf, so it seems unlikely that the scribe would have had the creative ability to present that section of text differently from how it appeared in the exemplar. Katie Hawks has described the Chetham's and Eton manuscripts as the two 'parent' manuscripts of the *Flores historiarum* tradition, but in design terms this is not the case.[23] Chetham's 6712 is the earliest *Flores* manuscript and stands alone as the manuscript that launched several separate visual dissemination strands.

Multiple occurrences of the same specific design features in manuscripts allow us to connect manuscripts via a shared exemplar, much in the same way that a textual approach does. A third manuscript contains the Anglo-Saxon heptarchy, British Library Arundel MS 96 [hereafter Arundel 96]. This manuscript differs in a number of ways from Chetham's 6712 and Eton 123, yet nevertheless the inclusion of this shared feature means that it must necessarily be related to them. In contrast to the other *Flores* manuscripts discussed earlier in this chapter, Arundel 96 is very large, with a page size of 261 × 373 mm and a text block of 186 × 297 mm; it is written in a single column of text compared to the two-column format of the Chetham's and Eton manuscripts. It was produced towards the end of the thirteenth century. Arundel 96 is a high-quality manuscript and was likely intended as a presentation-quality item, although it was never illuminated and retains large gaps for illuminations that were never completed. The chronicle in Arundel 96 covers the years up to 1284, compared to the more commonly encountered continuations that stop either at 1306 or around 1320. We can explain this with reference to Chetham's 6712, with which we know to connect Arundel 96 through the shared occurrence of the Anglo-Saxon heptarchy in eight columns. It seems probable, in fact, that Chetham's 6712 was its direct exemplar, because that manuscript was continued by ten different scribes at Westminster Abbey in an ad hoc manner, and 1284 coincides with a scribal break in these continuations.[24] Furthermore, the presentation standard and the political and geographic proximity of Westminster Abbey to the crown might indicate that the manuscript was planned as a present in relation to Edward II, who was born in that year. Here, then, studying the shared design features allows us to significantly narrow down the route of dissemination and identify potential exemplar manuscripts. Without the direct visual connection, it would not be immediately obvious that the Arundel and Chetham's manuscripts also share a connection through the continuation process, nor suggest reasons for the manuscript's creation.

The heptarchy design in the *Flores* tradition seems to span only one generation of manuscript and is found only in manuscripts from London and south-west England. It is a distinctive feature, but one that required significant effort from the scribe with limited benefit for the reader, so it is not surprising it was not replicated more widely. Only one other manuscript contains the Anglo-Saxon heptarchy in eight columns, BL, Cotton MS Nero D II [hereafter Nero D II], which was a heavily customised *Flores historiarum* from Rochester Priory, a manuscript that shares many characteristics with Paris' *Chronica maiora* due its institutional customisation. This is a complex manuscript, and there is not sufficient space to analyse it here, but Nero D II contains the same textual variant as Chetham's 6712, and when combined with the heptarchy design it therefore seems likely that these two manuscripts share a close connection.[25] Even without further research to understand the exact relationship between these two manuscripts, we may observe a close intellectual connection between St Albans and Rochester Priory as a consequence. These monastic institutions were sharing learning, texts and, importantly, visual culture too, and it is through this collection of shared knowledge that individual compilers such as Matthew Paris could develop their manuscripts and creative practice.

The *Flores historiarum* and the *Chronica maiora*

Expanding the comparison of design to manuscripts related to the *Flores historiarum* allows us to gain further understanding as to the different function and purpose of particular books. By studying some of the autograph manuscripts of Matthew Paris which remained at St Albans Abbey we can see that far from existing in isolation, Paris was instead part of a vigorously, creative environment. The rich holdings of the abbey library provided Paris with a basis from which to work and a source of visual templates.[26] The work of Matthew Paris was so much a part of the monastic community that he created chronicle books to fulfil particular functions at the abbey. As it is important to consider the whole manuscript, not just the text, so too is it important to look at manuscripts and their design within the wider context of production.

Only two of Matthew Paris' autograph manuscripts ever left St Albans Abbey, the Chetham's *Flores* in the thirteenth century and the *Historia Anglorum* (BL, Royal MS 14 C VII) in the fifteenth century, yet the manuscripts that remained are informative, complex and visually engaging volumes, distinctive for their highly personalised nature.[27] Furthermore, the works are visually divergent, suggesting that each manuscript had a different purpose, usage or audience. The rich illustrations, rare to this extent in medieval chronicles, have attracted the attention of many scholars, notably M. R. James, Nigel Morgan and Suzanne Lewis.[28] Paris' maps are also some of the earliest and clearest extant examples of medieval cartography.[29] His autograph manuscripts are a testament to medieval knowledge management and use of design: Paris' artistic skills allowed him to experiment with different layouts and presentation strategies. The importance of these manuscripts to our understanding of late medieval England, knowledge management and manuscript production should not be understated, but it is important to understand why these manuscripts differed and why they remained at the abbey. The manuscripts themselves offer clues to their usage; their inimitable and rich qualities reflected the prestige of St Albans at the time and for modern audiences these manuscripts act as a mirror in which to view the abbey's perception of itself.

Before looking at the differences in design between the *Flores* tradition and the *Chronica maiora* manuscripts, it is important first to acknowledge their similarities. Matthew Paris is best known for his *Chronica maiora* manuscripts, extant only in Cambridge, Corpus Christi College, MSS 16 and 26 [hereafter CCCC 16 & 26], a two-volume set of richly illuminated chronicles. These are large manuscripts, measuring 240 to 250 mm × 360 mm and with 151 and 286 folios respectively. The presentation standard of the text is very similar to that of the Chetham's *Flores*, though the parchment is of intermittent quality, perhaps because of the manuscript size. Both manuscripts contain sections written by Matthew Paris himself in autograph.[30] There are strong textual similarities too, as the *Chronica maiora* is based on the *Flores historiarum* text, merely a version of it that is customised with additions from other historical sources held at St Albans Abbey at the time. A handful of other history books at St Albans during this period would have provided Matthew Paris with sources, and Paris also made further collections of his own that represented records in different ways from the chronicle form.

The relationship between the *Chronica maiora* and the *Flores historiarum*, however, poses a problem. Modern historians have come to know these manuscripts as the *Chronica maiora*, but this title does not reflect the original identity of these collections in the monastic community at St Albans. The *Chronica maiora* was not the title given to CCCC 16 and 26 by their scribe and compiler; that title was the *Flores historiarum*, and, as highlighted by Richard Sharpe, the identity of medieval texts is multifaceted.[31] The titles that scribes gave their own works were very significant and in this instance indicate a connection that has not properly been explored (see Figure 10.2).

The glaring difference between the two sets of manuscripts is arguably one of perception, especially with regards to how the *Chronica*

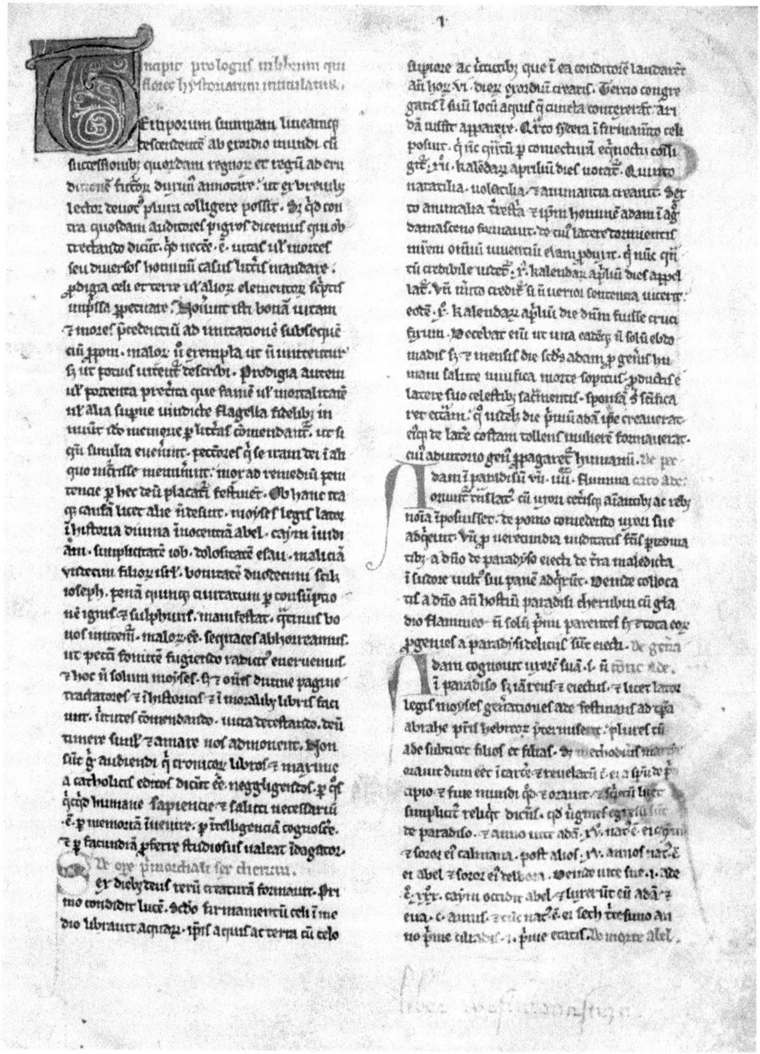

Figure 10.2 Titular incipits. (a) Manchester, Chetham's Library MS 6712, fol. 7ʳ. Reproduced with permission from Chetham's Library (b) Cambridge, Corpus Christi College, Cambridge, MS 26, fol. 1ʳ. © Parker Library, Corpus Christi College, Cambridge

maiora is viewed. There is nothing per se incorrect in naming CCCC 16 and 26 the *Chronica maiora*, except that it is just a descriptive term by which these manuscripts, not works, are commonly known and a way to

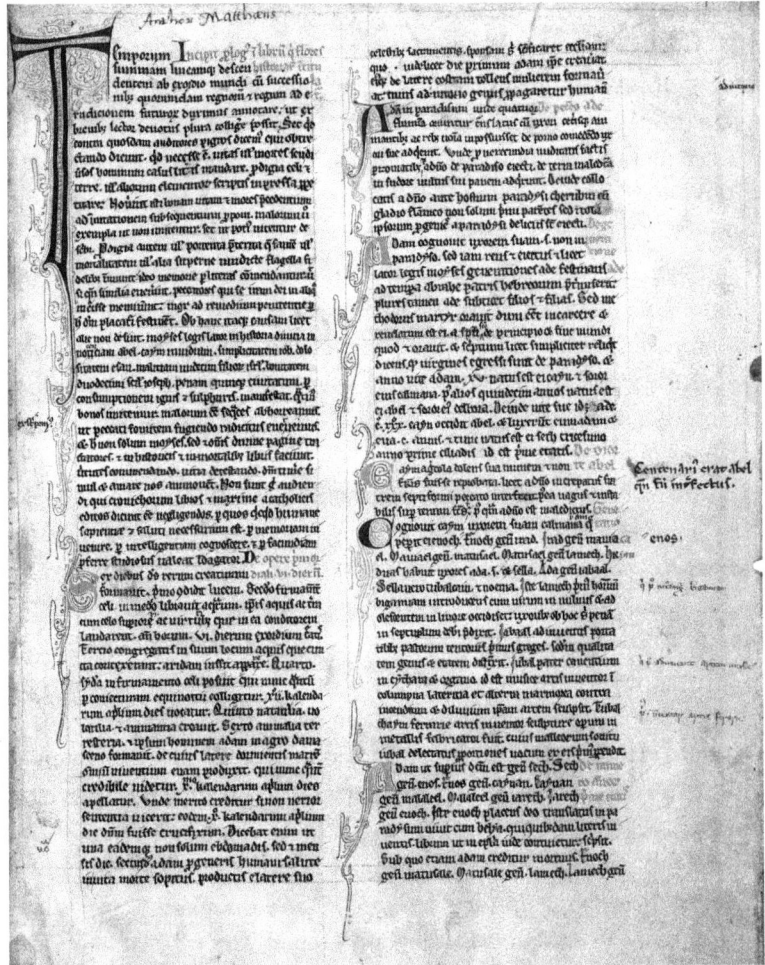

Figure 10.2 (cont.)

separate these from the numerous *Flores* manuscripts in wider circulation. Indeed, how these manuscripts have been approached by scholars, and the amount of attention these two manuscripts have received in contrast to the twenty-nine of the *Flores*, reflects the direct opposite of the *Flores historiarum* tradition. The *Chronica* manuscripts are two unique volumes with limited impact as a textual tradition, yet they have been elevated because of their special qxualities, including richness of content, artistic merit and distinctive approach.[32] By contrast the

Flores tradition is textually rich, but its materiality has been ignored, with Vaughan stating that the *Flores* tradition is 'of only incidental value'.[33] It is time, then, that these two elements were viewed together. As mentioned, the *Flores* provided a framework and base that could be adapted for different purposes or emphases. The Corpus Christi manuscripts are an extreme example of this, a set of heavily customised *Flores* manuscripts that remained at St Albans Abbey. This explains why St Albans was happy to gift Chetham's 6712 to another monastic house – the monastic library at St Albans had retained an expanded, illustrated and more detailed version of the *Flores historiarum* in the form of the *Chronica maiora*. From this perspective the highly customised *Chronica* manuscripts become the apex of the *Flores* tradition, rather than an independent work in their own right.

Matthew Paris' detailed illustrations offer an insight into the usage of the *Chronica maiora* at St Albans. Paris' autograph manuscripts are exceptional for their time: no other chronicle book compiled in England had hitherto been so heavily illustrated and in the same fashion. Prior to Paris' work, the illustration of histories in England was confined to a handful of pages in each book. Some manuscripts of Henry of Huntingdon's *Historia Anglorum*, which was circulating widely by the mid thirteenth century, contained sporadic marginal illustrations, such as BL Arundel MS 46. Several scholars have also drawn connections between Paris' work and the diagrammatic approach to historiography found in the rolls and manuscripts of Peter of Poitiers' *Compendium historiae*, for example in Eton MS 96.[34] It was the illustration of these earlier history manuscripts that laid the groundwork for Matthew Paris. Indeed, Paris' handwriting can be found in a historiographical miscellany manuscript from the abbey library that contains Huntington's *Historia Anglorum* (BL Royal MS 13 D V) and he was exposed to these wider historiographical and illuminated traditions both at St Albans itself and within the wider monastic culture of manuscript production.[35]

It seems likely that the *Chronica maiora* manuscripts carried a performative function at St Albans Abbey, one that saw these massive manuscripts on display. Lewis has claimed that Paris' marginalia were designed to accompany readings of his manuscripts, as their narrative function would support and elaborate on the chronicle content.[36] The style in which Paris produced his illustrations further suggests this connection: the inclusion of detail and movement combined with descriptive words was considered an important aid to memory in imagery, and all of these were common techniques employed by Paris.[37] In addition, it seems likely that such imagery was designed to appeal to a non-monastic audience and served an important role at a local level. An abbey as large as St Albans and in a prime location on the main arterial road out of London towards the north would have housed a high quantity of guests seeking monastic hospitality. Whilst it is challenging to know precisely what the abbey offered guests because of the paucity of evidence, Julie Kerr has suggested activities such as tours, library visits and an opportunity to view treasures of the monastery were common for more distinguished visitors.[38] The two *Chronica maiora* volumes were one such treasure at St Albans. If we also factor in the great size of each manuscript, then, it is more likely that the manuscripts were used as static display pieces than as practical, everyday reference books, much in the same way that impressive medieval manuscripts are on display in reference libraries and museums now. The *Chronica maiora* manuscript volumes are an illustrated history intended to interest and engage readers and viewers as well as to provide historiographical information. Furthermore, these were not manuscripts constructed by one person alone; they were the product of an active monastic scriptorium. Nine scribes wrote the two volumes of the *Chronica maiora*, which equates to a significant investment from the monastery itself. It is just as valid to think of this chronicle as an institutional work than as the output of one very creative individual.[39] It therefore seems probable that the *Chronica maiora* served a dual purpose at St Albans. The chronicle provided the abbey with a highly detailed and expanded version of the *Flores historiarum*, on the basis of which further historiographical works could be composed and continued, whilst also doubling up as a form of attraction or visitor entertainment. The *Chronica maiora* had little to no circulation outside of St Albans, but that is perhaps as the abbey intended; visitors had to travel to the abbey itself to view the chronicle.

St Albans Abbey, a Creative Hub

Manuscripts as rich as the *Chronica maiora* were the product of the wider creative community at St Albans Abbey in the thirteenth century, which was vibrant and dynamic. It is tempting to view Matthew Paris in isolation from this environment, but much of the inspiration for the design and illustration of his own manuscripts came from the rich holdings of the abbey library, which was estimated to contain 300–400 manuscripts by 1200.[40] Indeed, Paris' hand can be found in marginal annotation in the St Albans–owned manuscripts of Ralph Diceto's *Abbreviationes chronicorum* and *Ymagines historiarum* (BL, Royal MS 13 E VI) and a historical miscellany containing extracts from multiple different chronicles, including the *Historia Brittonum* (BL, Royal MS 13 D V).[41] Such creative inspiration and transference is also seen in the manuscripts of Paris' peers, such as his contemporary John of Wallingford (BL, Cotton MS Julius D VII), further indicating that the wider environment and sources available through the institution played a crucial role in fostering and developing creativity. John of Wallingford was at St Albans Abbey during the same period as Paris and served as *infirmarian* in the 1240s, but his one surviving manuscript is rich in detail and artistry.[42] Here again the importance of studying design is clear as it is only through direct comparison with other manuscripts from the monastic library or contemporary libraries that the breadth of influence can be seen. Furthermore, this helps to put the manuscripts of Matthew Paris and his peers into perspective. The level of skill involved in the illustration and design of Paris' extant manuscripts means that it is tempting to view him as prodigal figure in isolation, especially at St Albans, but this gives a one-sided picture.

In the thirteenth century monks at St Albans were producing manuscripts that experimented with how to present information, a characteristic of the monastery's production not commonly seen from other English religious institutions during this period. Matthew Paris was one of the first English compilers to make use of diagrammatic forms within his manuscript designs, which he did in the *Flores historiarum* (as seen with the Anglo-Saxon heptarchy) but also in his larger historiographical works, the extended *Flores historiarum* now commonly called the *Chronica maiora* and the *Historia Anglorum* (see Figure 10.3).[43] These unique approaches for the genre are what has made the manuscripts associated with Matthew Paris stand out. In the *Chronica maiora*, for instance, Paris includes itinerary maps alongside alternative presentations of the Anglo-Saxon heptarchy and various practical diagrammatic tables, as well as illustrations of

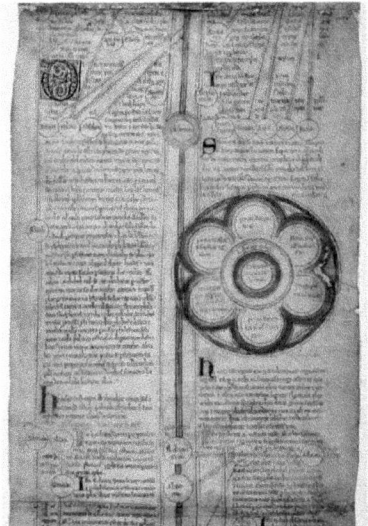 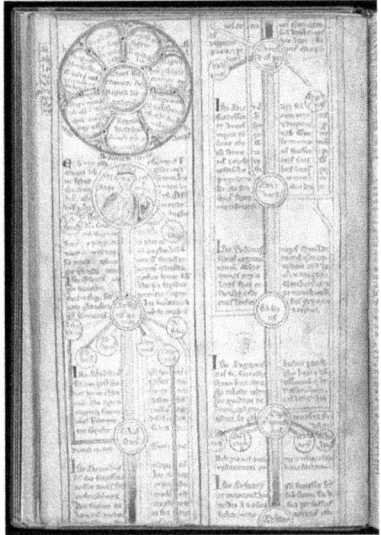

Figure 10.3 Diagrammatic forms. (a) Bodleian Lat. th. b. 1, membrane 3. © Bodleian Library (b) BL Cotton MS Claudius D VI, fol. 10ᵛ. © British Library

religious and national significance, such as the Virgin and child (CCCC 26, fol. viiʳ), and, famously, Henry II's elephant (CCCC 16, preliminary matter, fol. iiʳ). To support the *Chronica maiora* manuscripts Matthew Paris also created a separate manuscript to house additional items, evidence and sources, commonly called the *Liber additamentorum*.[44] Extant in a single copy (BL, Cotton MS Nero D I), this manuscript utilised a cross-referencing system seen earlier in the work of Ralph Diceto, and as mentioned, a copy of Diceto's chronicles was present in the Abbey library.[45] Cross references to the Nero D I continue to be found in St Albans collections into the fifteenth century, in the *Gesta abbatum* of John of Wheathampstead, as well as influencing other administrative documents at the Abbey, such as cartulary manuscripts.[46] The *Historia Anglorum* saw the use of a different feature – heraldry. As with the other elements, heraldry was rare at this point in manuscripts, let alone in historiographical manuscripts, and here too Paris was adapting a design feature seen elsewhere to provide innovative elements within his own manuscript. In this chronicle heraldry was used to highlight the death, birth or coronation of specific individuals, with the heraldic shields sharing who had been affected. His likely source of inspiration for this approach was his own work in compiling heraldry for the

Liber additamentorum.⁴⁷ While it is tempting to embellish Matthew Paris' contribution to wider manuscript culture based on the significance and creativity of his manuscripts that remained at St Albans Abbey, his creative ability and sense of design cannot be denied.

John of Wallingford's historical miscellany has received little attention, especially as a complete manuscript, yet it is instrumental in understanding how Matthew Paris' work related to the library at St Albans, demonstrating the extent of shared influences. It survives in a single manuscript, BL, Cotton MS Julius D VII, produced in the mid-thirteenth century, and contains miscellaneous historiographical material reflecting the varied historiographical interests of St Albans. The content has been documented by Vaughan and is eclectic, from tables to calculate the day of saints' feasts and complex infographics, to chronicles and devotional imagery, and in many ways resembles a personal commonplace book.⁴⁸

Despite the eclectic content, the Julius manuscript provides a more detailed window into the creative community at St Albans during this period, illuminating the ways in which scribes adapted elements from different manuscripts and genres. For instance, Wallingford's manuscript demonstrates direct connections to Paris' work. Julius D VII contains a heptarchy chart and a genealogy of kings starting from Alfred the Great (fols. 49ᵛ, 56ᵛ–59ᵛ), mirroring Paris' innovative diagrammatic design. This is an alternative presentation of the Anglo-Saxon heptarchy in a petalled roundel and is present in several other historiographical manuscripts associated with Matthew Paris.⁴⁹

Until recently Paris' diagrammatic representations of history have received little attention, again being dismissed by previous scholars like Vaughan as unimportant, though their significance is now being recognised.⁵⁰ Another shared feature is a series of decorative columns to frame the page, as found in BL, Cotton MS Claudius D VI, a manuscript of the *Abbreviatio chronicorum* which also contains the work of later historiographical compilers from St Albans. But some of the most exciting information design in Julius D VII cannot be found in Paris' manuscripts and instead connects other manuscripts held in the St Albans library. A unique approach is taken in Wallingford's miscellany to presenting Henry of Huntingdon's *Historia Anglorum*: instead of the usual single or double-columned layout, Julius D VII utilised presentation resembling a glossed manuscript. The St Albans library contained a beautiful manuscript copy of the glossed gospels produced at a similar time to Wallingford's work with precise and ornate text layout, extant in Cambridge, Trinity College, MS B.5.3 (see Figure 10.4). While the text layout in Julius D VII does not come close to that of the gloss, there is definite experimentation with textual layout that suggests a strong level of influence from a manuscript such as this one: the glossing style seems to be used to section off additional pieces of information, but not in a uniform fashion. On some pages the different sections are marked at the beginning with a symbol that acts as a way of cross-referencing this information in other parts of the text, while on other folia the main text seems to continue in these different sections. The layouts in which the text in the Henry of Huntington section were formatted did not exist in historiographical works, certainly not within any extant historiographical manuscript associated with St Albans Abbey. Instead, it seems most likely that this section, as with others in Wallingford's miscellany, were experimental forms, in this case a merging of chronicles and glossed gospels. Furthermore, it seems plausible that as a personal miscellany Wallingford made the most of

Figure 10.4 Glossed layout. (a) Henry of Huntingdon's *Historia Anglorum* BL Cotton MS Julius D VII, fols. 32^v–33^r. © British Library (b) Glossed gospel book from St Albans, Cambridge, Trinity College, MS B.5.3, fol. 23^v. © Master & Fellows of Trinity College, Cambridge

Figure 10.4 (cont.)

the opportunity to experiment and that the whole manuscript contains innovative approaches to different material, including adapting the unique output of colleagues like Paris in the creative community at St Albans.

Manuscripts contain remnants of their exemplar in the text and art copied, but also in the design. This quick glimpse into the wider manuscript culture at St Albans Abbey contextualises Matthew Paris' creative practice. Although we do not fully understand the role of figures like Paris in instigating, creating or perpetuating periods of creative production within the great manuscript-producing institutions, looking at similarities of design and influence can help to address this. By taking a design-based approach, these networks of influence are easier to see, especially important when some of the influences transcend formal genre boundaries. Manuscript design therefore should be a central consideration when trying to reconstruct such intellectual and creative communities.

Antiquarian Collectors and Their Manuscripts

Manuscript design is not only a useful tool for understanding medieval manuscripts or contemporary manuscript production; the value of this methodology can also be seen when analysing how later collectors used the medieval source material and fixed perceived problems presented by their texts, and when observing changing attitudes towards book production and authenticity in the age of print. Manuscripts copied from printed exemplars often retained the design of the book from which they were copied, in much the same way that design in manuscripts was transmitted.[51] Likewise, apparent gaps in the textual record of these manuscripts were filled with a range of different sources in the early modern period and it is through the design transmission that the source exemplar can be identified. This practice was driven, in part, by changes in attitudes towards exemplars, but there was also a shift in thinking about the permanence of text and book design. Such additions were fundamentally a product of the sixteenth-century collectors and their desire for completeness in the manuscripts that they collected. As custodians and acquirers of lost monastic heritage, the role of antiquarians was a significant one. This section will highlight the contrary nature of sixteenth-century antiquarianism, a form of scholarship that favoured the knowledge found in original material yet was happy to make modern additions to medieval manuscripts. Furthermore, it will debate the role of printed text in shaping attitudes towards the book and textual authenticity, and the texts associated with Matthew Paris and St Albans demonstrate a variety of approaches to book production during this period.

One such sixteenth-century collector was Matthew Parker, Elizabeth I's first archbishop of Canterbury. Parker was an avid collector of medieval manuscripts and of knowledge, and the dissolution of the monasteries, which was complete by 1540, provided him with the opportunity to accumulate these manuscripts in his own personal reference library. In part, these collecting habits were driven by a desire to rebuild the great monastic libraries, many of which had since and very quickly been torn apart; however, to Archbishop Parker the history and development of England, in particular its religious history, was just as important as he looked to reframe England's past.⁵² Although some modern scholars have found antiquarian manuscript collecting practices unpalatable, the reality is that without these collectors far fewer medieval manuscripts would have survived. By this point in time – the era of printed media – medieval manuscripts were old tech; they were antiquated, written in a script and language few people were used to reading, and covered topics no longer considered relevant. Parker, then, played a significant role. His reworking of medieval history, his creating and sharing the medieval sources, demonstrates the changing role and purpose of book production in the sixteenth century.

The *Chronica maiora* manuscripts were some of the jewels in the crown of Parker's medieval historiographical manuscript collection, most of which is still extant in the Parker Library at Corpus Christi College, Cambridge. Yet the second of these two manuscripts, CCCC 16, was incomplete. It is not clear when the gaps occurred, but they were prior to Parker's ownership. Antiquarian collectors like Parker used a mixture of manuscript and printed exemplars to fill in apparent gaps in the manuscripts they gathered, which indicates that they favoured completeness over any sense of textual authenticity. The source material used can be traced through the design of the additions. Two sixteenth-century additions have been added to CCCC 16 on folia 4^r–11^v and 233^r–234^v: one copied from the 1571 printed edition (see Figure 10.5) and the other from BL Cotton MS Nero D V.⁵³ Both sections appear to be written by the same scribe. The first section directly copies the layout of the printed book with very little change. The only real difference is that display initials are written in colour rather than black, suggesting a small tweak to try and make the addition sit more naturally with the medieval original. Otherwise, the features are predominantly those of the printed edition: a single column of text, a running head, the same marginal annotations and the same paragraph breaks in the text. The other addition is much closer in design terms to that of the original manuscript, as Nero D V is one of the few contemporary manuscript adaptations of the *Chronica maiora*. This is described as an adaptation as it is not a full copy of the *Chronica maiora*: in fact, the manuscript is closer in length to the *Flores historiarum* manuscripts. A shared presentation of the Anglo-Saxon heptarchy, though, which is different in CCCC 26 and Nero D V from the design in the *Flores*, confirms that it must nevertheless

10 Manuscript Design in Production and Transmission

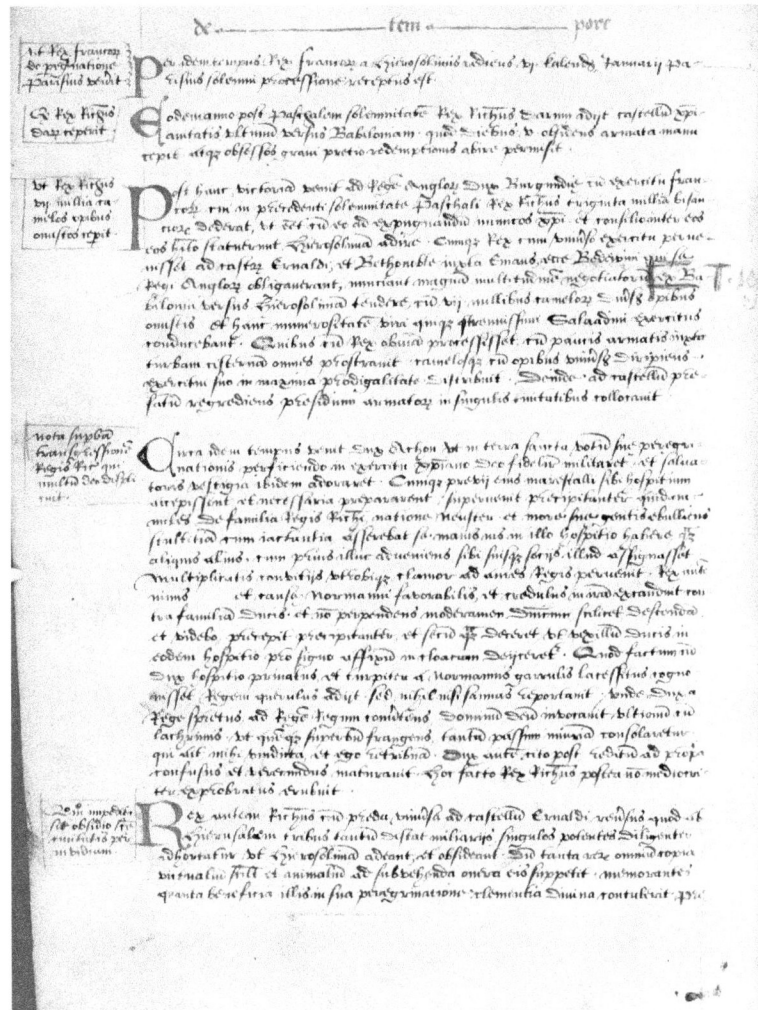

Figure 10.5 (a) The 1571 printed edition used as an exemplar for one of the additions in an autograph manuscript, Cambridge, Corpus Christi College, MS 16 (II), fol. 10ᵛ. © Parker Library, Corpus Christi College, Cambridge; (b) *Matthæi Paris, monachi Albanensis, Angli, Historia maior à Guilielmo Conquaestore, ad vltimum annum Henrici tertij. Cum indice locupletissimo.* (London: Reginald Wolf, 1571), 224. © The Library of Trinity College Dublin

224 MATTH. PARIS. HIST. ANGL.

inquit, & virum in foemina mecum admiramini. Accurrūt muliercule mulæ, & pretium panni quem ferebat vænalem, folerter inquirunt. Cumq̄ nihil responderet, vt qui Anglicanam non nouerat linguam: coeperunt inter se confabulari, & dolum suspicantes, manus iniecerunt in peplum, quo fauces tegebantur. Et summittentes à naso vsq̄ deorsum, faciem hominis viderunt nigram, & nuper rasam. Clamorem vtiq̄ ad sydera tollentes adinuicem: venite inquiunt, & lapidemus hoc mōstrum, quod sexum vtrumq̄ deformauit. Et factus est illico concursus virorum ac mulierum, extrahentium de capite peplum, & trahentium eum prostratum, ignominiose per masnicas & capicium, per arenam & saxa, non sine pōtificis læsione. Seruientes eius tandem occurrunt, se d non potuerunt. Nam populus cum insatiabili corde illum persequens, verbis, alapis & sputis dehonestatum, per plateas distractum in quodam cellario sub carcerali custodia includunt. Sic vtiq̄ factus est in derisum omni populo, qui vtinam se solum & non sacerdotium inquinasset. Tractus est, qui Archiepiscopum Eboracensem traxerat, captus qui ceperat, ligatus qui ligauerat, incarceratus qui incarcerauerat: vt secundum quantitatem culpæ, quantitas poenæ commensurabilis haberetur. Tandem spretis obsidibus atq̄ iuramento quod fecerat, se non recessurum à regno Angliæ, antequam castella redderentur, idem Cancellarius, quarto Kalendas Nouembris, in Normanniam trās fretauit.

Nota rem inauditam.

EOdem anno, iuuenis quidam de domo episcopi Londoniarum, Nisum quem habuit, docuit cercellas propensius affectare, itaq̄ ad sonitum illius instrumenti, quod à ripatoribus Thabur nominatur, subito Cercella quodam alarum perniciter remigio euolauit. Nisus autem illusus, Lupum quendam & Lucium in vndis natantem intercepit, inuasit, & arripuit, & super aridam, per spatium, sicut videbatur, quadraginta pedum sese cū noua præda recepit. Episcopus autem insoliti casus nouitate stupefactus, Nisum & lupum futuris sæculis memorabilem, vndecimo Kalendas Nouembris, Iohanni Comiti transmisit.

De morte Reginaldi Cantuariensis electi.

ANno Dominicæ Incarnationis. M.C.XCII. Reginaldus Bathoniensis episcopus, à Monachis Cantuariensibus in Archiepiscopum electus, decursis à die denominationis eius quadraginta 'noue' dieb⁹, Natiuitatis Domini die, diem clausit extremum. Sepultus est autem Bathoniæ in ecclesia sua, prope maius altare.

Vt Rex Franc̄ corum de peregrinatione Parisios venerit.

PEr idem tempus, Rex Francorum à peregrinatione rediēs, sexto Kalēdas Ianuarij, Parisiis solemni processione receptus est.

Quomodo Rex Richardus Darum ceperit.

EOdem anno, post Paschalem solemnitatem, Rex Richard⁹ Darum adījt Castellum Christianitatis vltimum versus Babyloniam, quod diebus quinq̄ obsidens, armata manu coepit, atq̄ obsessos graui pretio redemptionis abire permisit.

Vt Rex Richardus septem millia cætmelos opibus onustos cepertit.

POst hanc victoriam, venit ad Regem Anglorum Dux Burgundiæ cum Francorum militia, cui authoritate Regis Frācorum præerat, quasi dux & custos summus. Cui etiam in præcedenti solemnitate dederat Rex Richard⁹ triginta millia Bisanciorum, vt fideliter staret cum eo, ad expugnādum hostes Christi, & consilio inito, statuerunt irrefragabiliter Hierosolymam adire. Cumq̄ Rex Richardus cum vniuerso exercitu suo peruenisset ad Castrum Ernaldi & Bethonoble iuxta Emaus, ecce quidam Bedewini, qui se Regi obligauerant, nunciant maximam multitudinem negotiatorū

ex

Figure 10.5 (cont.)

descend from the *Chronica maiora*. The smaller addition taken from Nero D V is much more in keeping with the original manuscript presentation: the text is in two columns and summary rubrics appear at each new section with the display initials. This addition does, though, show the influence of print on the scribe. The rubrics are not included as part of the normal text block, as they were in most medieval manuscripts; instead, they float in a separate gap between the sections of text.

This suggests two possibilities. Either the scribe was not experienced in including rubrics in text, so left too much space and then just centred the rubrics, like in a print edition, or he deliberately chose to present it in this way; from the erratic sizes of the spaces left in the text block the former seems most likely. Although the second addition to CCCC 16 lacked much of the original medieval character, enough remains to see trace elements of the original manuscript design. Collectors like Parker and William Cecil had forgers on their staffs and most additions in medieval manuscripts demonstrate an attempt to match features like the script, although usually without much success.[54] In this instance, both sections clearly show the scribe was copying the layout of the exemplar from which they were working, rather than trying to adapt the material from the exemplar to the design of the *Chronica maiora* manuscript into which they were adding text. As one scribe wrote both sections, it would have been possible to create a unified look had that been the desire or had they had the skill to deliver it, yet this was not the case. Instead the influence of the exemplar can be seen. It is easier and quicker to copy that which is in front of one's eyes, which explains why transmission of design can be traced not only through complete manuscripts, but also later additions, and it is a further tool we can use to understand how collectors have adapted, altered and updated their manuscript collections.

A variety of sources were also used for creating contemporary manuscripts in the sixteenth century, and newly created manuscripts were produced during this time to expand the antiquarian collections. As with the additions to manuscripts, printed editions were considered a valuable exemplar for these contemporary manuscripts too, yet this use of hybrid sources by the manuscript producers has proven challenging to unpick. In many instances manuscripts copied from printed editions have been misidentified in later scholarship and instead connected to the manuscript exemplar of the printed edition. Frederick Madden, for instance, suggested that Cambridge, Corpus Christi College, MS 56 (CCCC 56) was a transcript of the *Historia Anglorum* (Royal MS 14 C VII), but it is actually a fusion of material copied from manuscript and print exemplars.[55] The manuscript contains several ownership marks, including Parker's *signa* on folio 1ʳ, which deliberately mimics the opening page of Parker's printed editions of these historiographical manuscripts.⁵⁶ A large portion of the manuscript may have been copied by one scribe from Royal 14 C VII: marginal annotations have been added and *signa* are included at appropriate points to signify the death or coronation of a monarch or noble, and these are not present in the printed edition. On folio 77ᵛ there is a copy of an illustration found at the bottom of folio 42ᵛ in Royal 14 C VII depicting the Templar seal of two knights riding on one horse posed next to a standard. Yet despite this section seeming to be a direct copy from the Royal manuscript, the influence of print is evident. Instead of creating rubrics with red ink, text is highlighted either by space on the page or by using thicker, bolder and bigger (but still black) script: all these approaches were created by printers to highlight text while saving on time and money by not using a different colour, which would have required a separate form for colour pages, doubled the time required and was a challenge to align correctly.⁵⁷ Print was changing how people approached the manual production of books, familiarising their audience with a different visual language that was then carried through into contemporary manuscript production.

Six entire quires in CCCC 56 were not copied from Royal 14 C VII at all, but from the 1571 printed edition, evident in the adoption of a particular layout and design features.⁵⁸ For example, during these sections the same marginal notations appear next to the text block that summarise what that section is about (not present in the original manuscripts). We also see the use of a running head (f. 145ʳ), and decorative line fillers (fols. 159ᵛ–64ᵛ). On folio 144ᵛ a short passage mimics the indented text found in the printed edition, although the final line was missed, and the marginalia are also identical; CCCC 56 therefore had two different exemplars. This manuscript is representative of book culture at the end of the sixteenth century: the combination of a traditional manuscript exemplar from a monastic library interspersed with sections copied from the printed edition, which was considered just as legitimate a source. As only one incomplete manuscript of the *Historia Anglorum* exists, without the addition of sections copied from the printed book CCCC 56 would be an imperfect copy, and this was not desirable. The printed edition was more accessible than the *Historia Anglorum* manuscript, both visually and geographically, and covered much of the same material whilst supplementing historiography with additional content. If anything, this marked the printed edition out as superior. Much as with the later additions to the *Chronica maiora* manuscript, then, continuity of design from exemplar to manuscript allows us to unpick the sequence of production. What is most interesting about CCCC 56 is that it demonstrates the change in attitude towards increasingly viewing printed texts as more authoritative sources than an original manuscript.

The interaction between medieval and contemporary book production in the late sixteenth century demonstrates how the advent of print shifted attitudes towards books quite significantly, at least with learned texts. The design of a printed book was established by the printer with inspiration from the original medieval source material, but once that was in place there was no need to change it, unless it was of practical or financial benefit for the printer themselves. Although antiquarians dabbled in their own manuscript production – an early form of living history that enabled them to better share collections – at no point do they seem to have considered, in the manner of their medieval predecessors, that they themselves as scribes could completely alter the manuscripts' design or presentation. Scribes no longer thought about book production in the same way as their medieval forebears – colour, decoration and marginalia gave way to space, font size and line numbers – and even when producing handwritten books this influence was evident. These were characteristics that became the norm through the consumption of printed books, where such changes were introduced as practical, cost-effective solutions. More significantly, though, the examples shown in this chapter demonstrate a real shift in what was considered an authentic source during this period. The edited printed editions appear to have been preferred as sources to the medieval originals, which may in part have been due to their availability. Manuscript books in this context became less of a freely creative space and place for exploring ideas, as Paris and his peers had regarded them in the thirteenth century, and more just a vessel for information. The work of Matthew Paris, then, had shifted over the course of 300 years, from being at the cutting edge of creative approaches to presenting information in the Middle Ages, to later being reinterpreted in very conventional and convenient means. In many respects, then, the early modern interaction with Paris' work produced manuscripts that were the antithesis of the purpose of the medieval originals.

This chapter has revealed the importance of design for understanding not only the first formation of a medieval manuscript but also the process of its transmission and reception as it passed from one reading context to another. Just as modern objects are carefully considered and their design tailored to usage and audience, so too were medieval manuscripts, and Matthew Paris' manuscripts were particularly significant in this sense. Although manuscripts were always unique, very rarely were moulds truly broken and real difference introduced at a scribal level. When this happened, as was the case with Paris' work, there should be a pause to carefully consider why, for whose benefit and for what purpose such singularity was demonstrated. Design allows us to see the intention hidden behind the creative display. Paris was actively involved in the creative community at St Albans and looked for new ways to present existing formats. In this instance Matthew Paris' richly illustrated *Chronica maiora* manuscripts were themselves intended as a treasure of St Albans Abbey, while his other manuscripts served different purposes depending on their design and interrelationship with other content in the monastic library. Design, then, provides an alternative view as to how to perceive the manuscript corpus attached to Matthew Paris and encourages us to look again at the traditions that are less visually arresting. Paris was redefining and experimenting with format and structure in his works with a view to creating historiography in a format accessible to a wider audience, but against such a background the *Flores historiarum*, the source historiographical tradition, has been lost. Yet a design methodology with the *Flores* corpus, of which one case study has been looked at here, illuminates the vibrant intellectual networks within which St Albans sat. Paris' works may not have continued to enjoy such creative reimaginings in the later iterations, but by this point in time the audience for Paris' work had significantly narrowed and the reason for creative solutions was no longer required. Manuscript and book design should therefore be considered an essential part of manuscript analysis, and charismatic individuals like Matthew Paris, who were prolific in their work and had a lasting legacy, provide an opportunity to greater understand the shifts and changes in book production and consumption over large periods of time.

Notes

1. Walker 1990, 23, 28.
2. Walker 1990, 22–37. For a wider definition of design see Kirkham and Weber 2013; Margolin 2017.
3. The content of this chapter draws in part upon material presented in my PhD thesis: Coatesworth 2021.
4. Mak 2011; Doležalová 2012; Kwakkel, McKitterick and Thomson 2012; Wakelin 2017; Kwakkel 2018.
5. Bately 1988; Nix 1994; Schipper 2003.
6. Martin and Vezin 1990; Chartier 1995; Hellinga 2010.
7. Tschichold 1928; Bringhurst 2005.
8. Approximate dates of manuscript production are given in brackets. Cambridge, Corpus Christi College: MS 264 (1345–1400), and Trinity College: MS R. 4. 2 (635) (1375–1425); London, British Library: Arundel MS 96 (1285–1300), Cotton MS Claudius E. VIII (1395–1400), Cotton MS Cleopatra A. XVI (1375–1450), Cotton MS Nero D. II (1300–50), Cotton MS Otho B. V (1350–1400), Cotton MS Otho C. II (1325–1400), Harley MS 641 (1350–1425), and Royal MS 14. C. VI (1305–30); Lambeth Palace: MS 188 (1200–1425) and MS 1106 (1310–45); Westminster Abbey: MS 24 (1310–30); Manchester, Chetham's Library: MS 6712 (1235–1300); Yale, Beinecke Library: MS 426 (1400–50); Oxford, Bodleian Library: MS Additional C. 22 [lost], MS Bodley 912 (1310–60), MS Douce 207 (1300–25), MS eMuseo 149 (1305–30), MS Fairfax 20 (1325–50), MS Hatton 53 (1310–60), MS lat. hist. d. 4 (1320–50), MS Laud. Misc. 572 (1295–1310), MS Rawlinson B 177 (1310–50), MS Rawlinson B. 186 (1375–1400); Paris, Bibliothèque nationale de France: MS Latin 6045 (1300–50); San Marino (California), Huntington Library: MS HM 30319 (1400–50); Windsor, Eton College: MS 123 (1300–20) and Oxford, All Souls' College: MS 37 (1375–1425). One of the manuscripts is now in private ownership but was formerly Dublin, Chester Beatty Library: Chester Beatty MS 70. By all accounts, this is a presentation-grade manuscript with rich illuminations. See also Chapter 15, 302, 307–8
9. Carpenter 2012b.
10. Vaughan 1953c, 384, 389–90.
11. Vaughan 1958c, 34; Gransden 1974b, 359, 364; Carpenter 2012b, 1355–56; Coatesworth 2021, 37–89.
12. Collard 2008, 444–45.
13. Gransden 1975, 370; Collard 2008, 452.
14. Spiegel 1983, 47–48; Kauffmann 1984; Sekules 2001, 126–30.
15. Chetham's MS 6712, Eton MS 123; London, British Library Cotton MS Nero D II and Arundel MS 96.

16. Luard 1890, xii–xvi, xxxv–xliii; iii. xiv–xix; Tout 1916, 450–64; Gransden 1974a, 439–41, 453–63, 473–74, 481–88.
17. Collard 2008, 443–44, 453.
18. Gransden 1974a.
19. Vaughan 1958c, 97.
20. Hawks 2023, 186–92.
21. Collard 2008, 441.
22. Hawks 2023, 186–87.
23. Hawks 2023, 179.
24. Folio 250^v. See also Luard 1890, i. xvii.
25. Gransden 1974a, 473.
26. Lewis 1987, 31–42.
27. London, British Library, Royal MS 14 C VII.
28. Wormald 1926; Marks and Morgan 1981; Lewis 1987; Collard 2010.
29. Gaudio 2000; Connolly 2009; Weiss 2013, 243–52.
30. Vaughan 1953b.
31. Sharpe 2003, 75.
32. Galbraith 1911; Galbraith 1944; Vaughan 1958c; Gransden 1974b, 356–79; Lewis 1987; Given-Wilson 2004; Connolly 2009; Weiler 2009.
33. Vaughan 1958c, 125.
34. Lewis 1987, 35–39; Collard 2010; de Laborderie 2013, 187–90.
35. García 2018, 127–29.
36. Lewis 1987, 45, 49–50.
37. T. Bradwardine, 'De memoria artificiali [On Artificial Memory]', Appendix C in Carruthers 1992, 282–83.
38. Kerr 2007, 17, 167–70.
39. García 2018.
40. Hunt 1978, 251; Thomson 1982, i. 5.
41. De Laborderie 2013, 187–90.
42. Vaughan 1958c, 66.
43. De Laborderie 2013, 70–75.
44. Keynes 1993. For Matthew's itinerary maps see also Chapter 12, 251–53.
45. BL Royal MS 13 E VI was produced at the beginning of the thirteenth century and would have been available when Paris compiled his manuscripts. Vaughan 1958c, 129; Gransden 1974b, 364; Lewis 1987, 43–45, 66–71; Martin and Thomson 2008, 401, 406.
46. BL Cotton MS Nero D I, fols. 30–73; BL Cotton MS Otho D III; Chatsworth House, Devonshire Collection Archives, St Albans Abbey Cartulary.
47. Nero D I, folios 171^r–172^r. For more on the heraldry see Wagner 1950, 1–3; Tremlett and Stanford London 1967, 2–86.
48. Vaughan 1958c.
49. BL Cotton MS Claudius D. VI, fol. 10^v and CCCC MS 26, fol. iv^v.
50. De Laborderie 2013; Collard 2024.

51. Lutz 1975; Janssen 2011.
52. Levy 1967, 80, 101–03, 117–23; Carley 2002, 339–43; Carley 2004, 96; Heal 2005, 111–15, 118, 128; Barr and Selwyn 2006, I. 367, 371–73.
53. [Matthew Paris] 1571. The section copied is from 211–27.
54. Page 1993, 7–8, 46–48; Graham 2006, 328–31.
55. Madden 1866–69, i. lxix–lxx.
56. Page 1993, 8.
57. For more on colour printing see Stijnman and Savage 2017.
58. Folios 123^r–71^v.

11

Matthew Paris and Heraldry

Heraldry owes an enormous debt to Matthew Paris, our first known compiler of coats of arms and our earliest heraldic artist. He was the right man, in the right place, at the right time to achieve both feats: an acute observer of life, an enthusiastic collector and recorder of information and a skilled artist. Heraldry (hereditary shield emblems) had existed in England for just over a century and had established its own technical language of description – blazon – so that shield designs could be accurately recorded and reproduced. This was normally in French, though Paris also uses Latin. If his blazons sometimes seem inadequate, we must remember that this monk of St Albans was one of the first to use blazon in such a comprehensive manner and that it was still in its infancy.

By the time Paris was writing in the mid thirteenth century, coats of separate families or lordships could be combined on one shield. This allowed heraldry to symbolically reflect a variety of family relationships and alliances. Paris provides us with possibly the first depiction in this country of a quartered coat: the castle of Castile quartering the lion of Leon. He also portrays a very early crest (upon a helmet) of a hammer for the Marshal family, plus some very early examples of a 'differenced' coat where the arms have been slightly altered to denote a close relationship or affinity to another coat.

Paris' heraldry is dispersed throughout his chronicles, though his earliest examples are probably contained in a single sheet of forty-two painted arms in his *Liber additamentorum*. This dates to in or before

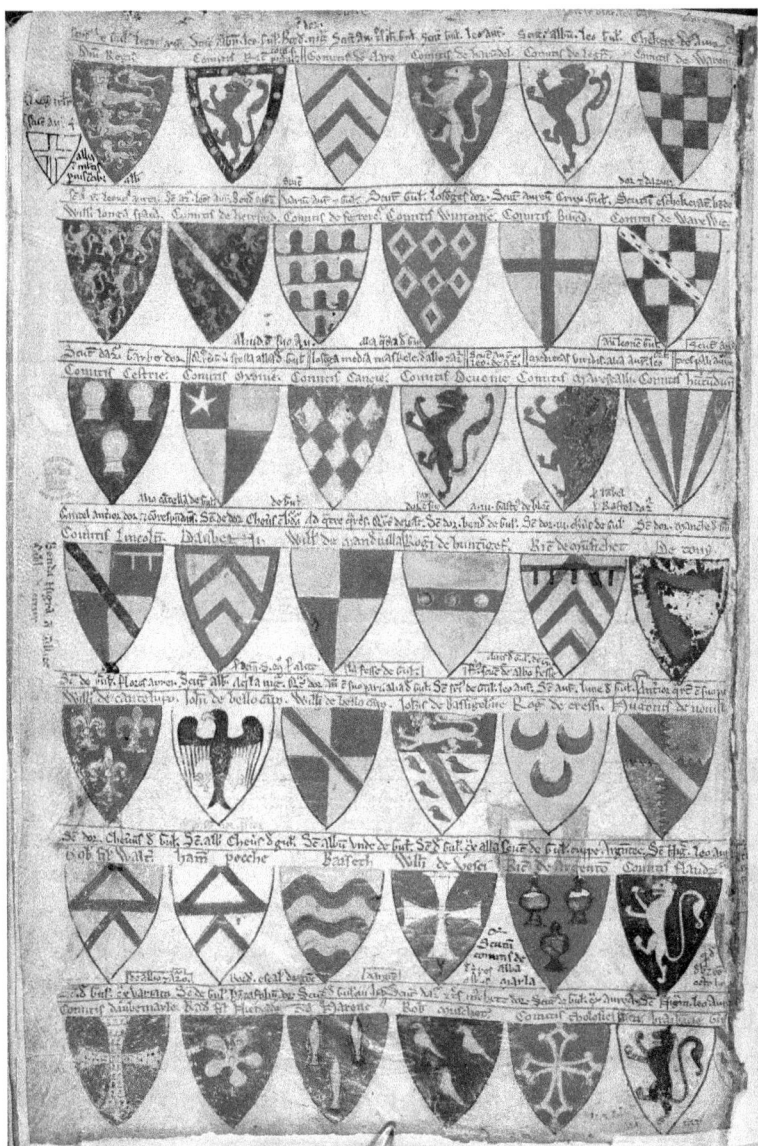

Figure 11.1 Heraldry in Matthew Paris' *Liber additamentorum*, British Library, Cotton MS Nero D I, fol. 171ᵛ. © British Library

1244 when Paris was in his mid-forties and had been a monk of St Albans for nearly thirty years. It is not known why he drew up these particular rows of painted shields, maybe as a reference tool for later works. Each shield is identified and blazoned beginning with the three lions passant guardant of Henry III, followed by his brother, the Earl of Cornwall, the other earls, and then knights. This armorial hierarchy was later used in other so-called rolls of arms (though Paris does not use long rolls of parchment), so it is just possible he copied them from another source. For now, however, the Matthew Paris shields in his *Liber additamentorum* and elsewhere remain our oldest English medieval roll of arms (see Figure 11.1).

Most of the 143 different coats of arms attributable to some 400 persons that Paris drew or painted feature in the margins of his later chronicles. Here they signalled the presence of an important event or person in the adjacent text. Of the 72 British coats, 27 appear for the first time. Reversed shields denote the death of their owner and one shield is rent asunder to symbolise the degradation of its owner.

If Paris was well placed in time he was also well placed in space. A visitor's book to his monastery at St Albans, a day's journey from London on the main road to the north, would have read like a current who's who. Not least amongst his various informants was the king himself, a frequent visitor. Nor was he isolated from the world outside. He may have studied in Paris and was very probably present at the marriage of Henry III and Eleanor of Provence at Westminster Abbey in 1236, and at York in 1251 for the wedding of their daughter, Margaret, to Alexander III of Scotland; both events would have been replete with heraldry. In 1248 he famously visited Norway and he includes the arms of Haakon IV.

Paris was clearly interested in heraldry. On two occasions he explains what he believed was the rationale behind a shield design. The first is that William I bore three lions because he was a king, duke [of Normandy], and ruler [*gubernator*] of England. William in fact never used this or any heraldic device since he predated heraldry. Paris' explanation owes more to his fertile imagination and weakness for a good story. His reasoning that Emperor Otto IV combined the lions of England with the imperial eagle 'for love of the king of England' is, however, probably true.

Paris drew or painted virtually all his shields, effortlessly recreating the cartoon-like character of heraldic birds and beasts with a few deft strokes of the pen. When towards the end he handed those tasks over to an assistant, the standard of artwork declined dramatically.[1]

Note

1. All the shields have been described and edited by Tremlett see *Aspilogia* 1967, 3–86. See also Vaughan 1958c, 250–53 and Lewis 1987, 174–81. To compare Paris' shields with other contemporary examples, refer to Woodcock, Chesshyre, Grant, Graham and Flower (1992–2014), where the arms are listed by shield design and indexed by name of owner; all four volumes should be checked to cover variations in design and use of two or more different coats by the same person.

12

Matthew Paris and His Maps

Matthew Paris has an important place in the history of mapping in the Middle Ages. Even the names of most medieval map-makers are unknown, and there is none before Leonardo da Vinci of whose life and work we know so much. To those who use his chronicles as a source for the history of his own time, the maps may seem a very minor adjunct to his work; in Richard Vaughan's seminal book on Matthew, discussion of the maps occupies no more than one of the four sections of the concluding chapter on his 'Other interests' beyond the chronicles, along with historical writing, lives of saints and artistic work.[1] However, in the history of cartography his maps are of great interest, for they throw an important light on the way maps were created and viewed by a highly inventive person of the thirteenth century, a man skilled in graphics.

The complete list of Matthew's maps is quite short: fourteen items representing seven constructs that we would call maps. They are:

a map of the Holy Land (the 'Oxford map')
a map of the world
a map of Britain ('map D')
another map of Britain in three versions ('maps A–C')
a map of the main Roman roads in Britain
another map of the Holy Land in three versions (the 'Acre map')
a strip map of the route from London to Apulia in four versions.

They are nearly all to be found in the pages of graphic material that are prefixed to the three manuscripts that contain his *Chronica maiora* and *Historia Anglorum*. However, they are not physically linked to the texts of the chronicles; in each case these introductory pages form a quire by themselves, added at the front at the volume. This means that we cannot use their association with the particular text as a guide to dating any of the maps, nor even to putting them in sequence. Nor are they linked intellectually to the chronicles: while inevitably many places mentioned in the texts are shown on one or other of the maps, there is no detailed correspondence. Many places named in the chronicles do not appear on the maps and vice versa.

We should see the maps, as Matthew himself must have seen them, in the same light as the other drawings prefixed to the chronicles: genealogical tables, church calendars, wind roses, portraits of the kings of England. They were all illustrations that would be relevant and interesting to the chronicles' readers. He will not have seen the maps as we do, in a class different from the rest; they were just topographical diagrams, one sort of diagram among others. Still less should we imagine – as has been proposed – that they contain sophisticated inner meanings, hidden messages in the manner of a Renaissance painting. However important the maps may be to modern historians of cartography, Matthew himself would probably say that Richard Vaughan is absolutely right: they are just one among many graphic forms that seized his imagination and his interest.

To see why they are important to historians of cartography we must see them in the context of other maps of the time. It cannot be too strongly stressed that medieval Europe was a society that managed almost entirely without maps of any kind. Whether a sketch map of a couple of fields or the line of a route, or the geographic outlines of countries or continents, they were most exceptional productions. Most people in thirteenth-century England will never have seen a map, nor will have had any clear idea of what a map was. Viewing Matthew's maps in this light, it is interesting to consider just what other maps he saw or may have seen, what lay behind the maps he drew, what gave him the ideas for them. To do this is to cast no doubt whatever on his originality and ingenuity; in the way he thought graphically he was a man of extraordinary imagination and inventiveness, and no part of his work shows this more clearly than the maps. But other maps he saw will have given him ideas and, indeed, in one way or another will have contributed to his own maps. We shall look at four different kinds of maps that he saw or may have seen – of two we can be certain, of the other two we can only guess.

Regional Maps

There can be no doubt that Matthew saw a regional map of the Holy Land because he copied it, and we know it only through his copy, the 'Oxford map', so called because it is in a manuscript belonging to Corpus Christi College, Oxford.[2] This is a Bible written at St Albans, partly, indeed, by Matthew himself, but although the parchment sheet with the map on it is bound into this volume, it is independent of it, a quite separate production. The heavy frame lines that dominate the map have nothing to do with it; they show through from the other side of the parchment, where they frame a pair of pictures of Christ's Deposition from the Cross and of the three Marys at the Sepulchre. These pictures were what was first drawn on the piece of parchment; they date from about the 1140s and are far from negligible as works of art. However, for whatever reason, they seem to have been discarded and the back of the parchment put to other uses. First, the sheet was folded into four, and one quarter used to copy two texts (in two hands, neither of them Matthew's) relating to a meeting of prelates and lay magnates at Westminster in March 1246. This left three quarters of the back of the parchment blank, and it was this L-shaped area that Matthew used to copy the map.

The oddness of the shape may explain some of Matthew's difficulties in copying. North is at the top, so the Mediterranean coast stretches along the left-hand side of the map. On the right, however, Matthew at the north end of the map had only half the space he had at the south end. It looks as if he first entered Damascus, with the Rivers Abana and Pharpar, as far to the right as he could at the top end of the map, then, filling in the other details between Damascus and the sea, found this did not give him enough room; he had to make the twin sources of the Jordan, the Jor and the Dan, flow through Damascus, adding a note that they did not really do this and should have been drawn nearer the coast.[3] This miscalculation affected the rest of the Jordan, so that the Sea of Galilee and the Dead Sea are both drawn too far to the south. However, from this point, the north end of the Sea of Galilee, the map exuberantly expands eastwards on to a still blank quarter of the parchment. The result is a pretty peculiar map, and we should see it not as Matthew's end product, but rather as a sketch from which he presumably intended to make a fair copy, a properly finished map of the Holy Land.

Whether he ever did this we do not know. It looks very much as if he had access only for a limited time to the map he copied; his copy shows every sign of having been drawn in haste on the first piece of discarded parchment he could lay his hands on. It is in the north-west corner that we are given most information – the distance between places in days' journeys, the sees of bishoprics, monasteries with their orders identified – and as we move from top left to bottom right it gets progressively sketchier. Throughout the map each place named is categorised as *civitas* (a town), *casella* (a village) or *castellum* (a castle), but these words are increasingly abbreviated to the ambiguous *cas* or even just to *c*, and a note that Matthew added to the map may be interpreted as a reminder to himself that *c* by itself stood for *civitas*. In the south-east quarter haste almost gave way to panic as the names of three Midianite rulers were turned into towns with a line around each and the letter *c*. In the Dead Sea three of the cities of the plain, Sodom, Gomorrah and Soar, are named, but the other two, Admah and Zeboiim, are just 'another', 'another' (*alia, alia*); perhaps Matthew found these less familiar names hard to read and left them to be looked up afterwards – he may well have been working in a bad light.

It is likely that the map Matthew copied was a very fine production. It will have been the only medieval regional map of Palestine known to us that was oriented to the north instead of the east, and we may guess that it was drawn and painted on parchment or cloth, so giving it portrait rather than landscape format would make it easier to hang on the wall. We may be fairly sure that Matthew's distinction between town, village and castle reflected not wording on the original map but three different symbols; a quite unrelated earlier map of Palestine uses two symbols to distinguish places, one of them coloured gold.[4] Where Matthew saw this map or who owned it we can only guess. He may well have seen it on a visit to Westminster Abbey or some other monastery, but one attractive possibility – again the merest guess – is that it belonged to King Henry III as a furnishing of his travelling household and that

Matthew saw it on one of the king's visits to St Albans; we know that some fifty years later Henry's son Edward I owned a world map that for a few years travelled with him as he moved around the country.[5] Matthew cannot have made his copy before 1246, the date of events already noted on the parchment, but it is not impossible that it introduced him to cartography, to the idea of a map; what few indications we have of the dates of Matthew's maps point to the later years of his life.

However, it seems more likely that Matthew was already familiar with the maps showing the whole of the inhabited world that were being drawn in thirteenth-century England and France, and he may have recognised that the basis of the map of Palestine was an extract from a world map. This will have provided coastal outlines, mountains, rivers and the principal towns, while further details will have been added from an account of the Holy Land that was circulating in several versions and in many manuscripts in the early thirteenth century.

World Maps

We have one world map in Matthew's own hand, and even if we had no other evidence we would know that he had seen not one but several world maps, because he tells us about them in a note that he added later to this map.[6]

> The layout of the world map of Master Robert of Mentley and of the world map at Waltham is set out in summary form. The world map of the king in his room at Westminster is shown in the ordinal of Matthew of Paris. Indeed, however, it is shown in that ordinal that it is like a cloak spread out. This is the shape of our habitable part according to the philosophers, that is, it is one quarter of the earth that is nearly triangular, for the body of the earth is spherical.

This calls for some explanation. Certainly, though, the concluding sentences are clear. It is a modern myth that the Middle Ages imagined the earth was a flat disc; educated persons then knew it was a sphere, but they thought it was rather smaller than it really is and that the tropical zone around the equator was so hot that no one could pass through it, so that the known inhabited world occupied only half of the northern hemisphere. This could be seen, inaccurately, as a triangle on the surface of the sphere and when projected on to flat parchment it would take the form of a semicircular cloak. Some medieval maps were drawn showing the habitable world in just that shape.

The king's map in his palace at Westminster was presumably part of the scheme of mural decoration in what was known as the painted chamber, on which work began in 1236.[7] It is unlikely that this map was itself in the shape of a cloak spread out, but Matthew's note could imply that he adapted it to this shape in the copy he made for the service book. It may seem an odd adornment for a liturgical book, but we have a miniature world map in a psalter produced at London in about 1265 and it has been suggested – though this can be only a guess – that this, like Matthew's map, was copied from the map in the painted chamber.[8] Certainly the psalter map is a miniature version of a circular world map of a style that developed in England and northern France in the twelfth and thirteenth centuries: coasts, rivers, mountains and cities formed a framework for pictures and inscriptions that presented a mass of miscellaneous information, on birds and beasts, mythological and biblical events, strange peoples and customs, making the map a kind of encyclopaedia arranged geographically. While we have a very few maps of this kind in books, drawn small to fit on the page, the genre consisted primarily of large sheet maps on parchment or cloth or, as in the king's room, painted on a wall.

Large sheet maps of any period have only a small chance of survival, and only one of these world maps remains to us, the map of about 1300 in Hereford Cathedral, a single sheet of parchment five and a half feet high and four and a half feet broad.[9] Another survived until 1943, when it was destroyed in an air raid on Hanover, but it has been carefully reconstructed from all available evidence. Some four times the size of the Hereford map, on thirty pieces of parchment, it was of about the same date but had probably been copied from a map of about 1240; it came from the nunnery of Ebstorf in Lower Saxony.[10] Of others we have only a draft or fragments or chance references in contemporary sources, and it is only through Matthew that we know of the map at Waltham Abbey and the map of Robert of Mentley, who was a clerk of the king and rector of Clothall, some seventeen miles from St Albans.[11] But it seems likely that there were quite a number of these maps in thirteenth-century England – perhaps not hundreds, for every one was the result of a great deal of work, but probably several dozen.

We can construct no line of development, no table of relationships, to link the few maps known to us, but we can infer that map-makers drew on what seems to be a common pool of information; within the basic outlines each seems to be a patchwork made up of details of which some appear in one map, some in another.[12] Thus in the map of Palestine that Matthew copied – itself developed from a world map – a bird is perched on Mount Gilboa; neither the Bible nor any other source provides a reason for this, but the same bird appears again on Mount Gilboa on a draft world map of English or northern French origin that is in Vercelli Cathedral in north Italy, and it may well be the same bird in different guise that appears on the Hereford map on the borders of the Holy Land as a phoenix. This does not mean that these three world maps were copied one from another; it is just that a bird on a mountain in Palestine was one of innumerable features that the map-maker, creating a map with more than one existing map as a model, might or might not copy into his new map.

We see the same phenomenon in the map of the Holy Land that Matthew designed himself, his 'Acre map', dominated by a plan of Acre disproportionately large; here too he took material from a world map and supplemented it from other sources that included the so-called Rothelin continuation of William of Tyre's chronicle of the crusades and probably first-hand information from some visitor to St Albans who was familiar with Acre. The Dead Sea is drawn with parallel lines across it, as though the River Jordan continued across it with uninterrupted flow – and we see just the same curious feature in the Sea of Galilee on the world map drawn about 1200 in a book that belonged to Sawley Abbey in Yorkshire. Again, there need be no direct relationship – it was just a feature that would turn up on one or another world map. Again, both on Matthew's Acre map and on the Ebstorf world map there is a two-humped camel east of Acre, but this could have arisen simply by chance, like the star at Bethlehem that appears on the same two maps or the crocodile on the Nile that Matthew's Acre map and the Hereford world map have in common.

In his four maps of Britain Matthew used the same technique: within a basic outline taken from a map of the world he added place names and further information taken from other sources. Certainly if we compare Matthew's outlines with those of Britain on the Hereford map or on the eleventh-century Cotton world map, drawn in a book, there is no obvious similarity, but when we look at these outlines point by point their relationships start to appear. On the Cotton map, as on Matthew's maps A, B and C, the Scottish coast slopes gently northwards from a point in the west, then straight along the northern shore, and, as on Matthew's maps A, C and D, the east coast slopes away from an inlet in southern Scotland, then in a straight line to the south-east tip of Britain. On the Hereford map, as on Matthew's maps A, C and D, Scotland is all but an island with a narrow land bridge while Wales is bounded by two deep inlets or rivers and, as on Matthew's map A, Cornwall is cut off by a narrow belt of water right across the peninsula. A map of the world was certainly the starting point for each of Matthew's maps of Britain, and it is most likely that map D, probably the first to be drawn, was based on one map, maps A, B and C on another.[13]

Itinerary Maps

It is beyond doubt that Matthew had seen at least one regional map and several world maps that he did not draw himself. It is possible that the regional map that he copied as his Oxford map of the Holy Land gave him the idea for his own regional maps: the Acre map of the Holy Land and his maps of Britain. However, in looking for a possible inspiration for his four itineraries, strip maps, from London to south Italy we are on much less sure ground.

They are a unique creation. While we are used to the idea of a map showing simply a single route, marking the places along it with names and pictures, people in the Middle Ages were not, and there is no known medieval parallel to Matthew's itineraries. Probably there is no need to look for a model or precedent: the written itinerary, listing places along a route, was a normal part of thirteenth-century life, and it would be entirely typical of Matthew's ingenuity and artistic imagination to present one in graphic form with little pictures of the towns, rivers and so on. It is not so different from the pictures and heraldry that he drew in the margins of his chronicles: we can see the same mind at work.[14]

All the same, we cannot help wondering whether Matthew may not have stumbled on something that gave him the idea – but what follows is the merest guesswork, just a remote possibility. The only detailed world map that we have from the Roman period is the Peutinger map, named after its sixteenth-century owners and now in the Austrian National Library in Vienna; drawn in or near south-west Germany in the twelfth century, it is copy of a map that probably originated around AD 300, with some slight revision in the ninth century. It is a map of routes covering the whole Roman Empire from, presumably, Britain in the west (its western end is lost) to India in the east. Lines with notes of distances join the staging points for journeys – cities, villages, inns and so on – that are marked with tiny pictures. It looks quite unlike any map we know, for everything has been compressed from north to south to turn it into a long strip, some twenty-three feet long and only fourteen inches deep; this has produced some strange juxtapositions, and while the places along each route are named in their correct order, the map is no guide to either direction or distance away from the drawn routes.

It has recently been shown that there was another copy of the Peutinger map, now lost, in fifteenth-century Padua, and Richard Talbert has suggested that there may have been a further copy in late medieval England; this could have provided the model – or inspiration – for the Gough map of Britain that likewise shows a system of routes, with distances marked, joining towns drawn as tiny pictures.[15] Like Matthew's itineraries, the Gough map has no known antecedent. The date of the Gough map is disputed; it was certainly later – probably very much later – than Matthew's itineraries, but we may wonder whether, if there was a copy of the Peutinger map in Britain when the Gough map was drawn, it was not there already when Matthew was at work at St Albans and that it was this that gave him the idea for his strip maps. That a copy of the Peutinger map might have found its way to England is perfectly possible: there were sufficient contacts between England and the part of the continent where our surviving copy originated. And that the copy in England should have failed to survive would be unsurprising; as we have seen, this has been the fate of most large maps in all ages. But while there is nothing impossible in all this, it can be no more than speculation, adding hypothesis to hypothesis. Matthew may well have seen a copy of the Peutinger map, but it is not necessary to assume he did in order to explain his strip maps – and even if he did, there is much in these maps that can have come only from Matthew himself.

Local Maps

Maps of any kind were rare in thirteenth-century Europe, but local maps, showing a limited area that the map-maker drew from his own knowledge, were all but unknown. From England we have only four that are earlier than the mid fourteenth century: a mid twelfth-century plan from Canterbury showing how water circulated in the Cathedral Priory, a diagram in the form of a cross of the Cistercian abbeys around Chester in about 1195, a plan of properties in Wildmore Fen in Lincolnshire that can be dated between 1224 and 1249 and a plan of the springs at Wormley in Hertfordshire that supplied water to Waltham Abbey, three miles away in Essex on the other side of the River Lea.[16]

This last is in a cartulary of the abbey, where it accompanies two written texts, the first a detailed account of how four skilled workers constructed the tanks that collected and cleaned the water at Wormley and laid the pipes along which it flowed to Waltham; this was in 1220–22 and the narrative was written soon after, or even while the work was still in progress. The second is a description of the works at Wormley: a tank into which the three springs fed, a pipe with perforated opening leading to another tank, whence one pipe, again with perforated opening, led to Waltham, another at the bottom of the tank was for draining sediment and a third, at the top, was an overflow pipe. This second text begins by saying, correctly, that all this is shown on the accompanying plan, and we can indeed see the text as explaining the plan rather than the plan as illustrating the text. Plan and description were probably composed later than the narrative, but not later than about 1230. However, what we have in the cartulary is a copy of the plan and the texts that probably dates from about the 1250s.[17]

We might reasonably say that all this has nothing to do with Matthew Paris and, indeed, there is not a shred of evidence to connect him with the plan of the Wormley springs. At the same time, Waltham is no more than fifteen miles from St Albans; we know that Matthew saw a world map there, and it is perfectly possible that he also saw this local plan. It is not even beyond the bounds of possibility that the plan was made at his suggestion; he entered St Albans in 1217 and by the late 1220s will have been well established there. In whatever role, he occasionally left his house: as early as 1220 he seems to have been at Canterbury for the translation of St Thomas Becket.[18] It is interesting, and may just possibly be significant, that one of our two local maps drawn in Matthew's lifetime comes from a neighbouring abbey that he is known to have visited.

In asking what maps Matthew will have seen, what maps may have contributed to the ideas behind his own maps, we have explored far beyond the known facts into areas of hypotheses, possibilities and guesses. It is hardly likely that they are all correct, but none of them is inherently unlikely. At the same time, there is no need for us to assume that Matthew needed any models or ideas other than those that sprang from his own imaginative and fertile mind. Whatever other maps he saw, his cartographic achievement is substantial and wholly original.

Notes

1. Vaughan 1958c, 235–50.
2. Oxford, Corpus Christi College, MS. 2* (formerly MS. 2), ff. 1v. 2r, most recently reproduced and discussed in Harvey 2012, chapter 7.
3. 'Istud propinquius est mari nec contingit damascum.'
4. Harvey 2012, chapter 5.
5. Harvey 2008, 52.
6. Cambridge, Corpus Christi College, MS. 26, f. vii verso, reproduced in Connolly 2009, plate II.
7. Brown et al. 1963–82, i. 495–97.
8. Described and reproduced by Peter Barber in Harvey 2006, 15–19.
9. Fully edited by Westrem 2001, reissued with the Folio Society's near-full-size reproduction, Harvey and Westrem 2010.
10. Reconstructed and fully edited by Kugler 2007.
11. Clutterbuck 1815–27, iii. 504; *CLR, 1260–7*, 64.
12. Discussed in Harvey 2006, 243–51.
13. Harvey 1992, 109–21.
14. The itinerary is described, illustrated and discussed by Vaughan 1958c, 247–50, plates XII, XIII, XV; Lewis 1987, 323–47; Connolly 1999, 598–622; Connolly 2009.
15. Dalché 2004, plates 1–3; Talbert 2010, 170–72.

16. The Chester diagram is published in Taylor 1912, frontispiece, 59; the other three are reproduced and discussed in Skelton and Harvey 1986, 43–81, plates 1–3.
17. BL Harley MS 391, fols. 1^r–6^r. The texts and plan are printed and discussed in Skelton and Harvey 1986, 59–70, plate 2.
18. Vaughan 1958c, 2–3.

MANUEL MUÑOZ GARCÍA

13

Matthew Paris as Scribe
Idiosyncrasy and Collaboration

The manuscripts of Matthew Paris are extraordinary in that for the most part, they were written and illustrated by the author himself.[1] There were other authors–scribes in medieval England – for example, William of Malmesbury (c. 1095–c. 1143) – but the combination of compiler, scribe and illustrator is quite unique.[2] The way Matthew Paris wrote, that is to say, his script, is also remarkable in that it is highly personal and displays a number of distinctive features that make it easy to identify while prompting debate on where it fits in the overall evolution of the style of formal script in thirteenth-century England. Particularly in his chronicle manuscripts, Paris was responsible for the entire production: compiling the text, writing most of it on parchment and illustrating it. This offers a rare opportunity to see a craftsman at work and to trace the development of his craft over time.

There are eighteen manuscripts that contain texts written in Matthew's hand, of which nine are his own works.[3] Well-known texts such as the *Chronica maiora*, *Historia Anglorum* or the *Life of St Alban* are among these nine, while the other texts, the work of other authors, bear witness to the wide-ranging interests of the St Albans polymath, including astrology, poetry, a Bible and different chronicle fragments.[4] In total, there survives the full text of five chronicles or abridgements of chronicles, six hagiographies (of which two are fragments), two works of local history, a genealogical tract and a collection of supporting documents for the *Chronica maiora*, called the *Liber additamentorum*.[5] These fifteen works offer us not only knowledge and insight, but also a unique opportunity to study the hand of Matthew Paris and its changes through time.

The way Matthew Paris has been studied has naturally shifted in post-medieval times. Up until the late nineteenth century, Paris – or rather, his works – were used and studied as historical sources, and the advent of printed editions perpetuated this concept. The first editions of some of Paris' works were published in the sixteenth and seventeenth centuries. The first to appear was Matthew Parker's edition of Paris' *Flores historiarum* in 1567, followed by a reprint in 1570; and of the *Chronica maiora* in 1571 (reprinted in 1589 and 1606).[6] The *Chronica maiora* was edited again by William Watts in 1641 (reprinted in 1644 and 1684).[7] The first partial translations of the *Chronica maiora* were published in 1841 and 1854, in French and English, respectively.[8] The nineteenth-century editions of Paris' works for the Rolls Series marked a turning point in the study of Matthew Paris' texts and manuscripts. Firstly, they introduced the reproduction of manuscript images in colour; secondly, they were prefaced by studies on each of the manuscripts, and also on Paris' life and more general discussions on authorship.

As part of the Rolls Series, H. R. Luard, F. Madden and T. D. Hardy produced the editions of the *Estoire de Seint Aedward le Rei*, *Chronica maiora*, *Flores historiarium*, *Historia Anglorum* and *Abbreviatio chronicorum*, which to this day are the only full editions available.[9] The Rolls Series editions started to address Matthew Paris as a scribe – even if as secondary to the study of the text – its sources and process of compilation. It was Luard who specifically discussed handwriting, identifying what he believed to be a 'St Albans hand'.[10] Matthew Paris had primarily been considered, in post-medieval times, as a historian and an author, and less as a scribe. The Rolls Series editions were the first step in understanding the handwriting of Paris' manuscripts, even though the editors assumed a relationship between handwriting and authorship that is problematic, in that Paris' hand appears in works that are not his.[11] The reproduction of Paris' hand in these editions, together with an indirect interest in the palaeography of his manuscripts, marked the first step towards a more comprehensive approach to the St Albans monk.

It was decades after the edition of Paris' works in the Rolls Series, in 1953, when the handwriting of Matthew Paris was newly reviewed and analysed under a different light. Richard Vaughan proposed a description of Paris' hand that would end the disputes that had started with the Rolls Series editors and had continued up to his own time.[12] Vaughan's intention with his article was twofold: he would provide an academic readership with a description of Paris' hand, while also listing and describing which manuscripts originating at St Albans contain this handwriting.[13] Apart from these, Vaughan also succeeded in settling the dispute over the attribution of certain manuscripts to Paris, particularly his hagiographies.

Vaughan's description of Matthew Paris' hand was a pioneering achievement in that it provided for the first time a guide to identify the hand and a list of manuscripts where it could be found. However, Vaughan's starting point was mainly the Rolls Series, and particularly Hardy and Madden's views on the attribution of some manuscripts to Paris. Vaughan set out to contest some of Hardy's conclusions by describing Paris' handwriting. However, as the author's method was to compare previous scholarship with his own findings, the description is done only from a comparative point of view. The general appearance of the script and letterforms are described, but the description omits important features. Vaughan's description of Paris' hand is based upon a description of aspect and of a number of characteristic letterforms (**a, d, g, s**), Tironian *et* and features of other letterforms such as the lobes of **b, p** and **g**; the shoulder of **r** and the ascenders of **b, h** and **l**.

Because Vaughan's description is based upon these principles, aspects of Paris' hand are not described, as they are not part of his 'general characteristics'. Apart from letterforms and Tironian *et*, Vaughan also provided a general description of Paris' *mise-en-page* and of his deployment of such features as rubrics and current titles. However, one of his major contributions in relation to Paris' hand is the acknowledgement of its evolution through time. This understanding of the evolution of the script led Vaughan to establish a relative chronology of Paris' manuscript. This idea was not new, since the Rolls Series editors identified some instances of Paris' hand as having been produced later in life based on changes in aspect. In this sense, Vaughan produced a more detailed description of the changes to the aspect of the hand, in the context of a general palaeographical and codicological description.[14] The description of Paris' hand and the acknowledgement of its changes through time was accompanied in 'The Handwriting of Matthew Paris' by some discussion on the participation of other scribes in Paris' manuscripts and an estimate of the number of hands that appear in them. This estimation – fifteen hands altogether – is not accompanied by descriptions.[15]

Vaughan's particular approach to Paris was expanded decades later by Suzanne Lewis' exhaustive visual study of the *Chronica maiora*. The physical study of the manuscripts initiated with the Rolls Series and taken further with Vaughan led to the study of Paris' next major output: art. From an art history point of view, Lewis' *The Art of Matthew Paris in the* Chronica maiora is still fundamental to understand Paris as an illuminator. Only few years earlier R. M. Thomson surveyed the manuscripts produced at St Albans between 1066 and 1235, which include some of Paris' manuscripts.[16] After Lewis, interest in Paris' manuscripts waned except for few publications related to his hagiographies.[17] As it happened, before Vaughan and Lewis the focus was on the content of Paris' works rather than the manuscripts, as Rebecca Reader's doctoral work shows in relation to Anglo-Saxon England and the Norman Conquest.[18] In 2004, a new entry for Matthew Paris in the *Oxford Dictionary of National Biography* gave an overview of Paris' scholarship until then, including manuscripts and script. A good number of publications dedicated directly or indirectly to Paris have appeared since, enriching our knowledge of Paris' relationship with art history, history writing, newsgathering and cartography, among other fields.[19]

The Hand of Matthew Paris: Characteristic Features

The period circa 1200–59 saw the development and consolidation of the Gothic scripts.[20] This is not to say that the Gothic scripts appeared in the thirteenth century. From the end of the eleventh century up to the early thirteenth century there was a transition between the script known as Caroline minuscule and the Gothic scripts. This period has been labelled the 'long twelfth century' and can be seen as a palaeographic dimension of the more widely known 'twelfth-century Renaissance' (1075–1225).[21]

In this transitional period, Caroline minuscule starts to show major changes in features and layout. As M. B. Parkes summarised, some of these changes are: changes to pen angle of writing, lateral compression, marking of serifs and feet, fusion of the lobes and stems of letters with opposing curves and changes in module and length of ascenders.²² Also, there is an increase in the differentiation between the handwriting used for documents and that used for books.²³ These changes that started to be apparent in Caroline minuscule have led to a large number of attempts to label it: the labels Late Caroline, Post Caroline, Early Gothic and Protogothic, among others, can be found in the literature, among which Littera Praegothica has been more successful.²⁴

In the 1220s there is a consolidated Gothic script known by the name Littera Textualis, Gothic Textualis or simply Textualis.²⁵ As can be expected, there are regional variants, named by Derolez Northern Textualis or Formata, and Southern Textualis or Rotunda.²⁶ Textualis, which started its evolution from high-quality copies of the Bible, is the most formal of the Gothic scripts.²⁷ Following G. I. Lieftinck's classification, we can identify the following Textualis key characteristics: two-compartment **a**, the ascenders of **b, h, k** and **l** without loops – that is, with flat tops – and **f** and straight **s** on the line without descenders.²⁸

New types of book scripts started to appear because of the will to write faster as well as changes in book production.²⁹ It is the birth of Gothic cursive scripts which, depending on the level of execution, can be either documentary or book scripts.³⁰ Again following Lieftinck, continental European cursive book scripts are characterised as having single-compartment **a**; loops at the right of ascender of **b, h, k** and **l**; and straight **s** and **f** with descenders dropping below the baseline.³¹ Derolez renames this 'cursive' Cursiva Recentior and adds a new category: Cursiva Antiquior, which displays a double-compartment **a**. In England, the variety of Cursiva Antiquior that developed towards the middle of the thirteenth century was named Anglicana by Parkes.³²

Anglicana – that is, English Cursiva Antiquior – is the only case in which Antiquior develops into a book script, something that can be seen from the middle of the thirteenth century and that is finalised circa 1270, lasting until the sixteenth century.³³ The most recognisable features of Anglicana are: the ascenders of **b, h, k** and **l**, which evolve from a hairline duplicating the top of the ascender of **f** and vertical **s** to bold ascenders ending in a loop to the right with an added horn to the left and a visible hairline, or marked forking; Caroline **a** with a large upper lobe, looping **d**, a small 8-like **g**, long **r** and sigma-like double-curve **s**.³⁴ This evolution of the Gothic scripts affects the way we can classify and understand Matthew Paris' hand, and also the hands of those who collaborated with him, as there are elements of Textualis and Cursiva – both Recentior and Anglicana – in them.

Matthew Paris' handwriting is both idiosyncratic and easily recognisable. Thus certain palaeographic elements are consistent throughout his manuscripts. However, Paris' hand is also quite variable. The overall appearance of his handwriting is spread out, uneven, lacking lateral compression, with a certain shifting of the axis of the letters that breaks the evenness of the lines. It is overall a hand that combines a relative morphological stability with variability of execution. Most importantly, it is a script that is neither Textualis nor Cursiva, but somewhere in between. Generally speaking, the hand tends to be more Cursiva than Textualis – and glosses or marginalia are much more cursive – but there is also a formal intention behind the main texts. This is a script that defies a definite label and rather shifts between the categories outlined previously in this chapter. However, following Derolez's classification – based on Lieftinck's – we can say Paris' script falls somewhere between Textualis and Hybrida.[35]

The most characteristic letterforms in Paris' hand are **a**, **g**, **d**, **e** and vertical **s**, which are the ones that present most variation. **a** is found in Caroline and round types: Caroline **a** shows some morphological variety from a well-proportioned letter to one with an exaggeratedly tall head curved at the top. This variation in shape and size can happen even in the same word, and it is this large head – often slanting to the left – that makes the identification of Paris' hand relatively easy. Round **a**, even though it is less common, also presents a certain variety, from a rounded type to a more angular version, or even one with the back protruding slightly above the lobe, which is often left opened.

g also displays a high degree of variability. The most common type joins the second and third strokes, forming an inverted-**s** shape that gives the letter a rounded appearance, resembling the shape of a flattened number eight. It can also present a more disjointed aspect, with the four strokes clearly visible, and some examples with a large loop to the left, similar to a Tironian *con*. These two types can be found regardless of the level of formality. Likewise, and echoing the case of **a**, **d** presents two different types, often appearing together in the same sentence or word. Uncial **d** can be found either with an angled ascender, or with a taller ascender curling to the right at the top, which when long closes in an enveloping stroke. The former tends to be used when the next letter has an opposite curve, as will be discussed later.

The next characteristic letterform in Paris' handwriting is **e**, the lobe of which can be disconnected from the main stroke, and/or the tongue. This gives the letter an open appearance, more of an elongated **c**. This upper body of the letter is also executed at times quickly, in a **z**-like stroke, making its overall appearance even more open, and – as in other letters – there is a certain tendency to angular shapes, particularly in the most cursive contexts. Lastly, vertical **s** often displays a particularity shared by other hands: the shaft has a protrusion to the left in the middle. The originality of this letterform is, however, the overall waviness of the shaft, creating what Vaughan called a 'broken-back appearance'.[36] The head is angular, and the shaft is generally footed. Although less common, double-curved **s** appears on occasion, particularly in final place, and it tends to either elongate the lower curve or substitute it with a downward stroke.

The combination of these features – from the exaggeratedly tall head of Caroline **a** to the Tironian *con*-like **g** – makes the script identifiable. These characteristics, together with the varying level of execution of the script, set the hand apart from contemporary scribes. Ascenders and descenders in Paris' script also play an important part in its overall definition. The ascenders of **b**, **h** and **l** are generally forked, which, added to the undulating of the vertical strokes, creates a sinuous effect. Also, the first line of writing on the page tends to have longer ascenders, but this is not always the case. **b**, **h** and **l** usually have forked ascenders on current titles and rubrics. However, the length and boldness of these forked ascenders do change, being generally smaller and thinner on notes and additions. Descenders also play a part, those of **h**, **x** and **p** – and also **g**, described above – being curved and sinuous, with the second stroke of **h** and **x** curving to the left. Letter **p**, on the contrary, curves to the right, creating a small but noticeable foot.

Other than specific letterforms, there are other aspects crucial to understanding the handwriting of Matthew Paris. In a script relatively lacking lateral compression like Paris', the way letters connect to each other becomes essential as these connections are less common. In 1897 Wilhem Meyer, through observation of Textualis script, summarised a number of fusion patterns between letters in order to date the development of the Gothic scripts.³⁷ Meyer's contribution continues to be highly influential, and the 'rules of Meyer' have been used as a conventional answer to the question of how fusions between letters work. However, they are not always followed, so their absence is not necessarily exceptional.³⁸

As discussed earlier in this chapter, Paris' hand varies greatly in execution, which affects the way fusions are carried out. In this sense, the degree to which his hand conforms to the rules of Meyer is relevant for the identification of the script, as the use of fusions in Paris' hand is uneven. The first rule – according to which two letters facing each other with opposing bows overlap – is not usually observed in Paris' hand. It is rarely observed when the first letter in the fusion is a **p** or a **d** – like in **po** or **do** – and other pairs do not usually fuse. The second rule – by which round **r** is used after a bowed letter – applies in most cases, particularly in **or** and **br**. The lack of fusions in Paris' hand is not a particularly striking aspect, considering that his script is not fully Textualis – to which the rules of Meyer are more strictly applicable – nor entirely cursive – where fusions of all types are commonplace. It is also relevant to note the presence of letters that, instead of sharing a central stroke, touch one another with their connecting strokes, forming what Erik Kwakkel calls 'kissing'.³⁹ Kwakkel associates the coexistence of both fusions and 'kissing' with the period before the full development of the Gothic script in the 1220s.⁴⁰ It is in the most formal hands in which fusions are more numerous, particularly in British manuscripts.⁴¹ However, the fact that Paris used fusions and 'kissing' between certain letters is remarkable as an identification feature, given that he continued to use fusions and 'kissing', simultaneously, beyond the 1220s.

Bearing in mind Paris died in 1259, the simultaneous use of fusions and 'kissing' until then makes the hand somewhat anachronistic. In the later Middle Ages, punctuation, which had been expressed through a great variety of symbols and systems, became more standardised. This meant most scribes used essentially four symbols: *punctus, punctus elevatus, punctus interrogativus* and *litterae notabiliores*.⁴² The *punctus* was the main punctuation mark and could indicate a pause, introduce a quotation, separate sections of text (as when distinguishing between

Roman numerals and letters), mark abbreviations and even introduce particular titles or names. The *punctus elevatus* and *punctus interrogativus* derive from the basic shape of the *punctus*, but indicate a more precise punctuation: *punctus elevatus* indicates a medial pause or colon, and the *punctus interrogativus* marks questions. Lastly, the *litterae notabiliores* were placed at the beginning of a *sententia* or paragraph, to differentiate it from the preceding text.[43]

The punctuation marks Matthew Paris used fit this general description, of which the *punctus elevatus* is the punctuation mark that shows most variation in shape. The *punctus* is usually found as a rounded dot at the base of the writing line, being used in all the aforementioned functions except for the introduction of names, when an initial, plain or coloured or with a splash of red or blue, is used instead. Against more formal hands, Paris' *punctus elevatus* is quite upwardly curved in its upper stroke or *virgula*, sometimes even resembling a reversed c.[44] However, there are instances in which the upper stroke looks more like a tick, more vertical than curved, but still within the usual shapes common in England in the first half of the thirteenth century.[45] The *punctus interrogativus* is present throughout Paris' manuscripts in its most recognisable shape: a dot and a diagonal upward stroke in the shape of a tight and slightly quadrangular s-like line. The second stroke is almost divided in two as the curve moves drastically from left to right, looking almost like an inverted ç. As with the other marks, the *punctus interrogativus* keeps a regular shape throughout the manuscripts in the corpus.[46]

As paragraph markers, Paris uses either coloured initials with pen flourishes (alternating red and blue), as in the *Historia Anglorum*, or just slightly enlarged letters with a splash of red or blue as in the *Chronica maiora*. Both systems are found working together, the flourished initials being used as paragraph markers and the highlighted letters as sentence markers. Both techniques are used together with rubrics, generally in red, and current titles, again alternating in colour. As rubrics became more important from the twelfth century, the traditional *notae* used as paragraph markers evolved and towards the end of the century the coloured *paraph* (¶) mark became commonplace.[47] Matthew Paris, however, used it mainly at the beginning of running titles in the verso of the folia. Its shape eliminates the lower stroke and instead extends the top stroke horizontally to the right, curving it at the end to the left.[48] The *paraph* is also used to introduce marginal additions to the main text. Although there are variants to this, as not all notes are introduced by a *paraph*, the marks ranging from none to diverse *signes de renvoi*.[49] Lastly, it is also used in lists of contents, such as in BL Nero MS D I, f. 166 r, as Vaughan observed.[50]

Rubrics, particularly in the manuscripts of the *Chronica maiora*, are used (in red) to introduce an episode or year, generally as part of the paragraph and on the right side. In comparison with the writing of the main text, rubrics show a slightly more disjointed handwriting, although in the same size. One of the signature features of Paris' rubrics, not described by Vaughan, is the curved line to the left filling the letter **D**, with which many of the titles begin. When the first letter of a rubric is not a **D**, it is generally a capital, and if it does have a tall ascender, it is prolonged and generally curved to the right.[51] There are instances in which Paris added a rubric to the margin, as there is no space in the text. In these cases, he would introduce it with a blue *paraph*.

Marginal notes in Paris' manuscripts are numerous, as the texts underwent a number of revisions. New information was added in the shape of notes that are introduced by *signes de renvoi* that refer to a specific place in the main text. If a block of text is being added, it is normally enclosed with wavy red lines. The shape of this text box varies from square to rectangular, or even trapezoidal. The use of *signes de renvoi* is rather common in Paris' manuscripts, and therefore understanding the way they work gives further grounds for identifying the script. There are two types of *signes* that can be found in Paris' manuscripts: the ones directing the reader to an addition, and the ones sending the reader to the *Liber additamentorum* (to be found only in the manuscripts of the *Chronica maiora*).[52]

Beyond letterforms, punctuation, rubrics and notes or additions, there is another aspect that is essential in defining handwriting: abbreviation. The way words are abbreviated reveals not only practices common at the time of writing, but also those common to the writer. Whether by contraction or by abbreviation sign, the patterns Paris followed when composing a text can be described and analysed to produce a list of the most idiosyncratic abbreviations that can aid identification and provide a better insight into Paris' graphic identity.

Starting with the most usual types of abbreviation, the general sign of abbreviation shows some variation throughout Paris' manuscripts, although it generally remains a line engrossed in the centre and with slightly curved ends. Although it is not a completely straight line, the curve is not too pronounced, although it sometimes starts to become diagonal towards the right. On the other hand, in less formal contexts – notes, additions, corrections – the general sign of abbreviation becomes much more pronouncedly curved, producing a nearly inverted **s** shape. Another abbreviation constant in shape and use is Tironian *et*, in the shape of a number seven, but with a small upward stroke, and ending in a foot to the right. The second stroke is always thick, which gives to the mark a bold appearance, and the diagonal third stroke slants to the left, right before the foot to the right. Even though it presents a stable shape, the level of cursivity of the text can make it look sharper, and the foot can be enlarged, almost connecting with the next letter. A rather important abbreviation sign in Matthew Paris' hand is Tironian *con*, which is generally written looping to the left, similar to his own looping **g**. Another Tironian sign is *est*, a horizontal stroke with two dots, one above and one below the stroke (which can sometimes be a comma), although this is not as commonplace as other types of abbreviation.[53]

Contractions occur frequently in Paris' handwriting, and they do so in the expected fashion.[54] Common words – like the demonstratives *ipse* and *iste*, pronouns, possessives and others like *omnis* – and *nomina sacra* are abbreviated by contraction on a regular basis, with a general sign of abbreviation over the word. Abbreviation marks other than the general sign of abbreviation are abundant in Paris' hand and they include a straight or slightly curved line for **m** or **n**; and a conventional crossed **r** for -*rum*. Also, and conventionally, the cursively traced **i** on top of letter **u** can be found in *ubi*. This superscript **i** can present a heavy serif stroke at the top left, which makes it resemble a number 7. Other signs include *us*, represented by an apostrophe-shaped symbol. Even though Paris' hand generally shows a great variety of letterforms, his abbreviation signs are quite stable. Other signs, more significant in context rather than by themselves, include the ones using **p** and **q**, like p*er*/p*ar*/p*or*, p*r(a)e* and p*ro*. This category includes the suspension sign for -b*us*, which can be either a distinct semicolon or a 3-like stroke that goes just below the baseline. A different category of abbreviation widely used by Paris is superscript vowels. Although sometimes they are difficult to distinguish from specific abbreviation signs, superscript vowels are present and are used distinctively. Letters **i**, **a** (open, almost like a **u** or a wavy line), **o** and, less frequently, **u** can be found throughout Paris' script. Superscript consonants are only represented by **t**, which is used to abbreviate third-person, indicative verbs ending in consonant + *it*, including *uit*. Despite the irregularity of Paris' hand his abbreviation and punctuation are quite consistent.

After the description of its general appearance, main letterforms, punctuation and abbreviation it can be concluded that the handwriting of Matthew Paris is, above all, idiosyncratic, which can aid in identifying and distinguishing it from that of other scribes. Paris continued using fusions and 'kissing' after, according to Kwakkel, they had stopped being used simultaneously (1225), developed a script that defies classification given its hybrid nature, and gave his script an appearance that sets it apart from those of contemporary scribes.[55]

The hand of Matthew Paris in the eighteen manuscript identified and listed by Vaughan is accompanied by other hands. As discussed earlier, Vaughan was the first to directly acknowledge the existence of a number of scribal collaborators in Paris' manuscripts, after the Rolls Series editors had discussed mainly the Paris' 'assistant' at the end of the third and last part of the *Chronica maiora*. Towards the end of this section, Matthew Paris is drawn in his deathbed, and a colophon informs the reader that the author has passed away. A few leaves before that, Matthew Paris' hand gives way to that of another scribe, who is entrusted with finishing the text and paying respects to the author.[56] Because of this 'final takeover' from Paris, this particular scribe received some attention in the edition of the *Chronica maiora*, although always in relation to Paris' hand or the aforementioned 'St Albans hand'. Apart from this particular scribe, the manuscripts of Matthew Paris contain several hands that are not that of the chronicler, and many participated in the copying of most of Paris' works, so their importance in the book-making process cannot be underestimated.

As part of my doctoral research on scribal collaboration in ten of Vaughan's eighteen manuscripts containing the hand of Matthew Paris, I endeavoured to identify and describe all non-Paris scribal hands in them. Thus I have estimated the number of scribal hands in those manuscripts to be thirty-four. Of these, there are three identified scribes who participate in more than one manuscript, and a further three unclear identifications across more than one manuscript.[57] By using digital and traditional palaeographic methods – including the award-winning Archetype framework – I have been able not only to describe these hands, but also to create a digital repository of images of those hands (in full and by letterform, abbreviation and punctuation), and to compare hands across manuscripts digitally. Overall, this analysis shows how unequal and inconsistent collaboration is in Matthew Paris' manuscripts, and how it is concentrated mostly in Paris' longer historical works. It poses intriguing questions with regards to the scriptorium and book production at St Albans in the first half of the thirteenth century; it dispels the idea that authors single-handedly produced their manuscripts, and it challenges the very idea of authorship. On the other hand, the thirteenth century is a rich and complex period from a palaeographical perspective, from the full transition from Caroline minuscule into Gothic that started in the previous century to the development of distinctive cursive scripts that are also used as book hands. The place the hand of Matthew Paris occupies in this picture is not just as an exceptional rarity, but as a significant example of the use, adaptation and evolution of script. The way Paris' hand fit – or does not fit – into the general characteristics of script in the first half of the thirteenth century; the features that it shows and where they come from and how they evolve, and the way his hand provides insight into cursivisation are all features of interest inside and outside the scholarship of Matthew Paris.

Notes

1. This chapter presents some of the findings of García 2018.
2. The study of the hand of William of Malmesbury also started with the Rolls Series; see Stubbs 1887–89; Ker 1944; Thomson 1978, 117–42.
3. Vaughan 1953b. These manuscripts are: Cambridge, Corpus Christi College, MS 16, Cambridge, Corpus Christi College, MS 26, BL Cotton MS Nero D I, BL Royal MS 14 C VII, BL Cotton MS Vespasian B XIII fol. 133, BL Cotton MS Nero D V, Trinity College Dublin, MS 177, Cambridge University Library, MS Dd. II. 78 and Chetham's Library, MS 6712.
4. Vaughan 1953b. Oxford, Bodl., MS Ashmole 304 is an astrological compilation that includes Bernard Sylvester's *Experimentarius*; Cambridge

University Library, MS Dd. II. 78 is a compilation of poems by Henry D'Avranches; Oxford, Corpus Christi College, MS 2 is a Bible, and BL Royal MS 4 D VII, BL Cotton MS Vitellius A XX, BL Royal MS 13 D V, BL Royal MS 13 E VI, BL Cotton MS Julius D VII and Cambridge, Corpus Christi College, MS 385 include texts from chronicles by John of Wallingford, Geoffrey of Monmouth and Petrus Comestor, among others.

5. For an outline of Matthew's historical writing see Chapter 1, 6-7.
6. For the first printing of Matthew's chronicles see Hardy 1862, i. xliv; iii. 399-414; Madden 1866-69, i. xxxiii-xxxvii; Luard 1872-83, i. ix; Vaughan 1958c, 155-56. See also Chapter 10, 230-35; Chapter 15, 319-21.
7. Watts 1640; Madden 1866-69, iii. xxxv-vi; Vaughan 1958c, 155.
8. Huillard-Bréholles 1840-41; Giles 1852-54.
9. In chronological order: Luard 1858; Hardy 1862; Madden 1866-69; Luard 1872-83; Luard 1890.
10. Hardy 1862, iii. cxxxiv; Luard 1872-83, i. xi; ii. x.
11. Vaughan 1953b.
12. Gilson and Poole 1928; Powicke 1941; Galbraith 1944; Powicke 1944, 18-21; Wormald 1946, 109-12; Vaughan 1953b; Vaughan 1958c.
13. Vaughan 1953b.
14. Vaughan also disputed the idea of the existence of a 'St Albans hand', a concept put forward by Luard, by identifying this 'house style' as Paris' hand itself: Vaughan 1953b, 384-86, in response to Hardy 1862, III, cxxxiv; Luard 1872-83, i. xi).
15. Vaughan 1953b, 384n8.
16. Thomson 1982.
17. McCulloch 1981; Morgan 1988.
18. Reader 1994; Reader 1996, 118-47.
19. Particularly relevant are: from a historical perspective: Weiler 2012; Cleaver 2018; Cleaver and Worm 2018; Greasley 2018 and 2021; Weiler 2018; Weiler 2019; Gaudio 2000; Pitocchelli (2024).
20. This section derives from my own doctoral work: see Muñoz García 2018, chapter 3.a.
21. Ker 1960; Benson, Constable and Lanham 1982; Bischoff 1990, 127; Derolez 2003, 56; chapter 3; Webber 2007, 139; Parkes 2008a, 110-20; Parkes 2008b, 93-94; Kwakkel 2012, 84-85; Brett and Woodman 2015.
22. Derolez 2003, 60-65; Parkes 2008a, 110-11.
23. Webber 2007, 164.
24. A discussion of terminology is found in Derolez 2003, 56-57 and it is also discussed in Bischoff 1990.
25. Bischoff 1990, 127; Derolez 2003, 71; Cherubini and Pratesi 2010, 431.
26. Derolez 2003, 72-122.
27. Derolez 2003, 73.

28. Derolez defines four subdivisions within Northern Textualis or Formata: Textus Quadratus, Textus Praescissus, Textus Semiquadratus and Textus Rotundus. These subdivisions differ from Lieftinck and Gumbert's Cartesian categories which distinguish between different levels of execution within Textualis: Formata, Libraria or Media and Currens. Southern Textualis or Rotunda is usually found in Mediterranean manuscripts. Differences within Rotunda are geographical, with variants in Italy, Spain and Portugal and southern France. Derolez also finds a different category mostly in Italy, although present in other Mediterranean areas: Semitextualis: Derolez 2003, 20–21, 74, 102–22; also see Lieftinck 1954, 15–34; Gumbert 1976, 47–49; Bischoff 1990, 127–45. A discussion on the elements that characterise Textualis can also be found in Cherubini and Pratesi 2010, 436–37.
29. Parkes 1969, xiii–xiv; Bischoff 1990, 137; Derolez 2003, 123; Parkes 2008a, 120–21; Parkes 2008b, 80.
30. Derolez 2003, 123.
31. Lieftinck 1964; Gumbert 1976, 46
32. Parkes 1969, xvi.
33. Parkes 1969, xiv; Derolez 2003, 134; Parkes 2008a, 130–31.
34. Derolez 2003, 135–36; Cherubini and Pratesi 2010, 502.
35. Derolez 2003, 130.
36. Vaughan 1953b, 386.
37. Meyer 1897, 12–16; Bischoff 1990, 130; Cherubini and Pratesi 2010, 436.
38. Derolez 2003, 77.
39. Kwakkel 2012, 100.
40. Kwakkel 2012, 102–04.
41. Derolez 2003, 78.
42. Parkes 1992, 42.
43. Parkes 2008b, 152.
44. In the manuscript of the *Historia Anglorum* (BL, Royal MS 14 C VII) there are several examples of the *punctus elevatus* with a certain variance on the same page, like in 10ra4m 4, 8 and 12. See in the *Chronica maiora* (Cambridge, Corpus Christi College, MS 16 II) in 16ra8 and 11.
45. Parkes 1992, 43.
46. For instance, BL, Royal MS 14 C VII, fos. 14ra, 18; Cambridge, Corpus Christi College, MS 16 (II), fol. 15^{vb2}.
47. Vaughan 1953b; Parkes 1992, 43.
48. The *paraph* mark in current titles is found all throughout the *Chronica maiora* (CCCC and BL MSS) and *Historia Anglorum* (BL, Royal MS 14 C VII), alternating blue and red.
49. An example of the use of the *paraph* in current title and a marginal note can be found on: BL, Royal MS 14 C VII, 13^v, current title and col. 1, left lower corner.

50. Vaughan 1953c, plate XV.
51. BL Royal MS 14 C VII, fol. 14^r, shows examples of different letters starting a rubric, with a *D* displaying an upwards inner stroke and other letters (like *W* and *U*) slightly prolonged.
52. Vaughan 1953b.
53. Thompson 1912, 89.
54. Cappelli 2011, xvii–xxii.
55. Kwakkel 2012, 102–03.
56. The transition between Matthew Paris and this scribal hand happens in 210r, c. 2.
57. Muñoz García 2018, chapter 4.

14

The Vernacular Culture of Matthew Paris

Matthew Paris in his monastery at St Albans was working and living in an environment where he was, in all probability, functioning in three different languages. Latin would have been part of his daily life as a monk, and his major works were, of course, written in Latin. Yet his writings in French are not insignificant and made an important contribution to the production of literature in French in medieval England. The most important of his writings in French are the four saints' lives attributed to him: *La Vie de Seint Auban*, *La Estoire de Seint Ædward le rei*, *La Vie de Saint Edmond* and *La Vie de Saint Thomas de Cantorbéry*, which survives only in fragmentary form.[1] He also used French for the notes, instructions and comments on some of his maps.[2] Although Matthew's famous and often reproduced map of Britain (BL Cotton MS Claudius D VI, fol. 12ᵛ) has notes in Latin,[3] other maps and itineraries, such as his complex map of the journey to the Holy Land, include instructions in French.[4] Similarly, some of the blazons above the shields in BL Cotton MS Nero D 1 use French terms, although the majority are in Latin.[5] French may have been the language of daily conversation between the Benedictine monks of St Albans and was clearly Matthew's language of choice when he expected a wider readership.[6] French at this time was still a real vernacular among the educated and the higher echelons of society in England – that is, it would have been for many a language learned at home informally, possibly a mother tongue; it was certainly a language of literary composition.[7] That Matthew's extensive notes on the maps of Acre which precede his Latin chronicle, the *Chronica maiora*, are largely in

French assumes that those who were literate in Latin would also be literate in French.

We do not know whether French or English was Matthew's first language; his name may appear to suggest a link with the city of Paris, but none has been established and it was not an uncommon surname in England, so it is not possible to infer from this that he was not native to England.[8] It is generally assumed he knew English.[9] Richard Vaughan, author of a monograph on Matthew Paris, deduced from a single comment in the *Chronica maiora* where Matthew describes a day 'which in common speech we call Hoke Day' – that 'he thought of English as his own language'. He also claimed to be able to translate an English saying uttered by the dying Edmund in his French *Vie de Saint Edmond* (ll. 1544–45). This is, however, slender evidence to suggest that English was his main vernacular, though it must be acknowledged that the majority of the population of England were anglophone.[10] It is likely, moreover, that there was little need for him to read English, and even less need for him to write it. Matthew himself records in the *Gesta abbatum* the community's discovery of ancient manuscripts written in a strange vernacular (i.e. in pre-Conquest English). While the factual truth of this anecdote cannot be confirmed, the account of the community's struggle to find someone capable of reading them testifies to a sense that the community itself had lost touch with the pre-Conquest written tradition. Only a few vernacular books have been associated with St Albans, and these were in French. Some monasteries, notably Canterbury and Worcester, retained earlier vernacular books but there is no evidence of this at St Albans. Reading material available to Matthew after his entry into the monastery would not have been restricted to the volumes in St Albans' own library; he would have been able to borrow books from neighbouring Benedictine institutions, particularly that at Bury St Edmunds.[11] Although we do not have a catalogue of the books and manuscripts St Albans owned in the middle of the thirteenth century, there is sufficient evidence for us to be confident that it possessed what has been described as 'one of the greatest libraries of medieval England'.[12] Indeed, the amount and quality of scholarship coming out of the abbey would lead us to that conclusion even if we had no further documentary evidence.[13] Interpreting the evidence that is available regarding what Matthew may have been reading is not straightforward as it is not always possible to tell what language a book was written in. For example, a codex included in a fifteenth-century list of books borrowed from St Albans may have contained Matthew's French *Vie de Seint Auban* and his *Estoire de Seint Ædward le rei*, but the list entry is in Latin.[14] Cambridge Trinity College MS 0.9.34, an illustrated manuscript of the Old French *Roman de Chevalerie*, is thought to have been made at St Albans and Matthew's use of vernacular literary traditions suggests he had some access to vernacular books.[15]

All of Matthew's hagiographies, Latin and French, deal with insular saints, enhancing his reputation for being 'Anglo-centric', a reputation otherwise based largely on his somewhat chauvinistic comments in the chronicles.[16] This emphasises that the choice of language during this period had little to do with national identity; French was used widely in parts of Europe and especially in England. Matthew could write with approval about Edward the Confessor dismissing 'with tact flatterers and foreigners' and do so in the language of some of those same 'foreigners'.[17] In *La Estoire de Seint Ædward le rei* Matthew commented on his own French in lines which have been considered 'an established topos of linguistic deprecation':[18]

> Or pri chescun ki lit e ot
> Cest treité, s'en aucun mot
> Mesprein, k'il l'amender voile,
> Kar n'est hom ki ne sumoile.
> Language par païs varie;
> Si language de France die,
> N'en doi estre a droit repris
> De gent de veisin païs.
>
> (89–96)

[Now I beg of each person who reads and hears this work that if in any word I make a mistake, let him correct it, for there is no man who does not sometimes doze. Language varies from land to land; if I speak the language of France, let me not be reproached for it by the people of a neighbouring country. Trans., 54.]

This can be read in the context of the nun of Barking's famous apology for her '*faus franceis d'Angleterre*'.[19] This apology has itself been reassessed in recent years and is not always taken as an acceptance of the inferiority of the French of England.[20] Matthew's comment is rather less ambiguous and arguably defends the right of insular writers of French to use French in their own way, since language usage varies from country to country. Matthew is presenting us with a modesty topos in that he encourages his readers and listeners to correct what he has written if necessary. He is not necessarily implying that his French is inferior to that of a neighbouring country; rather he acknowledges that it is different from the French of France, that every country has its own way of speaking; *language* does not necessarily mean 'language' in the English sense, but rather *langage* in French – that is, 'idiom' or 'way of speaking'. Matthew acknowledges that his way of speaking or writing French may be different from that of the French and defends his right to do so.

Texts and Patrons

Although there is now a general consensus that the four extant French hagiographic texts listed earlier in this chapter were written by Matthew Paris, it is worth briefly addressing the question of authorship before we consider the texts as works of literature. The discussions of attribution, which have dominated discussions of Matthew's vernacular texts, emphasise the connections between the texts, linking the four texts in three different ways: the handwriting, the patronage and the comment of the chronicler Thomas Walsingham that Matthew Paris had elegantly composed *Lives* of the saints Alban, Thomas and Edmund, which immediately connects three of our four texts.[21]

La Vie de Seint Auban
Trinity College Dublin manuscript 177 containing the *Vie de Seint Auban* is key to the attribution not only of this text, but of all four texts. Extensive work on the handwriting of Matthew Paris has contributed to the identification of this as a holograph manuscript, though more recent research by Christopher Baswell suggests Matthew was working with a team of scribes.[22] A note on the flyleaf gives an instruction requesting that Isabel Countess of Arundel should be asked to 'send the book about St Thomas the Martyr and St Edward which I translated

and illustrated and which the lady Countess of Cornwall may keep until Whitsuntide'.[23] This note affirms that Matthew was responsible for these two further saints' lives, of Sts Thomas and Edward, linking three of the four vernacular saints' lives attributed to him. Another note in Matthew's own hand in one manuscript of the *Chronica maiora* refers to a history of St Edward.[24]

La Vie de Saint Edmond

The attribution of *La Vie de Saint Edmond* to Matthew is not unanimously accepted but seems likely.[25] The writer names himself as 'ge, Maheu' in the text, uses Matthew Paris' Latin text and dedicates the work to the Countess of Arundel, named, as we have noted, in the flyleaf of the *Saint Auban* manuscript. Given the probable date of the manuscript (BL Additional MS 70513), all but the first quire of which is from the late thirteenth century, it is not unlikely that this was copied from an autograph manuscript.[26]

The history of the manuscript also adds to our understanding of the importance of women in the spread of the written vernacular as the manuscript contains an ex libris noting that the book was *deviseie a la prioroe de kanpseie de lire a mangier*. While there has been some discussion of the meaning of *deviseie* and whether the manuscript was made for or given to the nunnery at Campsey, an Augustinian religious house in Suffolk, there is a clear sense of purpose here – namely, a collection of metrical saints' lives in French for the edification of the nuns, who would be expected to be able to follow narratives read aloud to them in French.[27] As Wogan-Browne has noted, while manuscripts belonging to women at this time could be in English, French or Latin, or any combination of these, 'the bulk of manuscripts and texts from this earlier period of women's literary culture are in French'.[28]

La Estoire de Seint Ædward le rei

While the Countess of Arundel was patron of the *Edmond*, the *Estoire de Seint Ædward le rei* was dedicated to the highest lady in the land, Queen Eleanor of Provence, who married Henry III in 1236 (ll. 49–72). The extant manuscript of the *Estoire de Seint Edouard* may have been copied for a later Eleanor, Eleanor of Castile, who married Henry's son Edward in 1254.[29] As we have noted in connection with British Library

Additional MS 70513, female patronage seems to have been significant in the development of vernacular writing, so in this the works of Matthew Paris are typical of his time. However, once the translation was made or the poem composed, it did not necessarily pass out of Matthew's hands. The note on the flyleaf of *St Auban* demonstrates that, on the contrary, Matthew lent out copies of his poems and expected them to be returned to him. The *Vie de Seint Auban* bears the press mark of the Abbey at St Albans and, it is thought, probably remained in the possession of the Abbey until the dissolution of the monasteries in the sixteenth century.[30]

Vie de Saint Thomas

Although the note on the manuscript of *Saint Auban* had referred to a life of St Thomas, as does Thomas Walsingham, it was some time before Matthew's *Vie de Saint Thomas de Cantorbéry* was identified with the fragmentary text surviving in the fragments known as the 'Becket leaves' (Stokenchurch, Wormsley Library, MS BM 3750). The *mise en page* and style of illustration of the manuscript, echoing Matthew's autograph work in the St Alban's book, has led to the probable identification of this with the lost *Saint Thomas* of the flyleaf note.[31] The surviving fragments in four disconnected leaves, offer different ways of reading the same story, a feature, as we shall discuss, of other manuscripts of Matthew's French works. The upper section of each page contains illustrations with Latin rubrics in red ink, both above and within the frame of the illustrations and below each image seventy-six lines of Anglo-Norman verse in rhyming couplets.[32] This may be the manuscript referred to on the flyleaf of Trinity College Dublin, MS 177, lent to the Countess of Arundel.

Rubrics for Pictures of Saints

More uncertain is the attribution of the 'Rubrics for Pictures of Saints' in Trinity College Dublin MS 177, the codex which also contains *La Vie de Seint Auban*.[33] The hand is similar to that of Matthew and the pattern of an illustration and a rhyming couplet corresponds to what we have found for both the *Vie de Seint Auban* and the 'Becket leaves'. A similar set of illustrations and French rubrics seems to have been intended for the Countess of Winchester; instructions are found on the flyleaf to the *Seint Auban* manuscript.[34]

Matthew Paris as a Translator

In the sixteenth century the poet Joachim du Bellay would advocate translation from and imitation of the classics as a means of enriching the French language. Three hundred years earlier translation was already a significant factor in the growing use of French, as is evident from the extensive range of material being translated into French, from religious texts to scientific material, notably in Anglo-Norman. In 1215 the French version of Magna Carta had been the first political document produced in the French of England,[35] and translations of hagiography were increasingly common, often produced by religious – that is, by nuns as well as monks.[36] It is difficult to know how much of this growing body of material Matthew would have been familiar with, but his practice exemplifies the fertilisation of French through translation from Latin.[37]

The *Vie de Seint Auban* is perhaps the most interesting of Matthew's French texts as an act of translation in that we find within the same manuscript several versions of the same narrative: the Latin prose life of St Alban by another monk of St Albans, a certain William, probably written around 1178;[38] Matthew's narrative in mono-rhymed *laisses*; the illustrations to this narrative and the rubrics to the illustrations, rhyming couplets in French which themselves constitute a shorter poem repeating the narrative. In the widest sense of the term each is a *translatio*, a transposition, of another work. The manuscript which contains these texts was partly executed by Matthew himself and has been described as a 'compendium or dossier of the monastery's saint'.[39] This multi-text codex reinforces our understanding of the multilingual context of the monastery, with text in French and Latin and some Middle English, the voice of the mob, in one image (f. 36 r). Immediately preceding Matthew's *Vie* are his source, the Latin prose life (ff. 20–28), and a Latin poem in elegiacs by Ralph of Dunstable; all the other texts (all in Latin) relate to the life of the community at St Albans, being the lesson for the Feast of St Alban (22 June), a treatise on the invention and translation of St Alban and the charter for the foundation of the Abbey. Modern reading practice might expect one version of the *Life* in a single text codex, but a medieval codex is more like a shelf of a library, in this case one which groups together related texts. The juxtaposition of different texts on the life of the saint is reflected in the structure of Matthew's *Vie*, which offers the possibilities of more than one way of reading the narrative. The *Vie de Seint Auban* is effectively not one *Life* but three, offering the same reading patterns as the 'Becket leaves'. The main text of *Seint Auban* is not written in rhyming couplets, by then the established form for the writing of most genres of verse narrative, but in the irregular *laisses* of the *chanson de geste* (Old French epic). Accompanying the text in Trinity College Dublin, MS 177 is a full programme of images, and accompanying the images are rubrics which themselves form a 464-line narrative in rhyming couplets. The codex as a whole therefore offers five different readings of St Alban's life, all ultimately springing from the Latin life by the monk William. The juxtaposition of the French and the Latin and the narrative in images also allows different readers with different levels of literacy to comprehend the main narrative. The codex was clearly for use by the community, so we may speculate that the French versions and the images were there to help novices, boys being educated in the Abbey's school, or the less able in Latin, thus ensuring that everyone associated with the community knew the life of its patron saint.[40]

The *Estoire de Seint Ædward le rei* is also an appropriation of a pre-existing version of the narrative, this time Aelred of Rievaulx's *Vita Sancti Edwardi*. I use the term 'appropriation' since translation in the Middle Ages could cover a wide range of concepts with *ad verbum* translation at one end of the spectrum, but with more dynamic translation as the norm.[41] In the *Estoire*, in a prayer addressed to the royal saint, Matthew tells us how he expects text and image to be read:

>Or vus pri, gentilz rois Ædward,
>K'a moi pecchur eiez regard
>Ki ai translaté du latin
>Sulum mun sen et mun engin
>En franceis la vostre estoire,
>Ke se espande ta memoire,
>E pur lais ki de lettrure
>Ne sevent, en purtraiture

> Figuree apertement
> L'ai en cest livret present,
> Pur ço ke desir e voil
> Ke oraille ot, voient li oil.
>
> (3955–66)

> [Now I pray you, noble King Edward, to remember me, a sinner who has translated your story from Latin into French as my intelligence and skill allowed, so that the memory of you may be spread about. For laypeople who do not know how to read, I have also represented your story in illustrations in this very same book, because I want the eyes to see what the ears hear. Trans., 105].

The combination of texts and image is thus inclusive, the images supplementing what the illiterate can hear.[42] True to his declared aim to write for those who are not literate in Latin, Matthew translated even when quoting. We read in Matthew's account that when the pope absolved Edward from his vow to go on pilgrimage and granted instead that he build an abbey, the pope wrote a letter to him in Latin. What we find in the text is the *summe de lescrit* – that is, the essence of the writing – in French. The status of his French account is stressed in the repetition of the lines:

> Et tel est de l'escrit la summe
> Ki est en latin apert
> Noté, ke en seit chescuns cert.
> De l'escrit est tel la summe ...
>
> (1652–55)

> [Here is the entire text, set down clearly in Latin, so that everyone may be sure of it. The text is as follows ... Trans., 74]

I have given here the published translation but, excellent though it is, using a translation without reference to the original can be misleading: what follows is the essence of the Latin rendered into French – not 'the entire text'. The practice of quoting the text of the document, albeit in translation, is also indicative of the literary tradition Matthew is writing his text into, as it was normal to quote documents in chronicles; in the *Estoire* the document is simply translated into another language and into verse form.

Later, when Edward seeks confirmation from Pope Leo's successor, we are told that the 'request was entered fully in writing, first in Latin, then in French' (trans., 84), emphasising the complementarity of the two languages.[43] Latin may have carried more authority, but where he could Matthew evoked both languages. Citing the 'history of the Normans' as his authority for what he said about the previous dukes of Normandy, he referred to the accounts in 'Latin and in French', taken to be an allusion to Wace's *Roman de Rou* and various Latin chronicles.[44]

With the *Vie de Seint Ædward* we can see a process of translation with editing, not very different from the practice of the scribe as editor. The *incipit*, which runs across columns b and c of the first folio, tells us that it was translated from the Latin. The medieval translator was free to elaborate and abbreviate, and also to edit in to his 'translation' material taken from other sources. The *Seint Ædward* has been described as 'for the most part ... a free translation of Aelred of Rievaulx's *Vita Edwardi Confessoris*, with an introductory section derived from Ailred's *Genealogica regum Anglorum*'.[45] It also contains original material and some use of Matthew's own *Flores historiarum*.[46] In this Matthew's work exemplifies the technique and freedom of the medieval translator, a freedom shared by the chronicler, to draw upon a source extensively while also adding explanations and extra material. In a manuscript culture where the source text itself was not stable, the translator had what might be described as a licence to depart from the source text. Matthew Paris availed himself of this licence.

In that it offers more than one way to read Edward's life, the manuscript of the *Estoire de Seint Ædward* (Cambridge University Library Manuscript, MS Ee.3.59) resembles that of the *Vie de Seint Auban*.[47] Both manuscripts suggest that such texts were presented in this way to enable a manuscript to be used for different purposes and by different readers. Of the two this is perhaps most clear with the *Vie de Seint Auban*. It was, for example, clearly lent out to at least one aristocratic lady who could be expected to be able to read the French text, but not necessarily the Latin; one can only speculate about the coexistence of the different ways of reading the text. Might these manuscripts have been used not just for personal pleasure and enlightenment, but also for educational purposes, such as for teaching the young of the aristocratic ladies, as much as for teaching young monks? We know that Latin was taught through the medium of French.[48] In manuscripts offering more than one reading the pictures would aid the understanding of the French, which in turn could be used to help students understand the Latin. Baswell, in his discussion of the manuscript of *St Auban*, posits an evolving audience, with 'an initial, largely monastic audience of the two Latin *Vitae*' being enlarged to 'include and attract the aristocratic, even royal agents who were so much a part of the life and power of St Albans'.[49]

In his *Vie de Saint Edmond* Matthew translated his own Latin work, a life of Edmund Rich, Archbishop of Canterbury, but he did not do so without changes. His willingness to adapt can be illustrated by one simple instance. C. H. Lawrence, in his study of St Edmund, points out the presence in the Anglo-Norman of additional information about both Edmund and the bishop consecrating him: we are told of their masters in arts and theology.[50] In fact, more can be seen in this single example as Matthew also adapted the rhetoric of the Latin to the poetics of the French. In the Latin he used the rhetorical figure of polyptoton, using different cases of the same word to emphasise the resemblance between the two men (*sanctus a sancti, theologus a theologo*, etc.), while in the French he achieved the same effect through poetic anaphora, beginning successive lines with '*Andeuz*' (both; see lines 847, 848, 850, 852). That the translator was willing to alter the text casts a little more light on the way a medieval translator saw his task, not as a simple mirror of the source text, but producing a text fit for a different time or a different audience. Moreover, the very process of translating from Latin prose to French verse was far from straightforward, especially when, as we shall see, the translator chose to adapt and employ the various techniques of versification used in the target language.

The text in the 'Becket leaves' also owes its narrative to a Latin source, in this case the *Quadrilogus*, a composite text redacted between 1198 and 1199. Meyer, editor of the fragments, compared the texts and described the French text as 'une sorte de traduction libre de la compilation latine'.[51] Again we have a manuscript which offers different ways of accessing the narrative. The images which run across the three columns of text (two columns for fol. 2) are supplied with rubrics in both Latin and French, the Latin being above the miniature and the French below.[52]

Narrative Technique

All of these vernacular texts are hagiographies, but they are not all the same in their mode of writing. In his translations Matthew Paris adopted the modes of vernacular narrative, writing his texts into traditions of chronicle, hagiography and *chanson de geste*.

An early editor of the *Estoire de Seint Ædward* included his edition of part of the poem in a volume entitled *Chroniques anglo-normandes*.[53] We have also noted the use of chronicle-style incorporation of documents into the narrative, albeit translated into French. The text is entitled, in the manuscript, an *Estoire*, a term often used to designate a chronicle, and it resembles a chronicle in its structure, while its main source, Aelred's *Vita*, in both title and structure follows the conventions of hagiography. Kathryn Wallace, the most recent editor, has noted that the opening verses in particular, with their chronological list of Edward's predecessors, suggest the form of a chronicle.[54] The modus operandi of the chronicler can also be detected in the way he uses his sources, combining material from different sources, principally bringing together Aelred's *Genealogica regum Anglorum* and the *Vita*, and adding eyewitness observations where possible – for example, in the description of Edward's church at Westminster (2290–2323).[55]

French verse chronicles drew on other genres for their discourse and intertextual references, including *chansons de geste*. In the *Estoire* Matthew Paris restricted his overt intertextual allusions to texts which his contemporaries would have deemed histories. The frequency of the intertextual allusions throughout Matthew's vernacular texts reveals a familiarity with French vernacular literature. They are, moreover, also a point of contact with his lay readers. He had a distinct predilection for the heroic over the romantic. We have references to Alexander the Great (*Auban*, 355; *Ædward*, 746) and he referred several times to the foundation myth of Britain, *Brut*, though this would have been known in Latin as well as French. In *La Vie de Saint Edmond* the saint is described as not giving 'a chestnut' for the romances (i.e. texts in French) of Ogier or of Charlemagne (331–32); while this may seem to cast such texts in a negative light, texts a saint does not waste his time on, it also suggests a familiarity with these epic tales. It is perhaps appropriate in his biography of the English king St Edward that it is the legendary King Arthur (rather than Charlemagne) who is evoked alongside Edward's antecedents:

> Li autre forz e hardiz mutz
> Cum fu Arthurs, Aedmunz e Knudz.
>
> (9–10)
>
> [Others were strong and bold/ like Arthur, Edmund and Cnut. Trans., 53]

Such a forbear could be compared directly to Edward:

> Ne fu puis le tens Arthur
> Reis ki feist si grant honur.
>
> (908–09)
>
> [Not since the time of Arthur had there been a king who had done such great honour. Trans., 65]

Yet while the explicit allusion is to Arthur, the description of Edward's court could almost have been culled from Nithard's *Life of Charlemagne*, with its praise of the state of land under Charlemagne:[56]

> Lors est la terre en bon estat.
> Cunte e barun e li prelat,
> N'est nuls a ki li reis ne pleise.
> Tut sunt riche, tut sunt a eise,
> E li prince ki sunt veisin
> Tuit li sunt ami enclin,
> Des les muntz gesk'en Espainne,
> Nis l'empereres d'Alemainne.
>
> (*Seint Ædward*, 872–79)
>
> [The state of the country was good then! There was no one whom the king didn't please, no earl or baron or prelate. Everyone was rich, everyone was comfortable, and Edward's princely neighbours, from the mountains down to Spain were his willing friends including even the emperor of Germany. Trans., 65].

I am not suggesting that Matthew necessarily knew Nithard's text; no copy is recorded as being in the possession of the monks at St Albans. It does, however, seem likely that he knew this kind of literature. Again, while the emphasis is on his insular antecedents, it has been suggested there are in the *Estoire* echoes of *chansons de geste* in the action described. Notably the combat between Cnut and Edmund is seen as being similar to that between representatives of Christian and Saracen in many *chansons de geste*, but perhaps most famously for modern readers in the *Chanson de Roland*.

Earl Godwin is also evoked in terms which might recall the treachery of a Ganelon; Edward recalls the treason of Godwin in a prayer:

> Aï, Aedmund, quer de liun!
> E tu peris par traisun
> God[e]win li quens de Kent,
> Li losengers ki flote e pent,
> Par traisun, pecché e tort.
>
> (776–80)

> [Ah Edmund, lionheart! You perished by the treason of Godwin, earl of Kent, the deceiving opportunist who shifted with the wind, treasonously, sinfully, and wrongly. Trans., 63–64].

The way the intertextual allusions work in the *Estoire* is to recall a historic past to which the saintly king can be compared. In the *Vie de Seint Auban*, by contrast, it is the heroic *chanson de geste* which is evoked, both by the verse form (see the example that follows), and in some of the allusions in the text. Perhaps most significant is his evocation of the 'trinity' of pagan gods, Mahom, Tervagant and Apollo, familiar to readers and listeners of the *chanson de geste*. By the mid thirteenth century many would have had a much more accurate view of Islam and Matthew was not an uneducated man, yet he used the popular constructs to present his narrative.[57] The enemies of the Christians in this text are called 'Saracen', again as in the *chansons de geste*. There is even what may be a direct quotation of one of the most famous *chansons de geste*; when describing Auban's sufferings the narrator comments:

> Mut deit pur sun Seignur sufrir leal chevalier.
>
> (686)

> [A faithful knight has to suffer much for his lord's sake. Trans., 80]

This may be no more than an aphorism, but it carries an echo of the *Chanson de Roland*, where Roland asserts what a man should be willing to suffer for his lord:

Pur sun seignur deit hom susfrir granz mals.

[One must suffer great hardships for one's lord. *La Chanson de Roland*, 1117].[58]

The key difference between the two is that Roland was alluding to his earthly lord, and perhaps only indirectly by his service to his lord bringing service to his heavenly Lord; Alban is serving God. The heroic connotation would not be lost on listeners accustomed to hearing epic tales in this form, but by its contrast there is also a suggestion that true heroism is the heroism of the saint.

Linked to other aspects of generic marking in his texts, and important in a consideration of Matthew Paris as a writer, are the questions around his versification. Matthew's versification has been a subject of much discussion and no little criticism since the publication of the first edition of his *Vie de Seint Auban* by Robert Atkinson in 1876.[59] It has been part of an ongoing debate about Anglo–Norman versification with the irregular syllable count variously considered the result of careless copying, inept poets or the influence of English stress-based prosody and the Latin quantitative verse which many of the poets may have been more accustomed to.[60] At least one scholar rejected the attribution of the *Vie de Seint Auban* to Matthew Paris on the grounds of its irregular syllable count.[61] Vaughan describes his verse as 'characteristic doggerel of his day', while Baker, the editor of *St Edmond*, blames the copyist for what he sees as faults.[62] Indeed, as the editor of *Seint Ædward le rei* has pointed out, 'the widespread belief that Anglo–Norman poets were careless or incompetent versifiers is hard to stamp out'.[63] Meyer, in his analysis of the versification of *Saint Thomas*, apparently written in octosyllabic rhyming couplets, identifies one-third of the lines as being only seven syllables, with a much lower number of hyper-syllabic lines. He counts the 'false' lines as following:[64]

Folio 1: 112 lines: 43 short, 5 long
Folio 2: 66 lines: 22 short, 5 long
Folio 3: 132 lines: 54 short, 4 long
Folio 4: 122 lines: 44 short, 5 long

These proportions suggest to him that the short lines were as intended by the author, as no copyist would be likely to be that incompetent, while his analysis of the long lines suggests that only three could possibly be the result of errors on the part of the copyist and that other lines could have been articulated as being octosyllabic if an unstressed *e* is taken into account. Meyer goes on to point out that this mixture of seven- and eight-syllable lines is not unknown in Anglo–Norman poetry.[65] Wallace's analysis of the couplets of the rubrics of the *Vie de Seint Auban* reveals that about 33 per cent of lines are of seven syllables and 63 per cent of eight syllables with 'a few irreducible nine-syllable lines ... presumably because the author liked them as they were.[66] As Wogan-Browne and Fenster express it, 'variation seems to have been regularly permitted in insular verse', and Matthew certainly seems to be flexible in line length.[67]

Flexibility in the way the rhyme scheme is worked out is also a feature of Matthew's practice. Meyer further notes that the text of the *Seint Thomas* sometimes has the same rhyme over four or even six lines; the same practice can be observed in the *Vie de Saint Edmond*.[68] This again is not unknown in other medieval and specifically insular texts.[69] A taste for *rimes équivoques*, homophones rhyming for rhetorical effect, has also been highlighted – a practice condemned in classical French prosody but rather valued in medieval versification.

If the irregularity of syllable count is typical of Anglo–Norman texts of the period, another aspect of Matthew's versification is both striking and innovative. Matthew was experimental in his vernacular verse in using different verse forms for different kinds of text. By the middle of the thirteenth century the rhyming couplet was the standard form to use in storytelling, whether this was a chronicle, a romance or a saint's life. Admittedly chronicles by now were also being written in prose but the verse chronicle had not disappeared. The exception to this was the *chanson de geste*, which was written in *laisses*, strophes of irregular length united by rhyme or assonance, normally in lines of ten or twelve syllables with a caesura.

The *Vie de Seint Auban*, is, as we have noted, effectively not one *Life* but three. The main text is not written in rhyming couplets, but in the irregular *laisses* of the *chanson de geste*. The rubrics, written in rhyming couplets, offer a narrative with greater momentum. Harden, the editor of *Seint Auban*, posits the theory that this is 'a relatively early work which the author revised ... for the form in which it is found in the Trinity College manuscripts'.[70] The implication is that he would later go on to write more conventional rhyming couplets. Dominica Legge, noting that this is the explanation that has been offered for the choice of versification, adds a comment on the colophon, in which the text is referred to as '*Li rumantz del estoire de seint Auban*', that 'perhaps its metrical form had something to do with this appellation'.[71] The word *rumantz* still meant little more than 'narrative in the romance vernacular'; *estoire* is more significant in that, as in the *Estoire de Seint Ædward*, it suggests a chronicle. The only texts, apart from *chansons de geste*, which use *laisses* are a few insular verse chronicles, which probably adopt it for its heroic resonances.[72] Indeed, Legge herself would, in a later study, posit the idea that 'the epic form . . . suggests it was designed for a masculine audience', an idea refuted by Campbell, who points out that, as we have seen, the work was 'associated with the baronial women readers of the court of Eleanor of Provence (notably Isabel of Arundel)'.[73] The idea that the epic was monologically masculine is, in any case, a reductive one. The *laisses* of the *Vie de Seint Auban* vary in length but none is very long, and they do present as units of construction and structure as they would be in a true *chanson de geste*.

While Matthew did not use those aspects of *chanson de geste* discourse which most clearly link to oral dissemination – formulae, *laisses parrallèles, laisses similaires, reprise* – we do find other characteristics of the *chanson de geste*, notably extensive use of direct discourse: slightly more than 50 per cent of the lines of the *Vie de Seint Auban* have at least some direct discourse in them; this contrasts with the 'Becket leaves', which have only 34 lines of direct discourse in 310 lines of text, or the rubric couplets of the *Vie de Seint Auban*, which have even fewer lines of direct discourse: 15 lines in a text of 464 lines.[74] We also find instances of the *rhétorique populaire* such as we might expect in a *chanson de geste*: binomials, accumulation, anaphora, some use of alliteration, rather obvious similes and metaphors (e.g. line 281, trans., 72 'God had transformed the wild lion into a lamb'). Mixed with this is the more clerical rhetoric, in a way that is typical of the Anglo-Norman *chanson de geste*, with, for example, the neatly chiastic comment on the Trinity:[75]

> Ke un fust trois, e trois un senglement
>
> (194)

[That one is three and three only one. Trans., 70]

The beginning of *laisse* 9 can be taken as a typical piece of text for analysis; St Auban is recounting his vision of Christ:

> 'La nuit estoit peisible, li tens beus e seri.
> En mun lit fu chuchez e ferm fu endormi
> Avis m'ert ke li cels se desclot e uvri,
> Beus e delitables e purs e esclarci,
> U la gloire de Deu parut e resplendi
> Uns hom d'iluec en terre ça jus desendi;
> En terre fu vivant, en terre fu nurri.
> Un poples cuntre lui e cruel e hardi
> Vint, ki sa doctrine despit e eschivi ... '
>
> (222–30)

> ['The night was peaceful, the weather fair and calm. I had gone to rest in my bed and was fast asleep. It seemed to me that the heavens parted and opened, beautiful, joyous, pure and bright: God's glory appeared and shone resplendently. A man came down from above to earth: he lived on earth and was brought up there. A people both fierce and cruel, who hated and despised his teaching, arose against him ... '. Trans., 71]

Here in line 222 we find a line which, although not formulaic – in the sense that we do not find the same phrase elsewhere in the text – echoes the formulaic descriptions of a *chanson de geste*. The following examples are taken from the *Chanson de Roland*.

> Cler est la noit et la lune luisant.
>
> (2512)

> [The night is clear and the moon is shining.]

> Cler est li jurz e li soleilz luisant.
>
> (2646)

> [The day is clear and the sun is shining.]

Matthew Paris used the twelve-syllable line, which is more common in the later *chansons de geste*, rather than the ten-syllable line of the *Chanson de Roland*, but otherwise his line, with its strong caesura, would not be out of place in the epic text.

Continuing our analysis of *laisse* 9 we note alliteration in 'ferm fu'; line 225 is a list of adjectives; binary structures abound, but include the isocolon of line 228, which we would perhaps be more likely to meet in romance than in epic. Most surprising is the enjambment of lines 229–30 as this technique is rare in *chansons de geste*. We thus have a mixture – devices which give to the text an epic flavour and others which appear more like romance – a mixture which is also found in other insular texts in *chanson de geste* form.[76] It seems that Matthew was giving this hagiographic text a touch of the epic. Campbell has analysed the pattern of martyrdoms in this text, which includes not only the story of St Alban, but also the Passions of Sts Heraclius and Amphibalus. Campbell describes the way these accounts interrelate: 'Alban's martyrdom is seen alongside that of Amphibel and other Christian martyrs, a parity that establishes a sacrificial community reliant on *compagnonnage*: a spiritualized version of epic feudal relations.'[77] While his relationship with Amphibalus is more that of a disciple than an equal (or almost equal) companion, the stress on his vassalage and ascent to heaven does recall that of the great epic warriors, like Roland in the *Chanson de Roland*.[78]

The narrative voice also gives a *planctus*, a lament over the death of Alban:

> Ai! martir gentilz! Ki diable vencu as,
> Gloire du mund guerpis, ta char ne espernias,
> Tun cors a martire pur la lei Deu livras;
> Eu ciel ore regnes e tuz jurs regneras,
> Ki pur tes enemis curaument Deu prias
> Quant l'ewe lur secchis e luis la lur dunas.
> Pieté te preinne de nus tuz, pecchurs las;
> De ceus ki toi honurent n'eit ja part Sathanas !
> Ki primers Engletere par martire aurnas
> Pur nus proiez celui k'est verai Messias,
> Ki en croiz mort sufri, trahi ja par Judas,
> K'il nus ki sa faiture sumes ne perde pas,
> Mais nus saut; si en dient 'amen' e haut e bas!
>
> (923–35)

[Ah, noble martyr, who has conquered the devil! You renounced the world's glory, did not spare your flesh, and gave your body over to martyrdom for the religion of God. In heaven you now reign and will reign forever, you who prayed earnestly to God for your enemies when you dried up the water for them and then restored it. May pity seize you for all us wretched sinners, and may Satan have no part of those who worship you. You who first honoured England by your martyrdom, pray to him for us; for he is the true Messiah, who, betrayed by Judas, suffered death on the cross that he might not lose us, his creation, but rather save us: let us all say 'Amen!' to this, both high and low. Trans., 85].

Charlemagne laments the loss of Roland in the *Chanson de Roland*, but Matthew's *planctus* differs from that of a *chanson de geste* in that it turns it into a prayer in which the martyred hero, as a saint, intercedes for those left behind.

Given that in this text he also evoked the ideological framework of the *chanson de geste*, with the aforementioned allusions to the pagan gods and designation of the pagans as 'Saracens', Matthew's choice of verse form was entirely in keeping with the way he told the tale and with his configuration of Alban as an heroic character cast in the epic mould.

If we turn to the images and the narrative given in the rhyming couplets of the rubrics we notice several differences from the text in *laisses*. First of all, the narrative itself is different. The narrative in *laisses* ends on folio 50 with the passion of St Amphibalus; the images and rubrics in rhyming couplets (and with another series of rubrics in Latin) continue to include St Geneviève of Paris and Offa finding the relics of St Alban; the codex, as we have noted, also contains a Latin charter for the foundation of the abbey issued by Offa and Ecgfrith. The two French texts together thus cover much of the narrative materials found in the Latin texts in the same manuscript. The narrative in rhyming couplets is told very economically, lacking the dramatic use of direct discourse that we found in the epic format; indeed, there are only 15 lines of direct discourse in a text of 464 lines. Two of these lines include the one case of enjambment:

> Dient: 'Querum ceu crestien
> K'Auban converti ...
>
> (140–41)

[Let us seek this Christian who converted Alban].

The rhyming couplet narrative lacks many of the *chanson de geste* echoes. Although we find the word 'Saracen', the panoply of gods of the *chansons de geste* has gone; instead there are theological echoes, with allusion to the Pelagian heresy (304, 312). Far from being more popular in tone, as we might expect from the use of the commonplace rhyming couplet, this version is slightly less so.

We are thus offered three parallel narratives: one in images, one in rhyming couplets, one in epic *laisses*. The form of the text and the discourse used give the two French texts of *Saint Auban* quite distinct flavours, that of the epic and that of a romance, chronicle or saint's life. The choice of verse form is, I argue, deliberate and part of the complex texture of this three-stranded narrative.

While some of the rest of Matthew's vernacular output may recall the *chanson de geste*, the form is, as we have noted, that normally used in hagiography and in rhymed chronicle. Despite the irregularity of syllable count we have noted, it can be demonstrated that in places he is able to exploit the verse form for dramatic effect. For example, in the *Estoire de Seint Ædward* a combination of rhetoric and rhyme in direct discourse adds a dynamic force to the rhythm; King Edward is enumerating the acts of violence the country had suffered during his exile and the news he had received:

> Ore de Cnut, ore de Suan,
> Par queus sufristes tant d'ahan,
> Ocise, arson,
> D'aver rançun,
> Exil, servage,
> E prisun,
> Nuveles de la mort mun pere,
> Nuveles des noces ma mere,
> Nuvele de Aedmund mun frère –
> Ki pire fu ke la premere –
> Nuveles de mes nevusz,
> K'ocis furent par Daneis gluz . . .
>
> (1415–26)

[Sometimes it was about Cnut, other times it was about Swein, at whose hands you suffered so many troubles: murder, arson, your wealth spent in ransoms, exile, servitude and prison. There was news of my father's death, the news of my mother's marriage, the news of Edmund my brother (which was worse than the news of my father's death), the news of my nephews who were murdered by the greedy Danes. Trans., 71–72].

Lines 1417–20 could be set out as two eight-syllable lines, though lines 1419–20 only work if the mute –e in *servage* is pronounced; the way the lines are set out by the modern editor, however, emphasises the staccato rhythm of the text. The anaphora of the lines which follow again puts the accent on the rhythm, which, combined with the repetition, thus emphasises the accumulation of evil news reaching the exiled prince.

In the *Estoire* the use of parataxis and occasional statement out of narrative chronology, both common in Old French narrative, does leave some passages lacking clarity by modern standards. Thus the translator's comments that the statement that Æthelred fled to Normandy (201–02) precedes the information that he sent his 'wife Emma and his children to Richard of Normandy so that he might protect them' (233–35), which might mislead the reader into thinking that this was the order of events, whereas he sent his family ahead of him.[79] It was not uncommon in French narrative, particularly *chanson de geste*, for the sequence of events to be unclear, though this was less usual in a chronicle. The two lines narrating Æthelred's escape head the section, because the necessity of his flight is the key point in what follows; the narrative sequence is not diegetic.

If the 'Rubrics for Pictures of Saints' are to be attributed to Matthew (and the hand is similar), then we find here yet another verse form.[80] This one is particularly striking and may be our only piece of evidence that Matthew was aware of English verse forms, as the rubrics are written in tail rhyme, a verse form common enough in Middle English but more unusual in French.[81] Legge described its use in romance, as distinct from hymns, as 'peculiar to England'.[82] The attribution of these lines is uncertain; the lines are far from polished but we must be wary of falling into the same trap as our predecessors and assuming they cannot be the work of Matthew Paris but must be from a less skilled pen. It is worth giving some consideration to these lines, if only because they have been almost totally ignored in scholarship on Matthew's writings. In the manuscript the lines are set out almost like a play, with each apostle speaking in turn. Let us take the words of four apostles:[83]

> Jacobus: Sue merci Deus me eschoisi e apostle apela
> Johannes: Bien me out Deus cher quant à garder sa mere me livra.
> Andreas: En croiz me mist, lier me fist, Egée li felun.
> Thomas: Ki en Deu croit, pas nel voit, par moi ad beneiçun.

Setting each speech out without the names of the apostles, the tail rhyme can be more easily seen:

> Sue merci
> Deus me eschoisi
> e apostle apela.
>
> [In his mercy, God chose me and called me apostle.]
>
> Bien me out Deus cher
> quant à garder
> sa mere me livra.
>
> [God held me dear when he gave me the charge of His mother.]
>
> En croiz me mist,
> lier me fist,
> Egée li felun.
>
> [The felon Egeans had me bound to a cross.]
>
> Ki en Deu croit,
> pas nel voit,
> par moi ad beneiçun.
>
> [He who believes in God, [and] does not see, receives from me a blessing.]

The verses are of no great literary merit, except that they would be easily remembered. The short lines are mostly of four syllables; if the elision of *nel* is ignored, they are in fact regular. The longer lines are of six syllables. Such short lines are not common in Old French poetry and may suggest that these lines are particularly intended for the use of the young. This would be appropriate in a manuscript for the use of the whole community, including novices, and possibly the schoolboys.

Legge's comment on the use of tail rhyme comes in the context of her discussion of another St Albans writer, Beneit, who had himself composed a life of St Thomas Becket. Legge reasoned that Beneit, who wrote good French, adopted the English romance verse 'to provide a romance-loving public with something edifying, yet readable, and to do this he used the Devil's instrument and made use of the characteristic tail-rhyme'.[84] More recently Purdie, in her detailed study of the use of tail rhyme in England, has noted that '[The tail-rhyme romances] are designed to appeal to a broad and varied audience in that they offer elementary moral or spiritual lessons attractively packaged.'[85] Our short lines are certainly elementary. The existence at St Albans of another text in tail rhyme removes the need to assume that Matthew was reading English romances, but if these lines are to be attributed to him this choice of a different form reinforces our sense that he experiments with forms to engage lay readers. The same impulse that Legge attributes to Beneit, to make his narratives appealing and fit them into recognisable forms, may lie behind the variety of verse forms adopted by Matthew. The diversity of his verse forms, and even the variability of his syllable count, may be due to a willingness to innovate and experiment, to choose a form depending on the subject matter, and a rhyme scheme which can be used flexibly rather than having to be adhered to as would be the case in lyric rather than narrative poetry.

We must be careful of imposing on a medieval writer our sense of genre divisions, and to Matthew no doubt his hagiographies were also histories, but it seems that he was aware of the generic implications of using different verse forms and willing to experiment and use different forms for different subjects, his choice of form setting up certain expectations in the mind of the readers (and listeners) of his narratives.[86]

Matthew Paris should perhaps be considered above all as a storyteller using a range of modes of narration: when writing histories for the literate he wrote in Latin prose; when writing his narratives in French he used verse, still the natural way to tell a story in French in the middle of the thirteenth century. He also told his story in images, text and image complementing each other, bringing out different aspects of the narrative. His experimentation with the different verse forms and structure of thirteenth-century vernacular narratives are also indicative of his self-conscious literariness, using the familiar to engage his readers. He did not simply adopt a form or mode of tale-telling. He rather used and evoked a mode of narrative – history, epic, romance – each serving a different purpose. Like all creative writers he took a tradition and did something different, writing a *chanson de geste* where the hero is a saint rather than a warrior, a history where the king is also a saint and a saint's life where the saint is an archbishop. In all of his vernacular narratives the term which perhaps best sums up Matthew Paris' output is 'dynamic'. As a translator he operated in a way which we would now label as seeking 'dynamic equivalence' rather than 'faithful' translation; as a poet he exploited the possibilities of verse forms dynamically, rather than focusing on a strict adherence to ideals of prosody.

In some respects Matthew Paris epitomises the bilingual culture of the educated of his day, a culture in which clergy and some educated laity would move readily between Latin and French; Matthew employed the language and techniques appropriate for his readership and his subject matter, using Latin as his authority and enriching French literature by translating from Latin, thus broadening the textual community for these narratives. While such fertilisation across different languages is not untypical of the period, to have such a corpus from the pen of one man is exceptional, and no other named monastic writer has left us such a range of texts in French. It is time for his vernacular works to be brought out of the shadows.

Notes

1. *Auban* translated in Wogan-Browne and Fenster 2010; *Ædward*, also available online at www.anglo-norman.net/sources, translated in Fenster and Wogan-Browne 2008; Baker 1929; see also the translation of Matthew's Latin *Vita* in Meyer 1885; Lawrence 1996. Campbell 2008, 250–51 provides a useful timeline of early Anglo–Norman hagiographic texts showing clearly where Paris fits in to the tradition. I am grateful to Jocelyn Wogan-Browne for her comments on a draft of this chapter.
2. Harvey 2001, 165–77.
3. www.bl.uk/onlinegallery/onlineex/mapsviews/mapgb/large17694.html; see also Connolly 2009, plate X.
4. Connolly 2009, plate VI; fragments of a map survive on damaged leaves of a copy of Matthew's *Chronica maiora* in Corpus Christi College Cambridge MS 16, Corpus Christi College Cambridge MS 26 and especially British Library Royal MS 14 CVII; Dean and Boulton 2000, item 334, 183–84. See McKendrick, Lowden and Doyle 2011, 294–95.

5. Tremlett and Stanford London 1967, 7.
6. Short 1979–80.
7. There have been a significant number of studies about the uses of French in England; see for example William Rothwell, 'The Role of French in Thirteenth-Century England', https://anglo-norman.net/the-role-of-french-in-thirteenth-century-england; Short 1979–80; Wogan-Browne et al. 2009; Ingham 2010; Trotter 2011; Ailes and Putter 2014; Baswell, Cannon, Kerby-Fulton and Wogan-Browne 2015; for an annotated bibliography see https://frenchofengland.ace.fordham.edu/?page_id=100.
8. For Matthew's origins see Chapter 1, 15.
9. Vaughan 1958c, 1.
10. Vaughan 1958c, 1.
11. Thomson 1982, 41–42. St Albans is famously associated with the Hildesheim Psalter, which contains a copy of the *Vie de Saint Alexis* with a unique prologue in French prose. A twelfth-century list of books from the library of Bury St Edmunds includes no books in French, though prior to the Norman Conquest the Bury library had a good number of vernacular (Anglo-Saxon) manuscripts, Sharpe et al. 1996, 49–50. See also Chapter 3, 78.
12. Sharpe et al. 1996, 539.
13. Legge 1950, 19–43; Sharpe et al. 1996, 539; Thomson 1982, i. 3 considered that the lack of evidence means that a 'fully comprehensive and connected account of the growth of the Abbey library ... is out of the question'.
14. Sharpe et al., 1996, 50.
15. https://mss-cat.trin.cam.ac.uk/Manuscript/O.9.34.
16. Vaughan 1958c, 141–43.
17. *Ædward*, ll. 916–218; Fenster and Wogan-Browne 2008, 65.
18. Fenster and Wogan-Browne 2008, 118n18; see also Short 2013, 17–44.
19. Södergård 1948, l. 7; Legge 1950, 25, commented on the difficulty of interpreting the 'apology for the imperfections of language'.
20. See Short 2010, 35–55; O'Donnell 2011, 337–56; Russell 2012, 124; Wogan-Browne et al. 2015, 659–62; Wogan-Browne et al. 2016, 9–25; for a summary of the older interpretations of this see Rothwell 2001. Vising 1923, 26–27 took such apologies at face value: '*faus franceis* and *dreit engleis*'.
21. Baker 1929, 338; Vaughan 1958c, 19.
22. Vaughan 1953b; McCulloch 1981; Wallace 1983, xvii–xxi; Baswell 2010, 172–72, 177–79.
23. Fenster and Wogan-Browne 2008, 25; for a summary of arguments about attribution see 25–26. See also Wogan-Browne 2001, 151–88, especially 155–57. See also Chapter 16, 337.
24. Fenster and Wogan-Browne 2008, 25; Vaughan 1958c, 176.
25. Baker 1929, 338–39; Morgan 1982–88, ii. 15, 95–96.

26. On the manuscript, BL MS Additional 70513 see Vaughan 1958c, 168–78; Russell 2003; Campbell 2008, 182–83 and 235. See also Russell 2016.
27. Campbell 2008, 183n7.
28. Wogan-Browne 2001, 16; on women as translators of hagiography see Wogan-Browne 1994; see also Meale 1993.
29. Binski 1990; Fenster and Wogan-Browne 2008, 27–28.
30. Harden 1968, xv.
31. Backhouse and de Hamel 1988, 13–18. See Chapter 9, 201–7.
32. Dean and Boulton 2000, 284.
33. Dean and Boulton 2000, 282; see also Baswell 2010.
34. Wogan-Browne and Fenster 2010, 22–23.
35. Rothwell 1976.
36. Legge 1950; Wogan-Browne 2001.
37. So important was translation in the Middle Ages that one scholar described it as 'une vaste entreprise de traduction', Zink 2011, vol. 1, p. 9.
38. Wogan-Browne and Fenster 2010, 6.
39. Wogan-Browne and Fenster 2010, 15; for the manuscript and its background see Otter 1996, 23–26 and Baswell 2010.
40. The abbey had a grammar school established at a relatively early date; see Orme 1973, 167–79; Thomson 1982, i. 1.
41. 'Translated' can, as has been pointed out, mean 'transferred' or 'copied' as well as translated from one language to another, but in the multilingual context most frequently meant translation from one language to another; Fenster and Wogan-Browne 2008, 25.
42. Discussed by Legge 1950, 24.
43. Lusignan 2004, 155–217; Fenster and Wogan-Browne 2008, 137n178; on the complementarity of French and Latin see also Clanchy 1993, 196–223.
44. Fenster and Wogan-Browne 2008, 43n27, 119.
45. Lloyd and Reader 2004; see also Wallace 1983, xxiii–xxviii.
46. Lloyd and Reader 2004; see also Wallace 1983, xxiii–xxviii.
47. The manuscript is digitised and can be viewed at https://cudl.lib.cam.ac.uk/view/MS-EE-00003-00059/1; see also Baswell 2003 and the introduction to Fenster and Wogan-Browne 2008.
48. See Hunt 1991, i. 13. Orme 2006 states that 'French was used in schools for teaching Latin' (75), but also points to a few texts from the thirteenth century on which give some instruction in Latin for the learning of French (74).
49. Fenster and Wogan-Browne 2010, 185.
50. Lawrence 1960; for his discussion of the close relationship between the Latin and French texts see 74–78.
51. Meyer 1885, viii.
52. See facsimile in Backhouse and de Hamel 1988.

53. Francisque 1836–40. The extract included corresponds to ll. 4511–4638 of Wallace's edition.
54. Wallace 1983, xxiv.
55. Wallace 1983, xxvi; Wallace points out that archaeologists have used Matthew Paris' description to form a clear image of the old church at Westminster.
56. Nithard tells us that Charlemagne 'left the whole of Europe flourishing [the Franks and barbarians] dared do nothing in Charles' empire except what was in harmony with the public welfare' and later in his text he says that 'peace and concord ruled everywhere', Scholz with Rogers 1970, 129–30, 174.
57. There have been several studies of how much medieval scholars knew about Islam since Southern 1962; see for example Tolan 1996; Frassetto and Blanks 1999.
58. Brault 1978. All quotations and translations are from this edition.
59. Atkinson 1876.
60. Meyer 1885, xxxi. Much has been written on Anglo-Norman versification, much of it critical; see for example Vising 1923, 79–87, but cf. Johnston 1974; see also Johnston 1979; Johnston 1980; Pensom 2006.
61. Groeber, review of Atkinson's edition, cited in *Auban*, xi.
62. Baker 1929, 341; Vaughan 1958c, 181.
63. Wallace 1983, xxix.
64. Meyer 1885, xxxi.
65. Meyer 1885, xxxiv; Johnston 1980; see also Johnston 1979; Pensom 2006.
66. Wallace 1983, xxxi.
67. Essay on the language and versification of the *Vie de Seint Auban* in the introduction to the translation: Fenster and Wogan-Browne 2010, 41–50 at 45.
68. For example, ll. 23–26, 285–88.
69. Meyer 1885, xxxv, note 3 gives other examples. Legge 1950 picks up Meyer's analysis and that of M. R. James, pointing out that the same proportion of seven-syllable lines is found in the rhyming couplets of the *Vie de Seint Auban* rubrics.
70. *Auban*, xv; Legge 1950, 23.
71. Legge 1950, 23.
72. E.g. Johnston 1981.
73. Legge 1963, 268; Campbell 2008, 136, n. 24.
74. The *laisses* of the *Saint Auban* have 969 lines of direct discourse out of 1,846 lines; for a discussion of direct discourse in different genres see Marnette 1998, 115–36, on the *chanson de geste* see 124–27; Marnette notes that 'Les chansons de geste ... accordant beaucoup d'importance au DD ... les paroles des personnages reçoivent donc presqu'autant et parfois plus d'espace que celles du narrateur', 124.

75. Ailes 2009.
76. Ailes 2011.
77. Campbell 2008, 137.
78. Campbell 2008, 135–40; on Roland as God's vassal see Brault 1978, ii. 257–59.
79. Fenster and Wogan-Browne 2008, 120n32.
80. Legge 1950, 28–29; Dean and Boulton 2000, 282.
81. Purdie 2008, 34–65 discusses the use of tail rhyme in Anglo-Norman; with the exception of Beneit's life of St Thomas Becket, tail rhyme is found in lyric and, in particular, didactic literature.
82. Legge 1950, 20.
83. The lines are transcribed by Wallace 1983, xi–xii.
84. Legge 1950, 20.
85. Purdie 2008, 33.
86. Wogan-Browne and Fenster 2010, 3n9 comment that 'it is unlikely that Paris would have subscribed to modern genre divisions among historiography, romance and hagiography'.

JAMES G. CLARK

15

Afterlife

Medieval chroniclers were the servants of posterity. They wrote for the records of the past they had inherited and those of the present they had gathered for themselves to be preserved and together to pass to the next generation. For those living under a monastic rule, this act of service to the future was a necessary dispensation for a task which inevitably turned their attention from the eternal to the temporal. The humility and self-deprecation of their profession were at once threatened by the narration of humanity's deeds and words. Their defence was to connect their chronicle to their vocation – that is, to the practical and pastoral benefits they brought to the community of the faithful. 'What is more to the advantage of virtue or more conducive to justice', declared William of Malmesbury (d. 1143), than to read 'those things that, by the wonderful dispensation of God, have befallen . . . in recent times[?]'[1] 'I have been at pains to set down the things I have seen and heard', explained Jocelin of Brakelond (d. c. 1215) at Bury St Edmunds, 'certain bad things for caution, certain good which might be useful'.[2] If the limitations of their skill left the lesson unclear, then to the future they could look only for blessed forgiveness, as for 'poor little' Gervase of Canterbury (d. c. 1210).[3] If God's dispensation was not wonderfully demonstrated, the Winchester monk Richard of Devizes (d. c. 1200) directed, their work was 'only for the living'.[4]

Matthew Paris wrote to be read. He addressed the reader directly. 'I write this', he confided in his *Gesta abbatum*, 'so that the reader of this page may know the threat from our own enemies'.[5] Here he spoke for and to his own immediate colleagues in the monastic community, using the pronoun 'our(s)'. He wrote with an eye on other abbey records which he assumed would always be close at hand.[6] The tone of his contemporary history hinted at wider horizons. When he wrote of happenings at the abbey he named it: in 1251 thunderstorms struck the south of England and Matthew shared what he had witnessed 'at [*apud*] St Albans'.[7] Here there was no possessive, plural pronoun. Perhaps it would not be 'our' abbey for the reader. He anticipated an assiduous audience, either a 'critic' (*perscrutator*) or a 'diligent researcher' (*diligens indagator*) who would want to know, perhaps even to see the proof of his words.[8] Whether they came by way of his shorter history, *Historia Anglorum*, or his great chronicle, he assumed they would want to know more.[9] He also directed them to letter books and memoranda, to the abbey's liturgical books and in the life of Stephen Langton, to the scholarly resources of the abbey.[10] He imagined their point of view. Since they may not be a member of his own community or network of monks, he explained, he had spared them details of the internal divisions at Glastonbury and Winchester which had damaged their order and endangered their endowments.[11] Perhaps worldly (*saecularis*), he offered a warning to 'fear a fall into the hands of the living God' (Hebrews 10:31).[12] In the face of papal taxation, he hoped to stir them to respond by bringing them to the brink of tears (*quod lacrimas excutere debeat ab oculis audientium*).[13]

Matthew also looked to the future. When he was inclined to draw his chronicling to a close at the end of 1250, he affirmed that his purpose had been simply to write 'for the benefit of posterity' (*pro utilitate posteritatis subsecuturae*) so that current affairs are neither forgotten or obscured (*ne memoriam eventum modernorum vetustas aut oblivio deleat*). Readers other than his own St Albans colleagues were meant to recognise this, since he repeated it in his manuscript of *Flores historiarum*.[14] Here he also warned himself not to presume to reach into a future time he would never know (*nec ventura petas quae postera proferat aetas*).[15]

In his only preface to a chronicle, which opens his own copy of the *Gesta abbatum*, he echoed Jocelin's determination that the record of 'both good works and bad may be passed on to future times', to stir (*excitentur*) the one and to suppress (*coeceantur*) the other.[16] At times he broke off his narration to draw attention to what posterity should know (*ut sciant posteri*).¹⁷ Generally, these were lessons for the future which he had witnessed at first-hand: the 'poverty and slavery' (*miseria et servitus*) which appeared to be the aim of the crown in its approach to the monastic church; or how an election to the abbacy should be conducted.¹⁸ Just once he was tempted to offer up a judgement at a distance, urging the next generation to recognise, in Richard of Cornwall's election as the king of the Romans (1257), the capacity of the foolish English to be gulled by foreign cunning.¹⁹

His sifting of good and bad guided the shape of his records. He created a formula to capture the features of each passing year, a conclusion (*annalis conclusio*) which grew from observations on the weather and other conditions of daily life towards reflections on the fortunes of powers and their people, be it endangered, disturbed or embattled (*periculosus . . . procellosus . . . praeliosus*).²⁰ His closing summary for the year 1250 carried a word of foreboding, not to ask what the future might bring.²¹ In writing of the St Albans abbots he blended biography and obituary, holding only loosely to chronology so as to bring before the reader their personality, the remembered litany of their successes and failures (*praeconiis . . . et negligentiis memorati*) and their legacy as it was understood by the living community.²²

Matthew's approach was underscored by a concern to conserve his source material. He set down for his readers the form and origin of the century-old roll which he used as the basis for *Gesta abbatum*.²³ In the same manuscript he made a sequence of document transcriptions, presented as an appendix (*additamenta* was his chosen Latin term) to his chronicle of contemporary history, offering full proof of the business of monasteries that his annal reported. His ambition, perhaps, was to evidence the significant transactions both of St Albans and of its neighbours, although he found documentation did not always 'come to the notice of the writer of this book' (*ad noticiam praesentis libri scriptoris . . . non pervenerunt*).²⁴ In fact, he thought of his 'book of additional annals' (*librum additamentorum*) as garnering an authority which would reinforce any of his writing on recent times. In his life of Stephen Langton the reader was directed to 'come and inspect' the record of the archbishop's 'words, wisdom and virtues'.²⁵

This scholarly interest in the future value of his writing was matched by an impulse to attract personal acclaim. In his *Gesta abbatum* and in his contemporary history Matthew named himself as he 'who both copied and compiled' (*qui et haec scripsit et enarravit*).[26] Subjectivity was not unusual among the monastic writers of his time. At Bury, Jocelin and John of Taxter, a chronicler who was an exact contemporary of Matthew, placed themselves in their annals, noting their own position in the community at a given moment and their proximity to an event or its key protagonists.[27] But Matthew sometimes went so far as to cast himself as a character in the drama. Reporting table talk of the oppressions of the Poitevans in 1252, he entered the scene, sitting at the table (*ad commune parapsidem commensalem*) in the company of the very civil (*miles et literatus*) Sir Roger de Thurkeby. He reported his own speech (*recitaret, respondit et dixit*).[28] Matthew was at pains not only to be known as a witness but to be recognised for the quality of his testimony. When Bishop Grosseteste answered a question 'on the nail', not only did he hear it, but he was also able to record it word for word (*prout huius paginae audivit et verbo ad verbum satis dilucide scripsit*).[29] The story (1251) of the eight-day captivity of Thomas, a Norman monk of Sherborne, when overseas in the service of the king, he set out step by step (*seriatim*) because he judged it a worthy tale (*quia fide dignus erat [scriptor] plenius annotavit*).[30] Writing in French of King Henry and Queen Eleanor's devotion to the cult of Edward the Confessor, his affective description '*amer et cherir*' conveyed to the reader the intimacy of his own insight.[31]

Matthew magnified his presence in the craft of his manuscripts. He was not the only monk to write for himself, but his script departed so far from the typical style of his time that it was readily recognisable. His stints were surely traceable for readers until his texts were no longer a regular source of reference as new transactions for the abbey and the church had replaced the preoccupations of his own day.

He reached further than most who compiled and kept books by representing himself in a self-portrait. He showed himself kneeling before the Virgin Mary, the subject of a new devotional routine introduced for his generation of St Albans monks by his first abbot, William of Trumpington.[32] If the sacred image was meant to connect him with the present experience of all of his colleagues, nonetheless his own picture placed him in the hierarchy of the monastery with those masters and craftsmen whose commissioned works carried their name and in one instance another portrait, of the cellarer John of Wallingford, a patron, a compiler if not an independent writer of books.[33] At St Albans, creative investment purchased a personal memorial even for those professed to the practice of humility.

At the time of his death at the end of the 1250s Matthew Paris' writing was surely known within his own network, certainly at St Albans but also quite possibly across its dependent houses. There is no record of how many manuscripts made by Matthew Paris himself or with others were at his abbey at the time of his passing. What survives now may be almost all there was; there is no composition attributed to him of which at least a fragment has not been preserved. All of the survivors have lost their medieval bindings and all but a handful of their flyleaves, robbing them of valuable evidence of the context(s) in which they were kept. There is no early inscription that signals a new institutional setting and so it may be reasonable to assume that in the decades immediately following his death Matthew's manuscripts remained at St Albans. The condition of the leaves suggests continued handling although almost all of the notes in their margins are written in scripts which date from the next century and after.[34]

A clear indication of their currency for the community Matthew left behind is that his two largest works, *Gesta abbatum* and *Chronica maiora*, were continued by others in the next generation. His *gesta* of John de Hertford was completed after the abbot's death in 1263, the compiler weighing his strengths (*virtuta*) and weaknesses (*negligentis*) in same terms as Matthew had done for his predecessors. They acknowledged Matthew's own contribution to the annal, a 'reliable record of the past', piously representing it as an exemplum of the '*opus manuum*' to which they were all called under the Rule of St Benedict.[35] A precis of the deeds of twenty-three abbots (down to John de Hertford) may have been made at this time, if not initiated in the chronicler's lifetime.[36]

Matthew's chronicle of current events was extended for the remaining dozen years of Henry III's reign and, in due course, beyond. The earliest witness to this work now surviving was written to the end of one full quire in Matthew's own manuscript, BL, Royal MS 14 C VII. There it closed with the death of Henry III, but in later copies found in manuscripts with no direct connection to Matthew himself the narrative covers much of the following reign of Edward I. How many contributed to this continuing annal and at what intervals cannot be deduced from the partial copies preserved, but the first of them was conscious of Matthew and his legacy. They adopted his template for a summary of the passing year, echoed his words in giving a verdict on its fertile and fruitful harvest and, for a time at least, a litany of the notable obituaries. Those responsible for the text in the Royal manuscript made a visual memorial, a portrait of Matthew on his deathbed, painted in a style that recalled his own.[37] A fresh copy of the *Chronica maiora* narrative as far as 1250 was begun perhaps only a decade after Matthew death; a second part was completed close to the end of the century (now BL, Cotton MS Nero D V, Parts I and II). At the same time, a second copy of the *Chronica* was made (now, BL, Harley MS 1620).[38]

When there was no living memory of Matthew the awareness of and interest in his work at St Albans was as a source of reference for the recent past, for the church and the kingdom, and as the stem for the continuing task of record-keeping. At the end of the thirteenth century, to Matthew's sequence of document 'additions' was added a list of the abbey's tenants together with several transcripts of charters.[39]

There is no trace of any new copy of his own compilations having been made at the abbey or at one of its dependent communities after the turn of the fourteenth century. Notice of Matthew as a compiler of chronicles and histories in the *Catalogus* of Latin writers made after 1350 by Henry de Kirkstede may not be an indication that any, either original or new manuscript of his works had reached his own house at Bury St Edmund's.[40] Kirkstede consulted book collections beyond his own. He surely knew St Albans well. Thomas Wykes, a canon of Oseney (Oxfordshire), named Matthew alongside Bede and William of Newburgh, as among the 'most famous chroniclers of English affairs' but it is unclear where, directly or indirectly, he had discovered him.[41]

An outlier here is the solitary witness to a copy of a chronicle 'to the year 1252' attributed to Matthew in the University Library at Oxford at some time in the (presumably) first half of the early sixteenth century. It is among eighteen titles recorded in a list preserved among the papers of Cardinal Guglielmo Sirleto (1514–85). It has been suggested this was the manuscript containing the shorter *Historia Anglorum* (BL, Royal MS 14 C VII) since it had been presented to Duke Humfrey of

Gloucester (1390–1447) who was also a donor to the Oxford library. But it was not among those listed in the formal record of his gifts.[42]

Matthew's history of his own time did reach a wider readership in the years after his death through the development and dissemination of the universal chronicle known as *Flores historiarum*. His own version of a narrative originated by Roger of Wendover, his near-contemporary at St Albans, was written out with a sequence of illustrations in the manuscript now Chetham's Library MS 6712. The text for the years 1249–56 is the work of hands other than Matthew; almost all of the illustrations are the work of other artists.[43] On the evidence of the different orientation of the narrative it has been deduced that from 1256 as far as 1265 the book had passed to Pershore Abbey (Worcestershire).[44] Then it came into the possession of the monks of Westminster where perhaps the illustration of the coronation of Edward I was added.[45] It has been suggested that two turn-of-the century copies of *Flores* whose provenance is unknown, now BL, Arundel MS 96 and Oxford Bodl., MS Laud 572, were copied directly from the St Albans-Pershore-Westminster book.[46] A version of *Flores* finished at the turn of the fourteenth century also bears some similarities to the Chetham manuscript in its layout and image sequence. Marginal notes recording the succession of priors at Merton (Surrey) signal its ownership at that Augustinian monastery, although not necessarily its origin. Richard Vaughan posited that this copy was made from a St Albans copy of the Chetham manuscript which has since disappeared, although there is no tangible evidence of the reproduction of Matthew's *Flores* within the abbey.[47] A shorter version of the St Albans form of the *Flores* narrative was begun at Holm Abbey (Norfolk) also at the beginning of the new century and then continued at the Cistercian abbey at Tintern (Monmouthshire).[48]

This transmission was uncoordinated and certainly there is nothing to suggest that St Albans Abbey's affiliations carried any firm influence on the path taken by the text. Nonetheless, there was some slight awareness of Matthew's contribution to the compilation and his coverage of the events of his time. The late fourteenth-century compiler of the chronicle of Hyde Abbey (Hampshire) acknowledged Matthew by name.[49] He was named again as an historical source a century later in an anonymous genealogy of the kings of England added to a manuscript also containing Ranulf Higden's *Polychronicon*.[50]

Compilers who came after also found inspiration in the illustrations of the 'Westminster' manuscript. The coronations of kings from the legendary Arthur to the living Edward I appear to have acted as compositional template for the Merton Priory *Flores* and also appear to be echoed in a number of the subsequent copies.[51] The 'design' or 'mise-en-page' of the text was also imitated at least for certain distinctive entries, such as the diagrammatic representation of the Saxon heptarchy and the sequence of margin rubrics that run from the years 1069–1249 to explain each year's calculation for the date of Easter.[52]

The reception of *Flores* beyond St Albans was an exception to the general confinement of the illustrated manuscripts made by Matthew himself or others acting under his influence. One fifteenth-century miniature representation of the procession of the Holy Blood relic incorporated in the same royal genealogy that referenced Matthew appears to be a copy of his illustration for his Greater chronicle. Although it is conceivable it was derived from a fully illustrated copy of the St Albans book which has since been lost, it is most likely that it and the textual references were copied in situ at the abbey.[53] Since only fragments of the abbey's overall visual culture have been preserved, it is difficult to prove Suzanne Lewis' judgement that the monastery was 'no longer in the mainstream of Gothic art'. It is a possibility that the illustrations for the French lives of Edward the Confessor and Thomas Becket found the sole surviving manuscript witnesses were made by others in faithful homage to Matthew's work.[54] But this would have been when his own work remained in living memory. Later there is little trace of a direct stylistic influence.[55]

There may have been a larger readership outside St Albans for Matthew's hagiography. A faint note at the front of his collection of the cult texts for Alban and Amphibalus records the loan of the book, together with copies of the lives of Edward the Confessor and Thomas Becket to the countesses of Arundel and Cornwall.[56] Although there is no clear indication that a manuscript of Matthew's saints' lives was made for presentation as a gift to a lay patron, this signals that at least some of these texts did come into their hands. Surviving copies of any of the lives are scarce: those of Becket and Langton are found only in fragments, the Norman French Edward the Confessor in just one witness. But in itself this is not proof of a limited transmission.

Matthew's life of Edmund of Abingdon passed through the monastic network in the second half of the thirteenth century, no doubt propelled by the archbishop's early canonisation. By about 1300 it had reached Durham Cathedral Priory and entered into an existing collection of saints' lives.[57] The text was added to anthologies of saints' lives found at Christ Church, Canterbury and Campsey Abbey (Norfolk), where the collection was chosen for reading in the conventual refectory (*de lire a mengier*).[58]

By the turn of the fourteenth century, some five decades after Matthew's death, interest in his hagiography and history had faded. No copy of any of his saints' lives later than about 1325 is known to survive; nor is there a certain record of any of them in a book catalogue. The value of his narratives, even of the abbey and the abbots, had diminished over time. In the half-century between the accession of Edward I (1272) and the deposition of his son (1327) contemporary annals were kept at St Albans with an energy not seen since the age of Magna Carta and the First Barons' War. These annalists – of whom only William Rishanger can be identified with any confidence – acted with an awareness of their predecessors' work. They retained their template for a summary of each passing year; they showed a similar commitment to the transcription of key documents. At Tynemouth Priory they recalled Matthew's illustrative style, drawing inverted shields in the margin to mark the obituary notices of the notable.[59] A portion of Rishanger's narrative events from 1272 was used to extend the coverage of Matthew's manuscript, now BL Royal MS 14 C VII.[60] But generally these two (or more) generations felt no tie to the compilations of the past. Matthew's *Gesta abbatum* narrative was now continued in parallel lines which were kept apart: one a register of acts of the abbots at St Albans itself, another, found in a fragment of circa 1300, an annal of the administration of the dependent priory at Wymondham.[61]

Both Matthew's and Roger of Wendover's chronicles may have recaptured attention in the last years of their century when monasteries were called on to share their records of the Scottish crown. This may have been why a summary history of succession to the throne of Scotland was kept beside Matthew's work in BL, Cotton MS Claudius D VI.[62] An anonymous, unprovenanced compilation made at this time carries notes on the descent of the throne in Scotland taken '*ex cronicis sancti Albani*'.⁶³ But this search among the old authorities was ad hoc. No new audience for the abbey's records now arose, either for the chronicles of the age of John or Henry III or for those of Rishanger and his colleagues of the years from Rhuddlan (1282) to Bannockburn (1314). *Flores* also receded. By the second quarter of the fourteenth century, narratives associated with the old abbeys had given ground to those compiled in quite different contexts such as the *Annales* of the Dominican Nicholas Trevet, an 'immediate forerunner' of Ranulf Higden's *Polychronicon*, and the *Historia aurea* compiled by the secular clerk John of Tynemouth.⁶⁴

Patterns of reading and original writing (if any) at St Albans before the Black Death are difficult to discern. The abbey suffered collateral damage from the downfall of Edward II, who had shown more generous patronage than either his father or grandfather. During the abbacy of Richard of Wallingford (1327–34) books were sold to settle debts, among them at least one manuscript made by Matthew Paris.⁶⁵ Even so several other manuscripts show signs of care and close attention. It appears that the portion of the *Chronica maiora* contained in Cambridge, Corpus Christi College, MS 26 was now rebound as two leaves from an early fourteenth-century English canon law text, the first evidently used as a paste-down, are positioned as front flyleaves.⁶⁶ Judging from the style of the script before 1350 both BL, Cotton MS Nero D V and Trinity College, Dublin, MS 177 were given shelf marks assigning them to the first press (A) in the monastery's book room. Two others, BL, Cotton MS Nero D I, containing the *Gesta abbatum*, and the manuscript containing the *Historia Anglorum*, BL, Royal MS 14 C VII, were now marked with donation inscriptions '*dedit frater Mathaeus Parisiensis*'. It was the usual form of words to record a book, often a textbook, acquired by an individual monk for his own use and then assigned to the convent collection by him by choice or by default after his death. Now Matthew was remembered as a patron with choice possessions, not primarily as an author.

In the same period an anonymous compiler added a three-folio account of King Arthur to Nero;⁶⁷ an unknown reader of Dublin found a contradiction (*contractim*) between the text and that given in 'another volume [of history] from the beginning of the world to the advent of our Lord';⁶⁸ and a reader of Royal 14 C VII made notes on diverse topics, the Normans, the town of St Albans and the death of Roger Bigod.[69] Beyond the books themselves there is at least a hint of the lingering influence of Matthew's body of work. Probably it was at this time that an anonymous monk compiled stories of miracles at the shrine of St Alban witnessed at the time of the Battle of Bannockburn, presented in the mould of those Matthew included in the Dublin manuscript. They are found only in a manuscript from the turn of the fifteenth century (now BL, Cotton MS Claudius E IV), but their focus on Edward II and his knights suggests they were compiled some seventy-five years before.[70] A further continuation of his *Gesta abbatum* as far as 1307, covering the abbacies of John de Berkhamsted (1290–1301) and John de Maryns (1301–7), may also date from this time. The earliest of two extant copies was made in the middle years of the century.[71]

The final quarter of the fourteenth century saw a resurgence of interest in the figure of Matthew himself. His return to the minds of the monastic community may be attributed to an individual monk, Thomas Walsingham (c. 1340–c. 1422), precentor at the abbey from at least 1380 until 1394. His office was responsible for the convent's book collection, its distribution and use, repairs and new acquisitions. By his own account, Walsingham was placed in charge of a new 'writing-room' – a chamber in among the communal spaces of the monastery (chapter house, cloister) expressly equipped for the compiling and copying of manuscript books – which had been set up from scratch (*a fundamentis*) by Abbot Thomas de la Mare (1349–96).[72] Taking office after the monastery had been decimated by the Black Death, De la Mare took steps to restore religious life and to recover the position of St Albans as a cult church of national significance.[73] For this enterprise the abbey's archives, chronicles and saints' lives were a valuable resource enabling a new generation inside and out to discover the distinguished legends of the house. The manuscripts of Matthew Paris still found in the first book press were taken up again, now not only as sources of reference but also as templates for the making of new volumes whose contents might communicate the antiquity, sanctity and status of St Albans in the church and in wider society. Their words and pictures presented a monastery at the centre point of current affairs for centuries past time out of mind. Eternity is not time enough,

Walsingham declared, to praise such gifts to his church.[74] They were nothing short of a touchstone for the ambitions of Abbot De la Mare.

Walsingham began an anthology (now BL, Cotton MS Claudius E IV) which brought together the *Gesta abbatum* lives of St Alban and his co-martyr, Amphibalus, a sequence of miracles stories and transcripts of documents relating to the privileges and properties of the abbey. His selection was a blend of Matthew's book of the *Gesta* (now BL, Cotton MS Nero D I) and his own anthology of texts concerning the cults of the two patron saints (now Dublin, Trinity College, MS 177). Walsingham also compiled a new register of the abbey's benefactors (now BL, Cotton MS Nero D VII), drawing on Matthew's *Gesta* and 'Book of Additions' for his entries on the early abbots, royal and episcopal patrons down to the mid thirteenth century. From 1376, following Matthew's example, he kept a chronicle of current affairs which he continued for almost fifty years. Like Matthew, over time he revised particular passages and reproduced them elsewhere, not least in a history of Normandy which he dedicated to King Henry V.[75] The one surviving manuscript of Walsingham's chronicle which may have been made under his supervision (BL, Royal MS 13 E IX) was surely conceived as a companion volume to Matthew's own. The layout of the text echoes the earlier books and it appears there were meant to be pictures. Faint notes on the intended subjects can still be seen on the front flyleaves.

Walsingham was more impressed by the form and style of Matthew's manuscripts than he was interested in the substance of his writings. He used Matthew's *Gesta abbatum* as the foundation for his own version but expanded the narrative with sources overlooked by or unknown to his predecessor. He also incorporated occasional comments on changes in the abbey church which had occurred since his predecessor's time. He did not return to Matthew's Anglo–Norman life of St Alban but preferred to present a fresh prose history of the passion of Alban and Amphibalus which he identified as a Latin translation of another, unidentified French source. Nor did Matthew hold any influence over Walsingham's approach to the abbey's archival records. Walsingham's collection of documents to support his recent history of the abbey was comprehensive and, in contrast to Matthew's method, his transcriptions were verbatim. With formal responsibility for the written records of the monastery, unlike his predecessor, Walsingham made a compendium quite different in scale and scope to Matthew's appendices, a vast, two-volume cartulary which fully documented the fortunes of the abbey since its Norman restoration three centuries before. Walsingham did identify as an heir to Matthew's work as chronicler at the monastery, but he did not confine his own narrative to this St Albans context. An early version was transmitted, together with the attribution to 'Thomas Walsingham, precentor of St Albans, as a continuation of Ranulf Higden's popular universal chronicle, *Polychronicon*.[76]

Walsingham's compilations of chronicles and records may have given Matthew's own originals a new status in the monastery as valued relics. Abbot John of Wheathampstead (1420–40, 1452–65) recovered one of his manuscripts which had previously been sold. It was surely at his direction that Matthew's book of St Alban and St Amphibalus was displayed to King Henry VI when he visited their shrines, an event which was recorded on the first leaf of text.[77] This may have been done also because it was already close at hand, placed like other precious objects on one or other of the shrines of these patron saints. The same view of Matthew's work as among the treasures of the monastery led Abbot John at an unknown date to give up the manuscript of the *Historia Anglorum* to his friend and the abbey's patron, Humfrey, Duke of Gloucester. The new owner added an ownership inscription to the first leaf of text and appears to have given it some attention, marking a passage concerning Magna carta.[78]

In the generations that followed it was in this guise as rare artefact and artwork that Matthew's manuscripts found a readership. It may have been as a visitor to St Albans with Henry VI that his chaplain, John Blacman (c. 1407–85), viewed Matthew's picture of the procession of the Holy Blood and was inspired to reproduce it in his own version of *Flores historiarium*.[79] The manuscript given to Humfrey of Gloucester was consulted by Polydore Vergil (c. 1470–1555) in his preparation of his *Anglia Historia* first published in 1534. Arriving in England as a papal collector in 1503, he was appointed to the archdeaconry of Wells (Somerset) in 1508, although the cathedral context may not have been his source for Matthew's book. Vergil drew from the narrative in Matthew's manuscript from the first leaf, which included the marriage of Margaret of Wessex to King David I of Scotland (*c.* 1070). His reading of the source prompted reflections which he recorded in the margins. They fall thick and fast on the first leaves of the manuscript, effectively forming a commentary on the chronicle. At the Normans' defeat of the Scots he observed, 'the English profited' (*Angli profligavit*); in the struggle for succession between William Rufus and Robert, Duke of Normandy 'fraternal discord' (*discordia fratrum*); where Matthew saw Henry I's God-given good fortune, Vergil viewed him as 'ungrateful' (*ingratus princeps*). Occasionally, he challenged Matthew's assertions, such as concerning the orphan status of Princess Matilda of Scotland: '*errat hic auctor, nam parentes puellae mortui erant*'.[80]

At St Albans the interest of the monks now waned. In a commonplace book John of Wheathampstead compiled notes on the early history of the monastery taken not from Matthew's *Gesta abbatum* but from William of Malmesbury's *Gesta pontificum*. In the same volume he recorded verse epitaphs for Henry II and Bishop Richard Marsh of Durham, which he could have found in Matthew's history but may have come from elsewhere.[81] When he composed his own account of the history of England down to his own day as an entry for his encyclopaedia which he called *Granarium*, he made only a single, oblique reference to Matthew's work in retelling his story of the shooting of William Rufus as the result of the miraculous intervention of St Alban himself.[82]

The last readers of Matthew's work before the closure of his monastery in 1539 were outsiders. A copy of a portion of Matthew's chronicle was added to a manuscript anthology compiled by John Skewes (d. 1544) while he was in the service of Thomas Wolsey (1473–1530), the cardinal archbishop of York who was *commendam* abbot of St Albans from 1521 until he was stripped of his offices in 1529. Skewes acted as Wolsey's attorney general for the administration of the abbey's business, in which capacity he was on the premises more frequently than the cardinal himself.[83]

Perhaps before the end of Wolsey's tenure of the abbey, Edward Foxe (*c.* 1496–1538), the principal scholar responsible for researching historical and legal precedents to support Henry VIII's demand for a divorce from Catherine of Aragon, also consulted Matthew's chronicle to identify instances in which the English crown had exercised a governing authority over the church and its clergy. This surely accounts for the comment in the margin of the Royal manuscript: 'a byshop deposyd by the kynge and also put in by the kynge'.[84] The historical precedent passed into Foxe's treatise on the royal supremacy in spiritual matters published in 1534, where the case of Ralph d'Escures' investiture by Henry I (1114) was referenced as *'ut scribit . . . Matthaeus'*.[85]

Foxe may have been followed to St Albans by John Leland (c. 1503–52), chaplain to King Henry, encouraged (although not formally commissioned) to make a record of the significant holdings of the monasteries' libraries.[86] Leland recorded books he saw still in situ and occasionally copied excerpts from their contents. He continued to expand his record of what had belonged to this or that monastery as they passed out of their precincts and into other hands. Since no entry in his notebooks is precisely dated, his sighting of a particular manuscript can only be plotted across a period of a decade from the first of his searches made around 1533. At St Albans it seems he was told or shown a record of what the abbey book collection had once held, since he made a note of the fact that a beautiful manuscript of Matthew's chronicle had been 'stolen away' (*furto sublata*).[87] He surely saw the manuscript BL, Cotton MS Nero D I, still shelved as he copied extracts from Matthew's *Gesta abbatum* account of the abbey's foundation and its first, pre-Conquest abbots.[88] He read closely if not also transcribed his treatment of King Arthur. He was drawn to Matthew's description of the king's tomb at Glastonbury, the pyramids that stood sentinel beside it and the legend inscribed, lamenting that the chronicler could not record them.[89]

Presumably it was just as King Henry showed a close interest in the monasteries' holdings on history that Matthew's *Historia Anglorum* (BL, Royal MS 14 C VII) came into the possession of the crown. The manuscript was noticed in an inventory of the books kept at Westminster first compiled in 1542. Later it was passed to Henry Fitzalan, the twelfth earl of Arundel (1512–80), the king's chamberlain from 1544, although whether before or after the monarch's death in January 1547 remains unclear.[90]

At the break-up of the St Albans library, the remaining manuscripts of Matthew's writings made in his own lifetime appear to have passed into hands of those in or close to the abbey's internal, professional and social networks. The early edition of his *Gesta abbatum* found in BL,

Cotton MS Julius D VII was taken out of the monastery by the former prior, Thomas Kingsbury (d. 1545).[91] He presented it to John Conyngesby, who may have been of the same family that held the manor of North Mymms neighbouring the former monastery's estate; Humphrey Coningsby II (d. 1599), married the daughter of Sir Richard Lee, Surveyor of the King's Works at Calais, who was grantee of the site of the St Albans priory at Sopwell and later of a portion of the abbey site itself.[92] The manuscript written and illustrated by Matthew, which combined the shorter chronicle and the *Abbreviatio*, BL, Cotton MS Claudius D VI, came into the hands of Richard Hutton, who had been chaplain to the women of the St Albans priory at Markyate.[93] Cambridge, Corpus Christi College MS 26 was acquired by Edward Aglionby (1520–91?), until 1548 a fellow of King's College, Cambridge.[94] Another manuscript of the text, Cambridge, Corpus Christi College MS 16, came into the possession of Robert Talbot, prebendary of the new, reformed cathedral chapter at Norwich. Talbot was a collector of 'the best . . . strangest and rarest' of 'old written books' and it is possible that the book was brought to his attention by another former member of the monastic community at St Albans, Robert Catton, who had been the crown's appointed successor to Wolsey as abbot and after his removal held church livings in Bedfordshire and Norfolk.[95]

The first secular, clerical or lay owners of Matthew's works may have kept them with much the same point of view as the last generation of monks, as relics of their old abbey. But the legal student Aglionby's acquisition reflected a rising antiquarian interest in the archival and historical contents of these ancient manuscripts. Since all of them were rebound in the nineteenth and twentieth centuries, none of the survivors now retain all of the inscriptions and other marks of identification they have taken on after they left the monastery. Nonetheless, it is likely that in the decades following the last of the dissolutions they continued to pass between connoisseur collectors and scholars eager to catch hold of a trace of a past which had become visible only as it was being wiped away. This was the shared interest that led John Skewes to bequeath his anthology to Reginald Mohun, a Cornish Member of Parliament and descendent of two of the West Country's most influential aristocratic families.[96] Mohun's likely concerns were lineage and lordship, which had been the recurrent themes in Polydore Vergil's 'commentary' on Matthew. But these mid-Tudor antiquarians reached for these texts for their record not only of the people of the nation but also of its landscapes and places. John Leland had turned to monastic chroniclers as authorities on topography. He was matched in this by Prebendary Talbot, who investigated the earliest itineraries of the British Isles. The impulse to map the kingdom intensified interest in Matthew's manuscripts and their own unique schemes.[97]

Returning from exile at the accession of Edward VI (1547), the former friar John Bale saw Robert Talbot's manuscript of Matthew's chronicle; he also appears to have come across a copy of his *Gesta abbatum* and perhaps the account of the discovery of the relics of St Amphibalus as preserved in Dublin, Trinity College, MS 177. He consulted Talbot's copy of the chronicle closely enough to digest Matthew's criticism of the papacy. In his *Actes of the Votaryes*, a history of the forces which had brought reformation in the church first published in 1551, Bale directed the reader that for the 'full antichrist in length and breadth, in pryde and in all other ungodlynesse ... loke [to] Matthew Paris'.[98] He surely made a transcript of the chronicle and it may have been this or a subsequent copy which was shared with the Lutheran theologian Matthias Flacius Illyricus (1520–75). Writing in 1561 to Matthew Parker, Archbishop of Canterbury (r. 1559–75), of their mutual interest in authorities in church history, Flacius told of excerpts from Matthew's chronicle which he had received from a friend (*dudum per quondam amicum fueram consecutus*).[99]

Some of these same manuscripts were seen by scholars drawn to the opposite side of the Reformation divide. Talbot bequeathed his books to the dean of his cathedral, John Harpsfield, elder brother of Nicholas, the archdeacon of Canterbury from 1554 until his deposition in 1559. Nicholas Harpsfield (1519–75) knew Matthew's chronicle, perhaps from the Talbot copy, as well as his *Gesta abbatum*, and he made them primary sources for his planned history of the church in England published after his death as *Historica Anglicana ecclesiastica*.[100]

It was the champions of Reformation who now carried Matthew's manuscripts and their witness to a new audience. John Bale had urged 'the conservacion of Englandes antiquitees' to be put in print not only as 'the bewtie of our nacyon'[101] but also for their value as 'a clere mirrour' of the 'most detestable abuses' of the 'obstynate papystes' who 'dwell in the hate of hys heavenly word'.[102]

In exile he may have brought the testimony of England's chronicle tradition to the notice of the Magdeburg Centuriators, scholars committed to compiling an account of the continuity of a pure Christian faith through centuries of papist corruption.[103] At home he called for the publication of approved editions of these narratives, to 'emprinte' and 'bring fourth one noble author and other [after] an other'.[104] In fact, his hope was fulfilled after a prompt from Magdeburg. In 1560 the Centuriators dispatched an envoy to Queen Elizabeth requesting her help to secure copies of the works of English writers who condemned the corruption of the Church of Rome. They specified John Wyclif and Matthew Paris, whose name Bale had surely introduced to them. The request was passed from Sir William Cecil (1520–98), the queen's secretary of state, to Archbishop Parker, who acknowledged that he himself did not know the full extent of Matthew's writings. Parker corresponded with Flacius, who shared with him his chronicle excerpts; he also made himself known to the elderly Bale, now a resident prebendary of his own cathedral church. Bale provided a list of English works relevant to the Centuriators' enterprise and advised Parker of the last known whereabouts of some of his own dispersed book collection. Parker eventually recovered some of these, although by his own assessment none were useful to the present purpose. He admitted to the Centuriators, 'I am unable to satisfy your request as I could wish,' although their representative Bernard Schwartz did still visit him at Canterbury in the summer of 1561 to borrow the books he had been able to locate.[105] No work of Mathew Paris was among them. Rather, Schwartz himself presented the archbishop with sixty leaves of a transcript from a portion of Matthew's chronicle.

Parker's dealings with the Centuriators and with Bale left him with a general determination to recover historical records. He lobbied Sir William Cecil for a formal commission for the task, finally conferred on him in 1568. His new writ ran wide, covering 'aunciente recordes and monumentes written', but even before it was in hand, it seems Parker had attached a particular priority to Matthew's historical writing.[106] He was loaned a manuscript of the *Chronica maiora* held by Henry Sidney, Lord Deputy of Ireland (1529–1586), but retained it, making good most of its sequence of missing leaves with transcripts of his own.[107] He also took into his hands Aglionby's manuscript; again it was not returned.[108]

He borrowed a further authentic, St Albans witness to the chronicle, the manuscript made a generation after Matthew's death (now BL, Cotton MS Nero D V), which had been acquired by the London antiquarian John Stow (1524–1605). Around 1567, he commissioned a transcript of the Royal manuscript, cross-referenced with another contemporary manuscript (now Bibliothèque nationale, 6048B) which was in the hands of Secretary Cecil himself.[109] A second sequence of extracts from the same manuscript, reproducing Matthew's coverage of the years 1135–79 and 1259–72, was written out in a looping cursive hand apparently as a working copy for the archbishop.[110]

Parker reached beyond the chronicle which had captured the Centuriators' attention to trace the transmission of Matthew's original narrative in *Flores historiarum*. *Flores*' continuous coverage of Plantagenet fortunes from Edward I to Richard II had likewise drawn the attention of Stow and another acquisitive antiquarian, John Dee (1527–1609). Parker prepared a text which he first printed in 1567.[111] Here the history was offered without any frame of commentary or even any account of the manuscript sources from which it was transcribed. Nonetheless it not only fed but also fuelled an interest in the narrative, and just three years later a new edition was printed. Now he did address the reader with the preface. While the monk chroniclers who made *Flores* were undoubtedly 'barbarous' figures (*barbaros esse fateor*) from a dark age (*profundis tenebris et obscura nocte suscitavit*), he urged for them to be thought of as worthy servants of God, indeed instruments of divine design intended to have been spared eternal damnation in order to speak the truth of its wickedness to the power of the papacy (*ut pro veritate propaganda ... insolentiae et impietatis accusare non timescant*).[112] John Dee, at least, was inclined to agree. In his copy of the edition he marked passages which recorded the demands made by the papacy on crown and church in England and, in one instance, the 'superstition of the clergy'.[113]

The popularity of *Flores* persuaded Parker to plan a companion volume. 'I would turn [Matthew Paris' story] to the commodity of our country,' he confided to Cecil in August 1569.[114] His edition of Matthew's own chronicle narrative, to which he gave the title *Historia maior*, followed the new *Flores* within a year. He acknowledged the aid of manuscripts in the hands of four of his distinguished network of collectors, Edward Aglionby, now a Member of Parliament, the earl of Arundel, Lord Deputy Sidney and the secretary of state himself.[115] He did not identify John Stow, although he certainly consulted the manuscript (now BL, Cotton MS Nero D V) which he held.[116] Now there was no hesitation in its introduction. Already the work was highly praised (*opus laudatissimum sit*), he explained in the preface, and the author, if not yet known to his reader, merited equal recognition (*hunc authorem satis laudaturum*). He should be counted among the English chroniclers as an authority on the antiquities of 'this our England' (*in hac Anglia nostra*).[117] In times of fable and falsehood, he maintained a balanced and measured judgement (*tam aequabile tamen et temperatum judicium servaverit*), narrating the nation's affairs as he saw and heard of them, 'simply' (*simpliciter*).[118] What is truly admirable, Parker declared, was how often and openly (*tam saepe tam manifeste*) he made known the arrogance, envy, materiality, pride and tyranny of the Roman papacy. Such a challenge to a corrupt leadership was to be compared to the charge St Paul placed on the faithful in Christ in his second letter to the Thessalonians (2 Thessalonians 2:3–5).[119]

This was a valuable service to his own and all times, but the archbishop was eager for the reader to recognise him in the front rank of historians with Geoffrey of Monmouth and William of Malmesbury, not least because so much of what might have been the legacy of their histories had been damaged and wretchedly and wrongly destroyed (*mutilata et in multis locis misere et turpiter depravata*).[120] His place in the pantheon was affirmed on the book's title page, which carried a celebrated Ciceronian tag on the nature of history as the 'teacher of life'.[121]

For the first time since the dispersal of the St Albans book, Parker drew attention to Matthew's multiple arts and crafts, the skill of his scribal hand (*aptissima scriptione textuali ... manu*) and his painting (*in exquisita pictura*).[122] The page layout of his editions preserved a hint of the appearance of the original manuscripts giving rubrics and italicised and indented lines of verses, although nothing of their shorthand of symbols such as shields and swords.[123] He also made the first attempt to form a continuous thread of historical writing from the books and fragments of books from St Albans of which he was aware, establishing the abbey and its monks at the leading edge (*sed maxime ab illo ...*

Albanensi) of a tradition 'continually and studiously observed' at many monasteries. The abbey was, he wrote, 'a treasury (commune thesaurum) ... of all the historic acts of this realm (omnia historica gesta huius regni)'.[124]

Parker's printed editions did not stifle the transmission of Matthew's writings in manuscript. Parker's secretary, John Joscelyn (1529–1603), compiled a list of chroniclers and chronicles, naming Matthew, although he did not follow it with any transcript.[125] Cecil's household tutor from 1563, Laurence Nowell (*c*. 1530–70), made an abbreviated copy of Matthew's *Gesta abbatum*, which when he left England in 1568 may have been placed in the hands of William Lambarde (1536–1601) a legal scholar at work on a compendium of the laws of Anglo-Saxon England. Nowell may have studied Matthew's map of England presumably already a part of the manuscript, Julius D VII, where he met with the *Gesta* itself. He had impressed on Cecil the need to chart the kingdom more accurately.[126] Close to Cecil, Robert Beale, clerk to the Privy Council (d. 1601), collected excerpts concerning church and state from chronicles and manuals on common law in a book also containing a tracts on furthering the Reformation and 'the well usinge of the goodes of the church'.[127]

In 1575 John Stow copied entries from the *Abbreviatio* in the Claudius manuscript which had come into his possession, perhaps only recently since he had not shared it with Parker before publication of the printed chronicle.[128] Around this time he also compiled an anthology including several self-contained episodes in church history derived from Matthew's narrative, which he identified as 'Liber sancti Albani' and 'Oute of the booke of St Albones'. As these rubrics signal, his source text was the Royal manuscript continued after Matthew's death, and he added to his collection the account of the trial of the Templars. Stow followed the continuations further, translating the early portion of Thomas Walsingham's contemporary history into English.[129]

William Lambarde made his own manuscript copy of the same St Albans book and also took possession of one of Parker's own transcripts.[130] Selected transcripts appear in a manuscript by Lord Arundel, Henry Sidney.[131] Contemporary copies may also have been in the library of the gentleman book collector Henry Savile of Banke (d. 1622), and the Somerset herald Robert Glover (1544–1588), which may have been Beale's source.[132]

These antiquarians, more than a generation younger than Parker (b. 1504) and Bale (b. 1495), with no first-hand experience of the unreformed church or of its fall, did not attach the same imperative value to the critical voice in Matthew's writing. Nowell's principal interest in his *Gesta abbatum* appears to have been as a witness to pre-Conquest England.[133] Notwithstanding his involvement with Parker and his contribution to his two printed editions, it seems John Stow arrived at the settled view that Matthew Paris was no more than one of a number of authorities to be consulted for certain episodes in England's past. He turned to him for specific historical and topographical insights not recorded elsewhere, such as the 'great glorie' of the Temple which he 'crieth out on them for their pride', and the possible presence of a royal palace at Cornhill, where in 1232 Henry III sent Hubert de Burgh 'to answere all matters obiected against him'.[134] For this Stow overlooked Parker's printed edition, preferring to search 'a written [i.e. manuscript] copie of Matthew Paris his historie'.[135] What the archbishop had advanced as an invaluable witness to the wrongs of the Roman Church, Stow now regarded as of a more general, philosophical utility: 'it is a hard matter in my fansie for the Readers of Chronicles to pass without some colours of wisdom, invitements to virtue and loathing of naughty facts as it is for a well-favoured man ... walk[ing] up and downe in the hot, parching Sunne ... not to be ... sunburned'.[136] Lambarde, for his part, liked Matthew's style. 'Howe the king [John] came with bare and bleeding feete to Canterbury', he recalled, 'as Mathew Parise very pretely writeth it'.[137]

At a distance of five decades Matthew's standing as a stout defender of England against the rapacity of Rome was momentarily reasserted just as the personal rule of Charles I (1629–40) ended in the Long Parliament. A new edition of Parker's *Historia maior* was published by the London printers Miles Flesher and Richard Hodgkinson in 1639–40. They began to prepare the texts, recruiting the editor named on the main title page, William Watts, the rector of the city church of St Alban, Wood Street, when the work was already underway.[138] Watts had been encouraged to take up the study of Matthew's history by Sir Henry Spelman (*c.* 1562–1641), an antiquarian and parliamentarian firmly persuaded that for the foundations of English government 'let Matthew Paris . . . tell you the fashions of those time'.[139]

The purpose of the new edition was restoration: 'our Matthew, reprinted' (*Matthaeum Parisiensem nostrum . . . recusum damus*).[140] The preface was pointed: in fact, it was not only a reprint but also a correction, not through his own invention or conjecture but faithfully following the manuscripts (*non ex ingenio sive conjectura nostra; ast secundum manuscriptorum fidem*).[141] These Watts and his collaborators consulted at Corpus Christi College, Cambridge, which had taken the treasures of Aglionby and Cecil; these they supplemented with witnesses now in the library of Sir Thomas Cotton (1594–1662), son and heir of the collector Sir Robert (1571–1631), some of which were unknown to Archbishop Parker. They also returned to the manuscript (BL, Royal MS 14 C VII) which was still in the king's library but kept not at Westminster but St James' Palace.[142] Their research, the editors declared proudly, allowed them to polish the text, removing Parker's clumsy 'improvements', Aldemar where Matthew wrote Waldemar.[143] It also led them to offer the reader a new work, Matthew's *Gesta abbatum*, bound in with the *Historia maior* but showing a date of printing of 1639. This they met first in the Cottonian library, which held two copies, and were able to compare with another witness (now presumed lost) then in the library of Sir Henry Spelman (*c.* 1562–1641).[144]

Watts not only criticised Parker's text but also challenged his inclination to forgive, even to favour him as a voice for the Christian church. 'In our Matthew, I find more of use to the Romans [i.e. Catholics]', he concluded, 'than for us'.[145] Rather, he encouraged the reader to recognise the value of the chronicler's representation of worldly affairs. A consummate Englishman – no foreigner could claim him in spite of his name (*ab extero nemine pro populari vel compatriota suo vendicatus*) – zealously giving expression to the plight of England (*planctus Angliae*).[146] He even praised his Latin, the best of all our historians with the exception of Eadmer of Canterbury and William of Malmesbury; albeit hardly Ciceronian, his barbs struck all comers: kings, emperors, even the pope and the abbots of his own house.[147] An impression of a robust orator was captured in a frontispiece portrait made by the engraver Thomas Cecil (fl. 1626–40) apparently on sight of the original manuscript, showing the skirt of his habit gathered purposefully in the stance of a Roman senator.[148]

When the ensuing Wars of Religion were over, the churchman and scholar Thomas Fuller (1608–61), who had tried to hold the middle ground during the conflict, challenged Matthew's reputation. 'He seldome kisseth the pope's toe without biting it', he acknowledged in his *Worthies of England* (1662).[149] But his historical authority was derivative and unreliable. The first to explore Matthew's use of the chronicle compiled by Roger of Wendover, Fuller concluded that 'Matthew Paris doth quarter too heavily on the pains of Wendover, though a fabric built three stories high where of our Roger laid the foundations, Paris added the garet.'[150] In his *Churche-historie of Britaine* (1655) he criticised Brian Twyne (1581–1644), the keeper of the university archives at Oxford, for questioning the quality of Archbishop Parker's transcript of Matthew's chronicle, which 'can not be less than breach of canonical obedience against the memorie of so grave and godly a Prelate'. Yet tacitly he accepted that a 'suspicion of falsehood' and '*si vera sit*' (if it is true) might be directed if not at the printed book then at Matthew's 'most authentick manuscripts'.[151]

Still the familiarity of Matthew's name in the brief litany of England's early chroniclers did not fade. A popular history of Bad King John published in 1695 was presented to readers with 'Matthew Paris' on the title page. In Henry Fielding's novel *Amelia* (1751), his character Dr Harrison shared 'a pleasant story in Matthew Paris … as well as I remember it'.[152] In his *Anecdotes of Painting* (1762–71) Horace Walpole (1717–97) recalled 'the original copy of Matthew Paris with miniatures' which he had seen in the British Museum library opened three years earlier. 'Certainly', he concluded (mistakenly) '[it was] a present to [the] king [Henry III]'.[153]

Matthew's history was the anchor for a romantic epic, *St Albans Abbey*, composed by Anne Radcliffe (1764–1823), best known for her Gothic novels, which was published posthumously in 1826. The climactic scenes were of the battles which had run right up to the gate during the Wars of the Roses (1455, 1461) but the first canto conjured up the monastery and its monks, 'mong such … Matthew Paris stood / pious learned; wise and good, though shrouded in a bigot's hood'.[154] The monastic values of his world were contemptible to her, but like Walpole she celebrated the achievement of the scriptorium, 'written folio[s] rare', 'splendid ... fair', and since, 'closely kept and seldom viewed' then 'still fresh and glorious from century to century'.[155]

He was also the discovery of the young Edmund Burke (1729–97), future Member of Parliament and public philosopher, during his drafting of an *Abridgment of English History* which dates from 1757. The final chapter, a narration of the reign of John, kept close to Matthew's chronicle to tell of a 'people, grown desperate' and their challenge to the king which threatened 'that liberty which they had sacrificed everything to preserve'.[156] He did not name him among the 'writers of these times' he consulted, but both the course of events as he recounted it and his commentary echoed Matthew's own, on the crown – which 'instead of soothing [the] people ... sought to terrify them into obedience' – and the papacy – 'a prerogative ... not satisfied with ... supremacy [which] encroached on every minute part of [the] church'.[157]

A decade later Edward Gibbon (1737–94), author of the *History of the Decline and Fall of the Roman Empire* (1776–88), found Matthew 'afford[ed] many valuable materials'. He felt in his chronicle an affiliation to his own great theme: 'Matthew Paris has represented, from authentic documents, the danger and distress of Europe.'[158]

But the coming generation of narrative historians was circumspect about his reliability as an aid in their professional task. Preparing his epic six-volume *History of England* (1754–62), David Hume (1711–76) approached Matthew with caution. On the face of it he thought his reports of royal affairs were 'plausible' but only 'if [they] be true'.[159] In spite of his own faith and recusant family history, the seminarian John Lingard (1771–1851) was even more severe: '[since] fables ... abound in the pages of that writer', he advised readers of his *History of England* first published in 1819), 'therefore [he is] of no authority'.[160] Conscious he was known as a classic author in household libraries, he defended his damning verdict with care: 'it may appear invidious to speak harshly of this favourite historian: but this I may say that when I could confront his pages with authentic records or contemporary writers I have in most instances found the discrepancy between them so great as to give his narrative the appearance of a romance rather than a history'.[161]

Offering his *View of the State of Europe during the Middle Ages* (1818), Henry Hallam (1777–1859) showed more sympathy to the 'monkish chronicler'. He noted the mistakes and muddles of his 'prolix history', his own and those of his first editors, but he heard in Matthew's voice echoes of his own Whig values, a 'laudable zeal against papal tyranny' and a 'love of civil liberty'.[162] He traced an advance from the chroniclers who came before. In Matthew's day there was 'exited [an] energy of public spirit ... the strong man in the sublime language of Milton was aroused from sleep and shook his invincible locks ... we shall never find in the English writers of the twelfth century that assertion of positive and national rights'.[163] It was surely Hallam's judgement that caused Matthew's chronicle to be consulted as an authority in public affairs, in proceedings in a House of Lords' Privileges Committee to determine a claim to the Berkeley peerage (1858–61) and in a House of Commons debate on the persecution of Jews (1830).[164]

It was the outlook admired by Gibbon and affirmed by Hallam that led to a return to the text of the chronicle itself for the first time in almost three centuries. 'Occasional perusal ... of Matthew Paris' for Sir Walter Scott, pioneer of the historical novel, 'kept up a kind of familiarity with the [Latin] language ... in its rudest state'.[165] A translation into French was published in 1840–41 by Jean-Louis Alphonse Huillard-Bréholles (1817–71), a professor of history at Paris' Lycée Charlemagne. It was commissioned by Honoré d'Albert, duc de Luynes (1802–67), who introduced the text to readers as a narration of the age of Crusade, a 'grande chronique' to stand beside that of the French chronicler Jean de Joinville (1224–1317). It was a tale of monarchs afflicted, 'almost mad' (*une lâche demence*) in the face of church power, a *'supremitie sacerdotale'*.[166] Although he judged Matthew's expression poor and his preoccupations puerile, he was struck like Hallam by his bold assaults on the powerful, an *'esprit de censure hardie envers les grands'*.[167]

No doubt prompted by the Huillard-Bréholles' publication, an English text was commissioned from the Latin scholar John Giles (1808–84) for publication in the Bohn's Antiquarian Library Series. *Matthew Paris' English History* appeared in 1852–54, Giles observing that '[he is] too well known to the public to render any apology ... for publishing a translation'.[168] A new Latin edition of the chronicle text was not completed under the Record Commission Rolls Series for another four decades. It was the popular, English Matthew Paris which John Richard Green (1837–83) celebrated in his *Short History of the English People* first published in 1874, 'an annalist whose pages glow with ... outburst[s] of patriotic feeling ... his point of view is neither that of a courtier nor of a churchman but of an English man and the new national tone of his chronicle is but an echo of the national sentiment which at last bound nobles and yeomen and churchmen together into an English people'.[169] When the first volume of the Rolls Series Latin 'Greater chronicle' finally surfaced in 1872, Matthew was acknowledged by the editor Henry Richards Luard as 'perhaps the best known of all the mediaeval historians'.[170] Luard's aim was for his seven-volume text and notes finally 'to do [Matthew] justice', ensuring due appreciation of the originality and historical value of his narrative as '[an] authority for the contemporary history of [England and] other countries authority'.[171] 'He had in many respects the best means possible for collecting his materials and ascertaining the truth,' Luard declared. 'No-one can read [his] interesting and vivid accounts ... without feeling certain [about] the writer's information.'[172] What 'was ... familiarly known in England', affirmed William Stubbs in his *Constitutional History* (1874–78), 'is shown by ... Matthew Paris'.[173]

The scepticism, indeed, cynicism of the new twentieth century dulled the 'glow' with which Green and the previous generation had invested Matthew. A. L. Smith first dared to question the chronicler's fond reputation in his Ford Lectures delivered at Oxford in 1913. He pared back the Victorian varnish to reveal 'a hard hitter and a good hater' who was 'not above burking what he finds inconvenient or defending abuses if only they are old and vested'.[174] Either for [mainland] European or even English history, Smith judged him as wayward, 'rang[ing] in value from first-hand, priceless testimony to the most extravagant and worthless gossip'.[175] Tilting, at the same time at another more recent reputation, he declared him 'Macaulay minus the style ... in prejudice, wilful blindness, truculence and lack of spirituality'.[176] 'The modern historian', he concluded, 'is faced with the demoralising alternative whether he will be critical, cautious and dull or accept Matthew Paris and make a good story'.[177]

Smith associated many of Matthew's flaws with his monastic context and professed status, but in offering a definitive narrative of England's medieval monasteries, David Knowles set him apart from his kind. 'A certain lack of spiritual depth', Knowles argued, made him less like a monk and much more the embodiment of national (English) characteristics, such as 'fear of the unfamiliar and an instinctive dislike of foreign ways'.[178]

Knowles directed the doctoral research of Richard Vaughan, who was the first to take up Smith's challenge to 'set [Matthew Paris] straight before he can be safely used'.[179] Vaughan made a systematic study of the surviving manuscripts and reviewed the judgements of the nineteenth-century editors. Giving closest attention to the interrelationship of the different chronicle narratives they witnessed, he sought a 'solution' to the problems of authorship and manuscripts, of 'the definition and description of the material evidence'.[180] He unsettled the old assumption that they stood for a number of discrete compositions. Rather, he argued, '[they] are perhaps best regarded as editions of his main chronicle'.[181] Vaughan was more concerned with these matters of structure than the substance of Matthew's writing, still less his literary style. He treated Matthew's testimony to much the same breezy criticism as Smith and Knowles. Far from being the prophet of a post-Reformation England, Matthew was a prejudiced reactionary. He had beguiled posterity with his tricks.[182] Like them, he gave only glancing attention to Matthew's writing on devotional subjects, more or less dismissing the texts in Norman French as representative of a 'rather specialized culture'.[183]

Vaughan's thorough review of the manuscript evidence and trenchant remarks deterred further study for a generation and more, but perhaps the greater long-term result of his monograph has been the prompt it provided obliquely for Matthew's contributions in other genres, media and languages – those 'specialized cultures' – to be explored for the first time.[184]

The name, principal manuscripts and historical writing of Matthew Paris were known and studied after the dissolution of his monastery more frequently than any other from monastic England except Bede. Familiarity did not bring an understanding of his life, body of work or surrounding world. Rather it narrowed and over time distorted them. The observant monk with an equal fascination for past history and fervour for the cult of saints who like many Benedictines was drawn towards elite society was recast as an English everyman.

Notes

1. King and Potter 1998, 1.
2. Butler 1949, 1.
3. Stubbs 1879–80, ii. 3–4 at 4.
4. Howlett 1884–86, iii. 381–82.
5. Riley 1867–69, i. 378.
6. Lieberman 1879, 328. For the books of charters and 'supplements' referenced in the Gesta which he may have known see Riley 1867–69, i. 406, 458, 481.
7. Luard 1872–83, v. 264.
8. Luard 1872–83, v. 80, 246.
9. Madden 1866–69, ii. 440. For this didactic aspect see also Weiss 2012.
10. Riley 1867–69, i. 350; Luard 1872–83, iv. 518, 619; v. 254, 346, 384.
11. Luard 1872–83, v. 641.
12. Luard 1872–83, iv. 588–89.
13. Luard 1872–83, v. 241.
14. Luard 1872–83, v. 197–98 at 197. Retained in the *Historia Anglorum* and *Flores*: Madden 1866–69, iii. 97; Luard 1890, ii. 374–75.
15. Madden 1866–69, iii. 97; Luard 1872–83, v. 198; Luard 1890, ii. 374–75.
16. Riley 1867–69, i. 3.
17. Riley 1867–69, i. 307.
18. Riley 1867–69, i. 307–08.
19. Luard 1872–83, v. 626.
20. Luard 1872–83, iv. 283.
21. Luard 1872–83, v. 198.
22. Riley 1867–69, i. 299.
23. Riley 1867–69, i. 3.
24. Luard 1872–83, v. 446.
25. Lieberman 1879, 328.
26. Riley 1867–69, i. 242; Luard 1872–83, v. 129–30.
27. Butler 1949, 26, 36, 68, 128; Gransden 1964, xvii. See also Gransden 1974b, 381–85 at 382–83, 395–96.
28. Luard 1872–83, v. 317.
29. Luard 1872–83, iv. 644.
30. Luard 1872–83, v. 254.
31. *Estoire de Sent Aedward*, l. 76; Wallace 1983, 3.
32. BL, Royal MS 14 C VII, fol. 6^r. See also Collard 2015 and Chapter 8, 196–200 at 198.
33. BL, Cotton MS Julius D VII, fol. 42v. John compiled and part wrote this book and is identified as scriptor in the notice of his death at fol. 113v. See also Vaughan 1958a, 66; Vaughan 1958c, 229. See also Chapter 2, 34–37.

34. See 14th- and 15th-century marginalia in BL, Royal MS 14 C VII, fols. 14^v, 16^v, 43^v, with a cross-reference to another manuscript at 75^r.
35. Riley 1867–69, i. 394–95.
36. BL, Cotton MS Vitellius A XX, fols. 74ra–74vb. See also Clark and Preest 2019, 934–36.
37. BL, Royal MS 14 C VII, fol. 218^v. See also Chapter 16, 339.
38. Vaughan 1958c, 110, 153; Lewis 1987, 514.
39. BL, Cotton MS Nero D I, fols. 173^r–175^r.
40. Rouse and Rouse 2004, 360 [K 379].
41. Luard 1864–69, iv. 7; Vaughan 1958c, 153; Denholm-Young 1946.
42. Thomson with Clark 2015, 54–58 at 57 (UO3A. 11). See also Chapter 16, 342.
43. Collard 2008, 445–46.
44. Carpenter 2012b, 1350–56. See also Chapter 2, 37.
45. Collard 2008, 446; Carpenter 2012b, 1344–45. See also Coatesworth 2021, 43.
46. Luard 1890, i. xvii–xviii; Coatesworth 2021, 45–46, 51–52.
47. Now Eton College, MS 123. See also Luard 1890, i. xv–xvii at xvi; Vaughan 1958c, 101–02.
48. Now BL, Royal MS 14 C VI. Interestingly, the martyrdom of Alban and discovery of the relics of Amphibalus were highlighted in rubrics, and the abbey's founder, King Offa and the legend of the saint's role in William Rufus' death were noted by readers, fols. 44^r, 102^r, 158^{r-v}, 171^v.
49. Vaughan 1958c, 40.
50. Now Eton College, MS 213, fols. ix^r–x^v at x^r. See also Luxford 2009, 91.
51. Collard 2008, 452–57 (Merton copy), 457–64 (later copies).
52. Coatesworth 2021, 41–55. See also Chapter 10, 211–18, 224, 226, 230.
53. Eton College MS 213, fol. x^r. For the original image see Cambridge, Corpus Christi College, MS 16 (II), fol. 215^r; Luxford 2009, 96–100 at 97.
54. The manuscripts are Cambridge, University Library MS Ee3.59 and the Wormsley fragments. See also Morgan 1988; Slater 2018, 203; Kauffmann 2020, 186 and Chapter 9, 201, 205.
55. Lewis 1987, 436.
56. Dublin, Trinity College, MS 177, fol. 2r.
57. For the textual tradition see Lawrence 1960, 74–76; Sharpe 1997, 373. The Durham copy is BL, Cotton MS Julius D VI, fols. 123^r–151^v.
58. BL, Add. MS 70513, fols. 85^v–100^r, the reference to refectory reading at fol. 265^v. For this manuscript at Campsey see also Chapter 14, 276.
59. BL, Cotton MS Faustina B IX, fols. 185^r, 204^r.
60. For Rishanger see Gransden 1982, 4–6; Carley 1997.
61. Oxford, Magdalen College MS Lat. 53, pp. 1–5.

62. BL, Cotton MS Claudius D VI, fols. 138^r-84^r. See also Gransden 1974a, 443n.
63. BL, Cotton MS Vitellius A VIII, fol. 136^v.
64. Gransden 1982, 47, 56. See also Sharpe 1997, 334, 394.
65. Riley 1867-69, ii. 200. See also Chapter 16, 339.
66. Cambridge, Corpus Christi College Cambridge, MS 26, fols. bb^v-b^v.
67. BL, Cotton MS Nero D V, fols. 393^r-95^r.
68. Dublin, Trinity College, MS 177, fol. 75^r.
69. BL, Royal MS 14 C VII, fol. 161^r.
70. BL, Cotton MS Claudius E IV, fos. 59ra-70vb at 68^{ra-va} (miracles associated with Edward II's Scottish campaign).
71. Now, BL, Add. MS 62777, fols. 91^r-152^r. See also Clark and Preest 2019, 10-14.
72. Riley 1867-69, iii. 393.
73. Riley 1867-69, ii. 395-97, 401-9; iii. 384-85, 402-11. See also Clark 2002; Clark 2004; Clark 2006.
74. Riley 1870-71, ii. 302.
75. Riley 1876. See also Gransden 1982, 126; Clark 2004, 187-89, 265-66.
76. For Walsingham's approach to abbey history and archives see Clark and Preest 2019, 14-18; Clark 2001; Clark 2004. For his chronicle as a *Polychronicon* continuation see Oxford, Bodl., MS Bodley 462, fol. 141^v.
77. Dublin, Trinity College, MS 177, fol. 1^v.
78. BL, Royal MS 14 C VII, fol. 155^v. For Humfrey's reading and occasional marginal notation see also David Rundle's 'The library of Humfrey, duke of Gloucester and his reading habits', forthcoming in England and France before 1500. Essays in honour of Jenny Stratford, Harlaxton Medieval Studies, 34, (ed.). C. M. Barron and M. A. Michael (Donington 2025), 226-54.
79. Eton College MS 213. See also Luxford 2009, 91.
80. BL, Royal MS 14 C VII, fols. 14^v, 15^r, 36^v, 40^v. See also Madden 1866-69, i. 188-89 at 188.
81. Cambridge, Gonville and Caius College MS 230, fol. 55^v. For these epitaphs incorporated in Matthew's narrative see Luard 1872-83, ii. 344-45 (Henry II), 669 (John); iii. 112 (Richard de Marisco).
82. ' Qui ut beato Anselmi per visum ostensum fuerat graves contra eum exposuerat querelas super injuriis illatis ecclesie Anglicana vindicta sagittam Albano Anglorum protomartiri contulit: Oxford, Bodl. MS Bodley 585, 25^r.
83. BL, Harley MS 2258, fols. 31^r-315^r.
84. BL, Royal MS 14 C VII, fol. 10^v.
85. Foxe 1534, fols. 74^v-75^r.
86. Carley 2000, xliv.
87. Hearne 1715, iii. 163.

88. Hearne 1715, iii. 163–67 at 164–65.
89. Leland 1544, dedication, unfoliated, fols. 30^r.
90. Carley 2000, 185 (H2. 1041).
91. BL, Cotton MS Julius D VII, fos. 115v–121v. For Kingsbury's career before and after the dissolution of St Albans see Clark 2000, 315–16, 326–27. The probate inventory made at this death recorded 'books grett and smale' valued at '58', shillings and pounds not specified: Hertfordshire Archives and Local Studies, A25/26. I am grateful to Ailsa Herbert and Jon Mein for this reference.
92. BL, Cotton MS Julius D VII, fol. 1r: 'Constat Johanni Conyngesby ex dono magistri Kyngesbury'. His name repeated at 34r, 61r. For Humphrey Coningsby see https://www.historyofparliamentonline.org/volume/1558-1603/member/coningsby-humphrey-ii-1601. For Sir Richard Lee see https://www.historyofparliamentonline.org/volume/1509-1558/member/lee-sir-richard-15012-75. For the Coningsby property see Page 1908, 254.
93. For Hutton's position at Markyate see TNA, SP1/68, fol. 78^r; SP1/91, fol. 25^r. Perhaps he is to be identified with the rector of Higham Gobion (Bedfordshire), 1540–46: Clergy of England Database Person ID 146961.
94. For Aglionby see Wright 2004.
95. For Catton's career before and after the dissolution of St Albans see Clark 2000, 316–17, 321–23, 327–28.
96. McKisack 1971, 69.
97. For the strengthening of this impulse in the second half of the century see McKisack 1971, 126–54 at 134–54.
98. Bale 1551, fol. li^v.
99. Bruce and Perowne 1853, [Letter 99], 139–41 at 140.
100. Harpsfield's record of miracles attributed to the relics of St Alban and of the monastery's refusal to admit the twelfth-century scholar Alexander Nequam signal a knowledge of manuscripts and texts, notably *Gesta abbatum*, over and above what was then circulating in print: Harpsfield 1622, 12–17 at 15, 470–74 at 470.
101. Bale 1549, Fvii^{v-vii}.
102. Bale 1549, Aiiii^{r-v}.
103. Jones 1981. See also Chapter 16, 343.
104. Bale 1549, conclusion, unfoliated.
105. Jones 1981, 46.
106. For an account of Parker's commission see Garnett 2020, 75.
107. Cambridge, Corpus Christi College MS 16 (II), fols. 4^r–11^v, entries covering the years 1190–92 in the reign of Richard I, fols. 233^r–234^v, entries from the year 1250; McKisack 1971, 35–36; Graham 2006, 322, 331.
108. Cambridge, Corpus Christi College, MS 26.
109. Now Cambridge, Corpus Christi College, MS 56. See also McKisack 1971, 41.

110. Cambridge, Corpus Christi College, MS 348, fols. 1^r–62^v, 66^r–92^r.
111. [Anon.] 1567. For Dee's diverse interests see McKisack 1971, 71–74.
112. [Anon.] 1570, preface, unpaginated.
113. London, Royal College of Physicians, D1/19-e-7, 217, 228.
114. Bruce and Perowne 1853, [Letter 271], 352–53 at 353.
115. [Matthew Paris] 1571, fol. 3^v.
116. Geaman 2012, 120–21.
117. [Matthew Paris] 1571, fol. 4^r. See also Parker's characterisation in the preface to the first printing of *Flores*: [Anon.] 1567, fol. ii^v.
118. [Matthew Paris] 1571, fol. 2^r.
119. [Matthew Paris] 1571, fol. 2^v.
120. [Matthew Paris] 1571, fol. 3^r.
121. [Matthew Paris] 1571, title page.
122. [Matthew Paris] 1571, fol. 3^r.
123. For further reflection on the aesthetics of Parker's project see Chapter 10, 229–35 and Coatesworth 2021, 208–36.
124. [Matthew Paris] 1571, fol. 4^r.
125. BL, Cotton MS Nero C III, fols. 208^v–212^v. For Joscelyn's interest in medieval historical texts see McKisack 1971, 45–48.
126. San Marino, California, Huntington Library, HM 26341, fols. 91^r–104^r; BL, Lansdowne MS 6, fol. 54^r; Vaughan 1958c, 241. See also Clark and Preest 2019, 32. For Nowell, although not his interest in Matthew Paris, see McKisack 1971, 53.
127. BL, Add. MS 48066, fols. 12^r, 20^r–75^v.
128. BL, Harley MS 545, fol. 88^r–110^v. See also Luard 1890, iii. 156.
129. BL, Harley MS 247, fols. 173^{r-v}, 182^{r-v}, 184^r–185^v; BL, Harley MS 6217, fols. 3^r–21^v. Stow also added to a manuscript of Walsingham's chronicle, BL, Harley MS 3634, fols. 3^r–125ra, 195rb–250^r.
130. BL, Cotton MS Vitellius D II; BL, Add. MS 20709.
131. Now BL, Lansdowne MS 205/17.
132. Matthew's original manuscript, BL, Cotton MS Nero D V, had passed through the hands of both Glover and Savile. For Savile see also McKisack 1971, 62.
133. San Marino, California, HM 26341, fols. 91^r–104^r.
134. Stow 1598, 326.
135. Stow 1598, 155.
136. Stow 1580, iiii^r.
137. Lambarde 1576, 243.
138. Geaman 2012, 139–40.
139. Gibson 1698, 60.
140. Watts 1640, A2^r.
141. Watts 1640, A2^r.
142. Watts 1640, A2^v.

143. Watts 1640, A2^r.
144. Watts 1639, preface, unpaginated.
145. Watts 1640, A5^r.
146. Watts 1640, A3^{r-v}.
147. Watts 1640 A4^r.
148. Watts 1640, frontispiece.
149. Fuller 1662, 157.
150. Fuller 1662, 121 (original misprint for 135).
151. Fuller 1655, 14.
152. Fielding 1793, iii. 54.
153. Walpole 1762–71, i. 12n.
154. Radcliffe 1826, iii. 102.
155. Radcliffe 1826, iii. 102.
156. McLoughlin, Boulton and Todd 1997, 335, 528.
157. McLoughlin, Boulton and Todd 1997, 535–36, 550.
158. Gibbon 1776–88, vi. 239n.
159. Hume 1778, ii. 98, 159.
160. Lingard 1844, iii. 33n.
161. Lingard 1823–31, iii. 216.
162. Hallam 1872, ii. 207n, 302, 310.
163. Hallam 1872, ii. 310.
164. Nicholas 1829, 353, 357, 363; Hansard 1830, 1289; [A. Wood Renton] 1901, 342.
165. Lockhart 1837–38, i. 42.
166. Huillard-Bréholles 1840–41, i. xiv, xxvii.
167. Huillard-Bréholles 1840–41, i. lxi.
168. Giles 1852–54, i. v.
169. Green 1874, 142–43.
170. Luard 1872–83, i. ix.
171. Luard 1872–83, iii. xii.
172. Luard 1872–83, iv. vii–viii.
173. Stubbs 1874–78, ii. 128.
174. Smith 1913, 168.
175. Smith 1913, 170.
176. Smith 1913, 170–71.
177. Smith 1913, 169.
178. Knowles 1948–59, ii. 292–93.
179. Smith 1913, 170.
180. Vaughan 1958c, 261.
181. Vaughan 1958c, 110.
182. Vaughan 1958c, 151.
183. Vaughan 1958c, 181.
184. See especially Chapter 14 272–300.

16

Matthew Paris' Manuscripts
Working Books and Artefacts in Medieval and Early Modern Collections

The illustrated histories of Matthew Paris can appear almost untouched by the passage of time. It is not at once clear that the custodians of Matthew's books have altered them for reading, display and conservation. These include the monks of St Albans; connoisseurs such as Matthew Parker (1504–75) and Robert Cotton (1571–1631) who acquired manuscripts following the dissolution of the monasteries; and institutional libraries, who continue to conserve and present these objects in new ways.

While the works of most medieval writers must be pieced together from distant copies, so many autograph manuscripts of Matthew Paris survive that they form a corpus in themselves, encompassing both his own works and earlier books that he annotated. This directly reflects Matthew's relative obscurity before the sixteenth century and achieving fame through modern publishers, as well as early modern collecting priorities. Understanding the reception of widely copied works such as *Flores historiarum* and its continuations is a separate question. Vaughan identified seventeen manuscripts with the handwriting of Matthew Paris. Their story is an ideal example of the typical path that manuscripts produced in English monastic houses took through the later Middle Ages and after the dissolution of the monasteries in 1536–40, as extensive evidence survives for Matthew's books. A volume such as Matthew's *Historia Anglorum* (London, British Library, Royal MS 14 C VII) was borrowed and misappropriated during both the medieval and modern periods. Matthew's books also illustrate a gradual shift in collectors' attitudes from treating manuscripts as parts of a working library to be changed at will, towards the creation of modern conservation practice that treats them as artefacts.

As with all collections, surviving books reflect the interests of those who inherited them. Recent scholarship has emphasised Matthew's labours as a collective effort by the monks of St Albans, correcting an earlier focus on his individuality.[1] The shared nature of the process becomes even clearer when one considers the survival and reception of Matthew's artistic and written work. The monks of St Albans Abbey treated Matthew's manuscripts as artefacts worthy of exhibition, but the books they preserved were already a selection. The dissolution of the monasteries scattered them to the crown, scholars and nobility. Since that time, Matthew Paris' manuscripts have scarcely fallen from the gaze of collectors.

Collecting History at St Albans

Medieval writers were keenly aware of the rhetorical power of writing surfaces. Geoffrey of Monmouth's prologue to *De gestis Britonum* claims that the work translates 'a certain ancient book in the British language' (*quendam Britannici sermonis librum uetustissimum*). Citing and outdoing Geoffrey's example, William of St Albans (fl. c. 1178) introduces his *Passio sancti Albani* as a translation of a book written in early English (*liber Anglico sermone*). This work in turn presents itself as an interpretation of crumbling carvings on the walls of Verulamium.[2] Its author, who wishes to remain anonymous for fear of pagans who still rule the land, concludes with an intent to bring his book to Rome. Matthew Paris reflects this material orientation, referring specifically to his other manuscripts and reminding his readers to examine them.

The manuscript that best encapsulates Matthew's ability to combine individual craft and collaboration to create books of interest both to his fellow monks and lay audiences is the 'Book of St Albans', an anthology on Alban and Amphibalus (Dublin, Trinity College, MS 177). This volume was a work in progress, made from low-grade parchment and scraps rejected for other books. Its fluid character illustrates vividly how he conceived volumes with texts and illustrations as a unity, and where this vision could flounder when involving other scribes.[3] The book includes Matthew's *Vie de Seint Auban* based on William's work, as well as a versification by Ralph of Dunstable, liturgical lessons and the abbey's foundation charters. The abbey kept the book alternately in the abbot's study and at the high altar as an object of veneration.[4] A note added to the beginning of the manuscript in the fifteenth century states that the monks showed it to King Henry VI on his way to a great council at Westminster (fol. 1^v). The artefact links the abbey's saints to its own community.

Though the primary audience for the 'Book of St Albans' might seem to be purely monastic, it also shows how the abbey engaged its patrons and other contacts. The Dublin manuscript was likely a maquette or model for other copies: Cecilia de Sanford, a widow who became a benefactor of St Albans, and her protégées Eleanor Plantagenet and Joan de Munchensi, were likely recipients.[5] Surviving inscriptions show that Matthew's other manuscripts had similar audiences. A note on the flyleaf in Matthew's hand reads:

> Send word, if you please, to the lady Isabel, countess of Arundel, that she should send you the book about St Thomas the Martyr and St Edward which I translated and drew, and which the lady countess of Cornwall will be able to [keep] until Pentecost.[6]

This draft refers to a lost illustrated collection of saints' lives: the women named are Isabel de Warenne, countess of Arundel (1226 × 1230–1282) and Sanchia of Provence, countess of Cornwall (*c.* 1228–61). On the other side of the leaf is a note directing an illustrated book for a countess of Winchester.[7] Cambridge, University Library, MS Ee.3.59, a copy of Matthew's *Estoire de seint Aedward le rei*, was probably one of the books made from a St Albans model for a noble patron. The Benedictines of Westminster made this manuscript, with whom Matthew also collaborated for *Flores historiarum* (Manchester, Chetham's Library, MS 6712).[8] Such direct evidence for lay audiences of books produced in monasteries rarely survives.

Like the 'Book of St Albans', Matthew's manuscripts fall into the category of bespoke collections that writers produced at once personally and collaboratively in religious communities. The *Ormulum* (Oxford, Bodleian Library, MS Junius 1) is one of the most famous such books of this period, a collection of Middle English homilies written in the 1170s or 1180s by Orm, a canon of Bourne Abbey in Lincolnshire. The earliest

French-language autograph is a verse collection on Gregory the Great (Paris, Bibliothèque nationale de France, ms. Français 24766), made in 1212–14 by Frère Angier at St Frideswide's Priory in Oxford. He explicitly directs the work towards a lay audience, fitting a broader programme at the priory to encourage pilgrimage to its shrine.[9] At St Albans Matthew Paris was not the only monk creating original collections. John of Wallingford (d. 1258) created a collection of astrological diagrams, prayers, chronicles, notes on timekeeping and understanding the climate and other texts useful for daily life (London, British Library, Cotton MS Julius D VII).[10] John includes some leaves from Matthew's own hand and adapts some of his writing, such as his description of an elephant (fols. 114^r–115^r). When the creators of such collections asserted an individual identity, they often did so within a collaborative frame. Matthew's self-portrait in *Historia Anglorum* depicts him not so much as a writer as a devout member of a community.[11] These collections form unique books that creatively addressed specific needs, and their creators updated them with experience.

These collections were infinitely malleable, and Matthew constantly rearranged his work. He overhauled the arrangement of his anthology of Henry of Avranches at least once, leaving a labyrinth of codicological evidence.[12] This is a tame example in comparison to the *Chronica maiora*. Vaughan shows that Matthew originally conceived Cambridge, Corpus Christi College, MSS 26 and 16 as a single book.[13] He rearranged the gatherings as two volumes as he extended the chronicle. Conservation at Corpus Christi in 2003 showed that this happened before they were bound for the first time, as there is no evidence that the two volumes were ever sewn together.[14] Matthew records that he met King Henry III in 1247 at the translation of the relic of the Holy Blood at Westminster, and this year was pivotal for his expansion of the *Chronica maiora*.[15] In this year, he developed a *Liber additamentorum*, which had a shifting position within this evolving collection. It includes shorter historical works (notably *Vitae duorum Offarum* and *Gesta abbatum*), and especially charters, to which the term often refers.[16] This supplement enabled cross references to documents in the style of a cartulary, ending the need to copy them out in full. Matthew intended the collection originally as an appendix to a single *Chronica maiora* volume but separated it soon after 1250 as it became more unwieldy.[17] These documents form not merely official evidence, but part of the narrative, both visual and textual.[18] The collaborative and flexible manuscript culture of this period enabled Matthew's hagiographical, historiographical and poetic collections, both working within and innovating on established genres.

After Matthew's death, the monks at St Albans continued to value his books, but volumes strayed from the abbey library. Thomas Walsingham (c. 1340–c. 1422) used Matthew Paris' texts extensively for his own historical writing. By his time, book production at the abbey was in a more organised state.[19] Other members of the community looked to extract value from its library rather than expand it. The abbey allowed Richard Bury (1287–1345) to borrow fine books and had to buy them back from his executors.[20] The Bible to which Matthew contributed left the abbey by the fifteenth century, to judge from an inscribed price.[21] Abbot John of Wheathampstead (c. 1392–1465) presented the third part of the *Chronica maiora* to Humphrey, Duke of Gloucester (1390–1447) not long after Thomas Walsingham or an associate had extended the manuscript with a continuation.[22] It later came into the hands of John Russell (c. 1430–94), the bishop of Lincoln. The monks sought to recover it: he wrote a note in 1488 indicating that he wished to leave it to New College, Oxford, but would return it to St Albans if the abbey could prove that the book was its property.[23] It was again available for Polydore Vergil (c. 1470–1555) to annotate along with Matthew's copy of Geoffrey of Monmouth (Royal MS 13 D V). Polydore uses both in *Anglica historia*, finished by 1513 and first printed in 1534.[24] Few could have imagined the scale of the upheaval that would soon scatter the abbey's collections and put its remnants into private hands.

Collecting the Dissolution of the Monasteries

The modern period transformed Matthew Paris' collections both physically and intellectually. Documentation shows that St Albans Abbey still had a rich collection by the end of the medieval period.[25] The antiquarian John Leland (c. 1503–52) obtained a royal charter to examine the libraries of religious houses throughout England. He visited St Albans Abbey in 1533–34, where Thomas Kingsbury (d. 1545), the last prior of St Albans, showed him the library.[26] He saw the *Liber additamentorum* as well as a 'most beautiful history stolen by theft' (*pulcherrima historia furto sublata*) by Matthew Paris.[27] The latter might refer to the case of John Russell and Royal MS 14 C VII. King Henry VIII dissolved St Albans in 1539, scattering these books. Those that survived did so only because they caught the interest of a collector.

Leland and other scholars complained of the loss of books resulting from the monasteries' closure. Proposals from Leland and others to collect monastic libraries wholesale and set up a national library went unheeded. John Bale (1495–1563), a former friar turned Reformation polemicist, urgently called for 'one solempne lybrary'.[28] Nonetheless, hundreds of books from former religious communities flowed into the crown's libraries at Greenwich, Hampton Court and Westminster (Whitehall), soon merged into the last of these palaces.[29] The Royal Library did not take over entire collections but chose books reflecting interests of the day. Books about the history of the English crown were far more likely candidates than local chronicles. Leland had paid close attention to books in monastic libraries relating to marriage, and texts among the royal manuscripts collected as evidence for Henry VIII's 'great matter' still form a sizeable proportion of royal manuscripts on theological topics.

At least twenty-nine St Albans books entered the Royal Library, either directly from the abbey or via Thomas Wolsey. While holding the abbacy of St Albans *in commendam* between 1521 and 1530, Thomas Wolsey (1470/71–1530) commandeered at least two manuscripts that Matthew annotated among other books: a collection of British historians (Royal MS 13 D V) and Ralph de Diceto (Royal MS 13 E VI).[30] Following his fall from favour, Wolsey's books entered the Royal Library. There are no known intermediaries in the case of the *Historia scholastica* that Matthew augmented with Robert Grosseteste (Royal MS 4 D VII) and the third part of his *Chronica maiora* (Royal MS 14 C VII). The latter, which John Russell had already coveted, soon strayed from the royal collection. Bartholomew Traheron, Keeper of the King's Library between 1549 and 1553, lent the book to Henry Fitzalan, the twelfth earl of Arundel (1512–80). John Bale had seen the book there and alerted Matthew Parker of its anti-papal potential: 'It were muche pytie that that noble storye shulde perish in one coppye. For no chronycle paynteth out the byshopp of Rome in more lyuely colours, nor more lyuely decalreth hys execrable procedynges, than it doth.'[31] Parker borrowed the volume and had a transcript made that often attempted to imitate the script and illustrations of the original (Cambridge, Corpus Christi College, MS 56).[32] Parker sent the original back to Arundel, who kept it for himself: the book only returned through the library of John Lumley (c. 1533–1609), which Henry Frederick, Prince of Wales (1594–1612) integrated with the royal collection.[33] Though the old Royal Library did not collect as ambitiously as it might have and was not always managed with rigour, the collection survives in the modern British Library.

Far more monastic books went into private hands. Some former monks kept volumes from their libraries. They focused on utility, which meant that they took printed books just as often as manuscripts. Thomas Kingsbury kept John of Wallingford's miscellany (London, British Library, Cotton MS Julius D VII). He died within six years of the dissolution and passed it to another probable former monk, John Conyngesby. The last abbot of St Albans, Richard Boreman, also kept books, selling them to John Dee (1527–1609) in the 1550s.[34] Other books passed to collectors, through those who bought former monastic properties. The first generation of the secular collectors of Matthew's most impressive books had close connections to the court. Edward Aglionby (1520–91?) acquired the first volume of the *Chronica maiora* (Cambridge, Corpus Christi College, MS 26). He was an undergraduate at Cambridge during the dissolution and became a Member of Parliament beginning in 1547. Robert Talbot (1505/06–1558) is the first known owner of the second volume (Cambridge, Corpus Christi College, MS 16); the book caught his interest as an antiquary. The courtier Sir Henry Sidney (1529–86) later acquired it, probably viewing it on the level of collectable art, as was becoming fashionable in the Tudor court.

Though the crown had wiped away monastic communities, early collectors treated books in continuity with their medieval predecessors. Manuscript culture was still a living part of the circulation of texts, meaning that there was not a clean division between handwritten and printed volumes: they were all merely books that formed part of a working library. Readers valued books for being more legible or richly decorated: an author, for example, might commission a handwritten presentation copy for a patron. This approach protected Matthew Paris' illustrated books. Owners sometimes discarded manuscripts in favour of new printed equivalents, as textual criticism was nascent, and it was not yet fully clear that manuscripts were still valuable after the publication of a print edition. This attitude also entailed combining manuscripts with other volumes, a practice inherited from the Middle Ages. John Stow (1524/25–1605) owned the fair copy of the *Chronica maiora* (Cotton MS Nero D V) and likely Matthew's *Abbreviatio chronicorum* (Cotton MS Claudius D VI). Either he or Robert Glover (1543/44–88) combined Matthew's *Chronica maiora* with another copy from the later thirteenth century into one volume. The catalogue of Henry Savile of Banke (1568–1617) shows that the book was also once bound up with Arthurian materials, which Robert Cotton later moved into another volume (Cotton MS Julius B XII, fols. 67–82).[35] Early modern collectors did not preserve books as they received them, viewing them as functional items rather than artefacts, and they attempted to make them more useful through rebinding and rearrangement.

Following the dissolution of St Albans Abbey, Matthew Paris' manuscripts quickly passed into the hands of more than a dozen different collectors and scholars. Reformers also ransacked university libraries. Cardinal Guglielmo Sirleto (1514–85) saw a *Chronica maiora* or *Historia Anglorum* when he visited the University of Oxford in the sixteenth century, probably in Duke Humfrey's Library, which raises the possibility that Abbot John of Wheathampstead might have given another manuscript to the duke together with Royal MS 14 C VII, but it has disappeared.[36] Even more significant than the rearrangement of volumes was the selection process, resulting in losses but also giving Matthew a wider prominence he never held during the Middle Ages. The books that did not connect with early modern interests were often sold as waste material. Reformers often viewed hagiography as superstitious and inaccurate, but Matthew Paris' historiography became popular with early modern antiquarians in part because they viewed him as a proto-Protestant. John Bale presented these writings as supporting the anti-papal cause.[37] Matthias Flacius Illyricus (1520–75) printed *Historia Anglorum* excerpts in a collection of precedents for Lutheran theology probably sourced from the exiled Bale.[38] Matthew's entrance into the historical canon thus occurred through early modern battles over the interpretation of history.

Matthew Parker's Collections and Publications

John Bale and other polemicists brought Matthew Paris to the attention of Matthew Parker (1504–75), the archbishop of Canterbury, whose collection became the Parker Library at Corpus Christi College, Cambridge. He also published editions of historians including Ælfric, Gildas, Asser and Thomas Walsingham alongside Matthew Paris.[39] Parker sent books to Flacius Illyricus for the Magdeburg Centuries, a large project to gather sources for ecclesiastical history. Matthew Paris was among the writers the Magdeburg Centuriators wished to include but had difficulty obtaining.[40] Flacius Illyricus sent a copy of his extracts to the archbishop in 1561, commiserating on the problems of manuscripts in private ownership.[41] Parker also brought *Flores historiarum* into print in 1567 and 1570, but under the author 'Matthew of Westminster'. He did not know Matthew Paris' connection to the work and was not fortunate in his selection of manuscripts.[42] These publishing projects were core to Parker's collecting and treatment of manuscripts.

With monastic libraries closed, Parker could not obtain a copy of every work that he wished to publish. His solution was to 'borrow' manuscripts such as Matthew's from their private owners. In 1568 the privy council had given him powers to impel the owners of manuscripts to loan them for study.[43] In many cases, Parker never returned them, as for his partial edition of the *Chronica maiora* (1571), which used five manuscripts.[44] A letter of 1569 displays his techniques for requesting loans, appealing to William Cecil (1520/21–98) for his copy of Matthew Paris (Paris, Bibliothèque nationale de France, ms. Latin 6048B).[45] He borrowed the first part of the *Chronica maiora* from Edward Aglionby, and the second from Sir Henry Sidney (Cambridge, Corpus Christi College, MSS 26 and 16). He proudly announced the owners of the manuscripts in the resulting publication and praised their '*exquisita pictura*'.[46] As already noted, he had to content himself with a transcript of Royal MS 14 C VII after he learned of it through Bale. He had realised that the illustrations were Matthew's own through reading the St Albans *Liber benefactorum* (London, British Library, Cotton MS Nero D VII).[47] Parker argues that the scarcity of the *Chronica maiora* was the result of papist attempts to suppress the text, a sentiment he also expresses to Flacius, and he saw his work and collecting as addressing this injustice.[48]

Parker and his associates left distinct marks of their work. He sometimes convinced others to loan them books with the offer that he could improve them. He employed a man named Lyly to rewrite missing pages for manuscripts in an imitative script, presumably Peter Lyly (d. 1569), Parker's registrar.[49] He advertises in his *Chronica maiora* preface that he had replaced text missing from Sidney's manuscript (Cambridge, Corpus Christi College, MS 16). Leaves were missing after folios 3, 103, 116 and 232; he had new leaves made from the copy then belonging to John Stow (Cotton MS Nero D V). On folio 38ᵛ, he cleaned up a dark blotch by having a slip added on top with the text recopied. Following this, Reyner Wolfe (d. in or before 1574) used the book in his print shop as a copy text, leaving pages covered in ink stains and black fingerprints. His colleagues added notes comparing the text with the printed version, using the pagination of Parker's edition, directly into the margins. A printer even used an ink-stained wooden block to prop a page open.[50] It is not known whether Sidney ever saw the manuscript again, or whether he agreed to its staying in Parker's collection, but in 1574 the archbishop was still asking to borrow books with a proposal to 'enlarge them'.[51] In contrast to Parker's own cavalier treatment of manuscripts, the donation of his books to Corpus Christi College, Cambridge, came with strict guidelines for their use and handling.

Like the users of manuscripts of the Middle Ages, early modern readers treated all books, whether handwritten or printed, as part of a working collection. This is especially vivid in Parker's case, who saw custodianship as creating tidy-looking and above all complete volumes that he and his associates could use for daily scholarship.[52] Within this context, it was entirely acceptable, for example, to take Matthew Paris' copy of William of Conches' *Dragmaticon philosophiae* and combine it with other thirteenth- and fourteenth-century theological texts (Cambridge, Corpus Christi College, MS 385). The connoisseurship of Matthew Parker and other early modern collectors aimed to maintain books as reference books, but at the cost of obscuring historical evidence. Their new, straight, matching bindings looked impressive on a shelf, but carelessly trimmed off the edges of annotations and images. Nonetheless, Parker spread knowledge of Matthew Paris' work and brought his manuscripts to greater prominence.

Robert Cotton's Connoisseurship

Sir Robert Cotton (1571–1631), a Member of Parliament and antiquarian, was the last of the connoisseur collectors of Matthew Paris' manuscripts. Cotton was already acquiring and lending out books by the 1590s and soon developed his own library as a public resource. He used his position at court to acquire books from older collectors as they died, to borrow volumes and even to trade books with the Royal Library.[53] His fair copy of the *Chronica maiora* (Cotton MS Nero D V), for example, came from the sale of Henry Savile of Banke's collection in 1626.[54] Like Parker, he aimed to formulate books and archives into a working library, which meant rebinding and rearranging print and manuscript materials of every kind. Located in central London, Cotton's library was influential in English intellectual life of this period, and his collecting practices defined books as they now survive.

The annotations and records of loans from Cotton's library allow us to know some of the people who read Matthew Paris most actively in this period, such as Arthur Agarde (1540–1615), John Selden (1584–1654) and Sir Simonds D'Ewes (1602–50). Improved access to these books allowed scholars to continue raising Matthew Paris' profile and to build on the growing realisation that he had created his own manuscripts. The cardinals Caesar Baronius (1538–1607) and Robert Bellarmine (1542–1621) suggested that passages criticising the papacy were insertions by Matthew's Protestant editors, which led to the prohibition of Parker's *Chronica maiora* on the Roman *Index*. In response, Isaac Casaubon (1559–1614) examined Cotton MS Nero D I and Royal MS 14 C VII, showing that Matthew had written the passages in his own hand.[55] Access to this collection was not continuous: when Cotton's loyalty fell under question, King Charles I ordered the library's closure in November 1629, and it reopened only in 1633 under Cotton's eldest son, Sir Thomas Cotton (1594–1662). This enabled a new edition of the *Chronica maiora* by William Watts (*c.* 1590–1649), reprinting Parker's text with pages of variant readings, along with Matthew's *Gesta abbatum* and *Vitae duorum Offarum* (1639–40). Thomas' son Sir John Cotton (1621–1702) eventually arranged for the collection's sale to the nation and it formed part of the basis for the British Museum in 1753.

Cotton inherited the approach of treating books as a living archive, which he combined with the sense of connoisseurship that developed in the early modern period; as seen in Parker, he overhauled his books without hesitation. This has obscured the original form of books in the Cotton collection and erased their earlier history. Cotton bound manuscripts together that had similarities in content with the aim of making it easier to find related materials.[56] The only surviving copy of Matthew's life of Edmund of Abingdon is in Cotton MS Julius D VI, folios 123^r–156^v;[57] it is now bound with another life of Edmund that historically had no relationship to it. Cotton acquired the fair copy of the *Chronica maiora* (Cotton MS Nero D V) already combined with unrelated materials, modifying and splitting them up further to such an extent that it is not possible to reconstruct the relationship between the surviving materials.[58] Cotton MS Nero D I, the *Liber additamentorum*, came to Cotton still with loose leaves in the volume.[59] Cotton extensively rearranged the book and added new material.[60]

Cotton's connoisseurship extended to improving books by cutting out decoration from manuscripts that he considered less valuable and adding it to his books to give them openings and closings that fit his aesthetic sense. He took apart an illuminated psalter from the fourteenth century in 1612–16 and added its decoration to various manuscripts, especially on flyleaves. Cotton MSS Claudius D VI, Nero C V and Nero D I were among the manuscripts he dressed up with such additions. That was not the end: beginning in the 1870s, staff at the British Museum started to remove identified leaves and gather them into a new volume, Royal MS 13 D I*, as an appendix to a manuscript where more of the psalter can be found, though it has no relationship to the original Royal MS 13 D I.[61]

Cotton's most misleading creation among the Matthew Paris manuscripts is Cotton MS Claudius D VI. Along with Matthew's *Abbreviatio chronicorum*, it includes a chronicle of William Rishanger, one of Mathew's immediate continuators at St Albans. Without knowing anything of the manuscript's history, one would assume that the later section was designed to go with the *Abbreuiatio*, constituting an essential unity produced at St Albans after Matthew's death. The scribe even applies coloured borders in vertical bands to leaves, as one sees in Matthew's manuscripts. A closer look reveals Cotton's tracks. The manuscript is heavily trimmed, cutting off features such as the names of the kings that open the manuscript. The pages were once at least seventeen millimetres wider, as diagrams folded in on folios 28 and 40 show. Cotton's binder was presumably looking to match the smaller size of the William Rishanger manuscript. Cotton, with the cooperation of the royal librarian Patrick Young (1584–1652), had taken apart Royal MS 14 C I and exchanged parts of the two manuscripts to improve his own.[62] The *Abbreviatio chronicorum* historically had nothing to do with the rest of the volume. The harmony of this manuscript, and its convenient coverage of English history from around 1000 to 1324, is an illusion created by Cotton. This prompts questions on almost everything about the manuscript. The first eight leaves, a gallery of kings closing with a map of Britain, were not originally part of the manuscript: the following quire was marked as the first at the time of its creation. It is impossible to know whether they were added in Matthew's time. This illustrates that examination of material evidence and provenance of any manuscript is necessary before making claims about the intentions of its creators or the impressions of later readers.

Balancing Function and Conservation in Modern Libraries

The working library was the dominant rationale for access and preservation decisions well into the twentieth century, until the emergence of modern conservation practice in the 1970s. The British nation bought the Cotton library in 1702 and moved it in 1712 from the dilapidated Cotton House to Essex House, The Strand, alongside the Royal Library. After authorities declared this a fire hazard, it migrated in 1730 to Ashburnham House, near Westminster Abbey. This proved disastrous when a fire broke out on 23 October 1731, damaging both collections, but especially the Cotton manuscripts. A copy of Matthew Paris' *Vie de Saint Edmond* and *Vie de Seint Auban* in Cotton MS Vitellius D VIII was among the books that disappeared.[63] A restoration effort began at once. Staff cut apart the leaves of the most damaged books, which had shrunk during the fire. They placed leaves in paper frames, rebinding them in imitation Cotton bindings.[64] This procedure resulted in the modern shape of the *Chronica maiora* excerpts in Cotton MS Vitellius A XX, making it difficult to untangle the components of the composite manuscript that Cotton had created in this volume. While modern conservators make changes that are minimal and reversible, custodians of Cotton's books in the eighteenth and nineteenth centuries instead aimed to restore an idealised version of the collection, adding yet another layer of intervention and rearrangement.

Restoration work on the Cotton manuscripts lasted well into the nineteenth century and was a central concern of Sir Frederic Madden (1801–73). He continued the tradition of Matthew Paris scholars who were also responsible for the writer's manuscripts. Madden had become assistant keeper in the British Museum's Department of Manuscripts in 1828, heading the department from 1837 until his retirement in 1866. He put a strong emphasis on illuminated manuscripts and in 1837 introduced a system of 'common' and 'select' manuscripts to restrict the use of these books, which remains in use. These categories became crucial at the outset of the First and Second World Wars, when curators hurriedly expanded them to prioritise collections for evacuations.[65] Madden also taught Henry Octavius Coxe (1811–81) palaeography as his junior at the British Museum in 1833–39, following which Coxe spent the remainder of his career at the Bodleian Library. Coxe combined his experience of the two collections in his edition of Roger of Wendover's *Flores historiarum* with an additional volume on Matthew Paris.[66] The success of this work likely influenced Madden's decision in 1858 to accept the invitation of John Romilly (1802–74), Master of the Rolls, to edit the *Historia Anglorum* and *Abbreviatio chronicorum* for the Rolls Series. He found it difficult to complete the project alongside British Museum responsibilities and soon expressed regret in his diary for having accepted the commission, which he completed after hours.[67] The three volumes appeared beginning in the year of his retirement.[68] Madden's direct access to the manuscripts allowed him to pioneer much of what is now known about Matthew's life and work, and later scholarship largely confirmed his assessment of the author's handwriting.[69]

Madden's contemporary editor was Henry Richards Luard (1825–91), a clergyman and registrar of the University of Cambridge. He was also active at the University Library and one of the main contributors to its printed manuscripts catalogue.[70] Among other Rolls Series volumes, he edited *La estoire de seint Aedward le rei*, *Chronica maiora* and *Flores historiarum*.⁷¹ The editions of Madden and Luard stem from extensive experience with manuscripts and have yet to be replaced. They made it possible to analyse Matthew's historical writings independent of their manuscripts, but also divorced these works from their illustrations until reproductions became more widely available.

Advances in photography and printing enabled the creation of manuscript facsimiles, making it possible for anyone to gain a sense of their images without access to the original. Although Madden was critical of the growing trend of exhibiting manuscripts, he took part in the rapid introduction of photography at the museum. This gradually brought more manuscripts into the public eye.⁷² At first energy was focused on either selected photographic plates in publications or facsimiles, which are expensive and bulky but also allow readers to experience reproductions at their original scale, sometimes even their original format. James (1924) is an early example, reproducing much of Dublin, Trinity College, MS 177. Beginning in the early 1930s, the Library of Congress began to microfilm manuscripts in British libraries, beginning industrial-level reproduction of special collections and setting the basic expectations for digitising manuscripts, which focuses on single images of pages.⁷³ It became possible for an overseas reader to view black-and-white reproductions of almost the entirety of Matthew's work, but only through a single dimension framed by an anonymous photographer. During the second half of the twentieth century, libraries also sold thematic sets of thirty-five-millimetre slides of colour manuscript photographs for research and teaching, focusing on illustration. This process created new artefacts out of Matthew's manuscripts. It was far less destructive than early modern habits of physically rearranging books to make them more useful, but like these earlier patterns it resulted in both democratisation and decontextualisation.

Though the ideas of Parker and Cotton in prioritising an aesthetically pleasing working library now seem foreign, preserving reader access is still a key determiner in custodianship decisions. Libraries frequently rebound manuscripts until the early twentieth century with no records of what they replaced. British Museum staff removed maps and itineraries from Matthew Paris' manuscripts in the early twentieth century, framing them individually, making it possible to display these leaves outside the constraints of a tightly bound volume, but leaving blank sheets in their original locations. These detached leaves took, for example, a prominent place in a 2011–12 exhibition of the royal manuscripts, where the public could view them from either side.[74] A 1950s rebinding of Cambridge, Corpus Christi College, MSS 16 and 26 used inappropriate conservation techniques that resulted in unusably stiff bindings. The college decided to rebind the manuscripts again in 2003 after holding a symposium on the *Chronica maiora*, which discussed either assembling them based on how they were thought to have existed at Matthew's death or creating 'a structure more suited to modern purposes'. The library determined on splitting MS 16 into two parts on the basis that the preliminary leaves were not always part of the manuscript.[75] Microfilming and manuscript digitisation also influence decisions in the foliation, labelling and binding of books, sometimes resulting in a proliferation of reference systems. Curators and conservators continue to change manuscripts in small but often undocumented ways to meet new needs.

Scholars still hope to find more examples of Matthew Paris' work in manuscript fragments. Work in this vein has so far focused on identifications of artistic styles, which has proven contentious. Based on the sketchbook of Villard de Honnecourt (Paris, Bibliothèque nationale de France, ms. Français 19093), Lewis conjectures that Matthew kept a similar notebook and lists twenty-four leaves as part of this, mostly from the known corpus of Matthew's books.[76] One of the exceptions, London, British Library, Arundel MS 157, folio 2^r, is a leaf added to the front of a psalter written in the 1200s showing the Veil of Veronica, made for St Frideswide's Priory, Oxford.[77] Lewis attributes it to Matthew based on his illustrations of the same subject in the *Chronica maiora*.[78] Morgan shows instead that it draws on a broader English iconographical tradition, arguing against any association with St Albans.[79] Similarly, *Sol meldunensis* (Cambridge, University Library, MS Gg.6.42), a miscellany of the works of Alexander Nequam (1157–1217) made by his nephew Geoffrey Brito in 1246–60, includes an inserted leaf (fol. 5) illustrating a series of robed clerics featuring Francis of Assisi. Lewis and Morgan suggest a 'direct connection' to Matthew, but Zutshi rejects the possibility.[80] Backhouse and de Hamel present the 'Becket leaves' (Stokenchurch, Wormsley Library, MS BM 3750), fragments of an Anglo–Norman life of Thomas Becket, as copies of Matthew's work, though Morgan suggests that they might instead have been his model.[81] Art historians have largely abandoned the idea of a 'St Albans school' that was prominent in earlier literature. Libraries nonetheless hold thousands of uncatalogued manuscript fragments in which discoveries are still to be made.

The history of books often emphasises creation, but it is equally important to understand survival. Medieval readers treated books as fundamentally functional items, modifying and recycling them at need. The Reformation resulted in vast loss of books and art. The surviving manuscripts of Matthew Paris caught the intellectual or aesthetic interests of early modern collectors. It was many more decades, however, before they began to distinguish between printed manuscript books, or before medieval approaches to working libraries began to change. The sense of connoisseurship that figures such as Matthew Parker and Robert Cotton brought to books displaced their original form. Modern collections must still balance between ensuring that books can still be read and best conserving them as artefacts. In the past century, library staff have changed shelf marks, rearranged volumes, modified folio numbers and moved collections to new buildings. Reproduction at scale has made images of manuscript pages far more widely available, but also decontextualised collections and created the illusion that all evidence can be represented digitally. The ownership and adaptation of Matthew Paris' manuscripts, together with the creation of printed editions, created a different writer from the one that his contemporaries knew. The next eight centuries will pose more challenges and changes for Matthew's manuscripts, but also present new opportunities to make his work accessible to new audiences.

Appendix: Manuscripts Written by Matthew Paris

These manuscripts are Matthew Paris' own copies of his work as well as copies of other authors that he either wrote himself or annotated. They are no longer in the same form as Matthew knew them: their owners have since rearranged, expanded, rebound and sometimes combined them with formerly separate volumes. Their provenance shows that they began to circulate during Matthew's own lifetime: the lists here include any notes or inscriptions that can be linked to a specific person, as well as records of loans from Robert Cotton's library, showing that some of the most influential early modern antiquarians consulted these volumes.[82]

The critical studies cited include descriptions of manuscripts and codicological analysis, especially those supplementing Vaughan's 1953 and 1958 studies. The list omits works superseded by recent scholarship.

The sigla indicate the letters that the Rolls Series editors and Vaughan use to refer to the manuscripts. The contents lists are not exhaustive, noting only the most significant items.

Cambridge, Corpus Christi College, MS 16 (Siglum *B*)

A 2003 conservation programme split the volume into MS 16 (I) and MS 16 (II).[83]

Contents
Fols. i^r–v^v (MS 16 (I)): Preliminary material, including lists, maps, diagrams, and the illustration of the elephant given by Louis IX to Henry III.
Fols. 1^v–282^r (MS 16 (II)): Matthew Paris, *Chronica maiora*, part 2.

Extent
360 × 245 mm; 5 (16I) + 281 (16II) leaves. Refoliated since Luard's edition.

Provenance
Matthew Paris gave the volume to St Albans Abbey: inscribed, fol. 1^r.
Robert Talbot (1505/06–1558): inscribed, believing he has the *Liber additamentorum*, fol. 248^v.
Sir Henry Sidney (1529–86).
Matthew Parker (1504–75): borrowed from Sidney (Parker 1571, preface).
Reyner Wolfe (d. in or before 1574): used the manuscript directly in his print shop while publishing Parker's 1571 edition.[84]
Stephan Batman (*c.* 1542–84): names the annotation on fol. 248^v as Talbot's. Compare his similar note in Talbot's notebook: Cambridge, Corpus Christi College, MS 379, fol. 24^r.

Critical Studies
James (1912, 1:54–58); Morgan (1982–88, no. 88).

Cambridge, Corpus Christi College, MS 26 (Siglum *A*)

Contents
Fols. i^r–vi^v: Preliminary matter.
Fols. 1^r–141^v: Matthew Paris, *Chronica maiora*, part 1.
Fols. vii^r–ix^r: Added illustrations, diagrams and notes.

Extent
360 × 250 mm; 2 + 6 + 140 + 2 + 1 leaves.

Provenance
Edward Aglionby (1520–91?): inscribed, fol. ix^r.
Matthew Parker (1504–75): borrowed from Aglionby (Parker 1571, preface).

Critical Studies
James (1912, 1:50–53); Morgan (1982–1988, no. 88); Jefferson (2006).

Cambridge, Corpus Christi College, MS 385, Pages 89–212

Contents
William of Conches, *Dragmaticon philosophiae*, with some diagrams by Matthew Paris.

Extent
185 × 140 mm; 2 + 44 + 62 + 5 + 12 + 2 leaves.

Provenance
Matthew Parker (1504–75): combined four thirteenth- and fourteenth-century manuscripts into this volume.

Critical Studies
James (1912, 2:232–235); Ronca and Jeauneau (1997, xxxix–xl).

Cambridge, University Library, MS Dd.11.78

Contents
Fols. 1^r–238^v: Poems of Henry of Avranches, copied by Matthew Paris and others.

Extent

185 × 130–40 mm; 238 leaves.

Provenance

John Moore (1646–1714), Bishop of Ely: King George I acquired his collection and gave it to Cambridge University.

Critical Studies

Hardwick and Luard (1856–67, 1:469–476); Townsend and Rigg (1987).

Dublin, Trinity College, MS 177 (Formerly E. i. 40)

Some scholarship refers to this manuscript as the 'Book of St Albans'.

Contents

Fols. 3^r–20^r: Ralph of Dunstable, versification of William of St Albans, *Passio sancti Albani* (*BHL* 212).

Fols. 20^r–28^v: William of St Albans, *Passio sancti Albani* (*BHL* 213).

Fols. 39^r–50^r: Matthew Paris, *Vie de Seint Auban*.

Fols. 50^v–52^v: Liturgical readings for the invention and translation of Alban (*BHL* 215).

Fols. 52^v–62^v, 66^v–68^v: Invention and translation of Alban (*BHL* 216).

Fols. 63^r–66^r: Foundation charters of St Albans Abbey.

Fols. 68^v–69^v, 73^r–77^r: Invention and miracles of Amphibalus (*BHL* 396).

Fols. 70^r–72^r: Translation of Alban (incomplete).

Extent

242 × 165 mm; 77 leaves.

Provenance

St Albans Abbey: 'de armariolo A', fol. 3^r. Note by Matthew Paris on a loan of his lives of Thomas Becket and Edward the Confessor between Isabel de Warenne, Countess of Arundel (1226 × 1230–82) and Sanchia of Provence, Countess of Cornwall (*c.* 1228–61), fol. 1^r, along with directions on illustrations for a book to be given to the countess of Winchester, fol. 1^v, referring to a different volume (James 1920, 20–21; James et al. 1924, 15–16; Vaughan 1958c, 170; Henderson 1967, 75; Wogan-Browne and Fenster 2010, 32–33). Cecilia de Sanford, Eleanor Plantagenet and Joan de Munchensi may have been among the early intended readership for the *Vie de Seint Auban* (Slater 2018).

? Loaned to William Dolte, likely a monk of Wymondham Priory (Riley 1872, 1:147): St Albans borrowers' list, 1420 × 1437 (Sharpe et al. 1996, no. B87.†50a).
? Richard Boreman, last abbot of St Albans (1538–39): sold books from the abbey to John Dee in the 1550s (Carley 2002, 341).
John Dee (1527–1609): his mark, fol. 77^v, and notes at fol. 20^r, but apparently not in his catalogues (Roberts and Watson 1990).
James Ussher (1581–1656): his collection came to Trinity College in 1661.

Critical Studies
James (1924); Harden (1968); McCulloch (1981); Morgan (1982–88, no. 85); Colker (1991, 339–43); Crick (2007, 45–48); Colker (2008, 185); Baswell (2010); Quinn (2010).

London, British Library, Cotton MS Julius D VII

The British Museum removed folios 50–53 for exhibition, now Cotton MS Julius D VII/1.

Contents
Fols. 1^v–134^v: John of Wallingford, miscellany and chronicle; integrates some leaves created by Matthew Paris, including his drawing of John of Wallingford (fol. 42^v), a map of Britain (fols. 50^v–53^r) and an illustration of Christ in majesty (fol. 60^v).

Extent
200 × 165 mm; 138 leaves.

Provenance
John of Wallingford (d. 1258): inscribed, fols. 1^v, 112^v; John died at Wymondham Priory, a dependency of St Albans.
Thomas Kingsbury (d. 1545), last prior of St Albans: inscribed, fol. 1^r.
John Conyngesby, sixteenth century: given to him by Kingsbury, inscribed, fols. 1^r, 34^r, 61^r.
Philip Howard, the thirteenth earl of Arundel (1557–95): inscribed, fol. 46^r.
Sir Robert Bruce Cotton, first baronet (1571–1631): inscribed, fols. 10^v, 10^r, 46^r; loaned the manuscript to Arthur Agarde (1540–1615) in 1612–15.

Critical Studies
Planta (1802, 15–16); Vaughan (1958c); Morgan (1982–88, no. 91); Tite (2003, 97–98).

London, British Library, Cotton MS Claudius D VI, Folios 5-100

The British Museum rebound the manuscript in 1929 and removed folio 12 for exhibition, now Cotton MS Claudius D VI/1.

Contents
Fols. 5^v-98^v: Matthew Paris, *Abbreviatio chronicorum*.

Extent
320 × 217 mm (originally at least 15-20 mm wider); 221 leaves.

Provenance
? John Stow (1524/25-1605): extracts in London, British Library, Harley MS 545, fol. 186^r (*c.* 1575), which Madden (1866-69, 3:156) thought suggested ownership, but without firm evidence. John Joscelin (1529-1603) also made extracts, Cotton MS Vitellius E XIV.

Sir Richard Hutton (bap. 1561, d. 1639): inscribed, fol. 9^v.

Sir Robert Bruce Cotton, first baronet (1571-1631): inscribed, fol. 6^r; combined two manuscripts into a composite volume, with some parts of the second manuscript now Royal MS 14 C I; table of contents by Richard James (bap. 1591, d. 1638), his librarian (fol. 3^r). Cotton also decorated the manuscript with leaves from a psalter, removed in 1912 along with those from other volumes to Royal MS 13 D I* (Carley and Tite, 1992).

The Cotton library loaned the manuscript to Richard Bancroft (1544-1610) in 1608 via John Pory (bap. 1572, d. 1633); George Allington and Patrick Young (1584-1652), before 1611; 'Mr Colwell', John Selden (1584-1654), John Speed (1551/52-1629), or Augustine Vincent (*c.* 1584-1626) in 1621-22; and Sir Simonds D'Ewes (1602-50) in 1626.

Critical Studies
Planta (1802, 196-197); Watson (1979, no. 520); Morgan (1982-88, no. 93); Carley (1992, 57-60; 1997); Tite (2003, 127).

London, British Library, Cotton MS Nero D I (Siglum *LA*), *Liber additamentorum*

Cotton decorated the manuscript with leaves from the same psalter as that used in Cotton MS Claudius D VI, removed to Royal MS 13 D I* (Carley and Tite, 1992). The lower part of fol. 197 is now Cotton MS Vespasian B XIII, fol. 133. Vaughan (1958c, chapter 5) argues that fols. 168–69 originally fell before fol. 85, with fols. 145–47 following fol. 63.

Contents
Fols. 2^r–25^r: Matthew Paris, *Vita Offarum*.
Fols. 30^r–73^v: Matthew Paris, *Gesta abbatum monasterii sancti Albani*, in two parts, with attached documents.
Fols. 74^r–201^v: Miscellaneous historical documents, the earliest added by Matthew Paris, and others added up to the fifteenth century; includes Matthew's tract on the St Albans gems (fols. 146^r–147^r) and a fragment of his life of Stephen Langton (fols. 197^r, 198^r: Liebermann 1879). Cotton probably added or rearranged the leaves from folio 162 onward.

Extent
380 × 250 mm; 202 leaves. Vaughan (1958c, 79–80) diagrams the collation of quires 1–25. After his research, folio 120* was refoliated as folio 121, along with all subsequent folios, meaning that his references must be incremented by one after this point.

Provenance
Matthew Paris gave the volume to St Albans Abbey: inscribed, fol. 2^r.
'Symons Thomas', early fifteenth century: inscribed, fol. 199^r.
? Robert Talbot (1505/06–58): annotates Cambridge, Corpus Christi College, MS 16 (II), fol. 248^v, 'sunt librum additamentorum puto me habere'.
Edward Ferrers (1524 × 1527–64) and Henry Ferrers (1550–1633): their names inscribed alongside those of Christfar Comons, Thomas Ward, Henry Sengeord and William Bery, fol. 202^{r-v}.
Sir Robert Bruce Cotton, first baronet (1571–1631): inscribed, fols. 2^r, 162^r; table of contents by Richard James (bap. 1591, d. 1638), his librarian (fol. 1^{r-v}). According to Cotton's catalogue, there were loose leaves in the manuscript in his time (London, British Library, Harley MS 6018, no. 199: Tite 2003, 136).
The Cotton library loaned the manuscript to William Camden after Christmas 1604; Richard Bancroft (1544–1610) in 1608 via John Pory (bap. 1572, d. 1633); Arthur Agarde (1540–1615) in 1612–15; John Selden (1584–1654) in 1622 and 1638; William Watts (*c.* 1590–1649) before 1640 (no record, but see Watts 1640, preface); Isaac Casaubon (1559–1614) had access to this and Royal MS 14 C VII after moving to England in 1610 (Signaroli 2013).

Critical Studies

Planta (1802, 236–37); Watson (1979, no. 542); Morgan (1982–88, no. 87); Tite (2003, 136); Crick (2007, 49–51); Collard (2022).

London, British Library, Cotton MS Nero D V, Folios 162–395 (Siglum *C*)

Contents

Fols. 162–395: Matthew Paris, *Chronica maiora*, a fair copy of Cambridge, Corpus Christi College, MS 16; annotations from Matthew suggest that he oversaw its production (Vaughan 1958c, 110).

Extent

370 × 250 mm; 395 leaves.

Provenance

? Robert Glover (1543/44–88): possibly 'Y' in his list of books, London, British Library, Lansdowne MS 58, fol. 105^r (cf. Selwyn 1997).

John Stow (1524/25–1605): inscribed, fols. 2^r, 161^r; annotated, fols. 9^r, 20^r, 21^r, 192^v.

Henry Savile of Banke (1568–1617): his catalogue suggests that Cotton MS Julius B XII, fols. 67–82, was bound into the volume in his time (Watson 1969, 21).

Sir Robert Bruce Cotton, first baronet (1571–1631): combined several manuscripts into a composite volume (Madden 1866–69, 1:lxiii); inscribed, fol. 2^r.

The Cotton library loaned the manuscript to William Watts (*c.* 1590–1649) before 1640 for his edition of Matthew Paris (Watts 1639–40, preface). Madden (1866–69, 1:lxiii) identifies a note, fol. 1*r, as being in the hand of Thomas Gale (1635/36–1702).

Critical Studies

Planta (1802, 238); Watson (1979, no. 545); Tite (2003, 137).

London, British Library, Cotton MS Vitellius A XX, Folios 67–108 (Siglum *V*)

The Ashburnham house fire in 1731 damaged the leaves badly, now separated and mounted in paper frames.

Contents

Fols. 77ʳ–108ᵛ: Excerpts from the *Chronica maiora* and other historical documents, with some text and additions by Matthew Paris, probably written in 1246–59.

Extent

210 × 145 mm; 242 leaves.

Provenance

Tynemouth Priory: inscribed, fol. 67ʳ, as a gift of Ralph de Dunham (prior, 1252–66/67).
Sir Robert Bruce Cotton, first baronet (1571–1631): the contents list on fol. 1*v suggests that this composite volume was already bound together by the time it reached him.

Critical Studies

Planta (1802, 381–82); Smith (1696, 84); Watson (1979, no. 576); Tite (2003, 160).

London, British Library, Cotton MS Vespasian B XIII, Folio 133

Detached from Cotton MS Nero D I, fol. 197.

London, British Library, Royal MS 4 D VII

Predates Matthew Paris; he added folios 1ᵛ–2ᵛ, 232ᵛ–247ʳ.

Contents

Fols. 1ᵛ–2ᵛ: Additions by Matthew Paris, including two plans of Noah's Ark and the candelabrum in the Temple.
Fols. 3ʳ–181ᵛ: Petrus Comestor, *Historia scholastica*.
Fols. 182ʳ–232ʳ: Richard of Saint-Victor, *Liber exceptionum*.
Fols. 232ᵛ–246ᵛ: Robert Grosseteste, *Testamenta duodecim patriarcharum*, the work that Matthew Paris, *Chronica maiora* mentions (Luard 1872–84, 5:284–85; Thomson 1940, 42–44).
Fols. 246ᵛ–248ʳ: Robert Grosseteste, *De probatione uirginitatis beate Marie*, translated from *Lexicon Suida*: Matthew Paris indicates in a colophon that he used a copy from Robert himself.

Extent

385 × 260 mm; 249 leaves.

Provenance

Raymond (prior of St Albans, 1195–1214) commissioned the manuscript and William de Trumpington (abbot, 1214–35) later presented it to the abbey; pressmark 'B 8 gradus', fol. 1^r. Matthew Paris mentions the book in *Gesta abbatum* (Riley 1867–69, 1:233–34, 294).

Royal Library, Westminster: appears in the 1542 inventory, 'n° 1335', fol. 1^r (Carley 2000, no. H2.1335).

Critical Studies

Warner and Gilson (1921, 1:90); Watson (1979, no. 867); Thomson (1982, no. 28).

London, British Library, Royal MS 13 D V

Matthew wrote some of the rubrics (e.g. fols. 42^v–44^r) and annotates parts of the volume, sometimes extensively, showing his use of these historical works. See for example his notes on Offa (fol. 65^r, which Vaughan 1953b, plate xviii(e) reproduces).

Contents

Fols. 1^r–37^v: Geoffrey of Monmouth, *De gestis britonum*.
Fols. 38^r–45^r: *Historia Britonum* (here attributed to Gildas).
Fols. 45^r–50^v: Ralph of Coggeshall (?), *Visio Thurkilli*.
Fols. 51^r–142^r: William of Malmesbury, *Gesta regum Anglorum*, with the *Historia novella* added as book 6.
Fols. 142^r–151^v: Aelred of Rievaulx, *De genealogia regum Anglorum*.
Fol. 152^r: Short lists of the shires and dioceses of England; the genealogy of the counts of Flanders, as far as Robert II (1093–1111); and the kings of France, as far as Louis VI (1108–37).
Fols. 153^r–200^v: William of Malmesbury, *Gesta pontificum Anglorum*, second recension.

Extent

381 × 279 mm; i + 201 + i leaves.

Provenance

St Albans Abbey: lost and later recovered during the time of John of Wheathampstead (abbot, 1420–40, 1452–64) according to an inscription, fol. 37^v; pressmark, 'de almariolo B primus liber in primo gradu', fol. 1*v.

Polydore Vergil (c. 1470–1555): notes in his hand – for example, fols. 39^r–40^r, 44^v (see also Royal MS 13 D V).

Thomas Wolsey (1470/71–1530), abbot of St Albans (1521–30): 'TC' monogram, fol. 1^r.

Royal Library, Westminster: acquired before 1542, inventory 'n° 1138', fol. 1^r (Carley 2000, nos. H2.1138, H4.38, H4.44).

John Lumley, First Baron Lumley (c. 1533–1609): inscribed, fol. 1^r. Not in his catalogue (Jayne and Johnson, 1956).

Henry Frederick, Prince of Wales (1594–1612): added Lumley's collection to the Royal Library.

Critical Studies

Warner and Gilson (1921, 2:110); Schmidt (1978); Thomson (1982, no. 35); Crick (1989, 184–86).

London, British Library, Royal MS 13 E VI

Matthew referred to this manuscript in his *Historia Anglorum* and made additions (Vaughan 1953b, 381).

Contents

Fols. 1^r–48^r: Ralph de Diceto, *Abbreuiationes chronicorum*.
Fols. 49^r–136^r: Ralph de Diceto, *Ymagines historiarum*.

Extent

411 × 304 mm; i + 138 leaves.

Provenance

St Albans Abbey: pressmark 'A 6 gradus 2 p', fol. i^r.

Borrowed in 1209/10 by Richard de Morins (d. 1242), prior of the Augustinian house at Dunstable (Cheney 1969).

Thomas Wolsey (1470/71–1530), abbot of St Albans (1521–30): 'TC' monogram, fol. i^r.

Royal Library, Westminster: acquired before 1542, inventory 'n° 1044', fol. i^r (Carley 2000, nos. H2.1044, H4.18).

Critical Studies

Warner and Gilson (1921, 2:112–13); Thomson (1982, no. 38).

London, British Library, Royal MS 14 C VII (Siglum *R*)

The British Museum removed folios 2–5 for exhibition in 1952, now Royal MS 14 C VII/1.

Contents

Fols. 1ᵛ–8ʳ: Maps and other prefatory material.
Fols. 8ᵛ–156ᵛ: Matthew Paris, *Historia Anglorum*.
Fols. 157ʳ–218ᵛ: Matthew Paris, *Chronica maiora*, part 3.
Fols. 219ʳ–231ʳ: Thomas Walsingham (?), 1259–72 continuation.

Extent

360 × 245 mm; ii + 232 leaves.

Provenance

Matthew Paris gave the volume to St Albans Abbey: inscribed, fol. 6ᵛ. He began *Historia Anglorum* after 1250 (fol. 10ʳ). Pressmark 'A 19', fol. 1ʳ.

Humphrey, Duke of Gloucester (1390–1447): presented to him by John of Wheathampstead (c. 1392–1465), abbot of St Albans (Clark 2004, 97); inscribed, fol. 231ʳ.

John Russell (c. 1430–94), Bishop of Lincoln: declares in 1488, folio 1ʳ, that he will return the book to St Albans if proven to be the abbey's property, but otherwise bequeaths it to New College, Oxford.

St Albans Abbey presumably recovered the book, since Polydore Vergil had access to both this and Royal MS 13 D V for his *Anglica historia* (first version completed by 1513, printed 1534). Leland records a 'most beautiful history stolen by theft' written by Matthew Paris ('*pulcherrima historia furto sublata*': Sharpe et al., 1996, no. B91.10), which Madden (1866–69, 1:xvi) assumed to indicate a recently stolen volume, but which might refer to Russell's inscription (Carley 2010, lxxiii).

Polydore Vergil (c. 1470–1555): notes in his hand, folios 10ʳ–100ʳ; presumably used the book at St Albans, since he also had access to Royal MS 13 D V; he uses the *Historia Anglorum* in his *Anglica historia*, following Matthew's narrative, for example, of the peace between Stephen and Matilda (Madden 1866–69, 1:295; compare Vergil 1534, 205). Madden (1866–69, 1: xli) erroneously assumes that these borrowings occurred with the 1555 edition.

Royal Library, Westminster: acquired before 1542, inventory 'n° 1041', fol. 1ʳ (Carley 2000, nos. H2.1041, H4.17); John Skewys (d. 1544) probably made extracts from the book there, now London, British Library, Harley MS 2258 (Madden 1866–69, 1:xlii–xliii).

Henry Fitzalan, the twelfth earl of Arundel (1512–80): lent to him by Bartholomew Traheron, Keeper of the King's Library (1549–53), according to John Bale, who had seen it in the Royal Library (Graham and Watson, 1998, 29–30; Carley 2000, lxxviii–lxxix).

Matthew Parker (1504–75): lent to him by Arundel (Parker 1571, preface).

? John Minsheu (1559/60–1627): inscribed, fol. iiʳ.

John Lumley, First Baron Lumley (c. 1533–1609), son-in-law of Henry Fitzalan: inscribed, fol. 1ʳ, but not in his catalogue (Jayne and Johnson 1956).

Henry Frederick, Prince of Wales (1594–1612): added Lumley's collection to the Royal Library.

Critical Studies

Warner and Gilson (1921, 2:135–36); Watson (1979, no. 893); Morgan (1982–88, no. 92).

Manchester, Chetham's Library, MS 6712 (Siglum *Ch*)

Contents

Fols. 7ʳ–295ᵛ: Matthew Paris, *Flores historiarum*.

Extent

250 × 190 mm; iv + 295 + iv leaves.

Provenance

Passed between St Albans Abbey and Westminster Abbey, with both communities making additions to the text. The book was at Westminster until at least the fifteenth century: inscribed, fol. 1ʳ and elsewhere.

Nicholas Higginbotham of Stockport, 1657: inscribed, fol. iiiʳ.

Critical Studies

Ker (1969–2002, 3:348–50); Morgan (1982–88, no. 96); Carpenter (2012); Hawks (2023).

Oxford, Bodleian Library, MS Ashmole 304

Matthew Paris wrote the entirety of this manuscript apart from folios 53ʳ–55ᵛ.

Contents

Fols. 2ʳ–30ᵛ: Bernardus Silvestris (attrib.), *Experimentarius*, in two versions.
Fols. 31ʳ–40ʳ: *Prenostica Socratis Basilei*.
Fols. 40ᵛ–52ᵛ: *Prenostica Pitagorice consideracionis*.
Fols. 52ᵛ–55ᵛ: *Sortes duodecim patriarcharum*.
Fols. 56ʳ–63ᵛ: *Quaestiones Albedaci*.
Fols. 64ʳ–70ᵛ: *Diuinacio ciceronalis*.

Extent

172 × 127 mm; 72 leaves.

Provenance

Copies of this manuscript were made in the late fourteenth (Oxford, Bodleian Library, MS Digby 46) and seventeenth centuries (London, British Library, Sloane MS 3857).
'Thomas West', 1602: inscribed, fols. 1ʳ, 67ᵛ–68ʳ.
Given to the Ashmolean Museum by '— Vaughan' of Brasenose College between 1697 and 1709: note by Edward Lhuyd (d. 1709), fol. 1ʳ.

Critical Studies

Pächt and Alexander (1966–73, 3:40–41, no. 437); Morgan (1982–88, no. 89); Iafrate (2013, 2015).

Oxford, Corpus Christi College, MS 2

Fols. 1ʳ–2ᵛ now mounted separately as MS 2*.

Contents

Fols. 1ʳ–2ᵛ: Bifolium with two full-page miniatures on 1ᵛ–2ʳ, in a style suggestive of a psalter; on the verso, Matthew Paris wrote notes towards the *Chronica maiora* and a map of Palestine (fols. 1ʳ, 2ᵛ).
Fols. 3ʳ–369ʳ: Vulgate Bible, with Matthew Paris writing some rubrics and prologues.

Extent

360 × 240 mm; 2 (MS 2*) + 368 (MS 2) leaves.

Provenance

No longer at St Albans Abbey by the fifteenth century: inscribed 'Bryn[?] Chetwode' with price, fol. 369^v.

Morgan Kidwelly (d. 1513), lawyer: inscribed, right pastedown.

John Tyson, who studied law at Oxford in 1520s and 1530s (Emden 1974, 585): inscribed, fol. 3^r.

Critical Studies

C.M. Kauffmann (1975, no. 72); Thomson (1982, no. 59); Thomson (2011, 3–4)

Notes

* I am grateful to James Carley, Alexander Devine, Kathleen Doyle, Alexandra Gillespie, Anne McLaughlin and Jane Muskett for their help in the research for this chapter.
1. Weiss 2017; Weiss 2018; Weiler 2019.
2. O'Donnell and Lamon 2010, 139–40.
3. Kauffmann 2020.
4. Clark 2001, 222–23; Clark 2004, 85.
5. Baswell 2010, 181–82; Slater 2018.
6. Dublin, Trinity College, MS 177, fol. 1^r: '*Mittatis si placet ad dominam comitissam harundell' Isabellam vt mittat vobis librum de sancto thoma martire et sancto edwardo quem transtuli et protraxi que[mque po]terit domina comitissa cornu[bie retinere] usque ad pentecosten.*' The ink is rubbed away at the edge of the page: James 1920, 20–21 gives a more accurate reading than Colker 1991, 339.
7. Gransden 1974b, 358–59; Wogan-Browne and Fenster 2010, 32–33.
8. Morgan 1982–88, no. 123; Binski 1990; Binski 1991 argue for this attribution; Hawks 2023, 180–87 discusses *Flores historiarum*.
9. Dunning 2018, 286–89.
10. Vaughan 1958c; Vaughan 1958c.
11. BL, Royal MS 14 C VII fol. 6^r: Collard 2015.
12. Townsend and Rigg 1987.
13. Vaughan 1958c, 50–59.
14. Jefferson 2006, 77.
15. Greasley 2021; Collard 2022.
16. Ashdowne et al. 2018, s.v. 'additamentum'.
17. Vaughan 1958c, 66–71.
18. Cleaver 2018, 146–55.
19. Clark 2002, 842–44.
20. Cheney 1973.

21. Oxford, Corpus Christi College, MS 2, fol. 369^v.
22. Clark 2004, 97.
23. BL, Royal MS 14 C VII, fol. 1^r.
24. Hay 1952, 86.
25. Hunt 1978; Sharpe et al. 1996, 538–85.
26. Clark 2000.
27. Sharpe et al. 1996, no. B91.10; Carley 2010, chapter 249.
28. Wright 1951, 211.
29. Carley 1999.
30. Carley 2000, xxxi–xxxii.
31. Graham and Watson 1998, 29–30, 52; Carley 2000, lxxviii–lxxix.
32. McMahon 2023, 242–47.
33. Barron 2003.
34. Carley 2002, 341.
35. Watson 1969, 21.
36. Thomson 2015, 54–55 and no. UO3A.11.
37. Bale 1548, fol. 143; Bale 1557–59, 315–16.
38. Illyricus 1556, 593–625.
39. Wright 1951. See also Chapter 10, 230–35.
40. Jones 1981.
41. Bruce and Perowne, 1853, no. 99.
42. Madden 1866–69, i. xix–xxviii.
43. Bruce and Perowne 1853, 327–28; Robinson 1998, 1067–70.
44. Madden 1866–69, i. xxix–xxxi.
45. Bruce and Perowne 1853, no. 371.
46. Parker 1571, preface.
47. Clark 2006.
48. Bruce and Perowne 1853, no. 221.
49. McKisack 1971, 34–36; Graham 1994, 432; Woudhuysen 1996, 118; Parkes 1997, 123–27.
50. Cambridge, Corpus Christi College, MS 16 (II), fol. 82^v. See Page 1993, 59 and plates 45–47.
51. Collins 1746, i. 67.
52. Graham 2006; Grafton 2017.
53. Tite 1994.
54. Watson 1962.
55. Signaroli 2013; Hardy 2017, 109–10.
56. Summit 2008, chapter 4.
57. Lawrence 1960, 70–100, 222–89.
58. Tite 2003, 137.
59. Tite 2003, 136.
60. Vaughan 1958c, chapter 5.
61. Carley and Tite 1992.

62. Carley 1992, 57–60; Carley 1997.
63. Smith 1696, 92.
64. Prescott 1997.
65. Prescott et al. 1998, 131–32.
66. Coxe 1841–44: his edition is based on Oxford, Bodleian Library, MS Douce 207.
67. Ackerman and Ackerman 1979, 21, 69.
68. Madden 1866–69.
69. Vaughan 1958c, 156.
70. Hardwick and Luard 1856–67.
71. Luard 1858; Luard 1872–84; Luard 1890.
72. Harris 1998, 226–27.
73. Prescott 2019, 147–50.
74. McKendrick et al. 2011.
75. Jefferson 2006, 73.
76. Lewis 1987, 471–72.
77. Morgan 1982–88, no. 24; Dunning 2018, 290–92.
78. Lewis 1987, 127–29.
79. Morgan 2017.
80. Morgan 1982–88, no. 84; Lewis 1987, 483; Zutshi 2018.
81. Backhouse and de Hamel 1988; Morgan 1988.
82. From Tite 2003.
83. Jefferson 2006.
84. Page 1993, 59.

ESTELLE GITTINS,
ALISON RAY,
CAROLINE HARDING AND
CLAIRE MCNULTY

17

Digitising Matthew Paris
The 'Book of St Albans' (Dublin, Trinity College, MS 177)

The Matthew Paris 'Book of St Albans' (Dublin, Trinity College [hereafter TCD] MS 177) was digitised by the Library of Trinity College Dublin in 2021 and is available on the Library's Digital Collections platform. The digitisation was part of the Virtual Trinity Library programme and made possible with the support of Carnegie Corporation of New York. Creating a digital surrogate of TCD MS 177 posed a unique set of challenges which this chapter aims to address, providing insights into the processes involved in making this volume available online, from the interdisciplinary team involved, and serving as a case study which might shed light on digital processes elsewhere.

As perhaps the most anticipated step within the Manuscripts for Medieval Studies project, the digitisation of TCD MS 177 'Book of St Albans' by Matthew Paris was a multifaceted, dynamic and labour-intensive process. Curatorial lead Estelle Gittins identified TCD MS 177 as a vital manuscript within the library of Trinity College Dublin and noted that the creation of a digital surrogate would make a valuable contribution to the scholarship on Matthew Paris and St Alban, and to medieval studies more broadly. Following the dissolution of the Abbey of St Albans and the dispersal of the library in 1539, the 'Book of St Albans' came into the possession of John Dee and from there was acquired by James Ussher, Archbishop of Armagh. The Library of Trinity College Dublin received Ussher's collection in 1661, and it became the major founding collection of the Library. The only work by Paris in an Irish collection, TCD MS 177 was the last of the major Paris manuscripts to be digitised, joining those that had been completed at the Bodleian, Parker Library, Corpus Christi College, Cambridge, and Chetham's Library in Manchester.

TCD MS 177 is an example of how the greatest pictorial art of the medieval period can be found within the pages of its books. Measuring 24 by 16.5 centimetres, the manuscript is made up of seventy-seven leaves containing fifty-four illustrations, each a unique work of art. Illustrations accompany several parts of the manuscript, from folios 29^v to 63^r, and are most probably drawn by the hand of Paris. Where illustrations exist, they occupy roughly half of a given leaf and are accompanied by red descriptive rubrics in French. Paris highlighted his line drawings with tinted colour washes, and sometimes gold highlights, which have been brilliantly preserved within the pages of the manuscript. The framed narrative images take up a third of any given page and run left to right, illustrating the text as they might a modern graphic novel (as indeed Kathryn Gerry discusses in relation to the manuscript's pictorial narrative in Chapter 7). Excelling in the portrayal of figures and animals, Paris derived his characters from a wide social spectrum, such as saints and kings, soldiers and holy men, sailors, labourers, bell-ringers and grooms. Out of a shallow picture plane, sometimes feet, hats, spears or hooves break out of their frames, from their world into ours, creating a sense of hectic activity.

The illustrations are washed with a green hue, and this colour predominates across the manuscript. Paris' use of tinted line drawing may be placed within a wider early-to-mid thirteenth-century resurgence of this technique, at which Paris may have been at the forefront. From the frames of the illustrations to the figures they contain and the clothes in which they are draped, a shadowy green features in almost every illustration. Other paint colours include red for rubrication, brick walls and certain clothing items; grey and black for spears, swords and axes; blue for bodies of water, armoury, some horses and weapons; and brown for draped clothing. The wash on the drapery, however, is mainly green with some red and blue, along with gold highlights (fols. 51^r, 52^r, etc.). As discussed later in this chapter, capturing the combination of green hues and gold highlights presented a unique set of challenges for photography, such as the need for extra light to illuminate the gold highlights while avoiding flattening the pastels. Indeed, a number of the illustrations had been reproduced by the 1924 facsimile edition by M. R. James, though this was not an exact surrogate, reproducing only those folios which contained illustrations.[1]

Prior to the digitisation, the only way to study the book was to consult the facsimile or visit the Library in person. On the release of the digitised version on the Library's Digital Collections platform, more researchers accessed it online than had accessed the original manuscript in the period from 2010 to 2020, and more than 70 per cent of those were new users to the platform. Getting a manuscript online does not happen overnight – it requires a number of individuals with a unique set of skills, from conservators to curators and photographers to metadata cataloguers. The work involved in sharing such manuscripts includes many different capacities and expertise, and the processes involved intersect science, information technology and the humanities. The project team includes curators, archivists, conservators, photographers, systems services colleagues, digital programmers, metadata cataloguers and academic researchers. As project manager and archivist Dr Alison Ray noted, digitisation is an interdisciplinary and labour-intensive process which required the creation of workflows through which the process was managed, and this process was further complicated by the onset of the COVID-19 pandemic.

Beginning with conservation, TCD MS 177 was first assessed by specialist Dr John Gillis with the assistance of project conservator Laura O'Farrell to ensure the volume was in stable condition and could be safely handled for imaging. In fact, conservation is often the first step in the digital process whereby a manuscript is checked by experts before being passed to photographers for imaging. Previous conservation work on the manuscript is covered in Patricia Quinn's article on 'Alban Disbound', which states that TCD MS 177 bears evidence of two previous sewings, the earliest of which may have been on four cords, judging from the holes visible in the spine folds.[2] The manuscript contains skins that vary in quality, including some folia made up from pieces grafted together. Prior to the 1980s conservation, the manuscript was in a nineteenth-century tanned leather binding sewn on five recessed sewing supports. More recently, the manuscript was carefully disbound, wax and ink stains were reduced where they impaired the text, damaged backfolds were repaired and the manuscript was re-sewn on five flexible supports laced into cushioned oak boards covered in Italian tawed goatskin. Since the manuscript received a full conservation treatment in 1983/84, a review of the manuscript condition, binding and camera access to the margins and gutters was conducted in the light of the specific angles needed for optimum digitisation. When these checks were completed, TCD MS 177 was then imaged in its entirety by senior digital and project photographer Caroline Harding.

TCD MS 177 was shot on a high-resolution and high-performing camera. While digital medium-format cameras have been in existence since the early 1990s, this equipment has been constantly evolving, with marked improvements circa 2008 when digital cameras began to replace film. Moreover, the Digital Collections department currently uses a 150MP camera which requires only one shot to capture images at high resolution with more accurate colour rendition. As with most of the photography conducted within the Digital Collections studios at Trinity, a standard twin lighting set-up with one flash head was placed on either side of the subject positioned 90 centimetres above the subject and was placed at a 45 degree angle towards the subject plane. The standard lighting set-up was used for digitising the Life of St Albans manuscript. In addition, a large silver reflector was placed over the top of the camera, and over the top of the two flash heads, and directly above the subject plane. The large silver reflector covered the entire diameter of the subject area and lighting circumference. The large reflector was kept in place directly above the subject throughout the entire shoot. While shooting the miniatures with gold illumination, an extra light was placed in front of the subject and pointed directly upwards towards the large silver reflector; this light was also set to the lowest setting. The purpose of using the extra light while photographing the miniatures with the gold illuminations was to help bring out the gold highlights, which are often hard to capture with the standard lighting set-up alone. The purpose of the large reflector was to bring out the gold highlights within the miniatures. However, the reflector was kept in the same position throughout the shoot to maintain lighting and white balance consistency. The extra light was kept on the lowest setting also for this reason and to avoid flattening the green pastel colourisation seen throughout the manuscript.

There are some distinct features in the illustrations found in the Life of St Alban that are not easily seen by the unaided eye and are not obvious on the collotype facsimile. These hidden features are the modelling (creating the illusion of three dimensionality) of the surface on parts of the uncoloured vellum. According to Quinn, the 'modelling of the surface of the uncoloured vellum' is not captured by the 1924 facsimile. This modelling 'creates a fine relief effect' which can be seen on the folds of draped clothing and the necks and haunches of the horses (fol. 49^r, Figure 3b.3) as well as the brickwork of the Abbey Church (fol. 60^r, Figure 3b.4) and on the laths of the boat (fol. 62^r). Quinn posits that this effect may have been contrived by Paris, and this is visible to the unaided eye with the assistance of raking light. Quinn notes that the 'variegated surface textures may, however, result from the congealing of the surface of the vellum that follows the selective application of a clear or coloured wash'.[3] It appears as though Paris has created that modelling, or three-dimensional effect, by using both pigments and vellum to create a textured effect which can be seen by casting a raking light across the illustrations. The aim of the raking light set-up was to show the hidden texture and detailing in the tinted illustrations, which have hidden modelling effects that cannot otherwise be seen with standard lighting. When using the raking light, the raised parts of the parchment and detailing in the illustrations facing the light are illuminated while the parts facing away from the light are shadowed. This allows one to see how rough and rigid parts of the illustrations are, which can give researchers a better insight into the techniques used to create parts of the detailing in the illustrations.

To accompany the digital surrogates created by Harding, Ray expanded the catalogue records for TCD MS 177, building on the work of M. R. James and Marvin L. Colker, by examining the manuscript closely and researching its contents, decoration, physical features and provenance. Ray enhanced the descriptions of the physical features of the manuscript and decorative elements, which were not as detailed in previous records, with Colker focusing more on the textual content. Moreover, the manuscript had been rebound since the last description, so it was important to capture that information. The new description was distinguished from previous records in that it aimed

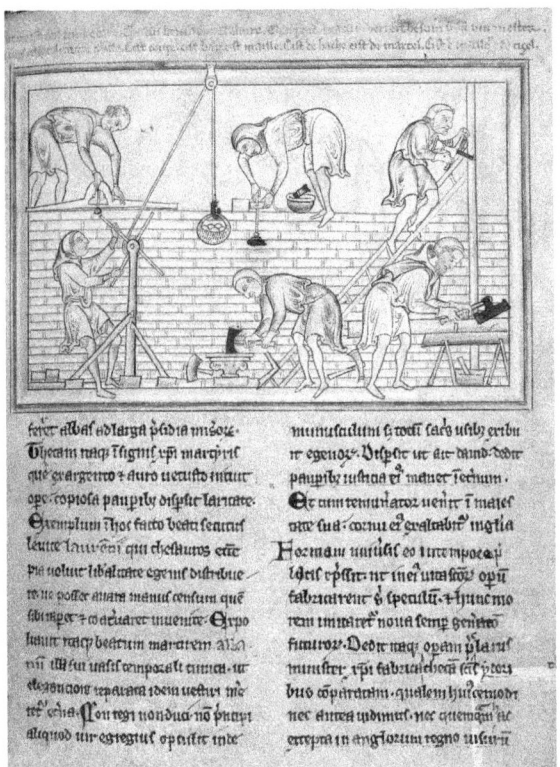

Figure 17.1 Modelling of the surface of the parchment creates a three dimensional effect for the brickwork of the abbey church. Dublin, Trinity College, MS 177 fol. 60ʳ. © The Library of Trinity College Dublin.

to describe the complete manuscript as a whole object. For example, Ray recorded the descriptions and placements of illustrations which were once present in the volume but are now missing. This information was then arranged alongside descriptions of surviving images to facilitate those researchers attempting to visualise the work and understand its production. One noticeable change was the addition of a separate catalogue entry for each of the folios which contain illustrations, which required significant input from Ray and metadata cataloguer Michelle Agar. As a result, each digital object has a specific image title so that it can now be searched according to the image title, which is a higher level of cataloguing than any other manuscript in Digital Collections for now. Agar then published the images together with the catalogue record for TCD MS 177 on the Library's Digital Collections website.

It is hoped that the digitisation of this manuscript, among others, will lead to new research insights, highlighting particular features of the artistry not easily seen by the unaided eye or allowing for a closer dating of the manuscript now available in its entirety. Analysis of digital versions opens up new perspectives, comparisons and lines of enquiry, and a powerful zoom function reveals layers of work not visible to the naked eye.

Notes

1. James et al. 1924.
2. Quinn 2010, 199.
3. Quinn 2010, 206–07.

References

Manuscript Sources

Amiens, Bibliothèque municipale	Lescalopier 30	Ambrose, *Hexaemeron*
Cambridge, Corpus Christi College		
	16 (I, II)	Matthew Paris
	26	Matthew Paris
	56	Matthew Paris
	264	*Flores historiarum*
	348	Chronicles
	379	Robert Talbot
	385	William of Conches
Cambridge, Gonville and Caius College		
	230	John of Wheathampstead
Cambridge, Trinity College		
	B.5.3	Glossed gospels
	O.1.64	Life of St Cuthbert
	O.9.34	*Roman de chevalrie*
	R.17.1	Eadwine Psalter
	R.4.2	*Flores historiarum*
Cambridge University Library		
	Dd.2.78	Henry of Avranches
	Ee.3.59	*Estoire de Seint Ædward*
	Gg.6.42	Alexander Nequam

Cologny, Fondation Martin Bodmer

| | 127 | Life of St Martin of Tours |

Dublin, Trinity College

| | 177 | Matthew Paris |

Edensor, Chatsworth House Devonshire Collection Archives

| | | St Albans cartulary |

Eton College

	96	*Flores historiarum*
	123	*Flores historiarum*
	213	Ranulf Higden, *Polychronicon*

Hertford, Hertfordshire Archives and Local Studies

| | A25/26 | Thomas Kingsbury Probate inventory |

Hildesheim, Dombibliothek

| | St Godehard MS 1 | St Albans Psalter |

London, Lambeth Palace Library

| | 188 | *Flores historiarum* |
| | 1106 | *Flores historiarum* |

London, British Library

	Additional 6164	William de Montibus
	Additional 20709	Chronicle transcripts
	Additional 28681	Map Psalter
	Additional 33943	Life of St Cuthbert
	Additional 48066	Chronicle transcripts
	Additional 62777	St Albans *Gesta abbatum*
	Additional 70513	Matthew Paris, *La Vie de saint Edmond*
	Arundel 46	Henry of Huntingdon
	Arundel 96	*Flores historiarum*
	Arundel 157	Psalter
	Cotton Claudius D VI	Matthew Paris

Cotton Claudius E IV	St Albans *Gesta abbatum*
Cotton Claudius E VIII	*Flores historiarum*
Cotton Cleopatra A XVI	*Flores historiarum*
Cotton Faustina B IV	Saints' lives
Cotton Faustine B IX	Chronicles
Cotton Julius B XII	Arthurian literature
Cotton Julius D III	St Albans sacrists' cartulary
Cotton Julius D VI	Saints' lives
Cotton Julius D VII	John of Wallingford & Matthew Paris
Cotton Nero C III	Chronicle transcripts
Cotton Nero C IV	Winchester Psalter
Cotton Nero C V	Psalter fragments
Cotton Nero C VI	*Flores historiarum*
Cotton Nero D I	Matthew Paris
Cotton Nero D II	*Flores historiarum*
Cotton Nero D V	*Chronica maiora*
Cotton Nero D VII	St Albans *Liber benefactorum*
Cotton Otho B V	*Flores historiarum*
Cotton Otho C II	*Flores historiarum*
Cotton Otho D III	St Albans cartulary
Cotton Titus D XVI	Prudentius, *Psychomachia*
Cotton Vespasian B XIII	Matthew Paris
Cotton Vitellius A XX	Chronicle excerpts
Cotton Vitellius D II	Chronicle transcripts
Cotton Vitellius A VIII	Chronicles
Cotton Vitellius D VIII (destroyed)	Matthew Paris

	Cotton Vitellius E XIV	Chronicle transcripts
	Harley 247	John Stow
	Harley 391	Waltham Abbey cartulary
	Harley 543	Chronicle transcripts
	Harley 545	Chronicle transcripts
	Harley 641	*Flores historiarum*
	Harley 1620	*Chronica maiora*
	Harley 2258	Chronicle transcripts
	Harley 3634	Thomas Walsingham, *Chronica maiora*
	Harley 6018	Catalogue Sir Robert Cotton's books
	Harley 6217	John Stow
	Harley Roll Y. 6	Guthlac Roll
	Lansdowne 6	Laurence Nowell
	Lansdowne 58	List of books of Robert Glover
	Lansdowne 205/17	Chronicle transcripts
	Royal 2 A XXII	Westminster Psalter
	Royal 2 F VIII	Peter Lombard
	Royal 4 D VII	Peter Comestor
	Royal 13 D I*	Psalter leaves
	Royal 13 D V	Geoffrey of Monmouth
	Royal 13 E VI	Ralph de Diceto
	Royal 13 E IX	Thomas Walsingham, *Chronica maiora*
	Royal 14 C I	William Rishanger
	Royal 14 C VI	*Flores historiarum*
	Royal 14 C VII	Matthew Paris
	Sloane 3857	Prognostication texts
London, Lambeth Palace Library		
	188	*Flores historiarum*
	1106	*Flores historiarum*
London, National Archives		
	JUST 1/82	Cambridgeshire eyre, 1261

	JUST 1/1187	Justiciar's roll of assizes, plaints & pleas, 1257-59
	SP1/68	State papers, Henry VIII (1531)
Los Angeles, J. Paul Getty Museum		
	Ludwig III 1[83. MC.72]	Dyson Perrins Apocalypse
Manchester, Chetham's Library		
	6712	*Flores historiarum*
New York, Morgan Library		
	M 638	Picture bible
	M 736	Life of St Edmund
Oxford, All Souls College		
	37	*Flores historiarum*
Oxford, Bodleian Library		
	Additional C 22 (lost)	*Flores historiarum*
	Ashmole 304	Prognostication texts
	Auct. F. 4.32	Dunstan classbook
	Bodley 462	Thomas Walsingham, *Chronica maiora*
	Bodley 585	John of Wheathampstead
	Bodley 912	*Flores historiarum*
	Digby 20	St Albans letters
	Digby 46	Prognostication texts
	Douce 207	Roger Wendover
	eMuseo 149	*Flores historiarum*
	Fairfax 20	*Flores historiarum*
	Hatton 53	*Flores historiarum*
	Junius 1	*Ormulum*
	lat. hist. d. 4	*Flores historiarum*
	lat. th. b. 1	Peter of Poitiers, *Compendium historiae in genealogia Christi*
	Laud Misc. 572	*Flores historiarum*
	Rawlinson B 177	*Flores historiarum*

	Rawlinson B 186	*Flores historiarum*
Oxford, Corpus Christi College		
	2*	Bible
Oxford, Magdalen College		
	Lat. 53	St Albans *Gesta abbatum*
Oxford, University College		
	165	Life of St Cuthbert
Paris, Bibliothèque nationale		
	Lat. 6045	*Flores historiarum*
	Lat. 6048B	Matthew Paris, *Chronica maiora*
	Français 19093	Villard de Honnecourt
	Français 24766	French verse
San Marino, CA, Huntington Library		
	HM 26341	Laurence Nowell
	HM 30319	*Flores historiarum*
Stokenchurch, Wormsley Library		
	BM 3750	Becket Leaves
Utrecht, Biblotheek der Rijksuniversiteit.		
	32	Utrecht Psalter
Westminster Abbey		
	24	*Flores historiarum*
Yale University Beinecke Library		
	426	*Flores historiarum*

Printed Primary Sources

Anderson, A. O., ed. 1908. *Scottish annals from English chroniclers, A.D. 500 to 1286*. London: David Nutt.

Anderson, M. O. and Anderson, A. O., eds. and trans. 1990. *Early sources of Scottish history A.D. 500 to 1286*. 2nd ed. 2 vols. Stamford, CT: Paul Watkins.

[Anon.] 1567. *Flores historiarum per Matthaeum Westmonasteriensem collecti, Elegans, illustris, et facilis rerum, præsertim Britannicarum, et aliarum obiter, notatu dignarum, a mundi exordio ad annum Domini 1307.* London: Thomas Marsh. STC (2nd ed.), 17652.

[Anon.] 1570. *Flores historiarum per Matthaeum Westmonsteriensem collecti praecipue de rebus Britannicis ab exordio mundi usque ad annum Domini 1307.* London: Thomas Marsh. STC (2nd ed.), 17653a.3.

Atkinson, R., ed. 1876. *Vie de Seint Auban: A poem in Norman-French.* London: John Murray.

Baker, A. T., ed. 1929. '*La Vie de Saint Edmond archevêque de Contorbéry*', Romania 55, 332-81.

[John Bale]. 1549. *The laboryouse iourney [and] search of Iohan Leylande for Englandes antiquitees given of hym as a new yeares gyfte to Kynge Henry the VIII in the XXXVII yeare of his reygne with declaracyons enlarged by Iohan Bale.* London: S. Mierdman for John Bale. STC (2nd end.) 15445.

[John Bale]. 1551. *The first two partes of the actes or unchast examples of the Englysh votaryes gathered out of their owne legenades and chronycles by Johan Bale and dedicated to our most redoubted souveraigne Kynge Edward the Syxte.* London: For John Bale. STC (2nd end.) 1273.5.

Barlow, F., ed. 1992. *The life of King Edward who rests at Westminster.* Oxford Medieval Texts. Oxford: Clarendon Press.

Brault, G., ed. and trans. 1978. *La Chanson de Roland.* 2 vols. University Park: Pennsylvania State University Press.

Bruce, J. and Perowne, T. T., eds. 1853. *Correspondence of Matthew Parker, DD, Archbishop of Canterbury comprising letters written by and to him, from AD 1535 to his death, AD 1575.* Parker Society. Cambridge: Cambridge University Press.

Butler, H. E., ed. 1949. *Chronicle of Jocelin of Brakelond concerning Samson abbot of the monastery of St Edmund.* Medieval Classics. London: Thomas Nelsons & Sons.

Byerly, B. F. and Byerly, C. R. eds. 1986. *Records of the Wardrobe and Household 1286-1289.* London: HMSO.

Carley, J. P., ed. and trans. 2010. [John Leland] *John Leland, De viris illustribus.* Toronto, ON: Pontifical Institute of Medieval Studies.

Carley, J. P., ed. 2000. *The Libraries of Henry VIII.* Corpus of British Medieval Library Catalogues 7. London: British Library and British Academy.

Cheney, C. R. and Powicke, F. M., eds. 1964. *Councils and synods with other documents relating to the English church. Vol. 2: A.D. 1205-1313.* Oxford: Oxford University Press.

Clark, J. G. and Preest, D., eds. 2019. [Matthew Paris] *The deeds of the abbots of St Albans. The* Gesta abbatum monasterii sancti Albani. Boydell Press: Woodbridge.

Collins, A., ed. 1746. *Letters and memorials of state, in the reigns of Queen Mary, Queen Elizabeth, King James, King Charles the First, part of the reign of King Charles the Second, and Oliver's usurpation*. 2 vols. London: T. Osborne.

Coxe, H., ed. 1841–44. [Roger of Wendover] *Rogeri de Wendover Chronica, sive Flores historiarum nunc primum edidit*. 5 vols. London: English Historical Society.

Coxe, H. O., ed. 1841. [Roger of Wendover]. *Rogeri de Wendover Chronica, sive Flores historiarum*. 4 vols. London: English Historical Society.

Coxe, H. O., ed. 1844. [Roger of Wendover] *Appendix ad Rogeri de Wendover Flores historiarum: In qua lectionum varietas additionesque, quibus chronicon istud ampliavit et instruxit Matthæus Parisiensis*. London: English Historical Society.

Crick, J. C., ed. 2007. *Charters of St Albans*. Anglo-Saxon Charters 12. Oxford: Oxford University Press for the British Academy.

Ellis, H., ed. 1859. *Chronica Johannis de Oxenedes*. Rolls Series 13. London: Longman, Brown, Green, Longmans and Roberts.

Fenster, T. S. and Wogan-Browne, J., eds. and trans. 2008. [Matthew Paris] *The History of Saint Edward the King by Matthew Paris*. Tempe: Arizona Center for Medieval and Renaissance Studies.

Fielding, H. 1793. *Amelia: In three volumes, embellished with engravings*. 3 vols. London: C. Cooke.

Francisque, M., ed. 1836–40. *Chroniques anglo-normandes: Recueil d'extraits et d'écrits relatifs à l'histoire de Normandie et d'Angleterre pendant les 11e et 12e siècles, publié pour la preimière fois d'après les manuscrits de Londres, de Cambridge de Douai de Bruxelles et de Paris*. 3 vols. Rouen: Librarie de la Bibliothèque de la ville.

Fry, T., ed. 1980. *RB 1980. The Rule of St Benedict in Latin and English with notes*. Collegeville, MA: Liturgical Press.

Fuller, T. 1662. *The history of the worthies of England. London. Who for parts and learning have been eminent in the several counties. Together with an historical narrative of the native commodities and rarities in each county*. London: Printed by J. G. W. L. and W. G. for Thomas Williams.

Galbraith, V. H., ed. 1937. *The St Albans Chronicle 1406–1420: Edited from Ms Bodley 462*. Oxford: Clarendon Press.

Giles, J. A., ed. and tr. 1852–54. [Matthew Paris] *Matthew Paris's English history, from the year 1235 to 1273*. 3 vols. London: H. G. Bohn.

Gransden, A., ed. 1964. *The chronicle of Bury St. Edmunds 1212–1301*. London: Nelson.

Grüner, H., ed. 1907. *Mathei Parisiensis Vitae duorum Offarum (saec. xiii. med.) in ihrer Manuskript-und Textgeschichte*. Kaiserslautern: Buchdruckerei P. Rohr.

Hansard's Parliamentary Debates: Forming a continuation of the work entitled, 'the Parliamentary History of England from the earliest period to the year 1805'. New Series; commending with the accession of George IV, VOL. XXIII, comprising the period from the ninth day of March to the seventh day of April, 1830 [Second volume of the session]. London: T. C. Hansard, 1830.

Harden, A. R., ed. 1968. *La vie de Seint Auban: An Anglo–Norman poem of the thirteenth century*, Anglo-Norman Text Society, 19 Oxford: Basil Blackwell for the Anglo-Norman Text Society.

[Nicholas Harpsfield] 1622. *Historia ecclesiastica Anglicana a primis gentis susceptae fidei incunabulis ad nostra fere tempora deducta et in quindecim centurias distributa*. Douai: Marc Wyon.

Harvey, P. D. A. and Westrem, S. intr. and comm. 2010. *The Hereford world map: Mappa mundi*. London: Folio Society, 2010.

Hearne, T., ed. 1715. [John Leland] *Joannis Lelandi antiquarii de rebus Britannicis collectanea*. 6 vols. Oxford: Clarendon Press.

Hewlett, H. G., ed. 1886–89. [Roger of Wendover] *Rogeri de Wendover liber qui dictum Flores historiarum ab anno Domini MCLIV annoque Henrici Anglorum regis secundi primo. The Flowers of History of Roger of Wendover from the year of our lord 1154 and the first year of Henry the Second, king of the English (ed.) Henry G. Hewlett*. 3 vols. Rolls Series 84. London: HMSO.

Hog., T. ed. 1845. [Nicholas Trevet] *Nicholai Triveti, Annales sex regum Angliae*. London: English Historical Society.

Hoskin, P. M., ed. *Robert Grosseteste as bishop of Lincoln: The episcopal rolls, 1235–1253*. Woodbridge: Boydell, 2015.

Howlett, R., ed. 1884–86. *Chronicles of the reigns of Stephen, Henry II and Richard I*. 4 vols. Rolls Series 82. London: Longman.

Huillard-Bréholles, A., ed. 1840–41. [Matthew Paris] *Grande Chronique de Matthieu Paris*. 9 vols. Paris: Paulin.

[Illyricus, Matthias Flacius] 1556. *Catalogus testium ueritatis, qui ante nostram ætatem reclamarunt Papæ*. Basel: Johannes Oporinus.

James, M. R., ed. 1920. *La estoire de Seint Aedward le Rei/The life of St Edward the Confessor reproduced in facsimile from the unique manuscript-Cambridge University Library Ee 3.59; together with some pages of the manuscript of the life of St Alban at Trinity College, Dublin*. Oxford: Oxford University Press for the Roxburghe Club.

Johnston, R. C., ed. 1981. [Jordan Fantosme] *Jordan Fantosme's chronicle*. Oxford: Clarendon Press.

King, E. and Potter, K. R., eds. 1998. [William of Malmesbury] *Historia novella: The contemporary history*. Oxford Medieval Texts. Oxford: Clarendon Press.

[William Lambarde] 1576. *A perambulation of Kent conteining the description hystorie and customes of that shyre*. [H. Middleton] for Ralph Newberie. London. STC (2nd end.) 15175.5.

Lawrence, C. H., 1960. *St Edmund of Abingdon: A study in hagiography and history.* Oxford: Clarendon Press, 222–89.

Lawrence, C. H., ed. 1996. [Matthew Paris] *The life of St Edmund of Abingdon by Matthew Paris.* Stroud: Alan Sutton.

[John Leland] 1544. *Assertio inclytissimi Arturiii regis Britanniae: Ioanne Lelando antiquario autore.* R. Wolfe for John Herford. STC (2nd ed.).

Liebermann, F., ed. 1879. [Matthew Paris] 'Matthaei Parisiensis Vita sancti Stephani archiepiscopi Cantuariensis. Fragment', in *Ungedruckte Anglo-Normannische Geschichtsquellen.* Strasbourg: Trubner & Co., 318–29.

Luard, H. R., ed. 1858. *Lives of Edward the Confessor.* Rolls Series 3. London: Longman, Brown, Green, Longmans, and Roberts.

Luard, H. R., ed. 1859. [Bartholomew Cotton] *Bartholomaei de Cotton Historia Angicana, AD 449–1298.* Rolls Series 16. London: Longman, Green, Longmans and Roberts.

Luard, H. R., ed. 1864–69. *Annales Monastici Volume.* 5 vols. Rolls Series 36. London: Longman, Green, Longmans and Roberts.

Luard, H. R., ed. 1872–83. [Matthew Paris] *Matthaei Parisiensis monachi Sancti Albani Chronica Majora.* 7 vols. Rolls Series 57. London: Longman & Co., Trübner & Co., also Parker & Co., Oxford, Macmillan & Co., Cambridge, A. & C. Black and Douglas & Foulis, Edinburgh and A. Thom, Dublin.

Luard, H. R., ed. 1890. *Flores historiarum.* 3 vols. Rolls Series 95. London: Printed for Her Majesty's Stationery Office by Eyre and Spottiswoode.

Madden F., ed. 1866–69. [Matthew Paris] *Matthaei Parisiensis, monachi Sancti Albani, Historia Anglorum, sive, ut vulgo dicitur, Historia Minor: Item, ejusdem abbreviatio chronicorum Angliae.* 3 vols. Rolls Series 44. London: Longmans, Green, Reader and Dyers.

Maxwell-Lyte, H. C., ed. 1916–64. *Calendar of liberate rolls.* 6 vols. London: Public Record Office.

McLoughlin, T., Boulton, J. T. and Todd, W. B., eds. 1997. [Edmund Burke] *The writings and speeches of Edmund Burke. Volume I: The early writings.* Oxford: Clarendon Press.

Meyer, P., ed. 1885. *Fragments d'une vie de Saint Thomas de Cantorbéry.* Paris: Société des Anciens Textes Français.

Mynors, R. A. B., Thomson, R. M. and Winterbottom, M., eds. 1998–99. *William of Malmesbury,* Gesta regum Anglorum: *The history of the English kings.* 2 vols. Oxford Medieval Texts. Oxford: Clarendon Press.

Pantin, W. A., ed. 1931–37. *Documents illustrating the activities of the general and provincial chapters of the English Black Monks 1215–1540.* Camden Third Series 45, 54. London: Royal Historical Society.

[Matthew Paris] 1571. *Matthæi Paris, monachi Albanensis, Angli, Historia maior, à Guilielmo Conquæstore, ad vltimum annum Henrici tertij. Cum indice locupletissimo.* London: Reginald Wolfe. STC (2nd. ed.), 19209a.

Powicke, F. M., ed. 1950. *The life of Ailred of Rievaulx by Walter Daniel*. London: Thomas Nelson and Sons.

Pryce, H. and Insley, C., eds. 2005. *The acts of the Welsh rulers 1120–1283*. Cardiff: University of Wales Press.

Radcliffe, A. 1826. *Gaston de Blondeville or The Court of Henry III keeping festival in Ardenne. A Romance. St Albans Abbey. A metrical tale; with some poetic pieces*. 4 vols. London: Henry Colburn.

Reeve, M. D. and Wright, N., eds. 2007. [Geoffrey of Monmouth] *The history of the kings of Britain: An edition and translation of* De gestis Britonum (Historia regum Britanniae). Woodbridge: Boydell.

Riley, H. T., ed. 1865. [William Rishanger] *Willelmi Rishanger, quondam monachi sancti Albani et quorundamanonymorum chronica et annales regnantibus Henrico tertio et Edwardo primo: AD 1259 1307*. Rolls Series 28/2. London: Longman, Green, Longman, Roberts and Green.

Riley, H. T. ed. 1866. *Chronica Johannis de Trokelowe et Henrici de Blaneforde, monachorum S. Albani, necnon quorundam anonymorum chronica et annales, regnantibus Henrico Tertio, Edwardo Primo, Edwardo Secundo, Ricardo Secundo, et Henrico Quarto*. Rolls Series 28/3. London: Longmans, Green, Reader and Dyer.

Riley, H. T., ed. 1867–69. *Gesta abbatum monasterii sancti Albani, a Thoma Walsingham, regnante Ricardo secundo, ejusdem ecclesiæ præcentore, compilate*. 3 vols. Rolls Series 28/4. London: Longmans, Green, Reader, and Dyer.

Riley, H. T., ed. 1870–71. [John Amersham] *Annales monasterii S. Albani a Johanne monacho ut videtur conscripti (AD 1421–1440) quibus praefigitur Chronicon rerum gestarum in monasterio S. Albani (AD 1422–1431) a quodam auctore ignoto compilatum*. 2 vols. Rolls Series 28/5. London: Longman & Co., Trübner & Co., also Parker & Co., Oxford, Macmillan & Co., Cambridge, A. & C. Black, Edinburgh and A. Thom, Dublin.

Riley, H. T., ed. 1872. *Registra quorundam abbatum monasterii S. Albani, qui sæculo XV^{mo} floruere* 2 vols. Rolls Series 28/6. London: Longman & Co., Trübner & Co., also Parker & Co., Oxford, Macmillan & Co., Cambridge, A. & C. Black, Edinburgh and A. Thom, Dublin.

Roberts, R. J. and Watson, A. G., eds. 1990. [John Dee] *John Dee's library catalogue*. London: Bibliographical Society.

Ronca, I. and Jeauneau, É. A., eds. 1997. [William of Conches], *Guillelmi de Conchis Dragmaticon philosophiae. Summa de philosophia in uulgari*. Turnhout: Brepols.

Rouse, R. H. and Rouse, M. A., eds. 2004. *Henry of Kirkestede Catalogus de libris autenticis et apocrifis*. Corpus of British Medieval Library Catalogues 11. London: British Academy and British Library.

Scholz, B. W., trans., with Rogers, B. 1970. *Carolingian chronicles: Royal Frankish annals and Nithard's histories*. Ann Arbor: University of Michigan Press.

Sharpe, R., Carley, J. P., Thomson, R. M. and Watson, A. G., eds., 1996. *English Benedictine libraries: The shorter catalogues.* Corpus of British Medieval Library Catalogues 4. London: British Academy and British Library.

Södergård, O. O., ed. 1948. *La vie d'Edouard le Confesseur: Poème Anglo-Normand du XII siècle.* Uppsala: Almquist and Wiksells.

Stevenson, J., ed. 1875. [Ralph of Coggeshall] *Radulphi de Coggeshall Chronicon Anglicanum.* Rolls Series 44 London: Longman & Co., Trübner & Co., also Parker & Co., Oxford, Macmillan & Co., Cambridge, A. & C. Black, Edinburgh and A. Thom, Dublin.

[John Stow] 1580. *Chronicles of England from Brute unto this present year 1580.* London: Henry Bynneman for Ralph Newberie, STC (2nd ed.) [23333].

[John Stow] 1598. *A survey of London contayning the originall antiquity increase modern estate and description of that citie, written in the yeare 1598.* London: [John Windert for] Iohn Wolfe. STC (2nd ed.) 23341.

Stubbs, W., ed. 1887–89. [William of Malmesbury] *Willelmi Malmesbiriensis Monachi De Gestis Pontificum Anglorum Libri quinque.* 2 vols. Rolls Series 90. London: HMSO.

Swanton, M., ed. 2010. *The lives of the two Offas.* Crediton: Medieval Press.

Talbot, C. H., ed. 1987. *The life of Christina of Markyate, a twelfth-century recluse.* 2nd ed. Oxford Medieval Texts. Oxford: Clarendon Press.

Tanner, N. P., Alberigo, A. and Jedin H., eds. 1990. *Decrees of the ecumenical councils.* Washington, DC: Georgetown University Press.

Taylor, J. Childs, W. and Watkiss, L. eds. 2003–10. *The St Albans Chronicle 1406–1422.* Oxford Medieval Texts. Oxford: Clarendon Press.

Taylor, M. E., ed. 1912. 'Extracts from the MS. Liber Luciani de laude Cestrie. Written about the year 1195 and now in the Bodleian Library, Oxford', Lancashire and Cheshire Record Society 64. Manchester: Record Society of Lancashire and Cheshire, 1–78.

Thompson, E. M., ed. 1902–4. *Customary of the Benedictine monasteries of Saint Augustine, Canterbury, and Saint Peter, Westminster.* 2 vols. Henry Bradshaw Society 23, 28. London: Henry Bradshaw Society.

Treharne, R. F. and Sanders, I. J., eds. 1973. *Documents of the baronial movement of reform and rebellion 1258–1267.* Oxford: Oxford University Press.

Tremlett, T. D. ed. 1967. *Aspilogia: Being materials of heraldry. II Rolls of arms of Henry III.* Oxford: Oxford University Press and the Society of Antiquaries.

[Polydore Vergil] 1534. *Polydori Vergilii Vrbinatis Anglicæ historiæ libri XXVI.* Basel: Johann Bebel.

Vaughan, R. ed. 1958. The chronicle attributed to John of Wallingford. Camden Society Third Series 90. London: Royal Historical Society.

Wallace, K. Y., ed. 1983. *La Estoire de Seint Aedward le Rei.* Anglo-Norman Texts 41. London: Anglo-Norman Text Society.

Walpole, H. 1762–71. *Anecdotes of painting in England with some account of the principal artists and incidental notes on other arts collected by the late Mr. George Vertue and now digested and published from his original MSS.* 4 vols. [Strawberry Hill]: Thomas Farmer at Strawberry Hill.

Wats, W. ed. 1639. [Matthew Paris] *Vitae duorum Offarum merciorum regum coenobii sancti Albani fundatorum et viginti trium abbatum sancti Albani una cum libro additamentorum.* London: R. Hodgkinson and Miles Flesher for Cornelius Bee and Laurence Sadler. STC (2nd. ed.) 19210.

Watts, W., ed. 1640. [Matthew Paris] *Matthaei Paris Monachi Albanensis Angli, Historia Majora juxta exemplar Londinense 1571, verbatim recusa.* London: Printed by Richard Hodgkinson for Cornelius Bee and Laurence Sadler.

Wright, T. ed. 1866–68. *The chronicle of Pierre de Langtoft: In French verse from the earliest period to the death of Edward I,* 2 vols., Rolls Series 47. London: Longmans, Green Reader and Dyer.

Webster, H. and Preest, D. ed. 2018. *The annals of Dunstable Priory.* Woodbridge: Boydell Press.

[A. Wood Renton] 1901. *The English Reports. Volume XI. The House of Lords. Containing House of Lords Cases (Clark's), Volumes 7 to 11.* Edinburgh: William Green & Sons; London: Steven & Sons, Ltd.

Secondary Sources

Abulafia, D. 1992. *Frederick II: A medieval emperor.* Oxford: Oxford University Press.

Ackerman, R. W. and Ackerman, G. P. 1979. *Sir Frederic Madden: A biographical sketch and bibliography.* New York: Garland.

Ailes, M. J. 2009. 'Fierabras and Anglo–Norman developments of the chanson de geste', in Epic Studies: Acts of the Seventeenth International Congress of the Société Rencesvals for the Study of Romance Epic. Storrs, CT. (July 2006). Ed. L. Z. Morgan and A. Berthelot. *Olifant,* Special Issue, New Series, 25:1–2, 97–110.

2011. 'What's in a name? Anglo–Norman romances or *chansons de geste*?', in *Medieval Romance, Medieval Contexts.* Ed. R. Purdie and M. Cochon. Woodbridge: Boydell and Brewer, 61–76.

Ailes, M. J. and Putter, A. 2014. 'The French of medieval England', in *La Francophonie européenne.* Ed. D. Offord and V. Rjeoutski. Bern: Peter Lang, 51–80.

Aird, W. 2004. 'Robert de Mowbray, earl of Northumbria (d. 1115/1125)', magnate. *Oxford Dictionary of National Biography.*

Alexander, J. J. G and Morgan, N., eds. 1982-88. *A survey of manuscripts illuminated in the British Isles. IV. Early Gothic manuscripts. Part 1 1190-1250. Part 2 1250-1280.* London: Harvey Miller.

Ashdowne, R. K., Howlett, D. R. and Latham, R. E., eds. 2018. *Dictionary of medieval Latin from British sources (Vols. 1-3).* Oxford: Oxford University Press.

Auslander, D. 2012. 'Clemence and Catherine: The *Life of St Catherine* in its Norman and Anglo-Norman context', in *Barking Abbey and medieval literary culture: Authorship and authority in a female community.* Ed. J. Brown and D. Bussell. Woodbridge: York Medieval Press, 145-63.

Backhouse, J. and de Hamel, C. 1988. *The Becket Leaves.* London: The British Library.

Baker, A. T. 1929. 'La vie de Saint Edmond Archevêque de Cantorbéry', *Romania,* 55, 332-81.

Baker, M. 1978. 'Medieval Illustrations of Bede's Life of St Cuthbert', *Journal of the Warburg and Courtauld Institutes,* 41, 16-49.

Bale, A. 2019. *Representing and Misrepresenting Jews in Medieval Culture.* Los Angeles, CA: J. Paul Getty Museum.

Bale, J. 1549. *Illustrium maioris Britanniæ scriptorum, hoc est, Angliæ, Cambriæ, ac Scotiæ Summarium.* London: John Overton.

Bale, J. 1557-59. *Scriptorum illustrium maioris Brytanniæ, quam nunc Angliam et Scotiam uocant: Catalogus (Vols. 1-2).* Basel: Johannes Oporinus.

Barlow, F. 1986. *Thomas Becket.* London: Methuen.

Barr, B. L. and Selwyn, D. 2006. 'Major ecclesiastical libraries: From reformation to civil war', in *The Cambridge History of Libraries in Britain and Ireland.* 3 vols. Ed. E. Leedham-Green and T. Webber. Cambridge: Cambridge University Press, 1:363-99.

Barrell, A. D. M. 2005. 'Scotland and the papacy in the reign of Alexander II', in *The Reign of Alexander II, 1214-49.* Ed. R. D. Oram. Leiden: Brill, 157-77.

Barron, K. 2003. 'The collecting and patronage of John, Lord Lumley (c. 1535-1609)', in *The evolution of English collecting: Receptions of Italian art in the Tudor and Stuart periods.* Ed. E. Chaney. New Haven, CT: Yale University Press, 125-58.

Barrow, J. 2011. 'Peter of Aigueblanche's support network', *Thirteenth-Century England XIII: Proceedings of the Paris conference.* Ed. J. Burton, F. Lachaud, P. Schofield, K. Stöber and B. Weiler. Woodbridge: Boydell, 27-40.

Bartlett, R. 1993. *The making of Europe: Conquest, colonization and cultural change 950-1350.* London: Allen Lane.

Baswell, C. 2003. 'King Edward and the cripple', in *Chaucer and the challenges of medievalism: Essays in honor of H. A. Kelly.* Ed. D. Minkova and T. Tinkle. Frankfurt: Peter Lang, 15-30.

Baswell, C. 2010. 'The manuscript context', in *The life of Saint Alban by Matthew Paris*. Ed. J. Wogan-Browne and T. S. Fenster. Tempe: Arizona Center for Medieval & Renaissance Studies, 169–94.

Baswell, C., Cannon, C., Kerby-Fulton, K. and Wogan-Browne, J. 2015. 'Competing archives: French and its cultural locations in Medieval England', *Speculum*, 90, 635–700.

Bately, J. 1988. 'Manuscript layout and the Anglo-Saxon chronicle', *Bulletin of the John Rylands Library*, 70, 21–43.

Bateson, M. and Costambeys, M. 2004. 'Thomas Wallensis [Thomas the Welshman] (d. 1255), bishop of St David's', in *Oxford Dictionary of National Biography*. Oxford: Oxford University Press.

Belting, H. (trans. M. Bartusis and R. Meyer). 1990. *The image and its public in the Middle Ages: Form and function of early paintings of the Passion*. New Rochelle: Aristide D. Caratzas.

Bennett, N. 2015. '"The face of one making for Jerusalem": The chapter of Lincoln during the episcopate of Robert Grosseteste', in *Robert Grosseteste and Lincoln Cathedral*. Ed. N. Temple, J. Hendrix and C. W. Frost. Farnham: Ashgate, 17–28.

Benson, R. L., Constable, G. and Lanham, C. D., eds. 1982. *Renaissance and renewal in the twelfth century*. Oxford: Oxford University Press.

Beverley Smith, J. 2010. 'Richard Earl of Cornwall, Prince Dafydd ap Llywelyn and Tintagel Castle', *Journal of the Royal Institution of Cornwall*, 31–42.

Binski, P. 1990. 'Reflections on the *Estoire de Seint Aedward*', *Journal of Medieval History*, 16, 333–50.

1991a. 'Abbot Berkyng's tapestries and Matthew Paris's life of St Edward the Confessor', *Archaeologia*, 109, 85–100.

1991b. 'Review of *The Art of Matthew Paris in the* Chronica majora by Suzanne S. Lewis', *Art Bulletin* 73:1, 141–44.

1992. 'The murals in the nave of St Albans Abbey', in *Church and city 1000–1500: Essays in honour of Christopher Brooke*. Ed. D. Abulafia, M. Franklin and M. Rubin. Cambridge: Cambridge University Press, 249–78.

2004. *Becket's crown, art and imagination in Gothic England 1200–1400*. New Haven, CT: Yale University Press.

2006. 'The faces of Christ in Matthew Paris's *Chronica Majora*', in *Tributes in honour of James H. Marrow: Studies in painting and manuscript illumination of the late Middle Ages and northern Renaissance*. Ed. J. F. Hamburger and A. S. Korteweg. Brepols: Turnhout, 85–92.

2024. 'The chronology of Matthew Paris's illustrated saints' lives', in *Tributes to Elly Miller: Opening manuscripts*. Ed. S. Panayotova, L. Freeman Sandler and T. Miller Wang. London: Harvey Miller, 22–32.

Binski, P. and Panayotova, S., eds. 2005. *The Cambridge illuminations: Ten centuries of book production in the medieval West*. Brepols: Turnhout.

Binski, P. and Sauerberg, M. L. 2006. 'Matthew Paris in Norway: The Faberg St Peter', in *Medieval painting in Northern Europe: Techniques, analysis, art history. Studies in commemoration of the 70th birthday of Unn Plahter.* Ed. J. Nadolny with K. Kollandsrud, M. L. Sauerberg and T. Frøysaker. London: Archetype.

Binski, P. and Zutshi, P. 2011. *Western illuminated manuscripts: A catalogue of the collection in Cambridge University Library.* Cambridge: Cambridge University Press.

Bischoff, B. 1990. *Latin palaeography: Antiquity and the Middle Ages.* Trans. D. O Cronin and D. Ganz. Cambridge: Cambridge University Press.

Blecker, M. 1984. 'The king's partners in Bracton', *Studi Sensei*, 96, 66–118.

Bocquet, D. 1995. 'Un idéal de théocratie monastique au XIIIe siècle: Mathieu Paris, *Chronica Majora*, 1235–1259', *Révue Mabillon*, New Series 6, 83–100.

Bolton, B. 1991. 'Too important to neglect: The *Gesta Innocentii* PP III', in *Church and chronicle in the Middle Ages: Essays presented to John Taylor.* Ed. G. A. Loud and I. N. Wood. London: Bloomsbury, 87–99.

Brand, P. 1992. *The making of the common law.* London: Hambledon.

2003. *Kings, barons and justices: The making and enforcement of legislation in thirteenth-century England.* Cambridge: Cambridge University Press.

Brault, G. J. 1978. *Song of Roland: An analytical edition.* 2 vols. University Park: Pennsylvania State University Press.

Breen, K. 2005. 'Returning home from Jerusalem: Matthew Paris's first map of Britain in its manuscript context', *Representations*, 89, 59–93.

Brentano, R. 1998. *Two churches: England and Italy in the thirteenth century.* Princeton, NJ: Princeton University Press.

Brett, M. and Woodman, D. A., eds. 2015. *The long twelfth century view of the Anglo-Saxon past.* Studies in Early Medieval Britain and Ireland. Burlington, VT: Ashgate.

Bringhurst, R. 2005. *The elements of typographic style, 3.1.* Point Roberts: Hatley & Marks.

Brooke, R. B. 2006. *The image of St Francis: Responses to sainthood in the thirteenth century.* Cambridge: Cambridge University Press.

Brown, J. N. and Bussell, D. A., eds. 2012. *Barking Abbey and medieval literary culture: Authorship and authority in a female community.* Woodbridge: York Medieval Press.

Brown, M. 2004. *The wars of Scotland, 1214–1371.* Edinburgh: Edinburgh University Press.

Brown, M. *Illumino: A history of medieval Britain in twelve illuminated manuscripts.* London: Reaktion Books, 2025.

Brown, R. A., Colvin, H. M. and Taylor, A. J. 1963–82. *The history of the king's works.* 6 vols. London: HMSO.

Budny, M. 1992. '"St. Dunstan's classbook" and its frontispiece: Dunstan's portrait and autograph', in *St Dunstan: his life, times and cult*. Ed. N. Ramsay, M. Sparks and T. W. T. Tatton-Brown. Woodbridge: Boydell, 103–42.

Bugyis, K. A.-M. 2016. 'Recovering the histories of women religious in England in the central Middle Ages: Wilton Abbey and Goscelin of Saint Bertin', *Journal of Medieval History*, 42:3, 285–303.

Burton, J. 1994. *Monastic and religious orders in Britain, 1100–1300*. Cambridge: Cambridge University Press.

Camille, M. 1996. 'The dissenting image: A postcard from Matthew Paris', in *Criticism and dissent in the Middle Ages*. Ed. R. Copeland. Cambridge: Cambridge University Press, 115–50.

Camp, C. 2015. *Anglo-Saxon saints' lives as history writing in late medieval England*. Cambridge: Cambridge University Press.

Campbell, B. S., Galloway, J. A., Keene, D. and Mitchell, M., eds. 1993. *A medieval capital and its grain supply: Agrarian production and distribution in the London region, c. 1300*. London: Institute of British Geographers, Historical Geography Research Group, Historical Geography Research Paper Series, Number 30, The Queen's University of Belfast and the Centre for Metropolitan History, Institute of Historical Research, University of London.

Campbell, E. 2008. *Medieval saints' lives: The gift, kinship and community in Old French hagiography*. Cambridge: D. S. Brewer.

Campbell, J. 1986. 'Bede I' in his *Essays in Anglo-Saxon History*. London: Hambledon.

Campbell, T. P., ed. 2002. *Tapestry in the Renaissance: Art and magnificence*. New York: Metropolitan Museum of Art.

Cannon, J. 2010. 'Kissing the Virgin's Foot: *Adoratio* before the Madonna and Child Enacted, Depicted, Imagined', *Studies in Iconography*, 31, 1–50.

Cappelli, A. 2011. *Dizionario di abbreviature latine ed italiane*. 7th ed. Milan: Ulrico Hoepli.

Carley, J. P. 1992. 'The Royal Library as a source for Sir Robert Cotton's collection: A preliminary list of acquisitions', *British Library Journal*, 18:1, 52–73.

1997. 'William Rishanger's chronicles and history writing at St Albans', in *A distinct voice: Medieval studies in honor of Leonard E. Boyle, O.P.* Ed. J. Brown and W. P. Stoneman. Notre Dame: University of Notre Dame Press, 71–102.

1999. 'The Royal Library under Henry VIII', in *The Cambridge history of the book in Britain, III*. Ed. L. Hellinga and J. B. Trapp. Cambridge: Cambridge University Press, 274–82.

2002. 'Monastic collections and their dispersal', in *The Cambridge history of the book in Britain, IV*. Ed. J. Barnard and D. F. McKenzie. Cambridge: Cambridge University Press, 339–48.

2004. *The books of King Henry VIII and his wives.* London: British Library.

Carley, J. P. and Tite, C. G. C. 1992. 'Sir Robert Cotton as collector of manuscripts and the question of dismemberment: British Library MSS Royal 13 D I and Cotton Otho D VIII', *The Library*, 14:2, 94–99.

Carpenter, D. A. 1980. 'The fall of Hubert de Burgh', *Journal of British Studies*, 19, 1–17.

1985. 'King, magnates and society: The personal rule of King Henry III 1234–1258', *Speculum*, 60, 39–70.

1990. *The minority of Henry III.* London: Hambledon.

1996. 'Matthew Paris and Henry III's speech at the Exchequer', in *The reign of Henry III.* Ed. D. A. Carpenter. London: Hambledon, 137–50.

1998. 'Abbot Ralph of Coggeshall's account of the last years of King Richard and the first years of King John', *English Historical Review*, 113, 1210–30.

2003. *The struggle for mastery: The Penguin history of Britain 1066–1284.* London: Allen Lane.

2007. 'King Henry III and St Edward the Confessor: The origins of the cult', *English Historical Review*, 122, 865–91.

2012a. 'Crucifixion and conversion: King Henry III and the Jews in 1255', in *Laws, lawyers and texts: Studies in medieval legal history in honour of Paul Brand.* Ed. S. Jenks, J. Rose and C. Whittick. Leiden: Brill, 129–48.

2012b. 'The Pershore *Flores Historiarum*: An unrecognised chronicle from the period of reform and rebellion in England, 1258–1265', *English Historical Review*, cxxvii, 1343–66.

2016. 'The secret revolution of 1258', in *Baronial reform and revolution in England 1258–1267*. Ed. A. Jobson. Woodbridge: Boydell, 30–42.

2021–23. *Henry III.* New Haven, CT: Yale University Press.

Carpenter, L., Shaw, S. and Prescott, A., eds. 1998. *Towards the digital library: The British Library's initiatives for access programme.* London: The British Library.

Carruthers, M. J. 1992. *The book of memory: A study of memory in medieval culture.* Cambridge: Cambridge University Press.

Carter, D. 2011. 'Matthew Paris's illustrated life of Edward the Confessor: History for the eyes and ears of a queen', *Athanor*, 19, 21–31.

2022. 'Illustrating the material past: A pictorial treasury in the later medieval manuscripts from St Albans Abbey', in *Lost artefacts from medieval England and France: Representation, reimagination, recovery.* Ed. K. Gerry and L. Cleaver. York: York Medieval Press, 136–57.

Carty, C. M. 1999. 'The role of medieval dream images in authenticating ecclesiastical construction', *Zeitschrift für Kunstgeschichte*, 62:1, 45–90.

2000. 'Dream images, *memoria*, and the Heribert shrine', in *Memory and the medieval tomb.* Ed. E. Valdez del Alamo and C. S. Pendergast. Ashgate: Routledge, 227–47.

Carruthers, M. 1998. *The craft of thought: Meditation, rhetoric, and the making of images, 400–1200*. Cambridge: Cambridge University Press.

Cavallo, A. S. 1993. *Medieval tapestries in the Metropolitan Museum of Art*. New York: Metropolitan Museum of Art.

Caviness, M. H. 1992. 'Biblical stories in windows: Were they Bibles for the poor?', in *The Bible in the Middle Ages: Its influence on literature and art*. Ed. B. S. Levy. Binghamton, NY: Center for Medieval and Early Renaissance Studies, 103–47.

Chartier, R. 1995. *Forms and meanings*. Philadelphia: University of Pennsylvania Press.

Cheney, C. R. 1936. 'The punishment of felonious clerks', *English Historical Review*, 51, 215–36.

1941. *English synodal of the thirteenth century*. Oxford: Oxford University Press.

1969. 'Notes on the making of the Dunstable annals, AD 33 to 1242', in *Essays in medieval history presented to Bertie Wilkinson*. Toronto, ON: University of Toronto Press, 79–98.

1973. 'Richard de Bury, borrower of books', *Speculum*, 48:2, 325–28.

1983. *Episcopal visitations of monasteries in the thirteenth Century*. 2nd ed. Manchester: Manchester University Press.

Clanchy, M. T. 1968. 'Did Henry III have a policy?', *History*, 53, 209–11.

1978. 'Highway robbery and trial by battle in the Hampshire eyre of 1249', in *Medieval legal records edited in memory of C. A. F. Meekings*. Ed. R. F. Hunnisett and J. B. Post. London: HMSO.

1993. *From memory to written record: England 1066–1307*. 2nd ed. Oxford: Blackwell.

2006. *England and its rulers 1066–1272*. 3rd ed. Oxford: Blackwell.

Clark, J. G. 2000. 'Reformation and reaction at St Albans Abbey, 1530–58', *English Historical Review*, 115, 297–328.

2001. 'The St Albans monks and the cult of St Alban: The late medieval texts', in *Alban and St Albans: Roman and medieval architecture, art and archaeology*. Ed. M. Henig and P. Lindley. Oxford: Wiley and British Archaeological Association, 218–30.

2002. 'Thomas Walsingham reconsidered: Books and learning at late-medieval St. Albans'. *Speculum*, 77: 3, 832–60.

2004. *A monastic renaissance at St Albans: Thomas Walsingham and his circle, c. 1350–1440*. Oxford: Clarendon Press.

2006. 'Monastic confraternity in medieval England: The evidence from the St Albans Abbey *Liber benefactorum*', in *Religious and laity in western Europe, 1000–1400: Interaction, negotiation, and power*. Ed. E. Jamroziak and J. E. Burton. Brepols: Turnhout, 315–31.

2020. 'St Albans Abbey and the people of St Albans: From the conquest to the dissolution', *Hertfordshire Archaeology History*, 18, 207–18.

Cleaver, L., 2018. *Illuminated history books in the Anglo–Norman world, 1066–1272*. London: Oxford University Press.

Cleaver, L. and Worm, A., eds. 2018. *Writing history in the Anglo–Norman world: Manuscripts, makers and readers, c. 1066–c.1250*. Woodbridge: York Medieval Press.

Clutterbuck, R. 1815-27, *History and antiquities of the county of Hertford*. 3 vols. London: Nichols, Son and Bentley.

Coates, A. 1999. *The Reading Abbey book collections from foundation to dispersal*. Oxford: Oxford University Press.

Colker, M. L., ed. 1991. *Trinity College Library Dublin: Descriptive catalogue of the mediaeval and renaissance Latin manuscripts (Vols. 1-2)*. London: Scolar Press.

Colker, M. L., ed. 2008. *Trinity College Library Dublin: Descriptive catalogue of the mediaeval and renaissance Latin manuscripts. Supplement one*. Dublin: Four Courts Press.

Collard, J. 2008. '*Flores historiarum* manuscripts: The illumination of a late thirteenth-century chronicle series', *Zeitschrift für kunstgeschichte*, 71, Bd. H4, 441–66.

    2010. 'Henry I's dream in John of Worcester's chronicle (Oxford, Corpus Christi College, MS 157) and the illustration of twelfth-century English chronicles', *Journal of Medieval History*, 36, 105–25.

    2015. 'Matthew Paris's "self-portrait with the Virgin Mary" in the *Historia Anglorum*. *Parergon*, 32:1, 151–82.

    2022a. 'Matthew Paris, metalwork, and the jewels of St Albans', in *Lost artefacts from medieval England and France: Representation, Reimagination, Recovery*. Ed. K. Gerry and L. Cleaver. York: York Medieval Press, 114–35.

    2022b. 'Memory and kingship in the manuscripts of Matthew Paris', in *Memorialising premodern monarchs: Medias of commemoration and remembrance*. Ed. G. Storey. Cham: Palgrave Macmillan, an imprint of Springer Nature, 197–220.

    2024. 'Matthew Paris, William of Conches, and the use of diagrams to observe the world', in *Medieval perceptions of magic, science, and the natural world*. Ed. A. Lawrence-Mathers, and C. Escobar-Vargas. York: Arc Humanities Press, 69–86.

Connolly, D. K. 1999. 'Imagined pilgrimage in the itinerary maps of Matthew Paris', *Art Bulletin*, 81, 598–622.

    2009. *Maps of Matthew Paris: Medieval journeys through space, time and liturgy*. Woodbridge: Boydell.

    2019. 'In the company of Matthew Paris: Mapping the world at St Albans Abbey', in *A critical companion to the English medieval* mappae mundi *of the Twelfth and Thirteenth Centuries*. Ed. D. Terkla and N. Millea. Woodbridge: Boydell and Brewer, 147–78.

Constable, G. 1996. *The reformation of the Twelfth Century.* Cambridge: Cambridge University Press.

Coss, P. R. 1975. 'Sir Geoffrey Langley and the crisis in the knightly class in thirteenth-century England', *Past and Present*, 68, 3–37.

Cowan, E. J. 1990. 'Norwegian sunset – Scottish dawn: Hakon IV and Alexander III', in *Scotland in the reign of Alexander III, 1249–86*. Ed. N. H. Reid. Edinburgh: John Donald, 103–31.

Cownie, E. 1998. *Religious patronage in Anglo–Norman England, 1066–1135.* Woodbridge: Boydell.

Crane, S. 1997. 'Social aspects of bilingualism in thirteenth-century England', *Thirteenth-Century England*, 6, 103–15.

Craster, H. H. E. 1907. *A history of Northumberland, Vol. 8: The parish of Tynemouth.* Edinburgh: Northumberland County History Committee.

Crick, J. C. 1989. *The Historia regum Britannie of Geoffrey of Monmouth, III: A summary catalogue of the manuscripts.* Cambridge: D. S. Brewer.

2001. 'Offa, Aelfric and the Refoundation of St Albas', in *Alban and St Albans: Roman and Medieval Architecture, Art and Archaeology*. Ed. M. Henig and P. Lindley. Oxford: Wiley and British Archaeological Association, 78–84.

Crook, D. 2015. 'Roger of Wendover, prior of Belvoir, and the implementation of the Charter of the Forest, 1225-27', in *The growth of royal government under Henry III*. Ed. D. Crook and L. J. Wilkinson. Woodbridge: Boydell, 166–78.

Cruse, M. 2006. 'Costuming the past: Heraldry in illustrations of the Roman d'Alexandre (Oxford, Bodleian Library, MS Bodley 264)', *Gesta*, 45, 43–59.

Dalché, P. G. 2004. 'Du nouveau sur la transmission et la découverte de la *Tabula Peutingeriana*: La "cosmographia vetutissim" de Pellegrino Prisciani (†1518)', *Geographia Antiqua*, 13, 71–84.

Davies, R. R. 1990. *Domination and conquest: The experience of Ireland, Scotland and Wales, 1100–1300.* Cambridge: Cambridge University Press.

2000. *The first English empire: Power and identities in the British Isles, 1093–1343.* Oxford: Oxford University Press.

de Hamel, C. 1986. *Western manuscripts and miniatures Tuesday 24 June 1986 at 2.30pm.* London: Sotheby's.

Dean, R. and Boulton, M. 2000. *Anglo–Norman literature: A guide to texts and manuscripts.* Anglo-Norman Text Society Occasional Series 3. London: Anglo–Norman Text Society.

Denholm-Young, N. 1946. 'Thomas Wykes and his chronicle', *English Historical Review*, 61, 157–59.

Denton, J. H. 1986. 'The making of the *Articuli Cleri* of 1316', *English Historical Review*, 101, 564–95.

Derolez, A. 2003. *The palaeography of Gothic manuscript books: From the twelfth to the early sixteenth century.* Cambridge: Cambridge University Press.

Dodd, G. 2007. 'Sovereignty, diplomacy and petitioning: Scotland and the English Parliament in the first half of the fourteenth century', in *England and Scotland in the fourteenth century: New perspectives.* Ed. A. King and M. Penman. Woodbridge: Boydell, 172-95.

Doležalová, L. 2012. *Obscurity and memory in late medieval Latin manuscript culture: The case of the* Summarium Biblie. Medium Aevum Quotidianum. Sonderband 29. Krems: Geschiche zur Erforschung der Materiellen Kultur des Mittelalters.

Duggan, A. 1982. 'The cult of St Thomas Becket in the thirteenth century', in *St Thomas Cantilupe Bishop of Hereford: Essays in his honour.* Ed. M. Jancey. Hereford: Friends of Hereford Cathedral, 21-44.

2008. 'Conciliar Law 1123-1215', in, *The history of medieval canon law in the classical period 1140-1234.* Ed. W. Hartmann and K. Pennington. Washington, DC: Catholic University of America Press, 318-66.

Duncan, A. A. M. 1975. *Scotland: The making of the kingdom.* Edinburgh: Oliver & Boyd.

2016. *The kingship of the Scots, 842-1292: Succession and independence.* 2nd ed. Edinburgh: Edinburgh University Press.

Dunning, A. N. J. 2018. 'St Frideswide's Priory as a centre of learning in early Oxford', *Mediaeval Studies,* 80, 253-96.

Egger, C. 2002. 'Henry III's England and the Curia', in *England and Europe in the reign of Henry III (1216-1272).* Ed. B. K. Weiler and I. Rowlands. Ashgate: Aldershot, 215-31.

2004. 'The growling of the lion and the humming of the fly: Gregory the Great and Innocent III', in *Pope, church and society: Essays in honour of Brenda M. Bolton.* Ed. F. Andrews, C. Egger and C. M. Rosseau. Leiden: Brill, 13-46.

Emden, A. B. 1974. *A biographical register of the University of Oxford, A.D. 1501 to 1540.* Oxford: Clarendon Press.

Flahiff, G. B. 1941. 'The use of prohibitions by clerics against ecclesiastical courts in England', *Mediaeval Studies,* 3, 101-16.

1944. 'The writ of prohibition to court Christians in the thirteenth century', *Mediaeval Studies,* 6, 261-313.

Foxe, E. 1534. *De vera differentia regiae potestatis & ecclesiasticae & quae sit ipsa ueritas ac uirtus utriusque. Opus eximium.* London. [STC 2nd ed. 11219].

Frame, R. 1988. 'Aristocracies and the political configuration of the British Isles', in *The British Isles, 1100-1500: Comparisons, contrasts and connections.* Ed. R. R. Davies. Edinburgh: John Donald, 142-59 (reprinted in R. Frame, *Ireland and Britain, 1170-1450.* London: Hambledon, 1998, 151-69).

Frassetto, M. and Blanks, D. R., eds. 1999. *Western views of Islam in medieval and early modern Europe: Perception of other.* New York: St Martin's Press.

Gabel, L. C. 1929. *Benefit of clergy in England in the later Middle Ages.* Northampton, MA: Department of History of Smith College.

Gabriele, M. 2003. 'Asleep at the wheel? Messianism, apocalypticism and Charlemagne's passivity in the Oxford *Chanson de Roland*', *Nottingham Medieval Studies*, 47, 46–72.

Galbraith, V. H. 1911. *The Abbey of St Albans.* Oxford: Oxford University Press.

1944. *Roger of Wendover and Matthew Paris.* London: Historical Association Pamphlet.

Galloway, A. ed. 2011. *The Cambridge Companion to medieval English culture.* Cambridge: Cambridge University Press.

Garnett, G. 2020. *The Norman Conquest in English history. Volume I: A broken chain?* Oxford: Oxford University Press.

Gaudio, M. 2000. 'Matthew Paris and the cartography of the margins', *Gesta*, 39, 50–57.

Geaman, K. 2012. 'Modernizing Matthew Paris: The standards and practices of the first printed editions', *Quidditas*, 33, 117–51.

Gerry, K. 2014. 'Picturing narrative and promoting cult: Hagiographic illumination at three English cult centres', in *Matter of faith: An interdisciplinary study of relics and relic veneration in the medieval period.* Ed. J. Robins, L. de Beer and A. Harnden. London: British Museum, 47–55.

2020. 'Extended shelf life: Manuscript consolidation in an English monastic library', in *Illuminating the Middle Ages: Tributes to Prof. John Lowden from his students, friends and colleagues.* Ed. L. Cleaver, A. Bovey and L. Donkin. Leiden: Brill, 207–23.

2021. 'Put it in writing (and drawing): Issues of loss and preservation in the works of Matthew Paris', November 2021, *14th annual Schoenberg symposium on manuscript studies in the Digital age.* Philadelphia/online, and is being edited for publication.

Gibbon, E. 1776–88. *The history of the decline and fall of the Roman Empire.* 6 vols. London: William Strahan and Thomas Cadell.

Gibson, E. 1698. *Reliquiae Spelmanniae: The posthumous works of Sir Henry Spelman, knt., relating to the laws and antiquities of England, from the original manuscripts.* Oxford: Awnsham and John Churchill.

Gibson, M., Heslop, T. A. and Pfaff, R. W., eds. 1992. *The Eadwine Psalter: Text, image, and monastic culture in twelfth-century Canterbury.* University Park: Pennsylvania State University Press.

Gibson, W. S. 1846–47. *The history of the monastery founded at Tynemouth in the diocese of Durham.* 2 vols. London: William Pickering.

Gieben, S. 1971. 'Robert Grosseteste at the papal Curia Lyon 1250: An edition of the documents', *Collectanea Franciscana*, 41, 340–93.

Giles, K. R. 1987. 'Two English bishops in the Holy Land', *Nottingham Medieval Studies*, 31, 46–57.

Gillingham, J. 1993. 'Conquering the Barbarians: War and chivalry in twelfth-century Britain', in *Haskins Society Journal*. Ed. R. B. Patterson, 4. Woodbridge: Boydell, 67–84 (reprinted in J. Gillingham, *The English in the twelfth century: Imperialism, national identity and political values*. Woodbridge: Boydell, 2000, 41–58).

Gilson, J. P. and Poole, H., eds. 1928. *Four maps of Great Britain designed by Matthew Paris about AD 1250: Reproduced from three manuscripts in the British Museum and one at Corpus Christi College, Cambridge*. London: British Museum.

Given-Wilson, C. 2004. *Chronicles: The writing of history in medieval England*. London: Hambledon.

Golding, B. 1986. 'Wealth and artistic patronage at twelfth-century St Albans', in *Art and patronage in the English Romanesque*. Ed. S. Macready and F. H. Thompson. Society of Antiquaries Occasional Papers New Series 8. London, 107–17.

Grafton, A. 2017. 'Matthew Parker: The book as archive'. *History of Humanities*, 2:1, 15–50.

Graham, T. 1994. 'A Parkerian transcript of the list of Bishop Leofric's procurements for Exeter Cathedral: Matthew Parker, the Exeter Book, and Cambridge University Library MS Ii.2.11', *Transactions of the Cambridge Bibliographical Society*, 10:4, 421–59.

  2006. 'Matthew Parker's manuscripts: An Elizabethan library and its use', In *The Cambridge history of libraries in Britain and Ireland. I to 1640*. Ed. E. Leedham-Green and T. Webber. Cambridge: Cambridge University Press, 322–42.

Graham, T. and Watson, A. G., eds. 1998. *The recovery of the past in early Elizabethan England: Documents by John Bale and John Joscelyn from the circle of Matthew Parker*. Cambridge Bibliographical Society Monograph 14. Cambridge: Cambridge University Library.

Gransden, A. 1974a. 'The continuations of the *Flores Historiarum* from 1265 to 1327', *Mediaeval Studies*, 36, 472–92.

  1974b. *Historical writing in England c. 550 to c. 1307*. London: Routledge & Kegan Paul.

  1975. 'Propaganda in English medieval historiography', *Journal of Medieval History*, 1, 363–82.

  1982. *Historical writing in England II c. 1307 to the early sixteenth century*. London: Routledge & Kegan Paul.

  2007. *A history of the abbey of Bury St Edmunds, 1182–1256: Samson of Tottington to Edmund of Walpole*. Studies in the History of Medieval Religion 31. Woodbridge: Boydell.

  2015. *A history of the abbey of Bury St Edmunds, 1257–1301: Simon of Luton and John of Northwold*. Woodbridge: Boydell.

Gray, J. W. 1966. 'Bishops, politics and the two laws: The *gravamina* of the English clergy, 1237-1399', *Speculum*, 41:2, 209-45.

Greasley, N. 2021. 'Revisiting the compilation of Matthew Paris's *Chronica majora*: New textual and manuscript evidence', *Journal of Medieval History*, 47:2, 230-56.

Green, J. R. 1874. *A history of the English people*. London: Macmillan.

Gumbert, J. P. 1976. 'A proposal for a Cartesian nomenclature', in *Miniatures, scripts, collections: Essays presented to G. I. Lieftinck* (Litterae Textuales). Ed. J. P. Gumbert and M. J. M. de Haan. Amsterdam: Brill, 45-52.

Hahn, C. 1990. 'Proper behavior for knights and kings: The hagiography of Matthew Paris, Monk of St. Albans', *Haskins Society Journal*, 2, 237-48.

    2001. *Portrayed on the heart: Narrative effect in pictorial lives of saints from the tenth through the thirteenth century*. Berkeley: University of California Press.

    2004. 'The limits of text and image? Matthew Paris's final project, the *Vitae duorum Offarum*, as a historical romance', in *Excavating the medieval image: Manuscripts, artists, audiences. Essays in honor of Sandra Hindman*. Ed. D. Areford and N. Rowe. Aldershot: Ashgate, 37-58.

Hallam, H. 1872. *View of the state of Europe during the Middle Ages*. 3 vols. London: John Murray.

Hanley, C. 2016. *Louis: The French prince who invaded England*. New Haven, CT: Yale University Press.

Harding, A. 2002. *Medieval law and the foundations of the state*. Oxford: Oxford University Press.

Hardwick, C. and Luard, H. R., eds. 1856-67. *A catalogue of the manuscripts preserved in the library of the University of Cambridge: Vols. 1-6*. Cambridge: Cambridge University Press.

Hardy, N. J. S. 2017. *Criticism and confession: The Bible in the seventeenth-century republic of letters*. Oxford: Oxford University Press.

Hardy, T. D. 1862. *Descriptive catalogue of manuscripts relating to the history of Great Britain and Ireland*. Rolls Series 26. London: HMSO.

Harris, P. R. 1998. *A history of the British Museum Library, 1753-1973*. London: British Library.

Harvey, B. 1993. *Living and dying in England: The monastic experience 1100-1540*. Oxford: Oxford University Press.

    2003. 'The monks of Westminster and the old Lady Chapel', in *Westminster Abbey: The Lady Chapel of Henry VII*. Ed. R. Mortimer and T. Tatton-Brown. Woodbridge: Boydell, 5-32.

Harvey, B., ed. 2001. *The twelfth and thirteenth centuries*. The Shorter Oxford History of the British Isles. Oxford: Oxford University Press.

Harvey, P. D. A. 1992. 'Matthew Paris's maps of Britain', in *Thirteenth-century England: IV*. Ed. P. R. Coss and S. D. Lloyd. Woodbridge: Boydell, 109-21.

2001. 'Matthew Paris's maps of Palestine', in *Thirteenth-century England: Proceedings of the Durham Conference, 1999*. Ed. M. Prestwich, R. Britnell and R. Frame. Woodbridge: Boydell and Brewer, 165–77.

2006b. 'The Holy Land on medieval world maps', in *The Hereford world map*, ed. P. D. A. Harvey. London: British Library, 243–51.

2008. 'Maps of the world in the medieval English royal wardrobe', in *Foundations of medieval scholarship: Records edited in honour of David Crook*. Borthwick Texts and Studies 36. Ed. P. Brand and S. Cunningham. York: Borthwick Institute of Historical Research.

2012. *Medieval maps of the Holy Land*. London: British Library.

Harvey, P. D. A, ed. 2006a. *The Hereford world map: Medieval world maps and their context*. London: British Library.

Hawks, K. 2023. 'Interflores, or Merton's meandering manuscripts', *Journal of Medieval Monastic Studies*, 12, 179–98.

Hay, D. 1952. *Polydore Vergil: Renaissance historian and man of letters*. Oxford: Clarendon Press.

Heal, F. 2005. 'Appropriating history: Catholic and Protestant polemics and the national past', *Huntington Library Quarterly*, 68, 109–32.

Hechelhammer, B. 2004. *Kreuzzug und Herrschaft unter Friedrich II: Handlungsspielräume von Kreuzzugspolitik (1215–1230)*. Mittelalter-Forschungen Band 13. Ostfildern: Janos Stekovic.

Hellinga, L. 2010. *William Caxton and Early Printing in England*. London: British Library.

Helmholz, R. H. 1981. 'The writ of prohibition to the court Christian before 1500', *Medieval Studies*, 43:1, 297–345.

2004. *The Oxford history of the laws of England, vol. 1: The canon law and ecclesiastical jurisdiction from 597 to the 1640s*. Oxford: Oxford University Press.

Henderson, G. D. S. 1967. 'Studies in English manuscript illumination', *Journal of the Warburg and Courtauld Institutes*, 30, 71–137.

Hennessy, C. 2023. 'Thomas Becket, Henry II, daughters and sons: A family affair', *Journal of the British Archaeological Association*, 176, 71–95.

Hershey, A. H. 2000. 'The rise and fall of William de Bussey, a mid-thirteenth-century steward', *Nottingham Medieval Studies*, 44, 104–22.

Hill, F. G. 2016. 'Magna Carta, canon law and pastoral care: Excommunication and the church's publication of the Charter', *Historical Research*, 89, 636–50.

Hilpert, H.-E. 1980. 'Richard of Cornwall's candidature for the German throne and the Christmas parliament of 1256', *Journal of Medieval History*, 6, 185–98.

1981. *Kaiser- under Papstbriefe in den Chronice majora des Matthaeus Paris*. Publications of the German Historical Institute, London, 9. Stuttgart: Ernst Klett.

1985. 'Zu den Prophetien im Geschichtswerk des Matthaeus Paris', *Deutsches Archiv für Erforschung des Mittelalters*, 41, 175–91.

Hodgson, J. C. 1904. *A history of Northumberland, Vol. 7: The parish of Edlingham, the parish of Felton, the chapelry or parish of Brinkburn.* Newcastle: Northumberland County History Committee.

Holcomb, M. 2009. *Pen and parchment: Drawing in the Middle Ages.* New York: Metropolitan Museum of Art.

Holdenried, A. 2006. *The sibyl and her scribes: Manuscripts and interpretation of the Latin 'Sibylla Tiburtina' c. 1050–1500.* Aldershot: Ashgate.

Holford, M. L. and Stringer, K. J. 2010. *Border liberties and loyalties: North-east England, c.1200 to c.1400.* Edinburgh: Edinburgh University Press.

Holmes, J. 1737. *The history of England.* London: A. Parker.

Holt, J. C. 1964. 'The St Albans chroniclers and Magna Carta', *Transactions of the Royal Historical Society*, Fifth Series, xiv: 67–88.

  2015. *Magna carta.* 3rd ed. Rev . G. A. Garnett and J. Hudson. Cambridge: Cambridge University Press.

Howell, M. 1998. *Eleanor of Provence: Queenship in thirteenth-century England.* Oxford: Blackwell.

Hume, D. 1778. *The history of England from the invasion of Julius Caesar to the revolution of 1688: A new edition with the author's last corrections and improvements.* 8 vols. London: T Cadell.

Hunt, R. W. 1978. 'The library of the Abbey of St Albans', in *Medieval scribes, manuscripts and libraries: Essays presented to N. R. Ker.* Ed. M. B. Parkes and A. G. Watson. London: Scolar Press, 251–77.

Hunt, T. 1991. *Teaching and learning Latin in thirteenth-century England.* 3 vols. Cambridge: D. S. Brewer.

Iafrate, A. 2013. 'Of stars and men: Matthew Paris and the illustrations of MS Ashmole 304', *Journal of the Warburg and Courtauld Institutes*, 76, 139–77.

  2015. *Le moine et le hasard: Bodleian Library, MS Ashmole 304.* Textes littéraires du moyen âge 39, Série Divinatoria 5. Paris: Classiques Garnier.

Ingham, R., ed. 2010. *The Anglo-Norman language and its contexts.* Woodbridge: York Medieval Press, Boydell and Brewer.

Ingledew, F. 1994. 'The Book of Troy and the genealogical construction of history: The case of Geoffrey of Monmouth's *Historia regum Britanniae*', *Speculum*, 69, 665–704.

James, M. R. 1903. *Ancient libraries of Canterbury and Dover.* Cambridge: Cambridge University Press.

  1912. *A descriptive catalogue of the manuscripts in the library of Corpus Christi College, Cambridge (Vols. 1–2).* Cambridge: Cambridge University Press.

  1925–26. 'The drawings of Matthew Paris', *Walpole Society*, 14, 1–26.

  1929. *Marvels of the East.* Oxford: Roxburghe Club.

James, M. R. with Lowe, W. R. L. and Jacob, E. F. 1924, *Illustrations to the Life of St Alban.* Oxford: Clarendon Press.

Jamroziak, E. 2013. *The Cistercian order in Medieval Europe, 1090–1500.* London: Routledge, Taylor & Francis.

Janssen, F. A. 2011. 'Manuscript copies of printed works', *Quaerendo*, 41, 295–310.

Jayne, S. R. and Johnson, F. R., eds. 1956. *The Lumley library: The catalogue of 1609.* London: British Museum.

Jefferson, M. 2006. *The conservation of Parker MSS 16 and 26, 'The Chronica majora'. Care and conservation of manuscripts 9: Proceedings of the ninth international seminar held at the University of Copenhagen, 14th–15th April 2005.* Ed. G. Fellows-Jensen and P. Springborg. Copenhagen: Museum Tusculanum Press, University of Copenhagen, 69–81.

Jenkins, C. 1922.*The monastic chronicler and the early school of St Albans: A lecture.* London: Society for Promoting Christian Knowledge.

Johnston, R. C. 1974. *The versification of Jordan Fantosme.* Oxford: Clarendon Press.

1979. 'Jordan Fantosme's experiments in prosody and design', in *Mélanges ... offerts à Pierre Jonin.* Ed. H. Duffaut. Aix-en-Provence: Presses Universitaires de Provence, 357–67.

1980. 'Matthew Paris, Jordan Fantosme and Anglo-Norman Versification', in *Mélanges ... offerts à Charles Foulon.* Rennes: Institut de Français, Université de Haute-Bretagne, 165–75.

Jones, N. L. 1981. 'Matthew Parker, John Bale, and the Magdeburg Centuriators'. *The Sixteenth Century Journal*, 12:3, 35–49.

Jotischky, A. 2004. 'Penance and reconciliation in the crusader states: Matthew Paris, Jacques de Vitry and the Eastern Christians', *Studies in Church History*, 40, 74–83.

Kauffmann, C. M. 1975. *Romanesque manuscripts, 1066–1190.* London: Harvey Miller.

1984. 'An early sixteenth-century genealogy of Anglo-Saxon kings', *Journal of the Warburg and Courtauld Institutes*, 47, 209–16.

Kauffmann, M. 2020. 'Seeing and reading the Matthew Paris saints' lives', in *Illuminating the Middle Ages: Tributes to Prof. John Lowden from his students, friends and colleagues.* Ed. L. Cleaver, A. Bovey and L. Donkin. Leiden: Brill, 182–206.

Kay, R. 1969. 'Wendover's last annal', *English Historical Review*, lxxxiv, 779–85.

Ker, N. R. 1944. 'William of Malmesbury's handwriting', *English Historical Review*, 59, 371–76.

1960. *English manuscripts in the century after the Norman Conquest.* Oxford: Oxford University Press.

1969–2002. *Medieval manuscripts in British libraries (Vols. 1–5).* Oxford: Clarendon Press.

Kelly, K. 1989. 'Forgery, invention, and propaganda: Factors behind the production of the Guthlac Roll', *Athanor*, 8, 1–13.

Kerr, J. 2007. *Monastic hospitality: The Benedictines in England, c. 1070–1250* Woodbridge: Boydell.

Kessler, H. 2019. *Experiencing medieval art*. Toronto, ON: University of Toronto Press.

Keynes, S. 1993. 'A lost cartulary of St Albans Abbey', *Anglo-Saxon England*, 22, 253–79.

Kim, K. 2000. *Aliens in medieval law: The origins of modern citizenship*. Cambridge: Cambridge University Press.

Kirkham P. and Weber S., eds. 2013. *History of design: Decorative arts and material culture, 1400–2000*. London: Yale University Press.

Kjaer, L. 2013. 'Matthew Paris and the royal Christmas', *Thirteenth-Century England*, 14, 141–54.

Kjølbye-Biddle, B. 'The Alban Cross', in *Alban and St Albans: Roman and medieval architecture, art and archaeology*. Ed. M. Henig and P. Lindley. Oxford: Wiley and British Archaeological Association, 85–110.

Knowles, D. 1940. *The monastic order in England*. Cambridge: Cambridge University Press.

    1948–59. *The religious orders in England*. 3 vols. Cambridge: Cambridge University Press.

Knowles, D. and Hadcock, R. N. 1971. *Medieval religious houses: England and Wales*. 2nd ed. London: Routledge & Kegan Paul.

Kugler, H. 2007. *Die Ebstorfer Weltkarte*. 2 vols. Berlin: Akademie.

Kuttner, S. and García y García, A. 1964. A new eyewitness account of the Fourth Lateran Council, *Traditio*, 20, 115–78.

Kwakkel, E. 2012. 'Kissing, biting and the treatment of feet: The transitional script of the long twelfth century', in *Turning over a new leaf: Change and development in the medieval book*. Ed. E. Kwakkel, R. Mckitterick and R. Thomson. Leiden: Leiden University Press, 79–126.

    2018. *Books before Print*. Leeds: ARC Humanities Press.

Kwakkel, E., McKitterick, R. and Thomson, R., eds. 2012. *Turning over a new leaf: Change and development in the medieval book*. Leiden: Leiden University Press.

Laborderie, O. de. 2013. 'Genealogiae Orbiculatae: Matthew Paris and the invention of visual abstracts of English history', in *Thirteenth century England XIV: Proceedings of the Aberystwyth and Lampeter Conference, 2011*. Ed. J. Burton, P. Schofield and B. Weiler. Cambridge: Boydell and Brewer, 183–202.

Lacey, S. 2018. 'Tinted drawing: Translucency, luminosity and *lumen vitae*', in *Colour and light in ancient and medieval art*. Ed. C. N. Duckworth and A. E. Sassin. New York: Routledge, 159–71.

Langmuir, G. I. 1972. 'The knight's tale of Young Hugh of Lincoln', *Speculum*, 47:3, 459–82.

Lawrence, C. H. 1960. *St Edmund of Abingdon: A study in hagiography and history*. Oxford: Clarendon Press.

  1984. *Medieval monasticism: Forms of religious life in Western Europe*. London: Longman.

  2004. 'Wyche, Richard of (d. 1253), bishop of Chichester', in *Oxford Dictionary of National Biography*. Oxford: Oxford University Press.

Laynesmith, M. 2018. 'The cult of St Alban of Verulamium, *c*. 400–*c*. 750'. London: Archbishop of Canterbury, Lambeth Palace.

Le Goff, J. 1996, *Saint Louis*. Paris: Gallimard, Bibliothèques des Histoires.

Legge, D. 1950. *Anglo-Norman in the cloisters*. Edinburgh: Edinburgh University Press.

  1963. *Anglo-Norman literature and its background*. Oxford: Clarendon Press.

Lehmann-Brockhaus, O. 1955–60. *Lateinische Schriftquellen zur Kunst in England, Wales und Schottland vom Jahre 901 bis zum Jahre 1307*. 5 vols. Munich: Prestel.

Lethaby, W. R. 1916. 'English primitives – I', *Burlington Magazine*, 29: 189–96.

  1917a. 'English primitives – V', *Burlington Magazine*, 31: 45–52.

  1917b. 'English primitives – VI', *Burlington Magazine*, 31: 97–98.

Levy, B. J. 1991. 'Autoportrait d'artiste, figure de poète: Le cas de Matthieu Paris,' in *Figures de l'écrivain au moyen age: actes du colloque du centre d'études médiévales de l'université de Picardie*. Ed. D. Buschinger. Gottingen: Kümmerle, 193–206.

Levy, F. J. 1967. *Tudor historical thought*. San Marino, CA: Huntington Library.

Lewis, E. 1964. 'King above law? "Quod Principi Placuit" in Bracton', *Speculum*, 39, 240–69.

Lewis, F. 1992. 'Rewarding devotion: Indulgences and the promotion of images', in *The Church and the Arts*. Ed. D. Wood. Studies in Church History 28. Oxford: Blackwell, 179–94.

Lewis, S. 1987. *The art of Matthew Paris in the* Chronica majora. Berkeley: University of California Press.

Lieftinck, G. I. 1954. 'Pour une nomenclature de l'écriture livresque de la période dite gothique', in *Nomenclature des écritures livresques du IXe au XVIe siècle*. Ed. B. Bischoff, G. I. Lieftinck and G. Batelli. Paris: CNRS, 15–34.

  1964. *Manuscrits datés conservés dans les Pays-Bas: Catalogue paléographique des manuscrits en écriture latine portant des indications de date*. 2 vols. Amsterdam: North Holland.

Lindquist, C. M. and Mittman, A. S. 2018. 'Aliens far and near', in *Medieval monsters: Terrors, aliens, wonders*. New York: Morgan Library and Museum in association with D. Giles Ltd., 78–121.

Lingard, J. 1823. *A history of England from the first invasion by the Romans to the accession of William and Mary in 1688*. 2nd ed. 10 vols. London: J. Mawman.

1823–31. *A history of England from the first invasion by the Romans.* 2nd ed. 14 vols. London: Printed for J. Mawman.

1844–45. *A history of England from the first invasion by the Romans to the accession of William and Mary in 1688: A new edition, corrected and considerably enlarged.* 13 vols. London: C. Dolman.

1855. *A history of England from the first invasion by the Romans to the accession of William and Mary in 1688.* A new edition. 13 vols. Boston: Phillips, Sampson & Company.

Liu, H. 2007. 'Matthew Paris and John Mansel', *Thirteenth-Century England*, 11, 159–73.

Lloyd, S. and Hunt, T. 1991. 'William Longespee II: The making of an English crusading hero', *Nottingham Medieval Studies*, 35, 41–69.

Lloyd, S. and Reader, R. 2004. 'Paris, Matthew (*c.* 1200-1259), historian, Benedictine monk, and polymath', in *Oxford Dictionary of National Biography*. Oxford: Oxford University Press.

Lockhart, J. G. 1837–38. *Memoirs of the life of Sir Walter Scott*. 7 vols. Edinburgh: Robert Cadell.

Logan, F. D. 2014. *University education of the parochial clergy in medieval England the Lincoln Diocese c. 1300-c. 1350*. Toronto, ON: Pontifical Institute of Mediaeval Studies.

Luard, H. R. 1879. 'A letter from Bishop Bale to Archbishop Parker', in *Cambridge Antiquarian Communications*, iii, 172–73.

Lunt, W. E. 1939. *Financial relations of the papacy with England to 1327*. Cambridge: Cambridge University Press.

Lusignan, S. 2004. *La Langue des rois au Moyen Age: Le Français en France et en Angleterre*. Paris: Presses Universitaires de France.

Lutz, C. E. 1975. 'Manuscripts copied from printed books', *Yale University Library Gazette*, 49, 261–67.

Luxford, J. 2009. 'A fifteenth-century version of Matthew Paris' Procession of the Holy Blood', *Journal of the Warburg and Courtauld Institutes*, 72, 81–101.

2019. 'Recording and curating relics at Westminster Abbey in the late Middle Ages', *Journal of Medieval History*, 45:2, 204–30.

MacKenzie, H. 1929. 'The anti-foreign movement in England 1231–1232', in *Anniversary essays in medieval history by students of Charles Homer Haskins*. Ed. C. H. Taylor. Freeport: Books for Libraries Press, 183–203.

MacLeod, W. 1980. 'Alban and Amphibal: Some extant lives and a lost life', *Mediaeval Studies*, 42, 407–30.

Maddicott, J. R. 1984. 'Magna Carta and the local community 1215–1259, *Past & Present*, 102, 25–65.

1994. *Simon de Montfort*. Cambridge: Cambridge University Press.

2010. *The origins of the English Parliament 924-1327*. Cambridge: Oxford University Press, 211–13.

Mak, B. 2011. *How the page matters*. Toronto, ON: University of Toronto Press.
Margolin, V. 2017. *World history of design*. 2 vols. London: Bloomsbury Academic.
Marks, R. and Morgan, N. 1981. *The golden age of English manuscript painting, 1200–1500*. London: Chatto & Windus.
Marner, D. 2000. *St Cuthbert: His life and cult in Durham*. London: British Library.
Marnette, S. 1998, *Narrateurs et points de vue dans la littérature française médiévale: Une approche linguistique*. Bern: Peter Lang.
Martin, G. and Thomson, R. M. 2008. 'History and history books', in *The Cambridge history of the book in Britain*. 6 vols. Ed. N. Morgan and R. M. Thomson. Cambridge: Cambridge University Press, ii:397–415.
Martin, H.-J. and Vezin, J. 1990. *Mise en page et mise en texte du livre manuscript*. Paris: Cercle de La Librairie – Promodis.
Matthew, D. 1997. *The English and the community of Europe in the thirteenth century*. The Stenton Lecture. Reading: University of Reading.
 2005. *Britain and the Continent, 1000–1300*. London: Hodder Arnold.
McCulloch, F. 1981. 'Saints Alban and Amphibalus in the works of Matthew Paris: Dublin Trinity College MS 177', *Speculum*, 56:4, 761–85.
McDonald, R .A. 1997. *The kingdom of the isles: Scotland's western seaboard, c. 1100–c. 1336*. East Linton: Tuckwell Press.
McKendrick, S., Lowden, J. and Doyle, K. 2011. *Royal manuscripts: The genius of illumination*. London: British Library.
McKisack, M. 1971. *Medieval history in the Tudor age*. Oxford: Clarendon Press.
McMahon, M. 2023. 'Ancient letters and old paper: How Matthew Parker (1504–1575) understood medieval books', *Book History*, 26:2, 237–73.
Meale, C. M., ed. 1993. *Women and literature in Britain 1150–1500*. Cambridge: Cambridge University Press.
Mellone, A. 1999. '*Vineam Domini* – 10 April 1213: New efforts and traditional topoi, summoning Lateran IV', in *Pope Innocent III and his world*. Ed. J. C. Moore. Aldershot: Routledge, 63–73.
Meyer, W. 1897. *Die Buchstaben-Verbindungen der sogenannten gothischen Schrift*. Berlin: Weidemannsche Buchhandlung.
Michael, M. A. 2004. 'Matthew Paris, Brother William, and St Marcella: Comments on the added leaf of the apocalyptic man in British Library MS Cotton Nero D.I', in *Prophecy, apocalypse and the day of doom* Ed. N. J. Morgan. Harlaxton Medieval Studies 12. Donington: Shaun Tyas, 239–49.
Mittman, A. 2015. 'Are the "monstrous races" races?', *Postmedieval: A Journal of Medieval Cultural Studies*, 6, 36–51.
Moll, R. J. 2003. *Before Malory: Reading Arthur in late medieval England*. Toronto, ON: University of Toronto Press.
Moore, J. C. 2003. *Pope Innocent III (1160-61–1216): To root up and to plant*. Leiden: Brill.

Morgan, N. J. 1982. *Survey of manuscripts illuminated in the British Isles: Vol. IV (1)*. London: Harvey Miller.

　1988. 'Matthew Paris, St Albans, London, and the Leaves of the 'Life of St Thomas Becket'', *Burlington Magazine*, 130, 85–96.

　1990. *The Lambeth apocalypse*. London: Harvey Miller.

　2011. *The Getty apocalypse*. London: The Folio Society.

　2017. '"Veronica" images and the Office of the Holy Face in thirteenth-century England', in *The European fortune of the Roman Veronica in the Middle Ages*. Ed. A. Murphy, H. L. Kessler, M. Petoletti, E. Duffy and G. Milanese. Brepols: Turnhout, 84–99.

Morgan, N. and Thomson, R., eds. 2008. *The Cambridge history of the book in Britain, vol. II, 1100–1400*. Cambridge: Cambridge University Press.

Morris, M. 2005. *The Bigod Earls of Norfolk in the thirteenth century*. Woodbridge: Boydell.

Morrison, E. and Hedeman, A. D. 2010. *Imagining the past in France: History in manuscript painting, 1250–1500*. Los Angeles, CA: J. Paul Getty Museum.

Muratova, X. 1986–90. 'Vir quidem fallax et falisidicus, sed artifex praeelectus. Remarques sur l'image sociale et littéraire de l'artiste au moyen age', in *Artistes, Artisans et production artistique au Moyen Age*. Ed. X. Barral I Altet. 3 vols. Paris: Picard.

Nederman, C. J. 1984. 'Bracton on kingship revisited', *History of Political Thought*, 5, 61–77.

　1988. 'The royal will and the baronial bridle', *History of Political Thought*, 9, 415–29.

Nicholas, N. 1829. *Report of proceedings on the claim to the barony of L'Isle in the House of Lords with notes and an appendix containing the cases of Abergavenny, Botecourt and Berkeley accompanied by observations on baronies by tenure*. London: William Pickering, Stevens & Sons.

Nisse, R. 2017. *Jacob's shipwreck: Diaspora, translation and Jewish–Christian relations in medieval England*. Ithaca, NY: Cornell University Press.

Nix, L. 1994. 'Manuscript layout and re-production of the text in Anglo-Saxon England', *Gazette du livre médiéval*, 25, 17–23.

O'Donnell, T. 2011. 'Anglo–Norman multiculturalism and Continental standards in Guernes de Pont-Sainte-Maxence's *Vie de Saint Thomas*', in *Conceptualizing Multilingualism in Medieval England c. 800 – c. 1250*. Ed. E. M. Tyler. Brepols: Turnhout, 337–56.

O'Donnell, T. and Lamont, M. 2010. 'The passion of Saint Alban by William of St. Albans', in *The life of Saint Alban by Matthew Paris*. Ed. J. Wogan-Browne and T. S. Fenster. Tempe: Arizona Center for Medieval & Renaissance Studies, 133–65.

Oman, C. 1932. 'The goldsmiths at St. Albans Abbey during the 12th and 13th centuries', *Transactions of the St Albans and Hertfordshire Architectural and Archaeological Society*, 215–36.

Oram, R. 2012. *Alexander II, King of Scots, 1214–1249*. Edinburgh: John Donald.

Orme, N. 1973. *English schools in the Middle Ages*. London: Methuen.

    2006. *Medieval schools from Roman Britain to Renaissance England*. New Haven, CT: Yale University Press.

Otter, M. 1996. *Inventiones: Fiction and referentiality in twelfth-century English historical writing*. Chapel Hill: University of North Carolina Press.

Pächt, O. and Alexander, J. J. G. 1966–73. *Illuminated manuscripts in the Bodleian Library, Oxford (Vols. 1–3)*. Oxford: Clarendon Press.

Page, R. I. 1993. *Matthew Parker and his books: Sandars lectures in bibliography delivered on 14, 16, and 18 May 1990 at the University of Cambridge*. Kalamazoo, MI: Medieval Institute.

Page, W. 1902. 'The St Albans school of painting, mural and miniature: Part I, Mural painting', *Archaeologia*, 2nd series, 8, 275–92.

    1908. *A history of the county of Hertford*. Vol. 2. London: Archibald Constable & Company.

Palgrave, F., ed. 1837. *Documents and records illustrating the history of Scotland, preserved in the Treasury*. London: Record Commission.

Papp Reed, Z. 2022. *Matthew Paris on the Mongol invasion of Europe*. Cultural encounters in Late Antiquity and the Middle Ages, 38. Turnhout: Brepols.

Parkes, M. B. 1969. *English cursive book hands 1250–1500*. Oxford Palaeographical Handbooks. Oxford: Clarendon Press.

    1992. *Pause and effect: An introduction to the history of punctuation in the West*. Aldershot: Scolar Press.

    1997. 'Archaizing hands in English manuscripts', in *Books and collectors, 1200–1700: Essays presented to Andrew Watson*. Ed. J. P. Carley and C. Tite. London: British Library, 101–41.

    2008a. 'Handwriting in English books', in *The Cambridge history of the book in Britain. Volume 2: 1100–1400*. Ed. N. J. Morgan and R. M. Thomson. Cambridge: Cambridge University Press, 110–35.

    2008b. *Their hands before our eyes: A closer look at scribes*. The Lyell Lectures delivered in the University of Oxford, 1999. Aldershot: Ashgate.

Pensom, R. 2006. 'Pour la versification Anglo-Normande', *Romania*, 124, 51–65.

Phillips, J. R. S. 1998. *The medieval expansion of Europe*. 2nd ed. Oxford: Oxford University Press.

Pitocchelli, B. 2024. *Matthew Paris, i Plantageneti, la crociata: Studio ed edizione dell'Iter de Londinio in Terra Sanctam*. Filologie medievali e moderne Serie occidentale, 29. Venice: Edizioni Ca'Foscari – Venice University Press.

Planta, J., ed. 1802. *A catalogue of the manuscripts in the Cottonian library deposited in the British Museum*. London: Hansard.

Poole, A. L. 1933. 'Outlawry as a punishment of criminous clerks', in *Historical essays in honour of J. Tait*. Ed. J. G. Edwards, V. H. Galbraith and E. F. Jacob. Manchester: Manchester University Press, 239–46.

Powell, J. M. 2001. 'Matthew Paris, the lives of Muhammad, and the Dominicans', in *Dei gesta per Francos: Études sur les croisades dédiées à Jean Richard*. Ed. M. Balard, J. Z. Kedar and J. Riley-Smith. Aldershot: Ashgate, 65–69.

Powicke, F. M. 1941. 'Notes on the compilation of the *Chronica Majora* of Matthew', *Modern Philology*, 38, 312–17

  1944. 'The compilation of the *Chronica Majora* of Matthew Paris', *Proceedings of the British Academy*, xxx, 147–60.

  1947. *Henry III and the Lord Edward*. Oxford: Oxford University Press.

  1959. 'Review of Richard Vaughan, Matthew Paris', *English Historical Review*, lxxiv, 482–85.

Pratesi, A. and Cherubini, P., 2010. *Paleografia Latin: L'avventura grafica del mondo occidentale*. Scuola Vaticana Paleografia, Diplomatica e archivistica, Littera antiqua 16. Vatican City.

Prescott, A. 1997. '"Their present miserable state of cremation": The restoration of the Cotton Library', in *Sir Robert Cotton as collector: Essays on an early Stuart courtier and his legacy*. Ed. C. J. Wright. London: British Library, 391–454.

  2019. 'Slow digitisation and the battle of the books', in *Slow scholarship: Medieval research and the neoliberal university*. Ed. C. E. Karkov. Cambridge: D. S. Brewer, 143–61.

Prescott, A., Brown, M. and Masters, R. 1998. 'The survey of illuminated manuscripts', in *Towards the digital library: The British Library's Initiatives for Access programme*. Ed. L. Carpenter, S. Shaw and A. Prescott. London: British Library, 30–147.

Prestwich, M. 1997. *Edward I*. Yale English Monarchs. New Haven, CT: Yale University Press.

  2005. *Plantagenet England, 1225–1360*. Oxford: Oxford University Press.

Purdie, R. 2008, *Anglicising Romance: Tail-rhyme and genre in medieval English literature*. : Cambridge: D. S. Brewer.

Quinn, P. A. 2010. 'Alban disbound: Codicological remarks on Matthew Paris's Life of St. Alban', in *The life of Saint Alban by Matthew Paris*. Ed. J. Wogan-Browne and T. S. Fenster. Tempe: Arizona Center for Medieval & Renaissance Studies, 195–212.

Radding, C. 1969. 'The origin of Bracton's *Addicio de Cartis*', *Speculum*, 44, 239–46.

Reader, R. 1996. 'Matthew Paris and the Norman Conquest', in *The cloister and the world: Essays in medieval history in honour of Barbara Harvey*. Ed. J. Blair and B. Golding. Oxford: Oxford University Press, 118–47.

  1999, 'Matthew Paris and women', *Thirteenth Century England*, VII, 153–60.

Richter, M. 1970–71. 'David ap Llywelyn, the first Prince of Wales', *Welsh History Review*, 5, 205–19.

Ridgeway, H. 1988. 'King Henry III's grievances against the council in 1261', *Historical Research*, 61, 227–42.

Rigg, A. G. 1992. *A history of Anglo-Latin Literature, 1066–1422*. Cambridge: Cambridge University Press.

Riley-Smith, J. 1995. *The Oxford illustrated history of the Crusades*. Oxford: Oxford University Press.

2014. *The Crusades: A history*. 3rd ed. London: Bloomsbury.

Robinson, B. S. 1998. '"Darke speech": Matthew Parker and the reforming of history', *The Sixteenth Century Journal*, 2:4, 1061–83.

Robson, M. P., ed. 2012. *The Cambridge companion to St Francis of Assisi*. Cambridge: Cambridge University Press.

2024. 'Francis of Assisi, Matthew Paris and his copies of the Franciscan rule of 1223', in *Pope, Bishops, Religious and Scholars: Studies in Medieval History presented to Patrick N. R. Zutshi for his Seventieth Birthday*. Turnhout: Brepols, 27–49.

Rothwell, W. 1976. 'The role of French in thirteenth-century England', *Bulletin of the John Rylands Library*, 58, 445–66.

2001. 'Stratford atte Bowe re-visited', *The Chaucer Review*, 36, 184–207.

Ruddick, A. 2013. *English identity and political culture in the fourteenth century*. Cambridge Studies in Medieval Life and Thought 4th Series 93. Cambridge: Cambridge University Press.

Russell, D. W. 2003. 'The Campsey collection of Old French saints' lives: A re-examination of its structure and provenance', *Scriptorium*, 57, 51–83.

2012. '"Sun num n'i vult dire a ore": Identity matters at Barking Abbey', *Barking Abbey and medieval literary culture: Authorship and authority in a female community*. Ed. J. N. Brown and D. A. Bussell. Woodbridge: Boydell and Brewer, 117–34.

2016. 'Matthew Paris, *La Vie de Saint Edmund, arcevesque de Canterbire/ The life of St Edmond, Archbishop of Canterbury*, 1250s', in *Vernacular literary theory*. Ed. J. Wogan-Browne, T. S. Fenster and D. W. Russell. Woodbridge: York Medieval Press, 120–27.

Sayers, J. and Watkiss, L., eds. 2003. *Thomas of Marlborough: History of the Abbey of Evesham*. Oxford Medieval Texts. Oxford: Clarendon Press.

Schipper, W. 2003. 'Style and layout of Anglo-Saxon manuscripts', in *Anglo-Saxon styles*. Ed. C. Karkov and G. Hardin Brown. Albany: State University of New York Press, 151–68.

Schulz, F. 1945. 'Bracton on kingship', *English Historical Review*, 60, 136–76.

Schmidt, P. G. 1978. *Visio Thurkilli relatore ut videtur Radulpho de Coggeshall*. Bibliotheca scriptorum Graecorum et Romanorum Teubneriana. Leipzig: Teubner.

Sekules, V. 2001. *Medieval art*. Oxford: Oxford University Press, 126–30.

Selwyn, P. M. 1997. 'Such speciall bookes of Mr Somersettes as were sould to Mr Secretary': The fate of Robert Glover's collections', in *Books and collectors, 1200–1700: Essays presented to Andrew Watson*. Ed. J. P. Carley and C. G. C. Tite. London: British Library, 389–401.

Sharpe, R. 1997. *A handlist of the Latin writers of Great Britain and Ireland before 1540*. Publications of the *Journal of Medieval Latin* 1. Turnhout: Brepols.

2003. *Titulus: Identifying medieval Latin texts*. Brepols: Turnhout.

Short, I. 1979–80. 'On bilingualism in Anglo-Norman England', *Romance Philology*, 33, 467–79.

2003. 'Language and literature', in *A companion to the Anglo-Norman world*. Ed. C. Harper-Bill and E. Van Houts. Woodbridge: Boydell, 191–21.

2010. 'Another look at "Le faus franceis"', *Nottingham Medieval Studies*, 54, 35–55.

2013. *Manual of Anglo-Norman* 2nd ed. Occasional Publication Series 8. Oxford: Anglo-Norman Text Society.

Signaroli, S. 2013. 'Isaac Casaubon and Matthew Paris', *Notes and Queries*, 6:1, 34–35.

Skelton, R. and Harvey, P. D. A. 1986. *Local maps and plans from medieval England*. Oxford: Oxford University Press.

Slater, L. 2018. 'Matthew Paris, Cecilia de Sanford and the early readership of the *Vie de Seint Auban*', in *Writing history in the Anglo-Norman world: Manuscripts, makers and readers, c. 1066–c. 1250*. Ed. L. Cleaver and A. Worm. Woodbridge: York Medieval Press, 189–212.

Smalley, B. 1974. *Historians in the Middle Ages*. London: Thames & Hudson.

Smith, A. L. 1913. *Church and state in the Middle Ages: The Ford Lectures delivered at Oxford in 1905*. Oxford: Clarendon Press.

Smith, B. 2001. 'Irish politics, 1220–1245', *Thirteenth-Century England*, 8, 13–22.

Smith, D. M. and London, V. C. M., eds. 2001. *The heads of religious houses: England and Wales, II. 1216–1377*. Cambridge: Cambridge University Press.

Smith, J. B. 2014. *Llywelyn ap Gruffudd: Prince of Wales*. 2nd ed. Cardiff: University of Wales Press.

Smith, T. 1696. *Catalogus librorum manuscriptorum bibliothecæ Cottonianæ*. Oxford: Sheldonian Theatre.

Southern, R. W. 1962. *Western views of Islam in the Middle Ages*. Cambridge, MA: Harvard University Press.

Spiegel, G. 1983. 'Genealogy: Form and function in medieval historical narrative', *History and Theory*, 22, 43–53.

Staniland, K. 1986. 'The nuptials of Alexander III of Scotland and Margaret Plantagenet', *Nottingham Medieval Studies*, 30, 20–45.

Steckel, S. 2015. 'Narratives of resistance: Arguments amongst the mendicants in the works of Matthew Paris and William of Saint-Amour', in *Authority and resistance in the age of Magna Carta: Proceedings of the Aberystwyth and Lampeter Conference.* Ed. J. Burton, P. Schofield and B. Weiler. Woodbridge: Boydell, 157–78.

Stehkämper, H. 1971. 'England und die Stadt Köln als Wahlmacher Ottos IV. (1198)', *Mitteilungen aus dem Stadtarchiv Köln*, 60, 213–44.

Stephenson, D. 2005. 'Potens et Prudens: Gruffudd ap Madog, Lord of Bromfield 1236–1269', *Welsh History Review*, 22, 409–31.

Stevenson, F. 1899. *Robert Grosseteste: Bishop of Lincoln.* London: Macmillan.

Stewart, S. 2000. 'What happened at Shere?', *Southern History*, 22, 1–20.

Stijnman, A. and Savage, E., eds. 2017. *Printing colour, 1400–1700: History, techniques, functions and receptions.* Leiden: Brill.

Stoneman, W. P., ed. 1999. *Dover Priory.* Corpus of British Medieval Library Catalogues 5. London: British Academy and British Library.

Stones, E. L. G. 1969–70. 'The appeal to history in Anglo–Scottish relations between 1291 and 1401. Part I', *Archives*, 9, 11–21.

Stones, E. L. G., ed. 1970. *Anglo–Scottish relations, 1174–1328: Some selected documents.* 2nd ed. Oxford: Clarendon Press.

Strickland, D. H. 2007.'The Jews, Leviticus and the unclean', in *Beyond the yellow badge: Anti-Judaism and Anti-Semitism in medieval and early modern visual culture.* Ed. M. B. Merback. Leiden: Brill, 203–32.

2022 'Antisemitism in medieval art', in *The Cambridge companion to anti-semitism.* Ed. S. Katz. Cambridge: Cambridge University Press, 248–70.

Strickland, M. 2016. *Henry, the Young King 1155–1183.* New Haven, CT: Yale University Press.

Stringer, K. J. 1994. 'Identities in thirteenth-century England: Frontier society in the far north', in *Social and political identities in western History.* Ed. C. Bjørn, A. Grant and K. J. Stringer. Copenhagen: Academic Press, 28–66.

Summerson, H. 1992. 'The king's *clericulus*': The life and career of Silvester of Everdon, bishop of Carlisle 1247–1254', *Northern History*, 28, 84–85.

Summit, J. 2008. *Memory's library: Medieval books in early modern England.* Chicago, IL: University of Chicago Press.

Talbert, R. J. A. 2010. *Rome's world: The Peutinger map reconsidered.* Cambridge: Cambridge University Press.

Taylor, A. 2017. 'Recalling Anglo–Scottish relations in 1291: Historical knowledge, monastic memory, and the Edwardian inquests', *Thirteenth Century England*, 16, 173–206.

Taylor, A. J. 1979. 'Edward I and the shrine of St Thomas of Canterbury', *Journal of the British Archaeological Association*, 3rd series 132, 22–28.

Taylor, J. 1968. *The universal chronicle of Ranulf Higden.* Oxford: Oxford University Press.

Temple, E. 1976. *Anglo-Saxon manuscripts 900–1066.* A Survey of Manuscripts Illuminated in the British Isles 2. London: Harvey Miller.

Thompson, E. M. 1912. *An introduction to Greek and Latin palaeography.* Oxford: Oxford University Press.

Thompson, S. 1991. *Women religious: The founding of English nunneries after the Norman Conquest.* Oxford: Oxford University Press, 56–61.

Thomson, R. M. 1978. 'The 'scriptorium' of William of Malmesbury', in *Medieval scribes, manuscripts and libraries: Essays presented to N. R. Ker.* Ed. M. B. Parkes and A. G. Watson. London: Scolar Press, 117–42.

1982. *Manuscripts from St Albans Abbey 1066–1235.* 2 vols. Cambridge: D. S. Brewer.

2011. *A descriptive catalogue of the medieval manuscripts of Corpus Christi College Oxford.* Cambridge: D. S. Brewer.

Thomson, R. M. with Clark, J. G. 2015. *The university and college libraries of Oxford.* Corpus of British Medieval Library Catalogues 16. London: British Library and British Academy.

Thomson, S. H. 1940. *The writings of Robert Grosseteste, bishop of Lincoln, 1235–1253.* Cambridge: Cambridge University Press.

Thomson, W. R. 1977. 'The image of the mendicants in the chronicles of Matthew Paris', *Archivum Franciscanum Historicum*, 70, 3–34.

Tierney, B. 1965. 'Bracton on government,' *Speculum*, 38, 295–317.

Tite, C .G. C. 1994. *The manuscript library of Sir Robert Cotton.* London: British Library.

2003. *The early records of Sir Robert Cotton's Library: Formation, cataloguing, use.* London: British Library.

Tolan, J. V. 1986. *Medieval Christian perceptions of Islam.* New York: Garland.

Tout, T. F. 1916. 'The Westminster Chronicle attributed to Robert of Reading', *English Historical Review*, 31, 450–64.

Townsend, D. and Rigg, A. G., 1987. 'Medieval Latin poetic anthologies (V): Matthew Paris' anthology of Henry of Avranches (Cambridge, University Library MS. Dd.11.78)', *Mediaeval Studies*, 49, 352–90.

Treharne, R. F. 1962. *The baronial plan of reform 1258–63.* Manchester: Manchester University Press.

Tremlett, T. D. and Stanford London, H., eds. 1967. *Rolls of arms, Henry III: The Matthew Paris Shields, c. 1244–59.* London: Society of Antiquaries.

Trotter, D. 2011. 'The (socio)linguistics of cross-channel communication', *Thirteenth-Century England*, 13, 117–32.

Tschichold, J. 1928. *Die neue Typographie: Ein Handbuch für zeitgemäss Schaffende.* Berlin: Bildungsverband der deutschen Buchdrucker.

Tyler, E. 2009. 'From Old English to Old French', in *Language and culture in medieval Britain: The French of England, c. 1100–c. 1300.* Ed. J. Wogan-Browne with C. Collette, M. Kowaleski, L. Mooney, A. Putter and D. Trotter. Woodbridge: York Medieval Press, 164–78.

Uglow, J. 2008. *Words and pictures: Writers, artists and a peculiarly British tradition*. London: Faber.

van der Horst, K., Noel, W. and Wüstefeld, W. C. M., eds. 1996. *The Utrecht Psalter in Medieval art: Picturing the Psalms of David*. Studies in Medieval & Early Renaissance Art History 19. Tuurdijk: HES Publishers, BV.

Vaughan, R. 1953a. 'The election of abbots of St Albans in the thirteenth and fourteenth centuries', *Proceedings of the Cambridge Antiquarian Society*, 47, 1–12.

    1953b 'The handwriting of Matthew Paris', *Transactions of the Cambridge Bibliographical Society*, 1, 376–94.

    1958a. 'The chronicle attributed to John of Wallingford', Camden Miscellany, 21. London: Royal Historical Society.

    1958b. 'The chronicle of John of Wallingford', *English Historical Review*, 73, 66–77.

    1958c. *Matthew Paris*. Cambridge: Cambridge University Press.

    1986. *Chronicles of Matthew Paris: Monastic life in the thirteenth century*. Gloucester: Alan Sutton.

Verstraten, F. 2003. 'Both king and vassal: Feidhlim Ua Conchobair of Connacht, 1230–65', *Journal of the Galway Archaeological and Historical Society*, 55, 13–37.

Vincent, N. 1996. *Peter des Roches: An alien in English politics 1205–1238*. Cambridge: Cambridge University Press.

    2001. *The Holy Blood*. Cambridge: Cambridge University Press.

Vising, J. 1923. *Anglo-Norman language and literature*. Language and Literature Series. London: Oxford University Press, Humphrey Milford.

Wagner, A. R. 1950. *A catalogue of English mediaeval rolls of arms*. London: Boydell.

Wakelin, D. 2017. *Designing English: Early literature on the page*. Oxford: Bodleian Library.

Walker, J. A. 1990. *Design history and the history of design*. London: Pluto Press.

Warner, G. 1928. *The Guthlac Roll*. Oxford: Roxburghe Club.

Warner, G. F. and Gilson, J. P., ed. 1921. *Catalogue of Western manuscripts in the Old Royal and King's Collections (Vols. 1–4)*. London: British Museum.

Watson, A. G. 1962. Sir Robert Cotton and Sir Simonds D'Ewes: An exchange of manuscripts. *The British Museum Quarterly*, 25:1/2, 19–24.

    1969. *The manuscripts of Henry Savile of Banke*. London: Bibliographical Society.

    1979. *Catalogue of dated and datable manuscripts, c. 700–1600, in the Department of Manuscripts, the British Library (Vols. 1–2)*. London: British Library.

Webber, T. 2007. 'L'écriture des documents en Angleterre au XIIe siècle', *Bibliothèque de l'École des Chartes*, 165, 139-65.

Webster, H. 2020. '*The Annals of Dunstable Priory*. From living memory to written record in a thirteenth-century textual community', *Journal of Medieval Monastic Studies*, 9, 147-73.

Weiler, B. 2000, 'Matthew Paris, Richard of Cornwall's candidacy for the German throne, and the Sicilian business', *Journal of Medieval History*, 26, 71-92.

2001. 'Henry III and the Sicilian business: A reinterpretation', *Historical Research*, 74, 127-50.

2008. 'Stupor Mundi: Matthäus Paris und die zeitgenössische Wahrnehmung Friedrichs II. in England', in *Herrschafsträume, Herrschaftspraxis und Kommunikation zur Zeit Kaiser Friedrichs II*. Ed. K. Görich, J. Keupp and T. Broekmann. Munich: Herbert Utz, 63-95.

2009. 'Matthew Paris on the writing of history, *Journal of Medieval History*, 35, 254-78.

2012. 'Matthew Paris in Norway', *Revue Benedictine*, 122, 153-81.

2018. 'History, prophecy and the apocalypse in the chronicles of Matthew Paris', *English Historical Review*, 133, 253-83.

2019. 'Historical writing in medieval Britain: The case of Matthew Paris', in *Medieval historical writing: Britain and Ireland, 500-1500*. Ed. E. M. Tyler, E. Steiner and J. Jahner. Cambridge: Cambridge University Press, 319-38.

Weiler, B. and Rowlands, I., eds. 2002. *England and Europe in the reign of Henry III (1216-1272)*. Aldershot: Ashgate.

Weiss, J. 2013. 'The itinerary and Palestine maps of Matthaeus Parisiensis: New input to a never-ending Discussion', in *Understanding different geographies*. Ed. K. Kriz, W. Cartwright and M. Kinberger. Berlin: Springer, 243-52.

Weiss, M. 2012. 'Text und bild. Lehrformen des Matthaus Paris in den *Chronica Majora*', *Das Mittelalter: Perspecktiven mediavistischer*, 17: 1, 66-75.

2017. 'M[atthaeus] Parisiensis, hujus scriptor libelli. Die Konstruktion des Matthaeus Parisiensis in den "Chronica maiora"'. In *Sprechen, Schreiben, Handeln: Interdisziplinäre Beiträge zur Performativität mittelalterlicher Texte* Ed. A. Bostelmann, D. Brandt, K. Skottki and H. B. Waxmann. Munster: Waxmann, 183-99.

2018. *Die Chronica maiora des Matthaeus Parisiensis*. Trierer historische Forschungen, 73 Trier: Kliomedia.

Weiss, R. 1945. 'Piero del Monte, John Whethamstede', *English Historical Review*, 60, 399-406.

Westrem, S. 2001. *The Hereford Map: A transcription and translation of the legends with commentary*. Terrarum orbis 1. Brepols: Turnhout.

Wild, B. J. 2012. 'Royal finance under King Henry III: The wardrobe evidence', *Economic History Review*, 65:4, 1380-1402.

Williams, D. 1991. 'Matthew Paris and the prospect of Asia', in *England in the thirteenth century: Proceedings of the 1989 Harlaxton Symposium*, ed. W. M. Ormrod. Harlaxton Medieval Studies 1. Stamford: Paul Watkins, 51–67.

Williams, G. A. 1962–64. 'The succession to Gwynedd, 1238–47', *Bulletin of the Board of Celtic Studies*, 20, 393–413.

Williel, R. T. 1977. 'The image of the mendicants in the chronicles of Matthew Paris', *Archivum Franciscanum Historicum*, 70, 3–34.

Wogan-Browne, J. 1994. 'Wreaths of Thyme: The female translator in Anglo-Norman hagiography', in *The Medieval Translator* 4. Ed. R. Ellis and R. Evans. Exeter: University of Exeter Press, 46–65.

  2001. *Saints' lives and women's literary culture: Virginity and its authorizations*. Oxford: Oxford University Press.

  2015. 'Competing archives, competing histories: French and its cultural locations in late medieval England', *Speculum*, 90:3, 653–73.

  2016. '*Faus franceis* and *dreit engleis*: On language', in *Vernacular literary theory from the French of England: Texts and translations, c. 1120–c. 1450*. Ed. and trans. J. Wogan-Browne, T. Fenster and D. Russell . Cambridge: D. S. Brewer, 9–25.

Wogan-Browne, J. with C. Collette, M. Kowaleski, L. Mooney, A. Putter and D. Trotter 2009. 'General introduction: What's in a name? The French of England', in *Language and culture in medieval Britain: The French of England, c. 1100–c. 1300*. Woodbridge: York Medieval Press, 1–14.

Wogan-Browne J., and Fenster, T. S., eds. 2010. *The life of Saint Alban by Matthew Paris*. Tempe: Arizona Center for Medieval & Renaissance Studies.

Wogan-Browne J., Fenster, T. S. and Russell, D. W., eds. 2016. *Vernacular literary theory from the French of medieval England: Texts and translations, c. 1120–c. 1450*. Woodbridge: D. S. Brewer.

Wolf, G. and Kessler, H., eds. 1998. *The holy face and paradox of representation: Papers from a symposium held at the Bibliotheca Hertziana, Rome and the Villa Spelman, Florence, 1996*. Bologna: Nuova Alfa.

Wood, D. 2002. *Medieval economic thought*. Cambridge: Cambridge University Press.

Wood, I. 2009. 'Germanus, Alban and Auxerre', *Bulletin du centre d'études médiévales d'Auxerre*, 13, 1–6.

Woodcock, T., Chesshyre, D. H. B., Grant, J., Graham, I. and Flower, S., eds. 1992–2014. *Dictionary of British arms*. 4 vols. London: Society of Antiquaries.

Wormald, F. G. 1926. 'The drawings of Matthew Paris', *Walpole Society*, 14, 18–21.

  1942–43. 'More Matthew Paris drawings', *Walpole Society*, 31, 109–12. Reprinted in his *Collected writings II: Studies in English and Continental art of the late Middle Ages*. Ed. J. J. G. Alexander, T. J. Brown and J. Gibbs. London: Harvey Miller, 1988, 70–74.

1946. 'More Matthew Paris drawings', *Walpole Society*, 31, 109–12.

1952. 'Some illustrated manuscripts of the lives of the saints', *Bulletin of the John Rylands Library*, 35:1, 248–66.

1953. *English drawings of the tenth and eleventh centuries*. New York: Praeger.

Woudhuysen, H. R. 1996. *Sir Philip Sidney and the circulation of manuscripts, 1558–1640*. Oxford: Clarendon Press.

Wright, C. E. 1951. The dispersal of the monastic libraries and the beginnings of Anglo-Saxon studies: Matthew Parker and his circle. A preliminary study. *Transactions of the Cambridge Bibliographical Society*, 1:3, 208–37.

Wright, S. 2004. 'Aglionby Edward (1520–1591?)', in *Oxford Dictionary of National Biography*. Oxford: Oxford University Press.

Young, A. 1997. *Robert the Bruce's rivals: The Comyns, 1212–1314*. East Linton: Tuckwell Press.

Zink, M. 2011. 'Préface', in *Translations médiévales: Cinq siècles de traductions en français au Moyen Age*. 3 vols. Ed. C. Galderisi. Brepols: Turnhout.

Zöllner, E. 1966. 'Das Projekt einer babenbergischen Heirat König Heinrichs III von England', *Archiv für Österreichische Geschichte*, 125: 54–75.

Zutshi, P. N. R. 2018. Images of Franciscans and Dominicans in a manuscript of Alexander Nequam's *Florilegium* (Cambridge University Library, MS Gg.6.42)', in *The Franciscan order in the medieval English province and beyond*. Ed. M. Robson and P. N. R. Zutshi. Amsterdam: Amsterdam University Press, 51–66.

Unpublished dissertations

Coatesworth, J. 2021. 'The historians and historiography of St Albans Abbey, 1200–1600'. University of Manchester, PhD.

Ellis, J. O. 1952. 'Gaston de Béarn: A study in Anglo–Gascon relations, 1229–90'. University of Oxford, DPhil.

García, M. M. 2018. 'The script of Matthew Paris and his collaborators: A digital approach'. King's College London, PhD.

Greasley, N., 2018. 'Matthew Paris's networks of information'. Aberystwyth University, PhD.

Reader, R., 1994, 'Matthew Paris and Anglo-Saxon England'. University of Durham, PhD thesis.

Index

Abel Valdemarsen, duke of Schleswig and king of Denmark (1250–52), 91
Aberdeen
  bishopric of, 158
Abgar, king of Edessa (d. 50), 91
Acre, 20, 244, 250–51, 272
Adam, cellarer of St Albans Abbey (fl. 12th cent.), 24
Æthelbert, king of Kent (589–616), 126
Æthelred II, king of England (978–1013, 1014–16), 10, 293
Ælfric, 343
Aelred of Rievaulx (d. 1167), 162, 279, 281, 283, 360
  De genealogia regum Anglorum, 360
  Genealogica regum Anglorum, 281, 283
  Vita Edwardi Confessoris, 281
  Vita Sancti Edwardi, 279
Agar, Michelle, 373
Agarde, Arthur (1540–1615), 345, 355, 357
Aglionby, Edward (1520–91?), 316, 318, 320, 323, 332, 341, 343, 353
Alan de la Zouche (d. 1270), justiciar of Ireland (1256–58), 150

Alan of Galloway (1190–1234), lord of Galloway, constable of Scotland, 149
Alban, St, 'protomartyr' of England, 7, 10–11, 41, 46, 73, 84, 107, 120–21, 145, 161, 167, 169–72, 174–76, 178–80, 182–89, 191–92, 195, 204–5, 256, 275, 277–79, 286, 290–91, 308, 311–14, 322, 330, 332, 336, 354, 368, 370, 372
d'Albert, Honoré (1802–67), 8th duc de Luynes, 326
Albigensian crusade, 103
Albigensians, 104, 114, 116
Aldenham (Hertfordshire), manor of, 84
Alexander de Stavenby, bishop of Coventry and Lichfield (1224–38), 71
Alexander II, king of Scotland (1214–49), 147–48, 150–52, 154–56
Alexander III, king of Scotland (1249–86), 62, 63, 145, 148, 151, 153–54, 157–58, 242
Alexander of Langley, monk of St Albans Abbey, 13
Alexander the Great, 114, 184, 283

Alexis of Rome (4th cent.), St, 10
  Life of, 28, 179–80, 193–94, 297
Alfonso X, king of Castile (1252–84), 92, 102
Alfred of Beverley (fl. 12th cent.), sacrist of Beverley, chronicler, 160
Alfred the Great, king of Wessex (871–99), 226
Alice de Lusignan (1224–56), countess of Surrey, 79
Al-Malik al-Kamil Nasir ad-Din Muhammad, 4th Ayyubid sultan of Egypt (1218–38), 93–94, 98–100, 103
Allington, George, 356
Amphibalus, co-martyr with Alban, 7, 10–11, 24, 110, 120–21, 169, 171, 178, 180, 183, 186, 195, 204, 290–91, 308, 312–13, 317, 330, 336, 354
Anglo-Saxon heptarchy, viii, 211–13, 215–17, 224, 226, 230, 308
Anglo-Norman language, 277, 287
Anketil, monk of St Albans Abbey, goldsmith, 195
Apollo, Roman god of music, 285
Arianism, 103
Armenia, 100, 111
  Armenians, 100
Arthur, legendary king of the Britons, 1, 160, 185, 284, 308, 310, 315, 342
Articuli Cleri (1314), 138
Ashburnham House, 347, 358
Asia Minor, 91
Asser, Bishop of Sherborne (c. 890–c. 909), 343
Athens, archbishop of, 91
Atkinson, Robert, 286
Alberic of Trois-Fontaines (d. c. 1252), 134
Augustinian monastic congregation, 276

Austria
  dukes of, 101, 115
Austrian National Library, Vienna, 252
Auxerre, bishop of, 135
Aymer of Valence (c.1222–60), bishop of Winchester (1250–60), 125

Backhouse, Janet, 350
Baker, A. T., 286
Baldwin de Redvers (1236–62), 7th earl of Devon (1245–62), 157
Baldwin de Vere of Addington (d. 1277), 78
Bale, John (1495–1563), Carmelite friar, bishop of Ossory (1552–53), 1–2, 195, 317–18, 322, 340, 342–43, 363
  Actes of the Votaryes, 317
Balliol, John (c. (1249–1314)), king of Scots (1292–96), 149
Bancroft, Richard (1544–1610), archbishop of Canterbury (1604–10), 356–57
Bannockburn, battle of (1314), 310–11
Barking Abbey (Essex), 17, 275
Barnabas, St, 68
Baronius, Caesar (1538–1607), cardinal priest of the Roman church, 345
Bartlett, Robert, 91
Basing, John (d. 1252), archdeacon of Leicester, 16
Basset, Fulk, bishop of London (1241–59), 121–22
Basset, Gilbert (d. 1241), 61
Baswell, Christopher, 184, 190, 192, 275, 282
Bately, Janet, 209
Bavaria
  dukes of, 101

Beale, Robert Beale (d. 1601), clerk to the Privy Council, 321–22
Beatrice (*c.* 1229–57), countess of Provence (1245–57), 76, 79
'Becket leaves', 176, 201–2, 205–6, 277, 279, 282
Becket, Thomas (1119/20–70), archbishop of Canterbury (1162–70), 7–8, 11, 107, 120, 145, 161, 169, 175, 178–79, 201–2, 204–6, 254, 275–77, 295, 300, 308, 337, 350, 354
Quadrilogus, life of, 282
Bede of Monkwearmouth (d. 735), xiii, 4, 41, 61, 306, 328
Bedford Castle, 16
Bedfordshire, 316, 332
Bellarmine, Robert (1542–1621), Cardinal, 345
Belvoir Priory (Leicestershire), 24
Benedict of Nursia, St (d. *c.* 547), 18, 108, 305
Benedict of Peterborough (d. 1193) Life of Thomas Becket, 294–95, 300
Benedictine order, i, xiii, 12, 17–18, 20–21, 25, 50, 68, 78, 84–85, 106, 108, 111, 117, 135–36, 149, 197, 272–73, 328, 337
Bernard of Clairvaux (1090–1153), 18, 268
Bernardus Silvestris (fl. 1148), philosopher, 16, 364
Bery, William, 357
Bethlehem, 250
Bible, 76, 91, 104, 109, 246, 250, 256, 260, 269, 339
Bible, Vulgate, 364
Bigod, Hugh (1211–66), justiciar of England (1258–60), 53
Bigod, Roger (*c.* 1209–70), 4th earl of Norfolk (1233–70), 152, 154, 164, 311
Bisset, Margaret (1179–1232), 19

Bisset, Walter (d. 1251), lord of Aboyne, 154–55, 159
Blacman, John (d. 1485), chaplain, 313
Bohn's Antiquarian Library, 326
Boniface of Savoy (*c.*1207–70), archbishop of Canterbury (1241–70), 45, 121, 124–25, 129, 135
Boreman, Richard, abbot of St Albans (1538–39), 341, 355
Brand, Paul, 53, 66
Bréholles, Jean-Louis Huillard (1817–71), historian, xiv
Bretache, John, 78
Brito, Geoffrey de, 350
Brown, Michelle, 190
Brut, Anglo Norman prose, 159
Brutus, 144–45
Burke, Edmund, MP (1729–97), 325
Abridgment of English History, 325
Burton-on-Trent Abbey (Staffordshire), 80
Bury St Edmund's Abbey, 10, 13, 20, 24–25, 57, 64, 72, 122, 273, 297, 301, 304, 306
Byzantines, 93, 98, 103, 109

Caesar, Julius (100–44 BCE), 76, 184
Cambridge
  Corpus Christi College, Cambridge, Parker Library, 220, 230–31, 323, 343–44, 369
  King's College, 316
  University Library, 175
Cambridgeshire, 15
Camden, William (1552–1623), antiquarian, 357
Campsey Abbey (Suffolk), 276, 309, 330
Canterbury
  archbishopric of, 7, 204, 229, 282

Cathedral Priory, 11, 21, 119, 121, 124–26, 133, 135, 161, 176, 182, 192, 194, 201, 253–54, 273, 309, 317–18, 323, 343
   city of, 322
   St Augustine's Abbey, 25
Carnegie Corporation of New York, 368
Caroline minuscule, 259–60, 268
Carpenter, David, 75
Carter, Deirdre, 183
cartography, xiv, 218, 244–45, 248, 259
Casaubon, Isaac (1559–1614), 345, 357
Castile, 240, 276
Cathars, 116
Catharine of Aragon (d. 1536), queen of England (1509–33), 314
Cato the Younger (d. 46 BCE), Roman senator, 77
Catton, Robert, abbot of St Albans (1530–36), 316
Caursines, 77, 127, 141
   moneylenders, 121, 123, 127
Cecil, William (1520–98), 1st baron Burghley, 233, 318–21, 323, 343
Cecil, Thomas (fl. 1626–40), 2, 323
Cecilia de Sanford, 19, 337, 354
Celtic language, 175
Chanson de Roland, 285–86, 289–91, 300
chansons de geste, 87, 279, 283, 285, 287–93, 296, 299
Charlemagne, Emperor of the Franks (800–814), 91, 95, 114, 283–84, 291, 299, 326
Charles I, king of England (1625–49), 322, 345
Chartier, Roger, 209
Chartwell (Kent), 37
Chaucer, Geoffrey (d. 1400), English poet, xiii

Cheshire, 15
Chester, 40, 150, 253, 255
Chetham's Library, Manchester, 210, 213, 220, 369
Chetwode, Bryn, 365
Chichester
   bishopric of, 11, 71, 110, 122, 124–25
   cathedral of, 110
Christina of Markyate (d. *c*. 1155), recluse, abbess of Markyate, 19, 24
Chroniques anglo-normandes, 283
Churchill, Sir Winston (1874–1965), Prime Minister (1940–45, 1951–55), 37
Cicero, Roman orator, philosopher (d. 43 BCE), 2
Cinthius the Roman, 128
Cistercian order, 18, 21, 110, 120, 123, 253, 307
Clerkenwell, 38
Cluniac, Benedictine congregation, 82
Cnut, king of England (1016–35), 24, 284–85, 292
Coggeshall Abbey (Essex), 72
Colker, Marvin L., 190, 372
Collard, Judith, 183, 186
Cologne
   archbishops of, 100
Columba, St (521–97), monk, 156
Colwell, Mr, 356
Comestor, Peter (d. 1179), 13, 20, 22, 31, 269, 359
   Historia scholastica of, 30, 340, 359
Comons, Christfar, 357
Comyn, Walter, earl of Menteith (1234–58), 150, 155, 158, 165
Connaught, 146
Coningsby, Humphrey II (d. 1599), 316
Conyngesby, John, 316, 341, 355

Cordoba, 102
Cornwall, 15, 36, 76, 115, 158, 251, 337, 354
Cotton, Sir John (1621–1702), 345
Cotton, Sir Robert (1570/71–1631), 1st baronet of Connington, 213, 217, 323, 335, 342, 345–49, 351–52, 355–59
    Cotton House, 347
    Cotton Library, 323, 356–58
    Cotton World Map, 251
Cotton, Sir Thomas (1594–1662), 323, 345
count of Flanders, Robert II (c. 1065–1111), 360
Coventry
    bishopric of, 71
Coxe, Henry Octavius (1811–81), 348
Crassus, Roman, 73
Crowland Abbey (Lincolnshire), 193
Crusades
    'Shepherds', 116
Cuthbert of Lindisfarne, St (d. 684), 10–11, 179–80, 191, 193
Cynthryth, queen of Mercia (d. after 798), 79

D'Ewes, Sir Simonds (1602–50), 345, 356
Dafydd ap Llywelyn, king of Gwynedd (1240–46), 146, 149, 152–54, 156, 161
Damascus, 246
Damietta, Siege of (1218–19), 98
Darius the Great (c. 550–c. 486 BCE), 76
David, biblical king, 184
David I, king of Scotland (1124–53), 314
de Hamel, Christopher, 350
De la Mare, Thomas, abbot of St Albans (1349–96), 311
Dead Sea, 246–47, 250

Dee, John (1527–1609), 319, 341, 355, 368
Derolez, Albert, 260
Devizes Castle (Wiltshire), 71
Devon, county of, 157
Diceto, Ralph de (d. c. 1202), dean of St Paul's cathedral and chronicler, 224–25
    Abbrevationes chronicorum, 224
    Ymagines historiarium, 224
Doležalová, Lucie, 209
Dolte, William, monk of Wymondham, 355
Dominican order, 64, 103–4, 106, 110, 310
Donatism, 103
Donatus, Aelius (315–80), Roman grammarian, 16
Dublin
    archbishopric of, 146
    canons of, 162
    Trinity College, 7, 167, 189, 275, 277, 279, 355, 368, 374
Dunstable Priory (Bedfordshire), 26, 32, 72, 166, 169, 175, 278, 337, 354, 361
Durham
    bishopric of, 314
    Cathedral Priory, 20, 55, 75, 179–80, 191, 309, 330
Durward, Alan (d. 1275), 158

Eadmer of Canterbury (d. c. 1126), 323
Eadwine, 192
Eadwine Psalter, 176, 192–93
Ealdred, abbot of St Albans, 182, 194
East Anglia, 12, 211
Ebstorf Abbey (Lower Saxony), 249
Ebstorf map, 250
Edgar, king of England (959–75), 151
Edith of Wessex, queen of England (1045–66), 79

Edmund of Abingdon (c. 1174–1240), archbishop of Canterbury (1233–40), 7, 11, 15, 18–19, 21, 61, 63, 70, 74, 81, 107, 110, 119–21, 126, 128, 132, 145, 161, 191, 204–5, 273, 275, 282, 309, 346
Edmund 'Ironside', king of the English (1016), 285, 292
Edmund, called 'Crouchback' (1245–96), 1st earl of Leicester, Lancaster and Derby, 94, 105
Edmund, king of the East Angles (855–69), martyr and saint, 10, 13, 20, 24, 72, 145, 179, 282, 284–85, 292
  Life of, 179
Edward I, king of England (1272–1307), 41, 45, 52, 59, 73, 97, 129, 156–57, 159–60, 165, 248, 277, 305, 307–9, 319
Edward II, king of England (1307–27), 217, 310–11
Edward the Confessor, king of England (1042–66), 7–8, 11, 49, 68, 72–73, 76, 79, 86, 93, 95, 97, 107, 121, 129, 140, 145, 161, 169, 175–76, 179, 204–5, 274–76, 280–81, 283–85, 292, 304, 308, 337, 354
  Vita Ædwardi regis, 72
Edward VI, king of England (1547–53), 317
Egypt, 93, 98–99, 124
Eleanor of Provence (c. 1223–91), queen of England (1236–72), 69, 72, 79, 92, 127, 153, 205, 242, 276, 288, 304, 337
Eleanor, countess of Leicester (d. 1275), 354
Elisabeth of Thuringia (1207–31), 30, 110
Elizabeth I, queen of England (1558–1603), 229, 318

Ely (Cambridgeshire), 10
Elyas le Evesk, Jew accused of crimes, 54
Emir, 82
Emma of Normandy (1002–35), queen consort of the English, 293
Eric IV, king of Denmark (1241–50), 91, 110
Essex, 211, 253
Edmund of Abingdon (c. 1174–1240), archbishop of Canterbury (1233–40), 119, 191
Etty, Claire, 160
Eustace of Fauconberg (1170–1228), bishop of London (1221–28), 71
Eustace IV (c. 1130–53), count of Boulogne (1146–53), 120, 132
Eustace of Faversham, hagiographer, 119
Eustace the Monk (d. 1217), mercenary and outlaw, 77
Evesham Abbey (Worcestershire), 25, 31

Falkes de Breauté (d. 1226), soldier, 71, 78
Feidhlim Ua Conchobair, king of Connacht (d. 1265), 162
Fenster, Thelma, 287
Ferdinand III, king of Castile (1217–52), 102, 110, 114
Ferrers, Edward (1524/27–1564), 357
Ferrers, Henry (1550–1633), 357
Fielding, Henry (1707–54), novelist, 324
  Amelia, 324
Fifth Crusade (1217–21), 20, 98, 115
First Barons' War (1215–17), 24, 309
Firth of Forth, 147
Fitzalan, Henry (d. 1580), 12th earl of Arundel, 320, 340, 363
Fitzwalter, Robert (d. 1235), 84
Fitzwilliam, Adam (d. 1238), king's escheator, 83

Flanders, 116
Flesher, Miles, printer, 322
Four Cantrefs of Wales, 150
Foxe, Edward (c. 1496–1538), bishop of Hereford (1535–38), 314–15
France, 13, 37, 39, 55, 57–58, 67, 73, 77, 91, 93, 106, 116, 193–94, 205, 248–49, 270, 274–75, 360
Franciscan order, 19, 57, 64, 104, 106, 122, 126
Frederick Barbarossa, Holy Roman Emperor (1155–90), 113
Frederick II, Holy Roman Emperor (1220–50), 70, 73, 77, 92–94, 96, 98, 100–2, 112, 114–16
French, 112–13
French language, xiv, 4–5, 7–8, 16, 26, 42, 82, 84, 90, 169, 174–76, 188, 240, 250, 257, 272–83, 287, 291–98, 304, 308, 312, 326, 328, 338, 369
Frère Angier, 338
friars, 16, 21, 43, 45, 63, 82, 104, 106, 109, 122, 134
Friars of the Cross, religious order, 134
Fuller, Thomas (1608–61), historian, 15, 324
Anglorum speculum or the worthies of England in church and state (1662), 324

Gaelic language, 146–47, 149
Galbraith, V. H., 32–33, 40, 60–61
Galloway, 145–47, 149, 155–56, 161–63
Galwegians, 147
Gascony, 38–39, 165
Genevieve (d. 502/12), Gaulish saint, 172–74, 291
Geoffrey de Gorron, abbot of St Albans Abbey (1119–46), 22
Geoffrey de Lizzino, 81

Geoffrey de Lusignan (d. 1274), lord of Jarnac, 35
Geoffrey of Monmouth (d. c. 1155), 31, 144, 146, 269, 320, 336, 339, 360
De gestis Britonum, 336, 360
Historia regum Britanniae, 144, 146, 160
George I, king of England (1714–27), 354
Germanus of Auxerre, bishop of Autissiodorum (d. c. 448), 171–74, 191
Germany, 77, 91, 96, 101, 158, 252, 284
Gerona, bishop of, 101
Gervase of Canterbury (d. c. 1210), chronicler, 301
Gibbon, Edward (1707–70), 325–26
History of the Decline and Fall of the Roman Empire, 325
Giessen (Hesse), 134
Gilbert de Umfraville (d. 1245), lord of Redesdale and baron Prudhoe, 78
Marshal, Gilbert (d. 1241), 4th earl of Pembroke, 78
Gildas, 343, 360
Historia Britonum, 360
Giles, John (1808–84), 326
Gillis, John, 370
Glastonbury Abbey (Somerset), 12, 302, 315
Glover, Robert (1544–88), 322, 333, 342, 358
Godwin, earl of Wessex (d. 1053), 285
Gough map of Britain, 252
Greece, 91
Greek language, 16, 104
Green, John Richard (1837–83), historian, 327
Short history of the English people, 327
Greenwich, 340

Gregory I, Roman pope (590–604), 131, 338
Gregory IX, Roman pope (1227–41), 21, 99, 108, 136
Grosseteste, Robert (1168/70–1253), bishop of Lincoln (1235–53), 14, 16, 19, 57, 71, 104–5, 108, 115, 122, 125, 127, 135–37, 141–43, 304, 340, 359
  De probatione uirginitatis beate Marie, 359
  Testamenta duodecim patriarcharum, 14, 359
Gruffydd ap Madog (d. 1236), lord Bromfield, 161
Gunnilda of Denmark, queen of Germany (1036–38), 95
Guthlac Roll, 182, 193–94
Guy of Warwick, 78
Gwynedd, 146, 152, 159
  princes of, 146

Haddington (East Lothian), 154
Hahn, Cynthia, 177, 184, 186–87, 191–92
Hailes Abbey (Gloucestershire), 20, 70
Håkon IV, king of Norway (1217–63), 69, 86, 95, 156, 242
Hallam, Henry (1777–1859), 325–26
Hampton Court (Middlesex), 340
Hanover (Lower Saxony), 249
Harden, 287
Harding, Caroline, 371
Hardy, Thomas Duffus, deputy keeper of public records (1861–78), 257–58
Harold, king of England (1066), 140
Harpsfield, John (1516–78), dean of Norwich Cathedral (1558–59), 317

Harpsfield, Nicholas (1519–75), archdeacon of Canterbury (1554–59), 317, 332
  Historica Anglicana ecclesiastica of, 317
Hawks, Katie, 216
Hellinga, Lotte, 209
Henry V, king of England (1413–22), 312
Henry of Avranches (d. 1260), poet, 16, 269, 338, 353
Henry de Kirkstede, monk of Bury St Edmund's, 306
  Catalogus of, 306
Henry Fitzalan (1512–80), 12th earl of Arundel, 315
Henry Frederick, prince of Wales (1594–1612), 341, 361, 363
Henry I, king of England (1100–35), 109, 314–15
Henry II, king of England (1154–89), 201–4, 206, 225, 314, 331
Henry III, king of England (1216–72), 1, 10, 17, 37–39, 44–46, 51, 53, 58, 59, 63, 68–69, 71, 73–83, 86, 92–94, 97, 99–100, 102, 105–7, 115, 120, 123, 127–29, 140–41, 144–46, 150–53, 155–57, 166–67, 187, 198, 205, 242, 247, 276, 304–5, 310, 322, 324, 338, 352
Henry of Bath (d. 1260), chief justice of common pleas (1245–51, 1256–58), 84
Henry of Huntington (d. *c.* 1157), chronicler, 227
Henry the Young King (1155–83), 201, 205
Henry VI, king of England (1422–61, 1470–71), 167, 189, 313, 337
Henry VIII, king of England (1509–47), 1, 26, 314–15, 340
Herakles, 184–85

heraldry, 8, 185, 211, 225–26, 238, 240–43, 240
Herbert of Bosham (d. 1194), clerk, 206
Hereford
　Cathedral, 249
　World Map, 249–51
Heribert, archbishop of Cologne (999–1021), 115
Higden, Ranulf (d. 1364), monk of Chester, chronicler, 160, 307, 310, 313
　Polychronicon of, 2, 310, 313, 331
Higham Gobion (Bedfordshire), 332
Hildegard of Bingen (d. 1179), abbess of Disibodenberg, 30, 110
Hodgkinson, Richard, printer, 322
Holt, J. C., 38
Holy Blood, relic of, 45, 60, 68, 72–73, 110, 308, 313, 338
Holy Land, 68–69, 78, 99–100, 102, 105–7, 109, 111, 130, 155, 244, 246–48, 250–51, 272
Honnecourt, Villard de, artist (fl. 13th cent.), 350
Howard, Philip, 13th earl of Arundel (1557–95), 355
Howden, Roger (d. 1202), chronicler, 75
Hubert de Burgh (1170–1243), earl of Kent (1227–43), 71, 77, 82, 96, 322
Hugh de Pateshull, bishop of Coventry and Lichfield (1239–41), 81
Hugh Neville (d. 1234), chief forester, 78
Hugh of St Victor (d. 1141), 22
Huillard-Bréholles, Jean-Louis Alphonse (1817–71), 269, 326
Hume, David (1711–86), 325
　History of England (1754–62), 325

Humfrey, duke of Gloucester (1390–1447), 306–7, 313, 331, 339, 362
Hungary
　kings of, 101
Hutton, Sir Richard, chaplain (d. 1639), 316, 332, 356

Iberia, 101
Illyricus, Matthias Flacius (1520–75), Lutheran reformer, 317–18, 342–43
Innocent III, Roman pope (1198–1216), 106, 130
Innocent IV, Roman pope (1243–54), 21, 78, 96, 102, 104–5, 108, 110, 115–16, 123, 149
Ireland
　'sub-kings' of, 146
Isabel de Warenne (d. 1282), countess of Arundel, 205–6, 275–77, 288, 308, 337, 354, 365
Isabella of Scotland (d. 1263), daughter of William I, king of Scotland, 92, 153, 164, 275
Islam, 20, 103, 187, 285, 299
Isle of Man, 146–47, 156
Italy, 82, 250–51, 270

Jacques de Vitry (d. 1240), bishop and cardinal, 20
James I, king of Aragon (1213–76), 101–3, 107, 110
James, M. R. (1862–1936), 190, 218, 299, 370, 372
James, Richard (d. 1638), 356–57
Jean de Joinville (1224–1317), chronicler, 326
Jean de Berry (1340–1416), duke of Berry and Auvergne, 192
Jerusalem, 11, 18, 94, 98, 100–1, 105, 110, 145
Jews, 57, 61, 129, 326

Joachim of Fiore (d. 1202), theologian, 134
Joan de Munchensi (c. 1230–1307), countess of Pembroke, 337, 354
Jocelin of Brakelond (d. 1211), monk and chronicler of Bury St Edmund's Abbey, 13, 301–2, 304
John de Gatesdene, 39, 77, 132, 142
John de Berkhamsted, abbot of St Albans (1290–1301), 311
John de Gray, 57
John de Hertford, abbot of St Albans (1235–63), 1, 12, 14, 17–18, 21, 23, 25, 84, 88, 124, 134, 225, 305
John de Maryns, abbot of St Albans (1301–07), 311
John Fitzgeoffrey (d. 1258), justiciar of Ireland (1245–55), 54, 66, 137
John of Basingstoke, 132–33
John of Lexington (d. 1257), knight, 78
John of Salisbury (d. 1180), 206
John of Taxter (fl. 13th cent.), monk of Bury St Edmund's, chronicler, 304
John of the Cell, abbot of St Albans (1195–1214), 12–13
John of Tynemouth (fl. 1350), chronicler, 310
  Historia aurea of, 310
John of Wallingford (d. 1258), monk and infirmarer of St Albans Abbey, 23–24, 29, 34–37, 47, 57, 224, 226, 269, 305, 338, 341, 355
John of Wheathampstead, abbot of St Albans (1420–40, 1452–65), 225, 313–14, 339, 342, 361–62
  Granarium of, 314
John the Baptist, 99
John, king of England (1199–1216), 14, 33, 51, 74, 76, 78, 106, 127, 153, 310, 322, 324–25, 331

John, suffragan bishop of Ardfert and Agdahoe (Co. Kerry, c.1217–24), 22–23
Jordan, River, 246, 250
Joscelyn, John (1529–1603), 356

Katharine of England (1253–57), daughter of Henry III and Eleanor of Provence, 79
Kauffmann, Martin, 175
Kenilworth (Warwickshire), castle at, 55
Kenneth II, King of Scots (971–95), 151
Kent, 65, 71, 211, 285
Kidwelly, Morgan (d. 1513), lawyer, 365
Kingsbury, Thomas (d. 1545), prior of St Albans Abbey, 316, 332, 339, 341, 355
Kjaer, Lars, 60
Knowles, David (1896–1974), historian, 328
Koran, 98
Kwakkel, Erik, 209, 263

Lambarde, William (1536–1601), antiquarian, 321–22
Lanfranc of Bec (1005–89), archbishop of Canterbury (1070–89), 192
Langley, Sir Geoffrey, 61, 156, 166
Langtoft, Peter (d. 1305), Augustinian canon, chronicler, 159
Langton, Stephen (c. 1150–1228), archbishop of Canterbury (1206–28), 7, 81–82, 107, 133, 302–3, 308, 357
Lateran, 4th council of (1215), 20, 25, 118, 120, 130–31, 133–37, 142
Latin language, 104
Laurence de Therbrugge, 84

Laurence, monk of Jerusalem, 11
Lawrence, C. H., 282
Lee, Sir Richard (1513–75), surveyor of the king's works, 316, 332
Legge, Dominica, 288, 294–95, 299
Leicester
   earl of, 137
Leland , John (c. 1503–52), antiquarian, 1, 315, 317, 339–40, 362
Leo IX, Roman pope (1049–54), 281
Leon, kingdom of, 240
Leonardo da Vinci (1452–1519), 244
Leonor of England (d. 1214), daughter of Henry II, king of England, 205, 207
Leopold V, 115
Leopold VI, 115
Lewis, Suzanne, 8–9, 135–37, 194, 218, 222, 259, 308, 350
Lexicon Suida, 359
Lhuyd, Edward (d. 1709), 364
Lieftinck, 260–61, 270
Lincoln
   bishopric of, 122, 124, 126–27, 132–33, 142, 339, 362
   cathedral of, 110
   clergy of, 124
   diocese of, 124, 132, 134–35
   earl of, 137
   Jews of, 61
Lingard, John (1771–1851), 325
History of England (1819), 325
Llywelyn ap Gruffudd, king of Gwynedd (1246–82), prince of Wales (1267–82), 146, 151, 156–57, 160–61
Lombard, Peter (d. 1160), 15, 22
London, 12, 24, 34–35, 38, 71, 73–74, 77, 80, 95, 104, 110, 121, 126, 128, 132, 140, 146, 150–52, 169, 189, 217, 223, 242, 244, 249, 251, 319, 322, 341, 345
   bishopric of, 71
   British Museum, 324, 345–46, 348–49, 355–56, 362
   Council of, 132
   Essex House, The Strand, 347
   St Alban, Wood Street, parish of, 322
   St James' Palace, royal residence, 323
   St Paul's Cathedral, 136
   St Thomas of Acre, hospitaller foundation, 38
Londoners, 53–54
Longespee wardship, 39
Lothian, 155
Louis IX, king of France (1226–70), 39, 42, 60, 62, 65, 73, 86, 96, 103, 107, 150, 352
Louis VI, king of France (1108–37), 360
Louis VIII, king of France (1223–26), 78
Lovell, Philip (d. 1259), lord high treasurer, 81
Lower Saxony, 249
Luard, Henry Richards (1825–91), 257, 327, 348–49, 352
Lumley, John, 1st baron Lumley (c.1533–1609), 341, 361, 363
Lusignans, 129
Lyly, Peter (d. 1569), 344
Lyon, Council of (1245), 77, 125

Macaulay, Thomas Babington (1800–59), historian, 327
MacDubhghaill, Eógan (d. 1268), lord of Argyll, 147, 152, 156
Madden, Sir Frederick (1801–73), 50, 58, 233, 257–58, 348–49, 356, 358, 362
Magdeburg Centuriators, 318–19, 343

Magdeburg Centuries of, 343
Magna Carta (1215), 38, 56, 58, 74, 107, 109, 121, 125–26, 140, 278, 309, 313
Mahom, pagan god, 285
Majorca, 102
Mak, Bonnie, 209
Malcolm III, king of Scotland (1058–93), 150, 166
Malden (Surrey), 79
Malory, Thomas (d. *c*. 1470), xiii
Mansel, John (d. 1265), chancellor of England, 60, 65, 71, 132, 150
manuscripts
    Amiens, Bibliothèque municipale, Lescalopier, 30, 200
    British Library, Additional MS 4806, 333
    British Library, Additional MS 20709, 333
    British Library, Additional MS 28681, 186
    British Library, Additional MS 39943, 179, 191
    British Library, Additional MS 62777, 331
    British Library, Additional MS 70513, 276–77, 298, 330
    British Library, Arundel MS 46, 222
    British Library, Arundel MS 96, 216–17, 237, 307
    British Library, Arundel MS 157, 350
    British Library, Cotton MS Claudius D VI, ix, 8, 162, 225–26, 238, 272, 309, 316, 321, 331, 342, 346, 356
    British Library, Cotton MS Claudius E IV, 311–12, 331
    British Library, Cotton MS Claudius E VIII, 237
    British Library, Cotton MS Cleopatra A XVI, 237
    British Library, Cotton MS Faustina B IV, 28
    British Library, Cotton MS Faustina B IX, 330
    British Library, Cotton MS Julius B XII, 342, 358
    British Library, Cotton MS Julius D III, 31
    British Library, Cotton MS Julius D VI, 191, 330, 346
    British Library, Cotton MS Julius D VII, ix, 29, 31, 57, 224, 226–27, 269, 316, 321, 329, 332, 338, 341, 355
    British Library, Cotton MS Nero C IV, 192
    British Library, Cotton MS Nero C V, 346
    British Library, Cotton MS Nero D I, 7–8, 28, 64, 66, 190–91, 194, 225, 237–38, 241, 265, 268, 272, 310, 312, 315, 330, 345–46, 356, 359
    British Library, Cotton MS Nero D II, 213, 217, 237
    British Library, Cotton MS Nero D V, 230, 232, 268, 306, 310, 319–20, 331, 333, 342, 344–46, 358
    British Library, Cotton MS Nero D VII, 27, 312, 343
    British Library, Cotton MS Otho B V, 237
    British Library, Cotton MS Otho C II, 237
    British Library, Cotton MS Otho D III, 238
    British Library, Cotton MS Titus D XVI, 194
    British Library, Cotton MS Vespasian B XIII, 190, 268, 357, 359

manuscripts (cont.)
  British Library, Cotton MS Vitellius A XX, 31, 269, 330, 347, 358
  British Library, Cotton MS Vitellius D II, 333
  British Library, Cotton MS Vitellius A VIII, 331
  British Library, Cotton MS Vitellius D VIII, 191, 347
  British Library, Cotton MS Vitellius E XIV, 356
  British Library, Harley MS 247, 333
  British Library, Harley MS 545, 333, 356
  British Library, Harley MS 641, 237
  British Library, Harley MS 1620, 306
  British Library, Harley MS 2258, 331, 363
  British Library, Harley MS 3634, 333
  British Library, Harley MS 6217, 333
  British Library, Harley Roll Y6. 193
  British Library, Lansdowne MS 6, 333
  British Library, Lansdowne MS 58, 358
  British Library, Lansdowne MS 205/17, 333
  British Library, Royal MS 2 A XXII, 192
  British Library, Royal MS 4 D VII, 31, 269, 340, 359
  British Library, Royal MS 13 D V, 31, 222, 224, 339–40, 360–62
  British Library, Royal MS 13 D I*, 346, 356
  British Library, Royal MS 13 E VI, 30–31, 224, 238, 269, 340, 361
  British Library, Royal MS 13 E IX, 312
  British Library, Royal MS 14 C I, 347, 356
  British Library, Royal MS 14 C VI, 237, 330
  British Library, Royal MS 14 C VII, iv, 27, 64–65, 160, 200, 218, 233–34, 268, 270–71, 296, 305–6, 309–10, 315, 323, 329–31, 335, 340, 342–43, 345, 357, 362, 365, 366
  British Library, Sloane MS 3857 364
  Cambridge, Corpus Christi College, MS 16 (I), 162, 352
  Cambridge, Corpus Christi College, MS 16 (II), vii, 56–57, 86–89, 113, 117, 166, 190, 219–20, 225, 230–31, 233, 238, 270, 296, 316, 330, 332, 338, 341, 343–44, 346, 350, 352, 354, 357–58, 366, 368–69
  Cambridge, Corpus Christi College MS 26, 8, 86, 220, 225, 230, 238, 254, 268, 296, 310, 316, 331–32, 338, 341, 343, 350, 353
  Cambridge, Corpus Christi College, MS 56, 233–35, 332, 341
  Cambridge, Corpus Christi College, MS 264, 237
  Cambridge, Corpus Christi College, MS 348, 333
  Cambridge, Corpus Christi College, MS 385, 269, 344, 353
  Cambridge, Gonville and Caius College, MS 230, 331
  Cambridge, Trinity College, MS B.5.3, 227
  Cambridge, Trinity College MS O.1.64, 191
  Cambridge Trinity College, MS O.9.34, 274

R.1.17, 176
R.4.2, 237
Cambridge, University Library, MS
    Dd.11.78, 268–69, 353
Cambridge, University Library MS
    Ee3.59, 169, 191, 281, 330, 337
Cambridge, University Library, MS
    Gg. 6.42, 350
Cologny, Fondation Martin
    Bodmer MS 127, 200
Dublin, Chester Beatty Library:
    Chester Beatty MS 70, 237
Dublin, Trinity College, MS 177, 8,
    27–29, 167–89, 194–95, 206, 268,
    277, 279, 310, 312, 317, 330, 336,
    349, 354, 365, 368–72, 374
Edensor, Chatsworth House,
    Devonshire Collection Archives,
    St Albans Abbey Cartulary, 238
Eton College, MS 96, 222
    MS 123, 211–16, 237, 330
    MS 213, 330–31
Hildesheim, Dombibliothek, MS St
    Godehard 1, 180
London, Lambeth Palace, MS
    188, 237
    MS 1106, 237
Los Angeles, J. Paul Getty Museum,
    Ms. Ludwig III 1[83.MC.72], 193
Manchester, Chetham's Library,
    MS 6712, 210–14, 216–18, 220,
    222, 237, 268, 307, 337, 363
New York, Morgan Library,
    MS M.638, 192
New York, Pierpont Morgan
    Library, MS M.736, 179
Oxford, All Souls College, MS
    37, 237
Oxford, Bodleian Library,
    Additional MS C. 22, 237
    Auct. F.4.32, 200
    MS Ashmole 304, 268
    Bodley MS 912, 237

Douce MS 207, 237, 367
MS eMuseo 149, 237
Laud MS 572, 307
MS Bodley 462, 331, 585
MS Digby, 20, 31, 46, 364
MS Fairfax 20, 237
MS Hatton 53, 237
MS Junius 1, 337
MS lat. hist. d. 4, 237
MS lat. th. b. 1, 225
MS Laud. Misc. 572, 237
MS Rawlinson B 177, 237
MS Rawlinson B 186, 237
Oxford, Corpus Christi College,
    MS 2, 31, 269, 364
Oxford, Corpus Christi College,
    MS.2*, 254
Oxford, Magdalen College MS
    lat.53, 330
Oxford, University College MS
    165, 180
Paris, Bibliothèque nationale de
    France, ms lat. 6045, 237
Paris, Bibliothèque nationale de
    France, ms lat. 6048B, 319, 343
Paris, Bibliothèque nationale de
    France, ms Français 19093, 350
Paris, Bibliothèque nationale de
    France, ms Français 24766,
    338
San Marino, CA., Huntington
    Library, MS HM 26341, 333
San Marino, CA., Huntington
    Library, MS HM 30319, 237
Stokenchurch, Wormsley Library,
    MS BM 3750, viii, 169, 202, 206,
    277, 191, 330, 350
Utrecht, Bibliotheek der
    Rijksuniversiteit MS.32, 192,
    194
Westminster Abbey, MS 24, 237
Yale, Beinecke Library, MS 426,
    237

Margaret de Beaumont (d. 1235), countess of Winchester, 278
Margaret de Burgh, daughter of Hubert, earl of Kent, 71
Margaret of England, queen of Scotland (1251–75), 63, 242
Margaret of Savoy, 157
Margaret, countess of Flanders (1244–78), 76
Margaret, Queen of Scots (1070–93), 150, 166
Margaret, sister of Alexander II, 152
Marie de France(fl. 1160–1215), poet, 78
Markyate Priory (Hertfordshire), 316, 332
Mars, Roman god of war, 77, 79
Marseilles, 101
Marsh, Geoffrey (d. 1245), 155
Marsh, Richard, bishop of Durham (1217–26), 314, 331
Marsh, William, 165
Marshal, Richard (c.1191–1234), 3rd earl of Pembroke (1231–34), 51, 119
Marshal, Gilbert (c. 1194–1241), 4th earl of Pembroke (1234–41), 78, 152
Marshal, William (d. 1219), 1st earl of Pembroke (1199–1219), 76, 78
Martel, Charles, Frankish prince (d. 741), 95
Martel, William, sacrist of St Albans Abbey, 14
Martin, Henri-Jean, 209
Martin, Master, a papal nuncio, 105, 124, 141
Matthew of Cambridge, clerk of works, St Albans Abbey
Medea, 76
Mediterranean, 246, 270
Melrose Abbey, chronicle, 158
mendicants. *See also* friars

Menelaus, Greek king of Sparta, 76
Mercia, 76, 79, 211
Merlin, 79, 96
Merton Priory (Surrey), 19, 211, 215, 307–8
Meyer, Paul, 263, 282, 286–87, 299
Meyer, Wilhelm, 262
Michael, Michael A., 182
Middle English language, 278, 293, 337
Midianite rulers, 247
Milton, John (1608–74), 326
Minorca, 102
Minsheu, John (1559/60–1627), 363
Mohammed (c.570–630), 98, 114
Mohun, Reginald (1507/08–67), Cornish MP, 316
Mongols, 93, 100–1, 109, 112, 114–15, 187
  invasion of 1244, 114
Montgomery, Treaty of (1267), 146
Moore, John (1646–1714), bishop of Ely, 354
Morgan Picture Bible, 192
Morgan, Nigel, 218, 350
Mount Gilboa, 250
Muslims, 77, 82, 97–103, 109, 111, 186–87

Nequam, Alexander (1157–1217), Augustinian canon, scholar, 186, 332, 350
Nestorian Christians, 103, 111
Nidarholm (Trondheim Norway), 12
Niger, Roger, bishop of London (1228–29), 121
Niobe, 76
Nithard (d. 844?), Frankish historian, grandson of Charlemagne, 299
  Life of Charlemagne, 284
Nix, Linda, 209
Noah's Ark, 91, 100

Norfolk, 12, 69, 82, 307, 309, 316
Normandy, 242, 281, 293, 312, 314
Normans, 174, 192
  Conquest of England, 174
North Mymms (Hertfordshire), 316
Northampton
  sheriff of, 83
Northumberland, 149, 151
Northumbria, 211
Norway, 15, 18, 36, 68, 107, 110, 146, 148, 152, 242
Nowell, Laurence (c.1530–70), antiquarian, 321–22, 333

O'Farrell, Laura, 370
Octavian, (d. 14), Roman emperor, 76
Odense (Denmark), 10
Odiham (Hampshire), castle at, 55
Offa, king of Mercia (757–96), 7, 10, 76, 79–80, 93, 95, 167, 171–72, 174, 177, 186–87, 191, 291, 330, 360
Offa, legendary king of the Angles, 75, 80. *See also* Offa, king of Mercia
Orkneys, 146
Oswine, king of Deira (c. 644–651), martyr and saint, 150
Otto of Tonengo (d. 1250/51), papal legate in England, Ireland and Scotland (1237–40), 78, 120, 132, 136–37, 148
Otto IV, Holy Roman Emperor (1209–18), 242
Ovid (d. 17/18), Roman poet, 74, 77–78
Oxford, 16, 48, 51–53, 55, 64, 67, 119, 244, 246, 251, 306–7, 324, 327, 338–39, 342, 350, 362, 365
  Council of (1222), 133
  Duke Humfrey's Library, 342
  New College, 339
  St Frideswide's Priory, 338, 350
  University Library, 306–7

Oxford Dictionary of National Biography, 259

Padua, 252
palaeographical features
  Anglicana script, 260–61
  Caroline script, late, 260
  Cursiva Antiquior, 260
  Formata, 270
  Gothic script, 259–60, 263
  litterae notabiliores, 263
  nomina sacra, 266
  paraph, 264–65, 270
  Prothogothic, 260
  punctus, 263–64, 270
  punctus elevatus, 263–64, 270
  punctus interrogativus, 263–64
  Textualis, 260–63, 270
  Textus Praescissus, 270
  Textus Quadratus, 270
  Textus Rotundus, 270
  Textus Semiquadratus, 270
  Tironian notes, 258, 261, 266
Palestine, 247–48, 250, 364
Papp Reed, Zsuzsanna, 114
Paris, 119, 174
  University, 18
Paris Matthew, 35
  Abbreviatio chronicorum, 6, 44, 56, 62, 148, 226, 257, 316, 321, 342, 346–48, 356
  'Book of St Albans', 8, 336–37, 354, 368
  Chronica maiora, 3, 7, 9, 17, 32–48, 50, 52–53, 56, 58, 60, 63–66, 90, 109, 118, 121–23, 125–27, 133–38, 140, 142, 144–45, 147–49, 152, 156, 158–65, 181, 195, 197, 217, 219–20, 222–25, 230–32, 233, 235–36, 244, 256–57, 259, 264–65, 267, 270, 272–73, 276, 305–6, 310, 318, 338–48, 350, 352–53, 358–59, 362, 364

Paris Matthew (cont.)
  Flores historiarum, 6, 17, 32, 37, 40,
    46–47, 56, 59, 61, 144, 146, 148,
    156, 160–62, 165–66, 210–13,
    216–19, 221–24, 230, 236, 257,
    281, 302, 307–8, 310, 313, 319, 329,
    333, 335, 337, 343, 348–49,
    363, 365
  Gesta abbatum, 6–7, 11–14, 21–27,
    80, 84, 88, 120, 126, 142, 182–83,
    186, 192, 225, 273, 301–3, 305,
    309–12, 314–17, 321–23, 332,
    338, 345, 357, 360
  Historia Anglorum, 6, 17, 40,
    44–45, 47, 56, 61, 63, 67, 71, 92,
    106, 118, 128, 137, 141, 144–45,
    149, 160, 165–66, 197–99, 218,
    222, 224–27, 233–34, 244,
    256–57, 264, 270, 302, 306, 310,
    313, 315, 329, 335, 338, 342, 348,
    361–62
  La estoire de Seint Ædward le rei,
    69, 86–89, 93, 95, 179, 181–82,
    191, 257, 272, 274, 276, 279–81,
    283, 285–86, 288, 292–93,
    337, 348
  La vie de seint Auban, 179, 191, 205,
    272, 274–75, 277–79, 281–82,
    285–89, 292, 299, 336,
    347, 354
  *La vie de saint Edmond archevêque
    de Contorbéry*, 272–73, 276,
    282–83, 286–87, 347
  *La vie de saint Thomas de
    Cantorbéry*, 179, 181–82, 191,
    202, 204–5, 272, 277, 286
  Liber additamentorum, ix, 7, 28, 32,
    35, 50, 53, 65, 75, 136, 138, 163,
    168, 182–83, 225–26, 240–42, 257,
    265, 303, 338, 340, 346, 352, 356
  Life of Stephen Langton, 190
  Vitae duorum Offarum, 7, 29, 75,
    95, 114, 191, 338, 345, 357

Parker, Matthew, archbishop of
  Canterbury (1559–75), 2–3,
  229–30, 233–34, 257, 317–24,
  332, 335, 340–41, 343–46, 349,
  351–53, 363
Parkes, M. B., 260
Parliament, 34, 36, 48–49, 51–52, 55,
  65–66, 75, 80, 88, 316, 320,
  341, 345
  House of Commons, 326
  House of Lords, 326
  Long Parliament, 322
  Oxford, 48, 51, 53, 55, 67
Parys, William, monk of St Albans
  Abbey, 22
Passelawe, Robert, 125
Patarenes, 104, 116
Patrick II (1232–49), 5th earl of
  Dunbar, 150
Patrick, son of Thomas of Galloway,
  Gall-Gaidhil prince, 149, 154
Pelagian heresy, 103, 135, 171, 292
Pembroke, earl of, 137
Pershore Abbey (Worcestershire), 37,
  47, 59, 64, 210, 307
Peter des Rivaux (d. 1262),
  courtier, 39
Peter des Roches, bishop of
  Winchester (1205–38), 101,
  107, 187
Peter of Poitiers
  Compendium historiale, 222
Peter II (*c*. 1203–68), count of
  Savoy, 129
Peutinger map, 252
Philip IV of Gascony, 165
Pietro della Vigna (d. 1249),
  chancellor and secretary of
  Emperor Frederick II, 77
Piper, Paulin, 78
Poitevans, 77, 81, 83
Pontigny Abbey (Burgundy), 21, 58,
  110, 120

Portugal, 270
Pory, John (d. 1633), 356–57
Prester John, 100, 111, 114
Priam, legendary king of Troy, 76
Princess Isabel, Holy Roman Empress (1235–41), 72
Privy Council, 321
Provence, 116

Radcliffe, Ann (1764–1823), novelist, 324
Ralph d'Escures, 315
Ralph de Diceto (d. c. 1202), dean of St Paul's cathedral and chronicler, 24, 31, 75, 340, 361
  Ymagines historiarium, 361
Ralph de Dunham, prior of Tynemouth Priory, 359
Ralph of Coggeshall (d. after 1227), Cistercian monk, chronicler, 360
Ralph of Dunstable, monk of St Albans Abbey, 169, 278, 337, 354
Ralph of Norwich, royal justice, 146
Ralph of Stanham, monk of St Albans Abbey and Whitby, 13
Ramsey Abbey (Cambridgeshire), 78, 135
Raymond, prior of St Albans, 360
Reading (Berkshire), 64
  abbey at, 17, 78
Reader, Rebecca, 259
Redbourn Priory (Hertfordshire), 22, 73, 110
Reymund, prior of St Albans Abbey, 22
Rhuddlan, Statute of (1282), 310
Richard d'Aubigny, abbot of St Albans (1100–19), 11, 14
Richard de Bury (1287–1345), bishop of Durham (1333–45), 339

Richard de Clare (1222–62), 5th earl of Hereford, 6th earl of Gloucester, 49–50, 55, 79
Richard de Morins (d. 1242), 361
Richard de Parco, 163
Richard de Potton, bishop of Aberdeen (1256–1270/72), 158
Richard I, king of England (1189–99), 114–15
Richard II, duke of Normandy (996–1026), 293
Richard of Croxley, abbot of Westminster (1246–58), 16
Richard of Devizes (d. c. 1200), monk of Winchester Cathedral Priory, chronicler, 301
Richard of Saint-Victor (d. 1173)
  Liber exceptionum, 30, 359
Richard of Wallingford, abbot of St Albans (1327–34), 310
Richard, 1st earl of Cornwall (1209–72), 16–17, 36, 39, 54, 58–59, 66, 70, 76–78, 93–96, 103, 115, 158, 205, 242, 303
Richard, Bishop of Bangor (1236–67), 151–52, 157, 161
rimes équivoques, 287
Rishanger, William (d. 1312), monk of St Albans Abbey, chronicler, 309–10, 330, 346–47
Robert II, count of Flanders (c. 1065–1111), 360
Robert Curthose (d. 1134), duke of Normandy (1087–1106), 314
Robert de Courçon (d. 1219), cardinal and papal legate, 20
Robert de Gorham, abbot of St Albans (1151–66), 24
Robert le Bougres, 106
Robert of Mentley, 248–49
Robert de Mowbray (d. 1125), earl of Northumbria, 11, 150, 163
Robert of Sotindon, 84

Robert of Torigni (d. 1186), Benedictine monk and chronicler of Mont St Michel, 148
Rochester Priory, 217
Roger de Quincy, 2nd earl of Winchester (1235–64), 147, 149, 156, 162
Roger de Thurkelby, justice of King's Bench, 71, 304
Roger of Poitiers, monk of St Albans Abbey, 13
Rolls Series, 5, 27, 32, 113, 257–59, 267–68, 326–27, 348, 352
Roman de Chevalerie, 274
Roman empire, 252
Romance literature, 78–79, 84
Rome, 10, 55, 70, 73, 81, 93, 120–21, 123–24, 130, 139, 162, 318, 322, 336, 340
  Lateran Palace, 137
Romilly, John (1802–74), master of the rolls, 348
royal ordinance of the Magnates, 54
Russell, John, bishop of Lincoln (1480–94), 1, 339–40, 362
Rustand, papal nuncio, 121

Sanchia of Provence (1228–61), countess of Cornwall, 205, 276, 308, 337, 354
Saracens, 103, 186, 285, 291
Satanists, 104
Savile, Henry (d. 1622) of Banke, 321, 333, 342, 345, 358
Savoyards, 129
Sawley Abbey (Lancashire), 250
Scandinavia, 91
Schwartz, Bernard, 318
Scotland, 14, 62, 63, 144–47, 149–54, 157–62, 164–65, 242, 251, 309, 314
  west coast of, 146

scribes, 50, 58, 176, 213, 217, 219, 230, 233–34, 256–57, 267, 281, 346
  cross-Channel, 22
Sea of Galilee, 246, 250
Selden, John (1584–1654), 345, 356–57
Seneca the Elder (54 BCE–39 CE), 77
Sengeord, Henry, 357
Seville, 102
Shere (Surrey), 54
Sicilian kingdom, 49, 123, 140
Sidney, Sir Henry (1529–86), lord deputy of Ireland (1565–78), 318, 320–21, 341, 343–44, 352
Simon de Montfort (d. 1265), 6th earl of Leicester, 39, 49–50, 55, 60, 64, 67, 77, 94, 103, 110, 122
Simon, abbot of St Albans (1166–83), 22
Sirleto, Cardinal Guglielmo (1514–85), 306, 342
Skewes, John (d. 1544), chronicler, 314, 316, 363
Smith, A. L. (1850–1924), historian, 327
Somerset, 313, 322
Sopwell Priory (Hertfordshire), 316
Spain, 270
Speed, John (1551/52–1629), 356
Spelman, Sir Henry (c. 1562–1641), 322–23
Siege of Damietta (1218–19), 98
St Albans (Hertfordshire), 71
St Albans Abbey, xiii, 1, 6–7, 9–15, 17–20, 22–26, 28, 32, 34, 37, 44–47, 57, 59–61, 63–65, 68–71, 76, 78, 83–84, 100, 128, 134–35, 142, 149–53, 159–61, 163, 166–69, 171, 174–76, 179–80, 182–83, 186, 191–94, 197, 200, 204, 209–10, 218–19, 222–29, 236, 240–42, 246, 248, 250, 252–54, 256–59, 267–69,

272–74, 277–78, 282, 284, 295,
297, 302–11, 313–16, 319–21,
324, 332, 335–43, 346, 350–52,
354–55, 357, 360–63, 365,
368, 371
  Book of Benefactors, 8
  Psalter, 193
St Davids (Pembrokeshire)
  bishopric of, 145
St Katherine, 69
St Thomas, 68
Stephen of Lexington, abbot of
  Clairvaux (1243–57), 95
Stephen of Segrave (d. 1241), chief
  justiciar (1232–34), 77, 80
Stigand, archbishop of Canterbury
  (1052–70), 140
Stow, John (1524–1605), antiquarian,
  319–22, 342, 344, 356, 358
Stubbs, William (1825–1901),
  historian, 327
Suffolk, county of, 276, 309
Sumercote, Robert, cardinal of San
  Eustachio (1239–41), 95
Surrey, earl of, 205
Sussex, 211, 214
Swereford, Alexander (d. 1246),
  baron of the Exechequer, 71, 76
Sylvester
  Experimentarius, 268

Talbert, Richard, 252
Talbot, Robert (1505?–58),
  prebendary of Norwich
  (1547–58), 316–17, 341, 352, 357
Templar, Knights order of, 38, 93,
  99–100, 102, 234, 321
Tervagant, pagan god, 285
Tewkesbury Abbey (Gloucestershire),
  25, 31, 50, 72, 80, 166, 206
Thame (Oxfordshire), 132
Thomas of Galloway (d. 1231), Gall-
  Gaidhil prince, 154

Thomas of Hortington, 82
Thomas de Moulton (d. 1240), 81
Thomas of Northumberland,
  archdeacon, 110
Thomas, monk of Sherborne, 304
Thomas, Symons, 357
Thomson, R. M., 259
Thweng, Robert, 127
Tintern Abbey
  (Monmouthshire), 307
Toulouse, 116
Tours, St Martin's Abbey, chronicler
  of, 134
Traheron, Bartholomew, 340, 363
Trevet, Nicholas (d. *c.* 1328),
  Dominican friar, chronicler, 310
  Annales Cambriae of, 39
  Annales of, 32, 310
Trojans, 112, 144–45
Trumpington (Cambridgeshire), 25,
  54, 194
twelfth-century renaissance,
  259
Twyne, Brian (1581–1644),
  antiquarian, 324
Tynedale, 151
Tynemouth Priory
  (Northumberland), 13, 149–51,
  163, 309, 359
Tyson, John, 365

Ussher, James (1581–1656),
  archbishop of Armagh
  (1625–56), 355, 368
Utrecht Psalter, 176, 192, 194

Valencia, 102
Vaughan, ____, of Brasenose College,
  Oxford, 364
Vaughan, Richard, 9, 32–34, 36–38,
  40, 42–44, 46–48, 50, 53, 55–58,
  66, 85, 212, 222, 226, 245,
  257–59, 262, 265, 267, 269, 273,

286, 307, 328, 335, 338, 352, 357, 360
Vergil Polydore (d. 1555), archdeacon of Wells (1508–46), 313–14, 316, 339, 361–62
Anglica historia of, 313, 339, 362
Veronica, St, 350
Verulamium, 182, 336
Vie de Saint Alexis, 297. *See also Alexis of Rome (4th cent.) St.*
Vincent, Augustine (*c.* 1584–1626), 356
Vitruvius (d. after 15 BCE), Roman architect, 16
Valdemar II, king of Denmark (1202–41), 96, 102, 110, 114

Wace (1100–75), 281
  Roman de Rou, 281
Wakelin, Daniel, 209
Walden Abbey (Essex), 21
Wales, 14, 39, 57, 82, 96, 120, 144–47, 149–56, 158–59, 161, 166, 251, 341
  marches of, 146
Wallace, Kathryn, 283, 287
Wallensis, Thomas, bishop of St Davids (1247–55), 145
Walpole, Horace (1717–97), 324
Walsingham, Thomas (*c.* 1340–*c.* 1422), monk and chronicler of St Albans Abbey, 8, 275, 277, 311–13, 321, 331, 333, 339, 343, 362
Walter de Cantilupe, bishop of Worcester (1236–66), 121, 132, 137
Walter of Colchester, painter at St Albans Abbey, 25
Walter of Rheims, monk of St Albans Abbey, 13
Waltham (Essex), 64, 248
  abbey at, 249, 253
Ward, Thomas, 357
Warin of Cambridge, abbot of St Albans (1183–95), 14

Wars of the Roses, 324
Washington, DC
  Library of Congress, iv, 349
Watts, William (*c.* 1590–1649), 257, 322–23, 345, 357–58
Weiler, Björn, 33, 43, 61, 160, 195
Wells (Somerset), archdeaconry of, 313
Wendover, Roger of (d. 1236), monk and chronicler of St Albans Abbey, 6, 9, 24–25, 31–33, 38, 40, 51, 56, 59, 61, 63, 74–77, 86–87, 110, 134, 136, 144, 148, 151, 161, 210, 307, 309, 324, 348
Wermund, father of Offa, of Mercia, 75
Wessex, 211, 314
West Cheap, 35
West, Thomas, 364
Westminster Abbey, 10, 12, 16, 25, 45–49, 68–69, 72, 82, 84, 86, 110, 166, 198, 210–11, 215–17, 242, 247–48, 283, 299, 307–8, 315, 323, 338, 347, 360–61, 363
  Abbot of, 57
  Psalter, 192
Westminster, parliament at, 48–49, 51–52, 55, 64–66, 246
  provisions of (1259), 66
Westminster, royal palace at, 71, 201, 249, 337, 340
  Royal library at, 360–61, 363
Whigs, 326
Whitby Abbey, 13
William, a Franciscan, 182
William de Raleigh, 137
William of Canterbury, 206
William of Newburgh (d. 1198), Augustinian canon, chronicler, 160
William of St Albans, monk of St Albans Abbey, 163
William de Bussey, 54

William de Forz (d. 1260), 4th earl of Albermale, 149
William de Haverhill (d. 1252), lord high treasurer, 81
William de Insula, 83
William de Montibus (*c.* 1140–1213), chancellor of Lincoln Cathedral and theologian, 23
William de Sisseverne, 84
William de Valence (d. 1296), 1st earl of Pembroke, 49, 52, 55, 63, 69, 73
William I, king of England (1066–87), 93, 140, 166, 214, 242
William II Longespée (d. 1250), 95
William II, called 'Rufus', king of England (1087–1100), 314, 330
William II, count of Holland and Zeeland, anti-king of Germany (1248–56), 77
William of Conches (*c.* 1090–*c.* 1154), scholastic philosopher, 344
  Dragmaticon philosophiae, 344, 353
William of Malmesbury (d. *c.* 1143), xiii, 40, 72, 86, 256, 268, 301, 314, 320, 323, 360
  Gesta pontificum Anglorum, 314, 360
  Gesta regum Anglorum, 360
  Historia novella, 360
William of Newburgh (d. 1198), Augustinian canon of Bridlington, chronicler, 75, 306
William of St Albans, monk of St Albans Abbey
  Passio sancti Albani, 336, 354
William of Savoy, bishop of Valence (1224–39), 69
William of Trumpington, abbot of St Albans (1214–35), 11–14, 17–18, 20, 22, 24–25, 28, 30, 73, 120, 130, 183, 194, 304, 360

William of Tyre, archbishop of Tyre (1175–86), chronicler, 250
William, king of Scotland (1165–1214), 164
Winchcombe Abbey (Gloucestershire), 20
Winchester
  Psalter, 192
Winchester (Hampshire), 71, 149
  bishopric of, 54, 63, 94, 101, 112
  Cathedral Priory, 21, 39, 52, 69, 72, 125, 147, 187, 301–2, 337, 354
Windsor, 36, 211
Withers, William, 127
Wogan-Browne, Jocelyn, 276, 287
Wolfe, Reyner, 344, 352
Wolsey, Thomas, cardinal archbishop of York (1514–30), 314, 316, 340, 361
Worcester, 11, 121, 273
  bishopric of, 132
Wormley (Hertfordshire), 253
Wulfstan, St, bishop of Worcester (1062–95), 10–11
Wyche, Richard (1197–1253), bishop of Chichester (1244–53), 11, 19, 71, 110, 117, 122, 125, 140
Wyclif, John (d. 1384), 318
Wykes, Thomas (d. *c.* 1292), canon and chronicler of Oseney Abbey (Oxfordshire), 51, 306
Wymondham Priory (later, abbey, Norfolk), 22, 57, 309, 355

Yarmouth (Norfolk), 12
York, v, 65, 117, 148, 151, 153, 184, 201, 242, 314
  archbishopric, 111, 314
Young, Patrick (1584–1652), 347, 356

Zutshi, Patrick, 350

For EU product safety concerns, contact us at Calle de José Abascal, 56–1°, 28003 Madrid, Spain or eugpsr@cambridge.org.

www.ingramcontent.com/pod-product-compliance
Ingram Content Group UK Ltd.
Pitfield, Milton Keynes, MK11 3LW, UK
UKHW021000250326
469333UK00019B/761